OTHER TITLES BY BILL GUNSTON

Avionics: The story and technology of aviation electronics

The Development of Piston Aero Engines

Faster Than Sound: The story of supersonic flight

Fighters of the Fifties

Giants of the Sky: The biggest aeroplanes of all time

Night Fighters: A development and combat history

Plane Speaking: A personal view of aviation history

Rolls-Royce Aero Engines

WORLD ENCYCLOPAEDIA OF AIRCRAFT MANUFACTURERS

From the pioneers to the present day

BILL GUNSTON

Naval Institute Press
Annapolis, Maryland

First published in 1993 by Patrick Stephens Ltd,
an imprint of Haynes Publishing,
Sparkford, Somerset BA22 7JJ, UK.

Published and distributed in the United States of America and Canada
by the Naval Institute Press, 118 Maryland Avenue, Annapolis, Maryland 21402–5035

Library of Congress Catalog Card Number 93–87264

ISBN 1–55750–939–5

Printed in Great Britain

Contents

Introduction

In this book I have attempted to list all the makers of what you might call 'significant aircraft'. Of course, such an undertaking is doomed to failure from the start. No sooner will this hefty tome hit the streets than someone will remind me of something I have omitted. I would like to think the omissions will be obscure. If I have left out any obvious name, I apologize. In any case, long as it is, this listing is merely the important centre of a grey area round the edges populated by many thousands of enthusiasts around the world. Once there was no aircraft industry, just enthusiasts. Today I have included many hundreds of people who, often working in a backyard or, like V.B. Shavrov, in their tiny apartment, have created worthwhile flying machines.

What aircraft?

I have listed producers of aeroplanes and rotorcraft—manned, powered aerodynes—from about 1852 onwards. Excluded are aerostats—balloons and airships—most microlights, hang gliders, unpowered gliders and sailplanes other than large transport gliders, and most replicas and restored aircraft (though scaled replicas made in quantity for sale or as homebuilts are in). In a few cases the product was a single aircraft which failed to fly but which was sufficiently famous to merit inclusion. Other worthy one-offs which never flew, such as Allen Wheeler's Slymph (which still exists after over 60 years), had to be omitted. There are limits!

What companies?

Obviously I have tried to include all companies whose primary business was making aeroplanes for sale. In the 'grey area' I have also included numerous enthusiasts who never formed a company, some of them being pioneers early in this century. Another part of the grey area is companies whose business is modification of existing aircraft, for whatever reason, and on a completely unquantifiable basis I have included those that seemed sufficiently important. At one extreme you have entries like Aero Spacelines and Satic; at the other are people who dope a length of cord along an aileron and hardly qualify. We in the West are familiar with the notion of an 'aircraft company', but not with how they used to do things in the former Soviet Union (called USSR here). Except for light aircraft, every design was carried out by an OKB (experimental construction bureau) which invariably also built and tested the prototype(s). The head of the bureau, usually with the rank (and uniform) of General Constructor, was often famous and entries appear under their names. They invariably had little say regarding which GAZ (state aircraft factory) would be chosen for series production, and the factories are not included. But today every factory manager is an aggressive capitalist, private factory companies are appearing almost daily, and the problems of the ex-USSR chronicler are self-evident!

What order?

For convenience, the entire book is in rigid alphabetical order by company or organization name, no matter what the product might be or where the entry may be located. Thus we find the sequence: Max Holste, Maximov, Maximum Safety, Max Plan, Maxson, Mayenberger and May, Harden and May. Some lexicographers say you must group organizations known by a set of initials in front of those having names, but this is often difficult. Where would you put Socata,

A–Z listings of aircraft manufacturers

AAA (International). Advanced Amphibious Aircraft was defined by Dornier and Alenia 1988; today participants are these plus HAI (Greece), Per Udsen (Denmark) and SDPR/SOKO (Serbia).

AAC: *See* Advanced (Aircraft Corp.), Aerostar Aircraft Corp., Aircraft Acquisition Corp., American Aircraft (Corp.), American Aviation Corp., Ateliers Aéronautiques de Colombes and Australian Aircraft Consortium.

Aachen Flugzeugbau (Germany). Built small series of trainers 1917–18, in 1920 gliders designed by Prof. Klemperer. Name changed 1921 to Aachener Segelflugzeugbau, but built FK light aeroplane, followed 1924 by 2-seat low-wing monoplane.

AAI: *See* American Aviation Industries.

AAI (Russia). Aviation Association 'Ilyushin' formed 1992 by AKI S. V. Ilyushin and VAPA to act as single customer interface for Il aircraft. Partners with KAL, V. P. Chkalov and other groups.

AAMSA (Mexico). Aeronautica Agricola Mexicana SA (1971–84) was a joint venture 30% owned by Rockwell, set up to take over from US company production of Quail Commander and Sparrow Commander ag-aircraft.

AAS (France). Ateliers Aéronautiques de Suresnes (Paris) was brief post-liberation organization at former Farman works which completed and tested He 274 prototype.

AASI (USA). Advanced Aerodynamics & Structures Inc., previously ASI, is developing Jet Cruzer 500 6-seat pusher turboprop (11 January 1989).

Abbott (UK). E. D. Abbott, Farnham, produced Mignet Fleas and Baynes Scud 1935–6.

ABC (UK). ABC Motors, Walton-on-Thames, produced piston engines, and prototype Robin high-wing single-seater 1929.

Abrams (USA). Produced Explorer (1936) twin-boom pusher survey/photo aircraft with fully glazed nacelle.

ACA (USA). Judith Wolkovich's company specializes in joined-wing research aircraft, aft-swept and forward-swept wings forming a diamond shape.

ACA Zeebrugge, ACAZ: *See* Zeebrugge.

Ace (USA). Successor to Corben (1923), with rights to Baby Ace, Heath Parasol and other homebuilts.

Acme (USA). Acme Aircraft Corp. established 1928 to build sporting biplanes.

Acme (USA). Air Craft Marine Engineering Co. formed 1954 Los Angeles to build Anser twin-jet 4-seat amphibian.

Acro Sport (USA). Markets plans/manuals for all versions of Poberezny-designed Acro Sport and Pober Pixie. By early 1991 over 1,300 Sport I and over 1,100 Pixies.

ACT (Philippines). Aviation Composite Technology formed 1990 to develop Apache 1 military trainer from Lancair 320 homebuilt.

A.D. (UK). Admiralty Air Department designed flying-boat, produced mainly by Pemberton-Billing, and prototype pusher interceptor, both in 1915.

ADA (India). Aeronautical Development Agency formed as instrument of government to manage Light Combat Aircraft; two prototypes funded INR 15,000,000,000 (*c*.US $872m) 1990, main contractor HAL.

Adam (France). Produced light aircraft 1948–55, especially RA.14 Loisirs high-wing 2-seater.

Adaro (Spain). Ing. D. Julio Adaro produced Chirta biplane trainer 1935.

ADC Aircraft (UK). Aircraft Disposals Co. formed March 1920 to manage conversion to money of vast stocks of wartime aircraft and engines. Did considerable conversion and modification to increase saleability but no intention of completely new design. Wound up 1930.

Ader (France). Clément Ader built steam-driven *Eole* monoplane which made 50 m (164 ft) uncontrolled hop 9 October 1890. 1897 *Eole II* failed to leave ground.

Adler (Germany). Adlerwerke vorm. Heinrich Kleyer formed Frankfurt am Main 1934, taking over Max Gerner, Gerner G.II.R becoming Adler G.II.Rb.

Advance: *See* Waco.

Advanced (USA). Advanced Aircraft Corp. was formed July 1983, took over production facilities of Riley and produced conversions of Cessna aircraft with PT6A turboprops.

Advanced Aviation (USA). Orlando, Florida, company supplying many hundreds of kits for 9 designs of microlight landplanes and amphibians.

A-DY (Ukraine). To increase collective strength, in 1991 ANTKI O.K. Antonov formed partnership, with joint board of directors, with enormous Dniepropetrovsk Yuzhyazhmash (Southern Heavy Machine Building Plant) which previously built giant ICBMs and space launch vehicles. First task is to arrange funding and provide production facilities for An-218 twin-jet widebody.

AEA (USA). Aerial Experiment Association formed at Hammondsport, NY, September 1907, by Dr Graham Bell (leader) and Mrs Bell (prime mover and financier), Glenn Curtiss and three others; 4 aircraft: *Red Wing* (Lt. T.E. Selfridge), *White Wing* (Canadian F.W. Baldwin), *June Bug* (Curtiss) and *Silver Dart* (Canadian J.A.D. McCurdy).

AEG (Germany). Giant electrical company, one of principal producers of aircraft in Germany 1910–19. Best known for large bombers (G.I to G.V), but in terms of numbers, chief products were 2-seat reconnaissance aircraft (B.I to B.III), 2-seat fighters (C.I to C.VIII) and armoured attack aircraft (J.I and J.II).

AEA 'Drome No. 4' Silver Dart (McCurdy), 23 February 1909.

AEG J.II of Deutsche Luft Reederei, April 1919.

AER (Italy). Established Orbassano February 1915 to produce Caudron G.3 under licence. Built 90, followed June 1916 by Caudron G.4. Later built Fiat (SIA) SP.3 and SP.4 and about 50 Ansaldo SVA. Closed February 1919.

Aerauto (Italy, 1950–53). Produced PL.5C 2-seat roadable monoplane (drivable on highways).

Aereon (USA, 1967–77). Produced Aereon 26 lifting-body airship, flown 1970.

Aerfer (Italy). Formed Naples 1955 by Aerfer parent and Meridionali. Produced parts of such aircraft as F-84F, F-104G and DC-9, and with Aermacchi developed AM.3 STOL military 3-seater. Merged into Aeritalia.

Aerial Distributors (USA). Formed 1967 to develop Distributor Wing DW-1 ag-aircraft, flown 1965.

Aerial Experiment Association: *See* AEA.

Aerial Service Corporation (USA). Formed 1920 to produce Mercury Liberty-engined inverted-sesquiplane mailplane. Became Mercury.

Aeritalia (Italy). Largest aerospace company in Italy, formed 12 November 1969 by equal share-holding of Fiat and IRI-Finmeccanica to group all Fiat aircraft (as distinct from aero-engine) activities, plus Aerfer and Salmoiraghi. Main aircraft works at Naples, Turin, Foggia, Venice and Rome, programmes including G91, G222, AM.3C and F-104S. Became Alenia.

Aermacchi (Italy). Original Macchi company adopted shortened name Aermacchi 1961; became aircraft-manufacturing subsidiary of Aeronautica Macchi parent, plant and airfield at Venegono outside Varese. Main products MB-326 (10 December 1957) and MB-339 jet trainer/attack aircraft. In 1959 Lockheed bought minority interest and Aermacchi built AL-60 Conestoga/Trojan. In 1983 Aeritalia bought 25% shareholding. Aermacchi has 23.8% of AMX programme. In 1992 transfer of SIAI-Marchetti fixed-wing programmes to Aermacchi was agreed to form single source for jet trainers. Risk-sharing partner on Do 328, assembling fuselage.

Aero (Czechoslovakia). **Aero Tovarna Letadel** was established outside Prague 1919, initially to build Phönix fighters under licence. These were followed by long series of indigenous designs, mainly led by Ing. Husak, notable for robust structures and good flying qualities. Included civil transports, fighters and bombers. Staple products were A.11 military 2-seat biplane (440 built), similar but Jupiter-engined A.32 (116) and bigger A.100 and 101 (137). Aero also built 124 Bloch 200 heavy bombers.

Aero A.300 bomber (2 × Mercury IX), 1938.

Aero (Czechoslovakia). On 1 December 1990 Aero Czechoslovak (now Czech and Slovak) Aerospace Industry Ltd, joint-stock management group, replaced former state-owned Aero. Factories and research centres became limited companies 1 January 1991.

Aero (Czech republic). After second World War, Czech industry was nationalized under central control, though Aero 45 and Super 45 light twins were marketed under that name. On 1 July 1953 a large factory was established at Vodochody outside Prague and, to perpetuate famous name, was later called **Aero Vodochody Národní Podnik.** In 1963–74 Aero delivered about 3,600 L-29 Delfín jet trainers, followed by 2,980 L-39 Albatros jet trainer and attack aircraft. L-59 derivative remains in production, with Ae 270 9/10-seat turboprop (1993).

Aero (USA). Original Aero company was formed in Culver City, Los Angeles, in December 1944 to design and build Aero Commander. In October 1950 it was re-formed as **Aero Design and Engineering Co.** in Oklahoma to build Commander in series. In October 1960 it became **Aero Commander Inc.,** a division of Rockwell.

Aero Boero (Argentina). Principal national builder since 1959 of light and agricultural aircraft, delivering (by 1993) 376 tough high-wing machines, plus a sesquiplane version.

Aerocar (USA). Moulton B. Taylor doggedly pursued his dream of a roadable aeroplane—in other words, a flying car—from 1948. Work is continuing on a 4th-generation version. Meanwhile, Mr Taylor has achieved great success with various homebuilt designs.

Aérocentre (France). When the French industry was forcibly nationalized in 1936, 2 firms, Farman and Hanriot, were grouped to form Société Nationale de Constructions Aéronautiques du Centre, known as SNCAC or Aérocentre. Products included NC.211 Cormoran heavy transport, NC.853 light 2-seater and NC.1080 naval jet fighter. In 1949 the group went into liquidation, its plants and work being shared by SNCAN (Nord), SNCASO (Sud-Ouest) and engine firm SNECMA.

Aero-Club Der Schweiz (Switzerland). This club's Ultimate EA230 aerobatic aircraft was built by Walter Extra, the design now being Extra's property.

Aero Commander (USA). Following Aero Design and Engineering (*see* above), Aero Commander Inc. was formed in 1960 as part of Rockwell. It formed the General Aviation Division at the original plant at Bethany, Oklahoma, producing single-engined low-wing and high-wing machines, and a wide range of high-wing twins with piston and turboprop engines. The singles were terminated in 1980. The final Shrike Commanders were phased out in the same year, and the Jetprop Commanders sold to Gulfstream American.

Aero Composite (USA). Aero Composite Technology Inc. Somerset, PA, have sold over 300 kits for Sea Hawker 2-seat amphibian.

Aero-Craft (USA). Established 1928 at Detroit, to produce Aero Coupe 3-seat biplane.

Aero Design: *See* Aero (USA); Aero Commander.

Aero Designs (USA). Have delivered about 180 kits for 2-seat Pulsar.

Aero Difusión (Spain). Company at Santander registered 1955 to build Jodel and Druine light aircraft under licence.

SNCA du Centre NC.211 Cormoran, January 1947.

Aerodis (USA). Aerodis America was formed in 1982 to build advanced light aircraft in collaboration with groups in Indonesia, Thailand and Hong Kong. Main products were to be AA200 Orion 4-seater, with propeller behind tail, and AA300 Rigel tandem jet trainer. Assets November 1991 to CRSS.

Aero Dynamics (N. America). Aero Dynamics Ltd, based in Seattle (USA) area, is subsidiary of North American Aero Dynamics of Vancouver (Canada). Produces Sparrow Hawk 2-seater in kit form.

Aerodyne (USA). Aerodyne Systems Engineering Ltd had brief existence in 1980s producing Wasp ag/utility helicopter and Hornet armed helicopter trainer, both based on Bell 47.

Aero Engines (UK). Aero Engines Ltd produced 'Douglas' motorcycle engines as used in Tipsy S.2 single-seater. Kingswood factory built 9 S.2 in 1937 under Avions Fairey licence, test flying at Whitchurch.

Aero-Ever (Hungary). In immediate post-war years, to 1951, this factory at Esztergom produced several types of light aircraft and gliders, mostly (numbered up to R.22) designed by Ernö Rubik.

Aerofan (USA). Abortive builder of SingleTwin pusher business aircraft, 1984–8.

Aero-Flight (USA). Long Beach company which in immediate post-1945 era built all-metal Streak tandem-seat low-wing monoplane with 85, 125 or 165 hp.

Aero Industrial: *See* AICSA.

Aero Industry: *See* AIDC.

Aeromarine (USA). Inglis M. Upperçu had small aircraft firm at Keyport, NJ, 1908, became Aeromarine Plane and Motor Corp. 1914. Chief engineer Charles Willard designed succession of flying-boats, seaplanes and a few landplanes, main product being Model 39 family of 100-hp trainers. Model 40F was 100-hp trainer flying-boat. AS (1919) and PG (1920) were fighters. Several F-5L flying-boats redesigned as post-war 12-passenger Type 75. Became Aeromarine-Klemm 1928.

Aeromarine-Klemm (USA). Built Klemm light

Aeromarine-Klemm AKL-26 (60-hp Le Blond), July 1929.

aircraft until killed by Depression 1930.

Aero Mercantil: *See* Gavilán.

Aeromere (Italy). Set up at Trento 1957 to produce under Aviamilano licence F.8L America, version of Super Falco for US market. Became Laverda in 1964.

Aero Mod (USA). Produces airframe conversions of Ag-Cat and Thrush ag-aircraft.

Aero Národní: *See* Aero (Czech republic).

Aeronasa (Spain). Constructora Aeronaval de Levante produced Piel Emeraude under licence 1960–67.

Aeronautica Agricola: *See* AAMSA.

Aeronàutica Ansaldo: *See* Ansaldo.

Aeronàutica d'Italia (Italy). Division of Fiat managing former Ansaldo factories (renamed 1925).

Aeronautical Development Agency (India). Formed 1990 to manage Light Combat Aircraft, *See* ADA.

Aeronautical Industrial SA: *See* AISA.

Aeronautical Syndicate Ltd (UK). One of world's first aircraft manufacturing companies, formed 1909 by Horatio Barber. Built about 29 Valkyrie tail-first monoplanes by December 1911; in 1911 Valkyries flew over 7,000 miles and carried over 150 passengers.

Aeronàutica Macchi: *See* Aermacchi.

Aeronàutica Umbra: *See* AUT.

Aeronautic Supply Co. (USA). Formed at St Louis October 1909, became Benoist 1912.

Aeronautics (India): *See* AIL.

Aeronca (USA). Incorporated as **Aeronautical Corp. of America** November 1928, first factory builder of light aircraft in USA, became Aeronca Aircraft 1941. First major product C-2 high-wing single-seater, followed by wide range of high- and low-wing successors including wartime O-58A Defender and L-3 Grasshopper. Post-war types included Tandem, Chum, Arrow and Chief, but staple product was Champion high-wing tandem-seater of which over 10,000 were built 1946–50 plus over 600 L-16 and 16A Army versions. Since 1950 Aeronca has been major subcontractor of airframe structures, e.g. for B-52, 747.

Aeronics (S. Africa). Licensed producer of Sequoia 300 and 301.

Aeronova (Italy). Aeronova Costruzioni Aeronàutiche formed 1941 to produce Pellarini roadable monoplane (flown 1948).

Aero-Reek (Russia). Private company formed 1991 at former GAZ at Gorkii (city now once again named Nizhni-Novgorod), expected 1993 to fly prototype Dingo multipurpose amphibian with air-cushion landing gear. Single pusher 850-hp turboprop, plus 250-hp turboshaft engine driving air-cushion fans. Intended as true 'go

Aero-Reek Dingo, 1992.

anywhere' vehicle, cruise 155 mph with 1,875-lb load; seeking partner and finance.

Aero Research (UK). Predecessor of CIBA (ARL) at Duxford, built de Bruyne light aircraft 1934-6.

Aero Resources (USA). Took over Jovanovich J-2, certificated 1970.

Aerosmith (Australia). Successor to Yeoman, 1970-71.

Aerospace (NZ). AESL (Aero Engine Services Ltd) and Air Parts amalgamated in 1973 to form New Zealand Aerospace Industries. Produced CT/4 Airtrainer, Airtourer and Fletcher FU-24. Became PAC (Pacific Aerospace) 1982.

Aerospace General (USA). Odessa, Texas, producer of one-man helicopters 1978-82.

Aerospace Industries of Malaysia: *See* AIM.

Aero Spacelines (USA). Established 1961 by A.M. 'Tex' Johnston, former Boeing chief test pilot, to build outsize carriers of space boosters, using B-377 Stratocruiser as basis. Produced entire Guppy family. Became Tracor 1974, selling Super Guppy rights to Airbus/Aéromaritime.

Aerospace Technologies: *See* ASTA.

Aerospatiale (France). Biggest aerospace company in France, formed 1 January 1970 by merger of Nord-Aviation, Sud-Aviation and SEREB ballistic missile and space group. About 29,500

Aerospatiale Caravelle VIR and 10B.

employees (1993), owned 93% by French government, with major plants at Toulouse, St Nazaire, Nantes, Marseilles–Marignane (Eurocopter-France). Socata wholly-owned subsidiary, partner in ATR (50%), Airbus (37.9%), Regioliner (25%) and Alliance SST; Euro-Hermespace on hold. Shareholdings in Helibras and aviation support firms in Morocco and Singapore. *See* also Sogepa.

Aerosport (USA). Formed 1970 in N. Carolina to produce Quail, Rail, Scamp (1973) and Woody Pusher. Scamp alone, 1,050 sets of plans.

Aerostar Aircraft Corporation (USA). Formed 1990 as offshoot of Machen to convert pressurized Aerostars to twin-jet propulsion (FJ44 underwing pods).

Aerostar SA (Romania). Former IAv Bacau factory renamed 1991. Designed Condor to replace Yak-52.

Aerostructures (Australia). Produced conversions of DHC-1 Chipmunk.

Aerostructures Hamble (UK). Former Folland, then Hawker Siddeley, then BAe, Hamble plant was set up 1989 as BAe subsidiary but acquired for £47m in management buyout 1992. Makes major parts for BAe, McDD, Saab and Westland.

AeroSud (S. Africa). Helicopter maintenance/repair organization, now marketing partner with RusJet and General Technologies in LCPT programme, with other products in prospect.

Aerotec (Brazil). Formed 1962, produced T-23 Uirapuru and developments. Major subcontractor to Embraer until 1984.

Aerotechnik (W. Germany). Developed unusual 4-rotor light helicopters 1963-75.

Aerotécnica (Spain). Established Madrid 1954 to develop Matra-Cantinieau helicopter, flown July 1956. Small production of two versions, AC-12 and -14.

Aero Tehnički Zavod (Yugoslavia). Produced V.55 tandem-seat high-wing aircraft, flown 1959.

Aerotek (S. Africa). Abbreviated form of Government Aeronautical Systems Technology,

Pretoria, which designed Atlas NGT trainer and is developing Hummingbird light 2-seater.

Aero Tovarna: *See* Aero (Czechoslovakia), 1st entry.

Aero Trader (NZ). Produced VW-engined trainer 1988.

Aero Union (USA). At Chico, California, since 1959 world's biggest converter of transports, bombers and patrol aircraft into firebombers.

Aero Vodochody: *See* Aero (Czech republic).

AESL (NZ). Established 1954, in 1967 acquired rights to Victa Airtourer, and merged into Aerospace 1973.

Afco (India). Boatbuilder which built gliders and, in 1960, RL.3 side-by-side 2-seater of own design.

AFG: *See* Memel.

AFIC (S. Africa). Formed 1967 at Kempton Park to produce RSA.200, modified version of Italian Partenavia P.64B high-wing 4-seater.

AFU (Switzerland). Aktiengesellschaft für Flugzeug-unternehmungen Altenrhein formed 1959 to continue development of FFA P-16 jet attack aircraft.

AGA (USA). Formerly Pitcairn-Larsen, became G&A, which *see*.

AGB (France). Ateliers Gérard Brobecker, in Alsace, produced several modified or original lightplanes in 1960s.

Ago (Germany). Formed 1911 as **Aeroplanbau G. Otto**, then (1912) **Aerowerke Gustav Otto** and (1912) **Ago Flugzeugwerke**. Important wartime producer of 2-seat reconnaissance biplanes, pusher and tractor. Closed 1920, but name resurrected 1934 for new factory at Oschersleben for production of designs by other companies. Ago Flugzeugwerke did, however, produce small series of its own Ao 192B Kurier light twin-engined transports, 1935–8.

Agos (USSR). AGOS, Department of Aviation, Hydro (Gidro) aviation and Experimental Construction, the design and manufacturing brigade within CAHI formed 1922 by Zhukovsky and headed with distinction by Tupolev.

Agricopteros (Colombia). Producer of Scamp B derived from Aerosport Scamp.

Agrupacíon Aviones: *See* FMA.

Agusta (Italy). Costruzioni Aeronautiche Giovanni Agusta was established 1907, re-formed 1923. Various fixed-wing designs built prior to 1939. Company resurrected 1952 and obtained exclusive European licence for Bell 47, leading to major series of follow-on helicopters. Licence-produced Bell 204, 205, 206, 212 and 412 and Sikorsky S-61 series. Own designs include A 106, A 109 and A 129 Mangusta. In 1977 Agusta Group was established, taking over Elicotteri Meridionali, SIAI-Marchetti and others. In 1980s two additions were BredaNardi and Caproni Vizzola. Brindisi (ex-Meridionali) produces CH-47 Chinook. Agusta is 50/50 partner in EHI, participates in NH90 and Eurofar and has 8 international affiliates plus links with FMA and Koc (Turkey). SAAC (which *see*) no longer exists. Giovanni Agusta is now called Cascina

Ago C.I armed 2-seater, August 1915.

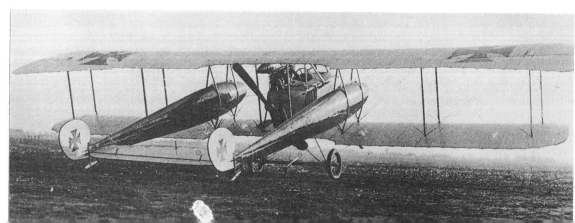

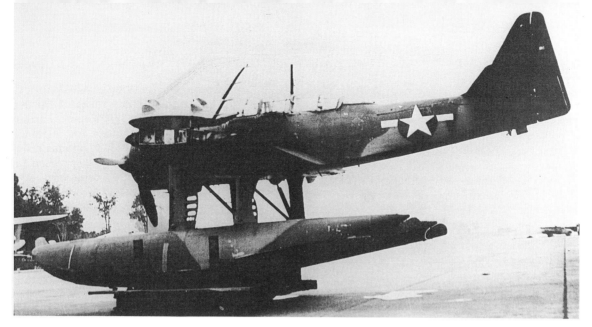

Aichi E16A1 after capture 1945 (wings folded, strut airbrakes shut).

Costa works, SIAI-Marchetti is Sesto Calende works, BredaNardi is Monteprandone works and Caproni-Vizzola has become Somma Lombarda works.

Ahrens (USA). Ahrens began design of AH 404 STOL utility transport, powered by 4 420-hp Allison turboprops, in January 1975. Prototype flew at Oxnard, California, December 1976, followed by first production AH 404 at planned production plant in Puerto Rico in 1979, but failed to finance through certification.

AIA (Australia). Aviation Industries of Australia Pty set up at Shepparton, Victoria, 1992 to take over MA-2 Mamba from Melbourne Aircraft.

AIAA (Algeria). As part of France prior to 1962, Algeria's limited industry built to French order. Atelier Industriel de l'Aéronautique d'Alger built about 240 Stampe SV.4C trainers 1948–50, and small batches of French types prior to 1960.

Aichi (Japan). Aichi Tokei Denki KK (Aichi Clock and Electric) began making aircraft at Funakata, Nagoya, in 1920. Major types (post-1935) included B7A torpedo/dive-bomber, D1A biplane bomber, D3A dive-bomber, E11A flying-boat, E13A and E16A reconnaissance seaplanes, H9A flying-boat, M6A submarine-based attack bomber and S1A twin-engined night fighter.

AICSA (Colombia). Aero Industrial Colombiana SA has assembled Piper aircraft since 1968 and PZL Mielec (Antonov) An-2 since 1989.

AIDC (Taiwan). Aero Industry Development Center established March 1969 as successor to BAI. First product PL-1B trainer derived from Pazmany PL-1. Next, 248 F-5E and 36 F-5F Tiger IIs made under Northrop licence. T-CH-1 turboprop trainer (23 November 1973), 50 series aircraft, followed by AT-3 twin-turbofan trainer/attack (16 September 1980), 60 series aircraft. Current programme Ching-Kuo Indigenous Defensive Fighter (28 May 1989): 256 planned including 40 2-seat.

AIEP (Nigeria). Aeronautical Industrial Engineering and Project Management Co. formed 1988 (60% holding by Dornier) to build Air Beetle trainer derived from Van's RV-6A. Production beginning 1992.

AIL (India). Aeronautics (India) Ltd formed as State enterprise August 1963 to make MiG-21; merged with Hindustan June 1964.

AIM (Malaysia). Aerospace Industries of Malaysia formed January 1985 as Government initiative. Signed agreement with British Aerospace 1987, but dormant.

AIR (USSR). All early Yakovlev designs were designated in honour of A.I. Rykov, numbered AIR-1 to AIR-18.

Air & Space (USA). Air & Space Manufacturing Inc., Muncie, Indiana, produced 68 Umbaugh 18A 2-seat autogyros 1964–5, but bankrupt 1966. *See also* next entry.

Air & Space (USA). Air & Space America Inc., Paducah, Kentucky, formed as manufacturing/marketing subsidiary of Farrington to restart production of slightly improved Umbaugh 18A. Deliveries from September 1990.

Airbus (International). Europe's great GIE (Groupement d'Intérêt Economique) set up December 1970 to manage A300 wide-body twin programme, and has since embraced many other designs. Shareholders: Aérospatiale (France) 37.9%, Deutsche Airbus (Germany) 37.9%, British Aerospace (UK) 20% and CASA (Spain) 4.2%. Fokker (Netherlands) is associate on A300 and A310, and Belairbus (Belgium) on A310, A319/320/321 and A330/340. Some DA work on A300/310 and A321 is subcontracted to Italy, Canadair supplies Aérospatiale with parts of A330/340, and many others have contracts.

Airco (UK). Aircraft Manufacturing Co. was established at The Hyde, Hendon, early 1912 by George Holt Thomas. In June 1914 Capt. Geoffrey de Havilland joined as chief designer, subsequently producing D.H.1–D.H.18. Holt Thomas sold Airco to BSA, which (there being little prospect of business) closed it in 1920. De Havilland formed his own company September 1920.

Airco (UK). Short-lived consortium formed 1958 by de Havilland, Fairey and Hunting to build D.H.121 (Trident).

Air Command Manufacturing (USA). Produces several versions of Commander single- and 2-seat autogyro, over 1,200 flying.

Airconcept (W. Germany). Airconcept Flugzeug

und Gerätebau set up 1976 to market VoWi 10 Airbuggy 2-seat ultralight as completed aircraft and in kit form.

Aircorp (Australia). Aircorp Pty Ltd produces Bushmaster light aircraft.

Aircraft Acquisition Corporation (USA). Bought Helio and Taylorcraft 1989. *See* New Technik.

Aircraft Dynamics (USA). Littleton, Colorado, corp. which has delivered many kits and plans for Nuwaco T-10 3-seat biplane.

Aircraft Hydro-Forming (USA). A major producer of airframe parts, this California company tried in 1968–70 to market Bushmaster 2000 based on Ford Tri-Motor.

Aircraft Manufacturing Co. (Canada). Formed 1917, no major production but did much overhaul/conversion, bought Boeing BB-1 flying-boat 1920 and produced several similar.

Aircraft Manufacturing Co. (USA). Short-lived (1949–51) company which bought rights to Johnson Bullet metal 4-seater and produced it as Texas Bullet.

Aircraft Mechanics Inc. (USA). Formed by management buyout of failed Alexander, produced new designs, ceased 1936.

Aircraft Technology Industries (International). Full name of Airtech.

Airdisco: *See* ADC Aircraft.

Air-Fouga (France). Briefly (1956–8) name of

Airbus A310–300, 1988.

former Etablissements Fouga, taken over as Potez Air-Fouga 1958.

Airliner Engineering: *See* Burnelli.

Airmark (UK). Brief existence (1969–72) building Cassutt and TSR.3 racers.

Airmaster (UK). Airmaster Helicopters was formed 1971 to develop cheapest possible 2-seat helicopter. Resulting H2-B1 flew February 1972.

Airmaster (USA). This Renton (Seattle) firm was formed 1980 to produce turboprop amphibians. Avalon 680 7-seater powered by 750-hp PT6A flew October 1983. Company failed to fly definitive Twin Star 1000 and military Guardian.

Air-Metal (W. Germany). Air-Metal Flugzeugbau und Entwicklungs was formed 1971 to produce STOL transports. Eventual design was AM-C-111, powered by 2 PT6A turboprops, but work stopped 1978.

Air New Zealand: *See* Murrayair.

Air Nova (S. Africa). Air Nova (Pty) Ltd had brief 1975 existence marketing plans and kits of Reed Falcon aerobatic biplane derived from Rooivalk.

Airod (Malaysia). Airod SDN BHD, Subang, has RMAF contract to rebuild and upgrade 34 S-61A Nuri helicopters.

AiRover (USA). AiRover Co. was formed August 1937 as subsidiary of Lockheed to build Unitwin Model 2 Starliner (April 1939) with patented twin-Menasco engines driving single propeller.

Occupied small building (previously Empire China Co.) next to Burbank plant. Under Mac Short then built pilotless drones, being renamed **Vega Airplane Co.** 1938, which *see*.

Air Parts (NZ). In 1957 this Hamilton company acquired local rights to Fletcher FU-24, and in 1964 purchased all rights to Fletcher ag-aircraft. Various developments produced before merging with AESL to form NZ Aerospace 1973.

Airplan (France). Produced single-seat monoplane with 40-hp Train engine in 1946.

Airplane (USA). Airplane Development Corp. formed January 1932 by Gerard Vultee when Lockheed (Detroit) failed. Finance by Cord Corp., which also owned Stinson and Auburn auto firm. *See also* Vultee.

Airspeed (UK). Airspeed Ltd began life in York, where AS.4 Ferry passenger biplanes were built 1932. Re-formed in Portsmouth as Airspeed (1934) Ltd, pioneered modern design in Britain with AS.5 Courier and AS.6 Envoy, with flaps and retractable landing gear. From Envoy was derived AS.10 Oxford multirole twin trainer, of which 8,586 were built 1938–45. Other great wartime type was AS.52 and 58 Horsa transport glider—3,799 delivered. BEA bought 20 AS.57 Ambassador airliners, and about 160 Oxfords were completed as AS.65 Consul light transports. Merged into de Havilland 1951.

Air Sud-Ouest (France). Also written Aérosudouest, 1947 builder of lightplanes, all with 75-hp Mathis or Regnier engines, including small run of ASO.1070 Grifon.

Airspeed Oxford I (built by Percival), 1942.

Airtech (Canada). Airtech Canada specializes in re-engining Otter and Beaver aircraft with Polish (Soviet design) engines.

Airtech (International). Joint company formed 50/50 in 1980 by CASA of Spain and IPTN of Indonesia to build CN-235 twin-turboprop transport.

Air Technical Bureau (Taiwan). Branch of Nationalist Chinese AF, predecessor of AIDC, which built original Pazmany PL-1 1968.

Air Tractor (USA). Olney, Texas, company founded 1978 by Leland Snow (*see* Snow). Major producer of piston and turboprop ag-aircraft.

Air Transport (USA). Air Transport Manufacturing Co. was active 1928–36 with mainly high-wing monoplanes with 1, 2 and 3 engines. Major type was B-6, with 2 engines on low stub wings.

AIS (Russia). Aviatsionnaya Ispitatelnaya Stantsiya, Morskaya Vedomstva, naval air test station, founded late 1916 at Petrograd Poly Inst., with seaplane base at Krestovsky Island. Engineers P.A. Shishkov and Sushenkov planned many aircraft, 2 being built. Shishkov produced torpedo carrier of Farman pusher-biplane type, 130-hp Clerget, made several flights of over 1 hour August 1917. Aist (t added to give word meaning stork) 2-seat seaplane, with 150-hp Sunbeam and 1 fixed and 1 pivoted machine-gun, complete autumn 1917.

AISA (Spain). Aeronautica Industrial SA established Madrid 1923. Built early Cierva autogyros, and subsequently many aeroplanes, including H.M. series of light trainers. AISA built Iberavia I.11 and I.115, in 1952 taking over Iberavia design department and building all 200 I.115 (E.6) trainers for Spanish AF. Last original AISA design unsuccessful GN autogyro (1982). Today shares in 18 programmes of others.

AJEP (UK). A.J.E. Perkins attempted 1974–7 to market Wittman Tailwind in kit form.

AJI (USA). American Jet Industries founded at Van Nuys 1951 to modify and repair transports; Turbo Star 402 and 414 are Cessna conversions with Allison 250 turboprops, and T-610 Super Pinto (1968) was Temco TT-1 Pinto strengthened for GE J85 engine. In 1978 purchased Grumman

American and became Gulfstream American of California (*see* Gulfstream).

AK (USSR). Alexandrov and Kalinin designed Soviet Union's first transport, AK-1, flown March 1924.

Akaflieg (W. Germany, Germany). All over Germany major universities and even technical high schools have aircraft design organizations, usually concerned mainly with sailplanes. Akaflieg in full is usually Akademische Fliegergruppe. Among biggest have been Aachen, Berlin, Braunschweig (Brunswick), Darmstadt, Esslingen, Hannover, Karlsruhe, München (Munich) and Stuttgart.

Akasamitra (Indonesia). Akasamitra Homebuilt Aircraft Association is concerned mainly with ultralights, but in 1984 produced prototype of ST-220 side-by-side trainer in 180-hp class.

Akron (USA). Akron Aircraft Co. was established at Ohio city of that name to produce Funk B light 2-seater. Became Funk Aircraft 1941.

AKYa. Aviatsionnaya Korporatisiya Yak: *see* Yakovlev.

Alagi KKUD (Hungary). Principal 1950–60 glider works, full title Alagi Központi Kisérleti üzem Dunakeszi, built 1 ultralight.

Al-Aire: *See* Talleres (Argentina).

Alan Muntz (UK). Formed at Heston 1937, chief designer L.E. Baynes, numerous often radical projects but only aircraft built was Youngman–Baynes high-lift research derivative of Proctor.

Alaparma (Italy). Company formed by Capt. Adriano Mantelli and Livio Agostini 1945 to produce tiny AM-8 pusher designed and flown by Mantelli 1942. AM.10 Tucano and AP.65 and 75 Baldo were refined versions.

Alaska (USA). Albuquerque, NM, company which in 1962 purchased rights to Luscombe Silvaire and also hoped to market improved version.

Albatros (Germany). One of chief aircraft companies in pre-1930 Germany, **Albatros Werke**

AG founded 1909 at Berlin-Johannisthal. Built Antoinettes under licence, but appointment of Ernst Heinkel as chief designer in 1913 led to very important 2-seat biplanes in B-series (reconnaissance) and C-series (general purpose fighter/attack). A different team under Dipl.-Ing. Robert Thielen produced single-seat fighters (D-series) noteworthy for their beautifully streamlined fuselages. Nearly all Albatros combat types were made in large numbers, often by several companies. Smaller numbers made of G-series bombers and J-series armoured close-support aircraft. Production of Albatros designs exceeded 10,300 by end of 1918. Work then began on civil types, numbered L 58–L 102. They included trainers, tourers and L 72 light transport and twin-engined L 73 and Jupiter-engined 73a used on international routes by Luft Hansa. New company, **Albatros-Flugzeugwerke GmbH**, formed 1925. In September 1931 Albatros was merged into Focke-Wulf Flugzeugbau GmbH in Bremen, Berlin works becoming Focke-Wulf Johannisthal. *See also* Memel.

Albert (France). Avions Albert formed 1926 to produce TE-1 (Tellier-Duhamel) light monoplane.

Albert Rinne: *See* Rinne.

Albree (USA). George Norman Albree designed numerous aircraft from 1912 characterized by no controls except ailerons. Most famous was Pigeon Fraser monoplane fighter: *see* Pigeon.

Alco (USA). Allison Airplane Co. established 1920 to build Allison Junior Coupe single-seater.

Alcock (UK). Flt. Lt. J.W. (later Sir John) Alcock designed and built Alcock Scout when serving at Mudros 1917, using parts of Sopwith Pup and Triplane. Taken prisoner by Turks, but in his absence Alcock Scout was flown successfully.

Alcor (USA). After collapse and sale of original Lockheed (as part of Detroit Aircraft) in 1932, Allan H. Lockheed formed Alhambra, later Alcor Aircraft Corp. Built small numbers of 2 fast transports, high-wing DUO-6 and low-wing, retractable-gear C-6. Novel feature of both was 2 250-hp Menasco engines side by side in wide nose, propellers splayed out to miss each other.

Alenia (Italy). Aerospace/electronics giant

Albatros W.4 for N Sea station defence, 1916.

formed by 20 December 1990 merger of Aeritalia and Selenia, both members of investment group IRI-Finmeccanica. Four divisions: Alenia Settore Aeronautico, Alenia Spazio, Alenia Sistemi Difesa and Alenia Sistemi Civili. Major own-design aircraft programme is G222 (USAF C-27A); others include EFA (21%), Tornado (15%), AMX (46.5%), ATR (50%), Falcon 2000, A321, Euroflag, Eurofar, Regioliner and AAA. Major modification of 707, DC-8, DC-10 and Nanchang A-5, assembly, test and support of AV-8B-Plus for Marinavia. Owns 60% Dee Howard and Partenavia, 25% Aeronautica Macchi and 22% FMA.

Alexander (USA). In 1924 Alexander Film Co., producer of short movies, found OX-5 Swallow such asset that they entered aircraft business, Alexander Aircraft being formed Denver, April 1925. August 1925 produced Eaglerock, 3/4-seat biplane (OX-5) designed by Daniel Noonan, later assisted by Albert W. Mooney. There followed 455 of over 30 variations by 1928, when moved to Colorado Springs. Produced redesigned A-series Eaglerocks with Whirlwind, Salmson, Hispano, Siemens and Comet engines. Despite 'largest commercial aircraft factory in USA' failed 1931, becoming Aircraft Mechanics.

Alexandrov–Kalinin: *See* AK.

Alexeyev (USSR). Semyon Mikhailovich Alexeyev (also written Alekseyev) was a chief designer for S.A. Lavochkin before setting up his own OKB (experimental construction bureau) in

1946. Produced series of twin-jet fighters and all-weather interceptors (I-211 to 215) and I-218 pusher armoured attack aircraft of 1948. Final type was Aircraft 150, based on Junkers EF 150 twin-jet heavy bomber. German designer Baade used this as basis of later passenger aircraft Type 152.

Alhambra (USA). Alhambra Airport & Air Transport Co. was original name of Allen Lockheed's company after failure of Lockheed (Detroit) in 1931. Became Alcor 1935.

Ali Viberti: *See* Viberti.

All American (USA). Small Long Beach company which in 1945 produced Model 10A Ensign side-by-side low-wing lightplane.

Allenbaugh (USA). Goodyear (under 200 cu in) racer of 1947.

Allgaier (Germany). Sepp Allgaier produced sailplanes after second World War, including H 30TS with BMW 8025 auxiliary turbojet.

Allgemeine: *See* Memel; ATG.

Alliance (International). General name for programme of study for future SST, more correctly SCTICSG (Supersonic Commercial Transport International Co-operation Study Group). Members (1992): Aerospatiale, Alenia, Boeing, British Aerospace, Deutsche Airbus, McDonnell Douglas and Society of Japanese Aerospace Companies (STDC).

Alliance (UK). Alliance Aeroplane Co. of Acton, London, took over Ruffy Arnell Baumann in 1919. Only original design P.2 Seabird with intended 21-hour endurance.

Allied (USA). Allied Aviation Corporation at Cockeysville, Maryland, produced LRA-1 troop-carrying amphibious glider 1943, followed in 1945 by Trimmer 3-seat twin-engined amphibian.

Allison (USA). Allison Division of General Motors delivered first Allison Convair re-engined with Model 501 turboprops in 1960. Subsequently designated Convair 580, deliveries continued until in 1969 programme was passed to Pacific Airmotive. Resumed 1984 as stretched Turbo Flagship ATF580S, plus conversions of

Beech Bonanza and T-34 Mentor with Allison 250 turboprop.

Alon (USA). Incorporated at Wichita 1963 to produce A-2 Aircoupe taken over from Ercoupe. In 1966 flew Alon Four or A-4 4-seater.

Alpavia (France). Factory at Gap (Hautes-Alpes) built Jodel D.117 1959–62, followed by Fournier RF 3 and RF 4, rights for latter being transferred to Sportavia in 1966.

Alpha (Poland). Aircraft branch of Marko-Elektronic formed to build Jaroslav Janowski's fifth design, glassfibre J-5, marketed in kit form; US distributor Alpha/USA Aviation.

Alpha (USA). Alpha Aviation produced Type 11D lightplane 1971.

Alter (Germany). Ludwig Alter-werke was active at Darmstadt 1915–18, prototypes including A.1 fighter.

Alula (UK). Not a company but name of patented wing design: *see* Commercial.

AM (France). In 1965 Ecole Nationale Supérieure d'Arts et Métiers at Cluny began considering a trainer. Result was AM-69 Georges Payre (6 May 1973), tandem wood monoplane. Planned metal version not built.

AMA (Hungary). Allgemeine Maschinen Aktiengesellschaft, Budapest, built Fokker fighters and various engines 1917–19.

Ambrosini (Italy). Formed 1934 as SAI (Società Aeronautica Italiana), becoming part of Ambrosini industrial group same year. Long series of mainly sporting and training aircraft designed by Sergio Stefanutti, most famous and successful being variants of S.7 high-speed tandem-seater (1939), including Supersette with 350-hp Gipsy Queen (1952). Out of normal rut, Sagittario swept-wing jet (1953) developed into transonic Sagittario II (1956) and ultimately Aerfer Ariete. *See also* SAI.

AME (Spain). Aeronáutica Militar Espanola formed 1916 at air force HQ at Cuatro Vientos, produced AME VI.A derived from Bristol Fighter, built 20 by 1927.

Ameco-Hawk (USA). Holding company Ameco

Ambrosini S. Sagittario, 1953.

joined Hawk International in 1989 to continue development of GafHawk turboprop utility freighter.

American: *See* American Eagle Aircraft.

American Aeronautical Corporation (USA). Formed 1928 Long Island City to build Savoia S.55 and S.56. Taken over by Dayton 1931.

American Aircraft (USA). American Aircraft Corp. unveiled Penetrator gunship conversion of Bell UH-1 December 1991 at Rialto, CA.

American Aircraft Co. (USA). Formed 1939 to take over manufacture of S-1B from Security.

American Airmotive (USA). Miami company which in 1954 marketed high-lift wings for Stearman ag-conversions, from 1957 selling complete rebuilds as NA-75.

American Airplane (USA). American Airplane Co. built single-engined high-wing monoplane transports, notably 10-passenger Pilgrim 1932.

American Aviation Corporation (USA). Incorporated 1950 at Freeland, Michigan, to market and support former Republic Seabee; merged into Downer 1960.

American Aviation Corporation (USA). Formed at Cleveland 1964 to produce AA-1 Yankee (Bede BD-1) 2-seater, other products later. Merged 1 January 1973 into Grumman American Aviation (later Gulfstream Aerospace).

American Aviation Industries (USA). Formed in California 1985 to re-engine JetStar, named FanStar.

American Eagle Aircraft (USA). Formed Kansas City 1925 to build American Eaglet, first 2-seater to be US certificated. Failed 1932, merged with Lincoln as **American Eagle-Lincoln**, then succession of purchasers attempted to restore operations 1945–65.

American Eagle A-129 dual-control 3-seater, December 1928.

American Gyro AG-4 Crusader, April 1935.

American General (USA). In June 1989 this Mississippi firm purchased from Gulfstream Aerospace rights to latter's light aircraft (Lynx, Cougar, Cheetah, Tiger). Cougar licence sold to TSPA.

American Gyro (USA). This company built 4 light aircraft, ending with twin-boom AG-4 Crusader 1935.

American Helicopter (USA). Company formed 1947 to produce light helicopters powered by tip ramjets. Purchased 1954 to form Helicopter Division of Fairchild.

American Jet Industries: *See* AJI.

American Multiplane (USA). Herbert F. Johns set up American Multiplane Co., Bath, NY, to build giant aircraft with 2 400-hp Liberty pusher engines on centre group of triplane wings,

preceded by biplane wings immediately in front and second biplane wings immediately to rear. Made hops 1919, then taken to Langley Field where alleged to have flown.

Ames (USA). Ames Industrial Corp. of Bohemia, NY, held US licence for French Microturbo small turbojets, and was awarded contract by NASA to build AD-1 (Ames/Dryden) slew-wing research aircraft (2 TRS 18-046 turbojets), first flown December 1979.

AMF (UK). AMF Microflight Ltd are in production with factory-built Chevron 2-32 side-by-side microlight trainers; 34 delivered by March 1992.

AMI (USA). Aero Modifications International produce stretched turboprop DC-3s.

Amiot (France). Formed as SECM (Société d'Emboutissage et de Constructions Mécaniques) by Félix Amiot at Colombes (Paris) 1916. There followed 20 years of unremitting development of 54 major designs, starting with trainers and tourers and in 1928 including Amiot 122 'Fat Julie', giant single-engined biplane bomber (nearly 100 built). In 1939 obsolescent Amiot 143 was most numerous French medium bomber, but beautiful Amiot 354 also in production. In 1940 Amiot became part of Junkers empire, assigned Ju 52 fuselage production, Colombes works in 1945 becoming Ateliers Aéronautiques de Colombes.

AMJ (Spain). Aviones Metallicos Junkers set up after 1919 to build the F13 and a handful of other types.

Amphibions Inc. (USA). Formed in Depression 1932 at Garden City, NY, built Privateer 2-seat

Amiot 143 bomber prototype, August 1934.

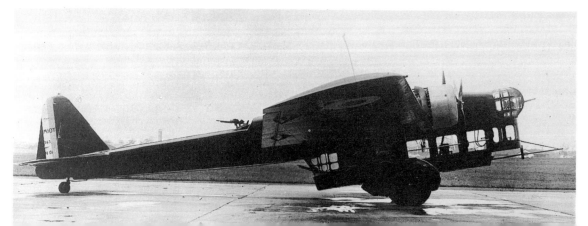

AMX (Italian single-seat version), 1985.

amphibian. *See* Spencer, 1st entry.

Amtorg (USSR). Organization formed to manage licensed US products, handled design and production of GST based on Consolidated 28 (PBY) 1936–43.

AMX (International). AMX International Ltd manages AMX close-support aircraft, work split being: Alenia (Italy) 46.5%, Aermacchi (Italy) 23.8% and Embraer (Brazil) 29.7%.

Anahuac (Mexico). Fabrica de Aviones Anahuac formed 1966 to produce Tauro ag-aircraft, initially 300 hp and finally (to 1978) 350 hp.

Anatra (Russia). Formed 1913 at Odessa by A.A. Anatra, initially to produce and modify Farman, Voisin, Nieuport and Morane aircraft. French designer E.A. Déscamps assisted design of Anatra D or Anadé; flown December 1915, variants mass-produced. Anatra VI (Voisin Ivanov) 1916, followed by Anatra DE twin pusher and Anadva Type VKh twin tractor designed by V.N. Khioni.

Anbo (Lithuania). Established at army factory (*see* Karo) outside Kaunas 1927 by Col A. Gustaitis, who designed series of monoplanes. Anbo I and II low-wing sport/training aircraft, Anbo III parasol advanced trainer, and Anbo IV (1932) parasol reconnaissance aircraft with 640-hp Bristol Pegasus. From IV derived 41, major production type. Anbo V and VI were trainers, and VIII a low-wing reconnaissance bomber.

Anderson (USA). PanAm 747 Capt. Earl Anderson designed and flew (1969) EA-1 Kingfisher 2-seat amphibian, marketed as homebuilt. *See* Warner.

Anderson-Greenwood (USA). Formed 1941, suspended during war, reopened 1945 and AG-14 flown 1 October 1947. Two-seat pusher, 5 built.

Andreasson (Sweden/USA). Bjorn Andreasson was wartime designer at AB Flygindustri sailplane works. In 1944 designed and flew BA-4 ultralight biplane, updated as BA-4B for home construction. In 1950s in San Diego designed and flew BA-6 low-wing single-seater and BA-7 shoulder-wing side-by-side sport/trainer, later produced as MFI, later Saab MFI-9/Safari/Supporter. Following BA-11 200-hp aerobatic biplane, Andreasson joined Malmo Flygindustri as chief designer.

ANEC (UK). Air Navigation and Engineering Co. was post-war (1919) name of wartime Blériot and Spad Manufacturing Co. at Addlestone, Surrey. In 1923–6 produced ANEC I high-wing ultralight, ANEC II high-wing 2-seater, ANEC III transport biplane and ANEC IV Missel Thrush 2-seat biplane.

ANF: *See* Mureaux.

Angkatan: *See* LIPNUR.

Anglin (USA). Anglin Engineering, N. Carolina, had by 1990 sold over 1,000 sets of drawings and

Ansaldo (Fiat) A 115 for reconnaissance, 1926.

50 kits for Spacewalker I, now joined by 2-seat Mk II.

Angus (UK). Aquila low-wing monoplane ultralight built 1931.

Ansaldo (Italy). Famed shipbuilding firm of Genoa, which was asked by Government 1916 to produce new fighter. Design of SV by Savoia and Verduzio (soon joined by Rosatelli), called SV.5 at first flight at Grosseto (March 1917), soon changed to SVA.5. Fastest fighter of its day, but inability to build in Liguria resulted in discussion with SIT, Turin, as result of which SIT became Cantieri Aeronautico Ansaldo. Built over 350 SVA, plus over 2,000 other SVAs and A.1 Balilla, and 299 A.300 recon-bombers. Plage & Laskiewicz built SVA and A.300 under licence. Merged Fiat 1925, losing identity.

ANT (USSR). Designation of all early designs by A.N. Tupolev, last being ANT-69 (Tu-8) of 1946.

Antoinette (France). Company formed 1900 by Jules Gastambide and named after his daughter. Designer Léon Levasseur created excellent water-cooled V-8 engine, used 1903 in graceful monoplane which failed to fly. Subsequently Gastambide-Mengin flew briefly February 1908, Antoinette II in August 1908, Antoinette III in September and Antoinette IV November. Antoinette IV a graceful classic design, followed by V, VI and VII, but company in liquidation 30 November 1911.

Antoni (Italy). Società Italiana Brevetti Antoni built variable-camber aircraft 1923.

Antonov (USSR, Ukraine). Oleg K. Antonov designed and built gliders from 1924, later designs becoming famous; RF (Red Front) series were most important competition sailplanes pre-1941 and over 2,000 built of US-3 primary. Over 400 A-7 military assault gliders built 1942, followed

Antonov An-124 (Volga–Dniepr), 26 December 1982.

by many hundreds of all-metal post-war sailplanes with butterfly tails. Powered aircraft included LEM-2 (OKA-33) light transport (1937) with payload of 2,822 lb on 100 hp, and OKA-38 derived from Fieseler Storch. SKh-1 (31 August 1947) led to An-2 multirole biplane of which over 18,500 produced in 5 countries. An-8 of 1955 was USSR's first large turboprop airlift transport, 100 built. Led to 4-turboprop An-10 series (over 200 built) and military An-12 (1,247). An-14 Pchelka light STOL transport (200-plus) led to An-28 produced by PZL-Mielec in Poland. Total production of An-24 and -26 twin-turboprop transports (not including China) 2,735, plus small numbers of An-30 (123) and 32 (231). Successors are An-72 and -74 twin-turbofan STOL transports now in production. First flown February 1965, An-22 Antei 4-turboprop airlifter was first Antonov giant (66 built). Four-turbofan An-124 flown 1982, 42 built to 1993. Six-engined derivative An-225 Mriya flown 1988, world's heaviest and most powerful aircraft of any kind, 1 only. An-70T military airlifter with STOL high-lift wing and 4 tractor propfans to fly early 1993. An-38, stretched and more powerful An-28, also flies 1993. An-180, 164 passengers with twin tractor D-27 propfans, flies 1995. An-218 widebody; *see* A-DY. Antonov died 4 April 1984, succeeded as head of **ANTKI O.K. Antonov** by Pyotr V. Balabuyev.

AOI (Egypt). Arab Organization for Industrialization set up November 1975 to provide basis for military industry. Three of 4 subsidiaries are aerospace: ABDCo, Arab British Dynamics; ABECo, Arab British Engine; and ABHCo, Arab British Helicopter. Planned production of Lynx and its Gem engine did not take place, and virtually all Egyptian aerospace production has been French, apart from Brazilian EMB-312 Tucano.

Applegate (USA). Applegate Amphibians built A-3 in 1945, followed by Applegate and Weyant Dart 2-seat landplane 1946.

Aqua (USA). Aquaflight Aircraft formed 1946 to build light amphibians, Aqua I (2x 125-hp) and Aqua II (2 × 190-hp), both 6-seaters.

Arado (Germany). After First World War Hugo Stinnes took over Werft Warnemünde for non-aero production. Meeting Ing. Walther Rethel in 1924, he decided to produce aircraft, forming **Arado Handelsgesellschaft** 1925. Next 8 years saw 15 prototype trainer and sporting aircraft, but in 1933 firm reorganized as **Arado Flugzeugwerke**, under control of RLM (air ministry), with Walter Blume as chief engineer (Rethel went to BFW). Then followed succession of aircraft produced in quantity, plus enormous production of such types as Bf 109, Fw 190, Ju 88 and He 177. Chief of company's own designs were: Ar 65 fighter biplane, Ar 66 biplane trainer, Ar 68 fighter biplane, Ar 95 biplane seaplane, Ar 96 advanced trainer, Ar 196 seaplane, Ar 232 transport, Ar 234 jet reconnaissance bomber, Ar 240 heavy fighter/reconnaissance aircraft and Ar 396 trainer, which became SIPA S.10. *See also* Blume.

Arbeits . . . , etc: *See* ARGE.

ARC (USA). ARC Special, 1946 racer designed by Art Chester, butterfly tail.

Arctic (USA). Arctic Aviation, at Anchorage, Alaska, has since 1979 produced improved versions of 1940 Interstate S1A, main version being S1B2 Arctic Tern.

Arado Ar 234C-3, abandoned 1945.

ARDC (USA). Aeronautical Research and Development Corp., based at Cambridge (Boston), bought rights to Brantly helicopters from Learjet in 1969. Intensive marketing and model development ceased 1970 when rights passed to Brantly Operators.

Area de Material Cordoba: *See* Fábrica Mílitar de Aviones (FMA).

ARGE (W. Germany). Several Arbeitsgemeinschaft (work group) partnerships were formed for specific programmes: **Arge 91** (Dornier, Heinkel, Messerschmitt) built Fiat G91R/3; **Arge Nord**, or Arge 104 Nord (Hamburger, Weser, Focke-Wulf, Fokker and Aviolanda) built F-104G; **Arge Süd**, or Arge 104 Süd (Messerschmitt, Heinkel, Dornier, Siebel) also built F-104G; **Arge Transall** (Blume, Hamburger, VFW (ex-Weser) and Nord-Aviation of France) built Transall C-160.

Argonaut (USA). Argonaut Aircraft built small series 1937–40 of Pirate 3-seat amphibian.

Ariel (USA). Ariel Aircraft Inc. formed by Glenn A. Stearman to build Ariel Models A (65 hp), B (75 hp) and C (80 hp) side-by-side low-wing cabin tourer. Work halted January 1942, company renamed Stearman Aviation Inc., Enid, OK, February 1942. Did not resume production.

Arkansas (USA). Arkansas Aircraft Co. formed Little Rock, December 1926, built first of 93 Command-Aire 3-seat biplanes January 1928. Designer Albert Voellmecke was ex-Heinkel, and he brought rights to Heinkel HD 40 (not taken up).

Arkhangyelski (USSR). A.A. Arkhangyelski led design of many early ANT (Tupolev) aircraft. When his chief was arrested he became *de facto* head of Tupolev OKB, and 1937–42 managed several major programmes, one of which (Ar-2 derived from SB-2) was designated for him. Other types were MMN and SBB, also advanced developments of SB-2. On Tupolev's release became first deputy designer, leading structure of all early Tu turboprops and jets.

ARL: *See* Aero Research.

Armella-Senemaud (France). Emerged at 1934 Paris airshow with 4-seat amphibian with twin pusher Gipsy Major, possibly not flown.

Armstrong Whitworth (UK). Merger in 1897 of rival engineering and shipbuilding firms resulted in Sir W.G. Armstrong, Whitworth, the comma later being forgotten. In 1912 declined to build Avro aircraft, and also failed to agree with Sir George White (British & Colonial) that its Italian subsidiary should make Bristol aircraft for Italy, but AW did agree to make ABC aero engines and Leitner hollow-steel propellers. In June 1913 Capt. I.F. Fairbairn-Crawford appointed manager of new Aerial Department, assisted by Dutch Frederick Koolhoven as designer. Built BE.2a, 2b and 2c at former skating rink at Gosforth (Tyneside), while Koolhoven designed FK.1 and flew it September 1914. FK.3 designed 1915 as improvement over BE.2c, 150 built plus 350 by Hewlett & Blondeau. FK.8 flown May 1916 as reconnaissance and army co-op, 1,652 built by November 1918. Numerous FK prototypes, often unconventional, until Koolhoven

Armstrong Whitworth FK.8 'Big Ack', December 1916.

went to BAT 1917, after which AW built 250 Bristol Fighters. In 1915–19 AW designed and built rigid and non-rigid airships at Barlow, Selby. Purchased Siddeley Deasey February 1919 and moved to Coventry, forming Armstrong Siddeley Motors and **Sir W.G. Armstrong Whitworth Aircraft**. Design team under John Lloyd initially at Parkside, factory at Whitley airfield, later joined by bigger plant at Baginton, all in or near Coventry. Staple products Siskin fighter (485) and Atlas multirole (446), plus trivial numbers of biplane and monoplane airliners for Imperial Airways. All fabric-covered metal, but Lloyd went all-metal with large AW.27 Ensign (14 built) and AW.38 Whitley bomber (1,814). AW.41 Albemarle was designed to avoid strategic materials, 600 built near Gloucester by *ad hoc* group called '**A.W. Hawksley**', AW having in 1935 been founder member of Hawker Siddeley Group. Also built 1,328 Lancasters and 281 Lincolns, and managed factories making Stirlings and Barracudas. Post-war took on all development and production of Hawker Sea Hawk (489) and Gloster Meteor night fighters (547), and built 133 Gloster Javelins. Own designs included 2 AW.52 experimental jet flying wings, 2 AW.55 Apollo turboprop airliners, followed by 16 civil and 56 military AW.650/660 Argosy freighters. AW.681, later HS.681, jet V/STOL freighter never completed. Mergers resulted in Whitworth Gloster in 1961 and Avro Whitworth in 1963, name vanishing into Hawker Siddeley Aviation 1 April 1965.

Arnoux (France). René Arnoux built at least 5 aircraft 1909–22, last being tailless Coupe Deutsch racer.

Arpin (UK). M.B. Arpin & Co. of West Drayton built A-1 2-seat pusher monoplane and flew it 1938.

Arrow (UK). Arrow Aircraft of Leeds built Active I single-seat sporting biplane 1931.

Arrow (USA). Arrow Aircraft & Motor Corp. set up 1928 at Lincoln, Nebraska. Over next 10 years at least 9 basic lightplane types, notably Sport and Sport Pursuit biplanes, and Model F and enclosed-cockpit G monoplanes with Ford V-8 car engines.

Arsenal (France). Arsenal de l'Aéronautique set up as state enterprise by 1936 nationalization of defence industries. Installed in factory at Villacoublay, expanded during war to Villeurbanne (Lyon) in then-unoccupied zone, and after war to main plant at Châtillon-sous-Bagneux (Paris). First major programme VG.30 light fighter, initials from director Vernisse and designer Galtier. This was followed by powerful fighters VG.31 to 39, all excellent but too late for 1940 campaign. VG.39 best fighter in France in June 1940. Design then in hand of VB.10 fighter bomber with contraprops driven by two HS12Z engines in tandem (7 July 1945). In 1939 began construction of Arsenal–Delanne 10 tandem-wing 2-seat fighter (18 October 1941). Post-war types included VG.70 jet research aircraft, VG.90 naval jet fighter, O.101 tandem-seat aerodynamic testbed, and series of sailplanes. Became SFECMAS 1952.

Arts et Métiers: *See* AM.

Arsenal O-101 for aerodynamic research, 1948.

Arup S-2 at 1933 Chicago races.

Artyumov (USSR). Mikhail Artyumov, usually partnered by Viktor Timofeyev, produced series of ultralights 1971–82.

Arup (USA). Arup Manufacturing Co. famed for series of 4 tailless monoplanes with wing of D-shape (straight leading edge) 1933–5.

ARV (UK). Land-speed record holder Richard Noble formed ARV Aviation 1983 to produce Super 2 lightplane, first flown 1985. Became Island Aircraft 1984.

Arvin: *See* Calspan.

ASC: *See* Aerial Service Corp.

ASI: *See* AASI.

ASJA (Sweden). AB Svenska Järnvägsverkstäderna was one of 2 Swedish manufacturers 1928–35. Took over Jaktfalk fighter programme, made Douglas 8A-5.

Asocíación Argentina: *See* AVEX.

ASRO: *See* Siemetzki.

Astra-Wright dual Type C, 1911.

ASTA (Australia). Aerospace Technologies of Australia formed 1986 to succeed GAF (Government Aircraft Factories) at Fishermen's Bend, Melbourne. Work includes F/A-18, PC-9, Black Hawk, 747, 757, 777, MD-80, MD-11, A320/330/340, CFM56 nacelle and assembly/test of SH-60 Seahawk.

Astec (USA). Advanced Systems Technology formed 1971 to undertake aerodynamic improvement, later converting Citation bizjets into Eagle SP.

Asteria (Italy). Founded about November 1909 at Via Salbertrand, Turin, by Francesco Darbesio and Ing. Origoni (initially in factory of Darbesio's Taurinia motor firm). First aircraft resembled Farman biplane. Nos. 2, 3 and 4 followed, all sound and strong pusher biplanes (without front elevators); No. 3 saw active service in Libya. MB 2-seat monoplane (May 1913) was last built by company.

Astra (France). Astra Société de Constructions Aéronautiques was major producer of balloons and non-rigid airships up to 1920. Licence to make Wright Flyers (1909) led to derived Astra-

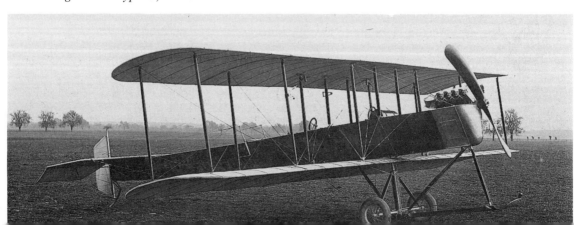

Wright C (commercial) and CM (military) biplanes, latter more powerful (usually 100-hp Renault). Both available on floats. Merged Nieuport 1921.

Astra (Romania). Chief national producer 1920 until after 1927. Built licensed designs and AS (Astra-Şeşefski) reconnaissance biplane.

ATAC (USA). Advanced Technology Aircraft Co. of Hanford, California, developed Model 480 Predator from Rutan 59; Rutan Scaled Composites built prototype, flown September 1984.

Atalante (France). GB.10 light 2-seater built 1946.

ATEL: *See* Aviation Traders.

Ateliers Aéronautiques de Colombes (France). Former Amiot company, nationalized on liberation 1945, continued building Ju 52/3m as AAC.1.

Ateliers Aéronautiques de la Côte d'Emeraude (France). Based at Dinard-Pleurtuit, built Piel Emeraude under licence.

Ateliers Aéronautiques d'Issy les Moulineaux (France). Former Avions Caudron-Renault, nationalized on liberation 1945, continued building Goëland and sailplanes.

Ateliers Aéronautiques de Suresnes (France). Former Farman company, nationalized on liberation 1945.

Ateliers de Constructions Aéronautiques Belges (Belgium). Formed Brussels 1933 to produce aircraft designated LACAB.

Ateliers de Constructions Aéronautiques Zeebrugge: *See* Zeebrugge.

ATG (Germany, W. Germany). Long-established Allgemeine Transportanlagen Gesellschaft Maschinenbau built transport equipment, but took over moribund DFW after 1918. Leipzig-Lindenthal factory transferred 1933 to Ju 52/3m production, Leipzig-Mockau added 1935, both adding Ju 88 and 188 production. In 1952 merged with Siebel to form SIAT.

ATL (China). Based in Hong Kong, Aircraft Technology Ltd is a major exporting organization of Chinese government (CATIC 40%), partnered by Lucas Aerospace (40%) and HK business interests (20%).

Atlantic Aircraft (USA). North American subsidiary of Fokker. Previously called Netherlands Aircraft Manufacturing Company of America, Atlantic Aircraft Corp. started operations at Hasbrouck Heights (Teterboro, NJ) in May 1924. Manager was R.B.C. Noorduyn (later planemaker in his own right), and though most early production was of established Dutch designs, Noorduyn designed Universal single-engined transport in 1925 which led to completely new products. One was Super Universal, also made in several versions by Nakajima. Swelling backlog required new factory at nearby Passaic and another at Wheeling, W. Virginia. Major types F.10, F.14, C-2, T.II and III, O-27 and F.32. Became Fokker Aircraft and bought by General Motors 1929, becoming successively General Aviation, North American and Rockwell.

Atlas (S. Africa). Atlas Aircraft Corp. of South Africa (Pty) Ltd formed 1963. Main facilities at Kempton Park manage aircraft, missile and engine programmes, major work being licensed-production of Impala (based on Aermacchi 326), manufacture of major parts for Mirage III and Mirage F1, and development and production of air-to-air missiles and Smart bombs. Original aircraft projects include: C4M Kudu STOL utility transport; XH-1 Alpha gunship helicopter based on Alouette III; CSH-2 Rooivalk combat-support helicopter derived from Puma, and Oryx and Gunship Puma conversions; family of Cheetah aircraft derived from Mirage III; and (with Aerotek) NGT turboprop trainer. *See also* Simera.

Atlas (USA). Atlas Aircraft Co. built H-10 all-metal 4-seater 1949.

ATR (International). Avions de Transport Régional is 50/50 Groupement d'Intérêt Economique formed by Aerospatiale of France and Aeritalia (now Alenia) of Italy, formally established 5 February 1982. First products ATR 42 and 72.

Aubert (France). First World War pilot Paul Aubert established **Aubert-Aviation** at Buc

ATR 72, 27 October 1988.

(Versailles) 1932, and produced prototype PA-20 Cigale side-by-side high-wing trainer 1936. In 1938 became **Avions Paul Aubert**, with large contracts halted by collapse 1940. PA-20 destroyed but design modified post-war as 4-seat PA-204, available to 1959 with various engines 140–180 hp.

Auster (UK). Having produced large numbers of wartime aircraft called Austers, Taylorcraft Aeroplanes (England) was replaced in March 1946 by Auster Aircraft Ltd, simultaneously moving from Thurmaston, Leicester, to nearby Rearsby. Production continued with large numbers of military AOP.6, T.7 and AOP.9, and civil J-1 Autocrat, J-2 Arrow, J-4, J-5B Autocar, J-5F Aiglet Trainer and variants. Final product was D-series (180 hp Lycoming), which continued briefly after company taken over by Beagle 1960.

Austin (UK). In 1916 Austin Motor Co. produced prototype Austin-Ball fighter. In 1917 set up aircraft design department. Two major products, both flown during war: AFT.3 Osprey triplane fighter, and Greyhound 2-seat biplane fighter, both excellent aircraft. In 1919 3 Whippet sporting single-seaters, concluding 1920 with 160 hp 2-seat Kestrel.

Australian Aircraft Consortium (Australia). AAC formed 1982 by Commonwealth Aircraft Corp., Government Aircraft Factories and Hawker de Havilland to produce A10 Wamira basic trainer for RAAF. In 1985 HDH bought out GAF share and acquired CAC as subsidiary, AAC ceasing to

be needed (and RAAF picked PC-9 anyway).

Australian Autogyro (Australia). Ted Minty began construction of Skyhook single-seat autogyro 1975, forming company 1984. Several variants and commercial sales.

Austrian Aviatik: *See* Aviatik.

AUT (Italy). Aeronautica Umbra Trojani, formed by Muzio Macchi 1935 at Foligno, south of Florence, built S.M.79 but never achieved major success with own designs despite several adequate prototypes. Best-known, AUT.18 fighter (1936), 1,000-hp Fiat radial. Remarkable MB.902 fighter (1942) had 2 1,475-hp DB605 in fuselage driving contraprops on wings, but destroyed before first flight. *See also* Umbra.

Autogiro Company of America (USA). Formed 1930 by Cierva (UK) to sublicense patents to Kellett and Pitcairn. Also dabbled in own AC-35 roadable autogyro.

Automobilove: *See* Mraz.

Avco (USA). Avco, Aviation Corp., formed 1929 when Averill Harriman and Lehman Bros underwrote stock issue, management including Juan Trippe and Sherman Fairchild. In 1931 linked with Cord Corp. to include Auburn, Cord and Duesenberg car companies, Stinson Airplane and Lycoming engines, adding Vultee in 1932 and (through Vultee) Consolidated in 1941. Resulting giant Convair was sold to Atlas Corp. 1947, and last aviation holding, Lycoming, sold to Textron 1984.

AVEX (Argentina). Asociación Argentina de Constructores de Aviones Experimentales is national organization like EAA. Numerous projects, some flying.

AVI (Argentina). Produced AVI 205 prototype 1963; single-engine multirole utility.

Avia (Czechoslovakia). Avia was biggest aircraft firm in country. Full title 'Avia' Akciova Spolecnost pro Prumysl Letecky, part of Skoda group, founded at Prague-Cakovice 1919. For next 7 years outstanding series of over 50 aircraft types designed by BH (Pavel Beneš and Miroslav Hajn). Initially mainly sporting aircraft, trainers and, especially, fighters, high proportion being

Avia BH.11, 1929 (L-BONI).

monoplanes. BH-25 airliner used by CLS and Romanian SNNA. B and H went to Praga 1928, replacement designers being František Novotný and Robert Nebesář. B.534 biplane fighter, first flown August 1933, was outstanding type, 566 built, many for export. B.35 and 135 were advanced monoplane fighters, and B.158 fast bomber. Avia-Fokker F.IX was 3-engined bomber, and B.71 Soviet SB-2 high-speed bomber. Lost identity during Second World War, through LD-40 (1954) and L-60 Brigadyr (1955) were originally given Avia name (because built at Cakovice) and licensed Il-14 transport was called Avia 14, ending 1960.

AVIA: *See* Azionari.

Aviamilano (Italy). Classic F.8 Falco 2-seater designed by Stelio Frati (June 1955), manufacture later passed to Aeromere. P.19 Scricciolo side-by-side trainer (December 1959), staple product along with several sailplanes. Final prototype Frati's F.250 (1964), sold to SIAI-Marchetti and led to SF.260 series. Following managing director's death 1968 firm liquidated, sailplanes going to Caproni-Vizzola.

Avian (Canada). Formed 1959 to develop 2/180 autogyro (spring 1960), failed to reach certification.

Avianautic (France). RA.14 high-wing tandem-seater (40-hp Train), flown early 1946.

Aviaspetstrans (Russia). This consortium was formed 1989 by Myasishchyev OKB and six other organizations to promote local air transport in Arctic and far east regions. First aircraft project (among other activities) is Yamal amphibian, 2t payload, twin turboshaft engines driving 6-blade prop behind tail.

Aviastar (Russia). Previously a mere GAZ (state aviation factory), the Ulyanovsk plant came

Tu-204-120. Tupolev designed it, Aviastar built it, RR power it and Bravia sell it (14 August 1992).

under its own capitalist management in 1991, its 40,000 people making UAIK (Ulyanovsk aviation industrial complex) largest for civil aircraft in the CIS. It markets its products as Aviastar, formed 1990, and is responsible for building Tu-204 and (forcibly transferred from Ukraine) An-124. Work confined to slow An-124 output and tooling for Tu-204 (no orders late 1992). Partner in Bravia and owner of Volga-Dniepr heavy cargo airline.

Aviasud (France). Aviasud Engineering SA at Fréjus is major producer of microlights, such as Mistral variants and Sirocco.

Aviat (CI/USA). Wholly owned by White International, Guernsey, Aviat Inc. of Delaware bought Christen Industries April 1991 and thus full rights to Pitts aircraft. Former Pitts plant at Afton also so far delivered 240 Aviat A-1 Husky utility aircraft.

Aviatechnica (Bulgaria). Set up at Plovdiv 1983 by VMZ as manufacturing and (mainly) R&D subsidiary. Now in partnership with Phönix (Russia), which *see*.

Aviatechnika (Russia). Co-operative design office, K-45 A/R-32, Moscow 103045, is producing over 100 kits annually of its twin-engined 2-seat biplane.

Aviatik (Germany). Automobil und Aviatik AG established Mulhausen 1910 (today called Mulhouse—Alsace-Lorraine now French). Quickly became one of most important constructors in Germany, moving to Freiburg 1914,

with head office and another plant at Leipzig. Austrian subsidiary, Öesterreichische-Ungärische Flugzeugfabrik Aviatik of Vienna, carried out much modification and original design, but built mainly parent firm's aircraft. Main 1914–15 production was B.I. and B.II unarmed reconnaissance 2-seaters. Austrian B.II had overhung control surfaces with large horn balances; Vienna also built B.III. Most important products were 2-seat scouts C.I to C.IX. Single-seat fighters D.II to D.VII remained prototypes, but Austrian D.I made in large numbers. *See also* Berg (Austria); Ö-UF.

Aviation Boosters (USA). Kansas City firm built Skyhopper ultralight monoplane 1945.

Aviation Corporation: *See* Avco.

Aviation Enterprises (UK). Partner of Ilyushin, investing in tooling for production of Il-103 multirole 4/5-seater at North Weald (*c*. August 1993).

Aviation Industries: *See* AIA.

Aviation Scotland (UK). Formed 1991 to take over production and further development of Super 2 from Island Aircraft; office Glasgow, plant Hamilton, marketing Malmesbury, Wilts.

Aviation Specialties International (USA). Produced turbine-engined conversion of S-55 helicopter at Mesa, Arizona, certificated 1971.

Aviation Traders (UK). Aviation Traders (Engineering) Ltd formed 1949 as design, manufactur-

Aviation Traders Accountant, July 1957.

Aviatka MAI-90, 1992,

ing and overhaul arm of larger group. Achieved some success marketing 7-seat conversions of Prentice trainer. Bigger undertaking was ATL.90 Accountant twin-turboprop airliner (9 July 1957). Last original design was ATL.98 Carvair. ATEL produced 22 of these DC-4 rebuilds with high 747-style cockpit above unobstructed interior with nose door for (typically) 5 cars and 22 passengers.

Aviatka (Russia). Joint-stock company created to manage production and marketing of light aircraft designed by MAI, notably MAI-89 light biplane (35 delivered 1992) and MAI-90 competition aerobatic aircraft.

Aviavnito (USSR). Name of design brigade at Kharkov Aviation Institute 1930–37.

Avibras (Brazil). Built A-80 Falcão, attractive 65-hp 2-seater, 1963.

Avid (USA). Avid Aircraft Inc., Caldwell, Idaho, have sold over 1,500 kits of Avid Flyer (600 + assembled 1993). Now marketing quite different Amphibian and 2 other types.

Aviméta (France). Major builder of military aircraft 1925–28, part of Schneider–Creusot armaments empire. Monoplanes predominated, including fighters, bombers and (Type 132, 1927) passenger transport, all featuring Alférium light alloy with corrugated skin.

Avioane SA (Romania). Former IAv Craiova factory, renamed 1991.

Avioes Mignet (Brazil). Set up 1952–4 by Henri Mignet to build advanced versions of 'Flying Flea'.

Aviolanda (Netherlands). Founded 1927 and built Dornier flying-boats and Curtiss Hawk fighters

Aviméta Type 92, May 1927

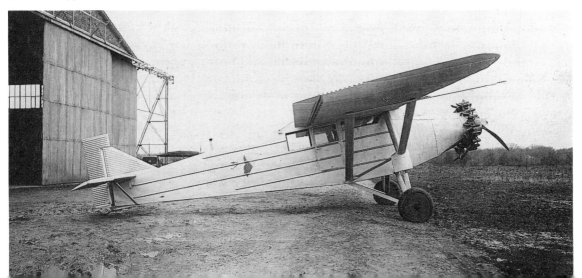

under licence. Major participant in production of Meteor, Hunter, F-104G and NF-5, before merged into Fokker-VFW 1970.

Aviolight (Italy). Formed 1988 by Partenavia and 2 other partners to produce P.86 Mosquito 2-seater. Now also producing more powerful P.66D Delta.

Avion: *See* Northrop.

Aviones de Colombia (Colombia). Cessna dealer 1961, then carried out assembly, now licence builder and also producer of AgTrainer modified locally with side-by-side seats.

Aviones Lockheed-Kaiser (Argentina). Set up 1960 to build LASA-60 utility aircraft.

Avions André Starck: *See* Starck.

Avions Claude Piel: *See* Piel.

Avions Fairey (Belgium). Fairey Aviation sold Firefly and Fox aircraft to Belgian government on condition future orders assembled in Belgium. Factory at Gosselies started March 1931 and SA Belge Avions Fairey registered 12 September 1931. Produced Fantôme and Féroce, while manager E.O. Tips produced lightplanes (see Tipsy). Licence-built Hurricanes, but destroyed 10 May 1940. Rebuilt after war, built Meteor 8 and

Hunter 4 and 6; shared F-104G and Mirage 5 and F1 components, briefly built BN Islander. Became SONACA (Sonaca) 1978.

Avions Fournier: *See* Fournier.

Avions A. Gatard: *See* Gatard.

Avions JDM (France). Established Neuilly 1948 to build Roitelet ultralight.

Avions Jodel: *See* Jodel.

Avions Marcel Dassault: *See* Dassault.

Avions Mudry: *See* Mudry.

Avions Pierre Robin: *See* Robin.

Avions Roger Druine: *See* Druine.

Avions de Transport Régional: *See* ATR.

Avis (Hungary). Avis I, II and III were actually designations of fighter prototypes built 1933–6 by army Central Repair Workshops, Székesfehévár-Sóstó.

Avro (UK). Alliott Verdon Roe was apprenticed at railway works, studied marine engineering, became engineer on merchant ships and then design draughtsman on cars! Won top newspaper

Avro Anson X (built at Yeadon, 1943).

prize 1906 for flying model aircraft, enabling him to build 24-hp man-carrying biplane which made 'hops' at Brooklands 1907. Next built triplane, despite only 9-hp flew well at Lea Marshes summer 1909. Summonsed for 'creating public nuisance', case dropped by Blériot's flight 25 July 1909, magistrates realizing a conviction (trial date 26 July) would not be popular! **A.V. Roe and Co.** registered 1 January 1910, and limited company 3 years later. Works moved from Brooklands to Manchester (Bullseye Braces factory), later vastly expanded at Mather & Platt works at Newton Heath, with (1916) second factory at Hamble, near Southampton; also flying school Brooklands 1910, moved 1911 to Shoreham. Prototypes included Types F and G of 1912, respectively world's first cabin monoplane and cabin biplane. Type 500 tandem trainer biplane of March 1912 led to Type 504 of July 1913, superb basic design and by far most important British trainer pre-1935; numerous versions totalled 8,970 in UK, of which Avro built 3,696 wartime and 630 post-war. Forced 1925 to find new airfield, bought New Hall Farm at Woodford, then Cheshire, major production centre to this day. Numerous 1920s prototypes, virtually no production. Roe sold his interest 1928 to form Saunders-Roe, control passing to J.D. Siddeley (including Armstrong Whitworth), who moved everything to Manchester, Hamble becoming Air Service Training. A few types found customers, including Avian light 2-seater, handful of high-wing transports derived from Fokker F.VII and, above all, powerful biplane trainers Tutor, Cadet and Prefect. All types had numbers beginning 500, thus Tutor was 621 and Prefect 626. Type 652 monoplane airliner of 1935 led to 652A Anson reconnaissance aircraft, built in many marks mainly as crew trainer to total by 1952 of 11,020. Type 679 Manchester heavy bomber was handicapped by unreliable engines (202 built 1939–42) but led to Lancaster, 7,377 built including 3,673 by Avro. This in turn led to York and Lancastrian, Lincoln, Tudor and Shackleton, Tudor leading to Ashton jet research aircraft. Type 707 delta research aircraft underpinned Type 698 Vulcan jet bomber (30 August 1952). Avro built seven prototypes and 15 production examples of Type 701 Athena advanced trainer. Types 720, 730 and 735 supersonic aircraft cancelled, and Type 748 transport (24 June 1960) became Hawker Siddeley. A.V. Roe was founder member 1935 of Hawker Siddeley, moving 1938 to giant shadow factory at Chadderton, north-east

Manchester, with experimental department at Ringway and assembly and flight test at Woodford, Newton Heath remaining in full production and being joined by Yeadon, today Leeds/Bradford airport, plus repair facilities Langar and Bracebridge Heath. Name retained in Avro Whitworth group 1961, but finally lost 1963.

Avro Canada (Canada). A.V. Roe Canada was formed by Hawker Siddeley Group 1945, taking over Malton (Toronto) plant of Victory Aircraft. Produced C-102 Jetliner, CF-100 all-weather interceptor (689 built), CF-105 Arrow advanced supersonic interceptor (cancelled January 1959 when 11 built) and Avrocar 'flying saucer'; gas turbine division became Orenda Engines.

A.V. Roe: *See* Avro.

Avro International Aerospace (UK/Taiwan). Name of company formed 50/50 by British Aerospace and Taiwan Aerospace Corp. January 1993 to design, produce, market and support BAe Regional Jet family.

Avstar (USA). Seattle firm trying with others to market updated Temco TT-1 Super Pinto trainer in China as T-100 Super Mustang.

Avtek (USA). Avtek Corp. formed 1982 to develop 400A canard twin-turboprop (17 September 1984); investors major firms in Denmark, Finland, Germany, Japan, USA. *See Also* EuroAvtek.

Aydlett (USA). Donald E. Aydlett briefly (1965–6) builder of light aircraft.

Ayres (USA). Ayres Corp. purchased rights to Rockwell Thrush ag-aircraft 1977 and has since produced piston and turbine versions; Vigilante armed surveillance aircraft abandoned.

Azcarate (Mexico). Mexican national factory (*see* Talleres [Mexico]) produced aircraft 1915–29. In final 2 years built aircraft of indigenous design, named for designer, Brig.-Gen. Juan Azcarate, chief of aviation staff. Both were sesquiplanes, O-E-1 bombing/recon and E training/sporting. Government stopped manufacture 1930.

Azionari (Italy). Formed 1939 by renaming

Vercellese as Azionari Vercellese Industrie Aeronàutiche. Continued to produce FL.3, again renamed 1947 as Lombardi.

B

BA (UK). British Aircraft Manufacturing Co. Ltd was British Klemm renamed. Works at Hanworth produced Swallow, Eagle, Cupid and Double Eagle 1935–8.

Baade: *See* VEB.

Babcock (USA). Developed light side-by-side monoplane 1935, used post-war as basis for Bartlett.

BAC (Australia). Buchanan Aircraft Corporation formed at Toowoomba, Qld, 1989; main product BAC/204 light 2-seater.

BAC (UK). British Aircraft Company formed 1928 at Maidstone, mainly to build gliders. In 1932 managing director C.H. Lowe Wylde fitted small engine to produce BAC Planette. Lowe Wylde killed in one 1933. Company taken over by Kronfeld, becoming Kronfeld Ltd 1936.

BAC (UK). British Aircraft Corp. Ltd formed February 1960 to comply with Government demand that TSR.2 attack bomber would be bought only from merged group. BAC grouped aircraft and missile interests of Bristol (20%), English Electric (40%) and Vickers (40%). Three wholly-owned operating subsidiaries retained identities: Bristol Aircraft, English Electric Aviation and Vickers-Armstrongs (Aircraft). These identities lost in May 1960, controlling interest acquired in Hunting Aircraft, adding Luton Division to 3 others: Filton (formerly Bristol), Preston (EE) and Weybridge (V). Apart from TSR.2, cancelled February 1965, products included Britannia, 188, 221 and Concorde at Filton, One-Eleven (assembled at Hurn), VC10/Super VC10, Viscount and Vanguard at Weybridge, Jet Provost/Strikemaster and H.126 at Luton and Canberra, Lightning, Jaguar and MRCA (later Tornado) at Preston. Merged into British Aerospace by nationalization of UK industry 29 April 1977.

BACC (USA). Business Air Craft Corp. formed July 1963 by merger of Howard and Alamo Aviation. Lost identity 1967.

Bach (USA). Bach Air Transport was high-wing 8-passenger airliner (3 P&W or Wright engines) built in small series 1928–9.

Bachem (Germany). Formed under Dipl.-Ing. Erich Bachem July 1944 to produce previously schemed Ba 349 Natter rocket interceptor, virtually manned missile.

Bacini (Italy). Bacini e Scali Napoletani began 1923 with repairs to marine aircraft and progressed to licence construction 1936.

Backstrom (USA). Al Backstrom produced ultralight 1977.

Bacon (USA). Erle L. Bacon Corp. built grossly modified 'Super AT-6' 1977.

BAe: *See* British Aerospace.

BAF (UK). British Air Ferries, Southend, rebuilding Viscount 800s to extend life 15 years.

BAG (Germany). Bahnbedarf AG, producer of railway equipment, produced light sporting aircraft E.1, D.1, D.11A at Darmstadt 1922–6.

Bagalini (Italy). Walter Bagalini built ultralight 1976.

Bahnbedarf: *See* BAG.

BAI (Taiwan). Bureau of Aircraft Industry formed 1946 in Nanking, China, moved to Taiwan 1948. First Taiwan-built Pazmany PL-1 completed October 1968 by Aero Research Lab, branch of BAI, which became AIDC 1 March 1969.

Bailey (USA). Built Avicar BF-8 light aircraft 1942.

BAJ (France). Boncourt-Audenis-Jacob at Lyon-Bron built Type IV fighter, officially called C2, 1918. Previously (1913–14) Audenis and Jacob had built 2 successful aircraft, but BAJ was first official grouping, lasting until Jacob killed in action.

Bakeng (USA). Gerald Bakeng, Edmonds, Washington, built and flew Duce tandem-seat parasol monoplane 1970, followed by 220-hp Double Duce biplane in 1972.

Baker (USA). Gil Baker, engineer with Chevrolet, built and flew BCA-1-3 2-seat amphibian May 1968.

Baker (USA). Marion Baker, flight mechanic at Wright-Patterson AFB, built and flew MB-1 single-seat delta sporting aircraft July 1960.

Bakshayev (USSR). Grigorii Ivanovich Bakshayev spent most of his career at NIAI, where particular forté 1930–36 was aircraft with telescopic extending wings (e.g. LIG-7/LK and RK-1).

Baldwin (USA). Gary Baldwin completed ASP-XJ (armed surveillance and patrol, experimental jet) in 1989.

Baldwin Aircraft Corporation (USA). Briefly acquired assets of Orenco to continue production.

Ball-Bartoe (USA). Ball-Bartoe Aircraft Corp., Boulder, Colorado, produced JW-1 Jetwing research aircraft flown July 1977.

B&B (USA). B&B Aviation built ultralight 1983.

Bannick (USA). Lester J. Bannick built Model T Copter, light autogyro, 1963; Models VW and C followed 1964–8.

Barbaro (France). René Barbaro built light aircraft 1966.

Barber (UK). Horatio Barber was pioneer constructor: *see* Aeronautical Syndicate Ltd.

Barclay, Curle (UK). Whiteinch, Glasgow, built BE.2c/2e and Fairey Campania 1916–18.

Baritsky (USA). Walter Baritsky built light aircraft 1967.

Barker (USA). Arthur Barker built B-2 ultralight 1971.

Barkley-Grow (USA). Barkley-Grow Aircraft Corp. incorporated 1935 to produce T8P-1 metal stressed-skin monoplane transport (2 Wasp Junior) with wheels, skis or floats.

Barling: *See* Engineering Division.

Barnett (USA). Barnett Rotorcraft have flown series of autogyros, available as plans or kits.

Barney Oldfield (USA). Company markets plans and kits for 3 versions of Baby Lakes sporting biplane scaled down from Great Lakes designed by Oldfield.

Barnwell (UK). Capt. Frank Barnwell, chief designer at Bristol, lost his life 2 August 1938 flying BSW.1 (Barnwell, Scott, Whitchurch).

Barr (NZ). Barr Brothers, New Zealand ag-company, partner in Flight Engineers assembling and part-building Transavia PL-12 Airtruk.

Barracuda (USA). Formed by Dr W.B. Buethe to take over Barracuda from Jeffair.

Barrett (USA). Barrett Aircraft Corp., lightplane builder 1982.

Barrón (Spain). Eduardo Barrón designed winning fighter 1919 at Hispano-Suiza factory, Guadalajara, aircraft commonly known as Barrón España. Later 2-seat recon.

Bartel (Poland). Major between-wars company, established Poznan 11 August 1923 as Wielkopolska Wytwórnia Samolotów Sp Akc. Chief designer Ryszard Bartel produced succession of sound Hanriot-derived biplane trainers (BM.2–BM.6) and one monoplane fighter (M.1 Maryla) 1924–31. Company liquidated 1931.

Bartini (USSR). Italian Roberto Bartini, Communist, emigrated to Soviet Union 1923 and devoted life to designing Soviet aircraft. Served Red Army to 1928; then joined OSS 'Stal', headed his own brigade; arrested 1938 but 1942 permitted to organize design bureau Siberia, finally closed 1948, Bartini later being appointed NII head of strategic planning. Designed VVA-14 Ekranoplan 1967, built by Beriev, but work withered on his death 6 December 1974.

Bartel M.B. 2, December 1926.

Bartlett (USA). Bartlett Aircraft Corp. formed 1945 to develop pre-war Babcock into Blue Zephyr, later produced in refined form as LC-13A Zephyr 150.

Barton (USA). Wayne F. Barton of Colorado built Sylkie One high-performance 2-seater, flown 1975.

Basler (USA). Basler Turbo Conversions market conversion of DC-3 to PT6A power.

Bastet (France). Raymond Bastet built light 2-seater 1962.

Bastianelli (Italy). Designer Filippo Bastianelli gave his name to PRB flying-boat, first product of Società Industriale per l'Aviazione 1918. Large biplane, civil or military, 4 300-hp Fiat in tandem pairs.

BAT (UK). British Aerial Transport Co. took on F. Koolhoven (ex-Armstrong Whitworth) as chief designer 1917. Products were F.K.22–F.K.28 (1919), all biplane or sesquiplane fighters, trainers or transport (F.K.26) except F.K.28 (underpowered ultralight monoplane). *See also* Koolhoven.

Bata (Czechoslovakia). Giant shoe firm, big user of aircraft, formed subsidiary in Zlin 1935 to produce tandem-seat cabin monoplane. Led to Zlin company.

Bathiat-Sanchez (France). Successors to Sommer, produced tractor monoplane and pusher biplane 1914.

Batwing (USA). Batwing Aircraft Corp. built 2-seat tailless monoplane (pusher Pobjoy) 1935.

Baumann (USA). Formerly with Lockheed, J.B. Baumann formed Baumann Aircraft Corp. at Pasadena 1945. His cousin flew B-250 Brigadier

Baumann Brigadier 250, June 1947.

5-seater (2 × 125-hp pusher Continental) June 1947. Later had 145-hp engines.

Bäumer Aero GmbH (Germany). Produced light aircraft 1925–7, when Bäumer killed.

Baumgartl (Austria). Paul Baumgartl produced 'strap-on' autogyro (Heliofly I) 1942, followed by Heliofly III counter-rotating helicopter (16-hp engine).

Baumgartl (Brazil). After 1945 Baumgartl went to Brazil and produced series of light rotorcraft, notably PB-60 towed rotor kite, PB-63 single-seat conventional helicopter and PB-64 driven by tip pulsejets.

Bay (USA). Bay Aviation Services, lightplane builder 1961.

Bayerische Flugzeugwerke: *See* BFW.

Bayerische Rumpler-Werke: *See* BRW.

Baynes (UK). L.E. Baynes, of Alan Muntz & Co., designed numerous aircraft but had no company of his own: *see* Abbott; Carden-Baynes; Slingsby; Youngman-Baynes.

Bayru: *See* BRW.

B.E.: *See* Royal Aircraft Factory.

Beachner (USA). Gem miner Chris Beachner built V-8 Special with modified Buick engine, flown 1978. Following Beachner's death, rights (kits, plans) bought by Mizell.

Beagle (UK). Beagle (British Executive & General Aviation Ltd) formed October 1960 as subsidiary of Pressed Steel Co. to build Austers and other light aircraft. Reorganized 1962, no longer linked with Pressed Steel, 2 subsidiaries being absorbed into new **Beagle Aircraft Ltd**. Former Beagle-Auster at Rearsby built Auster-type Husky, Terrier, Airedale and AOP.11. Former Beagle-Miles at Shoreham built newly designed B.206 and B.242 (derived from B.218) light twins. Bankrupt 1970, nationalized and owned by Government (Ministry of Technology). Auster assets sold to Hants & Sussex. Remaining work, production of Pup and derived Bulldog trainer, passed after collapse to Scottish Aviation.

Beal (USA). Airline pilot Thomas W. Beal built Bealine Sporty single-seater 1959.

Beardmore (UK). Shipbuilding and engineering firm William Beardmore & Co., Dalmuir, Scotland, built Austro-Daimler engines from early 1913, followed by licensed DFW and B.E.2c aircraft. G. Tilghman Richards then designed series of aircraft: W.B.I bomber, W.B.II to replace B.E.2c, W.B.III naval version of Sopwith Pup, and W.B.IV and V single-seat naval fighters. In 1923 contract for engines for R.101 airship; 1925 W.S. Shackleton designed W.B.26 2-seat fighter for Latvia; Air Ministry contract for 2 flying-boats (Inverness) and 1 giant landplane (Inflexible) all using Rohrbach stressed-skin construction. Seven civil prototypes ending with W.B.XXIV Wee Bee 1924.

Béarn (France). Constructions Aéronautiques du Béarn, at Pau (Pyrenées), built Minicab side-by-side 2-seater 1949, followed by small series and (1953) improved Super-Minicab, both designed by Yves Gardan.

Beattie-Fellers (USA). Ronald Beattie and Walter Fellers designed S-1 propeller-behind-tail racer in Los Angeles 1960.

Beatty (UK). American G.W. Beatty started school of flying at Hendon 1913; 3 years later built light biplane, 35-hp Anzani and later 60-hp Beatty.

Beaujon (USA). Herbert Beaujon claims Flybike, flown February 1975, is 'world's simplest and cheapest aircraft'.

Béchereau (France). Louis Béchereau, designer of SPAD fighters, gave his name to SAB C1 fighter built at Levasseur factory 1918. In 1926 Béchereau T.7 airliner was built by SRAP. *See* Kellner-Béchereau.

Becker (W. Germany). Horst Becker built light aircraft 1978.

Bede (USA). James R. (Jim) Bede (ex-NAA) and father James A. established Bede Aviation Corp. in Kansas 1960. BD-1 flown 1963 became AAI Yankee Trainer/Traveler, later Grumman. Subsequently by 1979 BD-2–BD-8, all attractive and very different, best known being family of BD-5 pushers including 5J jet versions.

Beechcraft 17R, November 1932.

Bedek (Israel). Bedek Aircraft established 1950 at Lod airport, carried out growing overhaul and modification and 1959 began to make Fouga Magister. Renamed IAI June 1960, of which Bedek Aviation Division handles military upgrades and modifications.

Bedson (Australia). Gordon Bedson and Associates produced Resurgam ultralight, but Bedson killed in it 1984.

Bedunkovich (USSR). Engineer-colonel Anatoli Georgievich Bedunkovich worked at NIAI Leningrad. Best-known designs LK-4 (NIAI-4) light biplane, P-3 (LIG-5) advanced trainer and SKh-1 (LIG-10) multirole transport and ag-aircraft, all 1934–9.

Bee (USA). Beecraft Associates formed by ex-Convair engineers 1946, built Wee Bee, claimed 'world's smallest aircraft'. Honey Bee single-seat parasol flown July 1952. Name changed to Bee Aviation 1954, and Queen Bee 4-seater flown 1958.

Beech (USA). Walter H. Beech was a principal of Travel Air, but resigned 1930 to design totally new Model 17 'staggerwing' high-speed cabin biplane. With wife Olive Ann Beech set up Beech Aircraft Co. in Wichita, Kansas, April 1932. Model 17 flew 4 November 1932, 748 built by 1948. Beech flew first twin-engined Model 18 on 15 January 1937, 7,091 built in 32 years of continuous production, all by Beech. V-tail Bo-

nanza flown 1946, over 17,000 by 1992 in various versions. Other major programmes included Mentor, Twin Bonanza, Musketeer/Sundowner, Baron, Duke, Queen Air, Debonair, Travel Air, King Air, Super King Air, Model 1900 Airliner, Model 400 Beechjet and Starship. Deliveries reached 50,300 by 1993. Beech also has substantial business in missiles and targets, and aircraft and spacecraft airframe subcontract manufacture. Became wholly-owned subsidiary of Raytheon 8 February 1980.

Beets: *See* G/B Aircraft.

Belairbus (Belgium). Formed by SABCA and SONACA to supply portions of Airbus A310, 320/321 and 330/340.

Bell (USA). Aerial Experiment Association, first formal heavier-than-air aviation group in USA, formed September 1907. Leader Dr Graham Bell, inventor of telephone; his wife was prime mover and financier. Bell's own multiplane flown briefly by McCurdy at Baddeck January 1909.

Bell (USA). Bell Aircraft Corp. formed October 1935 by former leaders of Consolidated on that company's move from Buffalo to San Diego, notably Lawrence D. Bell, Ray P. Whitman and chief engineer Robert J. Woods. Took over giant Buffalo plant, but won enough subcontract business to stay solvent. Woods built up design team and produced FM-1 Airacuda fighter (2 pusher Allison engines) in 1937 and P-39 Airaco-

Bell P-39F-1 Airacobra, 1942.

bra fighter (Allison engine behind pilot, with long shaft drive) flown April 1938. By 1944 P-39 deliveries reached 9,558, plus 3,302 improved P-63 Kingcobras. XP-59A Airacomet was first US jet, flown 1 October 1942, followed by later versions. Following XP-77 lightweight fighter and XP-83 heavy twin-jet came XS-1 (later X-1), world's first supersonic aircraft, exceeded Mach 1 14 October 1947. Other X-1 and X-2 versions followed, and X-5 was variable-sweep aircraft. Pioneer vectored-thrust VTOL was ATV of 1953, followed by X-14 twin-jet VTOL 1957 and X-22A VTOL of 1966 with 4 swivelling ducted propulsors. Bell operated giant government plant at Marietta, Georgia (today Lockheed), building B-29. Mid-1943 flew Model 30 light helicopter; from this stemmed Model 47, over 6,000 made in several countries. XH-40 of October 1956 won US Army contract, and as UH-1 'Huey' family reached production total exceeding 13,000 including Model 209 Cobra versions. HO-4 observation helicopter of 1960 led to Model 206 JetRanger and OH-58 Kiowa, total with licensees over 8,000. Grand total worldwide over 32,000 helicopters including later Models 212, 214, 222 and 230. On 5 July 1960 Textron Inc. began operating Bell's defence business via **Bell Aerosystems** at Buffalo and **Bell Helicopter Co.** at Fort Worth. In 1970 Textron was appended to names, and **Bell Helicopter Textron** became wholly-owned subsidiary 3 January 1982, Bell Aerospace ceasing to make aircraft. Partner with Boeing on V-22 Osprey tilt-rotor. To provide space at Fort Worth for this (at present haltingly

funded) programme, major product lines transferred to **Bell Helicopter Canada**. Chief licensees Agusta and Fuji; KBHC is joint partnership. Marketing/support companies in Singapore and Venezuela.

Bellanca (USA). In 1911 Giuseppe Mario Bellanca emigrated from Sicily to New York with nothing but degree in engineering. Flew monoplane built in Brooklyn basement, ran flying school and in 1919 joined Wright Aeronautical and designed CF cabin monoplane 1922. Wright-Bellanca WB.1 led to WB.2 *Columbia*, world records for endurance and distance 1927. Result was Bellanca Aircraft Corporation, 31 December 1927. Products mainly high-wing cabin monoplanes, CH-200 and CH-300 6-seaters, with wheels, skis or floats, led to Pacemaker 1929 and Skyrocket 1930, and larger (up to 15-passenger) Airbus, Aircruiser and Army C-27 of 1930–34. Models 28-70, 28-90 and 28-92 were long-range racers. Model 14 Junior (1938) was low-wing 3-seater, developed post-war into Model 14-13 Cruisair and Cruisemaster. Rights, jigs and tools sold 1955 to Northern Aircraft, Alexandria, Minnesota.

Bellanca (USA). Northern (*see* above) became Downer, then Inter-Air (making Viking, an improved Cruisemaster) and, in 1967, Bellanca Sales, subsidiary of Miller Flying Service. Bought Champion Aircraft 1970, name becoming **Bellanca Aircraft Corp.** Products included Model 7 Citabria (Airbatic spelt backwards),

Bellanca P-100 Airbus, May 1930.

Model 8 Decathlon and Scout utility versions, all at same Minnesota plant. Became wholly-owned subsidiary of Anderson, Greenwood, of Houston, Texas, 1978, and henceforth developed and marketed T-250 Aries high-speed 5-seater and Eagle ag-aircraft. Work stopped 1980, liquidation 1981, assets sold 1982 to Viking.

Bellanca (USA). Executives mainly from Miller Flying Service formed Viking Aviation 1982 to support large numbers of Viking and other Bellanca aircraft. Renamed Bellanca Inc., still at Alexandria, Minnesota, resumed Viking production 1984, and from 1985 supported Eagle ag-aircraft. Work stopped 1988.

Bellanca (USA). Losing its identity in 1959, original Bellanca company was restarted by G.M. Bellanca and son August in 1968, initially in W. Virginia and later Maryland. Concentrated on Model 19-25, later restyled Model 25, Skyrocket, outstanding glass-fibre 6-seater able to cruise 300 mph (483 km/h). Work stopped 1986.

Bellanger-Denhaut (France). Soc. Bellanger des Autos, motor company, built several aircraft 1920–22, notably Denhaut 22 patrol (later transport) flying-boat.

Bell Helicopter (Canada). Bell Helicopter Textron formed October 1983 as division of Textron Canada. Plant at Mirabel (Montreal airport) handles all non-licensed production of Model 206 JetRanger and LongRanger, 212 and 412. Except for Canadian sales, products sold to parent at Fort Worth.

Bell Helicopter (USA): *See* Bell, 2nd entry.

Belyaev (USSR). Viktor Nikolayevich Belyaev (or Belyayev) worked with many design brigades before designing twin-boom passenger transport 1934, developed into remarkable DB-LK bomber. EI pusher fighter destroyed 1941.

Ben Air (UK). Ultralight builder 1983.

Bendix (USA). Bendix Aviation Corp. tried to produce helicopters after Second World War, flying Model K single-seat coaxial in 1946 and Model J 4-seater a year later.

Benes-Mraz (Czechoslovakia). Benes & Mraz Tovarna na Letadla formed at Chocen February 1935 to produce efficient low-wing monoplane light aircraft. By 1939 Be 50, 51, 52, 53, 501, 51, 52, 550 and 156 had flown, most being in production. Post-war M1 Sokol, M2 Skaut and M3 Bonzo appeared. *See* Mraz.

Bengis (S. Africa). Bengis Aircraft Co. is producing TM20B Flamingo III (M-20 Mewa under PZL Mielec licence) and may assemble/produce An-28.

Bennett (NZ). Bennett Aviation of Te Kuiti built prototype PL.11 Airtruk designed by Luigi Pellarini. Became Waitomo Aircraft.

Benoist (USA). Previously Aeronautic Supply Co., Benoist Aircraft Co. registered St Louis 1912 and built numerous prototypes. One Type XIV Air-Boat 2-seat flying-boat operated world's first heavier-than-air scheduled service across Tampa Bay, Florida, from 1 January 1914.

Bensen (USA). Dr Igor Bensen, formerly of

Benoist XIV Air-Boat (first scheduled flight, 1 January 1914).

Kaman, set up Bensen Aircraft Corp. in 1952 at Raleigh-Durham airport, N. Carolina, concentrating on ultralight rotorcraft. Following tip-drive and engine-above-rotor helicopters, Bensen produced B-7 Gyro-Glider, B-7W Hydro-Glider and B-7M Gyro-Copter, latter (40-hp Nelson) leading to thousands of simple autogyros of B-8 family.

Bereznyak-Isayev (USSR). A.Y. Bereznyak and A.M. Isayev developed BI-1 rocket interceptor (15 May 1942).

Berg (Austria). Numerous designs of fighter and reconnaissance/bomber aircraft produced by Ö-UF Aviatik in 1916–18 were commonly known as Berg aircraft after designer Dipl.-Ing. Julius von Berg. *See* Aviatik and Ö-UF.

Berg (Norway). Finn Petter Berg built ultralight 1965.

Bergamaschi (Italy). Cantieri Aeronautici Bergamaschi formed at Bergamo 1926 to produce improved training aircraft, C.1 and C.2 biplanes. Became subsidiary of Caproni 1931, hence A.P.1 close-support monoplane, Borea, Ghibli and Libbecio received Caproni designations.

Berger (Switzerland). Franz Berger modified Erla 5D with VW engine 1968.

Berger (Switzerland). Hans Berger produced BX-50 single-seat and BX-110 2-seat helicopters 1973–5.

Bergeson (USA). John B. Bergeson produced light aircraft 1971.

Beriev (USSR). Georgii Mikhailovich Beriev began career with Aviatrust organization, working for Richard's design brigade. Following year formed marine-aircraft section within CCB.

Beriev MBR-2/M-17b, October 1934 type.

Launched own OKB at Taganrog 1932 to build MBR-2 flying-boat (1,330 built). Numerous other designs, nearly all seaplanes or flying-boats. Wartime LL-143 led to powerful Be-6, flown February 1949, followed by R-1 and Be-10 jet flying-boats and M-12 (Be-12) turboprop amphibian of 1960. Beriev died 1979, succeeded by A.K. Konstantinov. Major new programme A-40 Albatross ocean patrol and ASW amphibian, developed into Be-42 multirole civil aircraft, with planned Be-200 smaller civil partner. Now called **Taganrog tech centre named for G.M. Beriev**; General Designer Gennardi S. Panatov.

Berkmans (USA). Emile and Maurice Berkmans designed Speed Scout, attractive biplane fighter, 1916. Tested well but war ended and more powerful B-2 never built.

Berkmans (USA). Believed no relation, built light aircraft December 1947.

Berlin (Germany). Berlin Technische Hochschule had Flugtechnische Fachgruppe 1931–45 which produced research and experimental aircraft, notably AB.4 (Akaflieg Berlin No. 4) trim parasol single-seater 1931 and B 9 (built in partnership with DVL research organization) for prone-pilot research, 2 105-hp Hirth (1937).

Berlin Doman (USA). After Doman ceased trading 1961, Caribe Doman remained active on helicopter project and in 1967 formed Berlin Doman Aircraft to elect Don H. Berlin (former designer of Curtiss fighters) as Chairman.

Planned large BD-19 transport helicopter at Toughkenamon, PA, but money ran out 1971.

Berliner (USA). Famed inventor (of gramophone, etc.), Emile Berliner invented Gyro rotary aircraft engine 1911 and reasonably successful helicopters 1922–6.

Berliner (USA). Son Henry A. Berliner assisted with helicopters, formed Berliner Aircraft Co. 1926 at Alexandria, Virginia, and Potomac Flying Service. To operate this service produced attractive Parasol 3-seater (OX-5), 17 built in 1928. Designed prototype 4-seat 'all-vision monoplane' with fully glazed cabin; this was built by Berliner-Joyce.

Berliner-Joyce (USA). On his father's death 1929 Henry Berliner joined with Temple Nach Joyce, famed pilot and engineer, forming Berliner-Joyce Aircraft Corp., new plant at Dundalk, Maryland. Series of Army/Navy prototypes followed, starting with Navy XFJ-1 fighter flown May 1930. Only Army P-16 (later redesignated PB-1) 2-seat fighter and OJ-2 Navy observation biplane won production orders. In 1934 North American Aviation bought controlling interest, Joyce went to Bellanca and Berliner left to found Erco, plant becoming NAA B/J Division.

Bernard (France). Etablissements Adolphe Bernard formed April 1917, building SPAD fighters while Bernard designed first original product, AB.1 twin-engined bomber. In early 1918 Louis Béchereau left SPAD and joined

Berliner-Joyce 'All-vision' prototype, November 1929.

Bernard 60T (3 × GR radials), January 1930.

Bernard to design SAB fighter biplane made by Levasseur. EAB (Bernard) was dissolved 1922, replaced by SIMB **(Société Industrielle des Métaux et du Bois)**, but aircraft continued to be known as Bernard even though chief designer was Jean Hubert. Latter created succession of advanced cantilever monoplanes, initially wood and later stressed-skin metal. First was C1 fighter, later called Bernard 10, followed by simpler Bernard 12 fighter designed by Jean Galtier (later of Arsenal). V.1 and V.2 were racers, latter setting world speed record at 278.48 mph 11 December 1924. Bernard 14 and 15 were parasol fighters 1926, while 18T was 6-passenger transport. In 1927 SIMB was closed, and a new **Société des Avions Bernard** formed. Monoplane fighters, bombers, tourers, long-range record-breakers and Schneider racing seaplanes followed, but company failed 1935 prior to nationalization.

Bert (USA). Floyd S. Bert built light biplane 1959.

F.W. Berwick & Co. (UK). Built Airco DH.4/9/9A 1917–18.

Besneux (France). Alain Besneux built VW-engined light aircraft 1973.

Besobrasov (Russia). A.A. Besobrasov, F.E. Moska and V.A. Ponikovin built wierd triplane 1913.

Besson (France). Marcel Besson was designing aircraft before 1912. After 1914 he produced biplane and triplane trainers, followed in 1917 by triplane flying-boats powered by pusher engines of 180, 300 or 450 hp. Called LB, from being built by **Hydravions Georges Levallois et Levy**, they were made in small numbers. H.3–H.6 were flying-boats of 1920–21. Besson then built his own prototypes, calling them MB, best known being MB.26 fighter and reconnaissance seaplanes of 1925 and light MB.35 seaplane of 1926. Besson's lack of funds resulted in his becoming a division of ANF Les Mureaux, enabling him to finish big MB.36 transport flying-boat by 1930. Last design, MB.411 observation seaplane, escaped to Britain aboard parent submarine *Surcouf* 1940.

Bestelli (Italy). This Milan company built BN.1 Saetta, twin-fuselage fighter, designed by Nardi, completed 1939 but not flown until fitted with 2 1,350-hp DB 605. Bestelli-Colombo C.3 4-seat tourer with 2 135-hp Alfa-Romeo flown Arcore (Milan) 1940.

Beta (USA). Beta Aircraft formed to build light aircraft 1966.

Bezzola (Switzerland). Gion Bezzola built light aircraft 1978 and 1982.

BFW (Germany). Bayerische Flugzeugwerke established Munich 20 February 1916 as wholly-owned subsidiary of Albatros-Werke. Built parent designs plus 5 prototypes until 1919.

BFW (Germany). Bayerische Flugzeugwerke AG, unrelated to predecessor, formed 30 July 1926 by German transport ministry, Bavarian state and a banking house, taking over assets of Udet-Flugzeugbau at Ramersdorf, Munich, and factory of BRW at Augsburg. Produced Udet Flamingo, and to acquire design capability merged with Messerschmitt 8 September 1927, latter retaining design rights, but BFW bankrupt 1 June 1931.

BFW (Germany). Bankruptcy discharged and operations resumed May 1933. Enmity of Erhard Milch restricted company to licence production and private sale of light aircraft. Situation changed by Bf 108 and Bf 109, to such degree company name changed to Messerschmitt AG 11 July 1938. Aircraft designed after this date known as Me, not Bf.

BH (International). Loose association between Beech and Hawker to market 'BH-125' executive jet in N. America 1969–75.

BHEL (India). Bharat Heavy Electricals Ltd selected to construct 15 LT-1 Swati trainers (designed by Civil Aviation Dept Technical Centre) each year for Indian clubs; first flown 17 November 1990, BHEL approved as manufacturer 1991.

BICh: *See* Cheranovskii.

Biggs (USA). Floyd Biggs, Oklahoma, built light aircraft 1959.

Billman (USA). Billman Aviation Co. built light aircraft 1959.

Binder (W. Germany). Binder Aviatik, with Schempp-Hirth, built Piel Emeraude variant as CP 301S Smaragd 1963–6.

Bird: *See* Brunner-Winkle.

Bird (USA). Bird Corp., makers of medical respirators, built Innovator, PBY Catalina amphibian plus 2 × 340-hp Lycoming engines outboard 1967.

Birdman (USA). Birdman Inc. marketed kits/plans of TL-1A ultralight (122 lb [55 kg] empty) from 1975.

Bird Wing (USA). Bird Wing Commercial Aircraft Co., Mid-America Airport, St Joseph, MO, incorporated 1928 to make Imperial 3-seat biplane.

Birmingham Carriage & Wagon Co. (UK). Built Airco DH.10 Amiens and Handley Page O/400 1918–19.

Bishop (USA). Ray Bishop produced light aircraft 1972.

Bittner (Canada). Wilfred Bittner produced light aircraft 1976.

BK: *See* British Klemm.

Blackburn (UK). Civil engineer Robert Blackburn saw Wilbur Wright fly in France, threw up job as civil engineer in Rouen and designed monoplane built in Leeds and made brief hops on beach at Marske, near Filey, April/May 1909. Other monoplanes followed, and **Blackburn Aeroplane & Motor Co**. set up June 1914, with factory

Blackburn RB.3A Perth, 11 October 1933.

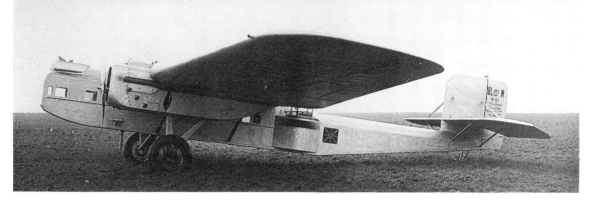

Blériot BL.137M multirole, December 1930.

in disused Leeds roller-skating rink. Wartime production included BE.2cs, Sopwith Babies and, at Sherburn-in-Elmet 12 miles east, Sopwith Cuckoos. To build marine aircraft new site chosen at Brough, on Humber west of Hull, which in 1929–33 replaced Leeds as main factory. Products included succession of lumpy carrier-based torpedo bombers (Swift, Dart, Velos, Ripon, Baffin and Shark), a series of large military flying-boats, and Bluebird 2-seat civil biplane and B-2 side-by-side trainer. Main products in Second World War were others' designs: 1,699 Swordfish at Sherburn, 250 Sunderlands at Dumbarton and 635 Barracudas at Brough. Company's own designs included Skua dive-bomber and Botha crew trainer; Firebrand torpedo bomber missed war. General Aircraft was taken over January 1949 forming **Blackburn & General Aircraft**, GAL.60 Universal being developed into Blackburn Beverley; licence production included Prentice and Balliol trainers. Most important of all was Buccaneer (30 April 1958). Robert Blackburn died 1955, company split into Aircraft, Engines and Electronics

companies 1959, and Blackburn Aircraft taken over by Hawker Siddeley Group, briefly becoming part of Hawker Blackburn Division before losing identity 1 April 1965.

Black Hole (Canada). Black Hole Investments produce Bücker Jungmann and Jungmeister aerobatic trainers.

Blair Atholl: *See* Dunne.

Blanchard (France). Société des Avions Blanchard produced several prototypes, nearly all flying-boats, 1920–24. One type, Brd.1 bomber/reconnaissance boat, equipped first such unit of Aéronautique Maritime 1923–6.

Blériot (France). Louis Blériot made large brass car headlamps. Also constructed unsuccessful ornithopter (flapping wing) 1901, and Voisin-Blériot glider seaplane 1905. Blériot III and IV made by Voisin. First successful machine was Blériot V pusher canard April 1907, followed by series of improved monoplanes leading to XIbis,

Blériot-SPAD S.91 light fighter, 1927.

Bloch 220 No. 2, January 1936.

or XI mod, cross-Channel 25 July 1909. This triggered massive orders, many civil and military variants, nearly 800 built in 1913 alone. Main factory at Suresnes, Paris, **Société Blériot Aéronautique** produced succession of undistinguished wartime aircraft, including 4-engined LIII (i.e., 53), 67, 73 and 74 4-engined bombers and derived 75 Aérobus airliner. Link with SPAD company August 1914, and takeover 1921, resulted after 1917 in SPAD designs being designated Blériot-SPAD, as noted later. Blériot's own designs, directed by André Herbemont, Léon Kirste and Filippo Zappata, included: 106 transport 1924, 110 long-range record-breaker 1930, 111 high-speed executive transport 1929, 115 airliner 1923, 118 fighter amphibian 1925, 125 twin-fuselage transport 1931, 127 multirole bomber 1926, 165 and 175 airliners 1926, 195 mailplane 1929, 290 3-seat amphibian 1931, and 5190 giant transport flying-boat 1933. When Herbemont replaced Béchereau as chief designer of SPAD in 1917 subsequent designs were called Blériot-SPAD: S.XIV fighter seaplane 1917, S.XX 2-seat fighter 1918 and 11 derived versions, S.27 light transport 1919, S.33 airliner 1920 and 17 derived versions, S.34 trainer 1920 and 13 derived versions, S.42 trainer 1921 and 3 derived versions, S.51 fighter

1924 and 3 derived versions, S.61 fighter 1923 and 13 derived versions, S.81 fighter 1923 and 6 derived versions, and S.91 fighter of 1930, from which stemmed S.510 used by Armée de l'Air 1937–40.

Bloch (France). Parisien Marcel Bloch was assigned to help manage production of Caudron G.III 1914, and 4 years later with Potez set up SEA (Société d'Etudes Aéronautiques) at Suresnes, producing outstanding SEA.4 2-seat fighter, but order for 1,000 cancelled at Armistice. Lack of demand for aircraft saw Bloch in furniture business, but formed Avions Marcel Bloch 1930, designers including B.-C. Vallières, Henri Deplante, Jean Cabrière and Lucien Servanty. Products included MB.60 and 71 mailplanes, 80 and 81 ambulance aircraft, 120 trimotor colonial transport, 130, 131, 134, 135, 162, 174, 175, 200, 210 and 211 bombers, 150–157 fighters and 161 and 220 airliners, all distinguished by being advanced stressed-skin monoplanes. With 1936 nationalization portions of company were handed to national groups, but main factory at Courbevoie, Paris, was deluged with work. Bloch arrested 1943 and sent to Buchenwald, contracting diphtheria and escaping hanging by minutes.

Blohm und Voss Ha 139B Nordstern, *May 1938.*

He survived to form Dassault, which *see*.

Blohm und Voss (Germany). Company started 4 July 1933 as **Hamburger Flugzeugbau GmbH**, subsidiary of Blohm und Voss of Hamburg, Germany's largest shipbuilding firm. Reinhold Mewes appointed designer and produced Ha 135 trainer, but then left to join Fieseler. Dr Richard Vogt came from Kawasaki and produced series of generally unconventional aircraft: Ha 137 dive-bomber, Ha (later BV) 138 reconnaissance flying-boat, Ha 139 mail seaplane, Ha 140 torpedo seaplane, Ha (later BV) 141 asymmetric reconnaissance aircraft and Ha (later BV) 142 transport. Renamed **Abteilung Flugzeugbau der Schiffswerft Blohm und Voss** September 1937. Large new plant at Hamburg Finkenwerder built Fw 200C and BV 222, and prototypes of BV 238 giant flying-boat and BV 40 glider fighter. BV 144 transport programme assigned to French industry. Company also produced air-launched weapons. Me 155 high-altitude fighter passed to BV for production; after arguments BV given responsibility to effect complete redesign as BV 155.

Blue Max (Australia). Microlight available in ready-to-fly form.

Blume (W. Germany). Dipl.-Ing. Walter Blume, former managing director and chief designer of Arado, set up design group post-war at Duisburg and had Bl 500 built by Focke-Wulf and flown 14 March 1957. Clean 4-seater, but production Bl 502 remained prototype.

BM: *See* Breguet-Michelin.

BMM (Nazi Bohemia-Moravia protectorate).

Böhmische-Mährisches Maschinenfabrik AG was one of 2 principal producers of Si 204D-3, absorbed into Aero after 1945.

BMS (W. Germany). BMS Flugtechnik and BMS Flugzeugbau active in light aircraft 1965–6.

BOAC: *See* Barney Oldfield (Aircraft Co.).

Bob Anderson (USA). Bob Anderson Sport Aircraft formed 1981 to market light homebuilt.

Bobba (Italy). Small company which built Gnome-powered monoplanes 1911–13.

Bock (USA). John Bock marketed Bock II ultra-light 1971.

Boden (USA). Edward Boden built 15ft-span biplane 1946.

Bodiansky (France). Little known of earlier types, but Model 16 was slatted/flapped 2-seat monoplane (June 1930) and Model 20 was low-wing 4-seat cabin monoplane (100-hp Renault), built at works of S. Poite with wooden wing made by Letord at Meudon, flew September 1931.

Boeing (USA). William E. Boeing, Yale graduate and Seattle timber merchant, flew in Curtiss seaplane 1914 and said to Cdr. G. Conrad Westervelt USN, 'I think we could build a better machine'. Result was two B&W seaplanes, first flown 29 June 1916—both had long career in New Zealand. Registered company as **Pacific Aero Products Co.** 15 July 1916, and quickly gained Navy and civil orders. Company re-registered **Boeing Airplane Co.** 26 April 1917, with growing business in landplanes and marine aircraft. In

Boeing 80B, 16 July 1930.

1920 low bidder for 200 Thomas-Morse fighters, and among prototypes earned money by building or modifying DH-4 versions, 298 by 1925. In 1923 built prototype fighter which led to Army PW-9, Navy FB-1, followed by numerous derivatives culminating in over 600 F3B/F4B/P-12 family 1928–33. Mail route operated 1 July 1927 by 25 Boeing 40A biplanes, followed by 16 3-engined Model 80 airliners from 1928. In 1929 joined with other companies in giant United Aircraft & Transport, among other things swallowing Stearman and setting up Boeing Canada. Air Mail Act 1934 forced break-up of UATC, leaving Boeing still owning Stearman. 'Bill' Boeing retired at this point, succeeded by Clairmont L. Egtvedt, former chief engineer, who masterminded move into stressed-skin cantilever monoplanes with Model 200 Monomail, B-9 bomber, Model 247 airliner (8 February 1933) and P-26/Model 281 fighter. Boeing Airplane Co formed **Boeing Aircraft Co.** 5 August 1933 as wholly-owned subsidiary to manufacture aircraft. Model 294 XB-15 remained giant prototype, but Model 299 (28 July 1935) led to 12,731 B-17 Fortress bombers and 10 Model 307 Stratoliners, first pressurized transport in service. Model 314 Clipper flew (later with 115-grade fuel, first in world) June 1938, and totally new Model 345 XB-29 (21 September 1942) led to 1,122 B-29A Superfortress bombers made at new Navy-funded Boeing plant at Renton, neighbouring city to Seattle, plus 1,644 from equally large new Boeing plant at Wichita (adjoining Stearman), plus 668

by Bell at Marietta, GA, and 536 by Martin at Omaha. From B-29 stemmed B-50, civil Model 377 Stratocruiser and C/KC-97 transport/tanker of which 888 were built. On 31 December 1947 Boeing Aircraft vanished on merger into parent. Willingness to adopt superior but high-risk solutions never more evident than in Model 450 XB-47 Stratojet (17 December 1947), leading to 2,272 of many versions. Model 464 XB-52 Stratofortress (15 April 1952) led to 744 of some of biggest and most powerful aircraft ever used by any air force, production being shared by Seattle (277) and Wichita (467). Under lawyer Bill Allen Boeing took crucial decision in 1952 to risk over $20 million, about net worth of company, on 4-jet Model 367-80 transport. This paid off, first with KC-135 tanker/transport for USAF (732 built at Renton, plus 88 C-135 variants), and secondly with commercial 707 and derivatives with bigger fuselage cross-section and, in most, larger airframe altogether (725 plus 153 lighter 720s), plus 125 derived military variants. During 1950s work diversified into wide range of missiles and spacecraft, gas-turbine engines and hydrofoil ships, reflected in name change to **The Boeing Company** May 1961. Giant gambles had to continue: 727 short-haul trijet (9 February 1963) broke all records with 1,852 sold; smaller 737 was even greater risk, launched on an order for 10 from a foreign airline, but today new record-holder with sales far exceeding 3,000. By far biggest risk of all—over $1 billion in 1966—launched 747 'Jumbo Jet'; but this has never had

Boeing Sentry E-3D, 1991.

a competitor, and today has gone well beyond 1,000 at up to $180 million each. Two further big gambles were narrow-body 757 and wide-body 767 twin-jets, both announced in 1978. In dollar terms greatest risk of all was launch of 777, world's biggest twin-jet, in 1990. Today largest operating unit is Boeing Commercial Airplane Group. On 2 January 1990 remainder of company formed into Boeing Defense & Space Group, main elements being Military Airplanes (Seattle), Product Support (Wichita), Helicopters (Philadelphia), Electronic Systems and Missiles & Space. Military Airplanes Division handles E-3, E-6, E-8 and 767-AWACS, and participates in Lockheed F-22A and Grumman A-X. Product Support Division handles KC-135 and 707 modification, A-6E wings, and support of B-1B, B-52 and other aircraft. Helicopters Division, former Piasecki/Vertol/Boeing Vertol, handles Chinook; with Sikorsky will produce RAH-66 Comanche and with Bell V-22 Osprey.

Boeing-Canada (Canada). Boeing-Canada Ltd set up 1929, and in 1937 began producing Blackburn Shark in new factory at Sea Island, Vancouver. Next came 312 PBY Catalina followed by 50 upgraded PB2B-2; by 1944 3 B-C plants were on B-29 and Mosquito components. New factory opened by **Boeing of Canada Ltd** near Winnipeg November 1971 to make 747 components, while Arnprior (previously Vertol) Division received 1980 contract to upgrade all CAF CH-113, and subcontracts on 757, 767, 777. On 31 January 1986 completed purchase of de Havilland Aircraft to form de Havilland Division; sold 1992 to Bombardier.

Boeing-Stearman: *See* Stearman, 2nd entry.

Boeing Vertol: *See* Boeing.

Bogardus (USA). Little Gee Bee built by George Bogardus said to be first homebuilt to fly across USA, August 1947.

Bohne (Germany). HTL Bohne completed EH.102C light 4-seater 1969.

Boillon (France). Assisted by Aéro-Club d'Auvergne, Jean Boillon completed Fulmo 2-seater 1963.

Boisavia (France). Société Boisavia set up 1946 and in same year flew B.50 Muscadet high-wing 3-seater. Developed into B.60 Mercurey 4-seater, series production including 240-hp tug version. Last design was B.260 Anjou light twin (2 June 1956), prototype only.

BOK (USSR). Bureau Osovikh Konstruktsii, bureau of special designers, set up October 1930 on initiative of P.I. Baranov as part of CAHI. BOK-1 pressure-cabin high-altitude (1936), BOK-2 high-lift 2-part wing (1935), BOK-5 all-wing tailless (1937), BOK-7 high-altitude 100-hour endurance (1938), BOK-8 again BOK-1-based for armament control system, BOK-11 high-altitude diesel-engined reconnaissance (1940), BOK-15, BOK-11 development.

Bolen (USA). Ralph Bolen built light aircraft 1981.

Bolkhovitinov (USSR). Viktor Federovich Bolkhovitinov was mercurial professor at VVA (Zhukovskii air force academy) 1932. Following year became head of group, in effect an OKB, with first task to design replacement for TB-3 heavy bomber. Result was DB-A, designation from long-range bomber, academy (5 March 1936). Two prototypes, one of which (N-209) vanished beyond N. Pole 12 August 1937. Second design, S, 2-seat fighter with 2 engines in tandem in nose 1939. Other projects incomplete.

Bölkow (W. Germany). Dipl.-Ing. Ludwig Bölkow formed civil engineering company at Stuttgart 1953, from which stemmed Bölkow Entwicklungen KG formed 1 May 1956, HQ at Ottobrunn, Munich. Began wide aeronautical research and production programme, beginning with Klemm Kl 107, produced as Bölkow Kl 107 versions and subsequently F 207 and Bö 207. Other products gliders, including Fauvel AV.36, Bö 103 light helicopter and Bö 46 high-power research helicopter (January 1964). Became Bölkow GmbH and merged with Messerschmitt AG 31 October 1968. *See* MBB.

Bombardier (Canada). Pronounced in French manner (rhyming with 'RDA'), Montreal-based industrial empire since 1986 moving strongly into aerospace by acquiring Canadair in that year, Shorts (1989), Learjet (1990) and de Havilland Inc. (51%, 1992). In 1992 formed Bombardier Aerospace North America to oversee Canadair, DH, Learjet.

Bordelaise Dyle et Bacalan DB.70, 1930.

Bond (USA). John Bond built Sky Dancer light autogyro, flown 1973.

Bonney (USA). Bonney Gull (180-hp Kirkham) experimental monoplane built to test concept of wings which quickly rotated to 90° when wheels touched on landing; flew 4 May 1928, crashed on landing.

Bonomi (Italy). Aeronàutica Vittorio Bonomi built several light aircraft 1926–30: *see* Bossi-Bonomi. Became Lombarda.

Borchers (USA). Lowell J. Borchers built light aircraft 1981.

Bordelaise (France). Société Aérienne Bordelaise, successor to Dyle et Bacalan, controlled by Nieu-port-Delage, built small numbers of twin-fuselage bombers and transports 1929–31.

Borel (France). Gabriel Borel produced series of monoplanes 1909–14, numbered Bo.1–Bo.19, most having superficial resemblance to Moranes except for 1913 pushers. Bo.11 served with Aéronautique Militaire and, as seaplane, with RNAS. Most made by Delacombe & Marechal. Conscription of workers closed Mourmelon factory, but restarted November 1915 as Etablissements Borel with 4 factories working on Caudrons, Nieuports and SPADs. Prototype Borel-Odier BoT twin-engine torpedo seaplane destroyed on first flight August 1916, but 91 later built and, in 1919, BoC 10-passenger version. In 1918 company restructured as SGCIM (Société Générale des Constructions Industrielles et

Borel 'Coupe Pommery' 1912 at Paris Salon.

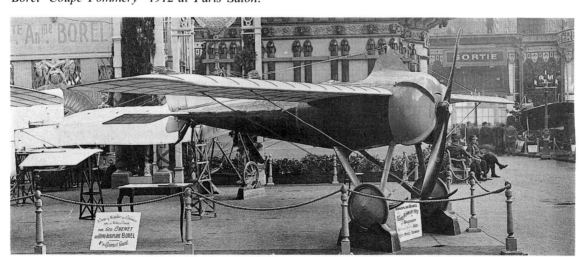

Boulton Paul Overstrand, 101 Sqn, Bicester, 1935.

Mécaniques), for which Paul Boccaccio designed C1 and C2 (Type 3000) fighters. C2 flew 1919, several times modified; outstanding performance (e.g. 162 mph) but war was over.

Borg (USA). Richard R. Borg built light aircraft 1981.

Borgward (W. Germany). Famous Bremen car company built Kolibri I 3-seat helicopter designed by Prof. E.H. Focke (8 July 1958).

Borovkov-Florov (USSR). Aleksei A. Borovkov and Ilya F. Florov set up OKB-7 early 1936, producing series of excellent small biplane fighters 7211, I-207 and I-207M. Fighter D, piston/ramjet, abandoned 1941.

Borzecki (Poland). Jozef Borzecki of Wroclaw built ultralight 1968.

Bossi (Italy). This company built at least 8 aeroplanes 1910–13. First appears to have been Bossi-Majoli biplane of 1911 with girder fuselage and chain reduction drive from low Gnome to high propeller. Hydroplane of 1913 said to be first Italian seaplane.

Bossi-Bonomi (Italy). Enea Bossi and Vittorio Bonomi built pioneer man-powered aircraft 1937, claimed flights near 1 km.

Botley (UK). Named after Hampshire town, Botley Aircraft purchased rights to Currie Wot, and marketed plans 1968.

Bottoms (USA). L.L. Bottoms built light aircraft 1966–7.

Bougie (Canada). Yvan C. Bougie built light aircraft 1976.

Boulton Paul (UK). Originally **Boulton & Paul**, long-established engineering firm in Norwich awarded 1915 contract for FE.2bs followed by many others. In 1917 set up design office under John Dudley North (ex Horatio Barber, Grahame-White and Austin-Ball). First design P.3 Hawk, later renamed Bobolink, narrowly beaten by Snipe as replacement for Camel. P.7 Bourges twin-engined bomber was looped, rolled and spun. This led to Bolton, Bugle and Bodmin, with wood structure replaced by steel, and hence to Sidestrand (1926) and Overstrand (1933) used by 101 Sqn. P.31 Bittern and P.33 Partridge fighters and P.64 mailplane remained prototypes, and only 2 P.71A passenger aircraft were built. In 1934 B&P formed new subsidiary, **Boulton Paul Aircraft Ltd**, and in 1936 this moved from Mousehold aerodrome, Norwich, to large new factory at Wolverhampton. First flown 11 August 1937, Defiant 2-seat fighter with power turret was a failure, most of 1,065 built being night fighters with radar or target tugs. Via 3-seat P.108 turbo-prop, 2-seat Merlin-engined Balliol T.2 was produced from 1951. P.111 and P.120 were subsonic delta jet research aircraft. BPA withdrew from aircraft manufacture 1954 and became world leader in flight controls and other systems, joining Dowty Group 1969.

Bounsall (USA). Eddie and son Curtiss Bounsall built Prospector light aircraft 1982 and Super Prospector 1989.

Bourdon (USA). Bourdon Aircraft Corporation, Hillsgrove, Rhode Island, built 6 Kitty Hawk 2-seaters powered by Ryan-built Siemens (5 May 1928).

Bourgois (France). Avions Légers Bourgois (not Bourgeois) produced AT.35 2-seat parasol monoplane 1928. AM.50 seaplane added lower wing.

Bowers (USA). Pete Bowers, well-known Boeing engineer, historian and writer, built Fly Baby monoplane 1960; now called Fly Baby 1-A, 4,900 plans sold, over 500 aircraft flown. In 1969 built Fly Baby 1-B biplane, over 20 more flown subsequently.

Bowker (UK). Bowker Air Service built light aircraft 1972.

Bowlus (USA). Major glider manufacturer, built CG-7 and CG-8 troopcarrier prototypes 1942.

Bowser-Barker (USA). Kenneth Bowser and Gailard Barker built light aircraft 1958.

Boyd (USA). Gary Boyd built light aircraft 1982.

Boyette (USA). Ernie Boyette built light aircraft 1982.

Brandenburg (Germany). Brandenburgische Flugzeugwerke established at Libau January 1914 by Igo Etrich, designer of original Taube monoplane. Heinkel joined as designer, but control passed May 1914 to Austrian commercial councillor and millionaire Camillo Castiglioni, who moved works to large facilities at Brandenburg am Havel and changed name to Hansa und Brandenburgische, which *see*.

Brändli (Switzerland). Max Brändli built BX-2 Cherry light aircraft 1982; 21 now flying.

Brandt (France). Michel Brandt, then chief engineer of Robin, built aerobatic aircraft 1976.

Branson (USA). Branson Aircraft, Denver, major modification centre.

Brantly (USA). N.O. Brantly began designing B-1 coaxial helicopter 1943, flown 1946. Replaced by simpler B-2, flown 21 February 1953, since mass-produced together with 5-seat Model 305. Successively became division of Lear Jet Industries, ARDC (Aeronautical R&D Corp), Brantly Operators Inc. and, on 1 January 1975, Brantly-Hynes.

Brantly (USA). Brantly Helicopter Industries USA formed 8 May 1989, James T. Kimura having purchased rights from Hynes. New company based Vernon, Texas.

Brantly-Hynes (USA). Michael K. Hynes acquired all rights to Brantly helicopters and formed Brantly-Hynes Helicopter Inc. 1 January 1975, at original location (Frederick, Oklahoma). Sold rights to Kimura March 1989.

Bratu (France). Formed Ateliers d'Aviation et Recherche, works at Juvisy, best known for Type 220 airliner for 10 passengers, high-wing monoplane with GR9 Jupiter on nose and pylon-mounted upper nacelle with 2 push/pull GR Titan (26 November 1930).

Bratukhin (USSR). Ivan Pavlovich Bratukhin ran OKB-3 at MAI 1940–51. Concentrated on helicopters with aeroplane tail and left/right girders or wings carrying an engine/rotor group. Omega, or 2MG, delayed by German invasion until 1943. Helicopters Omega II, G-3, G-4, B-5, B-9, B-10 and B-11 progressively better, last 5 designs having 550-hp or 575-hp AI-26GRF engines.

Braunschweig (Germany). Technische Universität Braunschweig (Brunswick) built 4 Zaunkönig (Wren) STOL ultralights, first flown June 1942, 2 flown post-war.

Bravia (International). Formed jointly by British and Russian interests to co-ordinate design, manufacture and marketing of Tu-204-220.

Breda (Italy). Società Italiana Ernesto Breda, Milan engineering company, was given 1916 contract to build Caproni bombers. Then followed profusion of original designs, covering many aircraft categories: A.2 cantilever

Breda Ba 65bis, October 1936.

monoplane 1921 for touring (130 hp) or reconnaissance (250 hp); A.3 4-engined heavy bomber; A.4 primary trainer (50 built); A.7 reconnaissance monoplane; A.8 twin-engined bomber; A.9 and A.10 advanced trainers; A.14 3-engined bomber; Ba.15 cabin tourer; A.16 long-range recon.; Ba.19 aerobatic trainer; Ba.25 mass-produced (719 plus over 30 exports) biplane trainer; Ba.27 monoplane fighter; Ba.28 aerobatic trainer; Ba.33 touring monoplane; Ba.39 and 42 touring monoplanes; Ba.44 twin-engined transport; Ba.64 attack/recon. monoplane; Ba.65 attack aircraft (275 built); Ba.75 attack/recon.; Ba.82 medium bomber; Ba.88 Lince attack aircraft; and Ba.201 dive-bomber. Company survived war and flew prototype Breda-Zappata BZ.308 airliner (August 1948) and Breda-Pittoni B.P.471 transport (1950).

BredaNardi (Italy). BredaNardi Costruzioni Aeronautiche formed Milan 15 February 1971 by Breda and Nardi in equal shares to build Hughes

(now McDonnell Douglas) 300C and 500C helicopters and derivatives. Became subsidiary of Agusta 1986 and lost identity 1990, becoming Agusta Monteprandone works.

Bredelet et Gros (France). Built BG-1 all-metal 4-seater 1985.

Breese (USA). Built 301 Penguin monoplanes for Army 1917 for fast taxi/hop, not flying training.

Breguet (France). Brothers Louis and Jacques, of famed Breguet clock and watchmaking family, collaborated with Prof. Charles Richet to build first helicopter to lift a man (19 September 1907). Improved Breguet-Richet II followed. First aeroplane was 60-hp biplane (28 June 1909) flown at Reims meeting. Breguet IV 'Coffee pot' carried 6 people August 1910. **Société des Avions Louis Breguet** formed 1911, starting 60 unbroken years of design and production. Early standard types included G.3 100-hp biplane once flown with 10

Breguet Bre 19B2, Lorraine 12Ed, Polish AF, 1925.

aboard, and series of C-U (Canton-Unné engine) types, one being a flying-boat. Many G.3 and G.4 biplanes were sold to military customers. German advance August 1914 resulted in evacuation from Douai factory and establishment of new works at Villacoublay. Here was completed first BU3 pusher bomber, mass-produced at Michelin works as BUM (Breguet-Michelin). Many variants, and Br.4, 5 and 12 were developments. Totally new design Br.XIV (21 November 1916) powerful tractor biplane was outstanding reconnaissance bomber and transport, 8,590 + built by 1926. Bre.16 and 17 were derivatives, but Bre.XIX (March 1922) was new design, with 3,280 sold worldwide by 1934. Bre.27 and twin-engined 41 had tail carried on slim boom to give rear gunner wider field of fire. Successful airliners were 280T single-engined and 393T 3-engined biplanes. Bre.521 Bizerte (September 1933) was large patrol flying-boat, 530 Saigon passenger version, Bre.730 (April 1938) giant monoplane flying-boat. Bre.462 Vultur bomber (1936) was cantilever monoplane, 470 Fulgur passenger version. Bre.690 prototype (23 March 1938) was outstanding high-speed twin-engined aircraft which, despite severe political delays, led to nearly 500 of several versions, mostly attack bombers, by June 1940. Breguet tried to avoid nationalization under 1936 law, and so had all priority in materials removed and 2 factories forcibly transferred to SNCAN and SNCAO. Wartime work included Ju 52/3m production, wings for Fw 189 and complete BV 144 transport programme. Bre.500 Colmar airliner designed during war, flown 1945. Bre.482 4-engined bomber flown 1948, Bre.76 Deux Ponts double-deck transport (12 Air France, 15 Bre.765 Sahara for Armée de l'Air) flown 1949 together with Bre.89-OH (2 Hercules) and 89-2S (4 Renault) Mercure transports, Type 900 sailplane and Type IIE helicopter (see next entry). Bre.960 Vultur anti-submarine aircraft with Mamba turboprop and Nene jet (3 August 1951) led to Bre.1050 Alizé with RR Dart turboprop (6 October 1956; still in service France and India). Br.1001 Taon twin-jet attack aircraft (26 July 1957); Br.1150 Atlantic patrol aircraft (21 October 1965), production handled by SECBAT. Br.121 was original French input to Anglo-French Jaguar produced by SEPECAT. Control of company passed by French government to Dassault 14 December 1971, forming AMD/BA (Avions Marcel Dassault, Breguet Aviation), which took control of Breguet/Dornier Alpha Jet. Identity lost in name-change to Dassault Aviation April 1990.

Breguet-Dorand (France). Breguet and René Dorand established Syndicat d'Etudes du Gyroplane 1931, building Gyroplane Laboratoire coaxial helicopter. Flown November 1933, regarded in France as first fully successful helicopter.

Breguet-Michelin, -Richet: *See* Breguet.

Bremen (W. Germany). Fluwag (Flugwissenschaftliche Arbeitsgemeineschaft) Bremen produced ESS 641 low-wing single-seat glider tug with 180-hp Lycoming (17 September 1971).

Brewster (USA). James Brewster formed company 1810 to make carts, wagons and coaches. Brewster Aeronautical Corp. 1932 built floats and airframe parts. Design began 1934 on carrier-based scout bomber XSBA-1 (15 April 1936), leading to 30 SBN-1 built by Naval Aircraft Factory. B-139 naval fighter first flew December 1937, led to US Navy F2A and RAF Buffalo—507 built including Dutch East Indies and Finland, but outclassed by enemy. SB2A Buccaneer (RAF Bermuda) naval scout bomber complete failure. Company's poor performance building F3A Corsair led to cancellation of all Navy orders 1944.

Bristol (UK). In 1909 aviation was not a polite subject for gentlemen to take seriously. Amazingly, at Bristol Sir George White Bt., brother Samuel and son George Stanley White decided to sink personal fortune in creating major aircraft company. One of their companies was Bristol Tramways, and the decision was announced at AGM in Grand Hotel 16 February 1910, emphasizing that not one penny would be taken from Tramways stockholders. Registered companies, chose name **British and Colonial Aeroplane Co.** Began by making French Zodiac (Voisin-type) biplane in tramways sheds at northern terminus at Filton. Unsuccessful aircraft, so G.H. Challenger produced improved version of Farman, result being Bristol Boxkite, 76 built. Flying schools established at Brooklands and Larkhill. First World War production included 371 agile Scout biplanes, 125 M.1C monoplane fighters and (including production by others) 5,252 of superb F.2B Fighter. Mainly to avoid excess war profits, business transferred 6 March

Bristol 188, No. 1 aircraft, January 1962.

1920 to *ad hoc* **Bristol Aeroplane Co.** (another registered 1910). At same time formed Engine Department to develop Jupiter and other engines designed by Roy Fedden formerly of Cosmos Engineering, and this business quickly became more important than aeroplanes. Most 1920s prototypes single-engined biplanes, by far most important being Type 105 Bulldog fighter (443 built 1927–34). Type 130 Bombay transport flown 1935, 50 built by Short & Harland. Type 138 height-record aircraft 1936. Type 142 high-speed transport, pioneer British stressed-skin monoplane (12 April 1935), leading to 142M Blenheim bomber (25 June 1936), 5,486 of several versions. Type 152 Beaufort torpedo bomber (15 October 1938), 1,380 plus 700 DAP Australia. Type 156 Beaufighter (17 July 1939), 5,564 plus 364 DAP Australia. In 1942–9 production included Type 163 Buckingham (123), 164 Brigand (147) and 166 Buckmaster (112). Only one Type 167 Brabazon flew (4 September 1949), but 214 Type 170 Freighters (2 December 1945) were built, and 178 Type 171 Sycamore helicopters (27 July 1947). Type 173 helicopter remained prototypes, and derived Type 192 Belvedere (26 built) was passed to Westland. Final designs were Type 175 Britannia (16 August 1952) long-range airliner (85 built) and two Type 188 supersonic research aircraft (1962). On 1 July 1944 overdue formation of Aircraft Division and Engine Division took place, and these became separate companies, **Bristol Aircraft** and Bristol Aero-Engines, January 1956. Former became 20% of British Aircraft Corp. February 1960. Latter became 50% of Bristol Siddeley Engines April 1959 (bought by Rolls-Royce 1966).

Bristol (USA). Bristol Aeronautical Corp. built 2 XLRQ-1 troopcarrying flying-boat gliders 1942.

Bristol Aerospace (Canada). Long-established Winnipeg producer of rockets, now handling upgrades of CAF Northrop CF-5 fleet.

British Aerial Transport: *See* BAT.

British Aerospace (UK). In 1977 Government determined to nationalize British industry and passed Aircraft and Shipbuilding Industries Act, as result of which on 29 April 1977 ownership of British Aircraft Corp., Hawker Siddeley Aviation, Hawker Siddeley Dynamics and Scottish Aviation was vested in corporation called British Aerospace, former companies continuing to trade under original names. On 1 January 1978 BAe was split into Aircraft Group and Dynamics Group. Aircraft Group was itself divided into 6 operating divisions: Kingston/Brough, Hatfield/Chester, Warton, Weybridge/Bristol, Manchester and Scottish. These divisions linked historical partners and had nothing to do with type of work. On 1 January 1981 all business of this nationalized corporation was vested in **British Aerospace plc** (public limited company) under British Aerospace Act; after share offer a month later ownership became: HM government 48.43%, shareholders 48.43%, employees 3.14%. In May 1985 HM government offered for sale all its remaining shares. Following further reorganization company operated as 8 divisions: Weybridge (Weybridge, Brough, Manchester, Dunsfold, Hamble, Kingston and Woodford); Civil Aircraft (Hatfield, Chester,

British Aerospace Jetstream 31s at Dayton, Ohio, 1990.

Bristol, Prestwick); Warton (Warton, Preston, Samlesbury); and 5 non-aircraft divisions. Further reorganization in 1989 resulted in all aircraft work being managed by 2 companies: **BAe (Commercial Aircraft) Ltd**, centred at Woodford (previously at Hatfield, being closed), and **BAe (Military Aircraft) Ltd**, centred at Warton. Further change in January 1992 split Commercial Aircraft into: BAe Airbus, making wings for all Airbus aircraft, mainly at Chester and Bristol; BAe Regional Aircraft, making BAe 146 and Jetstream 31, 41 and 61 (ex-ATP), and handling VC10 tanker and USAF F-111 support at Woodford, Prestwick, Bristol and elsewhere; and BAe Corporate Jets, making 125-800, BAe 1000 and Statesman at Hatfield and Chester. Also in January 1992 BAe Defence Ltd formed to combine Military Aircraft and Dynamics. Military Aircraft work includes Hawk in all versions and participation in EFA, Tornado, T-45A Goshawk, Harrier GR.7/Night Attack/AV-8B-Plus, Sea Harrier FRS.2 and TAV-8A, and update of Buccaneer and other aircraft. Dynamics produces air, army and naval weapons systems. Other aviation subsidiaries include Space Systems, Enterprises (managing Flying College, Prestwick) and BAe Simulation. Aerostructures Hamble sold (which *see*). Partner in Airbus (20%), Eurofighter (33%), Panavia (42.5%) and SEPECAT (50%). Member of Euroflag and Alliance. New company Avro Int. formed 50/50 with TAC/Taiwan government to develop and produce RJ regional jet at Woodford and Taichung. Total employees about 119,000,

including many non-aero (e.g. Rover cars, Royal Ordnance and Ballast Nedam). See Corporate.

British Aircraft: *See* BA.

British Aircraft Co.: *See* BAC, 1st entry.

British Aircraft Corporation: *See* BAC, 2nd entry.

British and Colonial: *See* Bristol.

British Army (UK). First recognized aeroplane flight in UK (16 October 1908) was made by S.F. Cody's biplane titled *British Army Aeroplane No. 1*.

British Burnelli (UK). Proposed company not formed: *see* Cunliffe-Owen.

British Caudron (UK). Subsidiary of French company, built B.E.2c, D.H.5 and Camel.

British Deperdussin (UK). Built original French aircraft plus (1913) Seagull twin-float seaplane.

British Klemm (UK). Success of German Klemm L 25 led to formation of British Klemm Aeroplane Co. early 1933, works at Hanworth, Middlesex, designer G.H. Handasyde. L 25 strengthened and further developed into Swallow (November 1933). Handasyde added new design B.K.1 Eagle, flown January 1934. Company renamed British Aircraft Manufacturing Co. 1935: *see* BA.

British Marine (UK). British Marine Aircraft Ltd, associate of British Aircraft, tooled up new factory at Hamble to build BM-1, version of Sikorsky S-42A flying boat; instead subcontracted for RAF Expansion Scheme.

British Nieuport: *See* Nieuport (UK).

Britten-Norman (UK). John Britten and Desmond Norman built BN-1 ultralight (1950), then studied BN-2 Islander light transport (13 June 1965). Developed as BN-2A, sustained major production, including improved BN-2B, BN-2T Turbine Islander, military Defender and Maritime Defender, and stretched 3-engined Trislander family. B-N suffered financial problems resulting in takeover by Fairey Group 1972. Fairey in turn went into receivership 1977, and in 1979 Pilatus of Switzerland purchased assets of Britten-Norman (Bembridge), including factory on Isle of Wight and former Fairey SA production at Gosselies, Belgium. Actual manufacture had been transferred to Romania (IRMA, then IAv Bucuresti, now Romaero). *See also* Pilatus Britten-Norman.

Brno (Czechoslovakia). Brno Transport Technical Institute produced XA-66 light autogyro, flown 16 May 1968.

Brobecker (France). Ateliers Gérard Brobecker built light aircraft 1967.

Brochet (France). Avions Maurice Brochet produced series of high-wing cabin aircraft simple enough for home construction. M.B.50 (1948) open cockpit; rest were 2-, 3- or 4-seat cabin machines designated M.B.60, 70, 71, 80, 100, 101, 110 and 120 by 1952.

Brock (USA). Ken Brock Manufacturing, division of Santa Ana Metal Stamping, has sold several hundred plans of KB-2 Freedom Machine autogyro.

Brodhead (USA). Arthur L. Brodhead built light aircraft 1972.

Brokaw (USA). Dr Bergon F. Brokaw, with Dr Ernest R. Jones, built Bullet, flown 18 November 1972, said to be fastest 2-seat homebuilt.

Bromon (USA). Bromon Aircraft Corp. formed 1987 to develop BR2000 twin-turboprop STOL transport, inspired by Ahrens 404 and likewise being built at Ramey AFB, Puerto Rico. Money ran out 1989.

Brooklands (UK). Brooklands Aircraft Co., based at Old Sarum, succeeded Optica Industries. Optica observation aircraft was designed by Edgley Aircraft, formed 1974 but failed 1985. Purchased from Receiver by A. Haikney of Aero-Docks, who formed Optica Industries which restarted production January 1986 until factory destroyed by fire 16 January 1987. Renamed Brooklands Aircraft 14 April 1987, but failed again March 1990 and bought by Lovaux. *See* FLS.

Broome County Aviation (USA). Bought rights to Dumod I and II in 1972.

Broughton-Blayney (UK). Produced 3 examples of Brawny ultralight at £195, 1936.

Brown-Mercury (USA). In 1927 pioneer pilot Lawrence W. 'Larry' Brown built Brown Mercury high-wing monoplane, which was basis for Kreutzer Air Coach. In 1931 he formed Lawrence Brown Aircraft to build racing aircraft to order. Famous *Miss Los Angeles* led to B-3 2-seat tourer 1936.

Brueggemann (USA). Clarence Brueggemann built light aircraft 1971.

Brügger (Switzerland). Max Brügger built Colibri 1 1965 and Colibri 2 1970, both single-seaters, over 260 Colibri 2 building or flying.

Brunet (France). André Brunet designed 2 parasol monoplane 2-seat fighters built by Ateliers des Mureaux and often referred to as Mureaux aircraft; 3C2 flew June 1927 and 4C2 1928. Latter served as basis for Mureaux 130 reconnaissance aircraft.

Brunner-Winkle (USA). Brunner-Winkle Aircraft Corp., incorporated 1928, built Bird 3-seat biplane.

Brunswick: *See* Braunschweig.

Brush (UK). Brush Electrical Engineering Co., later part of Hawker Siddeley, made Avro 504C/J/K and Short 184 and 830 1915–18.

Bücker Bü 133 Jungmeister (Mike Stowe's); prototype February 1935.

BRW (Germany). Bayerische Rumpler-Werke (Bayru) at Augsburg was Bavarian subsidiary of Rumpler Flugzeug-Werke at Johannisthal. BRW built various aircraft designed by parent firm and others, and among minor design tasks produced variant of Rumpler C.I adapted for training.

Bryan (USA). Leland D. Bryan spent 1955–63 developing roadable aircraft, Bryan 2, folded wings enclosing pusher propeller.

Bucciero (Italy). Alitalia captain Renato Bucciero, assisted by Gastone Canal, built SVIT training/touring aircraft 1969.

Buchanan: *See* BAC (Australia).

Bücker (Germany). Carl Clemens Bücker founded first SAAB company 1921. In 1932 he sold his shareholding and formed Bücker Flugzeugbau at Berlin-Johannisthal. Products were aerobatic sporting/training aircraft: Bü 131 Jungmann, Bü 133 Jungmeister, Bü 180 Student, Bü 181 Bestmann and Bü 182 Kornett. All outstandingly successful, many licensed to other countries.

Budd (USA). Edward G. Budd Manufacturing Co., famed for stainless steel products, especially railroad cars, built Conestoga stainless-steel cargo aircraft 1943; major contracts cancelled but 17 Navy JRB-3 built.

Buecker (USA). Carl H. Buecker built light aircraft 1961–2.

Buethe (USA). W.B. Buethe Enterprises sold 560 sets of plans of Barracuda high-speed sport 2 seater by 1992; about 60 flying.

Bugatti (France). Famed for cars and engines, Ettore Bugatti's company built at La Ferté Alais (but probably did not fly) 100P and 110P racers, 1933–4, each with 2 450-hp engines (not a single Bugatti twin-block King) driving nose contraprops, with canopy between spinner and engines; wing normally slight forward sweep, but pivoted to sweep slightly to rear in flight.

Buhl (USA). Buhl Aircraft Co., originally Buhl-Verville, established 1927 at Marysville, Michigan, continued production of versions of CA-3 Airster, followed by CA-5 Airsedan 5-seat cabin biplane. CA-6 was definitive 6-seat version and CA-8 had 8 seats or cargo. Sales were small, and to help survive in Depression LA-1 Bull Pup single-seater was built 1931 until closure 1933.

Buhl-Verville (USA). B-V Aircraft formed at Detroit March 1925 to build CA-3 Airster 2/3-seat biplane, recipient 1927 of Approved Type Certificate No. 1. Verville left 1927, company becoming Buhl.

Bulte: *See* Guldentops.

Bunyard (USA). K. Bunyard Aircraft Co. built small biplane flying-boat 1931, following with 3- and 4-seat amphibian prototypes 1946–7.

Burgess (USA). Entitled **The W. Starling Burgess Co. and Curtis** (no relation to Curtiss), this company was formed 1 February 1911. Initially built licensed designs by Farman, Curtiss, Grahame-White, Dunne and Wright, small numbers being sold to Army and Navy. Model I

Buhl-Verville CW-3 (OX-5 Airster), December 1925.

seaplane (60 hp, 2 pusher screws) used by Army in Philippines 1913–15. Six Model H trainers were Army's first tractor aircraft. More than 20 Model L and Model S trainers were built as land- and seaplanes before Burgess became division of Curtiss 1917.

Burgfalke (W. Germany). Burgfalke Flugzeug-bau, near Regensburg, built sailplanes after Second World War and, 1961, M.150 Schulmeister 2-seat pusher aerobatic aircraft.

Burkhart Grob: *See* Grob.

Burnelli (USA). Vincent Burnelli helped design various mainly unsuccessful aircraft during First World War, but always harboured dream of making aeroplanes with fuselages which

contributed to total lift. In 1920 he formed **Airliner Engineering Corp.** at Amityville, Long Island, in partnership with T.T. Remington. Built 2 RB-1 biplane transports and (1924) RB-2. Monoplanes followed: CB-16 (1928) built at Aeromarine plant for Sky Lines president Paul W. Chapman, aircraft also known as PWC; small GX-3 (1929) for Guggenheim competition; UB-20 transport (1930) made by Aeromarine Klemm, Inglis M. Uppercu president (hence designation UB) and Burnelli VP and chief engineer. Up-perçu-Burnelli then built UB-14 and UB-14B transports, latter also produced by Cunliffe-Owen. A-1 bomber (1935) not built, but design basis of XCG-16A troopcarrying glider built by General Airborne 1943. Final aircraft built was CBY-3 Loadmaster, by CanCar 1945. Numerous projects remained on paper.

Burgess HT-2, June 1917.

Buscaylet (De Monge) 7/4, September 1923.

Burns (USA). Burns Aircraft Co. built light aircraft 1967–8.

Buscaylet (France). Buscaylet et Cie produced aircraft under subcontract 1916–18. Reorganized post-war as Buscaylet Père et Fils-Bobin, hired Louis de Monge as designer and began with Buscaylet de Monge 5/2, parasol monoplane fighter first flown at Villacoublay early 1923. Based on de Monge 5/1 racer, and judged 'too modern' for service use. Advanced monoplane 7/4 (1923) and 7/5 (1925) flown but unsold.

Bush (USA). Bush Conversions specialize in tailwheel conversions of nosewheel Cessnas.

Bushby (USA). One of longest-running homebuilt programmes was launched when Robert W. Bushby flew Midget Mustang 1948; over 400 today and 800 being built. Side-by-side Mustang II flew 1966, over 350 now built and 1,300 plans sold.

Bushmaster (USA). Bushmaster Aircraft Corp., formed August 1970, purchased rights to Bushmaster 2000. Latter was updated Ford Tri-Motor designed by William B. Stout (*see* Stout, 1st entry) and built by Aircraft Hydro-Forming, flying 1966. In 1969 builder was purchased by Whittaker Corporation, which sold rights to Bushmaster 1970. No customers for aircraft.

Business Aircraft Corporation (USA). Formed San Antonio, Texas, July 1963 by merger of

Howard with Alamo. Howard subsequently styled Howard Aero Manufacturing Division (*see* Howard, 2nd entry).

Butler (USA). Butler Aircraft Co. built light aircraft 1970–72.

Butterworth (USA). G.N. Butterworth markets plans of 2/3-scale Westland Whirlwind, first flown July 1977.

Bylinkin-Jordan-Sikorsky (Russia/Ukraine). Having given up helicopters, Igor Sikorsky collaborated with 2 other students at Kiev Polytechnic Institute and built BJS.1 (or BIS, from Iordan) pusher biplane May 1910, and more successful BJS.2 June 1910, latter becoming basis for Sikorsky S.3.

C

CAARP (France). Coopérative des Ateliers Aéronautiques de la Région Parisienne, at Beynes, was a modification/repair centre until in 1965 it took over from Scintex manufacture of Super Emeraude. From this CAARP developed CAP.10 and 20 aerobatic aircraft, handling manufacture of latter and supplying CAP.10 fuselages to

Mudry, into which CAARP merged 1977.

CAC (Australia). Resulted from 1934 talks which led to syndicate to establish national capability in aircraft manufacture. Government was interested in independence of external military suppliers; October 1935 asked syndicate to form company, and Commonwealth Aircraft Corporation Pty Ltd registered 17 October 1936. Backers Broken Hill Pty, Broken Hill Smelters, General Motors Holden, ICI of Australia and NZ, Orient Steam Navigation and Electrolytic Zinc. Tugan Aircraft, just formed at Sydney Mascot by W/Cdr Lawrence J. Wackett, became subsidiary, Wackett becoming designer at new factory at Fishermen's Bend, Melbourne. Made N. American NA-16 version called Wirraway (755), and Wasp engine (680); CA-2 Wackett Trainer (200); CA-4 and -11 Woomera twin-engined bomber and Twin Wasp engine (870 engines); CA-12/13/14/19 Boomerang fighter (249); and 266 CA-17/18 Mustangs. Post-war 1 CA-15 Griffon-engined fighter, 62 CA-25 Winjeel trainers, 111 CA-27 Sabre fighters, 21 CA-28 Ceres ag-aircraft, 100 CA-29 Mirage III-O fighters, 85 CA-30 (MB.326) jet trainers and 56 CA-32 (Bell) Kiowa helicopters. By 1977 reduced to various subcontract and detail jobs, and in 1985 became subsidiary of Hawker de Havilland, losing identity.

CAC (China). Chengdu Aircraft Corp. formed 1958 as major centre for fighter development and production. CAC developed JJ-5 trainer based on J-5 (MiG-17), flown 8 May 1966 (1,061 built) and handled development of J-7 derived from MiG-21F-13 (17 January 1966) and many derivatives. Partnership with Grumman on Super 7 stopped by US Government 1989, now replaced by all-new J-9 fighter for year 2000.

CAC (Japan). Commercial Airplane Co. took over Japan's 767 work from CTDC July 1982.

CAF: *See* Changhe Aircraft Factory.

Cagny (France). Raymond de Cagny is haltingly developing Performance 2000 3-seater.

CAHI (USSR, Russia). Central Aero and Hydrodynamic Institute, Moscow, founded December 1918 by N.Ye. Zhukovsky. Provided aerodynamic basis of knowledge for all significant Soviet aircraft, and managed early rotary-wing programmes: 1-EA by Prof. B.N. Yur'yev (August 1930), 5-EA and 11-EA by Bratukhin, 2-EA autogyro by Izakson (1931) and outstanding A-4–A-15 used in Arctic and in Second World War.

CAI (Ciskei). Ciskei Aircraft Industries Pty Ltd was formed at Bisho's Bulembu airport but never managed to build Austrian HB aircraft under licence.

CAI: *See* Composite (S. Africa).

Cain (USA). Cain Aircraft Corp. incorporated at Detroit 1 January 1931 to build Cirrus-engined Cain Sport parasol 2-seater.

Cairns (USA). Cairns Development Co. October

CAC (Commonwealth) CA-14 Boomerang, with GE turbo, late 1942.

Cairns Model AW, 1930.

1928 became Cairns Aircraft Corp. August 1929, flew Model A stressed-skin monoplane April 1930.

CAL: *See* Aeronasa.

California Helicopter (USA). California Helicopter International owns rights to S-58T turbine conversion, and delivers complete S-58T helicopters or kits.

California Microwave (USA). Specialize in conversions for surveillance missions.

Call (USA). Members of Call family in Wyoming designed simple utility aircraft for neighbouring farmers and ranchers, 80-hp Model A flown 1940. During war Call Aircraft Co. registered at Afton, but production impossible until 1946. Model A-2 had 100 hp, A-3 125 hp, A-4 135 hp then 150 hp, A-6 180 hp, A-9 235 hp and B-1 400 hp. From this came even greater variety of CallAir aircraft, but in 1962 Call bought by IMCO.

Calspan (USA). Cornell Aeronautical Laboratory was academic seat of learning, part of Cornell University. Reflecting rapid growth in commercial contracting, changed name 17 November 1972 to **Calspan Corp**. Largest task at that time was Convair NC-131H TIFS (total in-flight simulator) under contract to USAF. Navy X-22A V/STOL was investigated, NT-33A flown for USAF Flight Dynamics Laboratory, and in 1981 a variable-stability Learjet was

added. Calspan became division of Arvin Industries 1978.

Calypso (USA). Calypso Airways, division of Calypso Engineering, markets modifications to Piper Tomahawk, including low tailplane.

CAM: *See* Carothers.

CAMA (USA). CAMA Manufacturing Co. built light aircraft 1957–9.

Camair (USA). Cameron Iron Works, Galveston, Texas, wanted twin-engined business aircraft and produced conversion of single-engined NAA/Ryan Navion. Flown early 1953, proved so successful it was produced for sale as Camair 480: *see* next entry.

Camair (USA). In 1966 all rights to Camair 480 purchased by newly formed Camair Aircraft Corp., Remsenburg, Long Island, aircraft being marketed as Camair Twin Navion (CTN) in versions CTN-A, -B, -C and -D, with engines increasing in power from 225 hp to 300 hp. Production ceased 1979.

CAMC: *See* Changhe Aircraft Factory.

CAMCO (China). Central Aircraft Manufacturing Co. established 1939 in new factory at Loiwing, initial task being to build Vultee V-12C. Bombed October 1940, tools and components sent to Hindustan Aircraft where most of remain-

CAMS 38 (1923 Schneider).

der completed and flown back to China. CAMCO undertook modification of various Curtiss, Grumman and Polikarpov aircraft.

Cammacorp (USA). Cammacorp formed El Segundo (LA) 1977 to manage major rework of DC-8 transports, including replacing engines by CFM56 turbofan, with McDonnell Douglas support. Total conversions 110.

Campbell (UK). Campbell Aircraft Ltd bought UK rights to Bensen autogyros 1959. Various projects failed to materialize, but 47 examples sold of basic version named Cricket.

CAMS (France). Major producer of flying-boats, Chantiers Aéro-Maritimes de la Seine formed November 1920 by Swiss engineer D. Lawrence Santoni to build seaplanes and flying-boats. Began building Italian SIAI-Marchetti S.9 and

S.13 under licence, their designer Rafaele Conflenti becoming CAMS technical director May 1922. CAMS.31 150-hp flying-boat standard French naval trainer; CAMS 31 300-hp fighter flying-boat; CAMS 33 (2 275-hp) recon/bomber; CAMS 36 racer; CAMS 37 (first by Maurice Hurel, who designed all subsequent) multirole 450-hp flying-boat or amphibian; CAMS 38 racer; CAMS 46 trainer; CAMS 53 (2 580-hp) transport, many built; CAMS 55 (2 500-hp) patrol bomber, many built; and CAMS 58 airliner. This took story to 1933, when CAMS purchased by Potez. For 141, 160 and 161, *see* Potez.

Canadair (Canada). In 1944, to increase Canadian-owned aircraft industry, Canadian government bought Canadian Vickers and awarded giant plant at Cartierville (Montreal) contracts for DC-4M conversions of DC-4 with

Canadair CL-28 Argus 1, July 1957.

Merlin engines (70 aircraft, military North Star and pressurized civil Argonaut). Crown company called **Canadair Ltd**, then sold to USA [!], becoming division of General Dynamics. Built 1,815 Sabres, 656 T-33AN Silver Stars and 33 CL-28 Argus derived from Britannia, but major programme for developed Britannias and Eland-engined Convairs killed by British cancellation of engines, leaving just Tyne-engined CL-44. In 1960s Canadair made 210 CL-41 Tutor jet trainers, 340 F-104G versions plus hundreds of F-104G parts, and major share of NF-5 Freedom Fighter programme with Fokker. Subsequent work included CL-84 tilt-wing V/STOL, CL-215, 215T and 415 fire-bombers, CL-600/601 Challenger business jets (8 November 1978) and derived RJ Regional Jet (10 May 1991) and Global Express (1996). In 1976 company was bought back from GD by Canadian government, coming under control of Canada Development Investment Corporation 1982. In 1986 sale agreed to Bombardier Inc. of Montreal, and on 5 August 1988 merged with parent to become Bombardier-Canadair, now part of Bombardier-Aerospace. Subcontract work includes parts of F-15, F/A-18 Hornet, 767, P-3C and A330/340.

Canadian Aeroplanes Ltd (Canada). Government company which took over former Curtiss Canada factory at Long Branch November 1916 to build Avro 504K.

Canadian Associated Aircraft (Canada). Formed 1938 to act as single interface with British government for CanCar, Canadian Vickers, Fairchild, National Steel Car, Fleet and Ottawa Car & Aircraft, until 1942.

Canadian Car & Foundry (Canada). Also known as CCF and, latterly, as Can-Car or CanCar, this firm was biggest Canadian manufacturer of railway equipment, but decided to set up aircraft business because of Spanish Republican interest in Grumman G-23 2-seat fighter. CCF obtained licence 1937 and assembled 51 using Grumman fuselages and Brewster wings/tails. CCF also built Gregor FDB-1 advanced biplane fighter (17 December 1938). Wartime production included 1,451 Hurricanes, 241 Ansons and 894 SBW Helldivers, while in 1952-4 output included 125 T-34 Mentors and T-6G Harvards. Subsequent work included wings and/or tails for DHC-6 Otter, CS2F-1 Tracker and CF-104 aircraft, all at Fort William plant to which company moved

1951. When Noorduyn ceased operations May 1946 CCF acquired rights and continued production to 1953. CCF acquired world rights to Burnelli (which *see*), built Loadmaster 1945 and set up Cancargo Aircraft Manufacturing Co. to produce both this and much larger developments. Became subsidiary of A.V. Roe Canada 1956, on airframe subcontract.

Canadian Curtiss Aeroplane Co. (Canada). Set up factory at Long Branch, Toronto, 1915 to build JN series trainers; taken over 1916 by Canadian Aeroplanes.

Canadian Vertol (Canada). Formed at Arnprior, west of Ottawa, February 1954, initial work centring on modifying Vertol 44 and H-21B helicopters to 42A standard. Became part of Boeing Canada 1960.

Canadian Vickers (Canada). Vickers Ltd established this company at Montreal St Hubert 1911 as engineering and shipbuilding works. In 1922 began assembling 8 Viking IV 6-seat amphibians, increasingly of local manufacture. W.T. Reid came from Bristol and designed Canadian aircraft, most succesful (61, 1924-31) being Vedette 3-seat flying-boat. Other types: Varuna transport flying-boat 1927, Vista single-seat flying-boat (1927), Vanessa 4-passenger seaplane 1927, Vigil observation landplane 1928, Velos twin-engined survey aircraft 1929. Subsequent production was of licensed designs, and from 1942 giant new Government plant at Cartierville produced 149 PBY-5A Canso and 230 OA-10A amphibians. This plant became Canadair 1944, Canadian Vickers abandoning aircraft manufacture.

Canary (W. Germany). Jack Canary set up Canary Aero Technik 1967 to build updated Bü 133 Jungmeister; programme continued by Hirth and Bitz companies after Canary's death 1968.

Cancargo: *See* Canadian Car & Foundry.

CANSA (Italy). Costruzioni Aeronautiche Novaresi SA, at Cameri, Novara, was subsidiary of Fiat. Among first designs were Lictor 90 (90 hp) and Lictor 130 (130 hp) low-wing cabin monoplanes of 1935. First production type was C.5 biplane trainer, 67 built 1939-41. C.5B and

CANSA (Fiat) L.C.20ter, January 1943.

C.6 were derivatives. F.C.20 high-speed reconnaissance aircraft (April 1941) led to F.C.20bis tank destroyer (also used unsuccessfully as bomber interceptor).

CANT (Italy). Formed 1923 as **Cantieri Navali Triestino**, sometimes rendered as CNT or Cant but correctly as CANT, wholly-owned subsidiary of famed shipyard Cantieri Navali di Monfalcone, also of Trieste. Appointed chief designer Rafale Conflenti, previously with Savoia and CAMS, who concentrated on flying-boats. Important early designs: CANT 6 bomber and 6ter 11-passenger transport had 3 engines; airline SISA used most of 22 CANT 7 trainers and at least 15 CANT 10 and 10ter 4-passenger boats, a few CANT 18 trainers and 10 CANT 22 8-passenger transports; Regia Aeronautica used several versions of CANT 25 fighter. CANT 26 and 36 were 2-seat landplanes.

CANT (Italy). New company formed 1931 as **Cantieri Riuniti dell' Adriatico** (CRDA), but products continued to be known by CANT title. Marshal Balbo persuaded Filippo Zappata to leave Blériot-SPAD and join as chief engineer. He produced few basic designs, but all outstandingly successful: Z.501 single-engined flying-boat (7 February 1934) named Gabbiano (Gull), 454 built by 1943; Z.506 3-engined 14-passenger seaplane flew 19 August 1935, 37 built; military Z.506B Airone (Heron) flown 1937, 322 built; Z.508 large 3-engined bomber flying-boat; Z.509 enlarged Z.506 for S. Atlantic mail route; Z.511 was world's largest twin-float seaplane (4 × 1,500 hp) for S. Atlantic route; Z.1007bis Alcione (Kingfisher) 3-engined landplane bomber flew 1938, 464 built by 1942. Z.1011 bomber remained prototypes, and Z.1018 Leone (Lion) could not be delivered in significant numbers before 1943 Armistice.

Cantilever: *See* Christmas.

Cantinieau (France). Jean Cantinieau developed helicopters with engine above cabin, first example

CANT Z.508 bomber flying-boat, 1936.

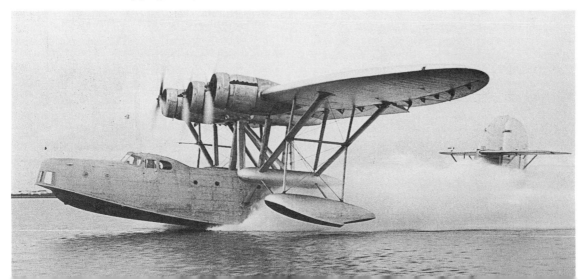

Caproni Ca 101 (1927) in Abyssinia, 1935.

actually built (by Société Matra) being Matra-Cantinieau MC.101, 1952. He then went to Spain: *see* Aerotécnica.

CAO: *See* SNCAO.

CAP (Brazil). Companhia Aeronáutica Paulista formed São Paulo 1944, quickly produced CAP.1 Planalto low-wing trainer, CAP.4 Paulistinha high-wing trainer/tourer (and 4B ambulance and 4C observation/liaison), and CAP.5 Carioca tourer. Money ran out 1948. *See* Neiva.

CAP: *See* CAARP; Mudry.

CAP: *See* Club Aviazione Popolare.

Capelis (USA). Single prototype XC-12 low-wing stressed-skin transport (2 × 525-hp Cyclone) built 1933 by Safety Aircraft. Designer, funding and builders were Greek.

Capital (USA). Capital Aircraft Corp. incorporated Detroit 1928 to produce 2-seat Capital Air Trainer monoplane.

Capital (USA). Capital Helicopter Corp. Built light helicopters based on Hoppi-Copter 1954–5.

Capitol (USA). Capitol Aviation Inc. built Capair light aircraft 1961.

Capitol (USA). Capitol Copter Corp. built single-seat cabin autogyro 1959.

Caproni (Italy). Count Gianni Caproni set up first of many companies and subsidiaries 1907, as qualified electrical engineer. Built large biplane at Milan (27 May 1910) and a year later with Agostini set up flying school at Vizzola, plus expanding factory which built monoplane (15 June 1911). Caproni suffered serious illness, Agostini replaced by Carlo Comitti who formed Società Caproni e Comitti late 1911, replaced mid-1912 by Soc. degli Ing. Caproni e Faccanoni (builder of first Italian aircraft January 1909). Government interest lukewarm, though 1 squadron equipped with excellent 1913 monoplane (80 hp). Breakthrough was prototype Ca 30 bomber of 1914, 2 tractor and 1 pusher propeller driven by row of 3 engines in central nacelle. This led to giant factory at Milan-Taliedo where by 1919 were built over 1,000 more powerful 3-engined bombers, used extensively by Italy, France, UK and USA, with additional licence-production in France and USA. Airline versions appeared from 1919, but newer designs were needed, supplied by Ing. Rodolfo Verduzio's Ca 73 of 1924, first of series of inverted sesquiplanes (big lower wing, small upper wing). Several bomber and transport versions, and scaled-up Ca 90 (6 × 1,000-hp) was world's largest/heaviest aeroplane early 1929. Ca 97 high-wing monoplane of 1927 (1 × 400/500-hp) was used for many roles, and substantial numbers also built of Ca 100 biplane trainer, Ca 101 3-engined monoplane bomber/transport and derived Ca 102 (4 engines) and Ca 111 (1 engine). Other types Ca 113 aerobatic trainer, Ca 114 biplane fighter, Ca 123 low-wing airliner, Ca 132 3-engined airliner and Ca 161 height-record biplane. Verduzio's Ca 133, flown Taliedo December 1934, was developed Ca 101 of which 417 were built, plus 135 improved Ca 148. Conflenti's Ca 164 biplane trainer was used by Regia Aeronautica (280) and French Armée de l'Air (100). By late 1930s Gianni Caproni controlled 28 main manufacturing companies, including Isotta-Fraschini engine firm. Few aircraft made by **S.A. Aeronautica Predappio** did not take Caproni name, but others did, as follow. **Compania Aeronautica Bergamasca**, at Bergamo, produced 'Caproni-Bergamaschi' types, designed by Cesare Palavicino. These began with PL.3 and Ca 301 of 1934, latter being enlarged into AP.1 attack aircraft, 66 built 1936–8. Ponte San Pietro (Bergamo) works was then allocated type numbers from 300, but major twin-engined bomber was designated Ca 135 as it was to have been produced at main Taliedo plant; but only 110 built, all at Bergamo. Ca 306 Borea light transport (7 built 1936) led to major series of upgraded derivatives: Ca 309 Ghibli recon/bomber (243 built 1936–43); Ca 310 Libeccio recon/bomber (193), Ca 311 (345), Ca 312 (39), Ca 313 (271) and Ca 314 (404, all for Regia Aeronautica). Ca 331 night fighter (2 × 800-hp) of 1942 remained prototype. **Officine Meccaniche 'Reggiane'** based at Reggio, Emilia, produced 'Caproni-Reggiane' aircraft, designed mainly by Roberto G. Longhi. Re 2000 fighter (24 May 1939) was influenced by Seversky, 147 built (and 192 by MAVAG); Re 2001 Ariete I, June 1940 (237); Re 2002 Ariete II, October 1940 (about 200, 20 destroyed by bombing before delivery); Re 2005 Sagittario, May 1942 (34 pre-series only). **S.A. Caproni-Vizzola**, at Vizzola Ticino, Varese, was noted for single original design: F.4 (F for designer F. Fabrizi), flown July 1940, having been overtaken by F.5 with different engine, flown February 1939; further different engines fitted to F.6M (1941) and F.6Z (1943). After Armistice several factories remained open; main factory produced Ca 193 5/6-seat pusher (2 × 155 hp), but cost of this prototype bankrupted company on 2 February 1950. **Caproni Trento**, at Gardolo, remained solvent, flying F.5 light jet trainer designed by Stelio Frati on 20 May 1952. Against all odds, **Caproni Vizzola Costruzioni Aeronautiche** also remained

solvent, mainly supporting military engines, and in 1969 began producing outstanding sailplanes designed by Ferrarin and Sonzio. These led to A.21J jet sailplane (January 1972) and from this to C22J side-by-side light twin-jet trainer (21 July 1980). Agusta bought Caproni Vizzola 1983, name disappearing.

Carden-Baynes (UK). Carden-Baynes Aircraft Ltd formed 1935 at Heston, gave name to Scud (*see* Abbott) and Bee (1936) ultralights. Terminated by Air Ministry takeover of Heston, but Baynes patented Heliplane (twin tilt-rotor VTOL, 365 mph) in 1937.

Cardoen (Chile). Industrias Cardoen Ltda, major producer of weapons, flew prototype C 206L-III multirole helicopter derived from LongRanger 1989. Narrower and stronger cockpit with flat transparencies, pilot on centreline. *See* Metalnor.

Caribe-Doman (Puerto Rico). Last company formed to try to get Doman helicopters into production, 1968.

Carley (Netherlands). J.D. (Joop) Carley established Carley's Aircraft Manufactory at Ede, Gelderland, 1921. C.III tandem trainer flew September 1922. S.1 single-seater with 20-hp Anzani flew 29 November 1923. Followed with C.II (100-hp Le Rhône) and C.12 (first 10-hp Indian, then 20-hp Anzani). Gave up own company but later designed transport for Werkspoor (which *see*).

Carma (USA). Carma Manufacturing Co. built light aircraft 1957–9.

CARMAM (France). Société CARMAM at Moulins, designers Jacquet and Pottier, produce sailplanes; also produced JP-20-90 Impala plastics racing aircraft (26 July 1971).

Carmier (France). Société Carmier flew Type 10 parasol single-seater 1946.

Carothers (USA). CAM Special aerobatic monoplane flew 1981.

Carr (USA). Walter Carr designed racers 1924 and 1927 and gave own name to 1932 Carr Racer (OX-5, then Warner 110-hp).

Carson (USA). Carson Helicopters specialized in

CASA 207 Azor (2 × Hercules), September 1955.

rebuilds of Bell and Hiller machines, with more power and (47G) 4 seats.

Carstedt (USA). Carstedt Inc., Long Beach, produced Jet Liner 600, stretched 19-passenger turboprop conversion of D.H.104 Dove, flown 1966.

CASA (Spain). Principal Spanish aircraft company, Construcciones Aeronáuticas SA was founded 3 March 1923 by Don José Ortez Echague. Work began 1924 at Madrid Getafe, primary aim being to produce metal aircraft for Ejercito del Aire. Major programmes included Breguet XIX (400), Dornier Wal (40) and Vickers Vildebeeste (27). After civil war second plant at Seville produced 25 Gö 145, 25 Bü 133 and 555 Bü 131, together with 170 Ju 52/3m (CASA 352L) and 200 He 111H-16 (CASA 2.111). Subsequent manufacture included Do 25 prototype, 50 Do 27 (CASA 127), 70 F-5A/B Freedom Fighters and 81 BO 105 helicopters. Among numerous other tasks are participation in EFA (13%) and Airbus (4·2%), as partner in each case; DC-10/MD-11 tailplane, B.757 flap, Falcon 100 wing, Mirage F1 centre fuselage, entire wing of Saab 2000, and major programmes in engines and avionics. First original design CASA.III 2-seat parasol tourer 1929. CASA.201 Alcotan twin-engined transport flew February 1949, 112 built. CASA.202 Halcón transport (2 × 775-hp) flew May 1953, 20 plus 1 much more powerful 202B. C.207 Azor transport (2 × 2,040-hp Hercules) flew September 1955, 22

built. Via SIAT, MBB and Hispano Aviación, CASA built 50 CASA.223 Flamingo trainers. Major new design C.212 Aviocar twin-turboprop transport flew 26 March 1971, total by 1992 459 including 114 licence-built by IPTN. Assisted by MBB and Northrop, CASA flew prototype C.101 Aviojet military trainer 27 June 1977, total late 1991 143 including 32 assembled by ENAER. Major new projects AX jet trainer/attack aircraft and 3000 twin-turboprop in 75-seat class, both possibly to fly 1996. For CN-235, *see* Airtech (International).

Casmuniz: *See* Cassio Muniz.

Caspar (Germany). Pioneer pilot/constructor Karl Caspar formed Zentrale für Aviatik October 1911 at Hamburg-Fuhlsbüttel—first German aircraft company. Among other things built Etrich and Rumpler type Taubes. *See* Hanseatische; next entry.

Caspar (Germany). Dr Caspar formed second company 1921, Caspar-Werke at Lübeck Trave-münde, appointing Ernst Heinkel designer. First product U.1 small observation seaplane, easily dismantled for shipboard use, 2 supplied US Navy and 2 to Japan 1922. Heinkel developed wartime W 29 seaplane into S.1 (Bücker got Heinkel to move this to Sweden, *see* SAAB, Caspar disputing rights to design, and Heinkel leaving May 1922). New designer Ernst Ritter von Lössl produced CLE.11 3-seat monoplane,

Caspar C.32 crop-duster, March 1927.

CLE.12 large 10-seater, CLE.16 3-seater, CJ.14 biplane fighter (1924), CS 14 larger fighter (1926) and C.17 light 2-seater. C.32 crop-dusting biplane (1927) was designed by Reinhold Mewes, and C.35 Priwall 8-passenger biplane by H. Herrmann. Company liquidated 1928.

Cassio Muniz (Brazil). To overcome import restrictions on light aircraft this company designed and built prototype Casmuniz 52 light twin, flown April 1953. Omareal was to produce in series.

Cassutt (USA). Long-lived programme for small racer, Cassutt Special I flown by airline captain Tom Cassutt 1954; won National championship 1958. In 1959 he completed even smaller Special II. In 1979 Cassutts took 1/2/3 at US Nationals. Over 160 flying, 2,000 + plans sold.

CAT (Italy). Costruzioni Aeronautiche Taliedo established 1937 at Milan. Produced Tm.2 transport glider 1939 (crashed 1946) and QR.14 Levriero tandem-seat monoplane with 2 130-hp Alfa 110bis engines and trousered landing gear designed by Queirolo (which *see*) and built by Caproni Taliedo (18 October 1947).

CATH: *See* Eurocopter.

CATIC (China). Abbreviation for China National Aero-Technology Import and Export Corporation, Beijing-based organization which,

under MAS, handles all international marketing.

Catron & Fisk: *See* Fisk.

Caudron (France). Gaston and René Caudron came from Picardy farming family, but seeing Wilbur Wright fly inspired them to build large twin-engined biplane; Farcot engines did not arrive and aircraft flown as glider December 1908. On 21 September 1909 made 4 good flights at Romoutier farm with smaller biplane (25-hp Anzani). In 1910 moved to foreshore at Le Crotoy, setting up flourishing school, with factory at Rue. Fifth biplane, Type B, established layout common to most of 113 aircraft of 20 types built 1910–14: biplane, 50-hp tractor Gnome, tail carried by booms which served as landing skids. April 1914 one set record 16 hr 28 min 56 sec. May 1914 Type G became standard trainer, 1,423 by Caudron, 1,027 other French companies, 233 British Caudron and 166 AER. German advance forced move to Lyon, and René opened second factory at Issy-les-Moulineaux. March 1915 G.4 reconnaissance/bomber was enlarged G.3 with 2 engines (80-hp or 100-hp), 1,358 in France, others British Caudron and AER. June 1915 R.IV (R.4) reconnaissance biplane replaced tail booms by normal fuselage, 249 built, one killing Gaston despite protestations by young Paul Deville that structure was weak. Deville appointed technical director and produced G.6 with normal fuselage (512), R.10 and R.11 twin-engined escort fighter (370), Type

Caudron-Renault CR.714 Cyclone fighter, August 1938.

O single-seat fighter, C.21 and 22 recon/bombers and C.23 heavy bomber. Post-war Deville produced C.23b airliner, C.25 20-passenger airliner, C.27 2-seater, C.31 4-seater, C.33 twin-engine 4-seater, C.39 seaplane (3 × 130-hp), C.43 transport (5 × 80-hp), C.47 (3 × 80-hp), C.51 trainer, C.57 advanced trainer, C.59 trainer (1,885 1923–8), C.60 trainer (64 Finland, 34 made there), C.61 airliner (3 × 180-hp or 2 × 260-hp), C.65 and 67 single-seaters, C.68 2-seater, C.74 transport, C.77 aerobatic trainer, C.81/82/83 derivatives of C.61, and C.91 4-seater. All this before Deville went to Dewoitine March 1923, when René Talpin designed C.92 transport, C.97 tourer, C.99/101/104 reconnaissance 2-seaters, C.109 parasol monoplane and C.120. Deville then returned, developed C.109 into 112/113/114/116/117, and designed C.127, C.161 and 168 2-seat biplanes, C.181 and 187 all-metal 3-engined high-wing monoplanes (first aircraft built at new factory/airfield at Guyancourt), C.190/191/192 low-wing monoplanes, C.230/232/233/235 2-seat biplanes, 725 of 19 versions of C.272 Luciole 2-seat biplanes, and over 240 of 26 versions of C.280 Phalène high-wing cabin monoplane. In 1933 Deville again left, and Caudron amalgamated with Soc. des Usines Renault. New chief designer gifted Marcel Riffard, manager of Renault Aviation, who put 'Caudron-Renault' on world map, especially with series of racing aircraft started with C.362, 1933, leading to C.450 and retractable-gear C.460 which set world class record 1934 at 314 mph. Late 1934 prototype, C.460 Goëland light twin-engined transport, led to many civil/military variants, total 1,702. Light types included C.480 Frégate high-wing 3-seater, C.510 Pélican ambulance/tourer, C.600 Aiglon tandem tourer (203, 1935–8), C.630 Simoun 4-seater (505, 1934–9),

C.640 Typhon mailplane with racer and bomber derivatives, and, derived from racers, C.690M fighter trainer, C.714 Cyclone (63 in combat by Finland and by Polish squadrons in France), and CR.760/770/780 prototypes. CR.770 was last to fly, just once, as German troops approached. C.810/811 gliders built 1946, but firm not revived.

Cavalier (USA). Cavalier Aircraft Corp. succeeded Trans-Florida 1967, taking over same business and facilities. Developed P-51 Mustang into Cavalier 2000 2-seater with tip tanks. Under USAF contract built F-51D Mustangs for MAP nations, using existing or new parts and with updated armament/avionics. In 1967 Mustang II counter-insurgency aircraft (more power, higher weights) led to Turbo Mustang III, first Dart then T55 engine. This bought by Piper as Enforcer.

Cavenaugh (USA). Cavenaugh Aviation, Houston, Texas, produces Cargoliner conversions of Mitsubishi MU-2/Marquise.

Cayley (UK). Sir George Cayley, Bt., Brompton Hall, Yorkshire, 1773–1857, published series of visionary drawings of fixed-wing aerodynes from 1791, including classic treatise 1809–10; published design of 'governable parachute' monoplane glider 25 September 1852, this reportedly flown with ballast, with small boy and with Cayley's coachman, thus first full-scale aerodyne in history.

CCB (USSR). Central Construction Bureau, also written TsKB.

CCE: *See* Colani.

CCF: *See* Canadian Car & Foundry.

CEA: *See* Centre Est.

Celair (S. Africa). Celair (Pty) Ltd is producing own-design Eagle 300 6-seater (4 April 1990). Design rights offered for sale 1993.

Centrair (France). SA Centrair produces sailplanes and parawing microlights. In 1980 work began on 6-seat propeller-behind-tail executive aircraft, in collaboration with Dassault and various technical schools.

Central (UK). Central Aircraft Co., 1917 subsidiary of joinery works R. Cattle Ltd, produced post-war aircraft of its own design: Centaur IV 3-seat biplane (8, 1919), and Centaur IIA 8-seater (2 × 160-hp), of which 2 were built.

Centrala Flygverkståderna (Sweden). Main maintenance depots of Royal Swedish AF, 1928–35 built C.V, Hart and Fw 44 under licence.

Centrala Industriala Aeronautica Romana: *See* CNIAR.

Central-Lamson (USA). Central-Lamson Corp. built light aircraft 1953–4.

Centralne: *See* CSS.

Central States (USA). Central States Aero Co. Inc. formed Davenport, Iowa, January 1927, to produce Monocoupe small side-by-side cabin monoplane designed by Don A. Luscombe. Trickle-built with 60-hp Air Cat 5-cylinder engine, a few with Cirrus, Siemens and Anzani. Failed 1928, restructured at Bettendorf, Iowa, as **Central States Aircraft Co.** Again failed 1930, despite much better sales due to 55-hp Velie engine, becoming **Mono Aircraft**.

Central Workshops: *See* Maestranza.

Centre de Recherches: *See* Jean St-Germain.

Centre Est (France). Centre Est Aéronautique formed at Dijon October 1957 by Pierre Robin and Jean Delemontez to develop 3-seat Jodel DR 100 Ambassadeur, leading to Sicile Record, DR 200 and DR 300. Name changed 1969 to Avions Pierre Robin.

Centro Técnico: *See* CTA.

Centrul National: *See* CNIAR; CNA.

Centrum: *See* CNPSL.

CERVA (France). Formed 1971 by Wassmer and Siren SA to produce CE.43 Guépard, metal version of Wassmer WA.4/21; 43 built when Wassmer liquidated 1977.

Ceskomoravska: *See* Praga.

Ceskoslovenské (Czechoslovakia). In 1949–60 all Czech motor and aviation industry was grouped as Ceskoslovenské Závody Automobilové a Letecké, later replaced by Omnipol.

Cessna (USA). Builder of more aircraft than any other company, Cessna Aircraft had origins in Blériot monoplane repeatedly crashed by Kansas farmer Clyde V. Cessna 1911. Eventually it was so modified it became first Cessna aircraft. Built 2 more aircraft at Jones Motor Car plant at Wichita 1916–17; then returned to farming until invited to head Travel Air 1925. Soon withdrew, forming **Cessna-Roos Aircraft Co.** 8 September 1927; changed after Roos's departure to **Cessna Aircraft Co.** 18 December 1927. First product Model A, clean cantilever high-wing cabin monoplane, 71 built in many versions. BW 3-seat, CW 6-seat and (1929) DC-6/6A/6B 4-seat. To keep going in Depression, Clyde and son Eldon produced CG-2 primary glider and EC powered version, but plant shut 1931. New company started: *see* Clyde V. Cessna Aircraft. But in January 1934 Cessna Aircraft reopened East Pawnee, Wichita, factory, with nephew Dwane Wallace as manager. Totally new C-34 flew June 1935, later voted 'most efficient airplane'—4-seater reached 162 mph on 145 hp compared with 148 mph for DC-6B on 300 hp. Developed through different models called Airmaster. On 26 March 1939 Wallace flew T-50 low-wing 5-seater (2 × 225 hp), leading to 5,399 wartime Bobcat/Brasshat/Crane variants. Also built 750 CG-4 troopcarrying gliders and major parts for B-29 and A-26. Traditional 'Cessna' resumed with 2-seat 120 (28 June 1945), total by 1950 2,164 plus 5,406 de luxe 140/140A. Cessna 190 (1947) cantilever 5-seater succeeded Airmaster, total 1,188 with 195 and LC-126. In 1948 braced 4-seat 170 led to biggest-selling series of all time, including 172, 175, Skyhawk, Skylane and USAF T-41, total when ceased December 1987 35,773. Model 305 won Army observation contest 1950:

The 100,000th Cessna single, a 1975 Skyhawk.

3,431 L-19 Bird Dog, plus licensed to Fuji Japan. Two new 1953 models were 180, more powerful 4-seater, and twin-engined 5-seat 310, leading to 6,432 Model 180 and 4,356 6-seat Model 185 Skywagon/U-17 and over 5,520 Model 310. In same year, unsuccessful attempt to market helicopter—CH-1 ex-Seibel—and first jet, T-37 USAF trainer, 1,268 plus 577 A-37B Dragonfly. Model 620 4-engined transport prototype only 1956. In 1957 return to 2-seaters with 150 and 152, ceased 1977 at 23,836. Model 210 Centurion introduced retractable gear to high-wingers, ceased 1987 at 8,504. Push/pull 337 Skymaster ceased 1980 at 1,821 plus 313 pressurized T337 and 501 USAF O-2A. Substantial numbers built of 6-seat Model 205, and twin-engined Model 402/411, 404 Titan, 414 Chancellor, 421 Golden Eagle, 425 Corsair (renamed Conquest I) and 441 Conquest II. AGwagon/AGtruck ag-aircraft 1965–85 total 3,901. Fanjet 500 business jet flew 15 September 1969, renamed Citation I, total by mid-1985 termination 691. Citation II 1976, total 623. Other variants Citation S/II and T-47A, Citation III, Citation V, VI, VII, X and Model 525 CitationJet, grand total close to 2,000. These remain in production, together with small numbers of Model 208 Caravan turboprop utility aircraft. Manufacture of all other types terminated by crippling US product-liability legislation, which explained 1985 sale of company as wholly-owned subsidiary of General Dynamics; resold 1992 to Textron for $600m. Total production just under 178,000 aircraft, but now increasing only very slowly. In 1960 Cessna bought 49% holding in Max Holste, later Reims, France, selling this February 1989. McCauley (propellers) is wholly-owned subsidiary.

CFA (France). When Paul Deville left Caudron he joined Salmson engine company, first product being Cri-Cri STOL 2-seater, made by Salmson and by 4 other companies under licence. Compagnie Française d'Aviation formed 1936 to undertake series production of Salmson aircraft. Built small number Cri-Cri Major post-war.

CFM (UK). Cook Flying Machines, trading as CFM Metal-Fax, produce large numbers of various versions of Shadow micros, mainly 2-seaters, and have worldwide licensees.

Chadwick (USA). Chadwick Helicopters built C-122S single-seat helicopter 1990.

Chagnes (France). Léo Chagnes built twin-jet version of VariViggen at Toulouse 1979.

Chambers (USA). Russell Chambers built R-1 Chambermaid race 1938, with Menasco Pirate, retractable gear and 13ft 8in span.

Champion (USA). Champion Aircraft Corp. formed at Osceola, Wisconsin, to build Model 7 Champion 2-seater, rights being purchased from Aeronca June 1954. Led to Traveler, Tri-Traveler, Sky-Trac, Challenger, Citabria and twin-engined Lancer. Assets acquired 30 September 1970 by Inter-Air (*see* Bellanca).

Champion (USA). In August 1982 B&B Aviation purchased rights to Champion aircraft from Bellanca. Company then renamed Champion

Aircraft Co. Inc. Tomball, Texas, produced Citabia, Decathlon and Scout to 1985.

Champion (USA). Kenneth R. Champion built J-1 Jupiter single-seater 1959, plans marketed.

Chance Vought: *See* Vought.

Changhe Aircraft Factory (China). CAF began producing commercial road vehicles 1974, but minor part of operations is responsibility within CHIC for Z-8 version of Aerospatiale Super Frelon.

Chantiers Aéro-Maritime de la Seine: *See* CAMS.

Chantiers Aéronautiques de Normandie (France). Name of former Amiot factory at Cherbourg, built Ju 52/3m and formed part of AAC.

Chantiers Navales de la Croisette: *See* Romano.

Chantiers de Provence Aviation (France). CPA.1 reconnaissance-fighter monoplane (2 × 400-hp Lorraine-Dietrich) flew Istres February 1926.

Charpentier (France). Jean Charpentier produced C.1 tailless aircraft with 45-m span (3 × 100-hp Hispano) flown Issy January 1935. Later Type 310-C1 fighter tunnel-tested December 1937, but not flown.

Chase (USA). Chase Aircraft Co., Trenton, NJ, formed 1943 to build assault gliders. In 1946 began building 2 all-metal XCG-18A gliders. These led to 5 YC-18As, 1 of which was converted into YC-122 with 2 R-2000 engines. Two YC-122As were followed by a 122B with Cyclone engines, and 9 similar YC-122Cs. Meanwhile much bigger XG-20 glider was fitted with R-2800 Double Wasps to become XC-123 Avitruc. A second was fitted with 2 B-36-type twin-jet pods to become USA's first jet transport (21 April 1951). USAF placed contract for 300 C-123B providers, passed to Kaiser-Frazer after K-F acquired majority interest in Chase 1953. Chase built first 5 C-123Bs at Willow Run, Detroit, but K-F ran into difficulties, contract was switched to Fairchild and Chase ended operations.

Chatelain (France). André Chatelain built light aircraft at Lyons 1966–71.

Chauvière (France). Famous propeller manufacturer built 2 biplanes to assist flight development. First, 2 pusher propellers, was at Doncaster meet 1910.

Cheetah Light Aircraft Co. (Canada). Clairco formed 1964 at St Jean, PQ, to build 4-seat metal Super Cheetah; prototype by Aircraft Industries of Canada flew September 1964.

Chengdu: *See* CAC (China).

Cheranovskii (USSR). Boris Ivanovich Cheranovskii pioneered tailless monoplanes, especially of 'parabola' form with curved leading edge. BICh-1 glider 1923, first powered aircraft -3 of 1926, successful. BICh-7 1929 unstable, rebuilt as -7A. BICh-10 and -14 twin-engined, -20 and -21 normal tapered wings, -26 projected supersonic fighter, Cheranovskii having previously tunnel-tested variable-sweep fighters with outboard pivots 1946–8.

Chester (USA). Art Chester designed and flew 8 racers 1936–48.

Chetverikov (USSR). Igor Vyacheslavovich Chetverikov joined Central Construction Bureau 1931 and soon appointed head of marine brigade at old Menzhinskii factory. Major task new long-range flying-boat for Morskaya Aviatsya. This flew as No. 11 on 14 January 1932, service designation MDR-3, led to Tupolev's ANT-27 MDR-4. SPL (OSGA-101) was small flying-boat foldable for carriage aboard submarine, complete December 1934 after Chetverikov opened OKB at Sevastopol to build ARK-3 Arctic flying-boat, flown 1936 but abandoned after failures. MDR-6 (Chye-2), high-performance patrol/bomber flying-boat, flown July 1937, was designer's only real success. TA 10-seat amphibian 1947 remained 3 prototypes, OKB closed 1948.

CHI: *See* California Helicopter.

CHIC (China). China Helicopter Industry Corp. has 3 members: Changhe Aircraft Factory, Harbin Aircraft Manufacturing and Helicopter Design and Research Institute.

Chichester-Miles: *See* CMC.

Chilton (UK). Chilton Aircraft formed 1936, built 4 D.W.1 and 1A single-seaters. Chilton Aircraft

Co. registered 5 June 1946, again at Hungerford, built Olympia sailplane which was passed to Elliotts of Newbury. Intended Chelsea Chilton, ARB-certificated D.W.1A, never materialized.

Chincul (Argentina). Chincul SA assembles and part-manufactures wide range of Piper aircraft (over 950 by late 1992) and assembles Bell 212 and 412.

Chiribiri (Italy). Antonio Chiribiri worked on cars, becoming chief engineer of Miller, Turin. Produced 40-hp engine made mainly of light alloy, and for this designed monoplane copied from Blériot (March 1911). Subsequently built improved No. 2, 3-seat No. 3, and 2-seat Nos. 4 and 5. In 1915–18 mass-produced Le Rhône engines.

Chkalov (USSR). Chkalov aeronautical college, Voronezh (named for famed pilot V.P. Chkalov), built C-12 tandem-wing ultralight 1968.

Chkalov: *See* KAL; V.P. Chkalov.

Chodan (USA). Ivan Chodan built light helicopter 1966.

Chrislea (UK). Chrislea Aircraft Co. formed Heston 1936 to build LC.1 Airguard trainer, flown 1938. Post-war flew CH.3 Ace high-wing 4-seater 19 August 1946, leading to Super Ace and tailwheel Skyjeep. Assets to C.E. Harper Aircraft 1952.

Christen (USA). Christen Industries occupies former Pitts facilities at Afton, Wyoming, building full Pitts range plus A-1 Husky 2-seat utility.

Chris Tena (USA). Chris Tena Aircraft Association built Mini Coupe (6 September 1971), kits and plans marketed; became Sport Air Craft 1978.

Christmas (USA). Dr William W. Christmas had medical practice but is famous—rather, notorious—for aircraft with flexible cantilever wings emulating those of birds. First aircraft allegedly flown September 1907 (burned later to protect secrets). Formed Christmas Aeroplane Co., Washington, 1911, built 2nd aircraft 1911, 3rd 1912. Fourth built by Continental Aircraft at Amityville under contract to Christmas, who later formed 'Cantilever Aero Co.' as subterfuge.

Army provided Liberty engine. Called Bullet, or Aero Bullet, shed wings and killed pilot on first take-off 14 January 1919. Second aircraft never flew, fortunately.

Chrysler (USA). Chrysler Technologies Airborne Systems produce major multisensor surveillance and special-mission aircraft; prime contractor for C-27A Spartan (based on Alenia G222). *See also* Electrospace.

ChUR (Russia). ChUR No. 1 got its designation from G.G. Chechet, M.K. Ushkov and N.V. Rebikov. Basically good-looking tractor monoplane, but with variable-incidence short upper wing, with ailerons, and strange main wingtips split into upper/lower parts turned up/down with 90° between them. Even tail also had auxiliary pivoted horizontal upper surface. First flight at Komendantsky aerodrome about 10 April 1912. Not repaired after heavy landing 5 July 1912.

Church (USA). Jim Church, designer of ag-machinery and elevators, used Heath Parasol as basis for mid-wing racers (about 4, 1928–9), with Heath Henderson engine (uprated) and spats.

Cicaré (Argentina). Cicaré Aeronáutica built series of 4 light helicopters 1972–81.

Cierva (Spain, UK). Don Juan de la Cierva was greatest pioneer of autogyro (his registered name: Autogiro). Convinced rotary wings could give safe non-stallable lift, he fitted contrarotating superimposed rotors to Deperdussin to produce C.I at Madrid 1920. Trial/error with C.I, C.II (2) and C.3 led to C.4 with rotor with 4 articulated blades; after changes made first successful flight at Getafe 9 January 1923. After similar C.5 Cierva received Spanish government assistance, but in 1925 he brought C.6, based on Avro 504, to England, and Air Ministry ordered 2 from A.V. Roe, Hamble. Cierva Autogiro Co. formed 24 March 1926 to hold patents and grant constructional licences. Latter went to A.V. Roe and to Parnall, Weymann-Le Père, Pitcairn, de Havilland, Westland, Comper, Focke-Wulf, Airwork, SNCASE, LeO and British Aircraft. Pitcairn perfected clutch for pre-spinning rotor by engine in 1932, and in same year Cierva company moved to Hanworth, while A.V. Roe moved to Manchester, Hamble becoming AST (Air Service Training) which handled Cierva

Cierva C.6c (Avro 574), 19 June 1926.

training and modification, though main Cierva school established at Hanworth. Principal production version was C.30 (1933), 66 by Avro and others by other licensees. Cierva ironically killed in DC-2 1936. Final model C.40 (Avro Rota) could perform direct jump take-off. From outset Cierva chairman had been Air Cdre J.G. Weir, who provided considerable financial backing. He had his own company G. & J. Weir at Glasgow, concentrating on helicopters. Companies merged 1943, and after war helicopters replaced autogyros: W.9 with tail rotor replaced by reaction exhaust jet; W.11 Air Horse, giant machine with 3 rotors driven by RR Merlin; and W.14 Skeeter 2-seater. W.9 unsuccessful, W.11 crashed, but W.14 developed via Saro Skeeter into production Westland Skeeter.

Cierva Rotorcraft (UK). Formed 1965 by original Cierva company and Rotorcraft Ltd at Redhill to develop CR Twin 5-seat coaxial helicopter, flown August 1969.

Cijan (Yugoslavia). Boris Cijan won 1946 air force contest for design of light trainer. C-3 Trojka flown October 1947.

CIL: *See* Composite (Australia).

Circa (Canada). Circa Reproductions, Edmonton, market plans of scaled reproductions of First World War fighters; over 800 sets sold for Nieuport XI alone.

Cirrus (USA). Cirrus Design Corp., Wisconsin, have sold many plans/kits for VK30 300-mph (483 km/h) 4/5-seater.

Ciskei: *See* CAI, 1st entry.

Citroën-Marchetti (France). Short-lived co-operative built light aircraft 1978.

Civil (India). Government Civil Aviation Department, Technical Centre, developed gliders and (1967–70) Revathi Mks I and II 2/3-seat cabin monoplanes.

Civilian (UK). Civilian Aircraft Co. formed 1928 at Burton-on-Trent. Works near Hull built 5 Civilian Coupé light 2-seat high-wing monoplanes.

CKD: *See* Praga.

Clairco: *See* Cheetah Light Aircraft Co.

Clark: *See* General Aviation.

Clark (USA). Clark Aircraft, at Marshall, Texas, flew Clark 1000 ag-biplane March 1956, redesignated Model 12 in 1960.

Clarke (UK). F/O J. Clarke (RAF) built Cheetah convertible monoplane/biplane 1929.

Classic (USA). Classic Aircraft Corp., Lansing, Michigan, produced updated Waco F-5 biplanes.

Claudius Dornier (Germany). Claudius Dornier Seastar GmbH formed at Immenstad 1982 to build Seastar multirole amphibian (17 August 1984). Company moved October 1985 to Oberpfaffenhofen: but filed for bankruptcy November 1989. *See* Dornier Composite.

Clayton & Shuttleworth (UK). Lincoln ag-machine firm which built Sopwith Triplane and Camel, HP O/400 and Vickers Vimy 1916–19.

Cleary (USA). Cleary Aircraft Corp. built CL-1 Zipper light aircraft 1983.

Clément-Bayard (France). Famed producer of airships, built pioneer welded-steel-tube aeroplanes including Santos-Dumonts and his own monoplanes. Sold out to Citroën 1928.

Club Aviazione Popolare (Italy). Built light aircraft 1983.

Clutton (UK). Eric Clutton built FRED 1963 and Clutton-Tabenor EC.2 1983.

CLW (UK). Cole, Levell and Welman built Curlew 2-seater at Bexleyheath 1936.

Clyde (UK). Name proposed for Clipper aircraft of Burnelli type 1935; Cunliffe-Owen OA-14 built instead.

Clyde V. Cessna Aircraft (USA). Formed by Clyde and Eldon Cessna during Depression 1931–3, rented space from Stearman to build advanced midget racers.

CMASA (Italy). Costruzioni Meccaniche Aeronàutiche SA new name 1930 for Società di Costruzioni Meccàniche di Pisa (*see* SCMP), became Fiat subsidiary same year. Long series of M.F. seaplanes and flying-boats, ending with RS.14 seaplane 1938–43.

CMC (UK). Chichester-Miles Consultants Ltd flew Leopard light business jet 12 December 1988, construction by Designability Ltd. Prototype 002 airframe mainly by Slingsby.

CNA (Italy). Compagna Nazionale Aeronàutica, established Rome to build own and licensed light aircraft and engines 1920–40.

CNIAR (Romania). Centrul National al Industriei Aeronautice Romane has since 1968 managed Romanian aeronautical manufacturing within Ministry of Machine Building Industry.

CNNA (Brazil). Companhia Nacional de Navegaçao Aérea, part of Henrique Lage group, built HL-1–HL-6 light aircraft 1936–51.

CNNC (Brazil). Companhia Nacional de Navegaçao Costiera, formed 1937 Ilha do Viana to make Muniz trainers for Army; 1942 became FBA.

CNPSL (Poland). PZL-Warszawa works at Okecie was prefixed 1976–82 by Centrum Naukowo-Produkcyjne Samolotow Lekkich = light aircraft science and production centre.

Coanda (Romania). Remarkable biplane built by Henri Coanda, powered by Gnome driving compressor feeding nose combustion chambers, i.e. form of jet engine; left ground under own power 10 December 1910.

Coates (UK). J.R. Coates built SA.11 Swalesong 2-seater 1973.

Codock (Australia). Cockatoo Dockyard & Engineering Co. set up aviation department 1932 under (then Flt. Lt) L.J. Wackett. Built twin-engined Codock for Kingsford Smith.

Cody (UK). Samuel F. Cody, flamboyant American (naturalized Briton 1909), built numerous man-lifting kites and gliders followed by (1907) powered aeroplanes. Six distinct aircraft before he was killed 7 August 1913; none built for sale.

Colani (Germany). Colani/Composite Engineering at Bochum sponsored by Tohshin of Japan, built Cormoran CCE-208 4/5-seater, not yet flown 1993.

Colden (USA). Milton Colden flew MWP (mid-wing pusher) September 1961.

Colemill (USA). This Nashville, Tennessee, company specializes in performance conversions of private aircraft, starting with Navajo 1980.

Colgate (USA). Gilbert Colgate's company at Amityville succeeded Spencer-Larsen in developing amphibian redesignated CL-15, but work stopped 1942 by war.

Commercial Aircraft Sunbeam C-1, 1930

Colli (Italy). Placido Colli built roadable 2-seater, single-boom pusher with folding surfaces (15 May 1947).

Collins (USA). Collins Radio Co. at Cedar Rapids had various advanced/unconventional aircraft ideas, only one to fly being X-112 Aero-foil Boat ram-wing ground-effect aircraft 1963.

Colomban (France). Distinguished by tiny twin nose engines, Michel Colomban's MC 15 Cricri first flew July 1973, today over 200 flown or being built.

Colonial (USA). Colonial Aircraft Corp., San-ford, Maine, formed 1946 to build Skimmer amphibian; 2/3-seat C-1 certificated 1955, 4-seat C-2 followed 1957, 17 of latter delivered 1959, rights then sold to Lake.

Commadaire (USA). Commadaire Aircraft Co., Little Rock, ARK, built Little Rocket racer (uprated Cirrus), won 1930 Cirrus Derby.

Command-Aire (USA). Formed July 1928 by renaming Arkansas Aircraft, Command-Aire Inc. continued production of biplane of same name until late 1930.

Commander (USA). Commander Aircraft Co., Bethany, OK, acquired 1988 rights from Gulf-stream for Rockwell Commander 112 and 114, and is producing improved 114B.

Commercial (UK). Commercial Aeroplane Wing Syndicate formed by A.A. Holle 1919 to fly his Alula wing on various aircraft.

Commercial (USA). Commercial Aircraft Corp., LA, produced Sunbeam passenger biplane in 1930.

Commonwealth: *See* CAC (Australia).

Commuter (USA). Commuter Aircraft Corp. built light aircraft 1981–3.

Compagna (Italy). Compagna Generale Brevetti Elettro-Domestici built light aircraft 1957–9.

Compagnie Française d'Aviation: *See* CFA.

Companhia Nacional: *See* CNNA.

Comper (UK). Flt. Lt. Nicholas Comper, previously designer of Cranwell CLA series, left RAF March 1929 and formed Comper Aircraft Co. at Hooton Park, Cheshire, to build CLA.7 Swift, derived from CLA.3, sporting single-seater, 41 built. Mouse, Streak and Kite 1933–4 remained prototypes. Became Heston Aircraft 1934.

Composite (Australia). Composite Industries Ltd has subsidiary, Eagle Aircraft Australia, develop-ing Eagle X 2-seater.

Composite (S. Africa). Composite Aircraft Indus-tries formed 1986 to build SE-86 8-seater (2 piston or turboprop engines).

Composite (USA). Composite Aircraft Corp.

Comper C.L.A.7 Swift, June 1930.

formed by Gerald P. Dietrick 1978 to take over Windecker Eagle. No finance for production.

Comte (Switzerland). Flugzeugbau A. Comte established Hargen, Zürich, 1923, built mainly German designs under licence. First original design AC.1 fighter, flown April 1927. Subsequent designs all prototypes or very short runs: AC.3 bomber/transport, AC.4 Gentleman 2-seater, AC.8 6-seater, AC.11 photo/mapping aircraft, and AC.12 Moskito 3-seater.

Comtran (USA). Comtran Ltd, San Antonio, markets Super Q complete modification and upgrade for Boeing 707.

Conair (Canada). Conair Aviation, Abbotsford, BC, produces Helitanker belly-mounted fire retardant tanks for numerous helicopters and conversions of CS2F Tracker to Firecat and Turbo Firecat and F27 Firefighter.

Conal (Brazil). Companhia Nacional de Avioes Ltda flew W-151 Sopocaba 5-seater 1964.

Condor (USA). Vero Beach, Florida, holder of plans of Shoestring racer.

Conroy (USA). Conroy Aircraft Corp. formed at Santa Barbara as successor to Aero Spacelines. Major project CL-44-O flew 26 November 1969; others included turboprop conversions of DC-3 (Turbo Three), Cessna 337 (Stolifter) and Grumman Albatross.

Consolidated (USA). Future giant was formed as Consolidated Aircraft Corp. by Major Reuben H. Fleet, organizer 1918 of first US air mail service and from 1922 manager of Gallaudet. Dayton-Wright, despite GM ownership, was also ailing, but Fleet had stature to gather finance and form these 2 companies into 1 viable unit. Operations started at former Gallaudet plant, making 20 TW-3 trainers designed for Dayton-Wright by Col. Virginius E. Clark. Fleet suggested Clark should design improved TW-3 with tandem seating. Resulting PT-1 (1925) was smash hit, leading to Army PT-3 Husky, Navy NY-2 and various export versions, to total

Consolidated PB4Y-2 Privateer, August 1944.

exceeding 800. Smaller version, Husky Junior, found few customers; Consolidated board proposed to drop it, so Fleet took it on himself, formed **Fleet Aircraft** (*see* Fleet) and in mid-1929 sold rights back to Consolidated, total built over 1,000. By this time Consolidated had moved into former giant wartime plant run by Curtiss at Buffalo. Here new designer Isaac M. 'Mac' Laddon designed Admiral (Navy XPY-1) monoplane flying-boat (3 Wasp), flown January 1929. Martin underbid for production, but Consolidated sold 14 civil Commodore derivatives to NYRBA airline. Also in 1929 bought Thomas-Morse, and in 1931 recruited Robert Wood from failed Lockheed-Detroit. He developed YP-24 2-seat fighter into later versions of which P-30A (PB-2A) went into Army service. Even in Depression production continued on fast Fleetster transports and mailplanes and Navy BY and B2Y bombers. Laddon produced P2Y flying-boat 1932, leading to 23 P2Y-1 and 23 P2Y-3, followed by XP3Y (Model 28) flown 28 March 1935, which led to PBY Catalina family, total 3,290 in N. America plus many (between 550 and 1,200) in Soviet Union—greatest of any marine aircraft. Under intense pressure Laddon's team designed Model 32 (XB-24) Liberator, flown 29 December 1939, leading to 19,203 of countless versions by 1945. In 1935 Consolidated moved from Buffalo to milder climate of San Diego, and during Second World War opened giant plant at Fort Worth, Texas. In 1940 took over Hall Aluminum Aircraft. In December 1941 Fleet sold 34% of Consolidated to Avco via latter's subsidiary Vultee, leading to complete merger March 1943 as Convair (Consolidated-Vultee Aircraft).

Consolidated (USA). Consolidated Aeronautics Inc. took over Lake 1962, continuing production of LA-4 amphibian.

Construcciones Aeronáuticas: *See* CASA.

Constructions Aéronautiques du Béarn: *See* Béarn.

Constructions Aéronautiques Stampe et Renard: *See* Stampe et Renard.

Constructions de Planeurs á Moteur Auxiliaire: *See* PAMA.

Constructora Aeronaval de Levante: *See* Aeronasa.

Continental (USA). Continental Aircraft Corp., Amityville, Long Island, made small numbers of aircraft 1917–19.

Continental (USA). Continental Copters Inc. Fort Worth, produced special ag-conversions of Bell 47 and other Bell helicopters 1959–81.

Continental (USA). Continental Inc. formed 1945 to develop Fulton Airphibian roadable aircraft.

Convair (USA). Consolidated-Vultee Aircraft Corp. (Convair) formed March 1943 as unit of Avco, linking Vultee (which incorporated Stinson) with Consolidated, managing 102,000 employees in 13 divisions: San Diego, Fort Worth, Vultee Field (Downey), Consairway, New Orleans, Miami, Stinson, Stout, Allentown, Nashville, Elizabeth City, Louisville and Tucson. Wartime production by Convair included 21 prototypes and 9,760 Liberators, 2,393 Catalinas, 216 Coronados, 1,531 Vengeances, 11,537 Valiants, 3,590 Sentinels, 500 Reliants, 180 Seawolves, 324 Vigilants, 739 Privateers and 27

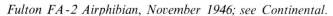

Fulton FA-2 Airphibian, November 1946; see Continental.

Privateer Express. But after VJ-Day employment slumped to 13,700 and Vultee, Stinson and Nashville closed. Work centred at San Diego on Convair-Liners (CV-240, 340, 440, total 1,068) and at Fort Worth on gigantic B-36 bomber, total 385. At lowest post-war point, 1947, Convair acquired by Atlas Corp., Floyd B. Odlum becoming chairman; but at height of Korean expansion, 1953, control bought by John Jay Hopkins as key element in General Dynamics. Other recent programmes included 875 F-102A Delta Dagger interceptors and 63 TF-102A, 277 F-106A Delta Dart interceptors and 63 F-106B, 2 XB-58 Hustler supersonic bomber prototypes, 28 YB-58A and 86 B-58A, and (a marketing and financial disaster) only 65 CV-880 and 37 CV-990 jetliners 1959–64. *See* General Dynamics.

Cook (USA). Cook Aircraft Corp. formed 1968 to develop JC-1 Challenger 4-seater. Two prototypes crashed 1970–72.

Coopérative: *See* CAARP.

Corben (USA). Corben Sportplane Co. Madison, Wisconsin, produced Ace, Baby Ace, Junior, Ace and Super Ace 2-seaters 1932–8 with Cirrus or Salmson engine.

Corby (Australia). John C. Corby markets plans for ultralight CJ-1 Starlet.

Corcoran (USA). R.S. Corcoran Co. produced 65-1 twin-engine biplane ultralight 1967.

Cornelius (USA). Cornelius Aircraft Co. built tailless aircraft with forward-swept wings, notably Mallard 4-seater 1943 and XFG-1 fuel-tank gliders 1945.

Cornu (France). Paul Cornu built tandem-rotor helicopter, flown 13 November 1907, generally given priority over Breguet as first helicopter flight.

Corporate Jets (UK/USA). Formerly part of British Aerospace, Corporate Jets Inc. and Arkansas Aerospace bought by Raytheon May 1993; 125 and 1000 marketing moving from Hatfield to Little Rock.

Corsini (Brazil). Ing. Romeu Corsini, lecturer at São Paulo university, built SP-18 light ag-aircraft 1969–74.

Coser-Oonk (USA). Joseph J. Coser and John H. Oonk built CO-2 Our Lady single-seater 1959.

Cosmic (USA). Cosmic Aircraft Corp. marketed F-23 (ex-Funk) ag-aircraft 1970–75.

Costruzioni Aeronautiche Giovanni Agusta: *See* Agusta.

Costruzione Meccaniche Aeronáutiche SA: *See* CMASA.

Cotter (USA). Doyle Cotter produced Cotter-Funk, re-engined Funk Model B, and supplied kits 1958–63.

Council (S. Africa): *See* CSIR.

Coupé-Aviation (France). Jacques Coupé, Azay-sur-Cher, built JC-01 light aircraft 1976, markets plans, and later produced JC-2.

Courier (USA). Courier Monoplane Co. Incorporated December 1928 to build 2-seat high-wing monoplane of that name.

Courtois-Suffit-Lescop (France). Roger Courtois-Suffit collaborated with Capt. Lescop in producing CSL.1 single-seat fighter built 1917–18 by SAIB at 49 rue St Blaise, Paris.

Coutant (France). Producer under licence of military aircraft 1915–18.

Couzinet (France). Société des Avions René Couzinet established 1926 to build (in Letord factory) 3-engined monoplane *Arc en Ciel* (rainbow) to fly N. Atlantic. Couzinet 10 destroyed, but led to improved Couzinet 30 and thus to second *Arc* Couzinet 70, flown across S. Atlantic by Mermoz 1933. Single examples also of 3-seat Couzinet 101 (3 × 85-hp) and 4-seat 110 (3 × 135-hp).

COW (UK). Coventry Ordnance Works, famed for aircraft 37-mm cannon, absorbed Warwick Wright 1911, built original designs to 1914, then produced BE.2/8/12, RE. 7/8 and Sopwith Snipe.

Cox (Canada). Cox Air Resources produced DHC-3T Turbo Otter 1978.

Cox (USA). Cox Aircraft Corp. produced light aircraft 1981–2.

Cox-Klemin (USA). Small company at College Point, Long Island, built aircraft under licence, imported several and also produced own design

Couzinet Type 101, 1932.

TW-2 (trainer, water-cooled) for Army 1922. In same year won Navy contract for 6 XS submarine scout seaplanes.

Cranfield (UK). Cranfield Aeronautical Services, approved to design and manufacture, handle major modification, such as 748 fire-bomber and One-Eleven auxiliary fuel system.

Cranfield (UK). Cranfield Institute of Technology carries out extensive commercial work ranging from feasibility studies through modification and manufacture to certification. *See also* Flight Invert Ltd.

Cranwell (UK). Cranwell Light Aeroplane Club built CLA.2, 3 and 4A for Light Aeroplane Trials and racing 1924–6.

Crawford (USA). Crawford All-Metal Airplane Co. incorporated Los Angeles 1928, built handful of small aircraft with corrugated Dural skin, notably Crawford 65 6-seater.

CRDA: *See* CANT, 2nd entry.

Croplease (UK). Croplease Ltd, Shannon, Ireland, purchased NAC.6 Fieldmasters; Croplease plc formed April 1989 to restart Fieldmaster/Firemaster assembly (parts from UTVA) and marketing.

Cropmaster (Australia). Cropmaster Aircraft Pty Ltd succeeded Yeoman in marketing Cropmaster and Fieldmaster until 1966.

Crosby (UK). Crosby Aviation, Knutsford, Cheshire, holds world rights for Andreasson BA-4B, and markets kits and plans.

Croses (France). Emilien Croses, Charnay-les-Macon, produced 9 prototypes from 1947, all tandem-wing and all certificated. Later types: Pouplume, Criquet, Tout-Terrain, Tourisme and Paras-Cargo.

Crosley (USA). Crosley Aircraft Co. incorporated Cincinnati 1929, subsidiary of radio corporation, producing C-1 2-seater and C-2 3-seater with interchangeable parts.

Crouch-Bolas (USA). Incorporated Rhode Island 1931 by Britons to build Dragonfly experimental twin-engined STOL biplane.

Crown (USA). Crown Aircraft Corp. incorporated 1930, division of Crown Motor Carriage Co., produced B-3 sporting biplane.

CRSS (Indonesia). Formed 1991, acquiring assets including prototypes of former Aerodis; is continuing to develop AA200 Orion fast 4-seat pusher and distributes (and may make) FFT Speed Canard.

Crusader (USA). Crusader Aircraft Corp. formed 1933 and built AF-4 twin-engined 4-seater. Taken over 1935 by American Gyro.

Cryoplane (International). DASA and ANTKI Tupolev are leading this German/Russian group which also includes Dornier, Lufthansa, Max-Planck Institut, MBB and MTU, plus KKBM (engine bureau) and NIAT research institute in Russia on future transport (possibly based on A310) fuelled by cryogenic fuel, either LH$_2$ or LNG.

CSIR (S. Africa). Council for Scientific and Industrial Research produced series of SARA (S. African research autogyro) aircraft 1971–82.

CSS (Poland). Centralne Studium Samolotów, aeroplane research centre, established 1946 to develop primary trainer, aerobatic trainer and light transport. First, CSS.10A, flown 3 September 1948; 2nd, CSS.10C, flown 25 April 1949; followed by 2 versions of more powerful CSS.11. Transport CSS.12 (2 × 440-hp Argus) flown 22 November 1950. CSS eliminated in political changes.

CTA (Brazil). Centro Técnico de Aeronáutica was set up by air ministry and comprised school (ITA) and R&D institute (IPD) which 1960–64 produced FG-8 Guanabara 4-seat derivative of Fokker S.12, and BF-1 Beija-Flor light helicopter. Bandeirante (1968) effectively replaced IPD by Embraer.

CTDC (Japan). Civil Transport Development Corp. formed 1978 to co-ordinate subcontract work by Fuji, Kawasaki and Mitsubishi on 767 programme, later adding 777. Work on 767 now co-ordinated by CAC, 777 by JADC.

Cuauhtemoc: *See* Servicios.

Cub (Canada). Cub Aircraft Corp. established at Hamilton 1937 to build Piper Cub and (1941) Harlow PJC-2.

Cubitt (UK). Croydon construction firm awarded contract for Airco D.H.9 1918.

Culver (USA). Culver Aircraft Co. formed from Dart Aircraft 1939, moving 1940 from Ohio to Wichita, Kansas. Single product Culver Dart GW, but designer Mooney soon produced Model L, later named Cadet (1939), production halted by war but developed into PQ-8 radio-controlled target and later PQ-14, made in large numbers. Post-war Model V flew 1946, excellent aircraft but Culver failed same year: *see* Superior.

Cunliffe-Owen (UK). Sir Hugo Cunliffe-Owen, chairman of British-American Tobacco, formed company called BAO 9 August 1937 to build Burnelli aircraft. Changed name to Cunliffe-Owen Aircraft May 1938, and at Eastleigh, Southampton, built 15-seat OA-1 (2 Perseus). Post-war W. Garrow-Fisher designed Concordia 10/12-seat transport (19 May 1947), abandoned after 2 built.

Cunningham-Hall (USA). Cunningham-Hall Aircraft Corp. formed 1928 at Rochester, NY, concentrating on light civil aircraft: PT-6 6-seat biplane, X-90(N) STOL 2-seater, GA-21M low-wing 2-seater with split trailing edges forming spoilers as well as flaps, GA-36 (improved GA-21) and, in 1937, PT-6F cargo version of company's original offering.

Currie (UK). J.R. Currie designed Wot ultralight biplane built by Cinque Ports Aviation 1937, together with Wot 2 destroyed by bombs May

Cunningham-Hall GA-36, January 1936.

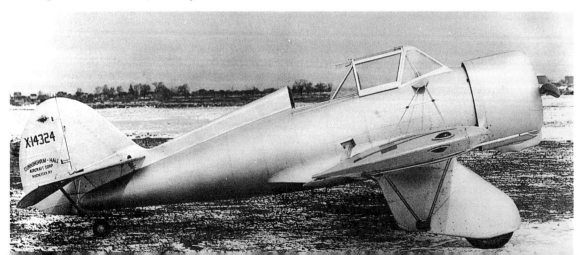

Curtiss HA mailplane (modified Dunkirk fighter), 1919.

1940, but 3rd aircraft built at Eastleigh 1958: *see* Hampshire.

Curtiss (USA). Glenn Hammond Curtiss, shy and reserved, was pioneer of aeroplane, formed what became world's largest aircraft company but then after Second World War withered with amazing swiftness almost to nothing. Bicycle-maker, then builder and racer of motorcycles including high-power engines. Provided engines for several airships and unsuccessful flying machines before becoming founder-member of Aerial Experiment Association 1 October 1907. Provided aircraft and engines for AEA members, and Curtiss' own *June Bug* won Scientific American prize for first officially observed flight exceeding 1 km (20 June 1908). On 20 March 1909 formed **Herring-Curtiss Co.** With Augustus Herring, first US aircraft company. Engaged 1908–13 in bitter and un-necessary litigation with Wrights. Took 63-hp machine to Reims August 1909 and won 2 major prizes; 29 May 1910 added $10,000 Pulitzer prize for flight down Hudson, Albany–NY. Set up flying schools and large team who toured US giving shows, one pilot (Eugene B. Ely) making first take-off from ship and later first landing. Substantial sales of Model D and 2-seat Model E landplanes, Types C and F flying-boats and various amphibians. **Curtiss Aeroplane Co.** formed at Hammondsport, NY, 1 December 1910; Curtiss Motor Co. 19 December 1911; merged into **Curtiss Aeroplane & Motor Corp.**

(adding another company, Burgess & Curtis, with one s) 13 January 1916. Curtiss started US naval aviation, training pilots and providing aircraft, and first major order was 144 of various subtypes of Model F trainer flying-boat. Built large flying-boat for transatlantic bid (thwarted by war) by Royal Navy officer John C. Porte, who imported giant Curtiss Wanamaker triplane and got H-4 adopted as standard RNAS patrol flying-boat, leading to large numbers of H-12 and H-16 boats and combined Curtiss/Porte F.2A and F-5L. In 1914 Curtiss lured B. Douglas Thomas from Sopwith to design Model J trainer, leading to JN-4 which trained over 95% of US wartime pilots and many Allied pilots, over 6,000 built. Other major wartime types were MF training flying-boat, R-2 and R-6 reconnaissance 2-seaters, R-6 torpedo bomber, N-9 trainer seaplane, and HS-1, -1L and -2L coastal flying-boats. By 1920 Curtiss had also flown 42 other types as prototypes, and in 1922 built 34 TS-1 fighters designed by Navy. Immediate post-war types included Model 17 Oriole 3-seater and Model 19 Eagle 3-engined airliner. Both had 160-hp inline engine derived from earlier Curtiss engines by Charles Kirkham; when Kirkham combined 2 cylinder blocks in K-12 result was world-beating 465-hp D-12, which later became Conqueror, up to 700-hp. Early recipients of this engine included Curtiss racers such as Army R-6 (won 1922 Pulitzer race and twice gained world speed record) and Navy CR-3 (won 1923

Schneider Trophy), R2C (1923 Pulitzer and world speed record) and R3C-2 (1925 Pulitzer and Schneider wins). Even more important, D-12 powered Army PW-8 fighter and all early Navy F6C Hawk fighters. These led to profusion of later Hawks, some with Curtiss water-cooled engines and others with Pratt & Whitney or Wright air-cooled radials, to total exceeding 340. Another major family were Falcon observation and attack aircraft (over 550 1925–32 including 100 for Colombia). Fledgeling trainer found civil and military buyers, Curtiss' own flying service using 109. Seahawks, Sparrowhawks, Falcons and Helldivers followed, same name often being repeated later for different designs. Hawk name was repeatedly used for new fighters, such as F11C and BF2C whose export versions were Hawk II (127) and Hawk III (137). Army also had a squadron of B-2 Condor heavy bombers, and civil Condor 18 (6) led to T-32 Condor II (57). No fewer than 769 Model 50 Robins were built, most 3-seaters, but only 14 twin-engined Kingbird 8-seaters. After 1918 Curtiss himself had other interests, remaining a design consultant but leaving most work to team headed by George A. Page Jr, at Garden City, NY, formerly engine factory. Another plant opened in 1928 at St Louis as result of formation of **Curtiss-Robertson Aircraft Corp.**, and this handled such civil production as Robin and Condor. On 8 August 1929 bitter old rivals Curtiss and Wright merged, to form huge **Curtiss-Wright Corp.**, Guy Vaughan becoming president and Burdette S. Wright v-p in charge of Airplane Division. One of first Army monoplanes was Shrike attack bomber of 1931, and one of last Navy biplanes SOC Seagull of 1934 (306). In 1930 Curtiss-Robertson merged with Travel Air to form **Curtiss-Wright Airplane Co**. as separate arm of Curtiss-Wright, products having CW designations. Major examples included CW-1 Junior, CW-12 Sport Trainer, various CW-14s, CW-19 fighter/trainers, CW-21 fighter and CW-22 (SNC Falcon) advanced trainer (591). Meanwhile, company's biggest single family began with Model 75 stressed-skin monoplane fighter designed by Don R. Berlin and flown 15 May 1935. This led to family of Hawk 75s with fixed landing gear, much bigger family of Hawk 75As and P-36s with retractable gear (RAF Mohawk) and even bigger family of Hawk 81 series P-40s (Tomahawk, Kittyhawk, Warhawk), to total by December 1944 of 13,738. Other production included SBC Helldiver biplane (349), SO3C

Seagull/Seamew (790 despite being almost unflyable), SB2C Helldiver carrier-based bomber (7,200), SC Seahawk (578), 3,341 C-46 Commando transports and 791 AT-9 Jeep twin-engine trainers. By 1945 Curtiss was huge empire with major plants at Buffalo, St Louis, Louisville, Kenmore and Columbus. Numerous projects, all of which collapsed. Last aircraft to bear Curtiss name was giant XF-87 Blackhawk 4-jet fighter (15 February 1948). Very last project was stillborn plan to make Doman helicopter. Later, after 1958, Wright Aeronautical plant at Wood-Ridge, NJ, built various multi-rotor VTOL devices.

Curtiss-Caproni (USA). Formed to build Caproni bombers and civil transports after First World War, did little business but bought 1928 by Canadian financier Clement Keys, merged into General Aviation Manufacturing 1933 and thence to NAA.

Curtiss-Reid (Canada). Formed 1928 by purchase of Reid Aircraft, continued light aircraft (Rambler biplane 1928, Courier monoplane 1932) but failed in Depression.

Curtiss-Robertson: *See* Curtiss.

Custer (USA). Made extravagant claims for so-called 'channel-wing' aircraft of which examples flown 1948, 1953 and 1964.

Cvjetkovic (USA). Anton Cvjetkovic built light aircraft in Yugoslavia 1951 and in USA 1962, 1965 and 1986, many sets of plans sold.

CWA (UK). CW Aircraft Ltd, Slough, formed 1935 by Chronander and Waddington to build Cygnet 2-seater and 8-seat Swan (2 × Wasp Junior). Latter incomplete, former flown May 1937 but CWA failed and Cygnet taken over by General Aircraft.

CWL (Poland). Central Warsztatach Lotniczych, central workshops of air force, built WZXN.1 2-seat fighter/recon biplane 1926.

CZAL: *See* Ceskoslovenské.

CZL (Czechoslovakia). Unlike CZAL, CZL was used as abbreviated form for new (1959) title of national aircraft industry, Ceskoslovenské Závody Letecké. Replaced 1962 by Omnipol.

D

DAA (International). German-registered joint-programme company, 1991, owned 50% by DASA and 25% each by Aerospatiale and Alenia. Became Regioliner.

Dabos (France). Test pilot Jean Dabos designed JD.24P d'Artagnan light twin, built 1963 by André Courtade of Auch.

Daedalus (USA). Daedalus Research Inc., Petersburg, Virginia, built GRP-350 'slaved tandem freewing' vectored-thrust turboprop 1989.

Daewoo (S. Korea). Daewoo Heavy Industries, Inchon, began making airframe components 1985 and now shares in 10 major programmes, main subcontractor to Samsung on KF-X (F-16C/D). Own programmes are KIT (Korean Indigenous Trainer) and ARCH (Agricultural Remote-Control Helicopter).

Daewoo-Sikorsky: *See* DSA.

Daimler (Germany). Daimler Motoren-Gesellschaft, Stuttgart-Sindelfingen, established aircraft division July 1915. Chief types biplane fighters, L6 (D.I) of which 20 produced, and

prototypes of L8 (CL.I), L9 (D.II), L11 and L14. In 1919 came L15 ultralight 2-seat with 7.9 hp but intended as glider, followed by L20 ultralight (20-hp Mercedes) designed by Hanns Klemm, leading to Klemm aircraft.

Dallas (USA). Dallas Aero Service developed Dalaero upgrades of Lodestar 1959–63.

Dalotel (France). Assisted by Soc. Poulet, Michel Dalotel built DM-165 aerobatic trainer 1969.

Damoure: *See* DFL.

Danton (France). Built pioneer aircraft 1911–13.

DAP (Australia). Department of Aircraft Production built 700 Beauforts and 364 Beaufighters 1942–5.

D'Apuzzo (USA). Nicholas E. D'Apuzzo produced Denight Special racer 1948, D-260 (*see* Parsons-Jocelyn) Senior Aero Sport 1964, Junior Aero Sport 1965 and now D-201 Sportwing.

DAR (Bulgaria). To establish national aircraft industry Bulgarian government formed Drjavna Aeroplane Robotilnitsa (state aeroplane workshops) at Bojourishte 1924. Began by repairing and then building German aircraft, DFW C.IV, and 42 Fw 44 Stieglitz; own designs (most prototypes or short runs only): DAR.1 trainer, DAR.2 recon biplane, DAR.3 Garvan recon bomber,

Daimler L.6 (D.I), November 1917.

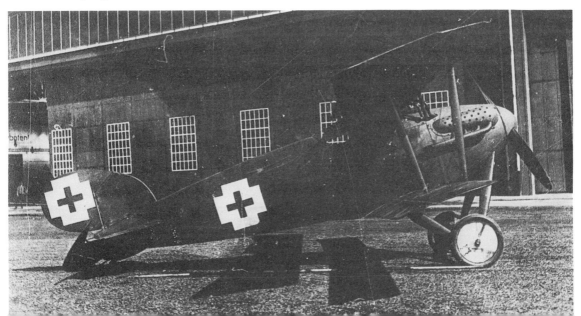

DAR.4 at Bojourishte, June 1932.

DAR.4 6-seater, DAR.5 aerobatic trainer, DAR.6 trainer, DAR.8 sport biplane, DAR.10 monoplane attack bomber and DAR.11 fighter (1941).

DARA (USA). Dayton (Ohio) Air Racing Association built *Miss Dara* racer (rebuilt B&B Special) 1958.

Darmstadt (Germany). Darmstadt Technischehochschüle (technical high school) established aviation society 1921 which to this day produces brilliant series of competition sailplanes. Between wars produced powered aircraft, notably D 18 (1928) cantilever cabin biplane, D 22 (1931) cantilever aerobatic biplane, and D 29 (1936) advanced high-performance tandem-seat monoplane.

Dart (UK). A.R. Weyl designed pusher ultralight 1935, built by Zander & Weyl at Dunstable and named Dunstable Dart. In 1936 company renamed Dart Aircraft Ltd, and aircraft renamed Pup. In same year built ultralight Flittermouse and Kitten.

Dart (USA). Dart Aircraft Co. formed 1933 by Albert Mooney and K.K. Culver at Columbus, Ohio, acquiring from Lambert Aircraft rights to Dart 2-seat monoplane, built in various versions. Company renamed Culver 1939.

DAS: *See* Dallas.

DASA (Germany). DASA, Deutsche Aerospace AG, formed 19 May 1989 to manage aerospace activities of Daimler-Benz group, simultaneously assuming 57.5% holding in Dornier and 100% in MTU engine company. Later acquired control (64.89%) of MBB and 100% of Deutsche Airbus, Elbe and TST (Telefunken). Control (51%) of Fokker being finalized late 1992. Programmes include Airbus (plus Satic and UHCA), Eurocopter Deutschland, Euroflag, Regioliner and Cryoplane. Combined workforce about 80,000.

Dashatou (China). Rosamonde I trainer/recon, believed first Chinese aircraft to fly, built at Dashatou repair works, Guangdong, by Yang Xian co-operative (July 1923).

Dassault (France). During Second World War Marcel Bloch's brother took resistance codename of d'Assault, and after war family adopted Dassault as new surname. Marcel convalesced from illness and privation caused by Buchenwald concentration camp, gathered his team (Vallières, Cabrière, Deplante) and set up Avions Marcel Dassault, with office at 46 ave Kléber, Paris, and factory at Talence, later augmented by larger works at Bordeaux-Mérignac. First products MD.315 Flamant light multirole transport and MD.450 Ouragan jet fighter. Sheer excellence of fighters and speed of development resulted in abandonment of other prototypes and concen-

Darmstadt D 18 (open cockpits), October 1928.

Dassault MD.320 Hirondelle, 11 September 1968.

tration on Mystère, Super Mystère B2, Mirage III/5/50 (1,422), Mirage F1 (745), Mirage IV bomber (62) and Mirage 2000 (510 orders by 1993). Arrogantly nationalist, Dassault did nothing to help sales of Jaguar, subject of 50/50 deal with Britain by Breguet, whom Dassault took over in December 1971 to form **Avions Marcel Dassault-Breguet Aviation, AMD-BA**. Declined to participate in EFA, instead building all-French Rafale. Etendard and Super Etendard naval attack aircraft made in small numbers, Breguet-designed Atlantic developed into Dassault Atlantique 2, Alpha Jet made in 50/50 deal with Dornier. Business jets began with Mystère 20 (Falcon 20) of 1963 and today Mystère-Falcon family have exceeded 1,000, but Mercure jetliner sold 10 only. French government acquired 20% stock January 1979, raised November 1981 to 45.76% with 54.7% of voting rights. AMD-BA renamed **Dassault Aviation** April 1990. Employees 1993 about 11,200. Government plan to integrate, not merge, with Aerospatiale. *See* Sogepa.

D'Astoux-Védrines (France). Famed aviator Jules Védrines assisted design of first of 2 d'Astoux & Cie aircraft 1916, triplane with 130-hp Clerget. Crashed Etampes early 1917.

Dätwyler: *See* MDB.

Davenport (USA). Bradley Davenport, Colorado Aero Technical College, built BD-2 Nuggitt single-seat aerobatic biplane 1967.

Davis (USA). David R. Davis not only founded Douglas but designed wing of B-24 Liberator and several other aircraft and in 1940 published patented plan for Manta fighter, with thick monoplane wing with downturned tips. Formed Manta Aircraft Corp., Los Angeles, but got no further than mock-up.

Davis (USA). Harold R. Davis, Hobart, Indiana, built Challis Special single-seat cabin monoplane 1956.

Davis (USA). Walter Davis formed Davis Aircraft Corp. January 1929 at Richmond,

Davis D-1 (ex-American Moth), 1930.

Dayton-Wright K-T Cabin Cruiser, 1920.

Indiana, to take over Vulcan Aircraft, thus American Moth became Davis Monoplane. Test pilot Louis Love shared in design of Love (Davis) Racer 1929; parasol later moved down to fuselage and engine fully cowled.

Davis (USA). Davis Aircraft Corp. formed March 1957 at Lake Village, Indiana, by Leeon Davis to produce DA-1 high-wing 5-seater. Followed with DA-2, DA-3 and DA-5A for homebuilders.

Davis-Douglas (USA). Formed 1920 at Santa Monica by wealthy sportsman David R. Davis and aircraft designer Donald Wills Douglas. Office behind barber shop on Pico Boulevard. Built Cloudster for Davis, then 38 DT-2 torpedo bombers. Re-formed as the Douglas Co. July 1921.

Dayton: *See* DARA.

Daytona (USA). Daytona Aircraft Construction Inc., Deland, Florida, formed 1990 to produce former Jamieson 2-/4-seater as D-120 to D-300, number indicating horsepower.

Dayton-Wright (USA). Formed March 1917 from original Wright company, Orville being appointed technical consultant though objective was to mass-produce to government specification. Three large plants, 2 at Dayton and 1 between nearby Moraine City and Miamisburg, mass-produced DH-4 and Standard J-1, but contracts slashed at Armistice. Control handed to General Motors 1920, depleted workforce built 40 XB-1A

(derived from Bristol Fighter) and numerous prototypes including K-T Cabin Cruiser, retractable-gear monoplane RB racer and PS-1 pursuit. Parent abandoned aviation 1923, assets bought by Reuben Fleet: *see* Consolidated.

Dean (USA). Herbert F. Dean killed on maiden flight 1961 of Delt-Air 250 pusher tailless delta.

de Bolotoff (UK). Only known product of de Bolotoff Aeroplane Works, Sevenoaks, was SDEB.14 2-seat biplane designed by Prince Serge de Bolotoff, flown August 1919.

de Bruyne (UK). Dr N.A. de Bruyne (pronounced broony), principal of ARL (Aero Research Ltd), Duxford, built 4-seat Snark 1934 and Ladybird ultralight 1936–7.

de Chevigny/Wilson (International). Explorer habitable aircraft funded by Bail Aviation, Lyon, commissioned by Hubert de Chevigny and designed Dean Wilson, flew April 1991.

Dee Howard (USA). San Antonio, Texas, owned 60% by Alenia, major upgrades of jet aircraft (One-Eleven, DC-8, 727, Learjet).

Deekay (UK). Deekay Aircraft Corp., Broxbourne, built Knight 2-seater 1937.

de Havilland (UK). Geoffrey de Havilland built motorcycle 1901 to commute to engineering school. Designed buses 1908, teamed with marine engineer F.T. Hearle, rented workshop off

de Havilland D.H.86 prototype, January 1934.

Bothwell St, Fulham, London, built biplane and tried to fly it at Seven Barrows, near Newbury, but wings broke. Repaired and improved biplane made good flight 10 September 1910. Flew for an hour at Farnborough 14 January 1911, two months after DH appointed designer and test pilot at HM Balloon Factory. Designed Factory aircraft (*see* Royal Aircraft Factory) until he joined Airco June 1914. Airco closed after war, and DH formed own company, **de Havilland Aircraft Co.**, 25 September 1920. Occupied 2 sheds at Stag Lane, Edgware, then north-west of London. Began with types designed at Airco, starting numerically with D.H.11 Oxford twin-engined bomber. From then a profusion of light aircraft, airliners, trainers, racers and a fighter (D.H.77) made first flights at Stag Lane, notably including D.H.60 Moth (22 February 1925), ending with D.H.86 4-engined airliner (14 January 1934). Stag Lane by then engulfed in London's urban sprawl, so moved to new site at Hatfield, where all subsequent prototypes built starting with D.H.87 Hornet Moth (9 May 1934). Numerically most important product D.H.82A Tiger Moth II, total including Queen Bee target version over 9,000; parent company built 1,150 pre-war and 795 during war. By far most important product D.H.98 Mosquito, 7,781 including 1,032 by D.H. Canada and 212 by D.H. Australia. D.H.100 Vampire jet fighter and trainer flew 20 September 1943, total 4,206 but over 1,000 overseas and nearly 1,200 by English Electric. D.H.104 Dove flew September 1945, 542 but attempts to produce successor failed. D.H.106 Comet, world's pioneer jetliner (27 July

1949), suffered structural problem and enjoyed only limited success. In 1948 large factory at Chester (called Hawarden or Broughton) taken over from Vickers-Armstrongs and tooled up for aircraft production, building successively Vampire, Venom, Dove, Heron, Comet, 125 and Airbus wings. Small run of DH.121 Trident built Hatfield. Gipsy engines led to D.H. Engine Co. 1 February 1944; 1935 licence for Hamilton Standard propellers led to Propeller Division which became D.H. Propellers Ltd 1946, which managed future missile programmes. Parent company de Havilland Holdings, formed 1955, purchased by Hawker Siddeley Group January 1960, forming de Havilland Division until 1 April 1965 when Hawker Siddeley Aviation operated as centrally controlled company. *See also* next 3 entries; Airspeed.

de Havilland Aircraft Co. Pty (Australia). Formed Melbourne 1927 to market, support and later assemble Moth; moved 1931 to Mascot, Sydney, then to Bankstown where growing factory built 1,085 Tiger Moth IIs, 87 Dragon Rapides and 212 Mosquitoes, engines and propellers. Prototype DHA-3 Drover flew January 1948, 20 built. In 1950s built Vampire Trainer. Became Hawker Siddeley subsidiary 1960, purchased Australian Bristol and Fairey companies and renamed Hawker de Havilland (HDH) 1963. Major producer of parts for foreign programmes.

de Havilland Aircraft of Canada Ltd (Canada). Formed January 1928 when assembly of Moths began in derelict warehouse at Mount Dennis,

de Havilland Canada DHC-4 (CV-2A) Caribou, December 1959.

DHC-1 Chipmunk, 1,657 DHC-2 Beaver I, over 480 DHC-3 Otter, 307 DHC-4 Caribou, 119 DHC-5 Buffalo, 835 DHC-6 Twin Otter, 115 DHC-7 Dash-7 and (by 1992) 388 DHC-8 Dash-8. Began making wings for DC-9 December 1965 until Malton plant was bought, first as Douglas Aircraft Co. of Canada, then as McDonnell Douglas Canada Ltd. Ownership transferred to Canadian government June 1974, and to Boeing January 1986, becoming Boeing Canada, de Havilland Division. Agreement April 1991 to sell to Aerospatiale/Alenia blocked by EC, so February 1992 sale to Bombardier 51% and Ontario government 49%, renamed **de Havilland Inc.**

de Havilland Technical School (UK). Intended for instruction rather than manufacture, produced single examples of light aircraft TK.1–TK.5 1934–9, all with single Gipsy engine (TK.2 190 mph, TK.4 244 mph).

de Lackner (USA). Donald de Lackner flew DH-4 Heli-vector, later called Aerocycle, January 1955, but market for simple 'platform' helicopter proved elusive.

Toronto. Moved 1929 to nearby Downsview, where wartime production included 1,520 Tigers, 1,032 Mosquitoes and 375 Ansons. Post-war built 100 CS2F-1 Trackers and own designs: 218

DelAero (Russia). Private OKB formed Moscow 1991 to develop T-101 Gratch STOL turboprop, T-401 Sokol light transport, T-501 turboprop trainer and T-602 Orel light twin. Became Rosk.

DelAero T-101 Gratch, with Myasishchyev Yamal beyond.

Delanne (France). Maurice Delanne built D.II light aircraft 1929, then adopted Nénadovich tandem-wing formula for series of fighter designs built by SAFRA and Arsenal 1937–9.

Delaunay-Bellville (France). Famed car company built at least 4 biplanes, most unusual being Coanda-designed SIA with twin 150-hp Hispano-Suiza amidships driving propeller behind twin-finned tail of beautifully streamlined fuselage. Crashed Etampes 1917.

Delemontez-Cauchy (France). DC-1 2-seater flew 1979.

Delgado (USA). Students at Delgado Trade School, New Orleans, built several aircraft 1932–7, including 2 trim low-wing racers. *Delgado Maid* was powered by Curtiss D-12 (June 1935), later Conqueror (about February 1936), unofficially 375 mph. *Delgado Flash* started 1933 but not finished until 1937 with fixed gear and 6-cylinder Menasco.

Delhamende (Belgium). André Delhamende took over Nipper ultralight from Fairey SA 1962.

Del Mar (USA). Bruce Del Mar established Del Mar Engineering Laboratories, Los Angeles, in 1940, main product a succession of Whirlymite ultralight helicopters.

de Marçay (France). Edmond de Marçay funded 1913 'sea monoplane', built SPADs during war and produced 2C1 high-speed fighter 1919. Thereafter 60-hp Passe-Partout ultralight, 60-hp single-seater and 2-seater limousine remained prototypes.

de Monge (France). Establissements Louis de Monge produced small prototypes 1922–5 and also M.101C2 2-seat fighter derived from Koolhoven FK.31 which firm built under licence 1925.

Denhaut (France). F. Denhaut took off from Seine at Juvisy 15 March 1912 in first flying-boat seen in Europe. Donnet and Lévêque formed company to build this and subsequent Denhaut designs. Denhaut designed BD.22 flying-boat for Bellanger 1922.

Denien (USA). Ralph R. Denien converted 1930 Hocker parasol monoplane into Sparrow Hawk biplane 1961.

Denight (USA). Ronald A. Denight built light aircraft 1983.

Denight (USA). William Denight built Goodyear-type racer 1949.

Denize (France). Robert Denize built light aircraft 1963.

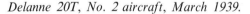

Delanne 20T, No. 2 aircraft, March 1939.

Deperdussin 1910 (Busson's, at Issy).

Denney (USA). Denney Aerocraft Co., Idaho, have sold over 1,200 kits for Kitfox Mks I, II and III 2-seaters, which are also licence-built in Australia, Brazil, Philippines, Portugal and S. Africa.

Denny (UK). William Denny, shipbuilding/engineering at Dumbarton, built BE.2c/2e 1915–17.

Departamento de Aeronaves (Brazil). Aircraft department of IPD: *see* CTA.

Department of Aircraft Production: *See* DAP.

Deperdussin (France). Société Pour les Appareils Deperdussin formed 1910 by silk merchant Armand Deperdussin at Béthery, Reims. Brilliant manager/designers Louis Bechereau and André Herbemont produced series of monocoque-fuselage monoplanes which won races and set world speed records until Deperdussin arrested for embezzlement August 1913. Company taken over by Blériot: *see* SPAD. Note: original

SPAD also said to stand for Soc. Provisoire des Aéroplans D., Soc. Parisienne des Avions D. and Soc. des Productions Armand D., and later for Soc. Anonyme Pour l'Aviation et ses Dérivés.

Descamps (France). Elisée Alfred Descamps built machine-gun-armed fighter 1913, designed for Aviatik at Mulhouse, became chief engineer for Anatra and then returned to France to build Descamps 27 fighter (May 1919) and 2 prototype bombers.

De Schelde (Netherlands). Koninklijke Maatschappij De Schelde, famed dockyard at Vlissingen (Flushing), took on most staff of Pander & Zonen 1935, including designer T.E. Slot. Produced S.12 4-seat monoplane, Scheldemusch and Scheldemeeuw light pusher biplanes, S.20 4-seat pusher and S.21 pusher fighter (which became so-called 'Focke-Wulf 198').

Desoutter (UK). Pioneer pilot Maurice Desoutter established Desoutter Aircraft Co. at Croydon

De Schelde S.20, March 1940.

1929 to build Koolhoven FK.41 3-seater under licence. Total 41 built in successive versions.

Despretz: *See* Jidey.

Detroit (USA). Detroit Aircraft Corp. was giant parent formed 1929 in era of conglomerates aiming at fast financial returns. In a few weeks purchased Ryan, Eastman, Lockheed, Blackburn, Aircraft Development, Marine Aircraft, Parks and Winton Engine Corporation. Failed 1931.

Deutsche Aerospace: *See* DASA.

Deutsche Airbus (Germany). Formerly MBB Transport Aircraft Group, 37.9% shareholder in Airbus Industrie responsible for assembly and test of A321. Also partner with Alenia/Aeritalia and Dornier on Advanced Amphibious Aircraft, with MBB and Dornier on DASA MPC-75 and for German share of Euroflag military airlifter. Now part of DASA.

Deutsche Flugzeug-Werke: *See* DFW.

Deutsche Forschungsinstitut für Segelflug: *See* DFS.

De Vore (USA). De Vore Aviation Corp. marketed Sunbird 2-seater 1986, based on British Ben-Air Sparrowhawk.

Dewey (USA). Jim Dewey built light aircraft 1981.

Dewoitine (France). Emile Dewoitine formed Constructions Aéronautiques Emile Dewoitine at Toulouse October 1920 to build metal monoplanes. D.1 fighter flew November 1922 and set pattern in achieving massive export success but rejected by French Aviation Militaire. D.7 ultralight followed by D.9 fighter (150 made by Ansaldo in Italy), D.21 (large sales to Turkey and licence-production Czech and Swiss firms), D.26 trainer for Switzerland and D.27 fighter (66 for Switzerland). Company liquidated January 1927, D.27 programme transferred to EKW, Switzerland.

Dewoitine (France). Emile re-established himself in France March 1928 with Société Aéronautique Française (Avions Dewoitine), office at Paris. SAF built 20 more D.27, 2 long-range D.33 record-breakers, D.37 fighters, D.332/333/338/342/620 3-engined airliners, over 380 low-wing fighters of D.500/501/510 series, and 478 D.520, regarded as France's best production fighter in 1940. Under 1936 nationalization law taken over by SNCA du Midi March 1937. This group liquidated January 1941, Dewoitine forming SIPA, which *see*.

DFL (France). MM. Damoure and Fabre, Aéro-Club d'Agen, produced DFL-6 Saphir 2-seater, flown 21 March 1960.

DFS (Germany). Central gliding research organization, formed Darmstadt 1933 from earlier (1925) organization. Produced DFS 230 troop-carrying glider (over 1,500 built) and various powered aircraft including all-wing pusher DFS

Dewoitine D.332 Emeraude, *at Croydon, September 1933.*

DFS (Lippisch) 39, Delta 4c, January 1937.

40 (1939), tailless rocket DFS 194 (which led to Me 163), DFS 228 high-altitude rocket-powered reconnaissance aircraft and DFS 346 supersonic aircraft (completed under Soviet management 1947).

DFW (Germany). Deutsche Flugzeug-Werke established by Bernard Meyer at Lindenthal, Leipzig, 1910, building Maurice Farman under licence and later Etrich and Jeannin Taubes. First original design Mars 2-seater in monoplane and biplane forms. Wartime designs mainly proto-types, but C.V armed 2-seater was major type

also made by Aviatik and Halberstadt. Biplane and triplane fighters included grotesque T.28 Floh (flea) of 1915, and 3 R-series giant bombers were also built. In 1920 a C.V was converted into 3-seat limousine, and there were plans to convert an R.II bomber into 24-passenger airliner. Lost identity on merger into ATG.

DH: *See* de Havilland.

DHC: *See* de Havilland Canada.

DHI: *See* Daewoo.

Díaz (Spain). Amalio Díaz designed single-seat fighter which competed unsuccessfully 1919 for air force order.

Dick, Kerr & Co. (UK). Electrical engineering company at Preston, built 110 F.3 flying-boats 1917–18, became part of English Electric.

Dietrich (Germany). Richard Dietrich built monoplane at Hanuske 1912; subcontracted in war but from 1921 produced DP.I, II, III and VII light aircraft. Failed 1927.

Dietrick (USA). Dietrick Sales and Service Co. produced light aircraft 1978.

Difoga (Netherlands). Designed and part-built during German occupation, Difoga 421 flown May 1946, pusher 2-seater with Ford V-8 engine.

Dil (Russia). Experimental reconnaissance biplane of 1917, wing incidence controllable from cockpit.

DFW Type I, built at Berlin-Johannisthal, 1912.

Dimanchev/Valkanov (Bulgaria). Georgi Dimanchev and Veselin Valkanov produced 2-seat ABC canard homebuilt (spring 1991).

DINFIA (Argentina). National aeronautical R&D and production organization, established 1957 having previously been FMA (1927), IA (1943) and IAM (1953). Major projects IA 35 Huanquero twin, IA 38 flying wing, IA 45 Querandi light transport, IA 46 Ranquel light ag/utility, IA 50 Guarani twin-turboprop and IA 53 ag-aircraft. Cordoba establishment again named FMA 1968.

Distributor Wing: *See* Aerial Distributors.

Dits (France). Les Etablissements Henri Dits set up 1912 to build to designs of Breguet pilot René Moineau; in 1915 original design with twin propellers driven by transverse engine in fuselage.

Dittmar (W. Germany). Famed sailplane designer/pilot Heini Dittmar flew prototype Motor-Möwe 2-seat light aircraft 1954. Small series included 3-seat versions.

Division of Aircraft Production: *See* GAF.

DMAV: *See* Dual Mode Air Vehicle.

DNP (France). MM. Duperron, Niepce and Fetterer made bomber in 1916, 3 × 200-hp Renault.

Doak (USA). Doak Aircraft Co. incorporated Torrance, Los Angeles, 1940, to research VTOL. Built Model 16 (US Army VZ-4) flown 1958. Assets sold to Douglas 1961.

Dobkevicius (Lithuania). Lt. Dobkevicius designed Dobi I, II and III trainer and reconnaissance aircraft at army factory 1922–5. He was killed 1926, successor was Gustaitis: *see* Anbo.

Doblhoff (Austria). Friedrich von Doblhoff pioneered helicopter with tip-drive rotor. Four prototypes 1943–5 with piston engine driving compressor blowing air through blades to combustion chamber and jet at tip. Patents taken by Fairey 1946.

Dockyard Constructional Unit (Malta). Built 18 Felixstowe F.3 flying-boats for RNAS 1917–18.

Doflug: *See* Dornier-Flugzeuge (Switzerland).

Dokuchayev (Russia). Moscow flight instructor Aleksandr Yakovlevich Dokuchayev built 6 aeroplanes. First, completed 1910, was biplane with pusher 50-hp Anzani, tested but possibly on ground only. No. 2 built 1912, sesquiplane version of Farman IV, 50-hp Gnome, said to have flown well. No. 3 again Farman type, but equal-span tandem trainer with 80-hp Gnome, flown late 1914. No. 4 again Farman type, sesquiplane trainer, 3 rudders, flown late 1915 on skis. No. 5 neat monoplane, much in common with LYaM, 80-hp Gnome, flown spring 1916. No. 6 reverted to Farman layout, 60-hp Gnome, flown with and without front elevator.

Doman (USA). Glidden S. Doman formed Doman Helicopters, Danbury, Connecticut, 31 August 1945, to develop helicopter with hingeless blades and enclosed self-lubricating hub. Rotor tested on Sikorsky R-6, led to various prototypes

Dobkevicius D.I, December 1924.

ending with 8-seat D-10B (Lycoming piston engine flat-rated at 400 hp) September 1958. Plans to produce in series in Italy and Puerto Rico came to nothing, as did twin-turbine BD-19 (Berlin Doman) project of 1967–70.

Dominion (Canada/USA). Former Boeing engineers formed Dominion Aircraft Corp. at Vancouver, factory at Renton, Washington. Prototype Skytrader utility transport (2 × 400-hp Lycoming piston engines) flew 21 April 1975. No production.

Domrachyev (USSR). Yuri Vladimirovich Domrachyev was brigade leader at NIAI 1934–40.

Donnet (France). Hydravions J. Donnet formed 1919 at Neuilly-sur-Seine after Percheron replaced Denhaut as designer. Built 6 HB3 civil flying-boats 1921–2.

Donnet-Denhaut (France). Having collaborated in Donnet-Lévêque company, Donnet and Denhaut formed new firm 1914 with factory on Île de la Jatte. Built series of excellent boats for anti-U-boat warfare, replacing FBA types from March 1916, total over 1,100 by 1922 including 58 for US Navy.

Donnet-Lévêque (France). Company formed 25 July 1912 to build flying-boats and amphibians to Denhaut's design, with original work on Seine at Juvisy but main factory Quai de Seine, Argenteuil. Standard product Type A 2-seater, originally 50-hp Gnome, later 80-hp. Donnet left early 1913, company briefly operating as Hydro-aéroplanes Lévêque until Schreck formed FBA.

Dorand (France). In 1916 Lt.-Col. Dorand, director of STAé (Section Technique de l'Aéronautique) issued requirement for 2-seat reconnaissance aircraft. Designed by Capt. Georges Lepère, AR was built in large numbers by STAé at Chalais-Meudon, and by private contractors, as AR.1 and AR.2 with differing engines and wing span. US Army used 142 as advanced trainers, and over 350 found (usually brief) civil use post-war. Took name of director, who had himself designed unsuccessful aircraft designated DO.1 in 1913.

Dormoy (France/USA). Etienne Dormoy was designer for, in succession, SPAD, US Army Engineering Division, Orenco, Verville and Buhl, producing Airster and Airsedan for last-named. Only aircraft to bear his name was Bathtub, strange and crude device which yet managed to win 1924 Rickenbacker Trophy.

Dorna (Iran). H.F. Dorna Co. established March 1989 to specialize in advanced composite-structure aircraft. Jet prototype homebuilt completed 1992.

Dornier (Germany). Prof. Dr Claude Dornier was a pioneer of all-metal structures. Joined Zeppelin Luftschiffbau 1910 working on airships, put in charge of research group set up 1914 at Lindau-Reutin and managed structural design of giant Rs series flying-boats: *see* Zeppelin. Dornier opened own design department at nearby Seemoos 1916 where several fighter (D) and attack aircraft (C, CL) were designed, first in world with true stressed-skin Duralumin structure. In 1919 Dornier transferred Lindau works to another lake-shore location, Manzell, renaming it Dornier

Dornier Do 217M-1 (May 1944) after capture 1945.

Metallbauten GmbH. Built C.II recon biplanes for Swiss, but large Gs.I transport flying-boat sunk by Allied Control Commission, so new Wal flying-boat (November 1922) was licensed to CMASA and SCMP Italy and to companies in Spain, Sweden, Switzerland and Japan, about 305 by 1931. Dornier's own production: Libelle 2-seat flying-boat, Delphin flying-boat (developed from 4 to 10 passengers 1921–4), Komet and derived Merkur landplanes (1921 5 seats, 1926 10), Do H Falke fighter, Do R Super Wal and giant Do X flying-boats and Do K freight landplane. In 1926 company set up in Switzerland (see below), built aircraft then proscribed in Germany, including prototypes which led to overt production in Germany of Do 11 and Do 23 heavy bombers from 1933. Firm restructured 1933.

Dornier-Flugzeuge (Switzerland). AG für Dornier-Flugzeuge set up 1926 at Altenrhein, with head office in Zurich marked Aero-Metall AG. Built Do D seaplane, Do E and Super Wal flying-boats, Delphin III 10-passenger boat and, by 1934, Do C3 (Do 22) torpedo seaplane, Do C4 fighter and Do Y 3-engined bomber. In 1939 built Bü 131 Jungmann.

Dornier-Werke GmbH (Germany). Main company renamed 1933, opening factories at Löwenthal, Allmansweiler and Wismar, latter (**Dornier-Werke Wismar GmbH**) becoming **Norddeutsche Dornier** 1940 with plants at Lübeck, Reinickendorf and Sternberg. In 1938 parent opened R&D centre at Oberpfaffenhofen, near Ingolstadt, became chief wartime development centre. Major types Do 18, 24 and 26 flying-boats (gigantic Do 214 not built), Do 17, 217 and 317 bombers and Do 335 Pfeil fighter, but main task production of He 111, Ju 88, Fw 190 and Me 410.

Dornier-Werke GmbH (Germany). Company re-registered 1954 at Friedrichshafen to build Do 25 then being designed by Oficinas Tecnicas Dornier (OTD) at Madrid, in collaboration with CASA. Do 25 developed into Do 27, over 600 built 1956–65. Then came Do 28A/B (120), and Do 28D/128 Skyservant (272). Do 29 and 31 V/STOLs were prototypes.

Dornier GmbH (Germany). Company restructured 22 December 1972, initially 65% Daimler-Benz but this holding since transferred to Deutsche Aerospace (DASA). All aviation activities managed by subsidiary **Dornier Luftfahrt GmbH**, partner in Alpha Jet and EFA, subcontractor to Airbus, upgrading UH-1D and Atlantic, integrated avionics for NATO E-3A. Sales of Do 228 twin-turboprop reached 205 by 1992, plus Indian licence (see HAL). Do 328 (6 December 1991) in development.

Dornier Composite (Germany). Formed 1990 by renaming Claudius Dornier Seastar, which had filed for bankruptcy previous year.

Doswiadczalne Warsztaty Lotnicze (Poland). Not normally abbreviated, aeronautical experimental works at Warsaw Okecie was put at disposal of Warsaw tech high school 1933 to produce school's designs: see RWD.

Douglas (USA). Donald Wills Douglas graduated US Naval Academy, graduated/lectured MIT, then chief engineer Glenn L. Martin. Moved LA and with sportsman David R. Davis formed **Davis-Douglas Co.** 22 July 1920, which see; 5 July 1921 formed **The Douglas Co.**, 2435 Wilshire Blvd, Santa Monica, great success with DT torpedo bombers, DWC world cruisers, M-2 and M-4 mailplanes, C-1 Army transport, T2D twin-engined torpedo land/seaplane, and above all O-2 observation aircraft, larger numbers than any other US between-wars type (over 900).

Douglas (USA). Company restructured as **Douglas Aircraft Co.** 30 November 1928, new location 3000 Ocean Park Blvd, Santa Monica, on Clover Field. Continued rapid expansion supported by observation, bomber, torpedo and civil aircraft. Company engineer John K. 'Jack' Northrop set up company 1932 operated as subsidiary: see Northrop. This took over former Moreland plant at El Segundo, another LA suburb, where Northrop and chief engineer Ed Heinemann produced Gamma, Delta, 8A/A-17 and BT/SBD Dauntless. In 1937 Northrop left, El Segundo becoming wholly-owned Douglas division responsible for Navy aircraft. Meanwhile Santa Monica chief engineer Arthur E. Raymond designed DC-1 airliner for TWA, flown 1 July 1933, leading to DC-2 (193) and DC-3 (10,655, mainly military and excluding 2,930 Soviet Li-2 and 486 Japanese L2D). This provided basis for 4-engined DC-4/C-54, DC-6 and DC-7. Heinemann's team produced fast attack prototypes leading to DB-7/Boston/Havoc/A-20, total 7,385, and A-26/B-26 Invader, 1,355 built 1944–5, and excellent DC-5. Navy programmes included SBD

Douglas DC-7B, October 1955.

Dauntless (5,936), AD (A-1) Skyraider (3,180), F4D (F-6) Skyray, A3D (A-3) Skywarrior, A4D (A-4) Skyhawk (2,980) and Mach 2 Skyrocket. Air Force programmes included C-74/124 Globemaster, C-133 Cargomaster and B-66 Destroyer. Wartime output 30,980 was second only to NAA, 9 major plants including Chicago, Long Beach and Tulsa, employment peak August 1943 at 157,200. Biggest gamble in company history was launch of DC-8 jetliner, no prospect of military order, on 7 June 1955; stretched Super Sixty series extended production to 556 by May 1972. From 1961 company gradually transferred all HQ services from Santa Monica to Long Beach, where DC-9 flew 25 February 1965. Severe cash-flow problem resulted in 28 April 1967 merger with McDonnell, forming McDonnell Douglas Corporation, which *see*. Douglas programmes include DC-10 large trijet (29 August 1970), 386 built plus 60 KC-10 Extender for USAF; MD-80 family of narrow-body twin-jets (18 October 1979), 2,000 sales; MD-90 twin-jet (22 Feb 1993) including MD-90-30T Trunkliner to be produced by SAMF in China; MD-11 improved derivative of DC-10 (10 January 1990), 180 orders late 1992; and C-17 airlifter for USAF (15 September 1991). Projects include high-capacity 4-engined MD-12, subject of long negotiations with Taiwan (*see* McDonnell Douglas), and MD-95 twin-jet to be developed jointly with Chinese industry. T-45A Goshawk transferred to McDonnell.

Downer (USA). Downer Aircraft Co., previously Northern Aircraft, purchased Bellanca assets at Alexandria, Minnesota, produced Downer Bellanca Cruisemaster from 1957 and Model 260 from 1959. Bought rights to Seabee.

Doyle (USA). Doyle Aero Corp. set up by Harvey Doyle at Baltimore 1929 to produce Oriole light aircraft.

Doyn (USA). Doyn Aircraft Inc., Wichita, specialized in uprating light aircraft (Cessna 172/175, Apache) with more powerful engines.

Dragon Fly (USA). Dragon Fly Aircraft Corp. formed at Chicago 1928 to produce 2-seat parasol monoplane of that name.

Driggs (USA). Driggs Aircraft Corp. incorporated February 1924 Dayton, Ohio, moving 1927 to Lansing, Michigan. Ivan H. Driggs had built aircraft 1915 and in 1924 Driggs-Johnson DJ-1 Bumblebee monoplane racers. Developed Dart 1 for Army high-lift research 1926, and Driggs Aircraft produced civil 2-seat version followed by Dart II and Skylark III. Driggs to Luscombe 1934, Dart rights to Phillips Aviation.

Druine (France). Roger Druine built first light aircraft 1938, followed by Aigle 1948 and single-

Druine D.31 Turbulent, January 1954.

seat Turbulent 1950, forming Avions Roger Druine in Paris. Tandem Turbi and side-by-side Condor followed, licensed to Rollason (UK), Stark (Germany/Spain) and Merville (France). Druine died 1958.

DSA (International). Daewoo-Sikorsky Aerospace Ltd formed 1988 to produce S-76 and H-76 at new plant at Chang-Won.

Dual Model Air Vehicle (USA). Arlington, Texas, company responsible for design and testing of TW-68 tilt-wing aircraft: *see* Ishida.

Dudakov-Konstantinov (Russia/USSR). Avro 504K used by White Russia, adopted by USSR, developed by V.I. Dudakov and V.A. Konstantinov into U-1 and 664 made at GAZ-3, plus 73 seaplane MU-1 1924–30.

Dudek (USA). Stanley Dudek built light aircraft 1958.

Dudley Watt (UK). D.W.2 tandem-seat biplane designed for Dudley N. Watt by K.N. Pearson and built Brooklands 1930.

Dufaux (Switzerland). Brothers Armand and Henri Dufaux built helicopter 1905 and triplane 1908 (1st Swiss aeroplane). Dufaux 4 still in Luzern museum, Dufaux 5 used army manoeuvres 1910.

Dufaux (France). Armand Dufaux formed Société pour la Construction et l'Entretien d'Avions, Paris, 1914, developed unconventional fighter with propeller rotating around fuselage behind wings, and Avion-Canon with 2 rotary engines athwartships in nose with bevel drive to propeller shaft around 37-mm Hotchkiss cannon, 1917.

Duigan (Australia). John R. Duigan made first flight in Australia, Mia Mia, July 1910, in aircraft built from photograph of a Wright biplane. Subsequently made other aircraft.

Duks (Russia). Joint-stock company founded by Yu.A. Meller in Moscow 1894. In 1910 bought licence for Farman and subsequently became largest aircraft company in Russia, by 1917 reaching 2,120 workers plus *c.* 300 staff. Chief engineer F.E. Moska based products on French, usually Farman or Nieuport. After Revolution

became GAZ-1, Moscow-Khodinka.

Dulkes (Netherlands). This company set up by brothers who often appear as Dijkman; in 1931 produced Bravo high-wing cabin single-seater with 750-cc DAF engine.

Dumod (USA). Dumod Corp. specialized in developments of Beech 18, originally called Infinité I and stretched Infinité II, later Dumod I and II. Rights bought by Broome 1964.

Dunai (Hungary). Dunai Repülögépgyár Rt (Danube aircraft factory) established by Germans at Horthyliget to mass-produce Me 210C, 267 delivered 1943–4.

Dunne (UK). Lt. John William Dunne produced man-lifting kites at HM Balloon Factory, Farnborough, following with D.1 biplane hangglider of tailless sweptback form. Experiments with added engines led to D.4, tested by *ad hoc* Blair Atholl Aeroplane Syndicate. Short Brothers built D.5, tested at Eastchurch 1910, leading to D.8, D.10 and derived designs by Burgess Aircraft. D.8 was excellent, inherently stable aircraft.

Dunstable: *See* Dart (UK).

duPont (USA). DP-2 twin-turbofan 30/44-passenger aircraft allegedly being built by duPont Aerospace Co., unconnected with chemical giant. Designers recruited 1979, no hardware seen by 1992.

Duramold (USA). Duramold Aircraft Corp. formed 1936 to develop plastic-bonded plywood construction patented by Col. V.E. Clark (previously designer of Clark aerofoils and Eng. Div. VCP and Gen. Avn. GA.43 aircraft). Built F-46A 1938 to test process which was used in such later aircraft as Fairchild XAT-13/14/21.

Durand (USA). Durand Associates, Omaha, produce Mk V metal 2-seat backstagger biplane, plans marketed (88 + sold).

Durant (USA). Durant Aircraft Corp. formed Oakland 1919 by Rex Durant to produce Durant-Standard J-1, wartime Standard J-1 trainer re-engined with 200-hp Hall-Scott (half Liberty).

Durban (S. Africa). Durban Aircraft Corp. formed September 1962 to continue production of Aeriel III, improved Piel Emeraude previously marketed by Genair.

Durenleau (USA). Rene Durenleau, Franklin, Vermont, flew A-1 Biddy Buddy single-seat biplane July 1959, plans marketed.

Duruble (France). Roland Duruble, with assistants, produced RD.02 Edelweiss 2-seater flown July 1962.

Dushkin (USSR). L.S. Dushkin led team developing various (mostly twin-chamber) liquid rocket engines, for BI especially; simple glider flown under rocket power 28 February 1940 referred to as Dushkin aircraft.

Du Temple (France). Félix Du Temple, naval officer, built what is believed to be first working model aeroplane 1857, publishing design same year. Subsequently built full-scale aeroplane which in 1874 was first in world to take off (down ramp) but then failed to fly.

DWL: *See* RWD.

Dybovskii (Russia). V.V. Dybovskii built streamlined Delphin 2-seat monoplane 1913.

Dycer (USA). Charles F. Dycer, owner of Dycer Airport, LA, built 90-hp 3-seat biplane 1926 and 160-hp monoplane 1930.

Dyke (USA). John W. and Jennie Dyke built JD-1 tailless delta 1964, and JD-2 Delta 1966; estimated 360 + Dyke JD.2 building 1992.

Dyle et Bacalan (France). Soc. Anonyme des Travaux Dyle et Bacalan, Bordeaux naval dockyard, started 1925 producing series of metal monoplanes, military/civil, land/sea. First 2 were DB.10 bomber and DB.20 armoured fighter, both with aerofoil fuselages carrying on leading edge 2 GR9 Jupiter engines.

Dynac (USA). Dynac International, NY, announced 1989 it had acquired rights to Lark Commander and planned to produce redesigned versions.

Dzerzhinski (USSR). Name of biplane built 1927 by S.D. Chernikhovskii.

EAA: *See* Eagle (Australia).

EAA (USA). Experimental Aircraft Association Inc., HQ Hales Corners, Wisconsin, has thousands of members in chapters worldwide. Among many services to members from 1955 developed aircraft for home construction, so far: EAA Biplane 1960, Acro-Sport I 1972, Super Acro-Sport 1973, Pober P-9 Pixie 1974 and Acro-Sport II 1978.

EAC (France). Etudes Aéronautiques et Commerciales SARL formed 1960 to build improved Jodels and market kits.

EAC (USA). Engineers Aircraft Corp. incorporated Stamford, Connecticut, 1929 to produce EAC-1 2-seat monoplane.

Eagle (Australia). Eagle Aircraft Australia, Fremantle, produced prototype EAA Eagle XTS 1988, all-composites 'three flying surface' configuration, primarily for farm applications: *see* EAI.

Eagle (USA). Eagle Aircraft Co., Boise, Idaho, reached agreement with Bellanca 1979 to produce latter's Eagle ag-aircraft.

Eagle (USA). Eagle Helicopter Corp. built prototypes of Eagle II 2-seat helicopter with 235-hp Evinrude V-6 engine blowing air to cold tip jets, and Eagle III with tip-mounted fuel-burning pressure jets (1980).

Eagle Wings (USA). This corporation at Boca Raton, Florida, flew Jaeger prototype September 1987, with folding tailbooms and choice of short- or long-span wings for high speed or extended gliding.

EAI (Australia). Eagle Aircraft International, Perth, formed 1991 as joint venture by Eagle and Malaysian government to build Eagle XTS.

EAL: *See* Ethiopian Airlines.

Earl (USA). Earl Aviation Corp., Los Angeles,

built small range of 2-seaters 1929–31.

Earthstar (USA). Earthstar Aircraft Inc., Santa Margarita, markets range of microlights and kits for homebuilts (Laughing Gull, Gull II, Ultra Gull).

Eastbourne (UK). Eastbourne Aviation Co. formed in that town 1913 by F.B. Fowler, built biplanes and monoplanes and, during war, Avro 504 and BE.2c.

East Coast (USA). East Coast Aeronautics, subsidiary of Barium Steel, built 2 XF-80C Shooting Stars using thick magnesium alloy to allow simplified structure.

Eastern Aircraft (USA). Division of General Motors formed March 1942 to use several car plants for aircraft production; delivered 1,060 FM-1 and 4,777 FM-2 Wildcats, and 2,882 TBM-1 and 4,664 TBM-3 Avengers.

Eastman (USA). Eastman Aircraft Corp. was one of those companies gathered up 1929 into Detroit Aircraft; made Flying Yacht, Sea Pirate and other small flying-boats and amphibians at Detroit. Original name (1926) the Beasley-Eastman Laboratories.

Eau Gallie: *See* EGHS.

Eberhart (USA). Originally Eberhart Steel Products, made wide range of aircraft/armament parts, and 50 SE.5E fighters 1922. Buffalo plant renamed the Eberhart Aeroplane and Motor Co. Inc. 1925, built Iroquois 3-seater and XFG-1 Comanche fighter, latter converted into XF2G fighter seaplane.

Ebershoff (USA). Over 5,000 sets of plans sold for Ebershoff-Steen Skybolt 2-seat aerobatic biplane.

Ecklund (Finland). Torolf Ecklund built TE-1 single-seat amphibian 1949.

Ector (USA). Ector Aircraft Co., Odessa, Texas, developed L-19 Bird Dog into Mountaineer and Super Mountaineer civil aircraft 1980–90.

Edgar Percival (UK). Capt. Edgar Percival (*see* Percival) started fresh company at Stapleford Tawney, Essex, 1954; built 21 E.P.9 utility aircraft before selling out to Samlesbury Engineering: *see* Lancashire.

Edgley (UK). Edgley Aircraft formed 1974 to produce Optica observation aircraft; company failed 1985: *see* Optica; Brooklands; FLS.

Edo (USA). Edo Aircraft Corp. incorporated 1925 at College Point, Long Island, producing seaplane floats. Produced 2 US Navy XOSE-1 seaplanes 1946.

Edwards (USA). William Edwards acquired rights to Spezio Tuholer sporting aircraft 1973.

EFW: *See* F + W.

EGAO: *See* Helwan Air Works.

EGHS (USA). Eau Gallie High School, Florida, produced Gull 2-seat research aircraft 1986.

Egrett (International). Team comprising E-Systems (USA), Burkhart Grob (Germany) and Garrett (USA) produced Egrett-1 proof-of-concept aircraft 1987 and D-500 surveillance aircraft 1989. Egrett II for service with Luftwaffe.

EHI (International). EH Industries Ltd formed June 1980 by Agusta (Italy) and Westland (UK)

EH 101 Merlin (foreground), Heliliner and utility, 1992.

EKW C-35, May 1937.

as 50/50 partnership to produce EH 101 helicopter. Programme managed by British MoD, except Merlin (Royal Navy version) by IBM/Westland team appointed 1991.

Ehmann (W. Germany). Rolf Ehmann built light aircraft 1984.

Eich (USA). James P. Eich built JE-2 2-seat autogyro 1977; plans marketed.

Eichmann (USA). Built Model A single-seat and Model B 2-seat metal flying-wing aircraft 1946–7.

Eidgenössiches: *See* EKW, F + W.

Eiffel: *See* Laboratoire Eiffel.

Eipper (USA). Eipper Industries, Temecula, California, one of world's largest producers of microlights (Quicksilver series) and kits.

Ekin: *See* WHE.

Eklund: *See* Ecklund.

Ekonomov (USSR). P.I. Ekonomov, at MAI 1936, built but did not fly Zhiroplan helicopter.

Ekström (Sweden). Staffan W. Ekström produces series of Humlan 2 light autogyros.

EKW (Switzerland). Eidgenössiche Konstruktions Werkstätte formed Thun 1914, built aircraft designed by Haefeli: DH-1 pusher (6), DH-3 2-seat tractor (110), DH-5 (60 in 1919) and DH-5A (22 in 1928). In 1932 produced Fokker C.V jointly with Dornier, and replaced this with C-35 flown 1935, 80 built 1937–9.

Elbe (Germany). Elbe Flugzeugwerke established in Dresden in DDR (E. Germany); in 1991 incorporated into DASA and assigned rear fuselage of Fokker 100.

Eldred (USA). D. Eldred, Willoughby, Ohio, built 2-seat seaplane with tail carried on floats 1946.

Electrospace (USA). Electrospace Systems, subsidiary of Chrysler Corp. at Richardson, Texas, undertakes specialist conversions for Dept. of Defense, e.g. DC-8 into EC-24A and 707s into EC-18D cruise-missile control platforms.

Elias (USA). G. Elias & Brother incorporated Buffalo 1881, but began making aircraft 1920: TA-1 Army trainer 1921, XNBS-3 bomber 1922, 6 EM-2 Marine utility land/seaplanes plus 1 EO-1 Navy observation version, AJE Air Express mail or ag-aircraft and, in 1927, EC-1 Aircoupe 2-seater. Failed 1930.

Elicotteri Helicopter: *See* EHI.

Elicotteri Meridionali (Italy). Formed with Agusta assistance at Frosinone October 1967, acquiring rights to CH-47C Chinook in 1968, producing this helicopter from 1970. EM remains affiliated to Agusta and CH-47C but lost identity as Sesto Calende (ex SIAI Marchetti) factory. Participates in all Agusta helicopter programmes.

Embraer EMB-120 Brasilia, 1983.

Ellehammer (Denmark). Pioneer aviator J.C.H. Ellehammer built monoplane 1905–6, added upper wing and achieved tethered flight round circular track 16 August 1906. Then built triplane (first flight in Germany 28 June 1908) and twin-rotor helicopter with cyclic pitch control (1912).

Elliotts: *See* Eon.

Elmendorf (USA). Leonard C. Elmendorf built light aircraft 1973.

Elmwood (Canada). Elmwood Aviation, Belleville, Ontario, markets plans of CA-05 Christavia 1 2-seater and CH-8 Christavia 4 4-seater, over 400 now being built.

Elston & Pruitt (USA). Built light aircraft 1974.

Elytroplan (France). L'Elytroplan built LB.20 2-seater 1946.

Emair (USA). Division of Emroth Co. at Harlingen, Texas, produced MA-1 ag-aircraft developed by Air New Zealand: *see* Murrayair.

Embraer (Brazil). Empresa Brasileira de Aeronáutica SA formed 19 August 1969 at São José dos Campos, and delivered over 4,500 aircraft in first 23 years. Shares were 63.81% government, but under 1992 privatization reduced to 20%, with 10% offered to Embraer employees, 30% local investors and 40% foreign. Major programmes EMB-110/111 Bandeirante, EMB-120 Brasilia, EMB-121 Xingu, EMB-145 jetliner, EMB-201 Ipanema and EMB-312 Tucano. Subsidiary **Neiva** builds Pipers. CBA-123 Vector is 67/33 programme with FMA and AMX is 29.7% share with Alenia/Aermacchi. Embraer makes MD-11 flaps and wingtips and fin fairings for 777.

Emigh (USA). Emigh Trojan Aircraft Co., Douglas, AZ, succeeded Emigh Aircraft Corp. and continued limited manufacture of A-2 Trojan 2-seater 1948–51.

EMIND (former Jugoslavia). New company at Erevik attempting to develop PPA-1 and -2 ag-aircraft with respectively 1 and 2 ducted propellers; thwarted by civil war.

Empresa Brasileira: *See* Embraer.

Empresa Industrias: *See* IAME.

Empresa Nacional: *See* ENAER.

Emsco (USA). Southern California industrialist E.M. Smith formed Emsco Aero Engine Co. 1928 to build 1,000-hp diesel, and in 1929 bought

Emsco Arctic Tern, 1931.

Zenith Aircraft to form Emsco Aircraft Corp., Downey (Los Angeles), producing trimotor Challenger, 2-seat Cirrus, 8-seat high-wing B-3, 9-seat B-3A, 2-seat B-7, fast Arctic Tern amphibian and incomplete B-10 STOL flying wing.

ENAER (Chile). Empresa Nacional de Aeronáutica de Chile is state organization formed 1984 from IndAer. Assembled 27 Piper Dakotas, used Piper components in T-35 Pillán trainer, assembles A-36 Halcón (CASA C-101) with increasing local content, upgrades Mirage 50 to Pantera 50C and is developing Namçu light aircraft.

ENET 1 (Argentina). Escuela Nacional de Educación Tecnica No. 1, one of several air force schools, produced Pazmany PL-4A and PL-2 in 1986–7 and prepared series production of developed PL-2 called PL-3 Guri, but funding inadequate 1990.

Engels (Russia). Evgenii Robertovich Engels, staff captain at artillery academy, built Orel cabin monoplane 1915, but killed testing MI flying-boat fighter of his design 1916.

Engineering Division (USA). Division of US War Department, Bureau of Aircraft Production, set up December 1917 on return of Cdr. R.C. Bolling from Europe where his team had investigated possibility of building Americanized European designs. Subsequently Engineering Division evaluated, investigated, designed and manufactured US Army aircraft, notably: LUSAC (Lepère US Army combat) series of fighters, USB/USXB based on Bristol Fighter, USD-9/9A versions of D.H.9, Pomilio FVL-8 fighter, VCP (Virginius Clark Pursuit), PW-1, TP-1 2-seat pursuit, GA-1 armoured ground attack made by Boeing, XNBL-1 'Barling Bomber', and Verville R-3 racer made by Sperry. Became Materiel Division, Air Corps, 1926, and in October 1927 moved from McCook Field to Wright Field, ceasing to design or build.

Engineering & Research Corporation (USA). Incorporated at Riverdale, MD, 1930, chairman H.A. Berliner and chief engineer Fred. E. Weick (*see* both). First major product Ercoupe, 1937, notable for pedal-less flight controls. *See also* Alon.

Engineers Aircraft: *See* EAC (USA).

English Electric (UK). EECo. formed 1918 by amalgamating Phoenix Dynamo (Bradford), Dick, Kerr (Preston) and COW, all of which had built aircraft, and 2 other large companies. Phoenix team continued to produce flying-boats, notably Cork, Ayr and Kingston. W.O. Manning designed Wren ultralight, covering 87.5 miles on 1 gal October 1923. Aviation Department closed 1926.

English Electric (UK). Urgent RAF expansion 1938 led to big order for HP Hampden bombers placed with EECo., at former Dick, Kerr works at Strand Road, Preston. Built 850, then 2,145 HP Halifaxes; tooled up for Folland F.19/43 but this was replaced by D.H. Vampire, nearly 1,200 delivered. Sir George Nelson and board decided to remain in aviation, collected design team under W.E.W. Petter in former bus garage in Barton St, Preston, and result was Canberra (13 May 1949), 1,352 built including 901 by EECo. P.1 supersonic aircraft (4 August 1954) led to Lightning interceptor (338). Vast new development/production centre grew at airfield at Warton, west of Preston, which together with guided-weapons division at Stevenage/Luton formed **English Electric Aviation Ltd** 9 January 1959. On 1 January 1960 this company became 40% of British Aircraft Corp., original name vanishing as BAC Preston Division 1 January 1964.

Enstrom (USA). R.J. Enstrom Corp. formed Menominee, Michigan, 1959 to produce F-28 3-seat helicopter flown as 'breadboard' prototype November 1960. Operations ceased February 1970, but restarted as **Enstrom Helicopter Corp.** 1971. Since then 915 helicopters delivered in 7 main versions, but company acquired successively by Pacific Airmotive, Bravo BVC (Netherlands), US group headed by Dean Kamen and Robert M. Tuttle (who is still president), and in 1990 by investment group based in LA.

Entler (Germany). Entler-werke formed Wilhelmshaven January 1922 by Victor Entler (ex-Sablatnig) and Hans Brand to produce all-metal corrugated-skin single-seat biplane (30-hp Haacke).

Entwicklungsring: *See* EWR.

Eon (UK). Elliotts of Newbury formed 1895 as joinery/furniture works; produced aircraft parts

1940–45, then flew prototype Newbury Eon 4-seater 8 August 1947. Also built Olympia and Baby sailplanes.

Epervier (Belgium). Epervier Aviation SA produce micro, ARV and observation versions of 2-seat Epervier (September 1990).

Epps (USA). Ben T. Epps Jr. built light aircraft 1971.

Equator (W. Germany). At Erbach, successor to Pöschel, who remained president; built P.300 5/6-seat STOL flown November 1970, followed by P.400 Turbo-Equator STOL amphibian 1977. Extensive redesign in 1980s.

Erco: *See* Engineering & Research Corp.

Ericson (Sweden). Hugo Ericson built light aircraft 1971.

Erla (Germany). In early 1933 Nestler und Breitfeld AG of Erla began building Erla 5 single-seater; name changed to Erla-Maschinenwerk GmbH 1934, HQ at Leipzig. Company expanded rapidly with orders for Ar 65 and 68 and He 51, and became major partner in Bf 109 production.

Ermolayev: *See* Yermolayev.

Erni (Switzerland). Hans Erni built light aircraft 1973.

ERNO (W. Germany). Entwicklungsring Nord formed Bremen 1961 by Hamburger and VFW (formerly Focke-Wulf/Weser) to manage major air and space projects; collaborated on Do 31 V/STOL.

Ernoul (France). Emil Dewoitine designed 2 aircraft for M. Ernoul, best-known being ED.3 civil

monoplane for 8 passengers with high monoplane wing and 2 × 250-hp Salmson side by side on nose (just far enough apart on pylons for propellers not to touch); built Toulouse (July 1922).

Escola de Engenharia (Brazil). Engineering school of University of São Paulo has produced succession of powered aircraft and gliders, with numbers prefixed IPT, SP or IPAI.

Escuela: *See* ENET 1.

Eshelman (USA). Cheston L. Eshelman Co. established at former GA/NAA plant Dundalk, MD, early 1942 to produce light aircraft with blended wing/fuselage. FW-5, commonly called Eshelman Wing, flown 1944; smaller Winglet flown 1946.

Esnault-Pelterie (France). Robert Esnault-Pelterie, commonly REP, was one of greatest pioneers of aeroplane, engines and rockets. Biplane gliders made first use of ailerons October 1904, but REP.1 with REP engine 1907 used warping. Subsequent aeroplanes progressively better. Parasol and Type N saw service in First World War. Founded Association des Industriels de la Locomotion Aérienne 1908. Vickers bought REP licence 1911.

Espenlaub Flugzeugbau (Germany). Gottlieb Espenlaub, famed glider pilot, formed company at Dusseldorf airport 1926. Most important early product Type 14 light 2-seat monoplane, produced in developed forms 1928–35.

Essex Aero (UK). Major producer of magnesium-alloy parts, flew Sprite 2-seat monoplane 1948 with all-Mg airframe.

Ethiopian Airlines (Ethiopia). Since 1986 has assembled Schweizer Ag-Cat Super B Turbine

REP No. 2, 4th rebuild, 1909.

(local name Eshet), with increasing local content.

Etrich (Austria). Igo Etrich, assisted by Franz Wels, built graceful tailless glider 1907. Led to bird-like Taube monoplanes made in large numbers 1909–16, initially by Etrich Flieger Werke, registered 1 November 1909.

Etrich (Germany). Etrich Flieger-werke GmbH established at Liebau 1912, building Taubes and other types, some very advanced. Taube also built by Rumpler (from 1911), Albatros, DFW, Gotha, Halberstadt, Jeannin, Kondor, Krieger, LVG and Lübeck-Travemünde.

Etudes: *See* EAC (France).

Euler (Germany). August Euler, pioneer aviator, bought Voisin licence 1910 and founded Euler-Werke at Niederrad, Frankfurt-am-Main. Produced 27 prototypes including biplanes, triplanes and a quadruplane, with small runs of types based on LVG and Nieuport. After Armistice ceased manufacture, founder appointed Sec. of State for Air.

EuroAvtek (Denmark). Avtek technology, production and marketing transferred October 1991 to EuroAvtek A/S owned jointly by Avtek, Per Udsen and Danish government.

Eurocopter (International). Helicopter divisions of Aerospatiale and MBB (now DASA) formed **Eurocopter SA** 16 January 1992 as holding company, HQ La Courneuve, Paris. Manufacturing arms are **Eurocopter France**, HQ Marignane, Marseilles, and **Eurocopter Deutschland**, HQ Munich. Tiger/Tigre/Gerfaut programme has own management: **Eurocopter Tiger GmbH**, Munich. All marketing by **Eurocopter International**, La Courneuve. **American Eurocopter Corp.**, Grand Prairie, TX, handles assembly, modification and support. **Eurocopter Canada** is subsidiary at Fort Erie marketing BO 105, exclusively making 105LS and sharing in new EC 155. Programmes include all existing Aérospatiale and MBB helicopters plus NH90 and Eurofar (which *see*), BK 117 (with Kawasaki), EC 150 (with CATIC and SA) and EC 120 Ibis (with Kamov). December 1992 agreement with Mil/Kazan/Klimov provides for design of Mi-38 cockpit, avionics and interior and management of export marketing.

Eurofar (International). Accord signed September 1986 by Aerospatiale, Agusta, Alenia, CASA, DASA and Westland to build European Future Advanced Rotorcraft, civil tilt-rotor convertiplane.

Eurofighter (International). Eurofighter Jagd-flugzeug GmbH formed by Germany 33%, Italy 21%, Spain 13% and UK 33% June 1986 to manage EFA (European Fighter Aircraft) programme, HQ Munich.

Euroflag (International). Euroflag srl formed April 1989 by Aerospatiale, Alenia, British Aerospace, CASA and Deutsche Airbus to replace FIMA in managing military airlifter

Eurocopter Tiger, 27 April 1991.

programme, title from Future Large Aircraft. In 1992 OGMA, Sabca/Sonaca and TAI joined.

Euro-Hermespace (International). Agreement signed 7 November 1990 by Aerospatiale, Alenia, Dassault and DASA to manage Hermès aerospace craft; shares Hermespace France (Aerospatiale 51, Dassault 49) 51.6%, DASA 33.4%, Alenia 15%. Other participants Austria, Belgium, Canada, Denmark, Netherlands, Norway, Spain, Sweden and Switzerland. In abeyance 1993.

Evangel (USA). Evangel Aircraft Corp. incorporated Orange City, Iowa, 1957 to produce tough transport for missionary groups, especially in S. America. Evangel 4500-300 flew June 1964, 7 production aircraft built 1969–74.

Evans (USA). Convair design engineer W. Samuel Evans produced Volksplane, simple single-seater, 1967. Since then 5,000 + sets of plans sold for VP-1 and several hundred 2-seat VP-2; today Evans Aircraft, La Jolla, CA, no longer sells VP-2 plans.

Evensen (USSR). P.A. Evensen (Ivensen) built parasol monoplane 1929.

Everett (UK). R.J. Everett Engineering, Sproughton, Ipswich, produce single-seat autogyro, first flown 1984.

Evergreen (USA). Evergreen Air Center, Marana, AZ, major modification centre, especially of powerful aircraft (e.g. bombers) to fire-bombers.

Evergreen (USA). Evergreen Ultralite produce Shadow I and II.

EWR (W. Germany). Entwicklungsring Nord: *see* ERNO. Entwicklungsring Süd formed 1960 by Bölkow, Heinkel and Messerschmitt to develop Mach 2 V/STOL; built VJ 101C prototypes.

Excalibur (USA). Excalibur Aviation Co. formed by Swearingen October 1970 to manage conversions of Beech Queen Air 65 and 80 to upgraded Queenaire standards.

Experimental: *See* EAA (USA).

Extra (Germany). Walter Extra's firm builds Extra 300 2-seat aerobatic aircraft.

Fabre (France). Henri Fabre built first seaplane, *l'Hydravion*, flown La Mède, near Marseilles, 28 March 1910. Later built landplanes, and floats for other builders.

Fabrica de Avioane: *See* SET.

Fábrica de Aviones Anahuac: *See* Anahuac.

Fábrica Brasileira de Aviòes (Brazil). Former army workshops at Ilha do Viana produced Muniz M-7 and M-9 Gipsy-engined biplanes and, from 1942, Fairchild M-62.

Fábrica do Galléão: *See* Galléão.

Fabrica Federale: *See* F + W.

Fábrica Militar de Aviones (Argentina). Established Cordoba 1927, built foreign designs until from 1932 produced original series of trainers, tourers and AeM.T-1 5-seat transport. Became IA in 1946, but reverted to original name 1 July 1956, became DINFIA 1957 and again reverted to FMA 1968. Most important recent projects IA.58 Pucará and IA 63 Pampa jet trainer, plus 33% share of Embraer CBA-123. Reorganization 1988 failed, but privatized April 1992 with 30% holding by FAA (air force).

Fábrica Nacional de Aéronaves (Chile). Company formed June 1953 at Los Cerrillos airport, later moved to Rancagua, built 50 Chincol trainers, did not complete jet prototype; known as Fanaero, wound up 1960.

Fábrica Nacional de Aviones (Peru). Established Lima May 1937 with Caproni assistance, built 25 Ca 100 trainers.

Fabrique Fédérale: *See* F + W.

Faccioli (Italy). Aristide Faccioli produced detailed book on propellers, rudders and wings 1895. Worked Turin where his N.1 triplane (13 January 1909) was powered by SPA/Faccioli engine with 8 opposed pistons in 4 cylinders. N.2 biplane (May 1909) flown by son Mario, led to

N.3 and improved N.4, gaining Mario first pilot licence on Italian aircraft. Last aircraft (1913) was N.6 high-wing monoplane.

Fahlin (USA). Fahlin Aircraft Co. produced several light aircraft 1933–6, notably Plymo-Coupe powered by converted Plymouth car engine.

Fairchild (USA). Sherman M. Fairchild, seeking suitable aircraft for photography and survey in 1924, decided to make them himself. Formed Fairchild Aviation Corp. with subsidiaries **F. Airplane Manufacturing**, F. Aerial Surveys and F. Camera and Instrument, HQ New York City, works at Farmingdale, Long Island. FC-1 high-wing 2/3-seater 1926 led to FC-2 with up to 5 seats, 220-hp Whirlwind or 450-hp Wasp, wheels/skis/floats, mass-produced and also by Canadian Vickers, leading 1928 to manufacture by **Fairchild Aviation**, Grand'mère, Quebec. Took over Kreider-Reisner (which *see*) 1929, but combined company taken over later that year by giant Aviation Corp. (Avco). Fairchild repurchased interests 1931 and ran Kreider-Reisner, being joined 1933 by Armand Thieblot from General Aviation, who became chief engineer. K-R, Hagerstown, MD, renamed Fairchild Aircraft 1935, and in 1936 **Fairchild Engine & Airplane Corp.** formed as parent of what in 1939 became **Fairchild Aircraft** and Ranger Engine Divisions. Most important 1930s product began as Kreider-Reisner C-8 high-wing monoplane, from 1932 called Fairchild 24, later C-61 Forwarder/JK/Argus, total 1,665. Most numerous of all was monoplane trainer flown as M-62 1939 and produced as PT-19/23/26/Cornell, total 9,260 including output by Fairchild Canada and licensees. Biggest task was C-82 Packet military freighter (220) followed by C-119 Boxcar (1,087). Fairchild also took over Kaiser-Frazer C-123

Provider (302). Licence to build Fokker F27 in 1956 led to 205 aircraft including 79 of Fairchild's own stretched FH-227, but 1966 licence for Pilatus Porter resulted in only 36 USAF AU-23A. Fairchild took over Hiller 1964 and Republic 1965, parent company becoming first **Fairchild Hiller** and in 1966 **Fairchild Industries**. **Fairchild Republic** built 721 A-10 for USAF, but following cancellation of T-46A Next-Generation Trainer and cessation of work on Saab (ex-Saab Fairchild) 340 company closed 1988. Fairchild Industries sold Metro Aviation (owning 97% Fairchild Aircraft) and sought protection against bankruptcy February 1990, purchase by Fairchild Acquisition Inc. approved by bankruptcy court 29 September 1990.

Fairchild (Canada). From St Maurice Valley Protection Association was formed Fairchild Aerial Surveys of Canada 1922, which opened manufacturing subsidiary **Fairchild Aircraft Ltd** 1929. Built FC-2 (parent firm design), 21 Model 71 7-seaters, 3 Super 71, 24 Model 82 and several prototypes including F-11 Husky (1946) sold to Husky Aircraft. Wartime production 160 HP Hampdens, 676 Bolingbrokes and 300 SBF Helldivers. Ceased aircraft manufacture 1948.

Fairey (UK). Young electrical engineer Richard Fairey made such good flying models he sold rights to A.W. Gamage's toystore 1910 and organized subsequent production. Joined Blair Atholl Syndicate (*see* Dunne) but poached by Short Brothers 1912 and became their factory manager and chief engineer. **Fairey Aviation Co.** set up 15 July 1915 with urgent order for 12 Short 827. Leased part of factory at Clayton Rd, Hayes, Middlesex, many workers Belgian refugees, bought field south of GWR railway to test landplanes, and tested 827s on Hamble River. Then followed F.2 twin-engined fighter, Campa-

Fairchild 24 (of fleet of 23 for US Dept. of Commerce), April 1934.

nia patrol seaplane, Hamble Baby (with variable-camber flaps), and Fairey III (1917) from which sprang other III versions, to total of 957 in 1930, plus 185 Gordons and 91 Seals with radial engines. New factory built 1918 at North Hyde Rd, Hayes, and designer Maj Barlow joined by Belgian refugees Marcel Lobelle and E.O. Tips. Post-war Fawn bomber to official specification so ungainly Fairey built streamlined Fox 1925, faster than RAF fighters. Only one squadron for RAF, but led to Avions Fairey, which *see*. For Fleet Air Arm 196 Flycatcher fighters built 1923–7. Company went public 5 March 1929, and in 1930 opened Great West Aerodrome at Harmondsworth, christened by first flight of Hendon heavy bomber November 1931. Major Second World War types were: Swordfish torpedo biplane (694 Fairey, 1,699 Blackburn), Battle land-based bomber (1,169 Fairey, 1,032 Austin), Barracuda torpedo bomber (1,161 Fairey, 692 Boulton Paul, 700 Blackburn, 18 Westland), Albacore torpedo biplane (800 Fairey), Fulmar 2-seat fighter (602 Fairey) and Firefly 2-seat fighter (1,702 Fairey). Massive complex operated comprising Hayes, Heaton Chapel (Stockport) and nearby Errwood Park, Austin at Longbridge, Hamble, Weybridge (ex-Saro), and 5 other Midlands plants plus Ringway (Manchester) flight development centre and Burtonwood (Warrington) repair and modification centre. Litigation 1945–64 finally compensated Fairey for conversion of Great West Aerodrome into London Heathrow Airport, Fairey moving to White Waltham, near Maidenhead, where Gyrodyne, Jet Gyrodyne and Rotodyne rotary-wing aircraft tested. FD.1 jet delta 1951 led to FD.2 which on 10 March 1956 increased world speed record by unique 310 mph to 1,132 mph. Final fixed-wing programme was Gannet anti-submarine and AEW aircraft (416). Growing diversification led to new parent **The Fairey Co. Ltd** formed March 1959, but government forced sell-out to Westland May 1960. Fairey-Clyde, later Fairey Aviation Co. of Australasia, and Fairey Aviation Co. of Canada handled repair, modification and conversion.

Fairey (Belgium). Richard Fairey's efforts to sell RAF Fox bombers powered by Felix (Curtiss D-12) engines, and single-seat Firefly fighter, all came to nothing. He persevered with these excellent aircraft and in 1930 won contract to supply 25 Fireflies to Force Aérienne Belge, plus 62 to be

Fairey IIIF Mk IV, 45 Sqn RAF, 1930.

built in Belgium. He accordingly set up branch factor at Gosselies, Charleroi. In January 1931 FAB ordered 12 Fox IIM bombers, and in 1933 separate Belgian company formed as **Avions Fairey SA**, building 177 Foxes of various marks by 1939. Factory destroyed 10 May 1940, reopened October 1946 and later enlarged to produce 67 Meteor F.8 and 240 Hunter F.4/6, and to play major role in production of F-104G, Atlantic, Mirage 5 and F-16. Took over assets of Britten-Norman and made Islander 1972, but company finally failed 1977, being restructured 1978 as Sonaca SA.

Fairtravel (UK). Formed by AVM Don Bennett 1962 to take over from Garland manufacture of Linnet derived from Piel Emeraude.

Falck (USA). William F. Falck produced Rivets midget racer, raced 1948–63.

Falco (Italy). Falco 376 low-wing cabin 2-seater with trousered landing gear (85-hp Fiat radial) designed and built by Capt. Enrico Ercolani 1939.

Falcon (USA). Falcon Aircraft Manufacturing Co. established 1958 at Tucson, AZ, to continue production of Baumann Brigadier.

Falconar (Canada). Falconar Aircraft, Edmonton, marketed wide range of plans including own developments AMF-S14 2-seater and Type 121 Teal light amphibian first flown 1967.

Fanaero: *See* Fábrica Nacional de Aéronaves.

Fane (UK). Capt. Gerard Fane set up Fane Aircraft Co. at Norbury, London, built F.1/40 AOP aircraft 1941.

Farman (SNCA du Centre) 222.2, July 1935.

Fanstar (USA). Fanstar partners 1988 designed 4-seat Fanstar 200T derived from RFB Fantrainer.

Farman (France). Henry, Maurice and Dick were sons of British parents living in Paris. Henry ordered improved Voisin biplane 1908, but Voisins sold this to Moore-Brabazon. Farman so incensed he set up his own small aircraft works at Mourmelon, flying classic Farman III 6 April 1909, setting world records and winning orders. Subsequent H.F. (Henry Farman) and M.F. (Maurice Farman) designs made at different factories until **Avions Henri** (French spelling) **et Maurice Farman** opened joint factory at Billancourt January 1912, this swiftly becoming largest aircraft factory in France. Major wartime types included M.F.7 'Longhorn' and M.F.11 'Shorthorn' pusher biplane trainers, H.F.20 multirole pusher (about 3,220 built in 5 countries) and F.40 reconnaissance pusher. In immediate post-war years, along with aero engines and quality cars, Billancourt built F.50 bombers and F.60 Goliath series, latter being made in 21 versions covering over 69 airliners and over 300 military. In typical French style prototypes appeared in profusion, over 50 distinct Farman types flying between 1918 and nationalization of industry in 1936. They included many light transports and private machines, some made in substantial numbers, and from 1932 a series of giant high-wing monoplane bombers, later versions of which had landing gear retracting into underslung push/pull engine nacelles. One member of final 'Farman' family, an NC.223.4, made 2,000-mile flight to bomb Berlin by circuitous route 7/8 June 1940. Designation NC reflected firm's enforced nationalization into SNCA du Centre, brothers retiring.

Farman (France). Original company purchased licence for Stampe SV.4. After Second World War Maurice Farman set up **S.A. des Usines Farman** at original works and developed series of Monitor monoplane trainers using SV.4 fuselage/tail, flown July 1952.

Farm Aviation (UK). Converted DH Chipmunks for agricultural use 1965–8.

Farner (Switzerland). Farner AG Flugzeugbau, previously an overhaul/modification centre, produced W.11 (W for designer Weber) light biplane 1933, followed by WF.21 (basically 4-seat version of Comte AC.4) 1935 and finally WF.12 2-seater 1943 with shaft drive from engine behind cabin.

Farnier (France). M. Farnier built and flew monoplane at Issy 1910, 50-hp Anzani, both foreplane and tailplane.

Farrington (USA). Farrington Aircraft, Paducah, Kentucky, took over 30 Type 18A 2-seat autogyros from bankrupt Air & Space, which *see* (both entries).

Faucett (Peru). Compania de Aviación Faucett founded Lima 15 September 1928 as civil operator, soon adding overhaul/repair and, in 1934, production of F-19 8-passenger transport. Manufacture discontinued 1947.

Fauvel (France). Charles Fauvel produced tailless sailplanes, adding powered versions, notably AV.45 (40-hp Nelson) May 1960. Other variant built in Germany by Bölkow. Later designs, up to M. Fauvel's death in crash 1979, were more like ultralight aeroplanes.

Fawcett (Australia). Fawcett Aviation Pty built light aircraft 1957.

FBA (France/UK). Registered at Charing Cross

Rd, London, January 1913 by Louis Schreck and Lt. Conneau (flying pseudonym André Beaumont). Called **Franco-British Aviation** because capital mainly British, but works at Argenteuil and also Juvisy and Vernon, all Paris region. Until 1918 produced series of light single-engined pusher flying-boats used for coastal and anti-U-boat patrol. Over 1,000 supplied to French navy of Type H alone, and Savoia in Italy built a further 982. Over 2,000 used by non-French Allied navies. For post-war *see* Schreck.

F.E.: *See* Royal Aircraft Factory.

Federal (Canada). Federal Aircraft Ltd, Montreal, was assembly centre for wartime production of local versions of Avro Anson: 1,832 Mk II followed by 1,050 Mk V.

Federal (Switzerland): *See* F + W.

Federal (USA). Federal Aircraft Corp. registered San Bernardino 1928, previously called Ryan Mechanics Monoplane Co. and formed by engineers who worked on Ryan NYP. Two products, both similar to NYP in general design: 5-seat CM-1 Lone Eagle and 3-seat CM-3.

Fedorov (USSR). Dmitri Dmitriyevich Fedorov returned from exile 1918 and designed DF-1 2-seat reconnaissance biplane. Prototype built at GAZ-15 under appalling conditions, flew May 1922 with 280-hp Maybach. Fedorov died December 1922 before 2nd DF finished.

Feigl & Rotter (Hungary). Budapest company which in 1920 built first post-war aircraft in Hungary (Feiro I 4-seater), followed by improved Feiro Daru and smaller Feiro Dongo 2-seater.

Feiro: *See* Feigl & Rotter.

Felixstowe (UK). Lt., later Sqn. Cdr., John Porte returned from Curtiss to England on outbreak of First World War and persuaded Admiralty to adopt Curtiss flying-boats. As commander of RNAS Felixstowe, location of HM Seaplane Experimental Station, decided 1915 to design improved single-step hull for Curtiss boats, resulting in F.1. This led to F.2 series, including about 100 F.2A, and about same number of improved F.3 and, starting in late 1918, F.5, standard RAF boat until 1925 and as Liberty-engined F-5L made in quantity in US and

Canada. British total F.2/3/5 about 513, almost all delivered 1918 or later. Other types, large Porte Baby (11 built) and even bigger Felixstowe Fury (September 1918).

Féllot-Lacour (France). Built ultralight 1946.

Feltrinelli (Italy). Instituto Tecnico Industriale Giacomo Feltrinelli built light aircraft 1959.

Ferguson (UK). Harry G. Ferguson made first flight in Ulster 31 December 1909 in monoplane built by J.B. Ferguson & Co., Belfast. Still being flown 1913.

Fernic (USA). Fernic Airplane Co., Westfield, NJ, built to designs of George Fernic (ex-Romanian AF): T-9 Cruisaire light transport 1929 followed by T-10 smaller test version 1930.

FFA (Switzerland). In 1948 AG für Dornier Flugzeuge, Altenrhein, became entirely Swiss FFA (Flug- und Fahrzeugwerke AG). Operated unchanged until in January 1987 aviation activity sold to Justus Dornier group, Zürich, name becoming **FFA Flugzeugwerke AG**. Developed Morane-Saulnier derived fighters until D-3803 (1946), when P-51 chosen instead. In 1948 Flugwaffe requirement for jet attack fighter resulted in P-16 (25 April 1955) but project cancelled 1958 (*see* SAAC [Switzerland]). Participated in licence production of Vampire, Venom, Pilatus P-3, Mirage III and F-5E/F. Following agreement with SIAI-Marchetti 1967 FFA build 34 AS 202/15 and 180 AS 202/18 Bravo trainers. FFA-2000 trainer has been transferred to Justus Dornier's FFT.

FFT (Germany). Gyroflug, formed August 1978 to produce factory-built Speed Canard based on Rutan VariEze, renamed FFT Gesellschaft für Flugzeug- und Faserverbund-Technologie mbH. Acquired by Justus Dornier group 1984 and moved to new factory complex at Mengen 1987–8. In production with manned and unmanned versions of SC 01 Speed Canard, and also took over from FFA development of FFA-2000, renamed FFT Eurotrainer 2000.

FFV Aerotech (Sweden). Arboga firm, not normally building complete aircraft, was to produce BA-14 Starling jointly with MFI (*see* Malmö, both entries).

Fiat G.59-2A, June 1951.

FFVS (Sweden). Embargo on export of US fighters October 1940 resulted in self-sufficient home fighter project led by Bo Lundberg, managed by Flygförvaltningens Verkstad (air board workshop). Resulting J22 fighter flew 21 September 1942 from Stockholm Bromma, 198 delivered 1943–6.

FFW (Switzerland). Occasionally used for Flug & Fahrzeugwerke, more often abbreviated FFA.

FGP (Nazi Bohemia-Moravia protectorate). Flugtechnische Fertigungsgemeinschaft Prague carried out research for German industry; built FGP 227 scaled version of BV 238 1942–4.

Fiat (Italy). Today vanished into Alenia, this giant group had its origin in formation 1908 of Fiat car company subsidiary to produce aero engines. From 1914 SIA (Società Italiana Aviazione) made aircraft at own factory at Turin to own and licensed designs, most important being SIA.7B (573) and SIA.9B (62). In 1918 SIA was merged into parent, directly under founder Giovanni Agnelli, and Ansaldo designer Celestino Rosatelli began famed Fiat career by upgrading SIA.7B into Fiat R.2, followed 1926 by more powerful R.22. Rosatelli's bombers began with BR and BR.1–4, all large single-engined biplanes, and ended with about 600 BR.20 twin-engined monoplanes. His fighters were more successful, beginning with CR.1 of 1923 (109 Fiat, 40 OFM, 100 SIAI), and developing via CR.20 (over 670), CR.30 (176), CR.32 (1,212) and CR.42 (1,781) biplanes, and out-of-sequence CR.25 twin-engined monoplane of 1939 (10 only). Designer Giuseppe Gabrielli produced even more varied list, in numerical (not chronological) order including G.2 trimotor transport, G.5 aerobatic/tourer, G.8 trainer biplane, G.12 trimotor transport (104 built 1940–49), G.18 twin-engined airliner, G.46 trainer (about 310 1946–52), G.49 trainer, G.50 fighter (778, 428 by old CMASA works, 1937–42), G.55 Centauro fighter (274 1943–4), G.59 advanced trainer (171 1950–56), G.80 and 82 jet trainers and G.91 light attack aircraft (724 all versions 1956–72 including 282 by Dornier). Fiat was chief company in Italian production of 80 Vampires, 221 F-86K and 205 F-104G. In November 1969 Fiat Aviazione became chief element in new aerospace group Aeritalia, which *see*.

Fibra (Sweden). Fibra AB at Vrena claim to be developing Fibra 8 turboprop proficiency trainer.

Fiereo: *See* Feigl & Rotter.

Fieseler (Germany). Famed fighter and display pilot Gerhard Fieseler worked for Raab 1926 and masterminded that company's Fieseler F1 Tiger-schwalbe. In 1930 purchased Segel-flugzeugbau Kassel, and 2 years later began building powered aircraft, changing name to **Fieseler-Flugzeugbau**. Factory at Kassel-Bettenhausen built Lippisch Delta IV as F3 Vespe, and tailed F4 and F5, latter leading to F5R with high-lift flaps. From 1935 company expanded, building 12 He 46, 200 He 51 and 30 He 72, while chief designer Reinhold Mewes produced Fi 97 STOL 4-seater, Fi 98 single-seat dive-bomber and, in early 1936, Fi 156 Storch STOL liaison/observation aircraft (at least 2,895 built by Fieseler, Benes Mraz and Morane-Saulnier). Several other designs remained prototypes, with singular exception of Fi 103 ('V-1') flying-bomb, though parent firm made only minor proportion of over 33,000 missiles produced (but all 175-odd piloted Fi 103R versions).

Fike (USA). William J. Fike, Anchorage, Alaska,

Fieseler F2 Tiger, January 1933.

built Models B, C, D and E light aircraft 1929–62.

Filper (USA). Canning-industry subsidiary Filper Research formed 1965 to develop rigid-rotor helicopter; single Beta 200 built (26 May 1966).

Finmeccanica (Italy). IRI-Finmeccanica is giant state corporation, parent of numerous companies including Aermacchi and Alenia.

Firestone (USA). Firestone Aircraft Co. formed 1946 by change of name of G&A Aircraft, purchased by Firestone Tire and Rubber 1940. Continued Model 45 helicopter as civil 45D, but abandoned 1947.

Firth (UK). Firth Helicopters, Thame, Oxon, built helicopter with twin lateral rotors 1954, using fuselage of second Planet Satellite. Not flown.

Fisher (USA). Fisher Aero Corp., Minford, Ohio, market kits (various build standard) for Culex twin and 3 other 2-seaters.

Fisher (USA). In 1942 Fisher Body division of General Motors proposed to USAAF to build large long-range escort fighter using parts of existing aircraft. Resulting XP-75 (2,600-hp Allison V-3420) flown November 1943. Five XP-75A with uncompromised airframe followed, but P-51 could fly mission better.

Fisher (USA). Fisher Flying Products, Edgeley, ND, markets plans of 7 homebuilts.

Fisk (USA). Edwin M. Fisk built first aircraft 1910, and from then until 1924 built 11 different types. Almost all were 2- or 3-seat open biplanes. In 1921 formed Catron & Fisk Airplane and

Engine Co., Ocean Park, California. Built CF-11 sport biplane and CF-14 triplane (3 Ford T, later 2 OX-5). Most important product F-17 International 3-seater (August 1924), distinguished like predecessors by 8-sided ply-covered fuselage. Reorganized as International.

Fixed & Rotary Wing Engineering (Australia). FRWE is completing 10 Trislanders acquired from IAC; unlikely to build Trislander from scratch.

Fizir (Jugoslavia). Croatian Rudolf Fizir produced AF.2 2-seat amphibian, 2 pusher 100-hp Walter radial, January 1931.

Flagg (USA). Claude Flagg worked for Consolidated at Buffalo, NY. Produced Flagg Snyder Special racer for 1930 Nationals; Cirrus-engined low-wing monoplane. In 1935, with other Consolidated engineers, formed Flaggship Co., building a second racer with Pobjoy engine 1937.

Flaglor (USA). K. Flaglor built long series of ultralights and near-replicas.

Flair (USA). Flair Aviation Co., division of AJ Industries, was Fletcher Aviation until 1960. Major producer of drop tanks and flight-refuelling hosereels, produced range of aircraft ending with FU-24 ag-aircraft.

Flanders (UK). L. Howard Flanders, pioneer British pilot, was also outstanding designer. Built 60-hp monoplane 1911, 4 monoplanes for War Office 1912 and biplane which flew 55 mph with 3 adults on board on 40 hp. Same aircraft, called B.2, delivered RNAS with serial 918.

Flèchair SA (France). Built aircraft to Payen design 1933–9.

Fleet (USA). As noted under Consolidated, that company declined to enter civil market 1928, causing Major Fleet to acquire rights for Husky Junior and form Fleet Aircraft at same Buffalo site. Six months later Consolidated bought this company and also opened Canadian subsidiary 1930. Fleet Aircraft Inc. produced series of trainer and sporting biplanes before losing identity in Consolidated 1934.

Fleet (Canada). Fleet Aircraft of Canada Ltd, Fort Erie, Ontario, produced large numbers of biplane trainers derived from original Consolidated design, notably 602 Finch for RCAF 1939–40, and also carried out original design, including 101 Fort monoplanes for RCAF 1941–2 and post-war Model 80 Canuck 2-seater. Latter caused cash-flow problem, rights being sold to Leavens Bros 1947: *see* next entry.

Fleet (Canada). Fleet Aircraft ceased aircraft work 1947 and became **Fleet Manufacturing Ltd**. In 1952 this acquired type certificate for Super V twin-engined Bonanza conversion, in 1953 began major subcontract for Avro/Canadair/DH Canada and Republic, in 1954 formed Doman-Fleet joint company to build helicopters and in 1955 began producing Courier under licence from Helio. Ceased operating 1957.

Fleetwings (USA). Incorporated Bristol, PA, 1929 to research stainless-steel aircraft structure, progressing to supplying complete wings. Occupied former Keystone plant 1934 and designed F-5 Seabird 5-seat amphibian (5 built). In 1939 supplied US Army XBT-12 trainer, 200 ordered but only 24 delivered as BT-12 Sophomore 1942. Single Model 33 light-alloy trainer followed. Acquired by Henry J. Kaiser 1943, and began bidding for big Navy contracts, e.g. XBTK (prototype flown but won by Douglas Skyraider) and XFK (also won by Douglas).

Fletcher (USA). Fletcher Aviation Corp. started 1941 at Pasadena, CA, building resin-bonded wood FBT-2 trainer, CQ-1A target control aircraft (not completed) and, 1950, FL-23 liaison/observation aircraft. Moved to Rosemead. FD-25 Defender light attack aircraft of 1953 led to FU-24 ag-aircraft of 1954, subject of agreement for assembly of 100 by Air Parts (NZ). Became Flair 1960; *see also* next entry.

Fletcher (USA). Fletcher Aviation Co., El Monte, formed 1961 by renaming Flair, remaining a division of AJ Industries, continued developing FU-24 without further success, becoming reliant on aircraft fuel equipment. Became Sargent-Fletcher 1964, in 1966 leaving FU-24 to Aerospace NZ.

Flettner (Germany). Anton Flettner pioneered rotating-wing aircraft. In 1932 tested machine with engine/propeller on each main rotor blade. Formed **Flettner GmbH** 1935, built Fl 184 autogyro, Fl 185 operable as autogyro or helicopter and Fl 265 helicopter with 2 intermeshing 'eggbeater' rotors (6 for German navy 1939–40). Led to Fl 282 Kolibri, first mass-produced helicopter in world (24 in service 1943, 1,000 ordered but factories bombed).

Fleury (France). Robert Fleury built Vedette light aircraft 1955 and RF-21 Trimard 1973.

Flight Dynamics (USA). Developed Flightsail VII 2-seat amphibian 1970.

Flight Engineers Ltd (NZ). Auckland firm assembled Transavia Airtruk 1973–80.

Flight Invert Ltd (UK). Non-profit company formed 1975 to manage Cranfield A1 competition aerobatic aircraft programme (23 August 1976).

Flight Refuelling (UK). Large and diversified company which converted many types of jet fighters and bombers into pilotless targets, developed original types of RPV and target and markets air-refuelling tanker/receiver conversion packages.

Fliteways (USA). Midget racer 2nd in 1947 Goodyear Consolation final.

Florine (Belgium). Nicholas Florine, Rhode St Genese, designed and built impressive helicopter with 200-hp engine driving nose/tail rotors, stayed aloft 9 min 58 sec in 1933.

Florov (USSR). I.F. Florov, co-designer on BI-1 (see Borovkov), produced 'No. 4302' rocket fighter flown 1947. No. 4303 never flown.

FLS (UK). Wholly owned by F.L. Shmidt Industries A/S (Denmark), comprises FLS Aerospace (near Winchester), FLS Engineering

Lovaux SAH-I Sprint, 23 August 1983; see FLS.

(Stansted, plus Bournemouth, Gatwick, Lasham, Manchester), FLS Lovaux (Bournemouth), FLS Aerospace Support (Horley) and FLS Nea-Lindberg (Copenhagen). FLS Lovaux produces Optica (ex-Brooklands) and Sprint (ex-Orca).

Flug- und Fahrzeugwerke: *See* FFA.

Flugwissenschaftliche Vereinigung Aachen (Germany, W. Germany). Aero research association of technical high school formed 1920 to concentrate on gliders; in 1959 flew FVA-18 40-hp 2-seater, or single-seat glider tug.

Flugzeug-union Süd (W. Germany). Formed 1956 by Heinkel and Messerschmitt to build Fouga Magister under licence; later managed German Fiat G91 programme.

Flugzeugwerft Lübeck-Travemünde GmbH (Germany). Formed at Travemünde Privall May 1914 to produce seaplanes. F.1 (3) and F.2 (11) were followed by 34 armed reconnaissance bi-planes with Bz IV engine 1917–18.

Flugzeugwerke Altenrhein (Switzerland). Briefly (1981–2) name of FFA; abbreviation FWA occasionally encountered.

Flygförvaltningens: *See* FFVS.

Flygindustri (Sweden). AB Flygindustri formed by Junkers December 1921 at Linhamm, Malmö, to evade Allied Control Commission prohibitions. Produced F13 and many Swedish-designed types: A20 (1923), G23, G24, K30C, W34, K37, K39, K47 and K53. Company liquidated July 1935.

Flygindustri (Sweden). AB Flygindustri, uncon-nected with previous, established at Halmstad 1937 to build Fi 1 sailplane. Gliders included 5 examples of Fi 3 troop transport 1944.

FMA: *See* Fabrica Militar de Aviones.

Focke-Achgelis (Germany). Formed 1933 by Heinrich Focke (ex-Focke-Wulf) and aerobatic pilot Gerd Achgelis. Developed what is often regarded as first successful helicopter, Fw 61, redesignated Fa 61 before first flight on 26 June 1936. Later produced Fw 186 autogyro, Fa 266 Hornisse and Fa 223 Drache (1,000-hp) helicopters, and Fa 330 autogyro kite towed by

Focke-Wulf (Germany). Focke-Wulf Flugzeug-bau AG formed by Heinrich Focke and Georg Wulf at Bremen 1 January 1924. Focke and Wulf had produced A5 single-seat monoplane 1912 and A7 Storch 2-seater flown November 1921, latter's demonstrations resulting in backing for formation of company. First Fw design A16 3/4-passenger transport (24) followed by A.17 Möwe 9-passenger airliner (10 Luft Hansa). Wulf killed 1927 testing canard F.19 Ente. Cierva autogyro licence 1931 led to Focke concentrating on rotating wings: *see* Focke-Achgelis. Kurt Tank (ex-BFW and Rohrbach) appointed designer and in 1933 technical director. Albatros taken over 1931, Fw continuing with short runs of private and light commercial transports until Fw 44 Stieglitz biplane trainer of 1932, over 2,500 built plus over 900 by foreign licensees. Tank's first design was Fw 56 Stösser advanced trainer (1933, 550 +), followed by twin-engined Fw 58 Weihe (1935, 1,299 plus 1,250 + by French and 162 in other countries 1940–42). Company reorganized as GmbH June 1936, with enormously increased capital from controlling shareholder AEG. Mass-produced Bf 109 and 110, while Tank designed Fw 200 Condor long-range transport and ocean patroller. Next came Fw 189 (1938, 853), followed by Tank's master-piece, Fw 190 fighter (1 June 1939, over 19,600 plus about 200 of final Ta 152 versions). By 1944 company administered 28,960 employees at 29

Focke-Wulf (ex-Albatros) W 102, 1932.

locations, and thousands more in small shops hidden in forests or city rubble.

Focke-Wulf GmbH (W. Germany). New company formed 1951 at 1–5 Hunefeldstrasse, Bremen airport. Made gliders, Blume 500 prototype and, from 1958, Piaggio 149D trainer. From 1960 assembled 375 F-104G as part of ARGE Nord. In December 1963 merged with Weser to form VFW, which *see*.

Fokker (Brazil). Fokker Industria Aeronautica SA formed 1954 at Rio's Galeão airport, assembled 100 S.11 and 50 S.12 trainers, works closed 1959.

Fokker (Germany). Anthony Herman Gerard Fokker, son of Java coffee planter, was sent to school in native Holland, avoided army conscription but cunningly got on aviation course at Bingen, Germany. Designed, built and flew aeroplane December 1910 at Baden-Baden. Was soon

paid display pilot, and making aircraft as 'Fokker-Aeroplanbau'. Company registered 22 February 1912 as **Fokker Aviatik GmbH** at Berlin-Johannisthal, mainly family finance, but larger firm registered 1 October 1913 as **Fokker Flugzeugwerke** with factory at Schwerin, near Baltic coast. Original monoplanes called Spin (spider) developed in many versions, civil for private sale and use at Fokker pilot school, military with M designations. Gradually Fokker delegated design to outstanding hires Martin Kreutzer and Reinhold Platz. Shown bullet-deflecting wedges on propeller of shot-down Morane in April 1915, Fokker quickly devised interrupter gear enabling machine-gun to fire ahead past blades of propeller. Tested on M.5k monoplane, led to E (Eindecker = monoplane) series, first effective fighter. Subsequent wartime designs included D biplane fighters, Dr. triplane fighter and various prototypes, plus 400 AEG C.IV trainers. After Armistice wily Fokker continued design and manufacture at Schwerin,

Fokker (Amsterdam) B.IV amphibian, June 1928.

Fokker T.5 (2 × Pegasus XXVI), October 1937.

including F.I and F.II passenger aircraft, latter flown October 1919. These in production at Schwerin and also by Grulich when Allied restrictions prompted move to own country. D.VII specifically named as every example to be confiscated, but Fokker smuggled to Amsterdam 6 trains of 60 boxcars each packed with D.VII hardware, drawings and material, plus 150 skilled workers!

Fokker (Netherlands). NV Koninklijke Nederlandsche Vliegtuigenfabriek (Fokker), office in Amsterdam and new and growing factory at Veere, Zeeland. Here aggressive global marketing—started amidst skulduggery and riots at 1920 Paris airshow, Fokker still being synonymous with 'enemy fighters'—led to company becoming world's largest planemaker, with large US subsidiary. F series high-wing airliners ended with F.XXII and XXXVI in 1935, unable to compete with DC-2 (for which Fokker obtained marketing rights and sold to KLM). Following 159 C.IV reconnaissance biplanes 1924–6 came 1,085 + C.V plus even greater number built by 8 licensees. Several hundred fighters built for export, and other important types included G.I heavy fighter/attack aircraft, T.IV and T.VIII seaplanes and T.5 bomber. Fokker died 23 December 1939, and factory at Amsterdam-Schiphol destroyed 10 May 1940.

Fokker (Netherlands). Original company restructured 1945, factory rebuilt and F.25 Promoter completed (November 1946) at Ypenburg factory of Frits Diepen; 20 built. S.11 Instructor also built at Ypenburg (18 December 1947)—100, plus 150 built by Macchi and 100 plus 50 S.12 by Fokker Brazil. S.14 Mach-Trainer (19 May

1951), 21 built. F.27 Friendship (24 November 1955), 786 delivered to 168 customers by 1986. F.28 Fellowship (9 May 1967), 241 delivered to 57 customers by 1986. F.27 succeeded by Fokker 50 (28 December 1985), 150 delivered by late 1992. F.28 succeeded by Fokker 100 (30 November 1986), orders by late 1992 over 280. Operating company **Fokker BV** has major share in global F-16 production programme, and makes parts for other aircraft. On 1 January 1969 became equal partner with VFW of W. Germany, renamed **Fokker-VFW**; this link ended by mutual consent 11 February 1980. Company restructured 1 January 1987 with corporate centre (bearing original name) and 6 operating companies, aircraft being made by **Fokker BV**. In 1992 DASA was to take 51% controlling interest and help fund Fokker 70 (reduced-capacity 100), and this should be finalized in 1993. Finmeccanica has 6.02% shareholding.

Fokker (USA): *See* Atlantic Aircraft.

Folkerts (USA). Clayton Folkerts designed for Central States and Mono, building on own account Cirrus-engined mid-wing racer 1930. Reached 142.14 mph in Nationals, but later modified as Folkerts Special, reaching 187 mph.

Folland (UK). Folland Aircraft Ltd formed May 1937 by renaming British Marine Aircraft, Hamble. Major subcontractor, and won contract to supply 12 large 43/37 engine testbed aircraft 1940–41. W.E.W. Petter joined as managing director 1950, designing Fo 139 Midge (11 August 1954) and Fo 141 Gnat (18 July 1955). Adopted by Finland, and by India which made 213 under licence and developed Ajeet. Only RAF interest was Fo 144 Gnat T.1 trainer; following enforced merger into Hawker Siddeley Group, 105 delivered 1959–65.

Ford, pre-1941: *See* Stout.

Ford (USA). In 1941 Ford Motor Co. built colossal plant at Willow Run, Michigan, which by termination on 1 August 1945 had built 6,915 B-24 bombers plus 1,894 shipped for assembly elsewhere. Factory at Iron Mountain, Michigan, produced 4,190 Waco CG-4A troop-carrying gliders.

Fornaire (USA). Fornaire Aircraft Co., Fort Collins, Colorado, was known as Forney Manufacturing Co. until 1959. Forney purchased rights to Ercoupe and marketed it as Aircoupe until rights sold 1960 to Carlsbad, NM.

Forney: *See* Fornaire.

Foster Wikner (UK). Australian Geoffrey Wikner built 3 sporting aircraft before coming to England May 1934 and setting up Foster Wikner Aircraft Co. F.W.1 high-wing cabin monoplane flew September 1936 with Ford V8 engine. Larger F.W.3 had Cirrus Major, but Gipsy Major powered 9 production G.M.1 built at Southampton 1938–9. All known as Wicko aircraft, RAF impressed name Warferry.

Fouga (France). Etablissements Fouga et Cie formed aviation subsidiary at Aire-sur-Adour 1936 to build gliders and, later, powered aircraft, designated CM from technical director Robert Castello and director/designer Pierre Mauboussin, who at that time had his own company. C.M.10 transport glider led to C.M.100 powered version, but it was sailplanes which, via C.M.8R Sylphe (14 July 1949) led to a succession of light jet aircraft culminating in C.M.170 Magister jet trainer (27 June 1951), 916 by Fouga plus 188 W. Germany, 62 Finland and 36 Israel. **Air Fouga** from 1956, purchased by Potez May 1958, becoming **Potez Air Fouga** until merged into Potez 23 September 1961.

Found (Canada). Found Brothers Aviation set up 1948 at Malton, Toronto, to build FBA-1A 4-seater. Flown 13 July 1949, led to 34 production FBA-2 versions, but company out of business July 1968 after certificating improved Centennial 100.

Fournier (France). René Fournier built RF01 single-seater 1960 with good soaring qualities. Development led to RF3 March 1963, production assigned Alpavia. About 95 built before superseded by RF4D, 160 built, mainly by Sportavia-Putzer. Established own firm as Avions Fournier at Montlouis to develop 2-seat version of 2 + 2 Sportavia RF6. Final (1982) product RF9 motor glider.

Frakes Aviation (USA). Specializes in performance modification and in turboprop conversions (Mallard, Ag-cat, Nord 262/Mohawk 298).

Francis-Allen (USA). Goodyear Class racer 1947.

Franco-British: *See* FBA.

Frankfort (USA). Frankfort Sailplanes built training gliders and designed troop-carrier, became aircraft division of Globe Corp. (unrelated to Globe Aircraft) during Second World War.

Fouga CM.88R Gemeaux I, 6 March 1951.

Friedrichshafen G.IIIa, FF.45 transport version, DLR, 1919.

Frankfurter (Germany). Frankfurter Flugzeugbau Max Gerner formed 1930 to produce G.I and
G.II light aircraft, became Adlerwerke 1934.

Frederick-Ames (USA). Produced EOS high-performance single-seater 1980.

Freedom Master (USA). Prototype FM-2 Air
Shark 4-seat amphibian flew 5 April 1985.

Freewing (USA). Washington DC firm developing light 2-seater with wings pivoted to reduce
effect of turbulent air.

Friedrichshafen (Germany). Flugzeugbau
Friedrichshafen GmbH established 1913 near
that city at Manzell. FF29 2-seat seaplane flown
late 1913 led to over 20 related types, including
FF33e (190), 33h (50), 331 (about 130) and more
powerful FF 49c (about 250). Other smaller types
included twin-engined torpedo carriers, pushers
and a few monoplanes. Most important products
were probably G-series heavy bombers, especially
G.III and IIIa of which some 340 built by subcon-

tractors alone. A few civil conversions of smaller
types were made in 1919.

Friesley (USA). Friesley Aircraft Corp., Gridley,
CA, built single Falcon, large transport biplane,
12 passengers, 2×400-hp Liberty, finished mid-
1920, not flown until 1921.

FRWE: *See* Fixed & Rotary Wing Engineering.

Frye (USA). The Frye Corp., Fort Worth,
formed 1955 by Jack Frye, former president of
TWA, to produce F-1 Safari STOL transport
with 4 piston engines, but never completed.

Fuji (Japan). In April 1952 permission was given
for resumption of aircraft manufacture in Japan.
As successor to Nakajima, Fuji Jukogyo
Kabushiki Kaisha (Fuji heavy industries)
established 15 July 1953 with main factory at
Utsonomiya. Licence-built Cessna Bird Dog and
Beech Mentor; latter developed into LM-1 Nikko
4-seater June 1955, leading to KM-2 and -2B
trainers. From 1962 built over 120 Bell 204

Friesley Falcon, 17 April 1921.

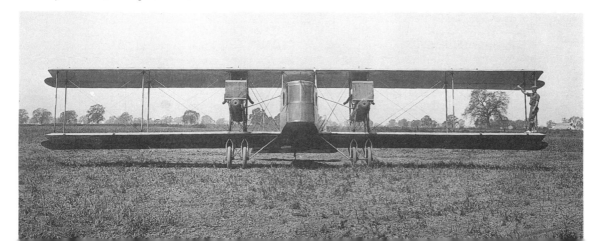

Fuji T1F2, later T-1A, February 1958.

helicopters, 60 T-1 jet trainers and 298 FA-200 Aero Subaru 4-seaters. Today Fuji builds Bell 205/UH-1H and AH-1S helicopters, KM-2Kai turboprop trainers and major parts for F-15J, 747, 757, 767 and 777, MD-11, P-3C, Fokker 50 and Kawasaki T-4. Partner in studies of SST (STDC), hypersonic transport and fan-lift VTOL transport (*see* NAL (Japan)).

Fukuda (Japan). Fukuda Kab. Kaisha was major glider firm, but planned large transport gliders never completed 1944.

Fulton (USA): *See* Continental, 3rd entry.

Fulton (UK). Fulton Aircraft Ltd, London Docklands, produced FA-1 side-by-side microlight trainer, flown in Canada August 1985.

Funk (USA). Brothers Howard and Joe Funk, Kansas City, developed Model B 2-seater, initially produced by Akron Aircraft, Ohio. Re-engined in 1941, production switched to Funk Aircraft Co., ending 1948 with over 300 built. Rights acquired 1962 by Thomas H. McClish.

Funk (USA). D.D. Funk Aviation Co. founded 1950 at Salina airport by former ag-pilot to produce F-23 low-wing ag-aircraft. Rights acquired about 1971 by Cosmic Aircraft.

FUS: *See* Flugzeug-union Süd.

FVA: *See* Flugwissenschaftliche Vereinigung Aachen.

F + W (Switzerland). Located at Emmen, government aviation R&D centre and, since 1934, also for production of military aircraft. At that time called EFW, from **Eidgenössiches Flugzeugwerke**. Prime contractor for Vampire, Venom, Hunter,

Alouette, Mirage and F-5. Three national languages resulted in 3 names, other 2 being **Fabrique Fédérale d'Avions** and **Fabrica Federale di Aeroplani**. This led to 'multilingual' title F + W from 1972. Assembled 19 of 20 Hawks, also makes components for A320, MD-80 and space launchers, and has important work in missiles and RPVs.

FWA: *See* Flugzeugwerke Altenrhein.

G

GA: *See* General Aircraft Corp.; General Aviation; Gippsland.

G & A (USA). Formerly AGA Aviation Corp., successor to Pitcairn-Larsen which in 1940 took over Willow Grove, PA, plant of Pitcairn. G&A acquired by Firestone 1943, did not complete 2 AGA CG-8 30-seat gliders but did build 627 Waco CG-4A. In 1945 produced XO-61, later redesignated XR-9B, 2-seat helicopter. Became Firestone 1946.

Gabardini (Italy). Former artist Gabardini of Turin built first aircraft 1909, but gained much publicity with 80-hp 3-seat monoplane (March 1913) used as trainer, over 250 built 1914–16 in former Rebus Co. factory, mainly for company's own school at Cameri. Company registered pre-1913 as **Società Incremento Aviazione**. Several 35-hp biplanes for competition 1920, followed by 300-hp G.8 and G.9 biplane fighters, latter modified by Filippo Zappata. Became Costruzioni Aeronautiche Novaresi, then absorbed by Fiat as Fiat-CANSA.

Gabriel (Poland). Gabriel Brothers produced several light aircraft 1924–30, notably P.5 parasol single-seater.

GAC (UK): *See* Gloster.

GAC (USA): *See* General Aircraft Corp.

GAC (USA). General Airplanes Corp. incorporated at Buffalo June 1928, aiming at already overcrowded market for 3-seat high-wing monoplanes. Built GAC-101 Surveyor, GAC-102 Aristocrat and GAC Mailplane sesquiplane before failing in Depression.

GACC: *See* Gulfstream.

Gadfly (UK). Gadfly Aircraft, Andover, built prototype Thruxton Gadfly 1968.

GAF (Australia). Government Aircraft Factories at Fishermen's Bend, Port Melbourne, had various names in former times, such as Beaufort Division, Department of Aircraft Production, and Aircraft Factories, Division of Aircraft Production, Department of Defence Production. Products included Avro Lincoln, EE Canberra and Mirage III-O, Malkara and Ikara missiles and Jindivik targets. Seeking civil business, factories decided on name GAF and produced Nomad twin-turboprop STOL utility transport, 170 built 1971–84. GAF reconstituted as private ATA (Aerospace Technologies of Australia Pty Ltd), effect from 1 July 1987. This again changed to ASTA, which *see*.

GAIC: *See* Guizhou Aviation Industry Corp.

Gail (USA). Gail Aircraft Engineering Co., Sacramento, flew prototype Model 202A Gold'uster (later Mantis) ag-aircraft 30 May 1956, no production.

Gakkel: *See* Hakkel.

GAL: *See* General Aircraft Ltd.

Galaxie (USA). Galaxie Engineering Co., PA,

formed by Glatfelter to continue development of G-100 single-seat helicopter. Flew June 1959, certificated February 1968.

Galaxy (USA). At Van Nuys, CA, markets turboprop conversions of light twins; at new plant in Oklahoma plans re-engined JetStars and is designing Star twin-turbofan STOL transport.

Gallaudet (USA). Major builder of seaplanes from 1913 at Norwich, Connecticut, and of Navy aircraft (Curtiss HS-2, DH-4) at East Greenwich, Rhode Island, from 1917. Particular feature of several designs was propeller revolving around rear fuselage, driven by 1 or 2 engines inside. Final designs were 1918 D-4 bomber seaplane, Chummy ultralight, 1920 5-seat tourer and 1922 PW-4 all-metal fighter. Factory taken over by Consolidated 1923.

Galleão (Brazil). Fábrica do Galleão, former naval air workshops, built aircraft for air force as well as navy 1937–48: 40 Fw 44, 25 Fw 58 and 48 Fairchild M-62.

Gallinari (Italy). Società Industrie Aeromarittime 'Gallinari' was subsidiary of Livorno (Leghorn) shipyard, with assembly/test at Marina di Pisa 1916–19. Assembled, and eventually constructed, Macchi flying-boats.

Gannet Aircraft (USA). Formed 1958 at Sun Valley, CA, to convert 24 SCAN 30 (Widgeon) airframes to Super Widgeon standard with R-680 engines.

Ganzavia (Hungary). Budapest company developing GA-K-22 Dino 2-seat multirole biplane.

Gallaudet DB-1B day bomber (700-hp ED 18-cylinder engine), 1920.

Gardan (France). Yves Gardan, designer of several of France's most popular light aircraft 1945–60, put his own name to GY.80 Horizon 4-seater flown 21 July 1960. Production by Sud-Aviation under 1962 agreement led to formation of Socata. Gardan's later designs produced from 1968 at his own company SITAR.

Garland (UK). Garland Aircraft Ltd successor to Garland-Bianchi 1959–60. Built 2 Linnets before Fairtravel took over.

Garland-Bianchi (UK). Formed 1955 by P.A.T. Garland and D.E. Bianchi to produce Linnet derived from Piel Emeraude. Prototype flew 1 September 1958, led to Garland Aircraft.

Garrett (UK). Richard Garrett & Sons, Leiston, Suffolk, built 60 FE.2b 1916.

Garrett (USA). Garrett General Aviation Services Division (Allied Signal Aerospace) is retrofitting Falcon 20 business jets with Garrett TFE731 engines.

Garrison (USA). Peter Garrison, LA, flew OM-1 Melmoth high-speed 2/3-seater 6 September 1973.

Gatard (France). Soc. des Avions Statoplan A. Gatard formed by Albert Gatard 1959 to test aircraft with large variable-incidence lifting tailplane. AG 01 Alouette experimental, followed 1961 by AG 02 Poussin and AG 03 Hirondelle intended for production.

Gatard Statoplan No. 02, October 1957.

Gates (USA). Gates Aircraft Corp. formed 1929 by Ivan R. Gates to produce Stampe et Vertongen RSV.18-100 and 26-100 under licence.

Gates-Day (USA). Gates-Day Aircraft Corp. formed 1927 at Paterson, NJ, to produce aircraft to Charles H. Day's design, starting with Standard J-1 (1917) and continuing with Standard G-D-24 5-seat biplane (December 1927). Became New Standard 1928.

Gates Learjet (USA). Gates Learjet Corp., Wichita, formed January 1970 following 10 April 1967 purchase by Gates Rubber Co., Denver, of all Mr Bill Lear's holding (about 60%) in Lear Jet Industries. Thus Learjet 23 antedated takeover, but Models 24, 25, 28, 29, 35, 36 and 55 primarily Gates Learjet products. Models 31A, later 55s and 60 are products of Learjet Inc., formed September 1987.

Gaunt (UK). Gaunt Aircraft, established at Southport 1910, flew Baby monoplane (later rebuilt as biplane) 1911.

Gauthier (USA). David Gauthier, Seattle, flew Sport Model 1 single-seater 13 June 1960.

Gavilán (Colombia). El Gavilan SA markets EL-1 utility 7-seater (7 November 1990).

Gazuit-Valladeau (France). St-Laurent company failed to produce planned versions of Gazelle 2/4-seater.

G/B Aircraft (USA). Glenn Beets markets plans of the G/B Special parasol (25 July 1973).

GCA: *See* Gruppo Costruzioni Aeronautiche.

GDL (Italy). Generale Gugliemetti e Ing Lamberto De Luca designed high-wing ambulance to seat 2 plus 2 stretchers, HM508D or CNA VIIIRC10 engine, built by Caproni Predappio (8 September 1943).

Gee Bee: *See* Granville.

Geest (Germany). Geest Flugzeugbau formed by Dr Waldemar Geest at Berlin-Oberschöneweide 1915, building several inherently stable monoplanes (Möwe patent) of vaguely Antoinette type. Did not participate in military production except for Aviatik-built prototype of biplane fighter 1917.

Genair (S. Africa). Common name for General Aircraft (Pty) Ltd, formed at Durban 1958 to fly Aeriel Mk II based on Piel Emeraude, flown October 1959. Work taken over by Durban.

Genairco (Australia). Common name for General Aircraft Co. Ltd formed at Sydney Mascot aerodrome 1929 to provide service/overhaul, but designed and flew Genairco 3-seat biplane 1930.

General Aeroplane Co. (USA). Incorporated December 1916 at Detroit; built series of light pusher aircraft including Alpha (possibly not flown), Beta flying-boat and Gamma L (landplane) and Gamma S (seaplane) biplanes.

General Airborne (USA). Los Angeles-based General Airborne Transport Inc. built prototype XCG-16A transport glider, with 40 troops or 4 tons cargo in lifting fuselage, in 1944.

General Aircraft Co.: *See* Genairco.

General Aircraft Corporation (USA). Incorporated 1941 at Astoria, Long Island, to build 'unspinnable' Skyfarer cabin monoplane. In 1942 switched to making 1,112 Waco CG-4A troop-carrying gliders, assigning Skyfarer rights to Grand Rapids.

General Aircraft Corporation (USA). Formed at Washington 1969, with Transport Division office at San Diego. Announced plans for 4-turboprop STOL transport, changed to twin-turboprop 1973, and then to production of Helio Super Courier, which in turn was abandoned 1975.

General Aircraft Ltd (UK). Formed at Croydon 1934 to take over assets of Monospar Wing Co., as result of great success of latter's ST.3 in 1931. Developed ST.4 and subsequent Monospar light twins until Croydon factory closed end-1933. GAL reorganized and refinanced, and moved to better factory at London Air Park, Hanworth, March 1934. Here Monospar ST.10–25 were produced, followed by GAL.38 Fleet Shadower, GAL.42 Cygnet/45 Owlet (taken over from bankrupt CWA), GAL.47 AOP, GAL.48 Hotspur training glider, GAL.49/58 Hamilcar heavy transport glider and powered freighter, and many other projects ending with GAL.60 Universal, which after January 1949 merger with Blackburn became Blackburn Beverley.

General Aircraft Pty: *See* Genair.

General Airplanes: *See* GAC, 3rd entry.

General Airplane Service (USA). FBO (fixed-based operator), Sheridan, Wyoming, specialist 1950–56 in conversion of various Pipers into ag-aircraft, often with extra wing and more powerful engine.

General Avia (Italy). Established 1970 at Pioltello, Milan, by Stelio Frati primarily to produce prototypes of his designs for production by others. Included F.15F, derivative of F.15E Picchio produced by Procaer, Canguru produced by SIAI-Marchetti and F.20 Pegaso high-speed twin, first flown 21 October 1971 and produced by Italair. General Avia also produced Jet Squalus (bought outright by Promavia), and F.22 Pinguino trainer/tourer family.

General Aviation (USA). GA Manufacturing Corp. formed May 1930 by yet another name change to company previously alternating between Fokker and Atlantic. Centred at Dundalk, Maryland, where A.H.G. Fokker oversaw design of XFA-1 Navy fighter flown early 1932. He returned to Holland late 1931, and subsequent designs withered. Limited production included AF-15 (ex-Atlantic Fokker) twin-engined Coast Guard flying-boats and G.A.43 (ex-American Airplane and Engine) high-speed airliners. Merged with North American Aviation 1933, and when 1934 Air Mail Act prohibited manufacture and operation, NAA chose to be a manufacturer, taking over assets and later moving to California, with generally new management.

General Dynamics (USA). GD, today a vast multifaceted corporation, was formed 1947 by John Jay Hopkins. At first a company, it became a corporation when on 25 April 1952 it bought Electric Boat Co., which in 1946 had purchased Canadair. GD purchased majority holding in Convair, which became a division 29 April 1954. CV (Convair) comprised 5 divisions: Convair (aircraft) and Astronautics (Atlas ICBM and spacecraft) at San Diego, Fort Worth (aircraft), Pomona (surface-to-air missiles) and Electronics (San Diego). Convair developed F-102 (with difficulty) and far better F-106 interceptors. Venture into civil jetliners with CV-880 and -990 was technically successful but a marketing disaster, returning a net loss exceeding $450m, then a record for a single product. Fort Worth ceased production of giant B-36 in August 1954 but for a further 8 years had extensive B-36 modification contracts; also handled challenging programme for B-58 Hustler supersonic bomber and, from 1960, F-111 swing-wing attack aircraft. In 1961 all divisions were separated, products receiving label General Dynamics; in 1969 Convair San Diego and Fort Worth were reunited into Convair Aerospace, but separated again in 1974. Astronautics became Space Systems, part of missile work was assigned, to new Valley Systems Division, and in March 1985 Cessna was purchased, resold to Textron 1992. A-12 Avenger II (joint programme with McDonnell Douglas) cancelled 1991, but GD shares in one of 5 possible A-X replacements. Largest programme is Fort Worth Division's F-16, plus share in F-22A whose prime contractor, Lockheed, purchased entire Fort Worth division 1 March 1993 for $1,500 m.

General Motors: *See* Eastern Aircraft; Fisher, 2nd entry.

General Technologies (Russia). Private joint-venture company set up 1991 as subsidiary of Marvol Projekt Consulting of Germany but with Russian shareholding. Major partner in LCPT programme with RusJet and AeroSud.

General Western Aero Corporation (USA). Built Meteor light 2-seat parasol monoplane at Burbank 1929–32.

Gepard (Switzerland). Carries out modification, notably design and fitting of multipurpose external payload pods.

Gérin (France). Jacques Gérin, Boulogne-sur-Seine, Paris, was a pioneer of aircraft with variable wing area. Seven years of research led to biplane flown March 1936, with unique wings along which additional leading and trailing edges could be extended, increasing area from 67.8 sq ft (6.3 m^2) to 280 sq ft (26 m^2).

Gerle (Hungary). Name of all early designs by MSE, even though designer was Banhidy. All were sporting aircraft.

German Bianco SA (Argentina). Large industrial firm founded 1891, which in 1944 set up division for aircraft repair and production of gliders. Built Macchi MB.308, first flying February 1959.

Germania (Germany). Germania Flugzeugwerke GmbH formed at Leipzig 1914, building small numbers of 2-seat biplanes of C (armed fighter/recon) series, and several prototypes including streamlined DB and JM fighters. Ceased manufacture 1919.

Gerner (Germany). Frankfurter Flugzeugbau Max Gerner GmbH formed in that city 1930, built prototypes of G.I and G.II light aircraft, taken over 1934 by Adler.

Geronimo (USA). Geronimo Conversions took over Vecto's work in upgrading Piper Apaches before it in turn became Seguin Aviation 1969.

Gillis (USA). Gillis Aircraft Corp. set up 1927 by C.H. Gillis at Battle Creek, Michigan, to build Crusader 4-seat biplane, built in small numbers until 1931.

Gippsland (Australia). Gippsland Aeronautics Pty Ltd formed 1971 at Latrobe Valley, Victoria, initially as modification centre but now as producer of own GA-200 family of ag-aircraft.

Glanard (France). Raymond Glanard built light monoplane 1966.

Glasfaser (Italy). Glasfaser Italiana srl, Bergamo-based sailplane firm, built prototype T-30 Katana competition aerobatic aircraft 1990.

Glatfelter (USA). Edward W. Glatfelter built light sporting aircraft 1961.

Glendening: *See* Glen-Lee.

Glen-Lee (USA). G.M. Glendening and A.L. Kennedy built Special 1, modified Stits Playboy, and Special 2, biplane of their own design, 1959. Glendening later began construction of side-by-side high-wing aircraft, believed not completed.

Glenny & Henderson (UK). Byfleet, Surrey, firm which built 3 single-seaters—Gadfly I, II, III— 1929.

Glenview (USA). Glenview Metal Products, Riverside, NJ, produced Flyride GMP-2 2-seat helicopter 1956, notable for supposedly simplified control system.

Global (USA). Global Helicopter Technology,

Fort Worth, specializes in adding sensor/weapon systems to Bell helicopters.

Globe (USA). Globe Aircraft Corp. incorporated at Fort Worth late 1940 as **Bennett Aircraft** to make aircraft from Duraloid bakelite-bonded plywood. Name changed early 1941 to Globe, which completed BTC-1 8-seat twin and then developed GC-1B Swift. This shelved during war, when Globe built 600 Beech AT-10 trainers and many other items, but GC-1A and -1B built in large numbers from 1945. Many built by Temco, which took over all rights when Globe failed 1947.

Gloster (UK). Urgent need to expand Britain's puny aircraft industry at start of First World War led to George Holt Thomas of Airco asking advice on capable woodworking firms from his chief supplier of spruce and ash, William Mallinson & Son. One company recommended was H.H. Martyn, at Sunningend Works, Cheltenham. Hugh Burroughes was sent to evaluate them in April 1915 and was impressed. Soon Martyn was deluged with work on Nieuport scouts and Bristol Fighters, and on major parts for many other aircraft. In 1917 Airco and Martyn discussed forming 50/50-owned company to rent expanding Sunningend factory and take over Airco's large subcontract business. As result **Gloucestershire Aircraft Co.** was registered 5 June 1917, and GAC soon became major unit in now large industry, drawing employees from throughout Gloucester/Cheltenham area. By 1918 it was producing 45 FE.2b, Fighter and Nighthawk aircraft per week, each towed 7 miles to Air Board acceptance park at Hucclecote, on other side of Gloucester. All contracts slashed at Armistice. Holt Thomas sold Airco, and many other firms shut down, including British Nieuport. Post-war contractual settlement imposed on GAC required firm to accept large quantities of Nieuport parts, especially for Nighthawk fighters. Nieuport's designer, Harry Folland, agreed to help GAC improve Nighthawk and modify these parts, and soon Gloucestershire aircraft were flying at remarkable speeds with Jaguar, Jupiter and Lion engines. One group, called Bamels (Bear/Camel), were racers, leading to Schneider Trophy contenders, while others, called Sparrowhawks, were important in setting up air arm of Japanese navy from 1921. In that year Folland was formally appointed chief engineer, starting 14-year period in which his radial-engined bi-

Globe Swift (1983, Buick engine).

plane fighters achieved great success, best-known types being Grebe, Gamecock, Gauntlet and Gladiator. But in May 1934 Hawker made takeover proposal which GAC—which from 1926 had spelt its name **Gloster** to help export customers—accepted, starting Hawker Siddeley Group. Folland left to set up his own firm, and successor W.G. Carter at once created excellent stressed-skin monoplanes but failed to win orders, firm being sustained by making Hawker aircraft: Hardy, Hart, Audax, all 200 Henleys, 2,750 Hurricanes and all 3,313 Typhoons. Carter did, however, win contracts for Britain's first jets, 2 E.28/39 testbeds being followed by F.9/40

Gloster Gladiator, preserved; prototype September 1934.

Meteor. Wartime expansion saw GAC with giant plants all round Gloucester. One was assembly building of fictitious firm **A.W. Hawksley**, set up to produce 600 AW.41 Albemarles. From 1943 GAC built 2,974 Meteors of 10 marks, night fighters being assigned to sister firm Armstrong Whitworth. Last GAC aircraft was massive Javelin night fighter, of which 302 were made by GAC and 133 by Armstrong Whitworth, the 2 firms becoming Hawker Siddeley's Whitworth Gloster division in October 1961.

Głowiński (Poland). First 3 Polish aircraft were monoplanes of general Blériot type constructed 1911–13.

Gluhareff (USA). Eugene M. Gluhareff was pioneer of simple tip-drive helicopters, flown 1957–8, but then concentrated on propane-burning jet engines.

Gnosspelius (UK). Major O.T. Gnosspelius designed Gull ultralight built by Short for 1923 Lympne trials.

Gobiet (Germany). Dietrich Gobiet formed aircraft company at Kassel before 1924, marketing by Bäumer Aero GmbH. Best-known products DP.IIa 2-seat biplane (75/80-hp Siemens) of 1923 and DP.VIIa parasol single-seater (55/60-hp Siemens).

Goedecker (Netherlands, Germany). Vliegtuigen Goedecker, Amsterdam, employed A.H.G. Fokker as designer-pilot until 1 December 1911; then transferred to Niederwallauf-am-Rhin, built small number of aircraft 1912–18 including steel-tube Taube.

Goetze (Germany). Richard Goetze made aircraft 1916–18 as subcontractor at 4 Berlin works, 1 in Berlin itself, 2 at Treptow and 1 at Johannisthal.

GOHL (China). Guangzhou Orlando Helicopters Ltd expect to assemble, and increasingly build, Orlando OHA-S-55 and 55T, and possibly S-58T, all named Panda.

Golden Eagle (USA). GE Aircraft Corp. incorporated 1929 in California to build Golden Eagle Chief high-wing trainer.

Golubkov (USSR). A.P. Golubkov led his own brigade 1939–40, many assignments but only original aircraft was SRB (high-speed recon bomber), never completed.

Goodyear (USA). Goodyear Tire and Rubber Co., Akron, Ohio, produced airships for US Navy in First World War and formed **Goodyear-Zeppelin Corp.** to build giant rigid airships post-war. Parent company formed **Goodyear Aircraft Corp.** 5 December 1939 to take over from G-Z all non-rubber aviation work. Built FG-1 Corsair and designed and built F2G. Post-war built Navy and commercial airships, GA-1 2-seat, GA-2 3-seat and GA-22 4-seat amphibians 1944–52, GA-400R light helicopter (9 May 1954), and Inflatable single-seat aeroplane with wing and rear fuselage of inflatable rubberized fabric 1956.

Gorbunov (USSR). Vladimir Petrovich Gorbunov was one of partners in development of I-22 and subsequent LaGG fighters 1938–42, producing his own improved LaGG as No. 105, prototype only 1942.

Gordon (UK). British Gordon Dove ultralights were designed by Buszard and built by Premier; no company named Gordon.

Gosport (UK). Gosport Aircraft Co. built FBA and Felixstowe F.5 flying-boats 1917–19. Planned G.9 post-war civil boat, designed by Porte on basis of Fury, abandoned 1921.

Gossamer: *See* MacCready.

Götaverken (Sweden). Giant shipyard and industrial concern at Gothenburg which opened aircraft department 1934 and from 1935 built Hawker Hart under licence and several types of

Gotha Go 150, October 1938.

light aircraft, notably GV.38 high-wing 2-seater.

Gotha (Germany). Gothaer Waggonfabrik AG was founded 1914, with factory and school at Gotha and seaplane school at Warnemünde, where several types of seaplane built 1914–16. Main factory concentrated on twin-engine biplane bombers, G.I–G.X (G.VI having 1 engine in nacelle on right and 1 on nose of offset fuselage); G.IV and G.V built in substantial numbers and bombed on all fronts, especially including London and south-east England. Oskar Ursinus designed a different G.I, built in small numbers 1916, and UWD twin-float version. Company closed 1919.

Gotha (Germany). Aircraft construction department of GWF reopened 2 October 1933, with design bureau under Dipl.-Ing. Albert Kalkert. Built Ar 66, He 45 and He 46 whilst designing Go 145 biplane trainer (9,929 by GWF and Ago, BFW and Focke-Wulf). Kalkert also designed Go 146 light twin, Go 147 tailless air observation post, Go 149 aerobatic trainer and Go 150 light twin. GWF also assisted design of DFS 230 and managed production and was by far chief source of Bf 110 twin-engined fighter (over 3,000). Go 242 assault glider (GWF built 900 of 1,528 total) was fitted with twin GR14M engines to become Go 244 (133, all conversions). Horten Ho IX twin-jet flying wing fighter was built as Go 229, Go 345 assault glider remained prototype, but 12 pre-production Go-Kalkert Ka 430 gliders were completed.

Goupy (France). Ambroise Goupy built first full-size triplane, first hop 5 September 1908, inspired A.V. Roe. Goupy II, built in Blériot factory (9 March 1909), generally accepted as first tractor biplane to classic formula shortly to become standard. Goupy II most successful, yet designer apparently stopped at that point.

Gourdou-Leseurre (France). In 1916 C.E.P. Gourdou and J.A. Leseurre worked on ways of reducing aircraft drag, and eventually encapsulated their findings in a patent filed 9 January 1917, describing a parasol-winged fighter. An order from Aviation Militaire followed, and GL Type a was built by Soc. Wassmer, who normally made propellers. Official testing resulted in demand for stronger wing, resulting in 20 GL 2C1 or Type b, made by Mayen and Zodiac, but order for 100 cancelled at Armistice. Partners decided to continue, and set up at 25 rue Krüger, St Maur les Fossés. First products GL.21 fighter and 22 trainer, Finland buying both (latter as ET). There followed a succession of fighters, trainers, recon aircraft and racers. In 1925 link with Ateliers et Chantiers de la Loire resulted in designations LGL, so new 1925 fighter was LGL.32. This became standard Armée de l'Air type, 479 being built at Loire dockyard, St Nazaire. By 1928 light seaplanes were on test, resulting in long series of shipboard reconnaissance types including one which folded for carriage aboard submarine *Surcouf*. GL and Loire parted 1929, latter forming its own aircraft department. GL rented 2 hangars at Villacoublay but from 1930 their only landplanes were prototype dive-bombers and a small night fighter.

Government: *See* GAF or under actual title in national language.

Grade (Germany). Hans Grade Flieger Werke

Gourdou-Leseurre CT (GL.1) racer, 1923.

established 1911. Grade built primitive triplane, first German flying machine, which made hops from October 1908. By 1911 aircraft, mainly monoplanes, were being sold to customers and used at Grade flying school. Factory sold to Aviatik after war broke out.

Grahame-White (UK). Claude Grahame-White achieved fame as early aviator, ran flying school at Pau (south-west France) and purchased land at Hendon and developed aerodrome, with its own schools and factories including his own. Built succession of aircraft 1909–19, almost all biplanes and early ones nearly all pushers, including Type X (Type 10) 5-seat passenger carrier for joy-riding and Type XV (15) trainer, of which about 130 built for RFC and RNAS. Post-war, GWE.6 Bantam and GWE.7 luxury transport. Last aircraft built was E.IV Ganymede bomber, with 2 fuselages and 3 engines, converted 1919 into GWE.9 airliner (2 × 450-hp Lion), scrapped 1920.

Grain: *See* Port Victoria.

Grand Rapids Industries (USA). Group of furniture companies around Grand Rapids which made large contribution to aircraft manufacture 1942–5; purchased rights to General Aircraft Skyfarer 1943, transferred later to Le Mars.

Granger (UK). Archaeopteryx single-seater was built 1926–30 by R.F.T. and R.J.T. Granger; no horizontal tail.

Granville (USA). Five Granville brothers, of Springfield, Mass., built series of Gee Bee racers from 1930 as Granville Aircraft Corp., most famous being Super Sportster R-1 (world landplane record 296.3 mph, 3 September 1932). Most were exceedingly tricky to fly. Company failed 1933; *see* next.

Granville, Miller and de Lackner (USA). Successor to above, built QED and R-6H to compete MacRobertson race; firm withered after Z. Granville, eldest brother, killed in crash 1934.

Great Lakes (USA). Great Lakes Aircraft Corp. established at Cleveland late 1928, initially to build unsuccessful *Miss Great Lakes* 8-seater derived from Martin T4M torpedo bomber. In contrast, 2-T-1 series of sport biplanes were a smash hit, many updated examples still being

built (*see* Barney Oldfield). Remarkably, Navy contract received for BG-1 carrier-based dive-bomber, 61 delivered from 1933. Upgraded B2G and XSG-1 amphibian remained prototypes.

Great Plains (USA). Acquired rights from HAPI Engines Inc. to market kits and plans of Sonerai I and II sport/racing homebuilts. Sonerai II, 550 + now flying.

Greek National (Greece). Blackburn Aeroplane and Motor Co. set up and ran Greek National Aircraft Factory at Old Phaleron navy yard near Athens 1924, producing Velos, AW Atlas and Avro 504 and carrying out much overhaul/repair. Produced 1 Chelidon (swallow) 2-seat biplane (11 February 1927). Greek personnel progressively took over, process complete 1938, but factory destroyed 1941.

Grega (USA). John W. Grega, Bedford, Ohio, developed modernized version of classic Aircamper designated GN-1, over 3,000 sets of plans sold by 1992.

Gregg (USA). Gregg Aircraft Manufacturing Co. built A-75 Rocket 2-seater 1945.

Gregor: *See* Canadian Car & Foundry.

Grenchen Flugzeugbau (Switzerland). Small company named for town where Farner located which built small number of latter's WF.21.

Gribovskii (USSR). Vladislav Konstantinovich Gribovskii became designer in his own right 1933, by 1950 producing 14 basic types of light aircraft and 17 gliders. Apart from G-25 biplane (with car engine in one form) all were monoplanes, most low-wing. Notable types included G-27 twin-engined crew trainer, G-28 racer and fighter trainer and G-29 (air force G-11) transport glider, about 100 of which were built 1941.

Grigorovich (Russia, USSR). Dmitrii Pavlovich Grigorovich was most important designer/constructor of pre-revolutionary Russia who continued work in Soviet Union. First 23 designs were in Russia, almost all being single-engined pusher biplane flying-boats starting 1912 with M-1 based on Donnet-Lévêque. Estimated 500 built of M-9 alone. After 5 years of civil war Grigorovich resumed work at GAZ-3 with upgraded flying-boats, but from 1924 added fighters (from I-1, I-2bis), civil transports (e.g. SUVP) and from 1927 large multi-engined monoplane flying-boats. TB-5 heavy bomber of 1931 was largest aircraft produced by first group of VT (internal prison) detainees, of whom Grigorovich was oldest and most senior. Most later designs were fighter and attack aircraft, ending with DG-58 (PB-1) dive-bomber of 1936.

Grinvalds (France). Jean Grinvalds produced all-plastics 4-seat prop-behind-tail Orion 1982.

Gripo (Italy). Light aircraft built 1959 by Compagnia Generale Brevetti Elettro-Domestici.

Grizodubov (USSR). Stepan Vasilyevich Grizodubov was pioneer Russian constructor/pilot, building series of biplanes in Wright or Voisin style 1910–12. Built motor-glider 1940.

Grob (Germany). Burkhart Grob Luft- und Raumfahrt GmbH, 8948 Mindelheim, has built over 3,600 light aeroplanes and gliders since being founded in 1972. Major powered programmes include G 109 motor glider, G 115 2-seater, GF 200 prop-behind-tail all-composites 4-seater and responsibility for airframe of Egrett international programme.

Groen (USA). Groen Bros., Salt Lake City, market Hawk I, II and V (single, 2- and 5-seat) factory-built streamlined autogyros.

Grokhovskii (USSR). Pavel Ignatyevich Grokhovskii formed design collective 1931 in Leningrad. Built succession of aircraft and pioneered air-drop of heavy loads. Six 1934 aircraft included rubberized-fabric inflatable *Naduvatsya*, tailless 35°-swept *Kukuracha* light aircraft and G-37 universal flying wing with 2×680-hp M-17 engines, twin booms and payload carried in detachable pod. G-38 twin-engined fighter/bomber was being built when team abruptly shut down December 1936.

Groppius (USSR). Ye. E. Groppius never completed pusher canard of 1923, but switched to conventional GAZ-5 (designated from Leningrad factory) biplane transport (300-hp) for pilot, mechanic and 4 passengers, completed autumn 1924.

Groupe Technique de Cannes: *See* SNCASO.

Grover Loening (USA). Grover Loening left Loening Aeronautical on its takeover 1928 and formed Grover Loening Aircraft Co. Inc. at Roosevelt Field, NY. Built small civil and Navy amphibians to 1936.

Grulich (Germany). Ing. Karl Grulich, technical manager of DAL (airline Deutsche Aero Lloyd) in 1922, was given free hand by Fokker to make F.II transport. DAL built a number of F.IIs as well as 19 improved Fokker-Grulich F.II with new cockpit, stronger main gears and redesigned cabin windows, all wings being made by Albatros. Production followed in 1923 of Fokker-Grulich F. III, and derived Grulich V1, V1A and V2. Grulich S.1 was original design for high-wing trainer 1925.

Grumman (USA). Leroy Randle Grumman graduated from Cornell, MIT and Columbia, served as Navy flying instructor and test pilot and then joined Loening, becoming chief engineer and managing director. When in 1928 Loening sold out, Grumman, Leon 'Jake' Swirbul and William

Grumman F3F-1 (VF-4, USS Ranger*), 1936.*

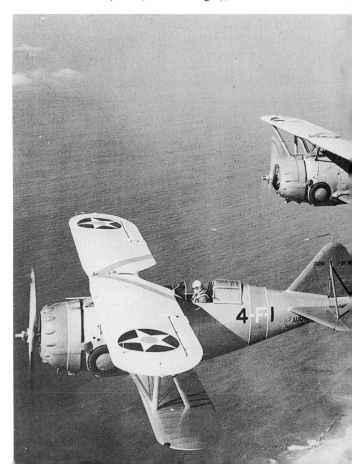

T. 'Bill' Schwendler decided to set up on their own. After handpicking Loening men and collecting funds (Loening put up $30,000 of the $77,250 launch capital), **Grumman Aircraft Engineering Corp.** was in business 6 December 1929 in derelict garage in Baldwin, Long Island, ostensibly to offer service support and repair for existing Loening amphibians, but also to market Grumman's own design of amphibious central float with fully retractable wheels, strong enough for catapulting and arrested landings. This led to first Grumman aircraft, Navy XFF-1 2-seat fighter (29 December 1931) with retractable landing gear, which proved to be 11 mph faster than Navy's latest single-seater. This in turn led to F2F and F3F single-seat fighters, so that during depth of Depression Grumman more than doubled in size annually, output also including J2F Duck utility amphibian and 2 neat twin-engined monoplane amphibians, Goose and Widgeon. In 1936 F4F biplane fighter was urgently redesigned as monoplane, leading to 7,898 Wildcats which, until mid-1943, carried almost entire burden of fighting naval fighter war. Meanwhile team under Bob Hall designed outstanding torpedo bomber, TBF Avenger, and Hall himself made first flight (7 August 1941). By this time Grumman had reputation for unbreakable aircraft, and TBF enhanced it, 9,939 being built (like F4F, jointly by Grumman and GM's Eastern Aircraft). On 26 June 1942 Hall flew XF6F Hellcat, and it was this fighter which dominated Pacific sky, Grumman's Bethpage, Long Island, plants delivering 12,275 in 30 months. The 4,000-hp F7F and agile F8F were made in hundreds rather than planned thousands, but with jet F9F Panther and swept-wing Cougar Grumman scored another smash hit, 3,370 being built. Other post-war types included Albatross multirole amphibian, Guardian search/strike aircraft, S-2 Tracker anti-submarine aircraft (with Tracer AEW and Trader COD transport versions), F11F Tiger supersonic fighter, Ag-Cat ag-aircraft (production entrusted to Schweizer, with lower overheads), OV-1 Mohawk Army observation aircraft and troubled XF10F Jaguar variable-sweep prototypes. On 14 August 1958 turboprop Gulfstream I opened new chapter with attractive purpose-designed executive transport, 200 being sold. This led to twin-jet GII (2 October 1966), which sold 256 by 1980. While building a solid bizjet customer base, Grumman's main support remained Navy and Marine Corps, which sponsored a twin-jet attack aircraft, A-6 Intruder, and a twin-turboprop AEW platform,

E-2 Hawkeye, both first flown in 1960. Orders for successive E-2 versions total 226 ending 1995; 684 A-6 Intruders of various marks, including many conversions, but future clouded by cancellation of advanced A-6F and G. A complete redesign of A-6 resulted in EA-6B Prowler 4-seat ECM platform, last of 164 in 1991, while C-2A Greyhound is COD transport derived from E-2. Grumman was GD's prime partner on F-111B, Navy fighter cancelled June 1968, replaced by F-14 Tomcat (21 December 1970). 557 F-14A followed by 38 F-14A (Plus) and 37 of planned 127 new-build F-14D when programme cancelled 1989, so last of 712 F-14 delivered 10 July 1992. Ray of hope for future is December 1991 study award for US Navy A-X strike aircraft to Grumman team with Boeing and Lockheed. In 1950–70 Grumman had considerable missile and space business, including prime contract for Orbiting Astronomical Observatory and complete Lunar Module. Other diversification included hydrofoil ships and aluminium truck and van bodies, of which it is world's largest producer. Gulfstream manufacture was moved 29 September 1967 to new plant at Savannah, Georgia, and in 1969 original firm split into **Grumman Corp.** (small holding company), **Grumman Aerospace**, Grumman Allied Industries and Grumman Data, all separate corporations. On 1 January 1973 American Aviation Corp. was merged into **Grumman American Aviation Corp.**, keeping office at Cleveland but switching production to Savannah. On 1 September 1978 Grumman sold entire general-aviation business to American Jet Industries, which later formed Gulfstream Aerospace, which *see*. By 1985 10 operating divisions proved unwieldy, and by 1991 company's shrinking operations were managed by **Grumman Aircraft Group**, Systems Group (which includes E-8A J-Stars), and 2 non-aero groups.

Grumman American: *See* Grumman; Gulfstream.

Gruppo Costruzioni Aeronautiche (Italy). GCA was group of Milan enthusiasts who in 1951–4 produced Pedro 2-seat cabin monoplane (60-hp) and Dumbo single-seater (23-hp).

Grushin (USSR). Pyotr Dmitryevich Grushin worked at MAI under Grigorovich 1931–4, building ultralight in spare time. First original design Sh-Tandem tandem-wing 2-seat attack aircraft (5 December 1937), followed by more advanced BB-MAI flown unknown date about October 1941. Gr-1 (IS) heavy twin-engined escort fighter evacuated from Moscow when about to fly October 1941, but wrecked, ending Grushin's KB (he joined MiG to design DIS).

Guangzhou Orlando Helicopters: *See* GOHL.

Gudkov (USSR). Mikhail Ivanovich Gudkov was manager of a GAZ (state aviation factory) September 1938 when he became partner forming LaGG. When this evacuated to Gorkii October 1941 Gudkov remained in Moscow and produced 2 LaGG derivatives, K-37 with 37-mm gun and Gu-82 with ASh-82 engine. Gu-1 (12 July 1943) was original design inspired by Airacobra; crashed and KB disbanded.

Guerchais (France). Known chiefly as designer of light aircraft, 1925–30 and 1946–7. Early group included T.9 cabin monoplane made by Hanriot. Post-war crop made by Roche Aviation included 2 low-wing cabin machines, 2-seat T.35 (140-hp) and 3-seat T.39 (175-hp).

Guillemain (France). Ing. J. Guillemain specialized in ambulance aircraft. JG. 40 high-wing all-metal machine for 4 patients completed Villacoublay with Salmson 9Ab5 but re-engined 120-hp Lorraine 5Pc before flight 7 March 1931 for Service Technique. JG.42, for emergency 6 patients, flew 1932 with 175-hp Salmson (Bloch design chosen).

Guimbal (France). Bruno Guimbal of Eurocopter France is developing Cabri G2 2-seat helicopter (11 April 1992).

Guizhou Aviation Industry Corporation (China). GAIC is diversified, chief aerospace programme being JJ-7 fighter trainer, counterpart of MiG-21U.

Guldentops (Belgium). Etablissement Jef Guldentops ran flying schools, and on sporadic basis produced 8 prototype light trainer and touring aircraft 1930–39; took over Société Bulte 1937 and later produced training biplane called Bulte-Guldentops.

Gulfstream (USA). Grumman sold Grumman American to AJI 1 September 1978. Business and plant unchanged at Savannah, but name changed 1979 to **Gulfstream American**. Grumman continued to develop Gulfstream III (GI II) under contract to Gulfstream, and received royalty on sales after 31 December 1979. Gulfstream American produced GAC-159C GI Commuter, GI I, GI II, the light series (Cheetah/Tiger/Cougar) and Super Ag-Cat, production of which was switched to Savannah from Schweizer May 1980. Meanwhile AJI (American Jet Industries), the parent, restyled itself **GACC** (Gulfstream American Corp. of California), and produced prototypes of Model 500 Hustler turboprop-plus-turbofan light business/utility transport (11 January 1978), Model 600 Peregrine side-by-side jet trainer (22 May 1981) and derived Peregrine II bizjet (1983). President Allen E. Paulson also took on production of former Rockwell Commander series, forming **Gulfstream Aerospace Oklahoma Operations** at Oklahoma City; but in 1985 announced termination of production, followed March 1985 by termination of Hustler/Peregrine and GACC (*See* Twin Commander). In August 1985 Gulfstream Aerospace

Guerchais-Roche Type 35, January 1946.

was purchased by Chrysler Corp., but Paulson and Forstmann Little & Co completed repurchase 19 March 1990. Current work centres on GIV and GV bizjets and doubtful partnership with Sukhoi on SSBJ (supersonic business jet).

GWF: *See* Gotha.

Gwinn (USA). Gwinn Aircar Co. formed 1935 at Buffalo to build Aircar allegedly stall/spin-proof cabin biplane.

Gyrodyne (USA). Gyrodyne Company of America, GCA, formed (originally as PC Helicopter Corp.) by partnership of Greeks 7 August 1946 at Fitzmaurice Field on Long Island. Built series of helicopters with coaxial rotors, including GCA-2 (5 seats, 450-hp) based on design by bankrupt Helicopters Inc., and from it produced GCA-7 with 2 outrigged engines with propellers. Amazingly, work continued and led to Navy/Marines evaluation of XRON-1 Rotorcycle, leading to mass-produced QH-50 pilotless anti-submarine RPV 1959–67.

Gyroflight (UK). Produced small number of ultralight autogyros and gyrogliders 1969–75.

Gyroflug: *See* FFT.

Gyroplan (France). Soc. Gyroplan produced G.20 light 2-seat helicopter 1946.

Gyroplane (USA): *See* Pennsylvania.

H

Häfeli (Switzerland). August Häfeli had worked for Farman and Aerowerke Gustav Otto before being appointed chief engineer of new aircraft department of K + W, Eidgenössisches Konstruktions Werkstatte (Ateliers Fédéraux de Constructions) at Thun in 1915. Six DH-1 2-seat pusher reconnaissance aircraft were followed by 6 tractor DH-2, 54 DH-3, 79 DH-3a, 59 DH-5 and 20 DH-5A, all 2-seaters used for training, recon and as mail carriers. Factory run down 1927.

Haerens (Denmark). Haerens Flyvertroppernes Vaerkstader (Royal Army Aircraft Factory), Kloeverkarksvej, Copenhagen, founded 1914, built mainly under licence, ending with Fokker C.VE and Gloster Gauntlet 1931–5.

Haessler-Villinger (Germany). Pioneer man-powered aircraft, built 1934, brief hops 1935.

Hafner (Austria/UK). Raoul Hafner achieved limited success with R.I. and R.II helicopters, built Vienna with Scottish finance. Moved to Heston, England, 1932 and designed A.R.III autogyro, built by **A.R.III Construction Co.** in Martin-Baker factory at Denham, 1936, complete success. Chief designer at AFEE (Airborne Forces Experimental Establishment) Beaulieu, 1942–5, developed Rotachute and Rotaplane (Spec. 11/42) for precision delivery of payloads and troops using air tow and free-spinning rotor. Extended idea to deliver Valentine tank, and as intermediate step built and flew Rotabuggy based on standard army Jeep, tested using Whitley tug. After war formed and headed Bristol helicopter department.

Hagiwara (Japan). Hisao Hagiwara formed company 1952 to develop light ramjet tip-drive helicopters (HCX-1 and -4) and, later, air-cushion vehicles.

HAI (Greece). Hellenic Aerospace Industry was formed November 1975, owned 87% by Government and 13% by Hellenic Industrial Development Bank; to be privatised 1993. Works at Schimatari comprise Aircraft, Engine, Electronics and Manufacturing divisions. Main activities include Atar/M53 engines, F-16 rear fuselage, A300 door frames and support of Mirage and C-130.

Haig (USA). Haig-K Aircraft Corp. flew HK-1 experimental light helicopter 1959.

Haines (USA). Frank Haines, Detroit, produced H-3 racer 1937 with Menasco and retractable gear.

Hakkel (Russia). Yakob Modestovich Hakkel (written Gakkel in Russian), electrical engineer, built 7 progressively better biplanes between March 1910 and July 1911, Hakkel III making first prolonged all-Russian flight 24 May 1910. Hakkel IX (1912) described as world's first parasol monoplane, good performance but burned in hangar.

HAL (India). Hindustan Aircraft Ltd formed Bangalore May 1940 to build aircraft for Indian market. Built and equipped large factory before shortages began to bite, producing Harlow PC-5 2-seaters (August 1941). Control and finance transferred to Government 2 April 1942, concentrating on support of US combat types. In 1948 set up design team under Dr V.M. Ghatage. Products included HT-2 primary trainer, HUL-26 Pushpak lightplane, HF-24 Marut supersonic attack aircraft, Gnat supersonic fighter (213 built under licence), Cheetah/Chetak versions of Alouette helicopters, Krishak AOP aircraft, HJT-16 Kiran jet trainer, HA-31 Basant ag-aircraft, 748 transport and other types. On 1 October 1964 merged with Aeronautics India to form **Hindustan Aeronautics Ltd**, since enlarged into 12 manufacturing divisions at 7 locations (Bangalore, Nasik, Kanpur, Koraput, Hyderabad, Lucknow and Korwa) with over 40,000 workforce. Bangalore produced Jaguar under licence (45 assembled from UK parts plus 31 built under licence), Cheetah and Chetak, and is developing 2 all-new helicopters, ALH (Advanced Light Helicopter, 30 August 1992) in partnership with MBB and LAH (Light Attack Helicopter). Kanpur is making HPT-32 multirole trainer and up to 150 Dornier 228 transports, and developing AWACS version of 748. MiG Complex (Nasik) built several hundred MiG-21s and is now building MiG-27M.

Halberstadt (Germany). Formed 1912 as Deutsche Bristol Werke, becoming Halberstädter

Hindustan Aeronautics ALH, 30 August 1992.

Flugzeugwerke early 1914. Chief designer Dipl.-Ing. Karl Theis produced series of military biplanes, all derived from B.I 2-seat trainer of 1914, via B.II (January 1915). One family were D.I–D.V fighting scouts, others being C.I–C.IX 2-seat recon and, most important of all, CL.II and IV armed 2-seaters.

Hall (USA). Hall Aluminum Aircraft Co. was formed 1927 to build all-metal aircraft for US Navy. Designer Charles Ward Hall produced metal wings for Curtiss HS-2L, prototype 2-seat Air Yacht and then important XPH-1 flying-boat based on Naval Aircraft Factory PN-11 (in turn based on British F.5). PH-1, -2 and -3 produced until 1940. Other prototypes were XFH-1 biplane shipboard fighter (1929), XP2H 4-engined biplane flying-boat (1931) and XPTBH heavy torpedo-bomber seaplane (1936).

Hall (USA). Robert Hall built Cicada 2-seat long-range racer for movie stunt pilot Frank J. Lynch, Hall coming 4th Unlimited in 1932

Halberstadt G.1, December 1917.

Nationals at 179.49 mph.

Hall (USA). Theodore P. Hall, chief development engineer of Convair, designed flying automobile in which wing, tail and 190-hp Lycoming were all attached on top of specially designed 4-seat saloon car. Convair funded development of proposed ConvAircar, flown successfully November 1947, but wrecked on third flight after taking off without refuelling. Rights reverted to Hall, who formed T.P. Hall Engineering Corp., but never achieved production status.

Halle (Germany). In 1933 Luftfahrtkommissariat asked Hanns Klemm to move to central Germany. Compromise solution was that Klemm stayed at Böblingen but opened subsidiary called Klemm Flugzeugbau Halle/Saale GmbH at Halle. Flugzeugbau Halle received major production contracts and also developed Klemm Kl 104 into Fh 104 light transport. As soon as possible (late 1936) Klemm handed over to majority shareholder Fritz Siebel, who renamed factory after himself.

Halpin (USA). Halpin Development Co. formed at Cincinnati 1925 to build Flamingo 6-seat high-wing monoplane. Assets passed 1928 to Metal Aircraft.

Halpin/Huf (USA). Richard Halpin and Tom Huf built H&H Special tandem parasol sport aircraft with 125-hp Lycoming 1968.

Halsmer (USA). Joseph L. Halsmer produced light aircraft 1966, 1970 and 1973.

Halton (UK). Halton Aero Club formed at RAF station 1925 produced 3 light aircraft: HAC.1 Mayfly biplane (32-hp Cherub) flown January 1927; HAC.2 Minus, same aircraft converted as parasol monoplane 1928; HAC.3 Meteor, remarkable tailless monoplane (2 × 36-hp Cherub) 1930.

Hamburger (Germany). Hamburger Flugzeugbau GmbH formed 4 July 1933 as subsidiary of Blohm und Voss (which *see*) shipyard. Designer Reinhold Mewes produced Ha 135 biplane trainer; his successor Richard Vogt produced Ha 136 advanced trainer, 137 dive-bomber, 138 3-engined flying-boat, 139 4-engined seaplane, 140 twin-engined torpedo seaplane, 141 asymmetric observation aircraft and 142 4-engined transport.

Ha 222 6-engined transport flying-boat was being developed when in September 1937 company was renamed Blohm und Voss, subsequent aircraft receiving BV designations.

Hamburger (W. Germany). Completely new company, HFB (Hamburger Fahrzeugbau GmbH) formed 1955 as subsidiary of Blohm und Voss, with rebuilt facilities at Finkenwerder. First work was manufacture of fuselage of Noratlas as part of Nordflug group. Subsequently member of ARGE Nord, building F-104G, with VFW in EWR Nord, partner in Transall programme, sole producer of HFB 320 bizjet (21 April 1964) and partner in F28 Fellowship. May 1969 merged with Messerschmitt-Bölkow to form MBB.

HAMC (China). Harbin Aircraft Manufacturing Co. was originally Manshu company formed by Japanese invaders 1938. Re-established from scratch from 1952, major assignments being production of H-5 (Il-28), Y-11 and -12 light transports, Z-5 (Mi-4, 545 built), SH-5 amphibian and Z-9A (Dauphin). Makes parts for BAe 146, Dauphin and Shorts 360.

Hamilton (USA). Thomas F. (Tom) Hamilton claimed in 1927 to have 'been responsible for production of 42 types of airplane in past 19 years', but design of many was work of James S. McDonnell, founder of McDonnell Aircraft. Formed **Hamilton Aero Manufacturing Co.**, Milwaukee, 1922, producing propellers, floats and various prototypes, all in Duralumin. H-19, 20, 21 and 22 were first built for sale, all single-engine high-wing with corrugated skin, by 1926 being sold with trademark Metalplane. H-43 and H-45 of 1928 were outstanding machines, latter Wasp-engined and 8 seats. Name changed 11 July 1927 to Hamilton Metalplane Co. Lost identity late 1928 in takeover by Boeing and United Aircraft, name surviving only in propeller company.

Hamilton (USA). Hamilton Aircraft Co. incorporated at Tucson 1961 to market Nomair conversions of T-28 trainers; later added various upgrades and rebuilds of Beech 18, finishing (as Hamilton Aviation) 1981 with Westwind and Super 580 stretched and upgraded turboprop versions.

Hamilton (USA). Hamilton Aerospace, San Antonio, Texas, produced 2-seat sport aircraft

Harbin (HAMC) Y-12 II, 16 August 1984.

1987, followed by HX-1 turboprop tactical development (pusher T800) and HXT-2 twin-turbofan trainer derivative.

Hammond (USA). Hammond Aircraft Corp. formed at Ypsilanti 1931 to take over production of Ryan Speedster from failed Detroit Aircraft. In 1934 Dean B. Hammond designed Model Y 2-seat pusher (*see* Stearman-Hammond).

Hampshire (UK). Members of Hampshire Aeroplane Club built 2 Wots (*see* Currie) 1958–9, but failed to complete HAC.2 Halcyon light twin.

Handasyde (UK). George Handasyde was partner in Martin & Handasyde, but set up Handasyde Aircraft Co. 1920. Produced 2 gliders and 1923 ultralight built by ANEC. He joined Desoutter 1929.

Handley Page (UK). Frederick Handley Page, born 1885, electrical engineer 1903–09, formed world's first *public* company solely for construction of aeroplanes, **Handley Page Ltd**, 17 June 1909. Moved from Woolwich to shed at (Barking) Creekmouth, making propellers and accessories, whilst lecturing at City & Guilds and later at Northampton Poly, London (now the City University). First aircraft, Type A *Blue Bird* monoplane (26 May 1910), led to improved Type D *Yellow Peril* (15 July 1911). Moved September 1912 to disused riding school at 110 Cricklewood Lane, N. London. Several further monoplanes and biplanes followed, with back-curved wings

Handley Page Victor K.2, 1975.

inspired by Weiss. On outbreak of war Cdr. Murray F. Sueter, Director of Admiralty Air Dept., asked HP to produce 'a bloody paralyser of an aeroplane'; result, O/100 bomber (17 December 1915). HP persuaded Admiralty to pay £20,000 on account; then persuaded his bank to lend same sum to finance 2 giant factory sheds at Claremont Road, Cricklewood. Here were built 46 O/100, followed by 320 O/400 and about 20 V/1500, both types also being produced by other contractors. Contracts cut at Armistice. Handley Page Transport began scheduled services August 1919 using converted O/400s followed by various purpose-designed W.8 airliners, leading to W.9 and 10 for Imperial Airways into which HP Transport merged 1924. Invention of slat 1919 (also patented by Gustav Lachmann, who became important HP aerodynamicist) brought increasing worldwide royalty payments. Encroachment of housing on airfield forced move to Radlett, Herts, 1929, Cricklewood factory remaining. Succession of fabric-covered biplanes continued until 1935. First production monoplane was H.P.54 Harrow bomber with fabric covering. Much superior H.P.52 Hampden was major wartime bomber/minelayer, 502 built plus 770 English Electric and 160 Fairchild Canada. H.P.57 Halifax heavy bomber flew 25 October 1939, total production 6,178 by HP, LAPG, Rootes, Fairey and English Electric. Post-war Halton civil conversion gave way to Hastings and Hermes transports and 50 Victor I (30 December 1952) and 34 Victor 2, both marks converted as tankers. HP himself knighted 1942. In June 1948 **Handley Page (Reading)** formed to take over former Miles

factory and projects, initially Marathon and later HPR.3/7 Herald. Main Cricklewood/Radlett complex tooled up for 15 H.P.137 Jetstreams per month, but Government showed no interest in company that refused to merge in 'shotgun wedding'. Sir Frederick died 1962, and after long struggle world's first aeroplane company collapsed 1970.

Han Jin (Korea). Han Jin Group of Republic of (South) Korea formed 1977; main subcontractor on Samsung F-16.

Hannaford (USA). Foster Hannaford Jr. bought rights to Rose Parrakeet 1948 and 10 years later offered plans/kits of improved version.

Hannover (Germany). Hannoversche Waggonfabrik AG, trademark Hawa or HAWA, long-established in rail rolling-stock, began building Aviatik C.I January 1915, followed by Rumpler C.Ia and Halberstadt D.II. Original design CL.II with biplane tail flew mid-1916, leading to series production of this and III, IIIa and V, and prototype IV, and post-war Civil Dreidecker (triplane) and F.3 limousine.

Hanriot (France). René Hanriot was pioneer constructor/aviator, retiring 1913. Returned after outbreak of war to form Aéroplanes Hanriot et Cie, first major contract being over 2,500 Sopwith 1A2/1B2 (1½-Strutter). Emile Dupont designed HD.1 single-seat fighter (June 1916) resembling Sopwith Pup, made in large numbers including 901 by Macchi. HD.2 seaplane version and larger HD.3 2-seat fighter followed. Post-war designs

Hannover CL.IIIa, about February 1918.

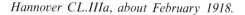

Hanriot H.35 FT.2, March 1925.

were mainly trainers and sporting aircraft, but included racers and various fighters including a large twin-boom pusher monoplane (H.110, 1933). H.18ØT (July 1934) 3-seat high-wing cabin monoplane was first of 346, plus many other variants, but H.220 and 232 twin-engined fighter/observation/trainer family made no contribution to war. H.220 was developed into NC.600, designation from SNCA du Centre which under 1936 nationalization law took over former Hanriot company and Bourges factory. *See also* Lorraine-Hanriot.

Hansa-Brandenburg (Germany). Brandenburgische Flugzeugwerke was acquired by Austrian millionaire Camilio Castiglioni May 1914, who confirmed Ernst Heinkel chief designer and changed name July 1914 to Hansa und Brandenburgische Flugzeugwerke GmbH. First production type was D 2-seat biplane (18 August 1914), followed by FD, then FB armed flying-boat, C.I reconnaissance aircraft (also made by

Phönix and Ufag in Austria), GW and GDW torpedo bomber seaplanes, CC fighter flying-boat (like several other H-B biplanes, with distinctive 'star' of multiple V-struts meeting at central point) and improved W.18 and 19, KD fighter and KDW fighter seaplane (with variants by Phönix), W/NW/GNW patrol seaplanes, W.12 fighter seaplane, W.13 and 20 patrol flying-boats, and outstanding W.29 and 33 2-seat fighter monoplane seaplanes. Company closed 1919 but W.29 continued in production in Denmark and W.33 in Finland and Norway.

Hanseatische (Germany). Founded as Zentral für Aviatik at Hamburg-Fuhlsbüttel 1911, renamed **Hansa Flugzeugwerke** 1913, merging 1914 with Brandenburgische. In 1916 Fuhlsbüttel factory separated to become **Hanseatische Flugzeugwerke Karl Caspar AG**. Built aircraft under licence, plus 1918 prototype of twin-engined cannon-armed fighter. About September 1918 bought Fokker factory at Travemünde, transferring activities

Hansa-Brandenburg W.33, July 1918.

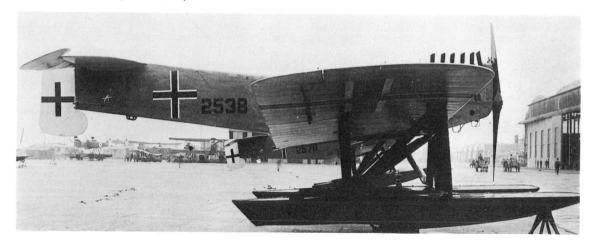

there and becoming Caspar Werke 1921.

Hants & Sussex (UK). H&S Aviation, Portsmouth, built Herald ultralight 1949; purchased all rights to Auster aircraft from Beagle 1968, but provided support only. Unsuccessfully tried to market Chipmunk with Rover turboprop.

HAPI (USA). HAPI Engines, of Eloy, Arizona, producers of VW conversions, own all rights to SF-2A Cygnet 2-seater, and market kits and plans.

Harbin: *See* HAMC.

Harlow (USA). Max B. Harlow, Professor of Aeronautics at Pasadena Junior College, organized PJC-1 4-seater as class project. Flew 14 September 1937, leading to PJC-2, certificated 26 August 1938. **Harlow Engineering Corp.** set up 1938 to produce PJC-2, taken over by **Harlow Aircraft Co.** 1939 to build PJC-2 and derived PJC-5 tandem trainer, of which sets of components supplied to HAL. Took over Interstate 1945 but ceased operations same year.

Harris & Sheldon (UK). Birmingham company contracted 1918 to produce 100 Bristol F.2B.

Hartman (UK). Sculptor Emiel Hartman designed man-powered ornithopter, built 1959.

Hartmann (USA). Hartmann Aircraft Co. took over rights to OW from Welch.

Hatfield: *See* HMPAC.

Hatz (USA). Hatz Airplane Shop had sold 313 sets of plans of CB-1 Biplane by 1985.

Haufe (USA). Walter Haufe built light aircraft 1962.

Havertz (W. Germany). Hermann Havertz, Essen, built HZ-3 light helicopter (4 December 1953), followed by HZ-4 (1965) and HZ-5 (1968).

de Havilland: *See under* de.

Hawa: *See* Hannover.

Hawk (USA). Hawk Industries Inc. found difficulty in transporting its oil- and water-drilling

equipment. In July 1977 design began of Gafhawk 125 turboprop STOL freighter (19 August 1982).

Hawk (USA). Hawk Aircraft Development Corp., Batavia, Ohio, expect 1993 to start producing 'clone of Cessna 172P' at former plant of Ayres.

Hawker (UK). Sopwith was put in hands of receiver 10 September 1920. Directors quickly registered new firm, picking on name of one of their number (the test pilot) and **H.G. Hawker Engineering Co. Ltd** registered 15 November 1920, acquiring Sopwith patents 'relating to the manufacture of motor cycles, cycles, internal combustion, and steam engines, and aircraft'. Factory at Canbury Park Road, Kingston (former roller-skating rink), produced cars and motor cycles, and received small contracts for Camel spares and Snipe refurbishment. On 12 July 1921 Harry Hawker died (it is believed of in-flight haemorrhage while in tight turn at low level), replaced by Fred Raynham and then P.W.S. 'George' Bulman. Chief designer Capt. B. Thomson produced unacceptable Duiker parasol monoplane observation aircraft (July 1923). In parallel he did Woodcock biplane night fighter (June 1923), completely redesigned by successor W.G. Carter as Mk II, 63 built. Yet another designer, Sydney Camm, produced Cygnet ultralight. Camm became chief designer 1925 and began to impress his stamp on his staff (then 40) and products, simultaneously introducing patented forms of metal construction with tubes formed from rolled sheet and joined by bolted fishplates. Series of single-engined military biplanes included Hart day bomber (June 1928) which led to more aircraft (3,020) of more variants (17) built by more companies (10) than any other British aircraft between wars. Ironically, first flight coincided with 20-year lease of huge Ham factory to Leyland. Hornet single-seat fighter (March 1929) led to production Fury and carrier-based Nimrod. Widespread licence-production of Hart spurred directors, notably Sopwith and Spriggs, to form large group. New company formed 18 May 1933.

Hawker (UK). Hawker Aircraft Ltd started 1933 with capital of £2 million, just 100 times as much as H.G. Hawker Engineering whose assets it took over. Within a year it purchased Gloster, and in 1934 formed Hawker Siddeley, which *see*. Camm abandoned Fury Monoplane in favour of High-Speed Monoplane with PV.12 engine (6 November 1935) from which was derived Hurricane, 14,231 produced by 1944 including 1,451 by Canada. Related Henley designed as dive-bomber, but 200 built by Gloster as target tugs. Typhoon fighter (24 February 1940) also transferred to Gloster (3,330), followed by Tempest (1,402) and Fury/Sea Fury (937). Jet P.1040 (2 September 1947) led to Sea Hawk, transferred to Armstrong Whitworth after 35th aircraft. P.1067 (20 July 1951) led to Hunter (1,972). P.1127 (21 October 1960) led to Hawker Siddeley Harrier.

Hawker Siddeley (UK). Purchase of Gloster Aircraft by Hawker in June 1934 was followed a month later by Sopwith's announcement of trust to acquire all shares of Armstrong Siddeley Development Co. Ltd and formation of public company known as **Hawker Siddeley Aircraft Co. Ltd**. Members were Hawker Aircraft, Gloster Aircraft and 4 new acquisitions: Sir W.G. Armstrong Whitworth Aircraft, Armstrong Siddeley Motors, Air Service Training and A.V. Roe. During Second World War, when 40,089 Group aircraft delivered, 'A.W. Hawksley' was invented to handle 100%-subcontracted Albemarle programme. Original name was replaced by **Hawker Siddeley Group Ltd**, which on 2 January 1955 added A.V. Roe Canada, Avro Aircraft, Orenda Engines, Canadian Steel Improvement and CanCar. Following intense pressure from Government, Folland was added September 1959, entire de Havilland enterprise January 1960, and Blackburn Aircraft 4 months later. Reorganized 1 July 1963 into major subsidiaries including **Hawker Siddeley Aviation**

(HSA) for aircraft and Hawker Siddeley Dynamics (HSD) for missiles, space, propellers and other activities. While Group HQ remained at 18 St James's Square, London, HSA was directed from Richmond Road, Kingston, which was former Sopwith Ham factory vacated after 20-year lease by Leyland 1948 and rebuilt with impressive new front offices. With surfeit of chief designers and chief test pilots, HSA organized itself into 3 divisions: Avro Whitworth (later Whitworth Gloster), de Havilland and Hawker Blackburn (including Folland). These divisions eliminated 1 April 1965, and on 29 April 1977 HSA and HSD themselves vanished in enforced merger with BAC and Scottish to form British Aerospace.

Hawker de Havilland (Australia). Unlike all UK companies, HDH has managed to survive machinations of successive British governments, and still exists profitably at Bankstown, Sydney, as member of Hawker Siddeley Group. Though major participant in RAAF/RAN programmes such as Black Hawk/Seahawk, Hornet and PC-9/A, principal activity is high-quality airframe subcontract for Airbus, Boeing and McDonnell Douglas. One recent risk-sharing agreement makes HDH responsible for supplying McDonnell Douglas with all airframes for Explorer helicopter.

Hayden (USA). Hayden Aircraft Corp. incorporated California 15 January 1955 to build Stout Bushmaster 15-AT 3-engined transport. Ceased operations 1958.

Hayes (USA). Hayes Aircraft Corp. formed at Birmingham, Alabama, spring 1951. Received

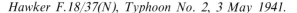

Hawker F.18/37(N), Typhoon No. 2, 3 May 1941.

numerous USAF and Army support contracts, and also converted 137 B-25s into TB-25s and 130 B-50s into jet-boosted KB-50J tankers.

HB (Austria). HB-Aircraft Industries Luftfahrtzeug AG produced HB-23 Hobbyliner side-by-side light utility aircraft and related Scanliner configured for observation/patrol purposes. Changed name to **HB Flugtechnik** 1992, ceasing manufacture.

HDH: *See* Hawker de Havilland.

Headberg (USA). Florida-based Headberg Aviation had by 1986 sold over 490 sets of plans for Flaglor Sky Scooter.

Heath (USA). Heath Airplane Co. of Chicago produced ultralights and aerobatic gliders from 1925, classic Parasol single-seater appearing 1926 ($750, or sold as ready-to-assemble kit $188). Ed Heath built many Parasol variations, plus at least 8 racers, some using Parasol parts. Most famous Cannonball 1930 and 115 Special 1932. Since 1960 Parasol resurrected by Ace and others.

HECC (USA). Helicopter Engineering and Construction Corp. produced prototype Model 100 single-seater for New York Aviation Show 1947. Never certificated.

Hegy (USA). R.C. Hegy flew 12ft-span *El Chuparoso* sport biplane 1 May 1959.

Heinkel (Germany). Ernst Heinkel, born 1887, joined LVG 1911 and was largely responsible for basic design of LVG wartime biplanes. Moved to Albatros 1913, and thence to Brandenburgische, later Hansa-Brandenburg. Work ceased at Armistice, but early 1921 joined Caspar-Werke. Decision of Sweden to procure S 1 seaplane of his design, and of Bücker to build Swedish factory to build his designs, prompted him to leave Caspar and set up **Ernst Heinkel Konstruktionsbüro** May 1922. Despite litigation by Caspar, formed **Ernst Heinkel Flugzeugwerke** 1 December 1922 at Warnemünde. For next 10 years profusion of designs prefixed HD, mainly military or naval single-engined trainers, observation or fighter landplanes, seaplanes and flying-boats for Sweden, Denmark, Japan and USSR. A 1930 order from latter country for 40 HD 55 flying-boats forced conversion to public company. By 1934 Heinkel had He 46 army co-op, He 51

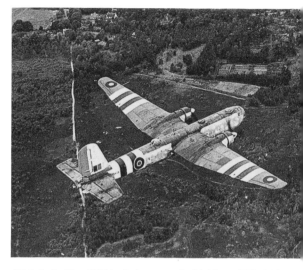

Heinkel He 177A-5 (captured 1945 as TS439).

fighter and He 59 and 60 seaplanes ready for production, but little productive capacity. Reformed as private company.

Heinkel (Germany). Ernst Heinkel AG formed as private company December 1935, moving from Warnemünde to much larger new factory at Rostock-Marienehe. Brothers Walter and Siegfried Günter had jointed as senior designers 1929, and their respective talents for aesthetic shape and mathematics, combined with capability of chief engineer Karl Schwärzler, resulted in series of aircraft beginning with He 70 (1 December 1932) whose aerodynamic perfection was envy of world. Rostock grew, but He 111 (24 February 1935) was needed in such numbers by new Luftwaffe that it was built by 4 other companies as well as by colossal purpose-built factory at Oranienburg managed by state-financed **Heinkel-Werke** (Heinkel being allowed only 3% holding). Repeated failure to displace Bf 109 as Luftwaffe fighter was major blow, and He 177 heavy bomber had most troubled history. He 178 was first turbojet aircraft (27 August 1939), but neither it nor He 280 twin-jet fighter had any influence on history. He 219 night fighter was outstanding but too late. He 162 jet fighter, flown 6 December 1944 just 90 days from initiation of project, was brilliant and formidable (in hands of experienced pilot) but planned 2,000 per month overtaken by final collapse.

Heinkel (W. Germany). Ernst Heinkel Fahrtzeugbau (soon changed to original Flugzeugbau) formed Speyer-am-Rhein 1955. Collaborated with Messerschmitt (unthinkable before war!) in production of Fouga Magister. Subsequently participated in G91 and F-104G programmes and produced Potez-Heinkel CM 191 4-seat derivative of Magister, but never built He 211 twin-jet transport. Merged into VFW 1964.

Heinonen (Finland). Juhani Heinonen, who designed at Valmet and then Finnair, produced HK-1 single-seater 1954 (flown non-stop from Madrid in 17 hr) and HK-2 2-seater 1963.

Heinrich (USA). Albert S. Heinrich designed Heinrich Pursuit, built by Victor Aircraft (which *see*) 1917 (115 mph on 80 hp).

Heinz (USA). Heinz Aircraft made several small biplane seaplanes 1924–8 with twin floats directly attached to lower wings.

Heli Air (USA). Member of Jaffe Group, markets Bell 222 and BK 117 re-engined with Allison C30Gs.

Helibras (Brazil). Helicopteros do Brasil SA formed 1978, owned Aerospatiale (now Eurocopter France) 45%, Bueninvest 30% and state of Minas Gerais 25%. Assembles with increasing local content HB 315B Gavião (SA 315B Lama), HB 350 and 355 Esquilo family (Ecureuil) and AS 565 Panther.

Helicom (USA). Helicopter Engineering Research renamed, still trying 1960–65 to certificate helicopter, now called H-1 Commuter.

Helicop-Air (France). This major helicopter operator displayed Girhel 2-seat winged autogyro at 1959 Paris airshow, never developed.

Helicop-Jet (France, Canada). Paris-Héliport-based company which designed helicopter powered by Palouste feeding air to cold tip jets, flown 1976. Second prototype with Astazou-driven compressor flown 1984. New management formed in Montreal to build pre-production machine with new engine, never completed.

Helicopter Engineering (USA). Helicopter Engineering Research Corp. formed 1954 by former aeroplane designer Harold E. Emigh. Renamed Helicom 1960.

Helicopter Manufacturing (S. Africa). Helicopter Manufacturing Co. founded by Marquand Vos to build Springbok 2-seat helicopter, demonstrated Cape Town July 1964.

Helicopteros do Brasil: *See* Helibras.

Helicopter Technik München (W. Germany). HTM formed to produce Skytrac helicopter (*see* Wagner). Abandoned for financial reasons 1975.

Heli-Europe (International). Heli-Europe Industries Ltd formed 31 May 1973 by Aerospatiale and Westland, registered UK but office Paris. Never heard of since.

Helio (USA). Helio Aircraft Corp. founded 1948 by Dr L.L. Bollinger of Harvard and Dr O.C. Koppen of MIT to build STOL aircraft. Courier (8 April 1949) led to over 500 Courier and 8/10-seat turboprop Stallion. Became division of General Aircraft Corp. 1969 and renamed **Helio Aircraft Co.** Subsequently passed into other hands as **Helio Courier** Ltd, **Helio Precision Products** and, in 1976, **Helio Aircraft** Ltd. This company acquired 1984 by Aerospace Technology Industries, and in turn purchased November 1989 by Aircraft Acquisition Corp. and restarted as **Helio Aircraft Corp.**, Morgantown, W. Virginia, active 1993.

Heliopolis Air Works (Egypt). English-language name of military factory set up 1950 to produce 6 marks of Goumhouria trainer, Bü 181D Bestmann made under licence.

Heliparts (USA). California company formed 1971 to produce Hiller 12E, initially using previously made (Fairchild) components. Renamed Hiller 1973.

Helitech (USA). New name in 1976 of Aviation Specialties.

Helitrans (W. Germany). Helitrans Hybrid-Flugzeugbau formed about 1983 to develop Helitruck transport system comprising helium airship fitted with 4 tilt-rotor lift/propulsion systems. Model displayed Hanover 1984.

Hellenic: *See* HAI.

Helmy (UK). Aerogypt I designed and built Heston 1938 by Egyptian S. Helmy, 4-seat trimotor with top of fuselage able to form long-chord slat. Flew February 1939, modified at White Waltham 1943 as twin with nosewheel. C. of A. issued 1946 but damaged beyond repair at start of planned flight to Egypt November 1946.

Helton (USA). Helton Aircraft Corp. formed Mesa, AZ, 1968 to produce 2 versions of Lark 95 aerobatic 2-seater developed 1965 from Culver Cadet.

Helwan Air Works (Egypt). English-language name of military factory set up 1962 by President Nasser to build Al Kahira (Hispano HA 200 twin-jet trainer) and Helwan-developed HA 300 supersonic fighter. Became aircraft unit in AOI.

Henderson (UK). One of 15 subcontractors building Avro 504K in 1917 was the Henderson Scottish Aviation Factory Ltd.

Henderson-Glenny: *See* Glenny & Henderson.

Hendy (UK). Hendy Aircraft Co. formed at Shoreham by Basil Henderson 1929 to build aircraft with cantilever monoplane wings. Model 281 Hobo single-seater flown October 1929, modified several times over long period. Hendy 302 tandem-seat cabin machine also built 1929 but by Parnall. Hendy 3308 Heck high-speed machine, with full-span slats/flaps, considered a Parnall aircraft because that company bought Hendy 1935.

Hennion (France). Working in Morocco (chief engineer, Casablanca aero club), Emile Hennion completed Type 11 28 August 1939; side-by-side low-wing monoplane (40-hp Train).

Henschel (Germany). Henschel und Sohn founded 1848 as major producer of locomotives. In 20th century added trucks, buses and machine tools. Discussed entering aviation, initially by abortive negotiations to take over ailing Junkers. Henschel Flugzeugwerke AG established 30 March 1933, initially Berlin-Johannisthal but late 1935 moving into large new factory at Berlin-Schönefeld. Produced Hs 121 fighter trainer, Hs 122 army co-op, Hs 123 dive-bomber, Hs 124 heavy multirole aircraft and Hs 125 advanced armed trainer, whilst building Ju 86 and Do 17 under licence. Chief types Hs 126 army co-op aircraft (over 600) and Hs 129 armoured anti-tank aircraft (879). Only 2 Hs 127 fast bombers were built, and 8-year effort on Hs 130 high-altitude bomber saw no reward. Hs 132 jet dive-bomber captured by Russians just before first flight. Henschel pioneered guided air/surface missiles, many hundreds being used 1943–5.

Henschel (W. Germany). Henschel und Sohn restarted operations 1954, mainly on railway work in Kassel. In 1955 joined Nordflug group to build Noratlas. Employed Prof. Heinrich Focke and bought licence for Sikorsky S-55 and S-58, but ceased operations soon after.

Hereter (Spain). Talleres Hereter SA at Barcelona was first major aircraft company in Spain, 1915. In 1917 built España fighter, almost SPAD

Henschel Hs 129B-2 (captured February 1944).

replica, designed by Eduardo Barrón. For 1919 Concurso de Aviones Heraclio Alfaro designed Hereter TH (also called Alfaro 8), also similar to SPAD.

Hermespace (France). Company formed (by Aerospatiale 51% and Dassault 49%) to be national 51.6% shareholder in Euro-Hermespace SA, prime contractor for Hermès aerospacecraft.

Herrick (USA). First flown 1937, Vertaplane was single-seat biplane whose top wing could be 'slipped' in forward flight to autorotate, converting machine into winged autogyro. Reappeared March 1947 as Herrick Convertaplane.

Herring-Curtiss: *See* Curtiss.

Herse (USA). This company made RWD.13 under licence 1937–9.

Heston (UK). Heston Aircraft Ltd formed August 1934 as reorganized Comper company, occupying same premises at Heston. Numerous wartime contracts, but only 4 original designs: Phoenix 5-seater (18 August 1935), T.1/37 military trainer (October 1939), Racer (12 June 1940) and A.2/45 observation aircraft (August 1947).

Heuberger (USA). Lawrence K. Heuberger built Doodle Bug light racer 1954, Stinger 2-seat tailless delta 1957, and Sizzler (with canopy starting just behind spinner) 1957.

Hewlett & Blondeau (UK). Major producer 1915–18, works at Clapham, London, building B.E.2 and 2c, works at Leagrave, Luton, building AD Scout, AW F.K.3, Dyott Monoplane and Dyott Bomber and Avro 504K.

HFB: *See* Hamburger, 2nd entry.

Higgins (USA). Higgins Industries of New Orleans, shipbuilder, formed Higgins Aircraft 1942 to build USAAF transports. First contract, for 500 C-76, was cancelled and replaced by contract for 500 C-46; this in turn was cancelled 1944, but 2 almost complete C-46 were delivered. In 1943 Higgins Industries formed Helicopter Division to develop helicopters designed by Enea Bossi; 2-seater was built and twin-engined 4-seater started when all work abandoned 1946.

Hild Marshonet (USA). Company formed early

1919 to produce HM Sportplane, single-seat biplane with 20-hp engine and tail carried on slim boom (2 December 1919).

Hiller (USA). Aircraft Division of Hiller Industries formed by Frank Hiller 1942 to develop small coaxial helicopters, Hx-44 Hillercopter prototype being demonstrated August 1944. UH-4 Commuter followed June 1946, but further work led to traditional layout with single main rotor incorporating control surfaces at 90° to main blades. This led to Model 360, certificated October 1948. In same year company reorganized and named **Hiller Helicopters Inc**. Subsequently staple product was Model 12 family (Army H-23 Raven) of which over 2,000 delivered by 1965. Less successful were XROE-1 Rotorcycle 1-man portable helicopter, YH-32 Hornet ramjet tip-drive 2-seater and VZ-1E Flying Platform; X-18 large tilt-wing VTOL (rebuilt YC-122) was never intended for production. Final product was OH-5A observation/liaison helicopter, which failed to win big Army contract but led to civil FH-1100. Company renamed **Hiller Aircraft Co.** 1959, became subsidiary of various others and from 5 May 1964 subsidiary of Fairchild, which became **Fairchild Hiller** and in 1966 Fairchild Industries, Hiller name disappearing.

Hiller (USA). In January 1973 Heliparts renamed itself **Hiller Aviation Inc.** and expanded to build new UH-12s as well as turbine-engined ET and E4T versions. In 1980 FH-1100 added to product range following purchase of rights from Fairchild. In April 1984 became subsidiary of Rogerson Aviation under Gerald Tobias, former president of Sikorsky, FH-1100 becoming RH-1100. In 1985 renamed **Rogerson Hiller Corp.** and moved to Port Angeles, Washington state.

Hill-Kemman (USA). Keith Hill and Roger Kemman built single-seat helicopter with tilting rotor devoid of cyclic control, completed 1959.

Hillson (UK). Manchester woodworking firm F. Hills & Son obtained licence for Praga E.114 side-by-side high-wing cabin ultralight and made at least 30 1936–7. Subsequently built single examples of Pennine cabin monoplane, Helvellyn open-cockpit trainer and Bi-Mono (1941) slip-wing research aircraft able to take off as biplane and fly mission as monoplane.

Hiro (Hirosho) Navy Type 15, H1H1, late 1925.

Hindustan: *See* HAL.

Hinkler (UK). H.J. Hinkler of Southampton, assisted by R.H. Bound (later of Dowty), built Ibis side-by-side high-wing machine (tandem 40-hp Salmson in upper nacelle) 1929–31, wing designed by Basil Henderson and built at Shoreham by Hendy.

Hioni: *See* Khioni.

Hiro (Japan). Imperial Navy 11th Arsenal at Hiro studied imported Felixstowe F.5 and built 60 under licence 1923–6, later designated H1H. Navy Type 89 (later H2H) was improved version, 17 built 1929–30. Rohrbach influenced Type 90 (H3H) 3-engined monoplane flying-boat, prototype only, and improved Type 91 (H4H) with 2 × 800-hp engines, of which 47 built 1932–4. Type 95 (G2H) landplane heavy bomber plagued by structure and 1,180-hp W-18 engines, only 6

Hirtenberg HS.9, probably 1936.

built by Hiro 1933–5 plus 2 by Mitsubishi, whose G3M took over.

Hirsch (France). René Hirsch produced MAéRCH.100 3-seat monoplane designed to fly smoothly through turbulent air, with 2 × 90-hp Regnier (15 June 1954).

Hirtenberg (Austria). Most famous of all Austrian aircraft companies, Hirtenberger Patronen Zündhutchen und Metallwarenfabrik AG formed by rename of bankrupt Hopfner 1935. Herr Hopfner was appointed director, and obtained licence to build Fw Stieglitz. Original designs led to 13 prototypes, often with military and civil versions of same basic type, including low-wing and high-wing transports, light aircraft and amphibians. One design, HS.9 tandem-seat parasol trainer/tourer, was produced in small series (about 40).

Hirth (Germany). Wolf Hirth, famous pilot and pre-war builder of sailplanes (continued today in Schempp-Hirth), supplied wood parts for many wartime aircraft, and restarted company post-war to support Bölkow programmes, now largely owned by DASA. From 1970 made small numbers of Acrostar aerobatic aircraft.

Hisao: *See* Hagiwara.

Hispano-Suiza (Spain). Aircraft works at Guadalajara established 1920 as subsidiary of Sociedad la Hispano-Suiza Fabrica de Automoviles SA of Barcelona. Built D.H.6 and D.H.9 under licence, followed by Nieuport-Delage

52C1, Fiat CR.32 and Messerschmitt Bf 109, all with Hispano-Suiza engines from Barcelona (109 later as HA 1112 with Merlin). Original designs E.30 parasol advanced trainer, E.34 trainer biplane, HS.42 advanced trainer (built Second World War with Bf 109 versions after move to large new works at Seville), HA.43 advanced trainer with retractable landing gear, HA.100 advanced trainer designed by Messerschmitt, HA.200 twin-jet advanced trainer also designed by Messerschmitt and HA.220 single-seat attack version (110 of both versions 1962–73). HA.500 attack aircraft never flown.

Hitachi (Japan). Hitachi Kokuki KK formed May 1939 to operate factories at Omori, Tachikawa and Tokyo-Haneda acquired by merger of parent Hitachi Seisakusho KK with Tokyo Gasu Denki Kogyo KK, which *see*. New plant built at Chiba became principal aircraft assembly centre. Aircraft built under licence included K2Y2, K5Y1, K9W1 and A6M2-K, and Hitachi was No. 3 among wartime engine producers. Original designs included TR.1 twin-engined light transport (Tokyo Gasu design) and T.2 biplane trainer.

HMPAC (UK). Hatfield Man-Powered Aircraft Co. produced successful Puffin (16 November 1961).

HOAC (Austria). Hoffmann Öesterreische Aircraft Co., Vienna, produced LF 2000 Turbo (16 March 1991), developing this into LF2 light 2-seater, changing name 1992 to **HOAC Austria Flugzeugwerke Wiener Neustadt GmbH**.

Hockaday (USA). Hockaday Aircraft Corp. formed Burbank October 1937 to produce Comet

2-seat cabin monoplane. Devoted capacity to wartime work, resuming construction of Comet April 1944, starting flight test 2 months later.

Hocker (USA). Hocker Sparrow Hawk ultralight parasol monoplane flown 1930. Resurrected 1958 by Ralph R. Denien, Indianapolis, converted to biplane **Hocker-Denien** Sparrow Hawk and flown 1961.

Hodek (Czechoslovakia). V. Hodek (not nationalized), produced HK-101 high-speed 2-seater (2 × Walter Minor), flown September 1947.

Hoefelmann (USA). Charles D. Hoefelmann, Mineral Wells, TX, produced CH-1 Schatzie single-seat biplane (February 1967).

Hoffman (USA). Edward C. Hoffman produced sporting single-seater 1960 and 2-seat flying-boat 1963.

Hoffmann (Germany). Wolf Hoffmann Flugzeugbau KG formed at Günzburg/Ulm to develop H 40 light side-by-side 2-seater (28 August 1988).

Hollandair (Netherlands). Hollandair TB, Katwijk, designed HA.001 Libel ag-aircraft, flown 1957.

Holste: *See* Max Holste.

Honey (USA). Ray Honey built sporting single-seater 1962.

Hönningstad (Norway). Engineer Birger Hönningstad formed company at Sköyen 1936. Produced Model A light utility transport 1938, but construction of C-5 utility transport seaplane

Hönningstad 5A Finmark (as flying-boat, 1949).

delayed by war, finally completed by Wideröe's 1948. Company moved to Oslo Fornebu 1946, and name changed 1947 to **Norsk Flyindustri A/S**, but best-known product, 5A Finmark 10/14-seat amphibian (17 September 1949), always known as Hönningstad 5A.

Hooper (UK). Chelsea coachbuilding firm Hooper & Co. built Sopwith $1\frac{1}{2}$-strutter, Camel and Dolphin 1916–18.

Hopfner (Austria). Flugzeugbau Hopfner, at Vienna Aspern, formed 1920 and produced S.1 3-seat monoplane, HV.3 4-passenger transport based on Fokker F.III, improved HV.6 (1928), HS.528 2-seat parasol and HA.1133 4-seat twin-engined amphibian before being taken over by Hirtenberger.

Hoppi-Copters (USA). Incorporated at Seattle 8 December 1945 to produce helicopter strapped to wearer's back. Second, called Model 101, added seat and landing gear. Models 102/103/104 followed, and 2 tested by MoS in Britain, but firm failed 1954, patents being taken over by Capital Helicopters, which tested version with tip pulsejets.

Horace Keane Aeroplanes (USA). Registered New York 1919 as successors to defunct Aircraft Engineering Corp. Produced Ace K-1 ultralight biplane to design of Alexander Klemin, consulting engineer to US Air Mail Service, though unable to carry mail.

Hordern Richmond (UK). Single Autoplane, 3-seat light twin, built at Heston 1936 by Heston Aircraft for E.G. Hordern and Duke of Richmond and Gordon. No pedals, rudder control by wheel as in Ercoupe.

Horn (USA). Mark Horn built sport aircraft 1958.

Horten (Germany). Brothers Reimar and Walter Horten formed Horten Gebrüder 1930 to produce gliders and competition sailplanes of tailless layout. First powered machine was Ho V (December 1942), followed by Ho VI, Ho VII produced in small numbers as Luftwaffe trainer and 60-passenger Ho VIII (never completed). Most ambitious was Ho IX fighter, powered by 2 Jumo 004B turbojets. Designed by Horten at Bonn, construction was assigned to Gotha at

Friedrichsroda as Go 229. Flown as glider, first powered prototype nearly complete when captured.

Hosler (USA). Russell Hosler built at least 5 racers 1928–38, including Cirrus-engined G&G Special (1930) with single wheel and retractable windscreen and 370-mph Fury 1938.

Howard (USA). Ben Howard built his first Damn Good Airplane, DGA-1, while working for Curtiss 1923. DGA-2 was racer built for 1930 Nationals, Howard by this time being airline pilot. Series of racers followed, and with DGA-6 *Mister Mulligan* Howard won all 3 major US races of 1935 despite its being a 4-seater. Series continued, and **Howard Aircraft Corp.** formed at St Charles, Illinois, 1 January 1937. Main product DGA-15 4/5-seater, and this led to US Navy GH-1 transport (31), GH-2 ambulance (131), GH-3 transport (115) and NH-1 instrument trainer (205). Army UC-70s were impressed civil aircraft. Howard also supplied DGA-18 trainers for Civil Pilot Training Program.

Howard (USA). Howard Aero Inc. formed San Antonio, Texas, by D.U. Howard 1947, swiftly becoming leader in business aviation. Manufacturing Division formed 1955 specialized in business conversions of Ventura, PV-1 and Lodestar into Howard 250, 350 and 500, with new airframe and systems, pressurized cabin and 350-mph cruise. On 15 July 1963 Howard merged with Alamo to form Business Aircraft Corp., San Antonio plant becoming Howard Aero Manufacturing Division.

HPK (USA). HPK Aircraft Associates, Bristol, TN, produced SP-1 single-seat sporting aircraft August 1957.

Hruby (USA). J. Hruby, Riverwoods, IL, produced Cayuse single-seat monoplane 1966, all fuel in tip tanks.

HS, HSA: *See* Hawker Siddeley.

HTL: *See* Bohne.

HTM: *See* Helicopter Technik München.

Huabei: *See* SAP.

Huff-Daland HD-4, January 1925.

Huey/Bulmer (USA). R.V. Huey and John W. Bulmer built light aircraft 1966.

Huff-Daland (USA). Huff-Daland Airplanes Inc. formed Bristol, PA, 1920. Began designing series of single-engined biplanes identified by names. In 1921 Huff-Daland Dusters (first ag-aircraft company) formed at Monroe, Louisiana, equipped with H-D aircraft, mainly of Puffer type. Small batches of trainers supplied to Army (mainly TW-5 and AT-1 and -2) and Navy (HN-1 and -2). Single XLB-1 Army prototype May 1923 led to most important heavy bombers of US Army 1925–34. Production LB-1 led to XLB-3 (2 × Liberty) and -3A (2 × Wasp), followed by XLB-5 and production LB-5 all with Liberty, senior designer from 1924 being James S. McDonnell, who later formed his own company. In December 1926 Mr Huff resigned, capital was increased to $1m, and on 8 March 1927 name changed to Keystone, which *see*.

Huffer (Germany). Flugzeugbau Dr Georg Huffer produced 5 prototypes 1923–8 including H.9 sporting biplane based on Fokker D.VIII and HB.28 parasol monoplane.

Hughes (Australia). Howard Hughes Engineering Pty Ltd major supplier of micros and homebuilts.

Hughes (USA). Howard Robard Hughes sponsored and largely designed Racer which gained world landplane speed record 13 September 1935. D-2 (July 1943) led to USAAF XF-11 photo aircraft. H-4 Hercules flying-boat, world's largest aeroplane (2 November 1947), still

on view at Long Beach. Giant XH-17 and smaller XV-9A were tip-drive helicopters. All were products of **Hughes Aircraft Co.** formed 1936 as subsidiary of oil-drilling Hughes Tool Co. Subsequently this company concentrated on advanced avionics, especially fighter radars and air-to-air missiles.

Hughes (USA). In 1970 Hughes Tool was reorganized as Summa Corp., and new subsidiary formed as **Hughes Helicopters**. This continued Models 269/200/300 and TH-55A piston-engined machines, OH-6 Cayuse Army observation, derived Models 500/530/Defender and prototype YAH-64 Apache attack helicopter (30 September 1975). AH-64 beat its rival and continues with other helicopters in production by MDHC (McDonnell Douglas Helicopters).

Hugo (USA). Adolph B. Hugo, Tulsa, built Hu-Go Craft light sporting biplane (19 April 1965), many plans sold.

Humber (UK). Humber Motor Co. produced series of monoplanes 1910–12, originally based on Blériot types. Particular models were designed by Hubert Le Blon, Roger Sommer (biplanes) and Capt. T.T. Lovelace.

Hunting (UK). In 1957 Hunting Percival Aircraft was renamed Hunting Aircraft, board seeing no reason to perpetuate famous name. In September 1960 controlling interest purchased by British Aircraft Corp. Cancellation of TSR.2 in 1965 meant closure of a factory, and, so that work could go to Warton, Luton (former Hunting

Hunting Percival Provost (Cheetah prototype), 23 February 1950.

factory) was shut, even though low-cost plant unconnected with TSR.2.

Huntingdon (USA). Huntingdon Aircraft Corp. started 1928 at Bridgeport, Connecticut, producing Huntingdon 11 2-seater and Huntingdon 12 Wasp-engined 4/6-seat amphibian.

Hunting Firecracker (UK). Hunting Firecracker Aircraft Ltd formed 1982 to produce Firecracker turboprop trainer. Responsibility reverted to Norman Aeroplane.

Hunting Percival (UK). In 1944 Percival Aircraft became part of Hunting Group, and name was changed to Hunting Percival Aircraft 1954. Production continued on Prince/Pembroke series and Provost trainer, and Jet Provost developed through successive marks. Renamed Hunting Aircraft 1957.

Hurd (USA). Aeronautical Division of E.P.

Hurel-Dubois H.D.34, February 1957.

Hurd, manufacturer of locks and chains, formed 1928 to produce HM-1 2-seat low-wing monoplane.

Hurel-Dubois (France). Avions Hurel-Dubois formed 1948 at rue Chappe, Paris, to develop Maurice Hurel's belief in wings of very high aspect ratio. H.D.10 research aircraft with aspect ratio 30 built by Pierre Levasseur, flown 1948. Company grew with government support for H.D.31 (2 × Cyclone) and 32 (2 × Twin Wasp) transports, respectively flown 1953 and 1955. Eight H.D.34 photo survey aircraft delivered to IGN 1957–9.

Hurleburt (USA). Formula racer at Cleveland 1947.

Hurry (USA). Le Roy Hurry built J-1 Sport using parts from Piper J-3 and PA-12 (11 November 1961.

Husky (Canada). Husky Aircraft formed at Vancouver 1955 to start aircraft manufacture on west coast and also put Leonides-Husky into production, a development of Fairchild F11-1 Husky.

Hussey (Canada). J.G. Harold Hussey, Calgary, produced Skyhawk 101 high-wing 2-seater (November 1959), followed by low-wing Skyhawk 400, both with quick-fold wings, car-tow attachment and wheel/ski gear.

Hutchinson (USA). William L. Hutchinson built WLH-1 light aircraft 1958–9.

Hydravions Schreck: *See* Schreck.

Hydroplum (France). Claude Tisserand, Corsica, markets this light amphibian; *see also* SMAN.

Hynes (USA). Hynes Aviation Industries was successor to Brantly-Hynes, formed 1 January 1975 and reinstating production of Brantly B-2B (as Hynes H-2) and 305 (as Hynes H-5). Assets put up for sale 1987 and bought by James T. Kimura, who formed Brantly Helicopter Industries USA.

Hyundai (S. Korea). Large automotive group expected to move into aerospace via collaborative link with Yakovlev (Russia).

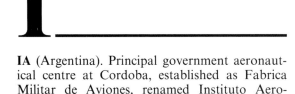

I

IA (Argentina). Principal government aeronautical centre at Cordoba, established as Fabrica Militar de Aviones, renamed Instituto Aerotécnico 20 October 1943. In 1952 incorporated into IAME.

IA: *See* Institutul de Aviatie. SA.

IABSA (Brazil). Indústria Aeronáutica Brasileira SA briefly produced prototypes of light aircraft 1966, including Premier 64-01 2-seater and Aerobatic 65-02.

IAC (Thailand). International Aircraft Co. Ltd formed to assemble Exec 90 helicopter kits supplied by RotorWay International.

IAC (USA). International Aeromarine Corp., Sanford, Florida, formed 1982 to certificate Thurston TA16 Seafire amphibian; company part-owned by Thurston.

IAC (USA). International Aviation Corp., Homestead, Florida, formed 1982 to assemble/manufacture Trislander; but incomplete aircraft bought by FRWE of Australia.

IAD (USA). In 1962–5 International Aircraft Deliveries produced so-called 126 10-2

IAe.33 Pulqúi II, 27 June 1950.

Modification to increase MTO weight of Beech C-45G/H from 8,750 lb to (3,969 kg) to 10,200 lb (4,627 kg) and enhance performance.

IAe (Argentina). Designation prefix of aircraft produced by Argentina's FMA/IA prior to 1952.

IAE (Brazil). Instituto de Atividades Espacias is space division of CTA.

IAF (Iraq). English-language abbreviation for Iraqi Air Force, manager of Adnan-1 and Baghdad-1 programmes.

IAI (Israel). Israel Aircraft Industries established 1953 as Bedek Aviation, changing name 1 April 1967. Operates 4 divisions: Aircraft and Bedek, both at Ben-Gurion International airport, and

IAI 201 Arava, early 1970.

IAR-823 prototype (then called 921), July 1973.

Electronics and Technologies. New Astra IV bizjet produced in partnership with Yakovlev Corporation.

IAM (Italy). Industrie Aeronautiche Meridionali formed at Brindisi with Agusta assistance and began to operate 1968 as Elicotteri Meridionali, changing name 1988. Manages Italian licence-production of Chinook at Sesto Calende and assists Agusta.

IAME (Argentina). Empresa Industrias y Mecánicas del Estado formed 28 March 1952 to take over all state activity concerning military or commercial aircraft, incorporating IA, formerly FMA.

IAR (Romania). Most important aircraft manufacturing organization in Romania was formed 1925 as Societate Anonima Industria Aeronàutica Romana, with Potez among share-holders. Works at Brasov produced aircraft and engines, chief series programmes being Potez 25, Morane-Saulnier 35, PZL P.11c and Fleet 10G. Numerous original designs, including CV.11 high-performance monoplane, IAR.12/13/14/15 monoplane fighters, 22 trainer, 23/24 cabin monoplanes, 27 trainer (225 built from 1937), 37/38/39 recon-bombers (325 from 1938) and 80/81 fighters (436 from April 1939). Changed name 1940, *see* Regia.

IAR (Romania). Soviet occupying power formed Sovromtractor 1946, which produced IAR.811 light 2-seater (May 1949). This led to 813, built in quantity, and smaller numbers of 814 light twin and 817/818 utility transports. Brasov factory known as URMV-3 in 1950–59. From 1968 renamed ICA-Brasov, but restored to original name 1991, *see* below.

IAR SA (Romania). Original Brasov works,

largely rebuilt and re-equipped, renamed IAR 1991. Major products Ka-126 (Russian licence), 330L Puma (Aerospatiale licence), 317 Airfox armed helicopter (derived from IAR-316B Alouette) and 828 ag-aircraft. IAR-503A turboprop trainer under development.

IAROM (Romania). IAROM SA chosen as 1991 name of former CNIAR, national management authority for aerospace industry.

IAv Bacau (Romania). Bacau factory, originally repair centre, drawn into manufacture to support One-Eleven and IAR-93; from 1979 produced complete Yak-52, No. 1,000 delivered early 1987 and 1,500 June 1990. May produce AG-6. Renamed Condor 1991, then **Aerostar SA**.

IAv Bucuresti (Romania). Known until 1980 as IRMA, part of URMV-3 at Brasov, most of which became IAR. Biggest of many programmes Rombac One-Eleven and Islander. On 20 November 1990 became **Romaero SA**.

IAv Craiova (Romania). Intreprinderea de Avioane Craiova (Craiova aircraft enterprise) formed to handle production of Romanian participation in IAR-93 with Jugoslavia; also handles development and production of IAR-99 Şoim jet trainer. Renamed Avioane late 1990.

Iberavia (Spain). Iberavia SA was a Madrid design office, working on equipment 1946 and complete aircraft from 1948: IP-2 glider, I-11 Peque side-by-side tourer and I-115 tandem trainer. These were built by AISA, which took over Iberavia 1954.

ICA (Romania). National aircraft factory at Brasov (IAR) renamed Intreprinderea de Constructii Aeronàutice of CIAR 1968. Products included IS-23A, -24 and -824 utility transports, Alouette III, Islander and sailplanes. Renamed IAR 1991.

ICAR (Romania). Intreprinderea Pentru Constructii Aeronàutice Romane formed Bucharest 1933. Built Raab Tigerschwalbe under licence, and small batch of unnamed 6-passenger high-wing transports first flown 1935.

ICS: *See* International Commuter System GIE.

ICX Aviation (USA). Washington DC company which in 1979 concluded agreement with Aviaexport to import Yak-40 and modify into 3 versions of X-Avia LC-3, to be produced at Wheatfield, NY.

IG JAS (Sweden). Industrigruppen JAS AB formed 1981 to represent activities of Saab-Scania, Ericsson, Volvo Flygmotor and FFV in JAS 39 Gripen programme. Acts as single industrial contractual interface with FMV (defence material administration).

Ikarus (Jugoslavia). First aircraft manufacturer in unified country, Ikarus Tvornica Aero i Hydroplana inaugurated 1924 at Novi Sad by German industrialist Hugo Stinnes, making SM 2-seat flying-boat designed by Josef Mickl. Produced Potez 25 under licence, followed by Avia BH-33, prototype of IM recon flying-boat and small batch of IOM. Ambitious IK fighter (22 April 1935) was built in small series in large new factory at Zemun, but all facilities destroyed in war. Zemun repaired 1946 sufficiently to overhaul Soviet military aircraft in Jugoslav service, but absorbed in anonymous nationalized industry.

IL (Poland). Instytut Lotnictwa (aviation institute) founded 1926, subsequently carrying out R&D in support of Polish industry. Managed design of a turbojet, but never a complete aircraft design until in 1979 team under Alfred Baron began design of I-22 Iryda trainer and close-support aircraft (3 March 1985).

Ilyushin (USSR, CIS-Russia). Sergei Vladimirovich Ilyushin, born 1894, chief of NTK-UVVS 1926, then CAHI, and deputy to Tupolev at KOSOS 1932, head of long-range bombers at CCB 1934; managed to relinquish Directorship of GUAP (top job in aviation ministry) 1938 and return to form his own OKB, which he led to his death 9 February 1977, since when general designer Genrikh V. Novozhilov. Following I-21 (CCB-32) fighter, bureau built CCB-26 long-range twin-engined aircraft (February 1936) which led via CCB-30 to DB-3 bomber (1,528) which in turn led to Il-4 (5,256). Parallel programme produced prototype CCB-55 or BSh-2 (30 December 1939), leading to Il-2 Stormovik (36,163, record for any single type), followed by Il-10 (4,966). Among civil types came Il-12 transport (9 January 1946, 663 built), leading to Il-14 (839 including licence production). Big Il-18 followed (30 July 1947) but Stalin terminated ('70 to 80 is too many to risk in one aeroplane'). So main effort switched to jet bombers: 4-jet Il-22 (24 July 1947) and totally new twin-jet Il-28 (8 July 1948, over 3,000), but Il-30, 40, 46 and 54 remained prototypes. A different Il-18 flew 4 July 1957, Stalin being dead (565, with many naval, military and research variants). Il-62 long-range jetliner flew January 1963 (265 by 1991 and continuing). Il-76 heavy airlifter flew 25 March 1971 (693 by early 1991 and continuing), with many versions plus derived A-50 early-warning

B-33 (Avia-built Ilyushin Il-10), 1948.

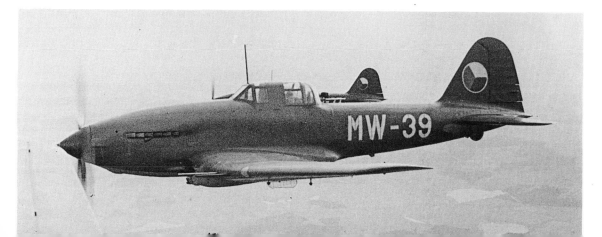

Ilyushin Il-78.

platform and Il-78 tanker. Il-86 wide-body flew 22 December 1976 (89 by early 1991 and continuing). More efficient long-range Il-96 flew 28 September 1988, planned to be developed in 6 new versions to cover spectrum 200/512 passengers over 4,000/13,500 km. Numerous new programmes and projects include Il-90 198/220-passenger liner with 2 underwing propfans, Il-114 60-seat twin turboprop (29 March 1990), 3 business/regional jets and 2 light aircraft (*see* Aviation Enterprises). Today's title **AKI** (Aviation Complex named for) **S.V. Ilyushin**. *See also* AAI.

IMAM: *See* Meridionali.

IMCO (USA). Intermountain Manufacturing Co., Afton, Wyoming, purchased CallAir 1962 and developed new ag-aircraft A-9 and B-1. In turn acquired by Aero Commander division of Rockwell 1966.

IML (New Zealand). IML Group briefly promoted Addax concept for STOL supersonic attack aircraft 1984.

IMP (Canada). IMP Group, Halifax, NS, handle major upgrades, e.g. role change for Sea Kings and rebuild (with turboprops) of Brazilian P-16E Trackers.

IMPA (Argentina). Compania Industria Metalúrgica & Plastica SA started aircraft department September 1941. Prototype RR-11 2-seater flew July 1942 and improved Tu-Sa-O in April 1943, as well as primary gliders.

INAv (Romania). Institutul de Aviatie SA, formerly major part of INCREST, now mainly private (holding company Orcas SA). Design authority for new aircraft including Aerostar AG-6, IAR-503A turboprop trainer and IAR-705 regional transport.

INCREST (Romania). Former national design authority, Bucharest; designed IAR-99 (*see* IAv Craiova) and managed Romanian participation in design of Jurom (*see* SOKO/Avioane).

IndAer (Chile). Industria Aeronáutica was manufacturing organization set up near Santiago 1980 by FAdeC (Chilean air force) with collaboration of Piper. Manufacture began at once on assembling 27 PA-28 Dakota, together with design of T-35 Pillán aerobatic/instrument trainer, using Piper parts where possible. First prototype flown by Piper in US 6 March 1981. Bigger challenge was assembly and manufacture under CASA licence of T-36 Halcón (C-101) jet trainer and to develop A-36 attack version. T-36 deliveries began 1983. In 1984 IndAer became ENAER.

Indaer Peru: *See* Industria Aeronáutica del Peru.

Indonesia Belalang: *See* LAPIP; LIPNUR.

Indústria Aeronáutica Brasileira: *See* IABSA.

Indústria Aeronáutica de Chile: *See* IndAer.

Indústria Aeronáutica del Peru (Peru). Indaer Peru's existence stemmed from wish to assemble Aermacchi MB.339 jets purchased by FA del P, 1980. Further study resulted in more modest objective of producing GA aircraft, starting with licence production of Aero Boero AB 115 and 180 and Pilatus PC-6 (these agreements not yet implemented 1993). Based on various US high-wing cabin machines, IAP-001 Chuspi was flown August 1987, now built in various versions for spraying, dual training and sport.

Indústria Aeronáutica Neiva: *See* Neiva.

Indústria Metalúrgica: *See* IMPA; Metalnor.

Indústria Paranaense de Estruturas: *See* IPE.

Industria Valtion: *See* IVL.

Industrie Aeronautiche e Meccaniche Rinaldo Piaggio: *See* Piaggio.

Industrie Aeronautiche Meridionali: *See* IAM.

Industrigruppen: *See* IG JAS.

Industri Pesawat: *See* IPTN.

Ingenieurburo Prof. Dipl.-Ing. C. Dornier Jr. (W. Germany). Operated by Claudius Dornier Jr. 1981–4 prior to formation of his own company Claudius Dornier Seastar.

Inland (USA). Inland Aviation Co., Kansas City, built Sport 2-seat parasol (19 July 1928) and more powerful Super Sport 1929.

Instituta LZS Branko Ivanus (Jugoslavia). Originally known as Letov works, this Ljubljana factory built sailplanes (notably Orao series), LK-1 Auster-like 4-seater (5 January 1955) and Debonair-like KB-11 Branko 1959. Merged into LIBIS 1960.

Institute of Science and Technology (Philippines). Formerly Bureau of Science, began 1952 to investigate possibility of aircraft manufacture in Philippine Republic, especially using local materials. XL-14 Maya high-wing 3-seater flew 1954, XL-15 Tagak utility aircraft 1955 and L-17 low-wing 2-seater 1957, all of wood construction.

Institute of Technical Research: *See* IPD.

Instituto Aerotécnico: *See* IA.

Instituto de Atividades Espacias: *See* IAE.

Instituto di Aeronautica Politecnico di Milano (Italy). Built light aircraft 1951.

Instituto Technológico de Aeronáutica (Brazil). Principal Brazilian aeronautical college, part of CTA, produces original design studies.

Institutul de Aviatie SA (Romania). Bucharest, produces original designs, most recent being AG-6 ag-biplane (prototype built by Condor) and IAR-705 50-passenger twin-turboprop, for which Craiova and Romaero expect to compete for manufacture.

Instytut: *See* IL.

INTA (Spain). Instituto Nacional de Tecnica Aeronáutica was Madrid design office responsible for H.M.1–H.M.9 training and touring aircraft produced by AISA 1943–53.

Inter-Air (USA). Formed by rename of Downer, continued development of Bellanca 14-19-3A.

Interavia (Russia). Created Moscow 1990 with support from Ministry of Aviation Industry to serve as Russian partner in international design and manufacturing partnerships. Minority partner in Phönix-Aviatekhnika. Launched aerobatic /utility/sport projects September 1992.

Interceptor (USA). Interceptor Corp., OK, formed 18 November 1968, among other things took over Myers 200B 4-seat turboprop, renamed Interceptor 400 (27 June 1969). Corporation failed, but reformed as Interceptor Co., Boulder, Colorado. Again failed, rights acquired by Prop-Jets.

Intercity (Canada). Intercity Airlines formed 1946 to develop Sznycer/Gottlieb helicopter (9 July 1947).

International (USA). International Aircraft Corp. formed by Ed Fisk (*see*) at Venice, CA, 9 February 1927. Built 32 F-17 (OX-5) in 1927 and 144 in 1928, later adding Whirlwind and Hispano versions, as well as F-18 Air Coach 6-seater. Moved Ancor, Ohio, and Jackson, Michigan, before failing 1930.

International (USA). A new International Aircraft Corp. formed 1930 at Cincinnati to take over assets of previous and continue same programmes.

Invincible 4-seater (170-hp Challenger), 1929.

International (USA). International Aircraft Manufacturing Inc., full name of Inter-Air.

International Aeromarine: *See* IAC (USA), 1st entry.

International Aircraft: *See* IAC (Thailand).

International Aircraft (UK). Capt. D.M.K. Marendaz and others formed International Aircraft & Engineering Ltd at Maidenhead 1935. Built at least 2 aircraft including first Marendaz Mk IIA, but Cordwallis Works destroyed by fire June 1937. Firm restarted as Marendaz.

International Aviation: *See* IAC (USA), 2nd entry.

International Commuter System GIE (International). Formed at Toulouse 1992 as marketing organization of Regioliner, owned equally by the 3 partners.

IPD Beija-Flor prototype, February 1959.

Interstate (USA). Interstate Aircraft & Engineering Corp. organized April 1937, El Segundo (LA), with fresh management August 1938. Produced mainly components and equipment, but in 1940 flew Cadet tandem cabin monoplane, developed as S-1B and Army XL-6.

Intreprinderea: *See* IAv, 3rd entry; ICA; IRMA.

Invincible (USA). Invincible Aircraft Corp. formed by Invincible Metal Furniture Co., Manitowoc, Wisconsin, 1929. One product, 4-seat high-wing cabin aircraft.

IPD (Brazil). Instituto de Pesquisa e Desenvolvimento, major group of CTA responsible for R&D, including design.

IPE (Brazil). Indústria Paranaense de Estruturas Ltda, Curitiba, developed IPE 06 Curucaca tandem ultralight, flown January 1990.

IPT (Brazil). Instituto de Pesquisas Tecnologicas, Sao Paulo, carried out mainly materials research, but also produced series of light aircraft IPT.0–IPT.17, 1940–52.

IPTN (Indonesia). By far biggest aerospace company in SE Asia, Industri Pesawat Terbang Nusantara inaugurated (as PT Industri Pesawat Terbang Nurtanio) 23 August 1976 when decision taken to centralize all nation's aerospace activities. Present name adopted 1985. Produces NC-212 Aviocar, NBO-105, NBK-117, NAS 332 and NBell 412 all under licence, and parts for 737, 767, Fokker 100, F-16 and P&W engines. Joint developer with CASA of CN-235 transport and is developing N-250 50-seat regional transport independently. N-442 helicopter is studied with DASA.

Iran (Iran). Iran Aircraft Industries, or IRGC

(Islamic Revolutionary Guards Corps), developed Fajr (February 1988), apparently Neico Lancair homebuilt.

↗ lookup

Iraqi Air Force (Iraq). Responsible for development of Adnan 1 AWACS and Baghdad 1 airborne early-warning conversions of Soviet-supplied Il-76 transports.

Irbitis (Lithuania). Designer Karlis Irbitis, responsible for almost all the series of VEF trainers and tourers, gave his name to I-16 prototype lightweight fighter, flown 1939. Single example flew with Soviet and then Luftwaffe markings.

Ireland (USA). G.S. Ireland was sales engineer for Curtiss. When in 1926 supplies of Jennies, Standards and Canucks ran out he decided to form Ireland Aircraft Inc., at Curtiss Field, Garden City, and market Ireland Comet (Oriole fuselage, OX-5 engine and new wings). Ireland Meteor and Neptune followed, latter being amphibian.

IRGC: *See* Iran.

IRMA (Romania). Intreprinderea de Reparat Material Aeronautiche was Bucharest section of URMV-3 (national aircraft component repair factory) 1959–68, during which period IRMA, besides repair, also constructed over 140 training, ambulance and ag-aircraft. Mainly became IAvB, later IAv Bucuresti.

Ishida TW-68, 1994–5.

Irwin (USA). Irwin Aircraft Co. registered 1916 at Corning, CA. First product M-T ultralight biplane, developed through M-T-2 and C-C-1, both with 25-hp Irwin engine and produced to 1929.

Isaacs (UK). John O. Isaacs specialized in scaled fighters; plans available for Hawker Fury (biplane) 7/10 linear scale, and Spitfire 6/10.

Isacco (USSR). Vittorio Isacco was Italian designer who, like Bartini, emigrated to Soviet Union. Arrested 1936 and worked in a VT 'special prison', continuing work on Isacco-4, rather clumsy helicopter with 80-ft 4-blade rotor with Gipsy engine on tip of each blade, plus Wright J-5 propulsion engine on nose. Severe troubles, never flew.

Ishida (Japan). Ishida Corp. of Nagoya has offices in Fort Worth and San Francisco, former handling major technical development of TW-68

Ireland N-2B Neptune, December 1927.

tilt-wing 16-seat transport, expected to fly early 1996, but firm seeking buyer 1993.

Ishikawajima (Japan). Ishikawajima Kokuki KK formed at Tokyo December 1924, with factory at Tachikawa. Built small batches of 2-seat biplanes: T-2/-3 recon, R-1/-2/-3/-5 trainers and light ambulance (later designated KKY). KKY with 130-hp Cirrus replaced by 150-hp Ha-12 or Kamikaze radial was developed as KS-1 for survey duty while company was being reorganized 1936 as Tachikawa.

Islamic: *See* Iran.

Island (UK). Island Aircraft, subsidiary of Taurus Aviation, was formed 1988 to take over development and marketing of Super 2 from defunct ARV. In turn failed 1991.

Israel: *See* IAI.

Issoire (France). Société Issoire-Aviation formed 1 February 1978 to take over premises at Issoire-le-Broc and other assets of Wassmer. Continued IA 80 Piranha and sought subcontract activities. Ceased trading 1980.

Italair (Italy). Italair SpA, Genoa, formed 1974 to develop range of GA aircraft. First product F.20 Pegaso light twin, designed by Frati and built by General Avia (21 October 1971). Rights reverted to General Avia 1975.

Itoh (Japan). Also known as C. Itoh & Co., Itoh Chu Kohku Seibi Kabushiki Kaisha formed Tokyo 1952; among many other activities developed N-58 Cygnet light cabin monoplane (1960) and N-62 Eaglet 4-seater (1966); converted various aircraft for film purposes.

IVL (Finland). Ilmailuvoimien Lentokonetehdas (aviation forces aircraft factory) established 1921 at Sveaborg, Helsinki. First product A-22 seaplane (Heinkel's Hansa-Brandenburg W.33), followed by Korka bomber-recon biplane, D.26 Haukka fighter (17 March 1927) followed by Haukka II, to replace Gamecock II which IVL built under licence. Also licence-built DH Moth. Merged into VL February 1928.

J

Jabiru (Australia). Since 1991 Jabiru Aircraft Pty Ltd has produced LSA (Light Sport Aircraft) high-wing 2-seat cabin machine at Bundaberg West, Queensland.

Jackaroo (UK). Jackaroo Aircraft formed 1956 as associate company of Wiltshire School of Flying, Thruxton, to modify Tiger Moth to multirole 4-seater or ag-aircraft. About 100 Thruxton Jackaroo kits produced 1958–60.

Jackson (USA). Lewis A. Jackson built sporting aircraft 1965.

Jacobs (USA). Jacobs Aircraft Engine Co., established 1929 at Pottstown, PA, formed Helicopter Division 1950 and flew simple prototype rig of Model 104 Gyrodyne October 1953.

Jacquet-Pottier: *See* CARMAM.

JADC (Japan). Japan Aircraft Development Corp. is successor to CTDC as co-ordinating body for national 20% share in Boeing 777. Also co-ordinates work on YSX 75-seater and (moribund) YXX/7J7.

Jaffe (USA). Jaffe Aircraft Inc., San Antonio, produced but abandoned SA-32T Turbo Trainer (31 May 1989). Comtran and Heli-Air are Jaffe companies.

Jameson (USA). Richard J. Jameson, Fullerton, CA, built Gypsy Hawk all-metal single-seater (1972), plans marketed.

Jamieson (USA). Mail pilot William L. Jamieson built 2 racers at Richmond, VA, second (1933) exceeding 300 mph on test. Jamieson's death on night mail route halted testing.

Jamieson (USA). Jamieson Aircraft Co. formed DeLand, Florida, 1947 to develop J-2-L1 Jupiter 3-seater. Renamed (unknown date) The Jamieson Corp., developed Jupiter into Take 1 and finally Model J with conventional (as distinct from butterfly) tail, certificated 1963.

Janowski (Poland). Jaroslaw Janowski, Lodz, built J-1 Don Quixote 1970 and J-2 Polonez 1976 single-seat ultralights, both powered by Saturn 2-stroke flat-twin of his design.

Janox (USA). Purchased assets of Navion 1970 but instead of continuing production sold to Cedric Kotowicz, who formed Navion Rangemaster.

Japan Aeroplane Manufacturing Co.: *See* NAMC (Japan).

Japan Aircraft Development Corporation: *See* JADC.

Japan Aircraft Manufacturing Co.: *See* Nippi.

Japan Experimental: *See* JEAA.

Jarvis (USA). Formed at Glendale, LA, 1945 to build VJ-21 Jaybird; taken over by Volmer and flown 1946 as Volmer-Jensen VJ-21.

Jarzab (Poland). Kazimierz Jarzab built light aircraft 1981.

JAS (Sweden). JAS Industrigruppen formed 1980 to manage JAS (then JAS 39) programme; today IG JAS. 1992 saw funding for further 110 JAS 39A plus 2-seat JAS 39B.

Jatho (Germany). Civil servant in Hanover, Karl Jatho built pusher biplane 1903 in which he made 'running jump' estimated 18m 18 August and a 60-m hop November; not claimed as true flights.

Javelin (USA). Javelin Aircraft Co., Wichita, formed by Dave Blanton 1 March 1953 to make simple autopilot, since became famed for fuel systems, conversions of auto (especially Ford) engines and modifications to PZL M-18 and many other aircraft. Marketed many hundreds of plans of Javelin Wichawk 2/3-seat sport biplane. Built BD-2 (11 March 1967) for WFI.

JDM: *See* Avions JDM.

JEAA (Japan). Japan Experimental Aircraft Association (EAA Chapter 306) produced numerous ultralights from 1968.

Jeaco (USA). Formed 1959 by Richard Johnston to build light aircraft.

Jeannin (Germany). Pioneer pilot and aircraft constructor, best known for *Stahltauben*, Taube-types built with steel-framed fuselage 1913–16.

Jean St-Germain (Canada). Centre de Recherches Jean St-Germain flew Raz-Mut ultralight 1976, several hundred being built.

Jeffair (USA). Jeffair Corp. (Geoffrey L. Siers), Renton, WA, flew Barracuda high-speed 2-seater 1975, over 350 being built by 1980.

Jensen: *See* Volmer.

JET (International). Project for Joint European Transport 1977–9.

Jetcraft (USA). Jetcraft (USA) Inc., Las Vegas, planned range of Executive Mk I and Mk II based on Vampire Trainer.

Jetcrafters (USA). Jetcrafters Inc., San Antonio, is Ed Swearingen company formed to market Taurus upgrade of Beech King Air 90.

Jidey (France). J. Despretz, Morlaix, built J-13 Flash tandem (backstagger) biplane (August 1964); name from French pronunciation of JD.

Jodel (France). Société des Avions Jodel formed at Beaune March 1946 by MM. Edouard Joly and Jean Delemontez to repair light aircraft and gliders; then produced D.9 Bébé-Jodel (January 1948), D.10 Jodel-Club, D.11, D.111, D.112 and D.140 Mousquetaire. Many licensees, about 5,500 flown (1993).

Johansen (Denmark). Dipl.-Ing. Carl Johansen produced CJ-59 4-seat twin-engined amphibian, flown 23 July 1967.

Johansen (USA). Johansen Aircraft Co. produced JA-1 and JA-2 light cabin aircraft 1936–8.

Johns: *See* American Multiplane.

Johnson (USA). Johnson Aircraft Inc., Fort Worth, developed Rocket 140 and 185. Reorganized 1947 as **Johnson Aircraft Corp.**, developed Rocket into 4-seat Bullet 125, which in turn built by Aircraft Manufacturing Co.

Johnson (USA). Johnson Airplane & Supply Co. Inc. established 1922 Dayton, Ohio, among other

Johnson Twin 60, October 1926.

things rebuilding DH-4 variants; 1923 began production of Hartzell (later of propellers) FC-1 and -2 biplanes; 1926 built Twin 60 utility biplane (2 × 32-hp Bristol Cherub), followed by 3-seat Canary and many other prototypes or small batches.

Johnson (USA). R.B. Johnson patented circular (disc) wing aircraft 1931, built Uniplane 1934 with 'fuselage' forming deep diameter across underside of circular wing with convex (downsloping) top; flown Harlem Airport, near Chicago, 1935.

Johnson (USA). Richard H. Johnson's sailplanes include small number of motorized or self-launch versions.

Johnston (Canada). Stanley Johnston produced 4 aircraft 1926–60, last being Special side-by-side tourer.

Johnston (USA). Richard Johnston, Jeaco, built light aircraft 1959–60.

Joint European Helicopter (International). JEH formed November 1986 to build Tonal based on A129 Mangusta, abandoned November 1990.

Jona (Italy). Produced small series of civil trainer/tourers 1930–39, almost all cantilever biplanes, designated J1 to J6s, one J6 being tilting-wing sesquiplane.

Jones (Canada). Daniel G. Jones built D-1 single-seat biplane 1979.

Jones (USA). Jones Aircraft Corp. formed by Ben Jones at Schenectady 1935 to build D-25 biplane, rights having been acquired from

Standard. In 1937 produced S-125 and -150 2-seat monoplanes.

Jordan Aerospace (Jordan). Company formed Amman 1989 to build Schweizer 330 helicopter for Mid-East and African markets, no hardware by 1992.

Joses (Brazil). Charles Rupert Joses built light aircraft 1982.

Joslin (USA). F.A. Joslin, Beaufort SC, built Chiisai Tanyoki 2/3 scale Mitsubishi A6M5 fighter 1969.

Joucques (UK). Joucques Aviation Co., Willesden, subcontractor on B.E.2b production 1914–15. Premises taken over by BAT 1917.

Jovair (USA). Jovanovich renamed Helicopter Engineering Research Corp. **Jovair Corporation** 1957, developing tandem-rotor JOV-3 into Sedan 4E, and building prototype J-2. Both taken over by McCulloch 1969.

Jovanovich: *See* Helicopter Engineering; Jovair.

J. Samuel White: *See* White, J. Samuel.

Jugoslav Government (Jugoslavia). Among several government projects of 1930s, most important aircraft to fly was Pionir monoplane for prone-pilot research, with 2 × 55-hp Mikron III, designed by Major Dragoljub at Beslin 1940. This was scaled up into Type 451, 2 × 160-hp Minor 6-III, built by Ikarus and flown 1951. This again modified into 451M light twin-jet. Resurrected industry 1946–60 wholly nationalized undertaking, though using facilities of former Ikarus, Rogozarsky and Zmaj, most important type being S-49 fighter based on Yak-3. Other types 213 and 522 piston-engined advanced trainers, 214 crew-trainer/transport and 452 baby twin-jet.

Junkers (Germany). Prof. Hugo Junkers (1859–1935) started **Junkers und Compagnie** 1895 making gas boilers and heating/ventilating installations. In 1910 patented concept of aircraft comprising large thick metal wing, with only vestigial nose/tail. Developed cantilever metal wings with corrugated Dural skin and used these on J1 cantilever monoplane (12 December 1915). Produced J2, J4 (in service as J.1 close-support aircraft), J7, J9 (in service as D.I fighter) and J10 (in service as CL.I armoured close-support aircraft). Lack of production capacity resulted in formation of Junkers-Fokker (which *see*), terminated 1918. **Junkers Flugzeugwerke** formed Dessau 24 April 1919. F13 single-engined all-metal cantilever monoplane transport flew 25 June 1919, total of 322 built over next 13 years. By 1921 work well advanced on giant G1 monoplane airliner of 125-ft span, but Allies ordered it to be scrapped. As result, 1923 saw formation of Junkers companies in Sweden, Spain and Soviet Union: *see* Flygindustri; AMJ; Junkers Fili. Aero-engine work led to formation of Junkers Motorenbau GmbH 1923, and airline Junkers-Luftverkehrs AG followed 1924, when G23 and G24 3-engined airliners appeared. In 1926 bigger G31 appeared, plus various postal, photo and military types, as well as W33 (199) and 34 (1,791) light transports. S36 transport led to K37 bomber, produced in Japan as Ki-2. Giant

G38, nearest to 1910 patent, flew 1929, 2 built plus 6 Japanese Ki-20 heavy bomber versions. Chief designer Karl Plauth killed in crash 1 November 1927, succeeded by Ernst Zindel who produced Ju 52 13 October 1930, developed into Ju 52/3m April 1931 (4,825). Many other types, but financial problems, and founder's anti-Nazi views, resulted in state takeover 1933, Dr Heinrich Koppenberg being appointed director-general. Amalgamation with engine company resulted in world's largest aircraft manufacturer, **Junkers Flugzeug- und Motorenwerke AG**. By 1945 controlled main works at Dessau and 17 other plants with 140,000 employees. By far biggest programme was Ju 88 (about 14,840). Others Ju 87 dive-bomber (at least 5,745), Ju 86, Ju 90/290/390, Ju 188/388 and Ju 252/352. After 1945 virtually all Junkers facilities were in Soviet hands. EF 131 jet bomber was used by Soviet Alekseyev bureau as starting point for Type 150 1946–50 (which led to East German VEF Type 152 airliner).

Junkers Fili (USSR). Junkers obtained concession from infant Soviet government, with civil war still raging 1923, to open design office and production factory in former RBVZ buildings at Fili north of Moscow. Arrangement to mutual advantage. Main types: Ju 20, based on A 20 (Soviet military R-2), Ju 21 (H 21) recon, Ju 13 (F13), PS-4 (W33) and JuG-1 (G24, Soviet military designations R-42, 42M and 42T). Junkers moved out 1 March 1927, factory becoming GAZ-22.

Junkers-Fokker (Germany). Junkers was unable

Junkers Ju 88A-5, captured at Chivenor 26 November 1941.

to fulfil first major production contract for J4 (Idflieg designation J.I). Junkers-Fokker-Werke formed at Dessau 20 October 1917, equal shares held by 2 principals. Built 227 J.I, 41 J9 (D.I) and 43 J10 (CL.I); impossible clash of personalities and Fokker walked out mid-1918.

Jurca (France). Marcel Jurca flew MJ.2 Tempête 27 June 1956, 45 since built, followed by large numbers of 15 further light designs all now supplied as plans (agent in USA).

Jurom: *See* SOKO/Avioane.

J.V. Martin: *See* Martin, 2nd entry.

K

KA: *See* Korean Air.

KAI: *See* Kazan.

Kaiser-Fleetwings (USA). Formed by takeover of Fleetwings 1943: *see* Fleetwings.

Kaiser-Hammond (USA). Formed Bristol, PA, 1944 to build updated Stearman-Hammond Aircar.

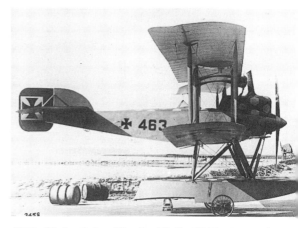

KW (Kaiserlicht Werft, Kiel) W.II, December 1916.

Kaiser-Hughes (USA). Company formed 1942 by Howard R. Hughes and Henry J. Kaiser to build 3 HK-1 'flying Liberty Ships'. Kaiser withdrew 1944 but Hughes completed 1 Hercules flying-boat.

Kaiserlicht Werft (Germany). Imperial navy yards at Danzig, Kiel and Wilhelmshaven all produced biplane seaplanes, known only by their serial numbers (sometimes with prefix KW), 1917–18. Designs original but very similar to others existing.

KAL (Uzbekistan). Privatized management organized 1992 for 3 large production facilities of KAL engineering works (previously GAZ-34, 184 and 243) at Tashkent where Li-2, Il-14 and over

Kaiser-Fleetwings XBTK-1, 1944.

1,100 An aircraft (8, 12 and 22) were built. Now producing Il-76/78, Il-114, An-70/77 and wing of An-124. Il-114 plant managed by **V.P. Chkalov Aviation Association**.

Kalinin (USSR). Konstantin Alekseyevich Kalinin directed aircraft repair factory 1923 and set up his own KB (GROSS) 1925, producing series of high-wing monoplane transports with elliptical wing, K-1 onwards. Most successful was K-5 (1929), 260 being built. K-7 was giant 7-engined bomber (1933), K-9 and -10 light sporting monoplanes and K-12 tailless twin-engined bomber (December 1936). In 1938 Kalinin caught up in Stalin's terror, accused of 'conspiracy' and executed.

Kalkert: *See* Gotha 2nd entry

Kaman (USA). Charles H. Kaman formed **Kaman Aircraft Corp.** December 1945 to develop helicopters with intermeshing rotors each fitted with servo-flap control. K-125A built 1947, K-190 in 1948 and K-225 (YH-22) in 1949. A K-225 with Boeing gas turbine was first turbine helicopter (10 December 1951). K-225 developed into HOK-1 and HTK-1, and adapted as remote-control drone. Further development led to over 200 HH-43 USAF rescue helicopters. With HU2K (H-2) Seasprite (2 July 1959) Kaman switched to conventional rotor arrangement; several hundred delivered and progressively upgraded and 97 SH-2G still being delivered. K-Max (23 December 1991) is multirole crane helicopter. Major producer of rotor blades and

Kaman HTK-1, October 1951.

subcontract airframe components. Diversified 1965 into Kaman Corp., Bloomfield, Connecticut, operations becoming first Aerospace Group and finally **Kaman Aerospace Corp.**, subsidiary of Kaman Corp.

Kaminskas (USA). Rim Kaminskas, Monrovia, CA, built Papoose Jungster I sport biplane (October 1962), Jungster II parasol monoplane (March 1966) and Jungster III aerobatic and racing biplane (September 1968).

Kamov (USSR, CIS-Russia). Nikolai Ilyich Kamov was locomotive engineer but 1928 qualified as pilot and worked on ROM-1 and other flying-boats under Grigorovich. Joined CAHI 3rd Brigade which created A-7 high-performance autogyro. In 1929–31 worked with

Kamov Ka-29TB, 1989.

N.K. Skrzhinskii on KaSkr-1 and -2 autogyros, and at start of war was developing observation autogyros. Evacuated near Lake Baikal (no problem, he was a Siberian). Switched during war to helicopters, despite problems, and in 1947 flew ultralight Ka-8. Followed with Ka-10, built in small series for ship observation duties. Ka-15 (1952) first real production cabin machine, like predecessors with coaxial rotors. Ka-18 (1957) was larger and roomier. Ka-22 Vintokryl totally unlike anything else, giant 11,000-hp compound helicopter with an engine/rotor/propeller group on each wingtip and with aeroplane tail. Ka-25 (1961) with 2 × 900-hp turboshaft engines adopted as standard ASW, target acquisition, missile-guidance and SAR helicopter of Soviet navy, 460 built 1966–75. Ka-26 multipurpose (2 × 325-hp piston engines) flew 1965, 850 built. Ka-27, growth version of Ka-25 (2 × 2,225-shp turboshaft) flew December 1974, led to many versions including Ka-28 (export), Ka-29 (assault transport and electronic warfare) and Ka-32 (civil), total over 300 end 1991 and rising. Ka-62 (1992) totally new single main rotor high-speed helicopter mainly for civil and export markets. Ka-118 (1993) high-speed NOTAR 5-seat helicopter. Ka-126 turbine derivative of Ka-26 assigned to IAR Romania. Ka-136 (1983) coaxial combat helicopter in limited production. Ka-226 (1990) twin-turbine utility and ag-helo planned for production with Allison engines. Ka-50 fast battlefield helicopter (27 July 1982) seeking Western partner and funding. Title **VNTKI** (helicopter scientific/tech complex named for) **N.I. Kamov**, General Constructor Sergei Mikheyev.

Kaproni Bulgarski (Bulgaria). So-called 'Avia factory' established 1926 at Kazanluk, becoming Caproni subsidiary 1930 and building that company's designs: KB-1 based on Ca 100 trainer, KB-2 (Ca 113) developed as armed 2-seater, KB-3, -4 and -5 all further developments, serving through Second World War. KB-11 (1941), 750-hp high-wing monoplane multirole, was original design.

Karhumäki (Finland). Veljekset Karhumäki O/Y established 1924 to build light aircraft under licence, adding Viri (Finnish club of aero engineers design) 1935. In 1941 moved into new factory at Halli to build Ilmavoimat (air force) trainers. Post-war designed Karhu 48B high-wing 4-seater on wheels, skis or floats.

Kari-Keen (USA). Kari-Keen Aircraft incorporated June 1928 at Sioux City, Iowa, as subsidiary of auto-accessory firm, producing K-K 90 high-wing cabin 2-seater.

Karo (Lithuania). Karo Aviacijos Tiekimo Skyrius was Lithuanian army aircraft factory at Kaunas (Kovno): *see* Anbo.

Karpeka (Russia). Pioneer constructor/pilot, built Voisin look-alike 1910.

Kasyanenko (Russia). Brothers Evgenii Ivanovich, Ivan and Andrei Kasyanenko were students at KPI (Kiev Polytechnic Institute) who in 1910–21 designed and built 6 increasingly original aeroplanes. No. 1 was pusher biplane of Farman style, which despite Anzani of only 15-hp made several short flights at Cherkassy. Modified as 1bis, front elevator removed and tail altered. No. 3 (next) built at St Petersburg with left/right biplane wings pivoted so that incidence of each side changed independently. Oerlikon 50-hp watercooled drove 2 tractor propellers via chains. Flight-tested October 1912. No. 4, tested by Nesterov summer 1913, deliberately low-powered monoplane, again with independent variable incidence on left/right wings; flown Kiev with 15-hp Anzani. No. 5, built at KPI and tested late June 1917, was unconventional biplane fighter, with variable-incidence left/right wings mounted on finely streamlined fuselage with nose gun and cockpit and 100-hp Gnome driving pusher 3-blade propeller (first in world ?) behind protective cruciform tail.

Katran (Australia/Singapore). Joint project for business jet; 1992 seeking venture capital.

Kawanishi (Japan). Kawanishi engineering works at Kobe established aircraft division 1921, building varied selection of types (mail-carrier, racer, passenger seaplane, trainer, fighter and planned trans-Pacific aircraft) as K-1–K-12 by 1928. In November 1928 Kawanishi Kokuki Kogyo Kabushiki Kaisha formed, moving to new factory at Narao 1930, gradually adding other factories at Konan and Himeji, all in Osaka/Kobe area. Among some 25 subsequent types, most important were E7K reconnaissance biplane, H6K and H8K 4-engined flying-boats and N1K1-J and 2-J fighters. Company reformed 1949 as Shin Meiwa.

Kawasaki (Japan). Kawasaki Jukogyo KK

Kawanishi F11K1, 1937.

(heavy industries) formed **Kawasaki Kokuki Kogyo KK** (aircraft engineering) subsidiary 1918, making aircraft and engines, but aircraft division made independent firm 1937 and engine subsidiary followed in 1939. Original factory Akashi near Kobe, but from 1935 huge second plant opened Kagamigahara (Gifu) near Nagoya. By Second World War 2 further sites building complete aircraft: at Ichinomiya, also near Nagoya, and Miyakonojo, on Kyushu island. Built 300 Salmson 2A2 and Dornier Wals, Do N bomber being basis of Type 87, first Kawasaki design by Richard Vogt (later of Blohm und Voss). Vogt then produced Type 88 recon biplane (707, including 187 by Tachikawa), Type 92 fighter (380), Ki-3 bomber (243) and Ki-10 fighter (580 +). First stressed-skin monoplane was Ki-32 bomber (854, 1938–40). During Second World War Kawasaki ranked third in airframe output, main types being Ki-61 and derived Ki-100

fighters, Ki-45, -102 and -108 twin-engined fighters, Ki-48 bomber, Ki-36 and -55 tactical/training aircraft and Ki-56 (Lockheed 14) transport.

Kawasaki (Japan). On 15 March 1954 former Kawasaki Kikai Kogyo KK and Kabushiki Kaisha Kawasaki Gifu Seisakusho were amalgamated as Kawasaki Kokuki Kogyo KK (same as pre-war), starting as major USAF overhaul facility, then building 210 Lockheed T-33, 48 P-2H (plus 82 own-design P-2J), 239 Bell 47 (plus 211 derived KH-4), 160 KV107 (derived from Boeing 107) and 133 McDD 500D. On 1 April 1969 company merged with Kawasaki dockyard and rolling-stock companies to form **Kawasaki Jukogyo** KK (Heavy Industries). Major programmes include Kawasaki T-4 jet trainer (29 July 1985), production with DASA (MBB) of BK117, support/mod of Kawasaki C-1 airlifter,

Kawasaki Type 88-1, May 1928.

production of 110 P-3C and 54 CH-47J, major parts for F-15J, 767 and 777, and large contracts for engines and space.

Kay (UK). David Kay formed Kay Gyroplanes Ltd 1929. First successful autogyro 1932, best-known was Kay Gyroplane, built at Eastleigh by Oddin, Bradbury & Cull 1935.

Kayaba (Japan). In 1939 Imperial Army imported Kellett KD-1A to learn about autogyros. Damaged in crash, this was transferred to Kayaba Seisakusho KK, Sendai, to assist development of Japanese 2-seat observation autogyro. Ka-1 (240-hp Argus) flew 26 May 1941; outstanding machine, about 240 built. Ka-1 KAI had tip rockets to boost capability; single Ka-2 had 240-hp Jacobs.

Kazan (USSR). Kazan Aviation Institute intermittently one of greatest SKBs (student construction bureaux) from 1934, supervisory designers being S.P. Gudzik and Z.I. Itskovich 1934–7 and M.P. Simonov 1956–66. Very first design, KAI-1 6-seat monoplane (2 × M-11) flown November 1934, was outstanding, and led to UPB bomber crew trainer. Apart from 10-passenger KAI-2 most subsequent types were trainers and gliders, though last known was 1967 VTOL with tilting ducted proprotors.

Kazan Gelikopter Kazan Helo Production Association joined with Mil, Eurocopter and Klimov engine bureau to produce Mi-38.

KB-7 (USSR). Construction Bureau 7 organized 1936 to create aerospace vehicles. Ten projects included R-05v fighter, but thinking so far ahead of practical technology caused designs to remain on paper.

KBHC (S. Korea). Korea Bell Helicopter Co. is joint venture which overhauls and inspects Bell helicopters, trains air/ground crews and makes parts for Daewoo and Samsung.

Keburiya (Russia, UK). Vissarion Savelyevich Keburiya built glider 1909, later bought Blériot which he repeatedly rebuilt (with changes) after crashes. Built second monoplane 1912, and No. 3 in 1913 similar to Morane but Nieuport-type undercarriage.

Keleher (USA). James J. Keleher, Fremont, CA,

built Lark sport/aerobatic monoplane, plans marketed from 1968 for revised 1B version.

Kellett (USA). Kellett Autogiro Corp. formed Philadelphia 1929 to operate Cierva licence obtained from Pitcairn. K-2, -3 and -4 were followed 1934 by KD-1 (Kellett Direct-control) built in small series including YO-60 for Army. Switched to helicopters with 'eggbeater' intermeshing rotors, XR-8 (1943) leading to XR-10 able to carry 6 stretchers (litters) in 1948.

Kellner-Béchereau (France). Louis Béchereau, pioneer constructor, devised patented form of lightweight monocoque construction, collaborated with Kellner (motor bodybuilders) and produced fuselages for Blériot-SPAD 510 fighter. Same partnership built 3 experimental aircraft with patented wing with forward fixed portion and abnormally large rear portion pivoted far below wing to serve as ailerons and as slotted flaps: E.1, E.C.4 and E.D.5, all 1936–7.

Kelowna: *See* KFC.

Kennedy (Russia, UK). Scotsman J.S. Mackenzie Kennedy built several primitive biplanes in St Petersburg 1909–14, using features of Wrights and Voisins. Returned to UK 1914 and with Hamilton Edwards formed Kennedy Aeroplanes Co. at Cromwell Rd, London SW, and obtained contract to build 'one Sikorsky, four 200-hp Salmson'. Resulting Kennedy Giant constructed by the Gramophone Co. and Fairey, both of Hayes, and assembled Northolt where it got mainwheels off ground 1917 but not tailskid.

Kensgaila (Lithuania). V. Kensgaila's Enterprise markets VK-8 ag-aircraft (assembled).

Kensinger (USA). E. Kensinger designed one of fastest Formula racers 1960.

Kentucky (USA). Kentucky Aircraft Corp. formed 1926 to produce Cardinal 3-seat biplane.

Kerr: *See* Dick, Kerr & Co.

Keystone (USA). Keystone Aircraft Corp., Bristol, PA, formed by name-change from Huff-Daland 8 March 1927. Continued as principal supplier of bombers to Army, including XB-1 Super Cyclops (2 × Packard), XLB-3 (2 × inverted Liberty), LB-5A Pirate

Keystone-Loening K-85 Air Yacht, 11 November 1930.

(2 × Liberty) and XLB-6 Panther. Army received 10 LB-5, 17 LB-6 and (1929–32) 25 B-4A, 27 B-5A and 39 B-6A, all with Wright or P&W radials. Other types included Navy XNK-1 Pup armed trainer, Pronto 3-seat land/seaplane, Pathfinder 10-passenger biplane, Patrician 19/20-passenger high-wing monoplane and Sign-Carrier with 90-ft lower wing for flashing neon signs and 8-hr endurance. Lost identity on takeover by Curtiss-Wright early 1933.

KFC (Canada). Kelowna Flightcraft Air Charter upgrades Convair 580 and related Canadair CC-109 Cosmopolitan.

KhAI (USSR, now Ukraine). Kharkovskii Aviatsionni Institut (XAI, in English written KhAI) was leading SKB (student construction bureau) in Soviet Union. Under Iosif Grigoryevich Nyeman produced KhAI-1 to -6 in 1932–7, plus various other types. KhAI-1 (8 October 1932) very clean low-wing monoplane transport, 201 mph with 6 passengers, 43 for Aeroflot, also bomber version. Another major programme was KhAI-5 tactical attack, 490 delivered as R-10. KhAI-2 was Flea, -3 a twin-engined flying wing and -4 a single-engined pusher flying wing. KhAI-6 and -52 were more advanced single-engined tac-recon and bomber aircraft. SKB resurrected 1960, produced KhAI-17 to -27 assisted by various senior designers, all light aeroplanes, helicopters or autogyros. No relation to XAPA.

Khioni (Russia, USSR). Vassili Nikolayevich Khioni was a lead designer for Anatra, small number of VKh Anasalya (Anadva-Salmson) bombers surviving Revolution. Khioni No. 4 (2 × 160-hp Salmson) flown 1922 but chaos of

civil war made production impossible. Likewise No. 5, named Konyek-Gorbunok, remained single trainer prototype at former Anatra works 1923–7, when 30 more were built as anti-locust dusters.

KIAT: *See* Korean Air.

Kindermann (W. Germany). Flugkapitän K.B. Kindermann built simple helicopter whose 3 blades were each attached to a cylinder of a rotary engine turning on a vertical axis, flown 1961.

King's (USA). At Orange City, Iowa, the King's Engineering Fellowship developed Model 44 Angel prototype (January 1984) from Evangel for missionary work; production start 1992.

Kingsbury (UK). At Kingsbury, Middlesex, built 150 D.H.6 1917. Designed large triplane seaplanes to carry Davis gun but cancelled 1918.

Kingsford Smith (Australia). Sir Charles Kingsford Smith established Air Service at Bankstown, Sydney, 1935, which became KS Aviation Service 1946, deciding 1955 to produce ag-aircraft to local requirements. Designer Pellarini produced Kingsford Smith PL.7 (21 September 1956), a sesquiplane with tail carried on booms, followed by more conventional KS.3 Cropmaster. Small number built when company taken over by Victa 1963, while Yeoman further developed Cropmaster. KSAS was agent for Auster and produced improved Autocrat as Kingsmith and improved Autocar as Bushmaster.

Kinner (USA). Established Glendale, LA, 1919 to produce radial engines. In 1926 produced Courier

2-seat parasol monoplane, followed by Sportster low-wing 2-seater and derived Sportwing, enclosed Playboy and larger 4-seat Envoy, built for Navy as RK-1 staff transports. Bankrupt 1939, rights for aircraft to Timm, while a totally new Kinner firm took over engines.

Kirby (UK). Kirby Kitten 2-seat monoplane registered G-ALGA November 1949, but never completed; was being built by well-known glider company.

Kirk (USA). Joe Kirk built light sporting aircraft 1967.

Kirkham (USA). Engine designer Charles B. Kirkham, wanting a fast aircraft to test K-12 engine, designed 18-T fighter, built by Curtiss and flown 5 July 1918. Soon captured national speed and height records. Often called Curtiss-Kirkham or simply Curtiss 18-T, but it was Kirkham aircraft subcontracted to Curtiss for manufacture. In 1920s Kirkham Products designed aircraft to order.

Kissinger-Crookes (USA). Curtis D. Kissinger and LeRoy Crookes, engineers with GE Schenectady, experimented in 1950s with circular-wing aircraft, ending with XK-1 piloted turboprop aircraft built at RPI (Rensselaer Polytechnic Institute).

Kistler (USA). J. Kistler owned and raced Skeeter (racing No. 31) designed by Wm. Statler of Lockheed.

Kitz (USA). Kitz Kopters developed kits for increasing Bell 47 payload, mainly for agricultural duties.

Kjeller (Norway). Acquisition from Spain of 5 Hispano-Suiza engines in 1918 prompted Haerens Flyvevaesen (Norwegian army flying service) to get a fighter designed to use them. Design office under Ing. Hellesen was started at Kjeller, and small factory grew, while requirement changed to 2-seat recon-fighter. Eventually FF6, called T.2 by customer, flew 1921, but poor performance. Subsequently Kjeller Flyfabrikk undertook major licensed construction of AW Scimitar, Fokker C.V and D.H. Gipsy Moth and Tiger Moth.

Klemm (Germany). Dr.-Ing. Hanns Klemm designed light aircraft for Daimler at Stuttgart 1919–1925, leaving 1926 to form **Klemm Leichtflugzeugbau** GmbH. First product was L 25 tandem-seat low-wing monoplane, direct successor to Daimler L 20 of 1924. Over 600 built in many variants, with at least 14 types of engine. Subsequently L 26–L 36 embraced over 40 subtypes, almost all built in series and with total of all variants of Kl 35 exceeding 4,600. Final types were Kl 105 ultralight, Kl 106 2-seater and Kl 107 side-by-side cabin machine; Kl 151 4-seater was stopped in 1940 and factory devoted to military production. Works destroyed but in 1955 **Hanns Klemm Flugzeugbau** registered and built Kl 107 prototype. Developed through 107B and 107C, rights acquired by Bölkow, which put Kl 107C into series production 1959.

Kleyer: *See* Adler.

Knoll (USA). Knoll Aircraft Corp. formed 1928 to build light aircraft designed by Felix Knoll, KN-1 and -2 metal 4-seat and 2-seat biplanes.

Knoller (Austria). Knoller Flugzeugbau produced small production runs of C.I and C.II 2-seat reconnaissance biplanes 1916–17.

Koberg (USA). Leslie R. Koberg built Mustang formula-type racer (28 June 1968).

Koc Holdings (Turkey). Through Kofisa Trading SA of Geneva, Koc Holdings is forming joint company with Agusta to promote aerospace, especially by starting helicopter industry.

Kochyerigin (USSR). Sergei Aleksandrovich Kochyerigin fought as pilot 1914–17 yet survived Revolution to become chief deputy to Polikarpov at OOS spring 1926. In 1930 head of recon brigade at CCB, with prolific and varied output even though never had his own OKB. LR and LR-2 were major redesigns of R-5; DI-6 2-seat fighter (his best-known design) served in various versions (about 330, 1935–8); SR and R-9 were modern recon/fighter/bomber monoplanes; BSh-1 and PS-43 were derived from Vultee V-11; and OPB-41 (1941) was dive-bomber able to reach 373-mph with 500-kg bomb.

Kokkola (Finland). Dipl.-Ings. Kalevi and Seppo Kokkola collaborated on light aircraft 1970.

Kokubun (Japan). Masanori Kokubun built light aircraft 1972.

Kokusai (Japan). Kokusai Kokuki Kabushiki Kaisha (International Aircraft Co. Ltd) formed Okubo 1936 to build foreign designs under licence. Remained very small until merged June 1941 into Nippon Kokusai. For most 'Kokusai' aircraft *see* Nippon Kokusai.

Kolb (USA). Kolb Co. Inc., Phoenixville, PA, markets kits for Twinstar III and Laser 2-seaters, as well as micros.

Kolesnikov (USSR). Dmitri Nikolayevich Kolesnikov designed gliders from 1930, collaborated with Romeiko-Gurko on RMK-1 and with Tsybin on KTs-20 troop-carrying glider 1940.

Kolpakov (Russia, USSR). Leonid Dyementyevich Kolpakov-Miroshnichyenko led design of several aircraft at Lebed company 1914–17. His own designs were: Kolpakov K-1 recon biplane (1916) with entire wing cellule variable incidence through 7°, Lebed XIV (or Lebed-Grand) twin-engined fighter (1917), and LB-2LD light bomber of 1926 developed from Lebed-Grand with crew of 4, delayed until after civil war.

KOMTA (USSR). Commission for Heavy Aviation formed spring 1920 under N.Ye. Zhukovskii, designed triplane transport named variously Komta or Kometa (comet). Two × 240-hp Fiat, normally 2 pilots and 6/8 passengers, flown March 1922, unsuccessful.

Kondor (Germany). Formed by Josef Suvelack (killed in air combat 1917) at Rotthausen aerodrome, Gelsenkirchen. Built various military types under licence. On Suvelack's death factory sold to city of Gelsenkirchen and **Kondor Flugzeugwerke** GmbH formed at Essen, importing designers Walter Rethel (later of Fokker, Arado and Messerschmitt) and Paul G. Ehrhardt from LVG. First Kondor aircraft was unsuccessful triplane fighter (October 1917). D.I fighter biplane again not impressive, redesigned by Rethel into D.II, flew well but too slow. D6 (D.VI) of 1918 had no upper centre section, again rejected. D7 was essentially a rebuild of the triplane, abandoned. Kondor E3, or D.I, was impressive cantilever parasol monoplane, widely regarded as best fighter of October 1918 competition. It was put into production and small numbers reached customers in Switzerland, Netherlands and other countries after Armistice.

Koninklijke: *See* De Schelde.

Koolhoven (Netherlands). Frederick Koolhoven, also called Frits and known to his friends as Cully, built first aircraft 1910 and then designed for British Deperdussin, Armstrong Whitworth and British Aerial Transport (BAT), latter company's aircraft having designations numbered FK.22–FK.28. After Armistice he returned to native land and became designer for NVI (Nationale Vliegtuigindustrie) at The Hague. In 1926 he set himself up as a freelance consultant at The Hague, and in 1934 he formed NV **Koolhoven Vliegtuigen** as a limited company

Kondor E 3a (D.I), September 1918.

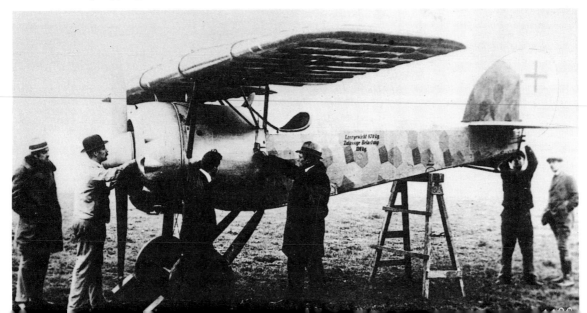

Koolhoven FK.58 prototype, 17 July 1938.

with offices and factory at Waalhaven aerodrome, Rotterdam. This was destroyed by bombing 10 May 1940. Major types included FK.29 cabin biplane with engine on hinged nose, FK.31 parasol recon-fighter, FK.41 and 43 cabin monoplanes, FK.46 biplane trainer, FK.49 and 50 high-wing transports, FK.51 basic trainer, FK.52 2-seat fighter, FK.55 experimental fighter, FK.56 basic trainer and FK.58 fighter used by Polish forces in France 1940.

Korea Bell: *See* KBHC.

Korean Air (S. Korea). KA's Aerospace Division was formed 1976 to develop and manufacture aircraft. Main income from manufacture of 80–90 Sikorsky UH-60P. Parts are made for 747, MD-11 and other US types; division has made 307 Hughes (McDD) 500D and 500MD helicopters, is developing Model 520MK, and its KIAT (Korean Institute of Aeronautical Technology) has produced microlights and Chang-Gong 91 4/5-seat cabin monoplane (22 November 1991).

Korolyev (USSR). Sergei Pavlovich Korolyev is revered as General Designer of GDL-OKB, creator of Soviet Union's powerful rocket engines and master architect of vast ICBM and space programmes. But in 1930 he was famed glider pilot, and in same year flew light aircraft he designed himself at Moscow School of Aviation, called SK-4, long-range ultralight. SK-7 was 1937 100-hp motor-glider with 5 passenger seats. RP-318 of 1940 was derived from SK-9 glider but with RDA-1 rocket engine. Korolyev's 1940 design for high-altitude pressurized rocket aircraft was halted by German invasion.

Korsa (Switzerland). Flugzeugbau Korsa, Alstettin, Zürich, known chiefly for Korsa I 50-hp 2-seat monoplane of 1927, several built.

Korvin: *See* Mikhelson.

Kosos (USSR). KOSOS, Bureau of Special Construction, formed 1929 within CAHI and led by Tupolev, Ilyushin and Sukhoi.

Kostovich (Russia). Ogneslav Stefanovich Kostovich, originally Hungarian, was pioneer of Russian aircraft, demonstrating models of helicopter, aeroplane and even ornithopter as early as 1879. Spent most time with dirigible *Rossiya*, and patented forms of plywood, but built 40-hp aeroplane 1911, seaplane 1914 and 100-hp amphibious monoplane 1916, though at least 2 of these were never flown.

Kotcherigin: *See* Kochyerigin.

Kozlov (USSR). Sergei Grigoryevich Kozlov was professor at VVA (air force academy) 1930–37. *Gigant* bomber (6 pairs of 730-hp engines) was never finished 1931. PS 'stealth' aircraft, low visibility and sound, flew 1936. EI fighter with variable-incidence wing was deliberately destroyed when factory evacuated October 1941.

Kramme & Zeuthen: *See* KZ.

Krauss (W. Germany). Dipl.-Ing. Peter Krauss built cabin autogyro with V-tail 1971.

Kreider-Reisner (USA). A.H. Kreider and L.E. Reisner formed company 1925 at Hagerstown, MD, building Midget racer 1926 and production

Kreutzer K-5 Air Coach, June 1931.

run of 10 versions of Challenger 3-seat biplane 1927–9, and a smaller 2-seater. Bought by Fairchild, retaining identity as wholly-owned division until 1935 renamed Fairchild Aircraft Corp.

Krenzer (USA). Frank J. Krenzer built WB-1 light biplane 1963.

Kress (Russia). Vasilii Vasilyevich (Wilhelm) Kress worked in Vienna where around 1900 he built an ambitious tandem triplane twin-float seaplane. On test it capsized, disaster blamed on ponderous weight of 35-hp Daimler engine.

Kreutzer (USA). Brown Mercury was used as basis 1929 for Air Coach built by **Joseph Kreutzer Corp.** on 2nd floor of Kreutzer Building in LA; 6-seater with 3 small engines, 1 only built.

Krier-Kraft (USA). Harold Krier built Acromaster, resembling Jungmeister, 1962.

Kristiansen (Norway). Aksel Kristiansen began building Norge B 3-seat monoplane during German occupation, flown (initially on floats) November 1946.

Kronfeld (UK). Robert Kronfeld took over British Aircraft Co. on Lowe Wylde's death May 1933, refining Planette into Kronfeld Drone. Company renamed Kronfeld Ltd 1936, building 33 Drones and 1 improved Kronfeld Monoplane (1937).

Krylov (USSR). Aleksei Aleksandrovich Krylov known only for R-II (also known as PP-1), 2-seat recon biplane built under difficulties 1923–5.

Krylov (USSR). V.Ya. Krylov (no relation) worked at GVF Leningrad with I.N. Vinogradov on AT-1 3-seat monoplane (1935), with several partners on ASK 4-seat amphibian for Arctic use with twin boat hulls (1935) and with V.F. Rentel on MA-1 6-seat amphibian (1939).

KuAPA (Russia). Kuibyshyev aviation production association, linked with ANTKI Tupolev, formed 1991, no longer builds Tu-95 or

KuAPA-built Tu-95MS 1991.

154, but took over work from XAPA.

Kudashyev (Russia). Aleksandr Sergeyevich Kudashyev, Kiev professor, flew at Nice with M.N. Yefimov February 1910, thereafter building 4 aeroplanes. Kudashyev 1 was at first glance like Voisin, but 35-hp Anzani drove tractor propeller. Other features: large ailerons on upper wing and simple (modern type) tail. Made first flight of any Russian aircraft 23 May 1910. Kudashyev 2 was larger, with 50-hp Gnome, flown autumn 1910. Kudashyev 3 was monoplane of Blériot type, but with pilot seated to look under wing. Flew winter 1910–11. Kudashyev 4 was improved 3 with 50-hp Gnome, even more like Blériot with pilot looking over wing; flew 2 April 1911.

Kuibyshev (USSR). Two distinct groups have built light aircraft. KuAI (aviation institute) built VIGR-1 helicopter with tip pulsejets 1965, Sverchok (cricket) 30-hp autogyro 1971 and both Strekoza (dragonfly) and Szmiel (bumblebee) ultralights 1977. KuPI (polytechnic institute) built light aircraft 1980. *See also* KuAPA.

Kumertaou (Russia). Kumertaou Aviation Production Association is a new production group, originally formed to manufacture wings for the Tu-154. Now builds Ka-26.

Kunming (China). One of 2 large military aircraft factories in China 1933–45, where several foreign types intermittently built under licence. Early 1941 began work on fighter loosely based on Curtiss Hawk 75A, result being X-PO (1942).

Kupfer (USSR). M.A. Kupfer built helicopter/autogyro trainer towed off ground with rotor spun by tethered cable 1953.

Kurchyevskii (USSR). Gun designer L.B. Kurchyevskii was authorized 1935 to form group to build fighters to use large recoilless cannon. IL designed by Lavochkin and S.N. Lyushin but never completed. BICh-17 by Cheranovskii was another fighter abandoned when Kurchyevskii arrested 1936.

Kuzakov (USSR). M.A. Kuzakov built light aircraft 1959.

Kyle-Smith (USA). Kyle-Smith Aircraft Co., Wheeling, became West Virginia Airplane Co. 1923, having made small number of sport biplanes.

Kyushu (Japan). Kyushu Hikoki Kabushiki Kaisha was Watanabe under new name May 1943, name being that of island where 3 small factories (later 6) were located. Main strength was trainers for Imperial Navy, notably K9W (derived from Bü 131), K10W (derived from NA-16) and K11W (own design). Also made Q1W Tokai original design of ASW aircraft. Licence production included E13A and E14Y seaplanes, A5M fighter and wings for G4M bomber. J7W fighter with pusher 6-blade propeller was single prototype at war's end.

KZ (Denmark). Founded as Kramme & Zeuthen A/S 1935, KZ produced KZ I single-seater. Became Skandinavsk A/S 1937: *see* SAI (Denmark).

L

Laboratoire Eiffel (France). Civil engineer (famed for his tower) Gustav Eiffel was also aerodynamicist. Among many other things he patented design of a clean low-wing monoplane 16 May 1917, resulting in construction of Laboratoire Eiffel monoplane, also called Breguet LE because Breguet did assembly, wings coming from SC de Levallois. Flew 28 March 1918, 140 mph on 180 hp. Service Technique wanted it rebuilt as biplane. Same design appeared post-war as LeO 9.

Labourdette-Halbron (France). Section Technique de la Marine built twin-hull triplane flying-boat 1917, (2 × 200-hp Hispano-Suiza); later fitted with 370-hp Lorraine, plus gunner nacelles on lower wing.

LACAB (Belgium). Les Ateliers de Constructions Aéronautiques Belges formed Brussels, with factory at Haren, 1932. Produced T.7 advanced trainer 1933, and in 1935 GR.8 twin-engined 4-seat multirole sesquiplane fighter.

LACEBA (Belgium). Les Ateliers de Construction et d'Exploitation de Brevets Aéronautiques built aircraft to others' designs 1934–40.

Lage (Brazil). Henrique Lage built at least 30 aircraft of many types, notably HL-8 light transport (3 × Lycoming O-290) 1943.

LaGG: *See* Lavochkin.

Laird (USA). Emil Matthew 'Matty' Laird built Model S ultralight biplane 1919, sold several and formed **Laird Airplane Co.**, 4500 W 83rd St, Chicago. First real product rebuilt JN-4 called Swallow, but sold design to Stearman as New Swallow. Fresh design 1924 LC (Laird Commercial) 3-seat biplane, about 30 built. Brother formed his own company (*see* below), so Matt formed **E.M. Laird Airplane Co.** at 5301 W 65th St, Chicago, concentrating on custom-built sporting and racing aircraft, notably Speedwing, Solution and Super Solution. Sesquiwing (1935), 6-seat sesquiplane, was attempt at comeback into commercial field. Final job was Roscoe Turner's LTR-14 Meteor racer 1936.

Laird (USA). Brother Charles L. Laird formed **Laird Aircraft Corp.**, Wichita, 15 November 1927, becoming chief engineer. To avoid confusion with brother's firm called product (large 4-seat cabin biplane) Whipporwill, and used this as trademark and headline everywhere.

Laister-Kauffman (USA). Glider manufacturer of St Louis, which in 1944 took over competitor Bowlus, produced XCG-10A assault glider 1944, 42 troops or 5 tons, 2 prototypes and 10 pre-production (possibly not all built).

LAK (Lithuanian SSR). Litovskaya Aviatsyonnaya Konstruktsiya formed 1969 to produce competition sailplanes and training gliders, in-

LACAB GR.8, January 1935.

cluding motor-gliders and self-launch sailplanes.

Lake (USA). **Lake Aircraft Corp.** formed Washington DC 1959 with factory Sanford, Maine. Obtained rights to Skimmer IV amphibian from Colonial October 1959 and produced as Lake LA-4. Developed 4 versions, and in 1962 became division of **Consolidated Aeronautics** (no relation to Convair), which later moved operation to Tomball, TX, where 1,000th (by this time called LA-4-200 Buccaneer) completed January 1980. Repeated changes of management led to **Lake Amphibian Inc.** formed 1983 in New Hampshire, followed by **Lake Aircraft Inc.**, Kissimmee, Florida, 1987, production by 1991 beyond 1,340 with 6-seat LA-250 Renegade and paramilitary Seawolf now added.

Lakes (UK). Capt. E.W. Wakefield formed Lakes Flying Co. 1911 and, after operating Roe-built Waterbird from Windermere, designed and built Water Hen as passenger carrier, flown intensively

Laird LC-R200 Speedwing (pilot C. W. Holman), January 1929.

until 1916. Gnosspelius-designed monoplane (13 February 1912) also flown until 1916, 2 years after takeover by Northern Aircraft Co.

Lambach (Netherlands). Hugh Lambach built HL I 1935 at Delft, formed company at Voorburg and built HL II aerobatic biplane 1937.

Lambert (USA). Lambert Aircraft Corp. formed July 1934 at Robertson, Missouri, by J.P.W. Lambert of Lambert Engine and Machine Co. to take over failed Mono Aircraft, henceforth making both aircraft and engines and retaining Monocoupe as trademark and marketing name. Failed 1936, designer Mooney joining Culver to form Dart Aircraft.

Lampich (Hungary). Builder of light aircraft, post-1920.

Lamson (USA). Lamson Aircraft Co., 1954 successor to Central-Lamson, continued production of L.101 Air Tractor ag-biplane until late 1955.

Lancair: *See* ACT.

Lancashire (UK). Lancashire Aircraft Co. formed 1960 out of Samlesbury Engineering, taking over production of former Edgar Percival EP.9 as Lancashire Prospector at Squire's Gate, Blackpool, as well as Samlesbury, until 1963.

Landgraf (USA). Fred Landgraf designed H-1 helicopter and then H-2 also with side-by-side rigid rotors with tip ailerons. Formed Landgraf Helicopter Co. at LA September 1943, flew H-2 2 November 1944 but ceased operations 1950.

L&P: *See* London and Provincial.

Langhurst (USA). Louis F. Langhurst, Mississippi, produced 7/10-scale Ju 87B (19 July 1976), several hundred sets of plans sold.

Langley (USA). Samuel Pierpont Langley's man-carrying *Aerodrome* of 1903 was first aeroplane built under government contract.

Langley (USA). Langley Aviation Corp. formed 1941 at 50 Rockefeller Plaza, NY, to build 85c cabin monoplane of 1938 design. Only original product was Twin 2-4-90 light twin, of resin-bonded plywood to avoid wartime metal short-age, flown 1942. Ironically it was resin that became unobtainable.

Lanier (USA). Lanier Aircraft Corp. of New Jersey formed 31 March 1943 to develop Paraplane STOL single-seater with large wing incorporating unusual slots and flap/ailerons. Despite flying 6 models and 3 full-scale aircraft, work abandoned 1962.

Lanzius (USA). Lanzius Aircraft Co. of New York formed 1916 and in 1917 flew L I 2-seat 'variable-speed biplane' for Army Signal Corps. Developed into L II (1919), single-seat fighter (350-hp Packard) with wings having variable camber and incidence.

LAPAN (Indonesia). Lembaga Penerbangan dan Antariksa Nasional (national aeronautics and space institute) established 1963, starting in 1977 to build XT-400 8-seat STOL transport (2 × 250-hp Lycoming piston engines).

LAPG (UK). London Aircraft Production Group formed 1942 to build Halifax bomber, members being: London Passenger Transport Board (Chiswick and Aldenham), Chrysler, Duple Bodies, Express Motor & Body and Park Royal Coachworks, final assembly being at Leavesden.

LAPIP (Indonesia). Lembaga Persiapan Industri Penerbangan, became LIPNUR, which *see*.

Larivièrre (France). Built AL 06 2-seat twin-boom pusher 1947.

Larkin (Australia). Formed 1919 as Larkin-Sopwith Aviation Company of Australasia, opening Melbourne's first aerodrome and building a factory on it. In 1921 became Lasco (Larkin Aircraft Supply Co.), making parts and, from 1927, producing aircraft under licence including 32 Gipsy Moths and at least one D.H.50A. In 1930 produced Lasco Lascoter all-metal 5-passenger transport (240-hp Puma), followed by Lasconder 6-passenger (3 × 165-hp Mongoose), but company run down from 1932.

Laron (USA). Laron Aviation Technology, Portales, NM, builds British CFM Shadow, 'world's smallest real light aircraft'.

Larsen (USA). John Larsen Aircraft Corp. formed New York 1917, built light aircraft post-

Latécoère 300 Croix du Sud, *September 1932.*

war, and JL-6 (Junkers-Larsen) Americanized Junkers F13 transports for US Post Office, Navy and other customers.

Larson (USA). Larson Aero Development, Concord, CA, produced D-1 ag-aircraft (30 March 1955) and F-12 Baby biplane (1961).

LAS: *See* Lockheed.

LASC: *See* Lockheed.

Lasher (USA). Lasher Renegade I Formula racer flew 1974, plans marketed by Southern Aeronautical, Miami.

Latécoère (France). Pierre Latécoère established **Forges et Ateliers de Construction Latécoère** May 1917, factory at Toulouse-Montaudron and office in Paris. Made over 800 Salmson 2A2 while producing Laté 1 2-seat fighter, Laté 3 postal and Laté 4 10-passenger airliner. Among many other early designs only Latécoère 15 was built in series, 9 of these 6-passenger machines (2 × 260-hp Lorraine) being used by Laté airline on

Casablanca-Oran sector from 1925. First really successful design was Laté 17 5-passenger parasol monoplane (300-hp Renault), 24 built in various versions. Laté 21, 23, 32, 34 and 501 were airline flying-boats, with bad safety record, whereas production of Laté 25 (improved 17) reached 61, and no fewer than 90 made of Laté 26 mail version, and 62 of stretched 8-passenger Laté 28. In 1922 company renamed **Société Industrielle d'Aviation Latécoère**, and in 1936 nationalization lost part of Toulouse plant to SNCA du Midi. Laté 29.0 torpedo-bomber seaplanes led to series-produced Laté 298 of Second World War. Giant flying-boats included 30.0, 301 and 302, 380 series, 6-engined 521/522/523 series, 611 (prototype fought 1940 but survived to 1947) and 9 examples of enormous Latécoère 631. Company survived at Toulouse as design and manufacturing centre for airframe parts, missiles and spacecraft; currently lead contractor for Super Flipper (*see* Satic).

Latham (France). Jean Latham, cousin of famed pre-war Antoinette pilot, opened **Société Latham & Cie** 1917, building 24 Lévy 40 flying-boats.

Latham L.1 (force-landed), 1923.

Three-engined bomber flying-boat was completed as transport, 4 built 1919–20, when company became **Latham et Cie, Soc. Industrielle de Caudebec.** Ten HB.5 flying-boats (4 × 260-hp Salmson) were followed by Schneider racers, followed by succession of biplane flying-boats with tandem engines: 42, 43, 45 and 47. Explorer Amundsen vanished along with 47.2 on 18 June 1928, after which company amalgamated with SECM, later Amiot.

Laverda (Italy). Laverda SpA, Trento, was Aeromere taken over 1964 by Dr Laverda, continuing to make Super Falco.

Laville (USSR). André Laville emigrated from France 1928 to work in Soviet Union, starting with Richard in OPO-4 where he drew fighter similar to Nieuport-Delage on which he had previously worked. Formed BNK (bureau of new designs) 1930, producing DI-4 2-seat parasol-wing fighter early 1933. BNK closed, but Laville produced PS-89, also called ZIG-1, 14-seat airliner, flown spring 1935. Then became journalist.

Lavochkin (USSR). Syemyon Alekseyevich Lavochkin worked in numerous brigades and groups, making detailed study of *delta* plastic-impregnated birch laminates. Convinced such material of great strategic importance, in releasing aluminium, obtained permission to build *delta* fighter, forming OKB-301 with V.P. Gorbunov and M.I. Gudkov and producing I-22 (30 March 1940). About 100 built as LaGG-1. Frantic improvement led to LaGG-3, total by August 1942 6,528 plus about 90 prototypes and incomplete (some lost in snowdrifts!). Switch to M-82 (ASh-82) radial engine resulted in greatly improved LaG-5 (March 1942), leading to La-5 built in several versions (about 9,920). In turn led to outstanding La-7, -9 and -11 with increasing switch to metal airframe. First jet fighter La-150 (17 September 1946) led via other prototypes to production La-15 (500) and La-15UTI trainer (500), and La-176 (supersonic in dive 26 December 1948) to La-200 2-seat night fighters, culminating in giant Mach 1.88 La-250 interceptor (16 July 1956). Lavochkin died 9 June 1960, bureau closed.

Lawhorn (USA). Jerry Lawhorn, Anchorage, Alaska, produced LA-3 two-seat twin-engined amphibian (3 July 1957).

Lawson (USA). A.W. Lawson's Air Line Co. of Milwaukee built C-2 Passenger Carrier December 1919 (2 × Liberty), with up to 18 seats plus 2 pilots. Even larger L-4 (sleeping berths and shower!) damaged before take-off 1924 and never flew.

Lazarov (Bulgaria). Many DAR aircraft are equally regarded as products of designer Zvetan (Cwietan) Lazarow (Lazarov), notably DAR-10 family. Started own design group 1946, producing LAZ-7M 2-seater, -8 4-seater, -10H helicopter, -11 ambulance and -12 single-seat aerobatic. Bureau closed 1961.

Lazor (USA). John Lazor and Prof. Robert Rautenstrach built advanced light aircraft 1959.

Lear (USA). Lear Inc. established Santa Monica 1930, becoming giant of hi-tech electromechanical and electronic industry. William P. 'Bill' Lear opened Aircraft Engineering Division 15 September 1953 to produce Lodestar-derived Learstar executive transport (19 May 1954), rights for which assigned PacAero Engineering 1957.

Learavia (USA). Learavia Corp., Reno, Nevada, was Bill Lear's last parent firm before his death 14 May 1978. Futura, later called Lear Fan, assigned to Lear Fan Corp. at Reno, for manufacture by Lear Fan Ltd.

Lear Fan (USA). Lear Fan Ltd formed 1980 to build (redesigned and renamed) Lear Fan 2100 twin-engine prop-behind-tail business aircraft. Parent firm Fan Holdings Inc. of Delaware, factory Aldergrove, Belfast Airport, UK. Production transferred to parent at Reno, Nevada, 1983, company in liquidation 1985.

Lear Jet (USA). **Lear Jet Corp.** formed Wichita, Kansas, 1962 by transfer of project from SAAC. Majority holding bought 1967 by Gates Rubber, company becoming **Gates Learjet.** This transferred operations to Tucson.

Learjet (USA). Majority holding in Gates Learjet bought by Integrated Acquisition Inc. September 1987, company renamed **Learjet Inc.** (Learjet one word) and returned to Wichita. On 22 June 1990 acquisition of Learjet by Bombardier of Canada completed, as wholly-owned subsidiary. Company continues as major airframe subcontractor to most large US aerospace constructors.

Model 45 launched 1992 with wing from DH Inc and body/tail from Shorts.

Leaven (Canada). Leaven Brothers built small number of Fleet Canuck 2-seaters 1965–6.

Lebed' (Russia). Vladimir Aleksandrovich Lebedev (commonly shortened to Lebed') was pioneer pilot, setting up aircraft factory at St Petersburg 1912. During war opened additional factories at Taganrog and Penze. In 1912–17 produced Lebed' VII (first original design, though copy of Tabloid), followed by VIII–XXIV, most being 2-seat recon biplanes often known by name Albatros plus engine type (Mercedes, Salmson, Sunbeam, etc.); XI, XII and XVII were made in greatest numbers, stopped by Revolution.

Lebouder (France). Robert Lebouder produced Autoplane, comprising side-by-side high-wing aircraft whose wing, rear fuselage and tail are removable, remainder converting into roadable car, 1973.

Le Bris (France). Sea captain J.M. Le Bris built full-scale gliders 1857 and 1868, and sought engine; broke leg in No. 2 in 1868.

Lederlin (France). Francois Lederlin built Pou-style tandem-wing 2-seater 1965.

Leduc (France). René Leduc devoted life to high-speed aircraft whose fuselage formed integral ramjet. Bench-tested ramjets at Argenteuil from 1929, starting construction of O.10 aircraft 1935 and flying it as glider October 1947 and under power 21 April 1949, in each case air-launched. O.16 added self-launch turbojets (8 February 1951), O.21 reached Mach 0.87 and over 65,000 ft (16 May 1953) and O.22 incorporated Atar turbojet and was planned as basis of fighter (26 December 1956), but funding was terminated.

Lee-Richards (UK). Cedric Lee and George Tilghman Richards built series of annular (circular)-winged biplanes and monoplanes 1911–14.

Lefebvre (France). Robert Lefebvre built MP.205 Busard formula-type racer (MP from Max Plan who provided original concept), flown 1971, plans marketed.

Leg-Air (USA). Garry LeGare's Leg-Air Corporation, Medford, Oregon (previously Aero Gare and related to Leg-Air of Canada), has marketed several hundred kits of Sea Hawker all-composites 2/4-seat amphibious biplane.

Legers (France). SA des Legers Bourgois produced AT.35 2-seat parasol monoplane 1928, and BT 3-seat low-wing monoplane 1930.

Legrand-Simon (France). Paul Legrand of SNECMA, helped by M. Simon of Breguet, built LS.50 side-by-side high-wing monoplane (13 January 1957), developed into LS.60 (27 April 1961).

Leichtflugtechnik: *See* LFU.

Leichtflugzeuge Entwicklung: *See* Mylius.

Leighnir (USA). William C. Leighnir built light aircraft 1958.

Leins (USA). Ballard Leins built Bal-Aire sport biplane (8 July 1960).

Leisure Sport (UK). Member of Ready-Mix Concrete group, Thorpe Park, Surrey, produce replicas of First World War fighters and other historic aircraft.

Lemaire (France). Built ARL.11 (January 1959) and ARL.20 light aircraft.

Le Mars (USA). Le Mars Manufacturing Co., Le Mars, Iowa, took over Skyfarer from Grand Rapids 1944.

Lembaga: *See* LAPAN; LAPIP; LIPNUR.

Lemberger (W. Germany). Karl Lemberger built sport aircraft 1972.

Lenart (USA). Lenart Aircraft Co., Dowagiac, Michigan, produced 2/3-seat biplanes, including wartime conversions, and PT-2 Zephyr monoplane, 1919–33.

Leningradets (USSR). Name of light aircraft produced at Leningrad (St Petersburg) 1962 by Sekinin, Tatsiturnov and Kostin.

Leningradskii: *See* NIAI.

Lenin Komsomol: *See* RIIGA.

Let L-200D Morava, May 1962.

LeO: *See* Lioré et Olivier.

Leopoldorff (France). MM. Leopoldorff and Levasseur built L.7 Colibri 2-seat biplane 1933, produced with various engines until 1949.

Lepère: *See* Engineering Division.

Lerho (USA). Lerho Laboratories produced light aircraft 1962–3.

Lesher (USA). Edgar J. Lesher produced light aircraft 1963–8.

Let (Czechoslovakia). Design office and factory 'Let' established Kunovice 1950, taking over programmes of Ceskoslovenske Zavody Auto-mobilove A Letecke, initially to produce C-11 (Yak-11), and later L-40 Meta-Sokol, M1 Sokol, M2 Skaut, Super Aero and Aero 145. Produced from scratch Z-37 Cmelák/Sparka ag-aircraft (29

March 1963), L-200 Morava light twin (8 April 1957), L-410 Turbolet airliner (16 April 1969, 1,222 delivered) and L-610 airliner (28 December 1988, certificated 1992). Original title Letecky Narodny Podnik, today Let Koncernovy Podnik, Bohemia-Moravia (Czech republic).

Letalski (Jugoslavia). Formed 1947 at Ljubljana as Letalski Konstrokcijski Biro at Higher Techni-cal School. Several prototypes and sailplanes plus KB-6 Matajur tourer/trainer. Merged 1960 with Institut 'Branko Ivanus' to form Letalski Institut 'Branko Ivanus' Slovenija, continuing production of KB-11 Branko, LK-1 and sailplanes and adding Czech L-200D made under licence.

Letord (France). Etablissements Letord founded 1908 at Chalais-Meudon to produce balloons and dirigibles. Expanded 1916 with second factory at Lyon-Villeurbanne, building aeroplanes de-signed by Col. Dorand (which *see*) of Service

Letord Let. 4 No. 5, March 1917.

Letov S-8 racer (Napier Lion), May 1924.

Technique de l'Aéronautique. Letord 1, 2, 3 and 4 were twin-engined backstaggered recon/bomber/fighter types, Letord 5 being sesquiplane, and 7 and 9 were large biplane bombers. Built 2 or 3 prototype or research aircraft 1919–23.

Letov (Czechoslovakia). Previously part of Austria-Hungary, Czechoslovakia started aircraft industry by forming Military Air Arsenal, also called Central Aircraft Works, Prague-Letnany, 1919, appointing Alois Smŏlik designer. Became **Vojenská továrna na letadla Letov** 1920. Types S 1–S 31 almost all single-engined military biplanes, but later (post-1930) included light aircraft and trimotor transports. Final product, S 328 2-seat biplane, flew 1932 but remained in production in Second World War (525 +).

Levasseur (France). Pierre Levasseur set up company known only by his name in Paris 1910, building propellers and, in 1913, aircraft designed

by others. First of his own designs was PL I 2-seat biplane, followed by PL 2 torpedo-bomber made in small series. Almost all Levasseur products (PL 3–15, with variations) were powerful single-engined biplanes for French Navy (PL 6 fighter was Army). On failure of Lévy, LB 2AM was produced by Levasseur. Final design was PL 400 STOL observation monoplane (December 1939).

Levi (UK). Renato Levi produced PL.3 Monsoon 2-seat monoplane 1960 (plans from Western Aircraft, Calgary, Canada) and PL.6 ultralight biplane 1974.

LeVier (USA). Lockheed chief test pilot Tony LeVier formed LeVier and Associates 1946 to build Formula racer, result being Cosmic Wind, 5 built.

Lévy (France). Constructions Aéronautiques J. Lévy was set up 1914 by financier Léon-

Levasseur PL 101.R3b, No. 60, December 1934.

LFG Roland G.I (1 × Mb IV), December 1916.

Georges Lévy mainly to build warplanes designed by others. First products were Lévy-Besson flying-boats and bombers, followed by Lévy-Lepen HB2 flying-boats. Company's own Lévy GL.40 flying-boat (November 1917) was very successful, 100 delivered. Trickle of Lévy-Biche designs ended with LB 2 shipboard fighter (1927), built in series by Levasseur after Lévy closed down.

Lewis (USA). Lewis Aircraft Corp. formed to market light aircraft 1981.

Lewis & Vought: *See* Vought.

Leyat-Jacquemin (France). Marcel Leyat and André Jacquemin produced several prototypes early 1930s, all with left/right wings with independent variable incidence. First, February 1933, resembled simple powered glider with 30-hp ABC Scorpion on nose, single seat and tandem wheels. Second was advanced high-wing machine with 35-hp Poinsard (6 November 1934).

LFG (Germany). First aviation construction company in Germany was **Motorluftschiff Studiengesellschaft**, Berlin, 1906, which later built Parseval airships at Bitterfeld. In 1909 formed **Flugmaschine Wright GmbH**, building Wright biplanes at Adlershof. This ceased trading 1912, whereupon financiers (notably Krupp) took over premises to found **Luftfahrzeug Gesellschaft**, or LFG. Confusion with nearby LVG resulted in company adopting Roland as tradename, title becoming **LFG Roland**. Initially built Albatros B and C types at Berlin-Charlottenberg, but Dipl.-Ing. Tantzen designed Roland C.II

(October 1915) with higher performance, about 320 built including 50 by Linke-Hofmann. Then followed D.I–D.XVII single-seaters, D.II and IIa being most important. Stralsund seaplane works produced various prototypes including V19 observation floatplane able to fold into hangar on U-boat. Post-war, Stralsund built or converted series of passenger seaplanes, named *Max* and *Moritz* (biplanes) and *Helene* and *Susanne* (monoplanes). Subsequently built handful of new-design V13 *Strela* biplane seaplane, V130 landplane version, V20 *Arkona* 4-passenger monoplane seaplane and V101 *Jasmund* metal version. Last-named used by Luft Hansa, others by LFG airline until liquidation 1928.

LFU (W. Germany). Leichtflugtechnik-Union GmbH formed 1963 by Bölkow (MBB), Pützer and RFB, one-third each. Produced LFU-205 4-seater (20 March 1968).

LIBIS (Jugoslavia). Initials from Letalski Institut 'Branko Ivanus' Slovenija: *see* Letalski.

Lignel (France). Produced light aircraft 1946–9, notably L.44 Cross-Country tandem-wing 2-seater 1947.

LiM (Poland). Licence-MiG designation of MiG-15 and -17 versions produced at Mielec.

Lincoln (USA). Ray Page formed **Nebraska Aircraft Corp.** at Lincoln 1922 to build 5-seat Air Coach. In 1923 added 3-seat Lincoln-Standard Tourabout. Acquired rights to New Swallow 1926 and January 1927 formed **Lincoln-Page Aircraft**, redesigning New Swallow into 3-seat

Lincoln-Page LP-3 (OX-5), January 1929.

LP-3. Lincoln-Page Trainer 1929, company then renamed **Lincoln Aircraft Co.**, building Playboy parasol monoplane 1931.

Ling-Temco-Vought: *See* LTV; Vought.

Linke-Hofmann (Germany). Made railway rolling stock at Hundsfeld, Breslau. In early 1916 began repairing and then building under licence Albatros and LFG Roland aircraft. Hired designer Paul Stumpf from AEG and produced R.I giant bomber with 4×260-hp Mercedes in incredibly deep fuselage driving propellers on wing struts (21 January 1917). Second R.I built alongside amazing R.II, colossal aircraft but with just 2 wheels, open cockpit amidships and 4 engines driving single propeller on nose! Span over 138 ft, propeller diameter 23 ft. Planned post-war passenger version not built.

Linke-Hofmann R.II (4 engines), January 1919.

Linn (USA). Charles C. Linn built L-1 Mini Mustang (14 January 1962).

Lioré et Olivier (France). LeO founded by Fernand Lioré and Henri Olivier as agricultural and general engineers at Levallois-Perret (Paris) 1906, building first aircraft 1908. Lioré helped form Witzig-Lioré-Dutheuil aero engineers 1911, but formed **Les Ateliers d'Aviation Lioré et Olivier** 6 March 1912. Built designs by 15 early aviators. From 1914 built over 2,000 Morane-Saulnier monoplanes and nearly 3,000 Sopwith $1\frac{1}{2}$-strutters. First major original design was LeO 4 recon biplane (September 1916), followed by post-war twin-engined 5, 3-engined 6 flying-boat and amphibian and 7 twin-engined bomber, 7/2 and 7/3 going into production. Four LeO 12s, one a passenger airliner, led to LeO 20, classic night bomber (February 1927), 311 delivered to

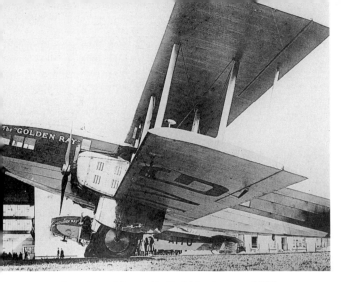

Lioré et Olivier LeO 213, August 1928.

Armée de l'Air plus 9 exported. Derived types were 21 18-passenger airliner, 21S ambulance for 10 stretchers and 214 trainer for 14 paratroops. Minor types included LeO 8 parasol monoplane night fighter (April 1923), LeO 9 low-wing fighter, H.180/193/194/197/198 single-engined flying-boats and amphibians and handful of licensed Ciervas. In 1930s LeO developed various single-engine biplanes, LeO 203/204/206 heavy bombers (4 × 350-hp in tandem pairs), LeO 300 giant bomber, various Cierva (Lepère-designed) autogyros, and tremendous variety of marine aircraft with prefix H, notably H.252–259 seaplanes derived from LeO 20, H.24 and 24-2 passenger flying-boats, H.43 shipboard observation seaplane, and H.47 and H.246 large 4-engined boats, designed for Air France but converted into ocean patrol bombers. Nationalization law transferred Argenteuil factory to SNCASE and Rochefort seaplane works to SNCASO. By far most important LeO was 45 twin-engined bomber (16 January 1937), outstanding aircraft, 1,783 ordered from SNCASE Clichy and Levallois plants, 452 delivered by collapse; Vichy government resumed production at SNCASE Ambérieu from April 1942, many LeO 451 used against Allies.

LIPNUR (Indonesia). National aircraft industry, run by department of air force, originally Departamen Angkatan Udara Republik Indonesia, Lembaga Persiapan Industri Penerbangan (dept of air force institute for development of national aero industry). Founded 1961, renamed after Air Marshal Nurtanio Pringgoadisurjo (died in crash 1966), institute renamed 1967, new name **Lembaga Industri Penerbangan Nurtanio**, or LIPNUR.

Lippisch (Germany). Never had his own company but masterminded many important aircraft at DFS, Messerschmitt (1942 patent for pivoted 'swing wings') and, post-war, Collins Radio. Aircraft designated for him included Lippisch DM-1 delta glider developed at Akaflieg Darmstadt and Akaflieg Munich 1944, Storch I–V and Delta I–IVb, LP 13a delta ramjet and various unbuilt projects.

Lisichkin (USSR). Brigade leader at NIAI, responsible for LK-1, also designated NIAI-1 (May 1933), 20 built.

Lisunov (USSR). Boris Pavlovich Lisunov masterminded Douglas licence for DC-3 and conversion into PS-84, later called Li-2 in recognition of his considerable redesign.

Lithuanian army: *See* Karo.

Liuchow (China). Liuchow Mechanical and Aircraft Factory, Kwangsi province, flew single examples 1937 of Type 2 biplane trainer and Type 3 derived fighter.

Livesey (UK). David M. Livesey built D.L.5 ultralight 1978.

LKB: *See* Letalski.

Lloyd (Austria-Hungary). Formed 1912 Budapest by Oblt Bier as branch of DFW, building DFW types under licence; titles (Hungarian) Magyar 'Lloyd' Repülögép es Motogyár, and (Austrian) Ungarische Flugzeug und Motorenfabrik 'Lloyd'. In 1913 built own-design C.I biplane (Bier set record 20,243 ft with 2 passengers). Subsequently built Hansa-Brandenburg C-types, while designers Wizina and von Melczer produced C.II and III recon biplanes, several hundred built, and C.IV and V (all 1914–16). In 1917 same designers produced prototypes of 40.15 fighter triplane and 40.16 fighter biplane, both with 185-hp MAG (Daimler).

LMSC: *See* Lockheed Missiles and Space Co.

LMZ (Russia). Luhovitskii Mashinostroitelnii Zavod, Moscow 101000, was major manufacturer in MiG-29 programme, now partner in Phönix-Aviatechnica.

Lobanov (Russia). Nikolai Rodionovich Lobanov

Magyar Lloyd (Ungarische Lloyd) C.I, June 1913.

was one of several students at Moscow Technical School who built early aircraft. Basically Farman type, but different undercarriage, control column pivoted down from upper wing and structure mainly steel tube. Four-blade propeller on 50-hp Gnome. About 100 flights in 1912.

Lobil (USA). Lobil Aircraft Co. did not finish prototype of 2-seat fighter monoplane 1938.

Lock Haven (USA). Arnold H. Andresen (ex-Piper) and William T. Piper Jr. took over former Piper plant as **Lock Haven Re-man Center** spring 1985 to refurbish various Piper singles and twins. In 1992 called **Lock Haven Airplane Co.**

Lockheed (USA). Allan Haines Loughead (pro-

nounced Lockheed) tore around Alma, south of San José, in homebuilt racing car at age 15 in 1904. In same year he studied a glider flown by Prof. James Montgomery of University of Santa Clara and became hooked on aviation. In 1910 found his half-brother Victor had 2 best-selling books in Chicago, *Aeroplane Designing* and *Vehicles of the Air*. Allan worked his way via motor race meetings to Chicago where he became mechanic to aviator Jim Plew and, when Plew failed to get airborne in deep snow, flew his Curtiss pusher without instruction! Returned to San Francisco, persuaded full brother Malcolm to join him, and built 3-seat seaplane, called Model G to hide fact it was their first effort. Very successful first flight 15 June 1913, and at Panama-Pacific Exposition in San Francisco 1915

Lockheed (Aircraft Co.), Model 3 Air Express, October 1928.

this seaplane carried 600 passengers and earned $4,000. This was more than double their borrowings from friends, with whom they formed **Alco Hydro-Aeroplane Co**. Accordingly this was liquidated and **Loughhead Aircraft Manufacturing Co.** incorporated March 1916 at Santa Barbara, to build large F-1 flying-boat (2 × 160-hp Hall-Scott) to carry 3,100-lb payload. Task of laying out hull and stressing wings given to young mechanic John K. Northrop. F-1 was again great success (28 March 1918), often carried 12 passengers, but war was almost over and Navy cancelled planned major order after contract for 2 Curtiss HS-2L. Post-war slump meant no customer for beautiful S-1 sport biplane, and firm suspended operations 1921. Malcolm devised superior hydraulic brake, from which sprang Lockheed Hydraulics, Bendix, Automotive Products and other giants. To help people get pronunciation right Allan had changed name to Lockheed 1918, and in December 1926 he opened **Lockheed Aircraft Co.** in small workshop at corner of Sycamore and Romaine in Hollywood, enticing Northrop back from Douglas. First result was beautifully streamlined Vega, flown 4 July 1927 from hayfield which became LA International. Hired test pilot Eddie Bellande said, 'You'll sell this airplane like hotcakes'; Lockheed built large new factory at Burbank and delivered 144 Vegas, setting 34 world records. In July 1929 Lockheed was one of 11 companies gathered into Detroit Aircraft by fast-buck financiers. At first Lockheed prospered, with Air Express, Sirius and Orion (6 passengers carried at over 200 mph). But Detroit prohibited

any investment or research, and, with obsolescing aircraft, company failed April 1932. Offered for $42,456, company was bought for $40,000 by Robert E. Gross, Harvard man who had formed Viking and helped Stearman. Company was continued unaltered, Gross chairman and treasurer, Carl B. Squier (who had been Detroit's man appointed to run previous company) as v-p sales and Cyril Chappellet treasurer. Gross hired young MIT engineer, Hall L. Hibbard, to help Stearman decide what to build, with Richard von Hake assistant designer. Rejecting a planned 'metal Orion', they built twin-engined Model 10 Electra (23 February 1934), a vital winner. Tunnel-testing was assigned to University of Michigan, where young Clarence L. 'Kelly' Johnson suggested a modified tail; he joined Lockheed and played increasingly crucial design role. Electra led to high-speed Models 12, 14 and 18, the 14 being turned almost overnight into Hudson for British Air Ministry (2,941) and various US Army versions, and 18 led to Ventura/PBO/Harpoon (3,028 all built at **Vega Airplane**, wholly-owned subsidiary which also built 2,750 B-17s). Extraordinary XP-38 interceptor (27 January 1939) led to P-38 Lightning (10,037 including 113 by Consolidated-Vultee and F-5 photo versions). XC-69 Constellation (9 January 1943) led to numerous civil and military Constellation and Super Constellation versions (856). XP-80 Shooting Star jet fighter (8 January 1944) led to 1,732 F-80 fighters, 851 F-94 night interceptors and 6,557 T-33 trainers (including 656 Canadair Silver Stars and 210 by

Lockheed (Aircraft Corp.), XF-90, 6 June 1949.

Kawasaki). P2V (later P-2) Neptune (17 May 1945) led to 1,181 of many versions. YC-130 Hercules (flown at Burbank 23 August 1954) led to production line at vast **Lockheed-Georgia** plant at Marietta which had previously built 294 B-47; non-stop production has delivered 2,080 as this book goes to press. Lockheed-Georgia also built 285 C-141 StarLifters and 81 C-5A and 50 C-5B Galaxies. L-188 Electra turboprop airliner (6 December 1957) led to 170, plus derived P-3 Orion maritime/ASW aircraft (659 at time of writing, with production being transferred to Marietta). XF-104 Starfighter (4 March 1954) led to 296 early versions for USAF plus 2,282 F-104G variants built in multinational programmes. U-2 (1 August 1955), first of 'Kelly' Johnson's 'black' programmes at secure Skunk Works, led to 104 amazing U-2 and TR-1 aircraft built in 3 groups 1955–89. JetStar (4 September 1957) ran to 204 examples. Numerous light-planes, helicopters and research aircraft did not support production, and L-1011 TriStar (17 November 1970) stopped at 247. A second giant secure programme at Skunk Works produced A-12 (26 April 1962), 12 research aircraft able to cruise at over Mach 3 at over 80,000 ft, followed by 4 YF-12 interceptors and 32 SR-71 recon aircraft. Burbank (**Lockheed-California**) built 187 S-3 Viking ASW aircraft 1972–8. Q-Star and derivatives were built by **Lockheed Missiles and Space**. Total restructure 1977 resulted in parent being renamed **Lockheed Corp.**, HQ moving from Burbank to Calabasas. Four giant groups formed, one being **Lockheed Aeronautical Systems Group** (LASG) at Marietta, to where P-3 line is being transferred. Latest known giant Skunk Works (now called **Lockheed Advanced Development Co.**, LADC) programme was Have Blue research into 'stealth', resulting in XST (December 1977) and production F-117A (18 June 1981), 59 built by July 1990. Even bigger programme led to YF-22 (29 September 1990) Advanced Tactical Fighter, announced as winner (with Pratt & Whitney F119 engine) 23 April 1991. Requirement for 2 YF-22, 11 F-22 proto-types and 648 F-22A Superstars to be assembled by LASG. LASG is member of A-X consortium with Boeing and GD (whose Fort Worth division Lockheed purchased in March 1993). LADC rumoured to have developed secret Aurora strategic recon aircraft. LAC (Lockheed Aeromod Center), Tucson, teamed with Swiss AVTEC on L-1011 rebuilds.

Lockheed Aircraft Service (USA). Since 1960 claimed to be largest independent aircraft modification and maintenance unit in world, at Ontario, California. Produced early digital flight recorders, cargo-converted almost every type of US transport, today major programmes concern C-130, P-3 and L-1011, LAS operating as division of Lockheed Technology Services Group. Opened major new facilities in California, Arizona, S. Carolina and Malaysia.

Lockheed-Azcarate SA (Mexico). LASA formed 1957 to produce LASA-60 (AL-60) utility aircraft, abandoned 1960.

Lockheed Brothers: *See* Alhambra; Alcor; Vega.

Lockheed-California (USA). Main operating arm of Lockheed Aircraft, based at Burbank, from June 1961. Later called Calac, eliminated in restructuring 1977.

Lockheed-Georgia (USA). Second of 3 Lockheed aircraft/space operating companies from June 1961, at Marietta. Later called Gelac, eliminated in restructuring 1977, but today LASG.

Lockheed-Kaiser (Argentina). Formed 1958 by Lockheed and Industrias Kaiser SA at Cordoba to build LASA-60 utility transport, abandoned 1962.

Lockheed Missiles and Space Co. (USA). Third Lockheed aerospace operating company from June 1961, LMSC proposed quiet surveillance aircraft and developed QT-2, Q-Star and YO-3A, 13 of latter being used in Vietnam 1970–72.

Lockspeiser (UK). Former test pilot David Lockspeiser spent 1965–85 working on LDA (Land Development Aircraft), tandem-wing utility aircraft with military potential; 70% scaled prototype flown August 1971.

Loehle (USA). Loehle Enterprises market kits for $\frac{3}{4}$-scale Mustang (200 + sold) and P-40.

Loening (USA). Grover C. Loening graduated from Columbia 1911, building monoplane flying-boat same year. Worked with Orville Wright and in US Army Signal Corps, then (1915) president of Sturtevant Aeroplane Co. Formed Loening Aeronautical Engineering Corp. December 1917. First product M-8 2-seat monoplane fighter with

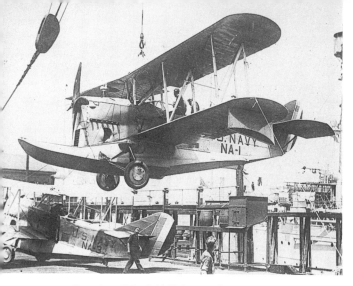

Loening OL-2 (440-hp Packard), December 1924.

many advanced features; such high performance Army ordered 5,000, but cancelled at Armistice. Despite biplane prejudice Navy bought 10 M-8-0 followed by 36 M-8-1 and 6 M-8-1S seaplanes. Small numbers followed of PW-2 single-seater for Army, and 2 PA-1s (first US fighters with radial engine), developed by Grumman, Swirbul and Schwendler (*see* Grumman). OL 2-seat observation biplane amphibian (1923) was classic design which led to 165 additional aircraft for Army and Navy, continued with agreement by Grumman J2F Duck family. Same formula led to civil Wasp (1927) and Air Yacht (1928). Merged with Keystone 1928, producing improved and upgraded Air Yachts to 1931. *See also* Grover Loening.

Lohner (Austria-Hungary). Jacob Lohner Werke und Sohn, Porzellangasse, Vienna, built 2-seat unarmed reconnaissance biplane 1913, basis for over 1,000 B series and armed C.I until 1917. In production 1918, AA single-seat scout and AB 2-seat (C class), both with 185-hp Austro-Daimler. Most important Lohner products were flying-boats with single pusher engine. About 40 E (85-hp Hiero, 1913) were followed by 160 + Lohner L (140- or 180-hp Hiero or Austro-Daimler), observer with gun on right of pilot. An L captured by Italy May 1915 gave rise to Macchi flying-boats. M was L built by Pola dockyard, R was recon variant (36), S were trainers (200). Post-war, many used for joyriding and mail transport in Switzerland, Ukraine and other countries.

Loire (France). Les Ateliers et Chantiers de la Loire, shipbuilders of St Nazaire, purchased Gourdou et Leseurre 1925, continuing production and development of latter's Type 32 fighter, now called LGL 32. LGL 33 and 34 had various different engines. L 2 shipboard seaplane (420-hp Jupiter) was followed by Loire 11 3-seat Type Colonial (1930) and Type 30 night recon monoplane (3 × 230-hp Salmson, 1932). Loire 43 fighter with high gull wing (17 October 1932) led via 45 to Loire 46 (1 September 1934) of which 60 for Armée de l'Air 1936–7 (5 clandestine to Republican Spain). Type 50 3-seat flying-boat (1931) led to 6 501 for Aéronavale. Type 60 and much bigger 70 flying-boats all had 1 pusher and 2 tractor engines, while 102 had 2 push/pull pairs and 130 (150 built) 1 pusher. Type 210 fighter seaplane (20 delivered 1939, 6 years after requirement) and 250 fighter landplane both first flew 1935. Gourdou et Leseurre was separated 1929, Loire opening new design office and test centre at La Baule-Escoublac. In 1933 Nieuport-Astra left SGA group and joined Loire, whose St Nazaire factory made profit from building Dewoitine 500/501/510 and Bloch 200. In 1936 nationalized

Lohner C.I, October 1915, in post-war Czech service.

Loire 102 Bretagne, *12 May 1936.*

into SNCAO, while designing Loire-Nieuport 161 fighter and 40 series dive-bomber (June 1938). Latter led to 40 LN.401 for Aéronavale and 40 LN.411 for Armée de l'Air; almost all shot down May 1940, but about 100 built by SNCASO (into which SNCAO merged 1941) at Issy les Moulineaux 1941–2. St Nazaire made major contribution to He 111 programme and also produced Ar 196A-3.

Lombarda (Italy). In 1931 Bonomi was retitled Lombarda (Aeronautica) SA, building light aircraft and gliders, but from December 1935 making contribution to military programmes.

Lombardi (Italy). AVIA (Azionari) was absorbed by Francis Lombardi late 1947, continuing production of F.L.3 and adding small numbers of L.M.5 Aviastar and 3/4-seat L.M.7. Ceased trading late 1949, assets acquired by Meteor 1953.

Lomonosov (Russia). M.V. Lomonosov produced first documented evidence of powered aerodyne 1 July 1754 with Russian Academy of Science report of spring-driven model helicopter.

London: *See* LAPG.

London and Provincial (UK). London and Provincial Aviation Co. formed October 1913, office in Edgware and flying school at nearby Hendon where built Caudron G.III trainer under licence. A.A. Fletcher joined from Martinsyde 1916 and designed Type No. 4 trainer (50-hp Gnome) and School Biplane (80-, then 100-hp Anzani), of which 12 + built 1916–17, excellent aircraft, 5 on post-war civil register.

Lonek (Czechoslovakia). Engineer J. Lonek designed Bata monoplane, formed company at Ostrokovice and built L.8 3-seat cabin monoplane (60-hp Walter radial) 1934.

Long (USA). J.C. Long built light aircraft 1965.

Longren (USA). Little-known, had one of longest careers in US industry, Longren Aircraft Inc. registered Topeka, Kansas, 1920. Sport biplane (1921) had vulcanized moulded-fibre fuselage and folding wings. Three experimental aircraft for US Navy (1923) had fuselages with parts stamped from compressed fibre sheets. Firm liquidated 1924, resurrected 1933 to build monocoque metal fuselage made in same way, 1 ordered by US Army. Liquidated a second time 1959.

Loose (USA). Chet Loose produced 9 racers 1930–47. All high- or shoulder-wing monoplanes; no designations known.

LoPresti (USA). LeRoy P. LoPresti formed LoPresti Piper Aircraft Engineering Co. at Vero Beach as Piper subsidiary but developing updated versions of Globe/Temco Swift: Swiftfire (Allison 250 turboprop) flew July 1988; LP-1 SwiftFury flew March 1989; SwiftThunder with nosewheel delayed by search for more capital.

Loring (Spain). Dr Jorge Loring, controlling shareholder of Compañia Española de Tráfico Aereo, founded company bearing his name in Madrid 1922, using army airfield at Cuatro Vientos. Built 20 Fokker C.IV under licence, but designer D. Eduardo Barrón produced original designs of single-engined biplane: R.1 recon (30), R.2 recon-bomber, R.3 recon-bomber (86), T.1

and T.2 trainers and C.1 fighter. Also built early Cierva autogyros under licence.

Lorraine-Hanriot (France). Original Aéroplanes Hanriot et Cie was replaced on death of René Hanriot 1930 by Lorraine-Hanriot, division of SGA (Société Générale Aéronautique). When SGA broke up 1933 son Marcel Hanriot formed new Compagnie des Avions Hanriot.

Loughead: *See* Lockheed.

Louis-Clément (France). Sole public appearance was at December 1919 Paris Salon: gull-wing monoplane racer and even more curious baby triplane with nose propeller driven by Anzani engine near tail.

Lovaux: *See* FLS.

Loving (USA). Neal V. Loving produced WR-1 Love single-seat racer built by Wayne Aircraft (7 August 1950), and Loving-Wayne WR-2 side-by-side pusher monoplane 1961.

Lowe (UK). Amateur F. Harold Lowe built HL(M).9 Marlburian monoplane (60-hp Gnome) at Newcastle upon Tyne early 1921.

Lowe-Wylde (UK). Built series of Planettes at Hanworth (1932), BAC VII gliders with 600-cc Douglas or Coventry Victor engines.

LTG: *See* Luft Torpedo GmbH.

LTV (USA). Chance Vought Corp. merged with Ling-Temco Electronics 31 August 1961 to form **Ling-Temco-Vought Inc.**, continuing aircraft operations at Dallas as Chance Vought, subsidiary of LTV, passing through series of reorganizations to become **Vought Corp.** 1976, **LTV Aircraft Products Group** 1986 and **LTV Aerospace and Defense Co.** 1990. Carried through entire VAX programme resulting in A-7 (27 September 1965), 1,545 built by 1983, and up-grade/modification programmes continue. Builds about one-third of B-2, aft fuselage/tail of 747, tailplane of 767, tail of 757, nacelles and tail of C-17 and nacelles of Challenger and RJ; still major programmes on T-38/F-5, completion of BAe C-29A, teaming on Panther and Pampa 2000. Renamed **Vought**, which *see.*

Lualdi-Tassotti (Italy). Two engineers produced

single-seat helicopter with 85-hp Continental (7 March 1954). By this time Lualdi had formed company, *see* next.

Lualdi (Italy). Aer Lualdi & C SpA formed Rome 1953, flying ES 53 helicopter with Hiller Rotor-Matic system plus Lualdi gyro system September 1953. Subsequently flew L.55, L.57 and L.59 (made by Macchi), each larger and more powerful than predecessor.

Lübeck-Travemünde (Germany). Flugzeugwerft Lübeck-Travemünde GmbH established at Travemünde Privall May 1914 to specialize in twin-float seaplanes. Originally related to Brandenberg, later bought by Carl Caspar, independent in brief post-war existence. F.1 (3), F.2 (11) and F.4 (34) were only production types; built one civil F.4 1919 for United Canning of Bergen.

Lubelska: *See* LWS.

Lublin: *See* Plage & Laskiewicz.

Lucas (France). Emile Lucas markets plans for L5 (13 August 1976) and quite different L6, L7 and twin-engined L10.

Luftfahrtzeug: *See* LFG.

Luft Torpedo GmbH (Germany). Luft Torpedo Gesellschaft (LTG) established Berlin-Johan-nisthal March 1915 mainly to develop aerial torpedo, but took on aeroplane subcontract, and 8 February 1917 received contract for 3 proto-types of fighter seaplane, FD 1; 6 seaplanes built (5 delivered) plus 1 landplane.

Luft-Verkehrs Gesellschaft: *See* LVG.

Lunds Tekniske (Norway). Arne Lund's company built Silhouette motor glider (3 July 1984), about 50 built to date with choice of span and engine.

LUSAC: *See* Engineering Division.

Luscombe (UK). Luscombe Aircraft Ltd, Lympne (Ashford) airport, produced various canard ultralights 1971–85.

Luscombe (USA). Don A. Luscombe designed Monocoupe (*see* Central States; Mono) before resigning as president of Mono 1933 and setting up **Luscombe Aircraft Engineering Co.** at Kansas City. Ivan Driggs designed Phantom, based on Monocoupe D-145 but all-metal (probably first stressed-skin lightplane), 125 built. Luscombe 4 (Model 90) 4-seater of 1934 led to Model 8a of 1938 (1,100) and generally similar 2-seat Silvaire, production of which was interrupted by war but reached 6,000 by 1961. A few low-powered Skybabies and post-war 4-seat Model 11A Sedans were built. Post-war company renamed **Luscombe Airplane Corp.**, Dallas, but failed 1949, assets being purchased by Temco which continued production under old name until in 1955 rights were sold to Silvaire Aircraft Co.

Luton (UK). Luton Aircraft Ltd's designer, C.H. Latimer-Needham, produced 1 Buzzard pusher ultralight 1936, 1 Minor parasol single-seater 1936 (followed by 3 modified built by Luton after move from Barton-in-the-Clay to Gerrards Cross and 10 modified homebuilts) and 1 2-seat Major (3 built elsewhere). Tandem-wing LA.2 not flown.

LVG (Germany). Luft-Verkehrs GmbH established December 1911 at Berlin-Johannisthal, operating and then constructing dirigibles and (early 1912) building Farmans under licence. First original design B.I 2-seat recon biplane (December 1912), classic design and prototype of virtually all subsequent B-series by all makers. Improved B.II made by LVG, Otto-Werke and Schütte-Lanz. Final variant B.III was strengthened for training. Armed recon C-series launched by LVG C.I (1915), modified into C.II (first aircraft to bomb London). Further increase in power (230-hp Benz) led to C.V and VI (1,100 plus). Designer Franz Schneider also produced fighters, starting with E.I 2-seat monoplane (1915) and several later D-series, other D-series being by Ehrhardt and Rethel, none in large numbers. Other original designs were twin-engined G.I and giant G.III triplane bomber, LVG also licence-producing Albatros fighters. Post-war LVG converted B.III and C.VI aircraft into Limousine, Kurier and Postal civil aircraft.

LWD (Poland). After Second World War Polish aircraft industry state-controlled, assigning production to PZL factories but permitting design and development to be undertaken by Lotnicze Warsztaty Doswiadczaine (LWD), or aircraft experimental workshops, Lodz. Staff under Tadeusz Soltyk produced first post-war Polish aircraft, LWD Szpak-2 (designed at Lublin

LVG D.IV, February 1918.

1945), 4-seat low-wing tourer. Developed into Szpak-3 (fixed tricycle gear), -4A open side-by-side aerobatic trainer and -4T improved 4-seater. Other 1947 aircraft included Zak-1 side-by-side trainer, Zak-2 open version and Zak-3 with Continental A50 replaced by Walter Mikron. In 1948 LWD flew Junak-1 (cadet 1) tandem military trainer, followed by Junak-2 (160-hp M-11FR) and Junak-3 with tricycle landing gear. Mis transport never completed, but 1 prototype flown of Zuraw (crane) STOL multirole aircraft (16 May 1951) before LWD closed.

LWF (USA). LWF Engineering Corp. established 1915 at College Point, Long Island, by Joseph Lowe, Charles F. Willard and Robert G. Fowler. Three principals left 1916, LWF then meaning Laminated Wooden (monocoque) Fuselage, patented 1914 by Willard. Converted 12 DH-4 into mailplanes and built twin-engined version. Competitive bids brought series production of Curtiss HS-2L and Douglas DT-1 for Navy and Martin NBS-1 for Army. Own designs included V-1 (1915) biplane trainer, developed into increasingly powerful V-2 and V-3 (201 delivered 1916–18). Post-war built ultralight and giant Owl (Model H) 3-engined triplane bomber. Built Army T-3 twin-engined transport but XNBS-2 metal bomber cancelled. Liquidation 1924.

LWS (Poland). Lubelska Wytwórnia Samolotów Sp Akc established Lublin 1935, taking over offices and factory of Plage i Laśkiewicz. First product actually built was LWS.2, high-wing ambulance designed by Zbyslaw Ciolkosz, prototype only 1937. LWS.3 Mewa (gull) was potentially important STOL recon and army co-op aircraft (730-hp GR 14M), first of 3 prototypes flown autumn 1937 but first production aircraft delayed until 2nd day of war. Ciolkosz had been working on PZL.30B transport, and this was continued as bomber called LWS.4. Outstandingly faulty design, with airframe designed for 450-hp Wasp engines yet actually fitted with 680-hp Pegasus. Prototype disintegrated 1937, but in panic programme 14 delivered before war, overweight, landing gear locked down and with other shortcomings. LWS.6 Zubr (bison), planned 'cured' version, remained prototype.

LYaM (Russia). Neat monoplane, reminiscent of Blériot, built at Aeronautical Society of Moscow by Russian pilots M.G. Lerkhe and G.V. Yankovski and Italian pilot-designer F.E. Mosca. Flew spring 1912 with 50-hp Gnome, set Russian height record 14 May 1912 at 1,775 m (5,823 ft). *See* Moskovskii.

Lyford (USA). Charles Lyford built light sporting aircraft 1968.

Maatschappij: *See* Aviolanda.

Mabley (Canada). J. Mabley built VW-engined ultralight 1961.

MAC (Australia). Melbourne Aircraft Corp. (trading as International Aircraft Corp. Pty Ltd) developed Mamba 2-seat STOL multirole aircraft (25 January 1989).

Macavia (USA). Macavia International markets Allison turboprop conversion of Cessna 207.

Macchi (Italy). Sig. Guilio Macchi was assisted by Nieuport in forming Società Anonima Nieuport-Macchi at Varese 1912, mainly to build Nieuport designs but also several original parasol monoplanes. From outbreak of war production of Nieuport scouts outstripped demand. Lohner L.40 flying-boat captured May 1915 was copied by Macchi within a month, giving rise to famous series of single-engine (nearly all pusher) biplane flying-boats which in turn influenced designers elsewhere. Several hundred built by 1918, notably including 244 M.5 fighter flying-boats, followed by at least 127 M.7ter fighter boats 1923-6. Company renamed **Aeronàutica Macchi** 1992. Over 70 civil M.18s were built, and over 56 big (tandem push/pull) M.24s, as well as a handful of military landplanes. Macchi's most famous products were Schneider seaplanes, M.39 (1926 winner), M.52, M.67 and MC.72 which missed 1931 race but in 1934 set speed record which still stands. Designer Mario Castoldi then produced series of large monoplane boats, followed by MC.200 fighter (24 December 1937), of which 400 built plus a further 753 by Breda and SAI Ambrosini. This led to MC.202 (10 August 1940, about 1,500 including 393 by Macchi) and MC.205 Veltro (19 April 1942, 262). Works rebuilt 1946 and produced aircraft to designs of technical director Ermanno Bazocchi, with MB. designations: 308 high-wing 2-seater, 320 light twin and 323 advanced trainer of 1952. For subsequent types *see* Aermacchi.

MacCready (USA). Dr Paul MacCready became famed glider pilot and record-holder before designing Gossamer Condor man-powered aircraft which won Kremer Prize, followed by Gossamer Albatross which crossed Channel 12 June 1979 and ultimately solar-powered Gossamer Penguin and Solar Challenger which made 5 hr 23 min France–UK flight 7 July 1981.

MacDonald (Canada). MacDonald Brothers, Winnipeg, built parts and finally assembled Anson V 1941–4. Also major parts Catalina, Norseman, Helldiver and Mosquito.

Macdonald (UK). D.J. Macdonald built ultralight 1976.

MacDonald (USA). Robert A. MacDonald built S-20 single-seater (9 March 1972), over 100 sets of plans sold by 1975.

Mace (USA). Harvey F. Mace built Macerschmitt sport racer 1960, followed by backstagger biplane.

Macchi M.C.99, March 1937.

Macera (Italy). Silvano Macera built light aircraft 1984.

MacFam (USA). Market plans for Cavalier (5,000 +), Jungster I biplane (1,500) and Jungster II monoplane (800): *see* McAsco.

Machen (USA). Machen Inc. has converted over 200 Aerostars to upgraded Superstar 650, 680 and 700.

Maestranza (Chile). Maestranza Central de Aviación, central workshops of air force, built first Chilean aeroplane, MCA Tricicolo, 1947, followed by HF.XX-02 2-seater 1952.

MAG (Hungary). Magyar Általános Gépgyár built Fokker D. VII with 210-hp MÁG-Daimler engine 1918–24, 2 on civil register until 1932.

Magni (Italy). Magni-Aviazione founded by Piero Magni in Milan 1919 for aeronautical research and manufacture to others' designs. Own aircraft included Vittoria single-seater and Bi-Vittoria 2-seater 1927, PM-3-4 Vale aerobatic single-seater 1937 and PM-4-1 Supervale 1939.

Magnum (USA). Claims to be completing by 1994 tilt-rotor based on marriage of Bell XV-15 and Mitsubishi MU-2.

Magyar: *See* Lloyd

Mahoney-Ryan (USA). Originally Ryan Airlines,

Piero Magni PM-3-4 Vale, 1937.

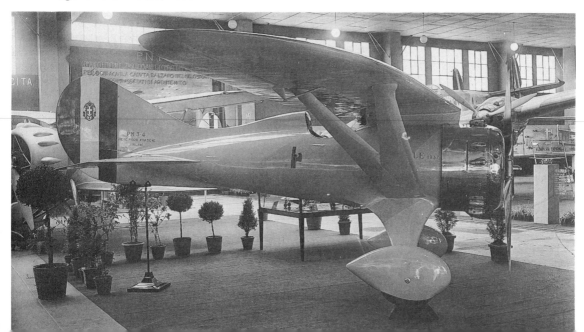

formed San Diego 1922, which in 1926 produced M-1 mailplane from which was derived Lindbergh's NYP. St Louis funding of NYP resulted in move to that city and formation there of B.F. Mahoney Aircraft Co. 1928, subsequently building Brougham. Merged into giant Detroit Aircraft 24 May 1929. *See* Ryan.

Mahugh (USA). G. Irvin Mahugh built Flying Bathtub 2-seat ultralight (15 May 1978), flown across USA later 1978.

MAI: *See* Mitsubishi (USA).

MAI (USSR). Moscow Aviation Institute was large and produced many graduates, taught by 13 of most famous Soviet designers, but produced paper designs rather than aircraft until baby delta MAI-62 (1962) and Kvant aerobatic aircraft (1967). Semurg bizjet not built; for MAI-890 (89-0) and MAI-90 *see* Aviatka.

Maillet (France). M.M. Maillet designed Maillet 20 3-seat monoplane 1936; *see* SFCA.

Maiss (W. Germany). Ulrich Maiss built Bayern II parasol monoplane to design of Frank Wiggins 1979.

Maj (Poland). Marian Maj built light aircraft 1969–70.

Makhonine (Russia/France). Ivan Makhonine, Russian emigré living in Paris, was pioneer of aeroplanes with variable wing area. His method was variable span, telescopic sections driven pneumatically. MAK-10 (480-hp, 11 August 1931) became MAK-101 (700-hp, 1935) and finally post-war MAK-123 (1,700-hp BMW 801).

Makina: *See* MKEK.

Malliga (Austria). Josef Malliga built light aircraft 1972–4.

Malmö (Sweden). AB Malmö Flygindustri (MFI) formed at Bulltofta 1959 as subsidiary of Trellborgs Gummifabric to produce aircraft and missile parts in rubber, plastics, glassfibre and laminates. Produced MFI-9 Junior (previously Andreasson BA-7, 10 October 1958) and Fi 10 (later MFI-10) Vipan STOL 4-seater (25 February 1961). Company acquired by Saab-Scania 1961, producing MFI-15 and -17 as Saab Safari and Supporter. *See also* next entry.

Malmö (Sweden). Björn Andreasson formed own company (which *see*) and later developed MFI-18, MFI-15 with all-composites wing, tested at a newly formed MFI (Malmö Forsknings & Innovations AB). Andreasson then designed MFI BA-14B trainer/utility aircraft as product of this new MFI (25 August 1988) in partnership with FFV Aerotech. MFI now switched to designer Hakan Langebro's LA-4 Vortex for home-building.

Malta (Malta). Dockyard Construction Unit built 18 Felixstowe F.3 flying-boats 1917–18.

Manchuria: *See* Mansyu.

Mancro (USA). Mancro Aircraft Co. built T56 turboprop conversion of C-123 (24 October 1980).

Mann & Grimmer (UK). Schoolboy R.F. Mann and his schoolmaster R.P. Grimmer formed company at Surbiton to build M.1 unconventional

Makhonine MAK-10, August 1931.

pusher biplane (19 February 1915).

Mann, Egerton (UK). Norwich motor manufacturers which in First World War built Short 184 (Type A) and own design Type B seaplanes, Short Bomber, Sopwith 1½-strutter, SPAD VII, D.H.9/9A, D.H.10 and own-design H.1 and H.2 fighters.

Manning Flanders (UK). W.O. Manning and Howard Flanders built MF.1 monoplane 1910.

Mansyu (Manchuria). Mansyu Hikoki Seizo K.K. established June 1938 by decree of occupying Japanese to incorporate all facilities at Harbin, in puppet state Manchukuo, where Hayabusa 6-passenger transport had been developed. In 1941 worked with Tachikawa to develop Ki-71 (improved Mitsubishi Ki-51), and in 1942 Mansyu developed Ki-79 advanced trainer (1,379, several versions). Ki-116 fighter was improved Ki-84, but Ki-98 attack aircraft never completed.

Manta: *See* Davis, 1st entry.

Mantelli (Italy/Argentina). Adriano Mantelli emigrated to Argentina 1949, taking Alaparma designs; produced AM-10 and AM-11 Albatross pusher 2-seaters.

Manzolini (Italy). Count Ettore Manzolini di Campoleone produced light coaxial helicopter Libellula (7 January 1952) followed by progressively more powerful II and III; Allison-engined IV not built.

MAPO (Russia). Moscow Aircraft Production Organization established 1991 by GAZ-155 (Mikoyan OKB) and 6 factories in greater Moscow area formerly involved in production of MiG-29 in order to act as single client interface and supply certified aircraft, spares, documents, training and after-sales support.

Maranda (Canada). In 1957 Maranda Aircraft Co. of Montreal acquired rights to Roger Adam RA-14 and RA-17 leading to Super Loisir, Falcon, Hawk, Lark and agricultural BM3.

Marchetti (Italy). Alessandro Marchetti designed outstanding MVT fighter 1919, designation from Marchetti and Vickers-Terni which built it. Unofficial world speed record. When Marchetti

joined SIAI ('Savoia') MVT became S.50.

Marchetti (USA). Frank Marchetti built light aircraft 1982.

March, Jones & Cribb (UK). Built D.H.5 and Sopwith Camel 1916–17.

Marcotte (USA). Kenneth Marcotte built light aircraft 1963–6.

Marendaz (UK). D.M.K. Marendaz designed Mks II and III high-speed 4-seaters built by International Aircraft at Maidenhead (not flown); then formed Marendaz Aircraft, Barton-in-the-Clay, and built second Mk III and single Trainer (11 December 1939).

Marinavia (Italy). Marinavia Farina SrL completed Qr.14 4-seater with 2 × 160-hp Alfa Romeo engines 1943. No flight possible until 1947 when re-engined with Gipsy 10.

Marinens (Norway). In 1915 Royal Norwegian Navy established Marinens Flyvebatfabrikk (naval flying-boat factory) at Horten, built various Farman, Hansa-Brandenburg, Douglas and Breda designs, plus own designs M.F.8 trainer, M.F.9 fighter, M.F.10 advanced trainer, M.F.11 reconnaissance and M.F.12 primary trainer, all float seaplanes.

Mario de Bernardi (Italy). Famed racing pilot built sport aircraft 1958.

Mark (Germany). Mark Abteilung Flugzeugbau was aviation subsidiary of Breslau engineering firm 1919–1930, building sports monoplanes and 4-seat R.V/23 named for designer Rieseler.

Märkische (Germany). Märkische Flugzeugwerke established 1916 at Golm in der Mark, produced Rumpler C.I and various trainers under licence and prototype Mark D.I fighter 1918.

Markwalder (Switzerland). A. Markwalder built light aircraft 1966.

Marmande (France). Marmande Aéronautique, member of Groupe Creuzet, is Microjet SA renamed, which took over programme from Microturbo and now produces Microjet 200B.

Marquardt (USA). Roy E. Marquardt formed his

company 1944 to produce ramjets. One piloted aircraft, M-14 pulsejet tip-drive helicopter (1950).

Marquardt (USA). Ed Marquardt markets plans of MA-5 Charger sport biplane.

Marrone (USA). Vincent Marrone built light aircraft 1958.

Mars (USA). Mars Manufacturing Co., Le Mars, Iowa, produced Skycoupe 2-seater 1946.

Marsh (USA). Marsh Aviation Co., Mesa, AZ, began by converting Rockwell Thrush Commander to Garrett turboprop and now has range of aircraft (Gulfstream Turbo Cat, Beech Turbo Mentor, Grumman S-2 Turbo Tracker) with Garrett power.

Marshall (UK). Marshall & Sons, Gainsborough, built 150 Arab-engined Bristol Fighters.

Marshall (UK). Marshall of Cambridge (Engineering) Ltd handle major conversions of transport aircraft and design/manufacture of parts for combat aircraft; no original design apart from Marshall MA.4 boundary-layer research rebuild of Auster T.7. Company changed name August 1992 to **Marshall of Cambridge Aerospace Ltd.** Under March 1993 agreement exclusive overhaul/repair centre Europe/Africa for Tupolev aircraft; further CIS deals possible.

Martin (UK). Single Martin Monoplane designed by Latimer-Needham and built by Luton Aircraft for F/O Martin Hopkinson 1937.

Martin (USA). Capt. James V. Martin designed tiny 45-hp biplane fighter, supplied to US Air Service as K-3 (May 1918) and 3 to Navy as K-IV (Navy KF-1) 1921.

Martin (USA). Glenn L. Martin started car repair business at Santa Ana 1905, and 2 years later flew homebuilt glider from beach. By 1909 taught himself to fly with homebuilt pusher aeroplane and, giving up business, set up as aircraft manufacturer, incorporated Santa Ana 1911 as **Glenn L. Martin Co.** Moved 1912 to larger premises on Griffith Park, hired several employees and went into production with variations on Model T tandem-seat tractor biplane land/seaplane. Army TT stayed aloft 7 hr 4 min with pilot and 2 passengers. September 1916 Wright and several other companies were merged with Martin to form Wright-Martin Co; this displaced Martin who withdrew October 1917 and set up under original name in large plant at Cleveland. Built 10 GMB (Glenn Martin Bomber), or MB-1, followed by Navy MBT and 20 MB-2 (plus 110 by rivals who underbid). Supplied Navy with SC scout bombers and T3M and T4M torpedo aircraft. Moved 1928 to even larger plant at Middle River, Baltimore, where produced stream of landplanes, seaplanes and flying-boats and, in January 1932, classic Martin Bomber. This stressed-skin cantilever monoplane had retractable gear, flaps, gun turret and performance higher than any Air Corps fighter; 359 built for Air Corps (most as B-10) and export. Large long-range Type 130 flying-boat for PanAm led to Type 156, Type 162 Mariner (PBM), JRM Mars, P5M Marlin and XP6M SeaMaster. Martin Bomber in many versions led to Type 167 Maryland, Type 187 Baltimore and Type 179 Marauder (B-26), latter also built by Martin Nebraska Co. at Omaha which also built 536 B-29s. Martin also delivered over 15,000 aircraft

Martin B-10B, January 1934.

gun turrets. Post-war built AM Mauler, XB-48 6-jet and XB-51 3-jet bombers, P4M Mercator, 202 and 404 civil transports and 403 B-57 derived from Canberra. When last P5M left factory 20 December 1960 President George M. Bunker said, 'Martin has sloughed off its emotional attachment to the airplane'. Renamed **The Martin Co.**, produced Titan ICBMs, missiles and space launchers, merging 1965 to form **Martin Marietta Corp.** which built X-23, X-24 and SV-5 lifting bodies.

Martin & Handasyde (UK). H.P. Martin and George Handasyde formed company at Woking 1908 to build aircraft at Brooklands. No. 1 1908 failed to fly with Humber car engine, but No. 2 monoplane was excellent and led to others including 1912 Military Trials monoplane, all owing something to Antoinette. In 1912 or early 1913 company re-registered as **Martinsyde** Ltd. Built S.1 scout biplane (October 1914), about 60 built, followed by larger G.100 and G.102 Elephant single-seat scouts (about 300). Following prototypes of F.1, 2 and 3 F.4 Buzzard 145-mph single-seat fighter was ordered in large numbers, but fewer than 62 delivered at Armistice.

Martin-Baker (UK). Capt. James Martin had workshop in Acton, London, where he developed aircraft structures of thin-wall steel tube with brazed, welded or, more often, bolted joints. In 1929 moved to derelict Army huts at Denham with 2 employees to build M.1 side-by-side 2-seater with Hermes engine behind cockpit with shaft drive. Forced to give up by Depression, but 1934 joined with Capt. Valentine Baker to form **Martin-Baker Aircraft Ltd**, producing MB.1 tandem 2-seater with engine in nose. MB.2 was remarkable fighter (3 August 1938) with Dagger engine and 8 guns; MB.3 (31 August 1942) had Sabre and 6 × 20-mm; MB.5 (23 May 1944) widely considered best piston-engined fighter of all. Company later famed for ejection seats.

Martinis (Italy). Martinis SRL built light aircraft 1965.

Martin Marietta: *See* Martin, 3rd entry.

Martinsyde: *See* Martin & Handasyde.

Martyn (Canada). Robert E. Martyn built West Wind ultralight (14 May 1960).

Marvel: *See* Parsons.

Marvin Patchen: *See* Patchen.

Maryland (USA). Maryland Pressed Steel formed Aircraft Department 1919, building Bellanca CE light sport biplane. Designer Bellanca went to Omaha Aircraft 1921.

Masarykova: *See* Zlin.

Mason (USA). Joe Mason flew 8/10-scale D.H.2 1 March 1974.

Massachusetts: *See* MIT.

Masschelein (Belgium). S. Masschelein and E. Verstraete flew man-powered aircraft May 1974.

Matra (France). Société des Engins Matra, major missile/rocket producer, flew M 360 Jupiter push/pull 4/5-seater 17 December 1963.

Matra-Cantinieau (France). Jean Cantinieau

Matra M 360 Jupiter, 17 December 1963.

(which *see*) designed MC.101 helicopter built by Matra 1952. He then went to Aerotécnica (which *see*) in Spain, but returned to France to work on Matra-Cantinieau Bamby 1963, but this never flew.

Mauboussin (France). M. Pierre Mauboussin set up private factory at Puteaux (Paris) 1931, building M.120 Corsaire light monoplane, followed by numerous derived types which from July 1934 were made by Breguet at Vélizy. In 1936 all rights purchased by Société des Etablissements Fouga, which built all types from M.123 to M.190, M.200 racer, M.300 6-seat light twin and unusual M.400 resembling pusher Rapide (1944). In 1945 Mauboussin became Director of Aircraft Department of Fouga, which *see*.

Maule (USA). Belford D. Maule flew M-4 high-wing 4-seater February 1957, and later set up Maule Aircraft Corp., Jackson, Michigan. Subsequently produced 6 variants of M-4 before moving 1968 to Moultrie, GA, to produce long series of M-5 Lunar-Rocket variants, company being renamed Maule Air Inc. 1984. Current range includes M-7 Starcraft with Allison turboprop.

MAVAG (Hungary). A major state aircraft manufacturer during Second World War, MAVAG built under licence 192 Caproni-Reggiane Re 2000 fighters as Héja II, and 43 WM-21 recon biplanes.

Maxair (USA). Maxair Aircraft have sold over 2,100 sets of plans for Drifter/ARV series.

Max Holste (France). M. Holste designed M.H.52 and 53 all-metal 2-seat monoplanes during Second World War, and formed Avions Max Holste 1947. M.H.152 high-wing observation/liaison aircraft (1951) led to M.H.1521 Broussard (17 November 1952), built in large numbers for French ALAT and civil customers. Reims factory next built M.H.250 Super Broussard (May 1959) which led to M.H.260 (2 × Bastan turboprops) and pressurized M.H.262, produced at Méaulte as Nord 262 after Holste was merged into Nord-Aviation. Before merger Cessna had bought large share of Holste, and on merger Reims was left private as Cessna subsidiary Reims-Aviation.

Maximov (USSR). Dmitri Sergeyevich Maximov (literally Maksimov) worked with aerodynamicist I.I. Drakin on SPS-89, fast passenger aircraft, at Gorkii (GAZ-89) 1937–9. Then GAZ-89 transferred to Yermolayev, and SPS-89 dropped 1940.

Maximum Safety (USA). This California firm built M-3 4-seater noted for 14° dihedral, 1928.

Max Plan (France). Head of supersonic tunnel at Meudon, M. Plan produced MP.204 racer (5 June 1952), later modified as 214.

Maxson (USA). Maxson-Brewster Corp. built 2 prototype XNR-1 twin-engined Navy trainers (1940).

Max Holste Broussard, November 1952.

Mayenberger (Germany). In 1925 built single-seat amphibian, 30-hp Haacke with tractor 4-blade propeller, pairs of wheels on each landing gear attached to sponsons.

May, Harden & May (UK). Subsidiary of Aircraft Manufacturing Co. with factory and slipway on Southampton Water. Built hulls for F.3, F.5, AD and Phoenix Cork and handled entire production of giant Porte Baby 1915–19.

Mayo (UK). Major Robert Mayo formed Mayo Composite Aircraft Co. 1935 to develop his concept of heavily loaded seaplane launched from back of lightly loaded flying-boat; resulting lower and upper components made by Short Brothers 1937.

MBB (W. Germany). **Messerschmitt-Bölkow-Blohm GmbH** formed May 1969 by merger of Messerschmitt-Bölkow and Hamburger Flugzeugbau, adding on 1 January 1981 all shares of VFW. Formed numerous groups and divisions, including Helicopter and Military Aircraft Group, major programmes Tornado, F-104G, F-4F/RF-4E, BO 105 and (with Kawasaki) BK 117, (with Aerospatiale) Eurocopter Tiger and (with HAL of India) ALH, and Transport Aircraft Group, major programmes Airbus family, Transall and Fokker 100. In September 1989 MBB was taken over by DASA (Daimler-Benz), which *see*.

MBB (Canada). MBB Helicopter Canada Ltd at Fort Erie formed 1984 to produce uprated BO 105LS helicopter. Now **Eurocopter Canada**.

McAsco (Canada). McAsco Aircraft Division, Calgary, are heirs to one of biggest homebuilt operations in world, previously Squaircraft, K&S and Macfam, all in USA; business now returned to MacFam (capital F) in USA.

McCandless (UK). Rex McCandless produced M4 light autogyro 1961; limited production from 1972 handled by Ekin: *see* WHE.

McCarley (USA). Charles E. McCarley, and later his widow, marketed plans of Mini-Mac aerobatic single-seater (1968) from Hueytown, Ala.

McCarthy (USA). McCarthy Aircraft Co. incorporated 1925 at Grand Rapids, Michigan, to build Air Scout 2-seat cabin monoplane and its Anzani engine.

McClish (USA). Thomas H. McClish purchased all rights to Funk 2-seaters 1960.

McCulloch (USA). Aircraft Division of McCulloch Motors Corp. developed MC-4 tandem-rotor helicopter with 200-hp Franklin engine (20 March 1951), later developing 4-seat MC-4E and J-2 (*see* Jovair) 2-seat autogyro, latter built in numbers 1962–6.

McDonnell (USA). James S. McDonnell graduated Princeton 1921, qualified pilot at Army (Brooks) San Antonio, obtained MIT Master's degree and spent inter-war years as designer—e.g.

McDonnell XF-88 Voodoo, 20 October 1948.

for Ford, Hamilton, Martin—before starting MAC (McDonnell Aircraft Corp.) on second floor of small building at Lambert Field, St Louis, 6 July 1939. With Garrett C. Covington (his former assistant at Martin) designed XP-67 fighter (6 January 1944) whilst building Fairchild AT-21 Gunners at Memphis. Navy awarded contract for XFD-1 twin-jet Phantom (26 January 1945) and F2H Banshee (11 January 1947, 895 built). Rotary-wing work included XHJD Whirlaway, in 1946 largest helicopter then flown outside Germany, XH-20 ramjet tip-drive, Army XV-1 (first aircraft to convert from rotor-supported to wing-supported flight) and Model 120 (1958) with payload 163% of empty weight. XF3H Demon (7 August 1951) was delayed by unsuitable engine but eventually matured as F3H-2/2M/2N. XF-88 Voodoo led to powerful F-101 Voodoo (29 September 1954) attack, recon and all-weather interception aircraft. Model 119 USAF UCX led to Model 220 4-jet executive aircraft, while new teams produced 1-man Mercury and 2-man Gemini space capsules and various missiles and decoys. XF4H-1 Phantom II (27 May 1958) led to biggest non-Soviet fighter programme since F-86 (5,157). While this was in full swing bid to merge with Douglas accepted, MAC becoming MCAIR, McDonnell Aircraft Company.

McDonnell Aircraft (USA). McDonnell Aircraft Co. formed on merger 28 April 1967. MAC appointed foster-parent to USMC Harrier 1970, and further work by MCAIR led to AV-8B

Harrier II and other variants produced in partnership with British Aerospace. Navy T-45 Goshawk was joint programme British Aerospace and Douglas but transferred 1989–91 to MCAIR St Louis. USAF FX requirement won by F-15 Eagle (27 July 1972), total 1,034 plus 191 made by Mitsubishi plus 200 (minimum) F-15E. Navy VFAX requirement won by partnership with Northrop producing F/A-18 Hornet (18 November 1978), total 1,157 (minimum). Many projects but hit by cancellation A-12 Avenger and non-selection YF-23A, so big effort to win Navy A-X (teamed with Vought) or Air Force MRF (multi-role fighter).

McDonnell Douglas (USA). MDC, McDonnell Douglas Corp., formed 28 April 1967. Some 115,000 employees in McDonnell Aircraft, Douglas Aircraft, MDHC (*see* next), MD Missile Systems and MD Space Systems. Cash-flow problems led to November 1991 MoU with Taiwan Aerospace to form joint company Douglas Global; this replaced May 1992 by Taiwan proposal to take debenture shares in Douglas, launch MD-12 and build fuselage and wing at new plant and purchase 20, not signed 1993.

McDonnell Douglas Helicopter (USA). Hughes Helicopters purchased by MDC and became wholly-owned subsidiary 6 January 1984. Company progressively moved from Culver City to Mesa, AZ, starting with AH-64 Apache production and following with MD 500/530 production 1986–7. Company name changed to

McDonnell Douglas MD-83, 1986.

McDonnell Douglas Helicopter Corp. (MDHC) 27 August 1985. Major new programme Explorer Notar (no tail rotor) 8/10-seat twin-engined helicopter (July 1992) in partnership with HDH (airframe) and Kawasaki (transmission).

McGregor (Canada). Wilmer McGregor built sport biplane 1962.

McKinnie (USA). McKinnie Aircraft Co. Inc. formed by Transocean Air Lines 1947 to build McKinnie 165 2-seater (10 August 1952).

McKinnon (Canada). McKinnon-Hickman began converting Grumman Widgeons into executive aircraft 1953, moving on to larger Goose as McKinnon Enterprises, which in 1978 became **McKinnon-Viking Enterprises** producing Super Widgeon with retractable tip floats and Turbo-Goose with PT6A engines.

MDB (Switzerland). MDC Max Dätwyler AG is major firm, mainly non-aero. Plant at Bleien-bach-Langenthal is major aircraft FBO, also creating own designs: MDC Trailer (1962) based on Piper PA-18, Lerche (1967) based on Jungmann and original MD3 Swiss-Trainer (12 August 1983). In 1991 all aero business gathered into new company, MDB Flugtechnik AG.

MDG (France). Instruments de Précision MDG exhibited LD.45 single-seat biplane 1946, followed by tandem-seat Midgy-Club (1948) built in small numbers.

MDHC: *See* McDonnell Douglas Helicopter.

Mead (USA). Mead Engineering Co. marketed plans for Adventure high-speed sport aircraft (1981–6).

Meadowcroft (USA). W. Meadowcroft built light aircraft 1960–61.

Mechanikai (Hungary). Mechanikai Laboratorium Dunakeszi, producer of sailplanes, also developed motor-glider and ultralights.

Melbourne: *See* MAC.

Melex (USA). Melex USA Inc. is subsidiary of Pezetel of Poland responsible for sale/support of M-18 Dromader in W. hemisphere. Also developed T45 Turbine Dromader and Water Bomber conversion.

Memel (Lithuania). To evade Allied Control restrictions in 1925, new Albatros company formed subsidiary outside Germany. Though actual title was **Allgemeine Flug-Gesellschaft** (AFG), products universally known by city where located. Chief product AFG.I (Albatros L 65) fighter.

Merckle (W. Germany). Merckle Flugzeugwerke, Bad Friedrichshalle-Oedheim, abandoned plan to produce Kiebitz 501 STOL 2-seater designed 1956 at Brunswick Technische Hochschule, but with government funds developed SM 67 5-seat turbine-engined helicopter 1959–63.

Mercury (USA). Mercury Air formed by Carl and Vincent Ast and Rodney Kreimendahl to build light aircraft 1959.

Mercury (USA). Mercury Aircraft Inc., Hammondsport, NY, was rename of Aerial Service Corp. Produced Mercury Junior 3-seat biplane 1925, Kitten 3-seat monoplane 1928 and T-2 Chic parasol trainer before failing 1930.

Mercury (USA). Mercury Aircraft Inc. formed at Menominee, Michigan, 1936 to build B-100 4-seat monoplane and BT-120 biplane trainer.

Mercury (USA). Film producer Cecil B. DeMille formed Mercury Aviation Co., marketing sleek Mercury Gosling designed 1919 by W.D. Waterman Aircraft.

Meridionali (Italy). Industrie Meccaniche e Aeronautiche Meridionali (IMAM) was formed 1936 by renaming SA Industrie Aeronautiche Romeo upon becoming part of Società Italiana Ernesto Breda. Continued Ro 37 recon biplane, Ro 41 fighter biplane, Ro 51 fighter monoplane (land/seaplane versions) and developed Ro 43/44 seaplanes, Ro 57/58 twin-engined fighters and STOL Ro 63.

Merkel (USA). Merkel Airplane Co., Wichita, produced Mk II aerobatic biplane (11 April 1973).

Mersey (UK). 'Mersey Monoplane' built for 1912 Army trials, killed pilot.

Messerschmitt (BFW) M.23c, January 1930.

Merville (France). Producing propellers from 1919, Hélice G. Merville added sailplanes from 1959 and D.63 improved Druine Condor with 105-hp Potez engine and tricycle landing gear (23 March 1962).

Messerschmitt AG (Germany). On 11 July 1938 Board of Directors of BFW voted to change name of Augsburg company to Messerschmitt AG, because of success of Bf 109, sole single-seat fighter in production for Luftwaffe. Designations Bf 108, Bf 109, Bf 110, Bf 161 and Bf 162 remained unchanged. Aircraft whose development began after spring 1937 were allocated air ministry 8-series numbers with prefix Me. These aircraft were: Me 209 racer; Me 209 (originally 209-II) fighter, a totally different design based on Bf 109G; Me 210 twin-engined fighter/bomber, a serious failure; Me 261 intended as long-range record-breaker; Me 262 twin-jet fighter; Me 263 rocket interceptor (later Ju 248); Me 264 long-range reconnaissance bomber; Me 309 fighter; Me 310 fighter/bomber; Me 321 Gigant glider and Me 323 powered development; Me 328 twin-jet bomber; and Me 410 fighter/bomber.

Messerschmitt (W. Germany). Prof. Messerschmitt re-registered company 1948, and began to rebuild Augsburg factory. One part, called Neue Technik GmbH, began to make prefab housing and commercial buildings. Messerschmitt AG restarted November 1949 to make Zick-Zack automatic sewing machine, P 511 advanced passenger car and KR 200 *kabinenroller* (bubble car). In 1951 Messerschmitt and design team moved to Seville, Spain, where they set up Hispano Aviaçion (*see* Hispano-Suiza). Augsburg factory expanded to repair railway rolling-stock, and from 1955 this extended to rebuild and overhaul

of T-6 and T-33 trainers for Luftwaffe. In 1956 Messerschmitt and Ernst Heinkel GmbH jointly formed **Flugzeug-Union Süd** to build Fouga CM 170 Magister under licence, and from 1958 Messerschmitt published civil projects which remained unbuilt. In 1958 Messerschmitt, Heinkel and Dornier began joint production of Fiat G91, Messerschmitt producing fuselage. In 1958 Messerschmitt, Heinkel, Dornier and Siebel formed Arge (Arbeitsgemeinschaft) Süd to build 210 F-104Gs, plus 32 TFs, Messerschmitt making forward fuselage and carrying out assembly and test at Manching, near Munich. In June 1958 Messerschmitt, Heinkel and Bölkow formed EWR (Entwicklungsring, development group) Süd to work on advanced jet V/STOL: *see* EWR. In 1965 Messerschmitt purchased all parts of former Junkers organization in Federal Germany, which was key move in formation in May 1969 of **MBB**.

Messier (France). Soc. Georges Messier, Soc. Française de la Matériel d'Aviation, built research aircraft July 1934 with bicycle landing gear to test various landing gears; all-metal low-wing (250-hp Hispano HS6).

Metalair (USA). Metalair Corp. formed 1931 by renaming Pittsburgh upon takeover by General Aviation.

Metal Aircraft (USA). The Metal Aircraft Corp. ('The' was part of title) formed 1928 at Cincinnati to take over assets of Halpin Development Co. and develop and manufacture Halpin Flamingo 6-seat monoplane (410-hp Wasp).

Metalnor (Chile). Formerly known as Indústrias Cardoen, claimed to cease weapon production and renamed 1992 **Indústria Metalúrgica del Norte Ltda.** CB 206L-III project appeared halted by USA 1992.

Meteor (Italy). Meteor SpA formed 1947 in Trieste, factory at Monfalcone building sailplanes and related equipment. Took over Lombardi (AVIA) and developed AVIA FL.3 into Meteor FL.53, 54 and 55. These further developed using engines of Meteor design, final models being Bis (110-hp) and Super (220-hp).

Metropolitan (UK). Metropolitan Waggon Co. built 100 HP O/400 bombers at Birmingham 1917–18.

Meyer (USA). Clair O. Meyer built light aircraft 1982–3.

Meyer (USA). Les K. Meyer built light aircraft 1982.

Meyer (USA). Meyer Aircraft formed at Corpus Christi, Texas, by George W. Meyer to market plans for Little Toot aerobatic biplane (5 February 1957).

Meyers (USA). Meyers Aircraft Co. formed at Tecumseh, Michigan, 1936 by Allen Meyers to produce OTW biplane trainer (10 May 1936), built in several versions. Post-war switched to low-wing cabin monoplanes MAC-125, 145 and 4-seat 200, latter flown 1953 and delivered from 1959. Taken over by Rockwell-Standard 1965, Meyers 200 becoming Aero Commander 200 made at Aero Commander Albany Division. Rights acquired 1977 by new Meyers company: see below.

Meyers (USA). Meyers Aircraft Manufacturing Co., Denver, Colorado, established by Carl Branson as division of Branson Manufacturing 1977 to produce Meyers 200D: see Branson.

MFI: See Malmö, both entries.

MFW: See Märkische.

MGZI (Russia). Moscow Helicopter Factory named for M.I. Mil is production and customer support adjunct of Mil OKB. Has delivered over 23,200 helicopters, currently working on Mi-26M, 28, 34M, 38, 40, 46 and 54.

Miami (USA). Miami Aircraft Corp. incorporated Hialeah 1929 to produce Miami Maid 5-seat amphibian.

Mickl & Consertn (Austria). Established July 1919 by 2 former naval officers who unsuccessfully attempted to set up production of multi-engined flying-boats.

Microjet: *See* Marmande.

Mid-Continent (USA). Willis Clinton Brown built aeroplane 1912, when he was 16; served US Air Service, and from 1923 flew Waco 7 and 9 as salesman around Tulsa, OK. Showed need for improved aircraft and in 1925 designed 3-seat biplane called Spartan (80-hp Le Rhône converted as static radial). Tested from 25 October 1926, so satisfactory Brown formed Mid-Continent Aircraft at Tulsa December 1926 to build replicas, most with Ryan-Siemens engine. Success attracted oil-tycoon W.G. Skelly, who with others bought company, later renaming it Spartan, which *see*.

Mid-Continent (USA). Mid-Continent Aircraft Corp., Hayti, Missouri, produces King Cat (Schweizer Super Ag-Cat with 1,200-hp Cyclone).

Midi: *See* SNCA du Midi.

Midwest (USA). Midwest Aircraft Co., Wyandotte, Michigan, produced 2 versions of Mercury high-wing 2-seater 1945.

MiG (USSR, CIS-Russia). Most famous OKB (experimental construction bureau) in Soviet Union, and probably best-known 'aircraft constructor' in world. Designation from surnames of Artyom Ivanovich Mikoyan and Mikhail Iosifovich Guryevich, former being General Constructor of OKB at GAZ-1 on formation 8 December 1939 and Guryevich chief deputy selected over other deputy V.A. Romodin. Reason for OKB was to build fighter K, later called I-200 (5 April 1940), leading to production MiG-1 (100) and MiG-3 (3,120 December 40–December 41). There followed 134 prototypes, hardly any two alike, including I-210/220/221/222/224/225/230 ultra-high-altitude fighters, various DIS (MiG-5) twin-engined fighters, N (I-250) piston/jet fighter, Zh (I-270) rocket fighter and Utka (MiG-8) canard research aircraft built for VVA academy. First Soviet jet

I-300 (24 April 1946) led to production of MiG-9 twin-jet fighter built in many versions including trainers. Arrival of Nene engines from Britain led to crash programme to build S-01 (I-310) with swept wings and tail (30 December 1947). This in turn led to MiG-15, many thousands built including 853 S-102 and 2,012 CS-102 trainers in Czechoslovakia, Poland (LIM-1) and China, and even larger numbers MiG-15bis including 620 Czech S-103 and LIM-2 in Poland. MiG-15bis-45° led via SI series to MiG-17 and 17F made in large numbers (total USSR production 8,400+, exported to 31 countries. I-320 twin-jet night fighters not built in series, but via SM-1 (I-340), supersonic I-350 and SM-2 (I-360) development reached MiG-19 supersonic twin-jet, again made in large numbers in many versions 1953–8. By this time major part of OKB work was development of large KS-1, K-10, K-20, K-22 cruise missiles, and modified fighters were used to develop guidance. Further 27 prototype and development aircraft led to MiG-21, USSR production 10,500+ in 3 plants, exported to 49 air forces. Meanwhile I-3/3U/3P, I-7/75, Ye-150/151 and various Ye-152 including 152M (Ye-166) record holder remained prototypes. After 1960 one team developed Mach 3 MiG-25 interceptor and recon bomber while others made totally fresh start on smaller fighters, studying jet lift with some (e.g. MiG-23PD) and variable wing sweep with others (e.g. 23/11). Latter won, leading to MiG-23 fighters (23 family) and MiG-23 and 27 attack aircraft, all Type 32 family, total 6,100+ in many versions. Via Ye-155 MiG-25 led to MiG-31 interceptor. Space brigade under G.Ye. Lozino-Lozinskii worked on many projects including 105-11 to investigate aerodynamic flight of aerospace-craft. A further fresh start resulted in MiG-29 multirole fighter (6 October 1977) with shipboard and trainer variants made in 2 plants,

total 1993 nudging 2,000. Grand total excluding licensees 55,200+. Guryevich retired on medical grounds 1964 and Mikoyan died in harness 1970, since when OKB has been **MMZI** (Moscow machine factory named for) A.I. Mikoyan. General Constructor is Rostislav A. Belyakov. French engines and avionics for AT jet trainer. In effort to build civil business new projects include 101M and 101N multirole utility twin-turboprops, 18-50 twin-jet and larger SVB twin-turboprop for hot mountainous regions. *See also* RusJet.

Mignet (France). Henri Mignet published book *Le sport de l'Air* 1928 and designed (presumably 13) aircraft before HM.14 (6 September 1933) which took world by storm as Flying Flea. Post-war continued to develop original (dangerous) design with workshop at São Paulo (formed company Avioes Mignet do Brasil 1952) producing HM.310; later returned to France, at Caen and finally (1961) St Romain de Benet, producing HM.290/293/351/360/380/381/390.

Mikhelson (USSR). N.G. Mikhelson was designer in pre-revolutionary Russia. At former Anatra works, Taganrog, 1921 began designing MK-1 fighter seaplane in partnership with Shishmaryev and Korvin (May 1923), prototype only. Went to GAZ-3 1931 and there, with Morshchikhin, produced U-3, refined and more powerful U-2, and U-4 in which higher performance attained solely by refinement. RV-23 further modified U-2 (August 1937) to attempt height record. Last aircraft, never completed, was MP unconventional high-speed torpedo aircraft with tilting engine.

Mikoyan: *See* MiG.

Mikoyan MiG-31, 16 September 1975.

Mignet HM.18, January 1936.

Mil (USSR, CIS-Russia, Siberia). Mikhail Leontyevich Mil (Siberian) assisted Kamov/Skrzhinskii 1929, Izakson A-15 and in 1936 deputy to Kamov. Chief rotary-wing brigade CAHI 1945, formed own OKB Moscow 1947, designs usually farmed out for production to Kazan or Ulan-Ude, some to Poland. Almost all classic helicopters with single articulated main rotor. Mi-1 (September 1948) basic 575-hp 4-seater, many versions, 1,200 + plus 1,700 + by WSK-Swidnik in Poland 1954–65. Mi-2 (September 1961) twin-turbine 8-seater, many versions, whole programme to WSK-Swidnik as SM-2, 3,970 +. Mi-4 (May 1952) large 1,700-hp piston-engined transport, 3,836 lb (1,740 kg) cargo or 14 passengers, 3,500 + plus 545 by HAMC China. Mi-6 colossal leap in helicopter technology with 114 ft 10in (35 m) rotor driven by 2 × 5,500-hp turboshaft, up to 26,450 lb (11,998 kg) cargo or 90 passengers (September 1957), 800 + 1961–81. Mi-8 (1961 with single 2,700-shp, September 1962 with definitive twin turbines standardized at 1,700-shp each) sustained huge programme of 10,000 + each with 8,820 lb (4,000 kg) cargo or up to 32 passengers. Many converted as Mi-17 (2 × 1,950 or 2,250-shp), 4,400 + by 1992 and continuing. Mi-10 crane version of Mi-6 (1960), 55 ending 1971. Mi-12, V-12, giant machine with side-by-side Mi-6 rotors, flew July 1968 but abandoned. Mil died January 1970, succeeded by Marat N. Tishchyenko, who dropped V-12 in favour of superb Mi-26 (14 December 1977), single 8-blade 105-ft rotor driven by 2 × 11,240-shp D-136 engines, payload 48,500 lb (22,000 kg) or 85 equipped troops, production since 1985. Mi-14 (September 1969) amphibious version of Mi-17 for ASW, MCM or SAR duties (3 versions), 250 +. Mi-24/25/35 family of armed helicopters with transport capability, first flown believed 1968, production assigned Arsenyev and Rostov, 2,300 by 1983, probably 2,700 + by 1993. Mi-28 (November 1982) outstanding all-weather combat helicopter, production 1991. Mi-34 totally new 4-seater (325-hp piston engine) flown 1986; Mi-34V (2 × 270-hp RC engines) to fly 1993. Mi-38 (2 × 3,200-shp) with unobstructed cabin for 5 tonnes cargo including vehicles or 32 passengers to fly 1993 and replace Mi-17. December 1992 agreement makes Kazan Helo responsible for production and Eurocopter for avionics, cockpit and interior and export sales. Tishchyenko replaced 1992 by Mark V. Vineberg. *See also* Rostvertol; USPA.

Miles (UK). Miles Aircraft Ltd formed October 1943 to continue business of Phillips & Powis Aircraft. Produced M.28 high-speed 4-seater, M.33 Monitor tug (2 × 1,700-hp Cyclone), M.38 Messenger STOL 2/3-seater (92), M.57 Aerovan light freighter (50) and M.65 Gemini light twin (170), as well as prototypes of M.60 Marathon airliner, M.68 Boxcar, M.71 Merchantman and M.75 Aries. M.52, which could have been a valuable supersonic aircraft, was cancelled January 1946. Like so many British companies, a wealth of talent and good products led to receivership November 1947. Handley Page took over assets.

Miles (UK). F.G. Miles Ltd formed Redhill, Surrey, June 1951, moving 1952 to Shoreham Airport, Sussex, directors including Mr and Mrs F.G. Miles and George H. Miles. Built up important business in plastics and electronics, and flew prototypes of HDM.105 Aerovan with

Miles (Phillips & Powis) M.2 Hawk prototype, March 1933.

Hurel-Dubois-type wing 31 March 1957 and M.100 Student twin-jet trainer 14 May 1957. Aircraft work absorbed into Beagle-Miles October 1960.

Militi (Italy). Bruno Militi built sport aircraft 1982–3.

Miller (Italy). Franz Miller, Turin, built biplane and several monoplanes 1908–11 as well as their 4- and 9-cylinder aircooled engines.

Miller (USA). Miller Aircraft Corp. formed February 1937 at Springfield, Massachusetts, to build range of Zeta 2-seaters with engines from 95 to 150 hp.

Miller (USA). J.W. Miller formed company at Marble Falls, TX, producing JM-2 high-speed single-seater with behind-tail shrouded propeller (1974) followed by Gem-260 2-seater version.

Miller (USA). Merle B. Miller, Savannah, GA, built sporting aircraft (3 June 1971).

Miller (USA). W. Terry Miller, Furlong, PA, built WM-2 sport aircraft (August 1972).

Miller (USA). William Y. Miller, Mesa, AZ, built W. Terry Miller's WM-2 and now handles sale of plans.

Millet-Lagarde (France). Société Millet-Lagarde began 1941 studying safety of small aircraft and in 1949 flew ML.10 3/4-seat pusher biplane with many unusual features.

Millicer (Australia). Henry Millicer, designer 1953 of Airtourer (*see*, e.g., Victa; Aerospace) produced high-speed Airmite 1977.

Milon (France). Pierre Milon, Brive, built PMB-78 Faucon sport aircraft (January 1979).

MIM (Brazil). Mauricio Impelizieri P. Moura built Esqualo 180 2/3-seater (6 February 1981) followed by Esqualo II 1989.

Mimi (Nazi Bohemia-Moravia Protectorate). Despite German occupation Czech Milos Mieik built Mimi-2-SS sport aircraft (7 August 1944); destroyed when Mieik joined partisans.

Minié (France). Establissements Victor Minié Aéronautique built light aircraft 1950–54.

Mini-Hawk (USA). Mini-Hawk International markets kits and plans of single-seat Tiger-Hawk (October 1974).

Ministry of Aero-Space Industry (China). Manages all aircraft factories and concludes international co-manufacturing agreements.

Minty (Australia). E.R. Minty built Skyhook light autogyro 1978.

Mission (USA). Mission Aviation Related Services built utility aircraft 1981.

Mitsubishi Ki-67-I Hiryu, June 1944.

Mississippi (USA). Mississippi State University built several boundary-layer control STOL research aircraft culminating in XV-11A Marvel 1966.

MIT (USA). MIT Manpowered Aircraft Association built Monarch B (1983), followed by Daedalus Project, completed new MPA, 4 world records, January 1987.

Mitchell (UK). Dr. C.G.B. Mitchell was original designer of Kittiwake I single-seater (23 May 1967).

Mitchell-Procter (UK). Mitchell-Procter Aircraft formed 1966, built Kittiwake I, partnership broke up October 1968; *see* Procter.

Mitchell Wing (USA). Mitchell Aerospace Co., Porterville, CA, market wide range of microlights, plus P-38 Lightning and larger AG-38 War Eagle, plus crop spraying or military equipment.

Mitrovich (Jugoslavia). M. Mitrovich was one of most famous designers in Jugoslavia 1928–40, one type built in modest numbers being MMS.3 light transport with tail carried on booms behind 2 × 130-hp Pobjoy Niagara.

Mitsubishi (Japan). Giant engineering company which in 1920 formed Mitsubishi Nainenki Seizo KK (Mitsubishi internal-combustion engine co.) at Kobe, a major task being production of aircraft. Early designs by Herbert Smith (ex-Sopwith) included 1MF fighter, 1MT1N torpedo bomber, B1M torpedo bomber, 2MR reconnaissance biplane and K3M high-wing monoplane crew trainer/transport, all for Imperial Navy. Alexander Baumann added 2MB1 (Type 87 bomber) and 2MR8 (Type 92 recon aircraft). Mitsubishi's own designers produced B2M biplane bomber, Ki-1 and -2 twin-engined monoplane bombers, and outstanding G3M long-range bomber (1,048) which led to G4M (2,446). Army types included Ki-21 bomber (2,064), Ki-30 light bomber (704), Ki-46 high-speed recon and interception (1,742), Ki-51 ground attack (2,385), Ki-57 transport and Ki-67 heavy bomber (698), while Navy types included F1M patrol seaplane (1,118), A5M fighter (788), A6M Zero-Sen fighter (10,450, of which 3,880 by Mitsubishi, plus 515 A6M-2K and -5K trainers made by others) and J2M Raiden fighter (476). In Second World War ranked No. 2 in number of aircraft produced but No. 1 in weight of airframes and number of engines. Reorganizations resulted in formation of separate Mitsubishi Kokuki KK (M. Aircraft Co.) 1928, which was absorbed 1934 into giant Mitsubishi Jukogyo KK (M. Heavy Industries Co.). Centre of aircraft activity always Nagoya but by 1944 Mitsubishi operated 6 airframe and 11 engine factories throughout Japan. Since 1921 built just over 18,000 aircraft, virtually all military/naval.

Mitsubishi (Japan). From December 1952 Shin Mitsubishi Jukogyo KK (M. Heavy Industries

Reorganized Ltd) rebuilt Komaki South and later Oye, Daiko and Komaki North to form integrated Komaki Aircraft Works. Overhauled USAF C-46, B-26 and later F-86, leading to selection to assemble 300 F-86F using 77% Mitsubishi parts. Built S-55 helicopter, followed by S-61 (185) and SH- and UH-60J. F-86 was followed by 140 F-4EJ, completed 20 May 1981. Prime contractor on F-4EJ update, 173 F-15J/DJ Eagles and next-generation FS-X based on F-16C. Own designs include MU-2 twin-turboprop (design from 1956, not flown until 14 September 1963), over 800 in many versions, T-2 supersonic trainer (20 July 1971) and derived F-1 attack fighter (3 June 1975) and MU-300 Diamond business jet (29 August 1978), *see* next entry. Mitsubishi also handled most of design of NAMC YS-11. Shin (reorganized) dropped from title 1963. Mitsubishi supplies airframe sections for 767 and 777, MD-11 (and has deal on MD-12), P-3C and other US aircraft, and makes engines, missiles, space launchers and spacecraft.

Mitsubishi (USA). Mitsubishi Aircraft International Inc. (MAI) established San Angelo, TX, 1965, to assemble and test MU-2. Developed and produced upgraded Marquise and Solitaire. Moved Dallas 1977, wholly responsible for Diamond business jet which in October 1985 was acquired by Beech and became Beechjet, MAI being closed.

Miyauchi (Japan). Miyauchi Manufacturing Co. produced light aircraft 1974.

MKEK (Turkey). Makina ve Kimya Endustri

Kurumu, state organization of mechanical and chemical industries, took over 1952 Ankara factory of THK, which *see*.

ML (UK). Founded 1935 as R. Malcolm Ltd, ML Aviation, White Waltham, took name from Mobbs/Lobelle, latter (ex-Fairey) chief designer. Main products RPVs and targets, produced Light Aircraft Mk 1 with inflatable wing 1956. Parent ML Holdings owns Slingsby.

MLD: *See* Mechanikai.

MLF (Austria). Motorluftfahrtzeug Gesellschaft, Vienna, oldest Austrian aircraft company (1911), producing Etrich Dove and various Lohner aircraft to 1921.

MMPL (India). IAF Maintenance Command Development Centre produced 190-hp Kanpur I and 225-hp Kanpur II (October 1961), high-wing 4-seaters.

Modern Wing (Canada). Richmond, BC, company rewinging DHC-2 Beavers.

Mod Squad (USA). Specialize in Thunderbird 211 modification of Mooney M20.

Mohawk (USA). Mohawk Aero Corp. established at Minneapolis January 1927 to produce Pinto 2-seat low-wing monoplane; reorganized as Mohawk Aircraft November 1927, produced Spurwing and Redskin.

Mohawk (USA). Mohawk Air Services, sub-

Mohawk Pinto prototype (Scarab), January 1928.

sidiary of Allegheny Airlines, updated fleet of Nord 262 to Mohawk 298 1975–6, actual conversion by Frakes.

Moiseyenko (USSR). Viktor Leonidovich Moiseyenko produced 2U-B3 trainer (185-hp BMW) 1926.

Mojaiski: *See* Mozhaisky.

Möller (Germany). Möller Flugzeugbau founded at Bremen 1935 by Hans Guenther Moller, built small numbers of Stomo 3 and Sturmer ultra-lights, former achieved 123 mph on 18 hp, 4 built.

Moller (USA). Moller International, Davis, CA, researches aspects of vehicle design, aerodynamics and noise, and in 1986 proposed to build series of advanced car-like VTOL flying vehicles powered by multiple ducted fans.

Molniya (Russia). Scientific and Industrial Enterprise which on 17 December 1992 flew prototype piston-engined 6-seater of same name.

Molyneux (Australia). Molyneux Helicopter Co. Pty never completed XM-1000 5-seat tandem-rotor helicopter 1957.

Monarch (USA). Monarch Aerial Corp. formed 1928 as sales organization of Schmuck Aircraft.

Monarch (USA). Monarch Aviation converted numerous 727, DC-8 and L-1011 to all-cargo.

Mong (USA). Ralph Mong sold numerous plans of Mong Sport biplane. Mong/Mortensen is uprated 209-mph version.

Monnett (USA). John T. Monnett formed company at Oshkosh to market plans and components of Sonerai I racer and Sonerai II 2-seat version. Rights passed 1986 to Inav Ltd which ceased trading within a year.

Mono (USA). Mono-Aircraft Inc. formed 1926 at Moline, Illinois, to produce Monocoupe light 2-seater designed by Dan Luscombe, using engine produced in same plant by former car manufacturer W. Velie. Successive models generally upgraded, ending 1934 with Monocoupe D-145 (145-hp Warner Scarab). In same year company taken over by Lambert.

Monocoupe (USA). Monocoupe Airplane and Engine Corp. was one of several companies picking up pieces after Lambert. Moved from Orlando to Melbourne and formed Monocoupe Aircraft of Florida Inc., producing Monocoupe Meteor 4/5-seat twin 1955.

Monospar (UK). Swiss H.J. Stieger developed monoplane wing of metal single-spar construction and designed light twin to test it; left Beardmore and formed Mono Spar Co. November 1928. Success of resulting Gloster-Monospar S.S.1 led to formation of General Aircraft, absorbing Mono Spar Co. 21 February 1931.

Monte-Copter (USA). Never succeeded in completing development of cold-jet tip-drive amphibious 3-seat helicopter, prototype completed February 1960.

Monocoupe (Florida) Meteor prototype, 1955.

Montee (USA). Montee Aircraft Co. formed at Santa Monica, CA, 1923, to build 4-seat open-cockpit monoplane; K.W. Montee killed 1926.

Mooney (USA). Al W. Mooney designed light aircraft from 1922, notably including entire Mono series, followed by Culver aircraft. In 1946 he designed M-18 Mite single-seater (25-hp Crosley), becoming M-18L Wee Scotsman (65-hp Lycoming). Mooney Aircraft formed with brother Art and 2 others at Wichita 5 July 1946, selling 300 before passing design on as home-builder kit. Four-seat M-20 followed (10 August 1953), selling 1,000 by 1962. In October 1967 acquired Alon, adding Alon Aircoupe as Mooney A-2A Cadet. Financial difficulties resulted in Mooney trading as Aerostar 1 July 1970 before being restructured as Mooney Aircraft Corp. as subsidiary of Republic Steel 4 October 1973. In 1984 Republic merged with LTV; various investors formed Mooney Holding Corp., until by 1985 control vested in MM Couvelair and Seydoux (both French) 70% and Lake Aircraft 30%. Based at Kerrville, TX, since 1954, Mooney still produces high-speed 4-seaters.

Morand (Switzerland). Ateliers de Précision Morand re-engined 25 ex-Flugwaffe Jungmann trainers 1974–6.

Morane-Saulnier (France). Léon and Robert Morane and Raymond Saulnier formed **Société Anonyme des Aéroplanes Morane-Saulnier** 10 October 1911 at Puteaux (Paris region). Vast output ensued of 140 different types, early designs being primarily braced monoplanes, leading to 2-seat Type G (1912), single-seat Type H and Type L (1913) and shoulder-wing Type N (1914). Various parasol monoplanes (notably Type AI, 1917, 1,210 built) and biplanes followed. Type AR parasol-wing trainer (1915) continued post-war as M.S.35 (400+ built), Type P reconnaissance aircraft (565) being similar. From 1920 MS concentrated on radial-engined parasol-wing fighters and trainers, several reaching 3-figure total and M.S.230 trainer (1929) exceeding 1,100 and M.S.315 trainer (1932) 346. M.S.405 fighter (8 August 1935) was low-wing monoplane with retractable landing gear, but outdated structure and only 860 hp, so production M.S.406 was no match for Bf 109E (1,081 delivered by June 1940 Armistice). M.S.470 Vanneau advanced trainer (22 December 1944) led to 500 of 3 versions. Single- and twin-engined light aircraft followed, ending with 165 M.S.760 Paris twin-jet 4-seaters (29 July 1954) and M.S.880 Rallye light 3-seater (10 June 1959). Company take-over by Potez 1963 as **Soc. d'Exploitation Etablissements Morane-Saulnier** was followed by reorganization May 1965 as subsidiary of Sud-Aviation, losing identity as part of SOCATA.

Moravan (Czechoslovakia, Moravia). Zlin company was renamed 1949 Moravan Národni Podnik (Moravian Aircraft National Corporation). For details *see* Zlin.

Moravko (Czechoslovakia). Moravko-Slezká Vazovká Tatra formed 1935 as subsidiary of Ringhoffer-Tatra automotive/rail conglomerate. Built biplane trainers: Avro 626 and Bücker Jungmann, followed by 700-hp Tatra T.126 of

Morane-Saulnier MS.730 No. 01, June 1949.

Morrisey 2150, January 1950.

own design. First original design was Tatra T.1 2/3-seat light monoplane. German control 1938 switched factory to other work. *See* Ringhoffer-Tatra.

Moreland (USA). G.E. Moreland formed company at El Segundo, LA, 1928, in following year offering Moreland Trainer, or M-1, to franchise distributors. Parasol monoplane, Trainer was first aircraft designed by Ed Heinemann.

Morgan (UK). Morgan & Co., Leighton Buzzard, were major producer 1916–18 including 504K, $1\frac{1}{2}$-strutter, DH.6 and BHP-engined Vimy.

Morin (France). Pierre Morin built light aircraft 1953.

Morrisey (USA). Douglas test pilot William J. Morrisey built Model 1000 Nifty tandem trainer (1948) for homebuilders, but formed Morrisey Aircraft Co. at Long Beach 1949. Reorganized 1952 at Long Beach as Morrisey Aviation Inc., began series production 1958 of Morrisey 2150. Rights passed to Shinn Engineering, in same plant, through 1964, and then to Varga Aircraft Corp., Chandler, AZ, which produced 2150A Kachina all-metal version until 1985. Bill Morrisey at Las Vegas built Bravo single-seater (30 June 1981), plans marketed.

Morrow (USA). Howard Morrow built factory 1941 at San Bernardino to build Model 1-L plastics-bonded plywood trainer.

Morse: *See* Thomas-Morse.

Mosca: *See* Moskovskii.

Moscow: *See* MAI (USSR).

Moser (USA). E.H. Moser built Aero Sportster single-seater 1984.

Moshier: *See* MTC.

Moskalyev (USSR). Aleksandr Sergeyevich Moskalyev produced 29 different types of aircraft, most at Voronezh and often in appalling conditions. Few built in series, though 37 SAM-5bis (1934) high-wing ambulance/utility and 200 5-2bis ordered, none delivered. Several SAM types were tailless, including SAM-7 Sigma 2-seat fighter (October 1935) and SAM-9 Strela with Concorde planform. Another fighter was twin-boom push/pull SAM-13 (1940). Final designs included assault gliders, flying-boat and rocket fighter.

Moskovskii (Russia). F.E. Mosca, Italian designer, left Savoia 1916 and set up Moskovskii Aviatsionni Zavod Mosca, Moscow Mosca aviation works. Built Morane monoplanes and Nieuport biplanes, and Mosca designed MB parasol monoplane 2-seater for reconnaissance and in early 1917 B-bis parasol fighter, both built in series.

Moss (UK). Moss Bros. Aircraft Ltd, Chorley, Lancs, built MA.1 and MA.2 2-seat monoplanes 1937 and 1939, often called Mosscraft.

Moth (USA). Moth Aircraft Corp. formed at

Lowell, Massachusetts, 1926 to build D.H.60 Moth, building 18 60G and 161 60M. Bought by Curtiss 1929, continued building Curtiss-Wright Moth 60GMW until 1931.

Motoimport (Poland). State organization formed 1956 to handle all sales of aviation products.

Motokov (Czechoslovakia). State organization formed 1948 to handle all sales of aviation products.

Motorluftfahrtzeug: *See* MLF.

Motor Products (USA). This company built several prototypes 1917–19, including William B. Stout's SX-6 Streamlined Monoplane.

Moura: *See* MIM.

Movo (Italy). Milan company (initials from 'modern aircraft organization') which built FM.1 Passero pusher ultralight designed by Stelio Frati (11 December 1947).

Möwe (W. Germany). Möwe-Flugzeugbau was later name of Heini Dittmar's company: *see* Dittmar.

Mozhaisky (Russia). Aleksandr Fedorovich Mozhaisky studied bird flight from 1856, and after prolonged model tests built large monoplane with rectangular wing 3,800 sq ft and 2 steam engines, 1 driving tractor nose propeller and other driving lateral propellers. Vast literature fails to record precise date (probably in August 1884) that he attempted to fly on military field at Krasnoye Selo near St Petersburg. First aeroplane to lift man off ground, but wrecked by uncontrolled roll to left. Died with more advanced aircraft incomplete.

Mozharovskii (USSR). Georgii Mironovich Mozharovskii was specialist in aircraft armament, teamed with Venyevidov to build MV Kombain armoured attack aircraft, abandoned 1941 because of success of BSh-2.

MPC (International). MPC Aircraft GmbH formed as result of 3 October 1985 Memo of Understanding between MBB (now DASA) of W. Germany (now Germany) and CATIC of China, to build jet in 100-seat class.

Mraz (Czechoslovakia). During Second World War Chocen factory of former Benes-Mraz built Fi 156 Storch and training gliders, and also prototype M.1C Sokol. Management reconstituted 1946 as Automobilove Zavody Mraz, with glider-making subsidiary at Nitra. Produced numerous M.1 Sokol and smaller numbers of M.2 Skaut and M.3 Bonzo, all low-wing cabin monoplanes, together with civilian Mraz Cap version of Storch. Lost identity on nationalization 1949, factory becoming CZ Automobilove A Letecke, later Let.

MSE (Hungary). The Gerle series of 29 types of sporting and training aircraft were produced by Müegyetemi Sportrepülö Egyesület, sport-flying association of technical university, at Budapest 1928–39.

MTC (USA). Moshier Technologies Corp. formed 1986 at Mountain View, CA, to continue development of unconventional VTOL aircraft.

MU-2 (USA). MU-2 Modifications Inc., Dallas, convert/modify long-body MU-2 aircraft.

Mudry (France). Avions Mudry et Cie established by Auguste Mudry at Bernay 1958, occupying former SAN premises and initially operated as extension of his CAARP, which was merged into Mudry 1978. Produces sporting/aerobatic aircraft, some in partnership with Sukhoi. US subsidiary is Mudry Aviation Ltd, Wappingers Falls, NY.

Müegyetemi: *See* MSE.

Muenzel (Germany/USSR). Also rendered Myuntsel, Christian names not recorded, German engineer responsible for MR-2 improved twin-float seaplane version of R-1 (derived from D.H.9a).

Müller (Germany). Jacob and Philipp Müller formed Boots und Flugzeugbau Gebr. Müller at Griesheim, Darmstadt, 1908, supplying Voisin parts to August Euler. Subcontractors in First World War, in 1920s formed Flugzeugbau Gebr. Müller, building GMG.II–GMG.V sporting aircraft.

Mummert (USA). Harvey C. Mummert, design engineer at Curtiss' Garden City plant, produced Baby Vampire sport single-seater 1921 with 25-hp

Mraz M.1C Sokol, December 1947.

Lawrence, followed by further biplanes and low-wing monoplanes, ending 1926.

Muniz (Brazil). Antonio Muniz, air force major in 1932, produced first Brazilian-designed aircraft, M-5, in 1932. Later, as Lt.-Col., produced M-7 and M-9 trainers, built in series by Fábrica Brasileira de Aviòes. As Colonel he set up Cassio Muniz SA at Botucatù, São Paulo, producing M-11 cabin monoplane, built by CNNA, and finally impressive Casmuniz 52 (April 1953) twin-engined 5-seater.

Mureaux (France). Les Ateliers des Mureaux formed at Les Mureaux 1918 to build landplanes and seaplanes, initially with few original designs; obtained licence for Vimy Commercial 1922, followed by Bre.XIVA2 and in 1926 Wibault monoplanes. M. Brunet designed Mureaux 3C2 (Hispano engine) and 4C2 (Salmson) 2-seat fighter/recon monoplane, which formed basis for staple products to 1940. In 1928 took over assets of Besson, building MB.35 shipboard seaplane. In 1930 amalgamated with railway firm Ateliers de Construction du Nord de la France, combined firm becoming Les Ateliers de Constructions du Nord de la France et des Mureaux, or **ANF Les Mureaux**. MB.35 developed into MB.411, and 3C2/4C2 into Mureaux 113, 115 and 117, all in major Armée de l'Air front-line service in 1939. Firm was nationalized into SNCAN 1 March 1937.

Murphy (Canada). Murphy Aviation market kits and plans for Renegade biplanes and Rebel 3-seat cabin monoplane.

Murphy (USA). Dick Murphy produced VM-7 Competitor aerobatic aircraft (March 1978).

Murray (USA). F.A. Murray built reduced-scale Curtiss JN-4 1961.

Murrayair (USA/NZ). Under contract to Murrayair of Hawaii, Air New Zealand built prototype Murrayair MA-1 ag-biplane based on Stearman 75 (27 July 1969). Subsequently marketed briefly by Murrayair.

Muscariello (Italy). Franco Muscariello was technical manager of Ali Viberti SpA (*see* Viberti). When that company ceased aeronautical work he continued to develop Musca, final (1953) version being 1°/2S.

MVT (Italy). Two prototypes, a fighter and a sport aircraft, produced 1918 and 1920 by Marchetti-Vickers-Terni, respectively designer, builder and location.

Myasishchyev 3MS, 1956.

MWG (Hungary). State (railway) Wagon Works, at Györ, built about 100 aircraft in Second World War including 60 WM-21.

Myasishchyev (USSR). Vladimir Mikhailovich Myasishchyev rose swiftly in Tupolev's brigade at CAHI, designing flush radiator system of R-6, rear fuselage/tail of TB-3, TB-4 and ANT-20 and whole design of DIP and ANT-41. Helped translate DC-3 drawings at Douglas until arrested 1938 and put to work in CKB-29 (special prison) as head of KB-102, where he produced DVB-102 high-altitude bomber (February 1942), delayed by evacuation to Irtysh. Followed with M-2, DB-108 (VM-16), VB-109 and DIS, all extremely fast and powerful twin-engined aircraft. New and larger OKB formed 1951 to build 3M M-4 long-range jet bomber which became 3MS and 3MS2 tankers. Next design even greater challenge of M-50 supersonic bomber/missile launcher (27 October 1959). General Designer, Valery K. Norikov, OKB title **EMZ 'Serp i Molot' I** (experimental machine factory Hammer & Sickle named for) V.M. Myasishchyev. Produced ultra-high-altitude M-17 and M-55 1981–90, current General Aviation projects SL 2-seater, Skif 4/5-seater, Gjel 5-seat turboprop, Yamal pusher turboprop amphibian and Delfine twin-pusher turboprops. Partner with Tec Avia on MM-1.

Myers (USA). H.H. Myers built Myers Special high-wing 2-seater with remarkable STOL performance, flight development 1950–65, and Model 145 2-seat sport aircraft.

VM-T Atlant, *rebuilt Myasishchyev 3M bomber used for carrying outsize loads, 1988.*

Myers (USA). New Ohio company formed to produce developed versions of Model 145 by original Myers company.

Mylius (W. Germany). Leichtflugzeuge-Entwicklungen Dipl.-Ing. Hermann Mylius built MY 102 Tornado single-seat sporting and aerobatic aircraft (7 July 1973) but failed to complete 2-seat MY 103 Mistral and 4-seat MY 104 Passat.

N

NAA: *See* North American.

NAC (UK). Northern Aircraft Co. formed 1914, took over Lakes Flying Co. at Windermere, operated school and built aircraft parts during war.

NAC (UK). The Norman Aeroplane Co. Ltd formed by changing name of NDN 22 July 1985, at same time moving to Barry, S. Wales.

NAC (USA). National Aircraft Corp. built light aircraft 1986.

NAF: *See* Naval Aircraft Factory.

Nagler (Austria/UK). Bruno Nagler and Raoul Hafner built R.I Revoplane, simple helicopter, Vienna 1929. Came to UK and built R.II 1932, followed by improved Helicogyro, able to fly as helicopter or autogyro, 1934. *See* next.

Nagler-Rolz (Germany). On outbreak of war Nagler joined with Frank Rolz to form Nagler-Rolz Flugzeugbau. Flew NR.55 (September 1940) with single rotor blade balanced by small engine/propeller group. Refined into NR 54 (1941), outstanding portable helicopter, but no production.

Nagler (USA). Emigrated to USA and formed Nagler Helicopter Co. Inc., building NH-160 helicopter (February 1955) and VG-1 Vertigyro able to fly in several modes: *see* Vertidynamics.

Naglo (Germany). Naglo Werft, Pichelsdorf

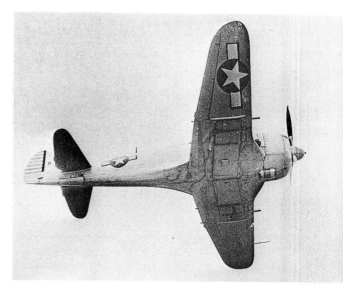

Nakajima Ki-44-IIb, captured 1944.

(Berlin), built biplane trainer and fighter, followed by D.II quadruplane fighter (spring 1918).

NAI (China). Nanjing Aeronautical Institute produced AD-100 Traveller composites canard ultralight (1985).

Nakajima (Japan). Formed 6 December 1917 by retired engineer (ex-Imperial Navy Lt.) Chikuhei Nakajima and Seibei Kawanishi as Nihon Hikoki Seisakusho KK (Japanese Aeroplane Manufacturing Work Co. Ltd). Partners split December 1919, Kawanishi forming own company; Nakajima obtained backing of mighty Mitsui in forming **Nakajima Hikoki KK** (Nakajima Aeroplane Co. Ltd). Continued unchanged during massive growth to become No. 1 producer in Second World War with 4 airframe plants (Ota, Koizumi, Handa and Utsonomiya) and 4 engine plants, but on 1 April 1945 transferred to state control as 1st Munitions Arsenal. In 1920–39 Nakajima built more than 6,000 aircraft, almost all for Imperial Army and Navy and including several licensed designs (Bre 14, Avro 504, NiD 29, W33, Gambet, etc.). Deliveries 1920–45 totalled 29,760. Major programmes for Second World War included Ki-27, Ki-43 Hayabusa, Ki-44 Shoki and Ki-84 Hayate fighters, B5N and B6N Tenzan torpedo bombers, C6N Saiun reconnaissance aircraft, Ki-49 Donryu heavy bomber, J1N Gekko escort and night fighter and E8N reconnaissance seaplane. Nakajima also made large numbers of aircraft

NAMC YS-11, 30 August 1962.

designed by others, notably A6M, Ki-21, G3M, P1Y and L2D, handling entire programme for A6M2-N fighter seaplane. Post-war, major assets were managed by Fuji.

NAL (India). National Aeronautical Laboratory supports national programmes, e.g. by developing carbonfibre rudder of Do 228, but no complete aircraft.

NAL (Japan). National Aerospace Laboratory handles major R&D programmes including Japanese Spaceplane, 100-passenger fan-lift VTOL and Asuka USB STOL aircraft.

NAM (Philippines). National Aero Manufacturing Corp. is subsidiary of PADC, formed to handle production of Islander and BO 105 and design/development of 4-seat utility aircraft. Closed 1982, these programmes subsequently handled directly by PADC.

NAMC (China). Nanchang Aircraft Manufacturing Co. formed 1951 to build CJ-5 (Yak-18 derived) trainer; built 379 and continues with improved CJ-6A. Produced J-6 (MiG-19 derived) and subsequently 997 Q-5 derived attack fighters. Handled Y-5 (An-2), building 727 before this transferred to SAP. Developing K-8 jet trainer (in partnership with Pakistan PAC) and N-5A ag-aircraft.

NAMC (Japan). Nihon Aeroplane Manufacturing Co. Ltd, English form of Nihon Kokuki Seizo KK, formed to manage short-range turboprop airline project agreed by Ministry of International Trade and Industry 1956. Six partners began design 1957: Mitsubishi (leader), Kawasaki, Fuji, Shin Meiwa, JAMC (Nihon Hikoki) and Showa. YSKK or TADA (Transport Aircraft Development Assoc.) formed May 1957, which in June 1959 was replaced by NAMC. Resulting YS-11 flew 30 August 1962.

NAMC/PAC (International). K-8 Karakorum 8 trainer (Garrett TFE 731 turbofan) developed by NAMC (China) and PAC (21 November 1990).

Napier & Miller (UK). Built BE.2c and 2e 1914–16 at Old Kilpatrick, Clyde estuary.

D. Napier & Son (UK). Famous engine firm produced numerous RE.7, RE.8 and Snipe aircraft 1915–18.

Naras (India). Naras Aviation Pvt Ltd, subsidiary of Naras Avionics of Miami, acquired rights to Brantly B-2B and 305 helicopters, plans to build presumably thwarted by new Brantly company in USA.

Nardi (Italy). Formed as **Fratelli Nardi** (Nardi Brothers) at Milan 1933 by Elio, Euste, Elto and Luigi Nardi to produce FN.305 advanced trainer (19 February 1935). Initial production handled by Piaggio until Nardi factory on Linate airport completed and company reorganized as **Nardi SA Per Costruzioni Aeronàutiche**. About 505 FN.305 built excluding 122 in Romania. Other trainers and tourers followed, notably FN.310, 315 and 316. Branch factory at Loreto destroyed, but Milan rebuilt post-war and FN.333 3-seat (later 4-seat) pusher amphibian designed (4 December 1952). Definitive production FN.333 all made under licence by SIAI-Marchetti. Surviving brother Dott. Elto Nardi established BredaNardi 1971, which *see*.

Nardi FN.305 (long-range single-seat version), January 1937.

NASA (USA). National Aeronautics and Space Administration is not in planemaking business, but has had many aircraft constructed or modified to support its research, including (e.g.) Fleep, QSRA, AD-1 slew wing and MAW F-111, and manages X-30 NASP (National Aero-Space Plane).

Nash (UK). Nash Aircraft, subsidiary of Kinetrol, produced Petrel 2-seater (8 November 1980).

Nash (USA). Paul L. Nash built light aircraft 1984.

National Aero Manufacturing: *See* NAM.

National Aeronautical Laboratory: *See* NAL (India).

National Aeronautics: *See* NASA.

National Aerospace Laboratory: *See* NAL (Japan).

National Aircraft Corporation (USA). Built light aircraft 1986.

National Aircraft Division (USA). Formed by American Airmotive Corp., which *see*, to produce NA-75 derivative of Stearman 75.

National Aircraft Factories (UK). Established 1916 by Ministry of Munitions: No. 1, Waddon, Surrey, built D.H.9; No. 2, Heaton Chapel, Stockport, built D.H.9 and 10; No. 3, Aintree, Liverpool, built Bristol Fighter.

National Airways (USA). National Airways

System, Lomax, Illinois, produced Air King 4-seat open-cockpit biplane 1926, marketed with choice of 4 engines.

National Dynamics (S. Africa). Formed 1975 by Air Nova to produce and market Explorer/Observer; *see* Patchen.

Nationale Vliegtuigindustrie (Netherlands). Formed 1920 at s'Gravenhage (The Hague) to produce Koolhoven designs, FK.23A, 29 and 31 in particular. Closed when Koolhoven left 1926.

National Steel Car (Canada). Malton (Toronto) railway rolling-stock firm which in 1940 switched major resources to building Westland Lysander I and NA Yale and Harvard. Became Victory Aircraft 1942.

Naugle (USA). At Latrobe, PA, built N-6 4-seater and N-12 Mercury 3-seater 1935–47.

NAV (Netherlands). Nederlandse Automobil en Vliegtuig Onderneming formed 1920 at Enykaaude, Maas. Only known product 4-seat Limousine, pilot in open rear cockpit, parasol wing, 220-hp Benz.

Naval Aircraft Factory (USA). NAF authorized 27 July 1917 not only to design and build aircraft but also furnish Navy with yardsticks for evaluating performance and costs of aircraft submitted by industry. Set up within perimeter of Philadelphia Navy Yard, built several thousand aircraft ending early 1945, including several types of Factory design. Built airship *Shenandoah*, TF tandem fighter flying-boats, various TS (turret scout) and TR landplanes and seaplanes, NW-1 and -2 racers, TG trainers, PT torpedo seaplanes, whole family of PN patrol flying-boats (many others built by contractors), PBN Nomad (upgraded Catalina) and, best-known Factory design, N3N Canary trainer seaplane (August 1935) which served at Naval Academy to 1961.

Naval Air Establishment (China). English title of government facility formed 1918 at Mamoi, transferred 1931 to Shanghai, producing handful of seaplanes including Chiang Hung 2/3-seater, Chiang Gaen 2-seat recon/trainer and Ning Hai single-seat shipboard recon.

Navion (USA). Navion Aircraft Co., Galveston, TX, formed 1959 to manufacture improved 5-seat 1,858-mile Navion Rangemaster (10 June 1960). Sold out to Janox.

Navion Rangemaster (USA). Previous company bankrupt 1962, assets purchased (via Janox) by Cedric Kotowicz who formed Navion Rangemaster Aircraft at Wharton, TX, intending production of improved Navion Rangemaster G (16 November 1974).

NB (USA). Nicholas-Beazley Airplane Co. Inc. formed 1921 at Marshall, Missouri, with many activities including limited production of (Barling) NB Trainer from 1929, Pobjoy Special racer 1930, and in 1934 single Swanson-designed cabin monoplane (prototype of Fahlin but with Pobjoy engine).

NDN (UK). NDN Aircraft Ltd formed at Goodwood/Chichester by N.D. Norman to develop and market NDN 1 Firecracker turbo-

prop trainer (26 May 1977) and subsequent designs. Did not succeed in objective, so name changed to NAC (Norman Aeroplane Co.) coincident with move to Barry: see NAC (UK), 2nd entry.

Neale (UK). J.V. Neale built series of aircraft at Bristol from July 1909. Howard Flanders joined as manager/pilot November 1909, testing several monoplanes and biplanes built for customers.

Nebraska (USA). Formed at Lincoln 1918, subcontractor to military programmes and until 1926 built many variations of Lincoln Standard 2-seat biplane.

Nederlandse: *See* NHI.

Neico (USA). Neico Aviation, Santa Paula, CA, produced Lancair (June 1984) high-speed side-by-side tourer/trainer. Several hundred kits delivered of original Lancair 200 and 235; more powerful and long-range Lancair 320 uses composite fuselages from ACT Philippines. Even more powerful 4-seat Lancair IV (cruise 333 mph) now in production.

Neiva (Brazil). Sociedade Aeronáutica Neiva built training gliders and sailplanes at Rio from 1954, but in 1956–8 moved to new factory at Botucatú, São Paulo, to build Paulistinha designed by CAP. Later produced improved Campeiro and Neiva-designed Regente (resembling 4-seat Cessna), Lanceiro and Universal (air force T-25). Built fuselages of Embraer Ipanema and on 10 March 1980 became Indùstria Aero-

Nicholas-Beazley NB-8, probably early 1930.

náutica Neiva, wholly-owned subsidiary of Embraer responsible for entire production of Minuano, Seneca III and Carajá and for major parts of Tucano and Bandeirante.

Nelson (USA). Ted Nelson produced small air-cooled engines from 1944 and by 1946 was fitting them to sailplane-like aircraft, usually of Bowlus design, including Bumblebee (1946) and Dragonfly (1948). Still produces engines.

Nennig (France). Edmond Nennig designed at least 8 aircraft between wars, built in shops at Porte de Châtillon. Three in 1925–6 had Anzani engines. Aircraft 01, of 1933, produced with André Maillet, achieved 290 km/h (180 mph) with 185-hp Regnier. Fastest was C.3 for 1935 Coupe Deutsch, with inverted 12-cylinder Salmson with Roots supercharger, 525 km/h (326 mph). Last, beautiful C.5, expected 290 km/h despite only 100-hp Minié.

Nesmith (USA). Robert E. Nesmith Inc., Houston, TX, produced Cougar side-by-side high-wing tourer (March 1957), many hundreds homebuilt.

Nesterov (Russia). Pyetr Nikolayevich Nesterov was most famous Russian pilot pre-1914, credited with first loop. Unlike contemporaries, recognized importance of banking in turns and invented (31 August 1911) complete control system with cams to warp wing. Rebuilt Nieuport IV with this system, rudder being removed.

Nestler (UK). F.C. Nestler Ltd formed 1912, office at 9 Greycoat St, Westminster, as British agents for Sanchez-Besa aircraft. From 1914 produced components, plus single Nestler Scout designed by M. Emil Boudot, probably built Hendon, flown prior to February 1917, crashed 26 March.

Nestler und Breitfeld (Germany). Formed January 1933 at Erla to produce ultralights designed by Justus Mehr. Renamed Erla 1934.

Neumann (USA). Harold Neumann produced at least 2 racers, including high-wing Special 1932.

Newcal (USA). Newcal Aviation, Little Falls, NJ, produce DHC-4T turboprop conversions of Caribou (16 November 1991).

New Standard (USA). In 1928 Gates-Day became

New Standard D-29, 9 June 1921.

New Standard Aircraft Corp., same address. Continued to produce G-D 24, adding fresh Day biplanes D-25 4-seat, D-26 2-seat and D-27 single-seat mailplanes, D-28 seaplane and D-29 trainer (Navy NT-1). Navy allotted NT-2 to 2 D-25A captured from prohibition smugglers.

New Technik (USA). New Technik Inc. formed 1990 at Morgantown, W. Virginia, by Aircraft Acquisition which had bought Taylorcraft; with WV University producing L-2M Tech 2 2-seat sport/trainer, Model 20 Tech 4 4-seater and Twin Tech 2-seat light twin.

New Transport: *See* NTT.

New Zealand (NZ). Aero Engine Services Ltd (AESL) and Air Parts (NZ) amalgamated 1973 to form NZ Aerospace Industries, building Fletcher, etc. Reconstituted 1 July 1982 as Pacific Aerospace Corp. (PAC).

NFW (Germany). National Flugzeug-Werke formed Berlin-Johannisthal prior to 1916, primarily to run flying school and handle repair and maintenance. Built E I fighting scout 1916 and more powerful E II 1917, both monoplanes.

NH90 (International). Programme to build multi-role tactical and naval medium helicopter launched in MoU September 1985 by France, West Germany, Italy, Netherlands and UK. UK pulled out, leaving as participants Agusta, Eurocopter France, Eurocopter Deutschland and Fokker, with HQ at Marignane, Marseilles. First flight 1995.

NHI (Netherlands). Nederlandse Helicopter Industrie RV formed 1955 at Papendrecht to continue work on SOBEH H-3 Kolibrie. Taken over by Aviolanda 15 May 1959.

NIAI (USSR). In September 1930 Leningrad LIIPS (institute for sail and communication engineers) formed UK-GVF (civil air fleet training organization) which in turn formed NIAI (Nauchno-Issledovatelskii Aero-Institut, scientific research aero institute) in 1931. From 1934 organized into design brigades led by G.I. Bakshayev, A.I. Lisichkin, A.G. Bedunkovich and Yu.V. Domrachyev. Produced at least 48 aircraft of 14 types, notably: NIAI-1/LK-1 by Lisichkin and V.F. Rentel, 4-seat blended wing/fuselage (May 1933), NIAI-4/LK-4 by Bedunkovich, 6 variants of STOL biplane (early 1934), LK tandem cabin monoplane by Bakshayev (1936), RK/LIG-7 by Bakshayev with telescopic variable-area wings 1936 (to lead to RK-1 fighter never built), P-3/LIG-5 family of biplanes (from 1936), LEM-3/LIG-6 10-seat 100-hp monoplane (1936) and SKh-1/LIG-10 multirole and ag-biplane (1937).

Nichi Koku KK (Japan). Established as Fiat subsidiary October 1939 with minority shareholding by Kanegafuchi cotton mill, to produce Fiat aircraft and engines. Supported 85 B.R. 20 bombers supplied earlier but these soon withdrawn and no new order.

Nicholas-Beazley: *See* NB.

Nickel & Foucard (France). Rudy Nickel and Joseph Foucard produce 001 Asterix unconventional 2-seater.

Nicollier (France). Avions H. Nicollier, Besançon, produce plans, kits and parts of sport monoplanes NH 433 Menestrel, 434 Super Menestrel and HN 600 Week-End single-seaters and HN 700 Menestrel II 2-seater.

Nielsen & Winther (Denmark). Copenhagen machine-tool firm, produced Type Aa single-seat fighter (21 January 1917), 6 served briefly with Danish army. Also prototypes of seaplane version Ac and 2-seat recon Ab.

Nieman: *See* KhAI.

Nieuport (France). SA des Etablissements Nieuport founded at Issy-les-Moulineaux, Paris, June 1910 by Edouard de Niéport, who used name Nieuport (to which he later changed his own) to avoid embarrassing his family. Niéport had built fast monoplanes from October 1908, first to carry designations being 30-hp 2N and 50-hp 2V (speed record 82.73 mph), both 1911. He was killed 15 September 1911, Henri Deutsche de la Meurthe reorganizing as limited company. By 1914 over 120 aircraft sold, many exported including to French, Italian and Russian armies. In 1914 Gustave Delage joined as designer and produced remarkable series of superior aircraft starting with Nie.10 2-seater (late 1914). From this stemmed over 10,000 aircraft of 16 basic types, notably including Types 11 and XVII agile lightweight V-strut sesquiplanes with rotary engines. This formula endured until Nie.28 (June 1917) which was conventional biplane. Delage also produced a triplane fighter and a monoplane. Post-war adhered to conventional biplanes, notably with Nie 29 (300-hp Hispano, June 1918) of which at least 1,220 built including many by

Nieuport-Delage NiD 52 (assembled in Spain), 1929.

French, Italian, Japanese, Belgian and Spanish licensees. Nieuport merged with Astra balloon/airship company 1920 to become **Nieuport-Astra**, aircraft being restyled Nieuport-Delage, with NiD designations. NiD 42 (1924) led to many versions of NiD 62 fighter (858). From 1930 most were parasol monoplanes. Delage retired 1930, and next design was thus designated Ni 140, 2-seat shipboard fighter dive-bomber with low cranked wing (March 1935). In 1934 company merged with Ateliers et Chantiers de la Loire, resulting **Groupement Aviation Loire-Nieuport** producing LN 161 fighter prototypes and production LN 40 dive-bombers.

Nieuport (UK). Nieuport & General Aircraft Co. established November 1916 at Cricklewood, London NW2, as one of group managed by Samuel Waring of Waring & Gillow, furniture manufacturers (others being Alliance and BAT). Original purpose to produce Nie.11 replaced by manufacture of Camel. After H.P. Folland and Major Heckstall-Smith joined early 1917, N&GA undertook design work, producing B.N.1 (initials from British Nieuport, though that was not firm's name), Nighthawk fighters and London bomber. Nighthawk served RAF post-war and was starting point for Gloucestershire company.

Nieuport-Astra: *See* Nieuport.

Nieuport-Macchi: *See* Macchi.

Nieuschloss-Sichtig (Hungary). Only known to have produced 2 different monoplane trainers 1923, designed by Bela Oravecz and Georg Szebeny.

Nihon: *See* NAMC (Japan); Nippi.

Nihon University (Japan). Led by Dr Hidemasa Kimura, students have built Okamura N-52, N-58 Cygnet, STOL N-62 (produced by Itoh as Eaglet), N-70 Cygnus, N-75 Cygnus II and 4 successful man-powered aircraft.

Nikitin (USSR). Vasili Vasilyevich Nikitin was architect who taught himself to design and fly aircraft. Worked under Grigorovich, Polikarpov and, finally, as deputy to Kamov. In 1930–39 produced series of successful prototypes. NV-1 small sporting monoplane (September 1933) improved into MV-2 (1935). NV-2bis enlarged and more powerful (1939), 200 ordered by VVS as fighter trainers but believed no production. NV-4 2-seat biplane amphibian (1936). MU-4 and -5 training biplane amphibians designed with N.G. Mikhelson. NV-5/U-5 led to series of U-5 biplane trainers (1937). LSh was more powerful U-5 (1942), prototype made over 600 front-line flights as staff transport. NV-6 (December 1940) tiny aerobatic biplane. IS-1 (6 November 1940) fighter took off as biplane, flew as monoplane, landed as biplane. Led to more powerful IS-2 (early 1941), but 447-mph IS-4 is believed to have been abandoned on evacuation of bureau. These folding-wing fighters often ascribed to Nikitin-Shyevchyenko, because original studies made by Nikitin's test pilot V.V. Shyevchyenko.

Nimmo (USA). Produced 2 Formula racers 1946–7.

Nipper (UK). Nipper Aircraft Ltd, East Midlands Airport, purchased rights 1966 to Tipsy Nipper. In liquidation May 1971; **Nipper Kits & Components** formed to support existing owners, still supplying plans and kits, over 70 flying.

Nippi (Japan). Nihon Hikoki KK, Japan Aircraft Manufacturing Co. Ltd, originally Nippi motor cycle firm, began 1959 overhauling US Navy aircraft in Japan and undertaking STOL research with series of modifications to Saab Safir. Grown to have 2 large plants, 1 (Atsugi) still mainly repair/overhaul, other (Sugita, Yokohama) with 30 major programmes including parts for 757, 767, 777, F-15, MD-11, T-4, P-3C, CH-47J, etc.

Nippon Kokusai (Japan). Nippon Kokusai Kokuki Kogyo KK formed June 1941 by merger of NKK and Kokusai Kokuki KK, main products being Ki-86 (licensed Bü 131 Jungmann), Ki-59 transport and Ki-76 STOL observation and liaison aircraft.

Nippon Kokyo: *See* next.

NKK (Japan). Nippon Koku Kogyo KK (Japan international air industries co.), Hiratsuka, produced several modest aircraft 1933–40, notably Ki-59 high-wing 8-passenger transport with 2 × 450-hp Hitachi (June 1939), production being by merged Nippon Kokusai.

Noorduyn (Canada). R.B.C. 'Bob' Noorduyn had lifetime of aircraft design in several companies

Nord 262 of Dan-Air, 1962.

before opening Noorduyn Aircraft Ltd (soon changed to Noorduyn Aviation) May 1935, occupying former Curtiss-Reid premises in St Laurent, Montreal. One product, Norseman utility transport (14 November 1935), initially with Wright Whirlwind or P&W Wasp Junior but main production all with 550-hp Wasp. Total by Noorduyn 896, including 749 UC-64A for USAAF. In 1946 assets sold to Canadian Car and Foundry, which built small number before selling rights 1953 to Noorduyn Norseman Aircraft which provided support to owners.

Noran (USA). Marketed Speedy Bat at San Francisco 1929 for $1,250.

Nord (France). Société Nationale de Constructions Aéronautiques du Nord formed January 1937 on enforced nationalization of defence industries, also known as SNCA du Nord or SNCAN. Took over CAMS, most of Potez, Les Mureaux and parts of Breguet and Amiot. Henry Potez was political animal, embraced nationalization and so was first Administrator of SNCAN. Continued existing programmes, and in Second World War produced Potez 63, Potez-CAMS 161, Do 24, Bf 108 and prototypes of Me 208. In 1945 continued Do 24, developed Bf 108 into Nord 1000 and began family of light aircraft continued with Me 208-derived 1100 Noralpha and 1200 Norécrin. Caudron-Renault was added 1945, Bourges factory of liquidated SNCAC 1949, Lyon-Villeurbanne factory of Arsenal 1953 and SFECMAS December 1954. Major

programmes of 1950s included NC.856 military liaison and 4-seat tourer, 1402 Gerfaut and 1500 Griffon supersonic research aircraft, 1400 Noroit patrol amphibian, 2501 Noratlas military freighter (*see* next entry), 3202 trainer and 3400 STOL observation aircraft. Called **Nord Aviation** from January 1958, group was augmented by agreement with Max Holste 1961 which effectively gave Nord former MH.262 programme. Produced wings for Dassault Mirage and major partner in Transall. Lost identity on merger into Aerospatiale 1 January 1970.

Nord (W. Germany). Upon adoption of Nord 2501 Noratlas for Luftwaffe, decision taken to buy 20 from Nord-Aviation and 117 from group formed as Nordflug, later changed to Flugzeugbau-Nord GmbH. Formed December 1955 by Hamburger Flugzeugbau, Siebelwerke-ATG and Weserflug.

Nordam (USA). Repair and mod centre, specialist in hushkitting 737-200.

Norman: *See* NAC (UK), 2nd entry.

Normande: *See* SAN.

Norman Thompson (UK). Douglas White (money) and Norman Thompson (Cambridge graduate) formed **White & Thompson Ltd** mid-1909 at Middleton-on-Sea, West Sussex, company registered June 1912. Built metal-skinned twin-engined biplane, pusher biplane and single- and twin-engined flying-boats 1912–13, followed by at least 8 No. 3 boats (150-hp Hispano). Built for RNAS 24 Short S.38 trainers 1913–14. After start of war F.P.H. Beadle joined as designer and produced tractor biplane (RNAS Type 1172 from first serial), believed first monocoque fuselage in production, 10 delivered. Company name changed 4 October 1915 to **The Norman Thompson Flight Co**, Bognor Regis. Built at least 50 NT.4 flying-boats (2 pusher Hispano), plus at least 150 NT.2B trainer flying-boats (pusher Hispano, Sunbeam or Beardmore), others built by S.E. Saunders and Supermarine. Prototype only of N.1B fighter flying-boat plus 2 N.2C developed from NT.4a. Company taken over by Handley Page 1919.

Norsk: *See* Hönningstad.

North American (USA). North American Aircraft is major division of Rockwell International Corp. Known as NA Aircraft Operations until 1990. Based El Segundo, production facilities Palmdale and Tulsa, main programmes X-30 NASP and ongoing work on B-1B Lancer (100 built 1985-88), OV-10B, F-111 Upgrade and AC-130U Spectre. *See* next; Rockwell.

North American (USA). North American Aviation Inc. formed 6 December 1928 by Clement M. Keys, former Editor *Wall St Journal*, as 'paper' holding company to manage proliferating empire of aviation acquisitions (at that time Curtiss, Wright, Curtiss-Caproni, Curtiss-Robertson, Travel Air, Keystone and Moth). In 1929 Ford Instrument, Sperry, Berliner-Joyce and Pitcairn were added, plus airlines Faucett, Cubana, Eastern, NY Airways and half TWA. NAA even bought into Douglas. After Crash, empire collapsed, and in 1933 29% of NAA was sold to General Motors, which itself had been building General Aviation around a rearranged Fokker Aircraft (Atlantic Aircraft plus Dayton-Wright). NAA disposed of most holdings, General Aviation took over Berliner-Joyce becoming General Aviation Manufacturing Corp. and began designing and making aircraft in former Curtiss-Caproni plant at Dundalk, MD: *see* General Aviation. General Motors sent Ernest R. Breech to run Dundalk as President of NAA. He imported numerous proven engineers including James H. 'Dutch' Kindelberger and John Leland Atwood. In 1934 Air Mail Act

North American YF-86K Sabre, 15 July 1954.

prohibited aircraft manufacturer from running airline and vice versa, so NAA decided to build aircraft only. Breech appointed Kindelberger President and Atwood VP and chief engineer. Continued GA-43 transport and 43J seaplane, developed GA-15 observation aircraft into Army O-47 and quickly produced prototype GA-16 (NA-16) monoplane basic trainer (8 April 1935). Army pilots thought it best of several contenders, and after changing from Whirlwind to Wasp and fitting enclosed canopy Army ordered 42 as BT-9. On strength of this single order NAA moved to California, building new plant at Mines Field, Inglewood (today LA International Airport). Original 148 employees grew over next 10 years to over 91,000, building numerous BT-9 derivatives (notably AT-6/SNJ, Texan, Harvard and Yale) for 87 customers, plus 9,817 B-25 Mitchell bombers, 15,586 Mustang/P-51 fighters, P-82 Twin Mustangs and even B-24s, at Inglewood, Dallas and Kansas City. Post-war recession made General Motors pull out, Kindelberger becoming Chairman and being replaced by Atwood. Move into light aircraft with Navion lost money (though aircraft itself was good, made by Ryan and others). FJ Fury, AJ Savage, B-45 Tornado and T-28 Trojan were all major programmes, but dwarfed by XP-86 (1 October 1947) which led to 6,933 F-86 Sabres plus 2,458 by licensees. Many Sabres were made at Government plant at Columbus, Ohio, which had been last home of Curtiss. New Columbus team produced Navy FJ-2/3/4 (AF-1) Furies, AJ-2 series and rebuilt T-6, while Inglewood produced F-100 Super

Northrop N-1M, 3 July 1940.

Sabre (24 April 1953). Columbus built 359 of 2,294 F-100s, whilst developing XA3J Vigilante, packed with new technology (31 August 1958), leading to A-5A/B and RA-5C production versions. Columbus continued with T-2 Buckeye and OV-10 Bronco, but F-107, F-108 and XB-70 remained prototypes. NAA became leader in giant missiles and rockets, Rocketdyne division (1955) still having monopoly in biggest liquid-propellant engines. Inglewood produced X-15 aerospace-craft, and manager Harrison Storms went on to manage Apollo lunar programme. Kindelberger died in harness 1967 and on 22 September 1967 NAA merged with Rockwell-Standard of Pittsburgh (which among other things had taken over Aero Commander) to form North American Rockwell. In turn this was merged 16 February 1973 with Rockwell Manufacturing to form Rockwell International Corp.: *see* preceding entry.

North American Rockwell (USA). Formed 22 September 1967 by merger of North American Aviation and Rockwell-Standard. Comprised Aerospace and Systems Group (military/naval aircraft and Sabreliners) and Commercial Products Group (Aero Commander Division and others). Disappeared on reorganization 1973.

Northern Aircraft: *See* NAC (UK), 1st entry.

Northern Aircraft (USA). Northern Aircraft Inc., Alexandria, Minnesota, purchased rights and assets to Cruisemaster 14-19 from Bellanca 1956,

also supporting former Republic Seabees after merger with American Aviation Corp.

Northrop (USA). John Knudsen (Jack) Northrop designed wings of Loughead F-1 and produced other Loughead designs. Joined Davis-Douglas 1923, but moved to Lockheed 1926 and designed Vega. Lockheed did not wish to embrace stressed-skin construction nor all-wing designs, so in 1928 set up own small **Avion Corp.** with Ken Jay at Burbank to build undesignated flying-wing aircraft tested at Lake Muroc. Clearly no market (yet) so accepted W.E. 'Bill' Boeing's suggestion that he should form **Northrop Aircraft Corp.** as division of huge United Aircraft & Transport Corp. UAT wanted Northrop's knowledge of metal stressed-skin structures, and Northrop quickly produced Alpha (May 1930), first such modern structure to go into production. Beta (200 mph on 300 hp) followed 1931, but decision of UAT to merge Northrop into Stearman at Wichita resulted in break, Northrop instead forming **Northrop Corp.** with D.W. Douglas, latter's Douglas Aircraft holding 51% of stock. New plant at El Segundo, LA, had briefly housed Moreland, whose designer, Ed Heinemann, joined Northrop as chief engineer. Major types that followed included Gamma (1933), XFT-1 fighter (1934), Delta and 3-A fighter (1935), BT-1 dive-bomber (1936) and A-17A, also known as Douglas 8A (1937). Douglas pressured Northrop to merge fully into Douglas, but Northrop increasingly wanted design freedom, result being amicable separation 5 April 1937, Northrop

Corp. becoming Douglas El Segundo division, Northrop assisting Heinemann in initial design of what became DB-7 bomber. Chance meeting spring 1939 with TWA official La Motte T. Cohu resulted in formation August 1939 of **Northrop Aircraft Inc.**, Cohu Chairman and General Manager, Northrop President and Chief Engineer, staff of 18 housed in Hotel Hawthorne, LA, until plant completed February 1940. Built 24 N-3PB seaplanes, tails for PBY and nacelles for B-17 while designed P-61 Black Widow (21 May 1942) and gigantic flying wing XB-35 (25 June 1946). N-1M, N-9M, XP-56, MX-324 and XP-79 were research or prototype flying wings of Second World War. XB-35 led to 8-jet YB-49 and 6-jet YRB-49A, and P-61 led to F-15. Various cruise missiles ended with intercontinental SM-62 Snark. USAF bought 23 C-125 Raider STOL transports, 1,050 F-89 Scorpion interceptors, 1,189 T-38 Talon supersonic trainers and 2,614 F-5 light fighters (a further 776 F-5 made in Canada, S. Korea, Spain, Switzerland and Taiwan). YF-17 (9 June 1974) led to F/A-18 Hornet produced jointly with McDonnell Douglas (following dispute, latter took over rights to F/A-18 8 April 1985) and same partners developed YF-23 Advanced Tactical Fighter (27 August 1990). In giant computer-run programme B-2 Advanced Technology Bomber was developed at new B-2 Division, Pico Rivera, CA (17 July 1989). Since 1966 made all 747 fuselages. Commercial Aircraft Division formed 1992.

Northwest (Canada). Northwest Industries (NWI), Division of CAE (mainly electronic group), is large Edmonton centre for modification, overhaul, etc., especially in support of CAF.

Noury (Canada). Noury Aircraft produced Tourer, resembling Taylorcraft, May 1940, and derived T-65 Noranda (6 February 1946). Company bought by CanCar June 1946.

NRC (Canada). National Research Council tested flying-wing glider with variable-incidence outer panels 1946–9.

NST (Germany). Norbert Schwarze Maschinenbau produced Minimum and Ministar ultralights 1986.

NTK-UVVS (USSR). Scientific and Technical

Committee of VVS (air force), c. 1925–60.

NTT (Germany/Indonesia). New Transport Technologies, by MBB/IPTN April 1984, to produce N-442 4-seat helicopter, active work suspended 1990.

NUD (Turkey). Nuri Demirag Tayyare Fabrikasi formed 1937 at Istanbul, produced gliders and NU D.36 biplane trainer in series and prototype NU D.38 6-passenger transport.

Nuri Demirag: *See* NUD.

Nurtanio: *See* LIPNUR; PT Nurtanio.

Nuvoli (Italy). Ing. Nuvoli, Turin, produced N.3 2-seater, 40-hp Salmson AD9 (30 October 1931), open-cockpit N.3S (Fiat A50) and larger N.5R, 75-hp Pobjoy (11 April 1933).

NWI: *See* Northwest.

Nyeman: *See* KhAI.

Nyevdachin (USSR). Vyacheslav Pavlovich Nyevdachin (not Newdashin) produced series of *Burevestnik* light monoplanes 1924–9.

Nyge (Sweden). AB Nyge-Aero, Nyköping, built VLA-1 light 2-seater 1984.

Oakland (USA). Oakland Airmotive specialized in conversion, e.g. PV-2 to Centaurus executive aircraft and Bonanza to twin-engined Super V.

Oakley (UK). Built 3 Sopwith Triplanes 1917 at Ilford of 25 ordered.

Oberlerchner (Austria). Josef Oberlerchner Holzindustrie woodworkers delivered 4,000 sailplanes 1941–61, as well as Bf 109 tails and He 162 wings, plus original-design JOB 15 3-seat low-wing monoplane (December 1960).

Occidental (USA). Occidental Aircraft Corp.,

Washington DC, did not complete Model 100 STOL 100-passenger transport based on Burnelli formula 1970.

Oddin, Bradbury & Cull (UK). Southampton (Eastleigh) firm which built several prototypes under contract including Kay Gyroplane.

OEC: *See* Orenco.

Oeffag: *See* Öffag.

Oertz-Werke (Germany). Max Oertz built both Kaiser Wilhelm II's yachts, but added aircraft from 1910, starting with Gnome monoplanes and during war concentrating on biplane pusher flying-boats, 1914 with 160-hp Daimler and from 1915 with geared 240-hp Maybach. Oddball 1916 was Flying Schooner, 2 × 240-hp and tandem sets of biplane wings.

Öffag (Austria). Österreichische Flugzeugfabrik AG, Wiener-Neustadt, financed by Skoda, built Albatros aircraft and Austro-Daimler engines under licence 1915–20. Only original design Type CF triplane fighter 1918.

Oficinas Gerais: *See* OGMA.

ÖFW (Austria). Österreichische Flugzeugwerke GmbH built light aircraft 1958–9.

Ogden (USA). Ogden Aircraft incorporated 1929 to build versions of Osprey racer (also 4- or 7-passenger) monoplane (3 × 90- or 125-hp Menasco).

OGMA (Portugal). Founded 1918 at Alverca, never changed name or location, built 12 types under licence and many engines. Oficinas Gerais de Material Aeronautico is air force establishment which supplied Aerospatiale with rotor parts for Lama and other helicopters. Major repair/overhaul centre.

Ohm-Stoppelbeim (USA). Richard V. Ohm and Gordon Stoppelbeim built Formula racer (21 August 1950).

Ohnishi (Japan). Yuichi Ohnishi, Tatebayashi, Gummi Prefecture, produced OG-2 high-wing ultralight (10 February 1967).

Okamura (Japan). Okamura Seisakusho KK, branch factory of Nihon, built N.52 2-seat monoplane to design of Prof. H. Kimura (7 April 1953).

OKL (Poland). Osrodek Konstrukcji Lotniczych, aircraft construction centre, set up at WSK Warsaw-Okecie 12 October 1957 to take over all Polish aircraft design (previously handled by IL). Main projects MD-12 20-passenger airliner (4 × 330-hp WN-3, 21 July 1959) and TS-11 Iskra jet trainer, plus many light aircraft, but excluding designs by WSK Mielec and Swidnik.

OKO (USSR). Bureau of Special Construction, Kiev, headed by Tyrov (which *see*).

Oldfield (USA). Andrew Oldfield designed scaled-down Great Lakes Sport Trainer to produce Baby Great Lakes 1962: *see* Great Lakes.

Ogden Osprey (Menasco engines), December 1933.

Olkhovskii (Russia). Capt. Vladimir M. Olkhovskii (or Ol'khovsky) rebuilt Morane-Saulnier L and then built original Torpedo monocoque monoplane (6 March 1917).

OM (Italy). Officine Moncenisio formed pre-1914 at Condove, Turin. Produced aircraft from January 1916 with SAML Aviatik followed by Pomilio PD and SAML S.2, total 616 by end 1918.

OMAC (USA). OMAC Inc. founded 1977 Reno, Nevada, to build OMAC 1 canard pusher turboprop business aircraft (11 December 1981). Modified second prototype was called Laser 300 (19 February 1983). Company moved to Albany, GA, in 1985, money ran out 1989.

Omareal (Brazil). Oficina de Manutençao e Recuperaçao de Avioes handled testing of Casmuniz 52 (*see* Muniz) but planned production never started.

Omega (USA). Omega Aircraft Corp. formed December 1953 by B.W. Sznycer (which *see*) to build BS-12D helicopter (26 December 1956). Development continued with 4 prototypes to 1964.

Omnionics (USA). Formed 1965 Merritt Island (Cape Canaveral) to build Dolphinair glassfibre 20-passenger twin-jet amphibian with telescopic outer wings. Failed to complete.

Omnipol (Czechoslovakia). Omnipol Foreign Trade Corp. handles all aviation exports; prior to 1955 Motokov, prior to 1952 Kovo.

Omni Titan (USA). Produce Turbo Titan, conversion of Cessna 404 with PT6A engines.

Omni Weld (USA). Produce Omni Questor pop-riveted aluminium single-seater (1983).

OMOS (USSR). Dept. of experimental marine aircraft design formed 1925 at Leningrad under Grigorovich. Products known by name of designer (Grigorovich, Syedelnikov, Gimmelfarb, Korvin, Mikhelson, Samsonov, Shavrov, Vigand) except KR-1 reconnaissance flying-boat derived from Heinkel HD 55 (1930).

O'Neill (USA). O'Neill Airplane Co., Carlyle, Illinois, formed 1962 to produce and develop Waco W Aristocraft, but this replaced by all-new

Model J Magnum (1982) 8-seat utility with 4 landing-gear legs; gave up 1987.

Ong (USA). Ong Aircraft Corp. formed 1936 at Kansas City to build M-32W 4-seat high-wing monoplane.

On Mark (USA). On Mark Engineering Co. formed 1954 at Van Nuys, CA, mainly to produce rebuilt B-26 versions: Marketeer executive transport, Marksman pressurized variant and B-26K Counter Invader attack bomber. Also built first 377PG for Aero Spacelines.

ONTZ (Russia/Siberia). Omsk scientific-technical factory in process of privatization 1992, produces An aircraft (e.g. 72, 74) and parts.

OOS (USSR). Section for experimental aircraft construction formed 1930 at VVA under Zhukovskii to manage existing Stal (steel) programmes for aircraft with minimal aluminium. Stal-2 and -3 were high-wing cabin aircraft, -5 flying wing, -11 high-speed low-wing light transport and Aviatourist small twin-engined racer mainly of Bakelite-ply.

Opel-Sander (Germany). First rocket aircraft was primary glider called RAK 1, fitted with 20 small Sander powder rockets as publicity stunt for car-maker Opel (30 September 1929).

Operation Ability (UK). Formed 1984 to convert P.149D trainer for pilot 85% paralysed.

OPO (USSR). OPO-1–OPO-4 were experimental sections within OMOS from 1927.

Optica: *See* Edgley; Brooklands; FLS.

Orca (UK). Orca Aircraft, Bodmin, took over SAH-1 trainer in buy-out of Trago Mills (Aircraft Division). Excellent aircraft, in liquidation 1989, but now *see* UTVA; FLS.

Ord-Hume (UK). Arthur Ord-Hume helped redesign Luton Minor and Major, built or restored 11 aircraft, produced English plans for GY.20 Minicab and produced all-wood O-H.7 ultralight.

Ordnance Engineering: *See* next entry.

Orenco (USA). Ordnance Engineering Corp.

Orenco D-1 No. 1, November 1918.

founded mid-1916 in New York City, with plant at Baldwin, Long Island, to build aircraft for US Army and other customers. Type A side-by-side trainer (February 1917) found no takers. In June or July 1917 Etienne Dormoy, experienced SPAD designer and member of Mission to USA, designed Type B fighter (early 1918), built in small numbers. This led to 3 versions of Type C, and thence to D (300-hp Hispano, January 1919). Outstanding fighter, but Curtiss underbid and got contract for 50. To avoid confusion with Army Ordnance Branch, company at this point coined acronym Orenco. Attempts to develop D further led nowhere and neither did 6 planned post-war models.

Orlando (USA). Orlando Helicopter Airways formed 1964 at Sanford, Florida, to update and remanufacture Sikorsky helicopters. Seven versions of S-55 including Mi-24 lookalike and 3 versions of S-58. *See also* GOHL.

Orliński (Poland). Roman Orliński's RO-7 Orlik (Eaglet) sport monoplane flew 22 February 1987, plans marketed.

Orlogsvaerftet (Denmark). Royal Dockyard at Copenhagen built Hawker Dankok, Fokker C.V and Farman Jabiru transport, as well as locally designed HM.1 reconnaissance seaplane which was really Heinkel He 8 under other name.

Orta Saint-Hubert (Belgium). Founded 1919 as St Hubert flying school by Capt. José Orta, manufacturing about 25 light aircraft of 5 types 1924–33.

OSA (Italy). Officina Sommese Aeronautica produced several light aircraft in 1930s, notably OSA.135 side-by-side low-wing cabin tourer with 130-hp Alfa 110/1 (January 1937).

Osprey (USA). Osprey Aircraft, Sacramento, CA, formed to market plans of Osprey I 2-seat flying-boat (pusher 90-hp Continental) first flown August 1970, designed and built by interior decorator George Pereira. Very successful evaluation by US Navy as X-28A 1971. Developed to Osprey II (April 1973), over 1,480 sets of plans sold in 50 countries, 300 + flown by 1992. GP4 high-performance long-range 2-seat landplane added 1984.

Osrodek: *See* OKL.

Österreichische: *See* Öffag; ÖFW; Ö-UF.

OTD: *See* Dornier-Werke GmbH, 2nd entry.

Ottawa (Canada). Ottawa Car and Aircraft Ltd built AW Siskin and Atlas, Avro Prefect and 626, AS Lynx and Cheetah engine and, during Second World War, assisted production of Anson, Hampden and Hurricane.

Otto (Germany). Gustav Otto Flugmaschinenwerke built for German army 6 M1912 pusher observation biplanes, plus small number of other aircraft.

Ouest-Aviation (France). Formed by changing name of SNCASO 1 September 1956. Main product SO.4050 Vautour; still working on

SO.1221 Djinn and SO.9050 Trident; made wings and rear fuselage for Mystère II and IVA, and Martin-Baker seats under licence. Acted as agent and parent-firm for French Vertol H-21C, but did not take up licence option. Amalgamated with Sud-Est to form Sud-Aviation 1 March 1957.

Ö-UF (Austria). Österreichische-Ungärische Flugzeugfabrik was wartime subsidiary of Aviatik, building German parent's B.I and B.II. Produced single-seat version of C.I (so-called Berg Scout, from designer Julius Berg), 700 and possibly 1,200 produced 1917–18.

P

PAC (NZ). Pacific Aerospace Corp. Ltd, Hamilton, formed 1 July 1982 by renaming NZ Aerospace Industries. Produces Fletcher FU-24 and Cresco turboprop derivative; until 1977 produced CT4 Airtrainer. Shares: ASTA of Australia 75.1%, Lockheed 24.9%.

PAC (Pakistan). Pakistan Aeronautical Complex is MoD facility between Islamabad and Peshawar comprising Mirage Rebuild Factory, F-6 (Shenyang) Rebuild Factory, and Aircraft Manufacturing Factory. AMF builds Mushshak (Saab Safari/Supporter), 217 delivered late 1991.

PAC (Philippines). Philippine Aircraft Co. Inc. produces Skyfox, i.e. Denney Kitfox.

PAC (USA). Pacific Airmotive Corp. formed 1953 and bought Lear Engineering Division, Burbank (see PacAero). Produced Tradewind (rebuilt modernized Beech 18), Nomad (T-28) and Convair 580, agent and completion centre for Dassault Falcon, Citation, Learjet, failed to build PAC-1 own design 28-seat commuter transport. Briefly owned Enstrom (1968–70), new parent Purex sold facilities 1972.

PacAero (USA). PacAero Engineering Corp. formed 1957 as subsidiary of Pacific Airmotive at Santa Monica to produce Learstar executive transports based on Lodestar, convert T-28A to Nomad and convert CV-340 and 440 to Allison power.

Pacer (USA). Pacer Aircraft Corp. Perth Amboy, NJ, produced Pacer Monoplane, 4-seat open-cockpit parasol aircraft 1927–30, and STOL B-1.

PACI: See PAC (Philippines).

Pacific Aero Products: See Boeing.

Pacific Aerospace: See PAC (NZ).

Pacific Airmotive: See PAC (USA).

Pacific Airplane & Supply Co. (USA). Formed 1920 at Venice, LA, to build Hawk 6-seat biplane (2 × 90-hp), followed by C-1 racing monoplane (90-hp OX-5), both designed by Otto Timm.

Pacific & Western (Australia). Pacific & Western Aviation built prototype Air Tourer (winning design in 1953 Royal Aero Club competition by Henry Millicer): see Victa.

Pacific Standard: See Rogers.

Pack (USA). Garland Pack and Associates, Nashville, produced Formula racers 1949–59.

Packard Lepère (USA). Packard Motor Co. of Detroit was awarded production of 30 LUSAC-11 fighters designed by Capt. Georges Lepère of French Aeronautical Mission; further orders and re-engined LUSAC-21 and -25 cancelled. See Engineering Division.

PADC (Philippines). Philippine Aerospace Development Corp. is government agency which builds Islander (PB-N licence) and BO 105 (MBB licence), making all GFRP parts for both. Has assembled 18 S.211 jet trainers and may produce SF.260 and Sukhoi S-80. Has helicopter service subsidiary, and air-freight business in partnership with TNT.

Paine (USA). Sim Paine built light aircraft 1959.

Pakistan: See PAC.

PAMA (France). Constructions de Planeurs à Moteur Auxiliaire, Drancy, formed 1934 from Albert-Aéronautique (in liquidation). Produced single-seater (20-hp Poinsard), later (1937) prototype 2-seater (40-hp Poinsard).

Panavia (International). Panavia Aircraft GmbH

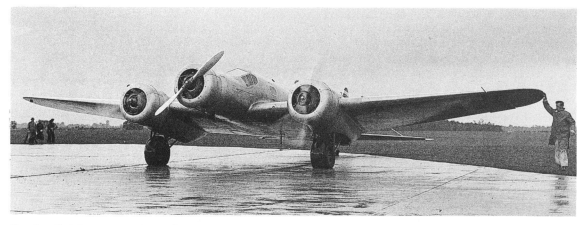

Pander S.4 Postjäger, 6 October 1933.

formed 26 March 1969 as single contractor to manage MRCA (later Tornado) programme; shareholding Aeritalia (later Alenia) 15%, British Aerospace 42.5%, MBB (later DASA) 42.5%; office Munich.

Pander (Netherlands). Furniture-maker Henk Pander took over defunct factory August 1924. Formed Nederlandse Fabriek van Vliegtuigen H. Pander & Zonen (H. Pander and Son) and developed Holland H.2 light monoplane into Pander D (16 November 1924). Pander E 2-seat sesquiplane (18 February 1926) built in numbers, but only handful of later types including 1 Postjäger (6 October 1933) long-range racer/mailplane (3 × 420-hp) which crashed during MacRobertson race 1934. Company into receivership, assets to De Schelde including designer T.E. Slot.

Panstwowe: *See* PZL, both entries.

Paragon (UK). Paragon Aircraft took over Jackaroo Aircraft at Thruxton 1961, continued Tiger conversions but did not build planned Plover and Paladin. Assets to Hampshire School of Flying 1964.

Paramount (USA). Paramount Aircraft Corp. formed 1928 at Saginaw, Michigan, briefly producing Cabinaire 4-seat biplane.

Parent (France). Norbert Parent markets plans for NP 2 Baladin side-by-side monoplane.

Parker (UK). CA.4 parasol monoplane (G-AFIU) believed flown 1938.

Parker (USA). Calvin Y. Parker, Chicago, flew remarkable Tin Wind ($500) 1962, followed by Teenie and (1969) Teenie Two for which, from Coolidge, AZ, over 4,100 sets of plans sold, possibly 400 flying.

Parks (USA). Parks Aircraft Inc. formed 1928 to build aircraft for Parks Air College and Parks Air Lines. Taken over by conglomerate Detroit Aircraft 1930, Parks designs assigned to Ryan, and P-1H biplane built by Hammond 1933.

Parmentier (UK). Wee Mite 2-seat ultralight built by Noel and Parmentier in Guernsey (hops April 1933, real flight September 1933).

Parnall (UK). Woodworking firm **Parnall & Sons**, Mivart St, Bristol, obtained contracts for 50 Avro 504B, 200 504J, 250 504K, 130 Fairey Hamble Babies and 20 Short 827s. Built prototypes of Parnall Scout and Puffin. In 1917 Harold Bolas, released by Admiralty, joined as chief designer and produced Panther carrier-based recon biplane. Firm sold to W. & T. Avery who refused Panther production contract (cut at Armistice from 300 to 150) and firm made no more aircraft. *See* next entry.

Parnall (UK). Most of original aircraft team, including Bolas, were gathered 1920 to form **George Parnall & Co. Ltd**, Park Row, Bristol, with works and airfield nearby at Yate. There followed remarkable demonstration of survival without production, Parnall producing prototypes of 18 different designs including civil and military biplanes and monoplanes, landplanes and flying-boats with engines from 20 to 1,000 hp.

Parnall (UK). In May 1936 George Parnall, Hendy Aircraft (*see* Hendy) and Nash and Thompson Ltd merged to form **Parnall Aircraft Ltd.** Hendy Heck became Parnall 3308 Heck, and Parnall 382 was open-cockpit derivative.

Parque de Aeronáutica (Brazil). Central (Rio) base of FAB included workshops where Waco EGC-7 was built under licence 1938–44. Became Fábrica Militar de Aviões.

Parsons (USA). Parsons Corp., Traverse City, Michigan, built parts for many aeroplanes and helicopters, plus 1 complete research STOL aircraft: XV-11 Marvel designed by Mississippi State University (US Army 65-13070).

Parsons-Jocelyn (USA). PJ-260 aerobatic biplane (28 July 1960) built by Rodney Jocelyn for Capt. Parsons to design of Nicholas E. D'Apuzzo, several more followed.

Partenavia (Italy). Partenavia Costruzioni Aeronautiche formed 1949 at Naples to build light aircraft to designs by Luigi Pascale: P.48B Astore, P.52 Tigrotto, P.53 Aeroscooter (option of adding 'safety rotor'), P.55 Tornado, P.57 Fachiro (4-seater, 7 November 1958, first built in numbers), P.59 Jolly, P.64 Oscar (metal P.57, 2 April 1965, several versions including P.66 Charlie), P.68 Victor (6/7-seat light twin, 25 May 1970, over 400 of many versions) and P.70 Alpha (24 April 1972). In July 1981 control of Partenavia passed to Alenia, and in 1992 to Piaggio, which assembles all company's aircraft.

Pashinin (USSR). Mikhail Mikhailovich Pashinin, deputy on fighters to N.N. Polikarpov 1931–9, formed own brigade to produce I-21, or IP-21, high-speed fighter (18 May 1940). Five prototypes abandoned April 1941.

Pasotti (Italy). Legnami Pasotti SpA formed about 1950 at Brescia, producing F.6 Airone (2 × 105-hp Walter Minor in prototype) and F.9 Sparviero, ending 1957.

Pasped (USA). Pasped Aircraft Co. formed about 1934 at Glendale, LA, building modest number of Skylark side-by-side low-wing monoplanes.

PAT (USA). Piper Advanced Technology, subsidiary formed 1981 to manage new programmes, was eliminated on sale to Lear Siegler 1984.

Patchen (USA). Marvin Patchen Inc. c/o *Aero* magazine, produced Explorer/Observer 4-seater (200-hp tractor Lycoming on pylon, November 1972). *See* Thurston.

PATS (Philippines). Philippine Air Transport & Training Services Inc. with National Science Development Board, briefly (1977–80) studied 7307En and XG-001 aircraft constructed from local material, especially bamboo.

Paulhan (France). Louis Paulhan was pilot, not designer, but several of his aircraft bear his name,

Paulhan-Tatin Torpille, June 1911.

notably Paulhan-Fabre biplane and Paulhan-Tatin monoplane 1911.

Paulista: *See* CAP (Brazil).

Paumier (France). Maurice Paumier produced MP 2 Baladin refined side-by-side monoplane February 1961, became Parent NP 01.

Pavlov (USSR). Aleksei Nikolayevich Pavlov, famed Orenburg instructor, built sporting monoplane 1929, crashed fatally after several impressive flights.

Payen (France). Around 1930 Roland Payen conceived futuristic configuration comprising forward wing with ailerons and flaps and rear 67° delta wing with elevators and flaps. PA 100 (380-hp GR 7Kdr, 1933) flew well until heavy landing at Istres. PA 22 (180-hp Regnier) was tested in Chalais-Meudon tunnel, flew at Villacoublay October 1942 but destroyed in air raid. PA 112, tandem engines, not built, nor various Flèchair fighter designs, but after war Payen produced Pa 49 baby jet (22 January 1954), series of Pa 61 Arbalète pushers and various projects.

Payne (USA). Vernon W. Payne marketed versions of Knight Twister, which he designed, from 1933 until 1985. All were single-seat aerobatic biplanes of 75-145 hp with 3 sizes of wing.

Pazmany (USA). Convair design engineer Ladislao Pazmany produced PL-1 2-seater (23 March 1962) and formed Pazmany & Associates, later incorporated at San Diego as Pazmany Aircraft Corp., selling 395 sets of plans by 1977, and 35 built by Nationalist Chinese AF. Developed PL-2 (4 April 1969) was adopted by air forces of China,

Payen Pa 49/B Katy, 22 January 1954.

Indonesia, Vietnam, Sri Lanka, S. Korea and Thailand, and over 400 sets of plans sold to private individuals. PL-4A single-seater (12 July 1972) adopted by Air Cadets of Canada and other groups, plus 460 plans sold by 1975.

PC Helicopter (USA). Peter Papadakos formed PC Helicopter Corp. In New York 7 August 1946, soon changing name to Gyrodyne.

PDQ (USA). Wayne Ison formed PDQ Aircraft Products at Elkhart, Indiana, to market plans of PDQ-2 ('pretty damn quick') single-seater (30 May 1973). Over 2,000 plans sold by 1980, 60 flying with wings of wood/fabric, metal or wood/polyurethane foam.

Pearson (USA). C.R. Pearson produced several lightplanes and racers in 1930s at Venice, LA. Best-known Pearson-Williams *Mr Smoothie* racer 1938.

Pearson-Pickering (UK). Ultralight monoplane with Pearson rotary ailerons and no fin or rudder, designed by K.N. Pearson, built by G.L. Pickering at Hanworth 1933.

Pecheron (France). Etablissements Pecheron, Neuilly-sur-Seine, produced various prototypes 1922–6, notably including P.18 2-seat biplane twin-float seaplane with 400-hp Lorraine, flown early 1925.

Pegler (UK). Pegler & Co. Ltd, Doncaster, Yorks, built Camels and Cuckoos 1917–18.

Pegna (Italy). Pegna Rossi Bastianelli formed 1920 to produce PRB flying-boat designed by Giovanni Pegna, and small monoplane. This soon taken over by Pegna & Bonmartini of Rome. In turn this taken over by Piaggio 8 August 1923, marking latter's return to aviation.

Pemberton-Billing (UK). Noel Pemberton-Billing was great character in pioneer days pre-1910, carrying out flying (mainly kite) experiments from 1903, learning to fly in one day; also MP, naval officer, author, visionary and businessman, starting design and manufacture of aircraft at Woolston, Southampton, June 1913. Coined 'Supermarine' as telegraphic address, aircraft known by this name, starting with Supermarine PB.1 flying-boat March 1914. Formed

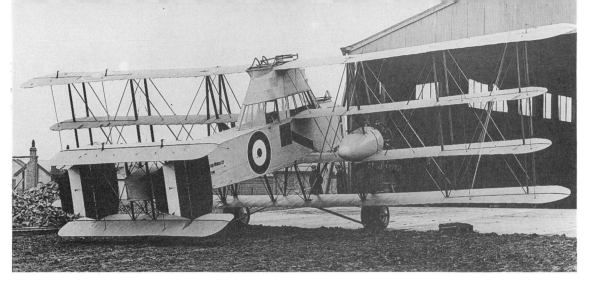

Pemberton-Billing (Supermarine) P.B. 31E, February 1917.

Pemberton-Billing Ltd June 1914, and when war broke out 4 August 1914 designed PB.9 fighting scout in one day and had it in air 7 days later (and very successful). PB.23 pusher fighter (August 1915) led to production PB.25. PB.29 anti-airship aircraft (1915) led to PB.31 Night Hawk (early 1916) quadruplane packed with remarkable features. From late 1916 company renamed **The Supermarine Aviation Works Ltd.**

Pemco (USA). Former Hayes International acquired and renamed by Precision Standard, Birmingham, AL, cargo conversions of 747, Tri-Star, 146, DC-9, 737.

Pena (France). Louis Pena produced 2 Capena high-performance aerobatic monoplanes (24 July 1984).

Penhoët (France). Chantiers et Ateliers de la Loire (Penhoët) produced marine aircraft from 1925, notably 5-engine flying-boat 1926. Designer Richard (which *see*) went to Soviet Union, and company merged 1931 with Wibault, forming Wibault-Penhoët.

Pennsylvania (USA). Pennsylvania Aircraft Syndicate formed 1933 to develop autogyro originally patented in Germany 1926 by Walter Kreiser and Walter Reiseler. Four-blade rotor with opposite blades rigidly joined, so as advancing angle of attack decreases retreating AOA increases. Trade name Gyroplane, called Wilford Gyroplane from company treasurer. Abandoned 1936.

Pentecost (USA). Original name 8 December 1945 of what in 1949 became Hoppi-Copters Inc.

Percival (UK). Australian Capt. Edgar W. Percival, purchaser of Hendy 302, was struck by impact of this modern monoplane and got R.H. Bound to design Gull 3-seater, 130-hp Cirrus Hermes, built by Parnall at Yate (3 July 1932). Percival and Lt.-Cdr. E.W.B. Leake formed **Percival Aircraft Co.**, 20 Grosvenor Place,

Penhoët RP, 6 March 1926.

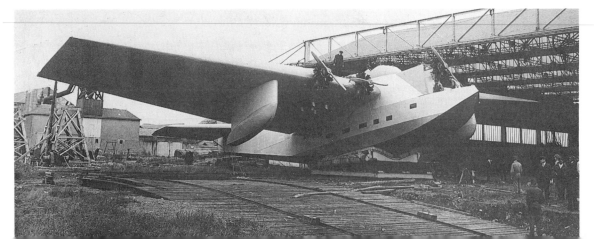

Percival Proctor IV prototype, May 1943.

London. Further Gulls made (24 at Yate in 1933), but June 1934 Percival's own factory opened at Gravesend airport, with A.A. Bage as designer. Immediate production of Gulls with various engines was interspersed 1935 with 6 Mew Gull racers and, from December 1935, 4-seat Vega Gull. Company restructured as **Percival Aircraft Ltd** and moved to larger factory at Luton October–November 1936. There built Q.6 twin, Proctor (wartime production 1,117, many by F. Hills & Sons), Prentice trainer (432), twin-engined Merganser prototype and Prince (24) leading to Sea Prince and Pembroke (187) and Provost (461). Percival became part of Hunting Group 1944, and name was changed 1954 to **Hunting Percival Aircraft**, founder immediately leaving to form his own company.

Perman (UK). E.G. Perman & Co. Ltd, Brownlow Mews, Guildford St, London WC1, built Mignet Fleas, and in May 1936 produced much safer ultralight Perman Parasol, construction No. EGP.56.

Pescara (Italy). Sig. Pateras Pescara, with Alessandro Guidoni, built high-wing monoplane seaplane of 62 ft 4 in (19 m) span with 200-hp Gnome BB19 (October 1914).

Pescara (Spain). Marquis de Pescara pioneered coaxial helicopter, building 3 1919–23, No. 3 being first controllable rotary-wing machine. Moved to France, where No. 3 further developed with articulated rotor with cyclic, collective, drag and flapping hinges, and provision for autorotative descent.

Peterborough (UK). Peterborough Aero Club ordered Guardian side-by-side cabin monoplane, with nosewheel, designed by J.H. Payne; left not quite finished 1939, subsequently to Slingsby, never flown.

Petlyakov (USSR). Vladimir Mikhailovich Petlyakov became world leader on aluminium-alloy structures, especially wings, and played major role in Tupolev (CAHI) TB-1, TB-3 and other programmes, managing entire design of TB-4 (ANT-16) and ANT-20. Appointed chief of ZOK to manage ANT-42 heavy bomber, later called Pe-8, but arrested 1937 on similar nonsensical charges to Tupolev, imprisoned at TsKB-29 where he created VI-100 which led to Pe-2 bomber (18 November 1940), 11,427 built of many versions. Pe-8 heavy bomber (27 December 1936) led to only 79, ending 1941. Petlyakov killed in crash of Pe-2 12 January 1942; replaced by Izakson, Putilov and finally Myasishchyev before OKB shut 1946.

Petrolini (Argentina). Petrolini Hermanos, Societa Anonima Industrial y Comercial, Departamento Aeronáutico, at Moreno, built 160 El Boyero 2-seaters (designed by IA) for clubs and schools on Government contract 1949–52.

Petters Ltd (UK). Formed 7 July 1910 at Yeovil mainly to produce oil engines but in April 1915 began move to new site where large factory was built to produce aircraft, Robert Bruce joining as designer, factory being called Westland Aircraft Works. Initial production was under licence: Short 225, Short Canton-Unné, Sopwith 1½-Strutter, D.H.4, D.H.9 and Vimy. Petter's own designs began with N.16 and 17 fighter seaplanes (October 1917) but these, and all successors, were commonly known as Westland aircraft, which *see*, even though company name did not change until 4 July 1935.

Peyret (France). Louis Peyret, Courbevoie (Paris), produced early gliders (won *Daily Mail* £1,000 prize Itford 1922), and several light aircraft including Albessard tandem monoplane (*see* SFCA) and Le Prieur seaplane, before becoming designer for Mauboussin.

Pezetel (Poland). Previously Motoimport, formed 1972 to handle all export sales, becoming limited company Pezetel Foreign Trade Enterprise Co. Ltd 10 February 1983.

Pfalz (Germany). Pfalz Flugzeug-werke GmbH established October 1913 at Speyer-am-Rhein, initially building Morane-Saulnier Types H and L monoplanes under licence. After start of war accelerated output of Pfalz version of H, forming family of Eindeckers (E.I–E.V) similar to Fokker and likewise from late 1915 fitted with 1 or 2 synchronized guns. With these obsolescent, company switched 1916 to licence-production of LFG Roland D.II, and this led to company's own D.III (14 May 1917) and IIIa, over 600 built. Many other fighter biplanes and a triplane failed to be made in quantity, but outstanding D.XII (spring 1918) was in many respects judged better than Fokker D.VII, about 350 delivered by Armistice.

Phalanx (USA). Long Beach company published details of fantastic MP-18 Dragon VTOL combat aircraft; predicted first flight 'early 1988' still awaited.

Pheasant (USA). Pheasant 3-seat open biplane (1 of 19 such types in USA 1927) was produced that year by Lee R. Briggs, who operated airport/school at Memphis, MO. Briggs killed 1928, development taken over by Wittman, formed Pheasant Aircraft Co., Fond du Lac, Wisconsin, 1928. Production of 4 variants, plus Traveler single-seat cantilever high-wing 1929.

Phelps (USA). William W. Phelps produced Li'l Spitfire sporting 2-seater (31 May 1961).

Philippines: *See* PAC; PADC.

Phillips (UK). Horatio Phillips pioneered efficient aerofoil profiles from 1878, but his aircraft, built at Sydenham and Harrow 1902–07, tended to have multiple wings, best known having 20.

Phillips (USA). Phillips Aviation Co. formed 1937 Los Angeles to produce Type 1B 2/3-seat monoplane and CT-1 and -2 trainer biplanes.

Phillips & Powis (UK). F.G. and G.H. Miles designed and built Martlet biplanes themselves, but even smaller Satyr was built by Parnall at Yate. On a flight from Yate to his base at Shoreham F.G. Miles stopped at Reading (Woodley) for lunch. He fell into conversation with Charles Powis, of Phillips & Powis, car and cycle dealers who owned Woodley aerodrome. Upshot was that Miles enterprise became part of Phillips & Powis January 1933, moving to Woodley. Here prototype Hawk 2-seat monoplane was produced (29 March 1932), selling at £395, first of many thousands of Miles aircraft built at Reading. Original tentative **Phillips & Powis Aircraft (Reading) Ltd** was replaced March 1935 by public company **Phillips & Powis Aircraft Ltd.** In 1936 Rolls-Royce acquired interest, A.F. (Sir Arthur) Sidgreaves becoming chairman. This eased previous severe cash shortage, but enormous orders for aircraft, especially Master advanced trainer, enabled Miles to take over RR interest 1941 and form new all-company board. This was followed October 1943 by change of name to **Miles Aircraft**.

Phoenix (NZ). Phoenix single-seat sporting monoplane was actually work of William S. Dini, Christchurch, based on a Heath Parasol wrecked 1929; flown 1933, improved 1935.

Phoenix (UK). Phoenix Aircraft Ltd was formed 1958 at Cranleigh, Surrey, to produce updated Luton LA.4a Minor and LA.5a Major, adding 2/4-seat Majorette 1969. Latter never built,

Pfalz D.XV, September 1918.

Phönix D.III (Swedish, 1919).

company out of business 1972, Minor plans henceforth marketed by Popular Flying Association.

Phoenix Dynamo (UK). Bradford electrical company which from 1916 built Short 184, Short Bomber, Maurice Farman Longhorn, Armstrong Whitworth FK.10, Felixstowe F.3 and F.5 and own-design P.5 Cork flying-boats. In 1918 Phoenix joined with others to form English Electric Co., whose management retained Phoenix capability in aircraft and sanctioned several later flying-boats including 3 marks of Kingston and Ayr, ending 1926.

Phönix (Austria-Hungary). Formed about October 1913 by Dr. Ing. M. Gabriel who, though he started Albatros in Germany, was himself Austrian. After start of war he returned to Vienna and arranged for Ö-Albatros to handle design and Phönix to produce in quantity. By 1915 Phönix had added licence manufacture of Brandenburg aircraft, and upshot was that

Phönix C.I was derived from Hansa-Brandenburg (Heinkel) D.II and Phönix D.I was a supposedly improved Hansa-Brandenburg D.I. Phönix built 110 C.I and 158 D-series (D.I, II and III), almost all with Hiero engines. Works closed 1919.

Phönix (Russia). Moscow-based company formed 1990 as subsidiary of Interavia to collaborate with Bulgaria in development and manufacture of General Aviation aircraft: *see* next entry.

Phönix-Aviatechnica (International). Limited-liability joint venture formed 1991 by Bulgaria (VMZ 46%, Metalhim 5%) and Russia (LMZ 25%, Interavia 24%). Thus Bulgarian financial control but president based in Moscow. First projects LKhS twin-engined STOL utility biplane (1993) and SL-90 Leshii 2/3-seat STOL multirole (1990, certificated 1990). Other designs (one by UK subcontractor) planned.

Piaggio (Italy). This famous firm was started by Rinaldo Piaggio, industrialist and politician, who

Piaggio P.23R (re-engined with P.XI radials 1938).

began December 1915 producing parts for Caproni bombers at Genova (Genoa) Sestri factory. By mid-1916 complete Capronis were being made, adding FBA and Macchi flying-boats at Finale Ligure 1917–18. Closed down after Armistice. In 1923 took over Pegna & Bonmartini and reopened Sestri Ponente factory, Giovanni Pegna remaining chief engineer for 25 years. Early designs mainly prototypes, including P.2 monoplane fighter, P.3 biplane bomber and very unconventional P.7 Schneider racer, though Navy bought 15 P.6 spotter biplanes. From 1933 Pegna concentrated on monoplane bombers with 2 engines, 3 engines, 4 engines in push/pull or 4 engines all tractor. The latter won, 163 P.108B heavy bombers being built 1941–3 plus 16 P.108C civil transports. Inactive late 1943.

Piaggio (Italy). Piaggio & Co., Società per Azioni was formed 1946 and began by converting C-47s into civil airliners. Production of P.140 airliner derived from P.108C wisely dropped, and instead new P.136L 5-seat amphibian (2 × 215-hp Franklin pusher) flown late 1948 and built in fair numbers. P.148 and 149 trainers won major orders from many air forces, Focke-Wulf making 190 149D under licence. Collaboration with Douglas on PD-808 light twin-jet (29 August 1964) led to a mere 29 aircraft, but P.166 has been successful: *see* next entry.

Piaggio (Italy). Company restructured 29 February 1964 as Industrie Aeronautiche E Meccaniche Rinaldo Piaggio SpA, reflecting Rinaldo's replacement of former joint managing directors Armando and Enrico Piaggio. Main product P.166, upgraded landplane derivative of P.136, substantial production in many versions initially with Lycoming piston engines and currently with 600-hp Lycoming turboprops. In 1982 development started with Gates Learjet of P.180 Avanti corporate transport with up to 10 seats, 2 × 1,485-shp PT6A-66 pusher turboprops (23 September 1986); Learjet withdrew, and Piaggio has makings of excellent programme with first 10 delivered by February 1992 and 10 more by 1993. Shareholding by Alenia 0% to 1988, 31% to 1992, 24.5% today (1993) but to rise to 31.5% later.

Piasecki (USA). Frank N. Piasecki formed company 1941 as PV Engineering Forum, incorporated in Pennsylvania 1943, making parts for PBY and for radars. Increasing design effort devoted to single-seat experimental helicopter, PV-2 (11 April 1943), leading to various NACA contracts and award of Helicopter Pilot Certificate No. 1 to Mr P. In February 1944 Navy contract for large transport helicopter led to PV-3 (8 March 1945) with banana-like fuselage with 41-ft (12.5 m) rotor at each end. This led to production HRP Rescuers, and restructuring as **Piasecki Helicopter Corp.** with large plant at Morton, Philadelphia, September 1946. HRP led to PD-22, Army H-21, Navy HRP-2, redesigned smooth metal fuselage, 554 being produced by 1959. Smaller PV-14, again tandem-rotor, led to over 400 HUP Retriever and H-25 Army Mule. In May 1955 'as result of bitter managerial disagreement Mr Piasecki was relieved of his positions' and with many associates resigned and formed a new company. Original had to be renamed, becoming Vertol in March 1956.

Piasecki (USA). Frank N. Piasecki started afresh June 1955 as **Piasecki Aircraft Corp.** at Philadelphia airport, expanding a year later with Delaware Division occupying former Bellanca plant. Subsequently carried out numerous contracts, many of research nature, including re-entry vehicle design, Navy RPVs, VZ-8P Flying Jeep VTOL (12 October 1958) and, in particular, 16H Pathfinder high-speed helicopter (21 February 1962). Over 10 years of effort on combined airship/rotor lift systems ceased 1989, but 16H Pathfinder continues 1992 with civil and military proposals lacking nothing but proper funding.

PIC (Canada). Promavia International Corp.: *see* Promavia.

Pickering: *See* Pearson-Pickering.

Pidek (Canada). Joseph Pidek built JP.2B light helicopter (2 × 50-hp) 1962, modified into Pi-4 1964.

Piel (France). Claude Piel produced light aircraft from 1949, most famous being CP.30 Emeraude (1952), marketed in many variants in form of plans, kits and complete aircraft by Ateliers Aéronautiques de la Côte d'Emeraude, Société Ouest de Constructions Aéronautiques and (250 +) Scintex-Aviation, by Fairtravel (as Linnet) in UK, by Durban Aircraft (as Aeriel II) in S. Africa and as Aeronasa in Spain. Scintex collaborated with Super Emeraude, and from

1972 Avions Claude Piel suddenly proliferated with Diamant, Beryl, Zef, Pinocchio and even tandem-wing CP.500. Emeraude led to CAARP (Mudry) products, while Piel ceased factory manufacture and, despite death of founder, remains major source of kits/plans.

Pietenpol (USA). Bernard H. Pietenpol Air Camper tandem-seat parasol monoplane (1929) led to numerous homebuilts, including improved GN-1 by John W. Grega and Elmer Niebecker (November 1965). Donald Pietenpol continues to market plans.

Pigeon (USA). After USA joined war April 1917 George N. Albree (which *see*) designed monoplane fighter (100-hp Gnome) in style of Fokker Eindecker of 1914; 2 built by Pigeon Hollow Spar Co., East Boston, were delivered to Signal Corps, known as Pigeon Fraser. Tested December 1917, considered 'old-fashioned, unreliable, too slow', but until 1978 Albree insisted he was victim of unfair conspiracy.

PIK (Finland). Polyteknikkojen Ilmailukerho (Helsinki University flying club), famous for sailplanes, also produced powered aircraft starting 1953 with PIK-11 single-seater; PIK-15 tug 1964, PIK-19 tug/trainer 1972, PIK-21 Formula racer 1982.

Pilatus (Switzerland). M.E. Bührle, owner of Oerlikon Group, formed syndicate 1938 leading to wholly-owned subsidiary Pilatus

Flugzeugwerke December 1939, hiring as chief engineer H. Fierz, formerly with Alfred Comte. Prototype SB-2 Pelikan STOL 5-seater (May 1944) led to P-2 and P-3 advanced trainers, P-4 5-seater and PC-6 Porter (4 May 1959), initially piston-engined, later turboprop, 500 of many variants by late 1991. Turboprop trainers began with PC-7 (12 April 1966), 460 delivered by 1993, leading to PC-9 (7 May 1984), 190 + 1993. Major risk is massive investment in PC-12 pressurized turboprop business transport or 9-passenger airliner (31 May 1991). Company never changed name or location (Stans, near Luzern), purchased assets of Britten-Norman 24 January 1979.

Pilatus Britten-Norman (UK). As noted, Pilatus purchased assets of Britten-Norman (Bembridge) January 1979, including Fairey SA assets in Belgium. Immediately formed operating company **Pilatus Britten-Norman Ltd**, subsidiary of Oerlikon-Bührle Holding Ltd, continuing production of all versions of Islander and Defender at Bembridge. About 2 per month from Romaero. Total 1993 about 1,200.

Pilcher (UK). Percy Pilcher, disciple of Lilienthal, would probably have been first aeroplane pilot had he not been killed gliding in 1899. He had become proficient pilot, and was expecting to fly with a petrol engine in 1900.

Pilgrim (USA). Short-lived Pilgrim Manufacturing gave name to several high-wing transports 1927–8, biggest a 10-seater which became

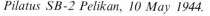
Pilatus SB-2 Pelikan, 10 May 1944.

Pilatus Britten-Norman Islander BN-2B-26, 1992.

Fairchild F-100 in 1929. After Avco takeover this came briefly under American Airplane & Engine Corp., occupying previous Fairchild plant on Long Island, which also developed fast low-wing American Pilgrim 150, designed by Clark. This in turn became Clark GA-43: *see* General Aviation.

Pintsch (Austria). Julius Pintsch AG, Vienna engineering company, organized aircraft department January 1934 and built small numbers of Raab Schwalbe II and Tigerschwalbe II training biplanes.

Pioneer (USA). Pioneer Aircraft Corp. produced small numbers of single-seat Pioneer Sport biplane with 40-hp Pioneer engine.

Piper (USA). W.T. 'Bill' Piper was secretary/treasurer of original Taylor Aircraft Co.; when this ran into financial difficulty 1936 Piper

took it over and reorganized it as Piper Aircraft Corp., moving from Bradford to Lock Haven, PA, W.T. Piper Jr. becoming secretary and assistant treasurer. Produced original J-3 Cub in increasing quantities, ending 1946 with 14,125 civil and 5,703 military. Subsequent types included PA-18 Super Cub, PA-22 Tri-Pacer, PA-23 Apache/Aztec twins, PA-24 Comanche, PA-25 Pawnee and PA-36 Pawnee Brave ag-aircraft, PA-28 Cherokee family, PA-30 Twin Comanche, PA-31 Navajo family, PA-32 Cherokee Six/Lance/Saratoga, PA-34 Seneca, PA-38 Tomahawk, PA-42 Cheyenne, PA-44 Seminole and PA-46 Malibu. River often flooded Lock Haven, and Piper found new site at Vero Beach, Florida, which from 1957 was R&D centre, Cherokee being designed there and also built there. In 1971 came licence agreement with Chincul in Argentina, 1974 Embraer in Brazil and 1977 PZL Mielec in Poland; 100,000th Piper

Piper Skycoupe (130-hp Franklin), August 1944.

produced 1976. In 1978 took over Ted Smith, adding Santa Maria, CA, to Lock Haven, Piper and Renovo in Pennsylvania, and Vero Beach and Lakeland in Florida. Bill Piper Sr. died 1970 and sons Bill jr., Howard and Thomas were ousted in stock fight, company becoming subsidiary of Bangor Punta Corp., and then of Lear Siegler effective 1 March 1984. Product liability litigation progressively forced cessation of production and closure of plants, and M. Stuart Millar bought Piper 12 May 1987 as subsidiary of Romeo Charlie Inc., closing all product lines except Cheyenne and pressurized Malibu Mirage, whose prices are high enough to absorb otherwise crippling product liability insurance. Bankruptcy court sought buyer 1991–3, all plants closed, but Congress Finance made loan 1992 which enabled 66 outstanding orders to be completed and 250 workers rehired. Piper aircraft now made only by Bengis, Chincul, Neiva and PZL Mielec.

Piper North (USA). Formed by John R. and William H. Piper 17 November 1989 at Lock Haven as subsidiary of Romeo Charlie Inc., intending to build Navajo Chieftain and possibly SwiftFury (*see* LoPresti), but loan guarantees not forthcoming late 1991.

Pippart-Noll (Germany). Established 1913 Mannheim, building modified Etrich Taube under licence.

PIRT (Hungary). Pestlőrinci Ipartelepek RT, at

Pest, produced Ju 52/3m 1943–44.

de Pischoff (France). Emil de Pischoff built biplane (June 1907), first to use either Anzani engine or Chauvière propeller; set up factory at Billancourt with Koechlin where at least 8 biplanes and tandem monoplanes built (most for customers) by 1910.

Pishchalnikov (USSR). Engineer at OMOS, built light aircraft 1926.

Pissarenko (USSR). Viktor Osipovich Pissarenko built VOP-1 light monoplane (27 November 1923), followed by Model T high-speed (near 186 mph) single-seater 1925.

Pitcairn (USA). Harold F. Pitcairn, of Pittsburgh Plate Glass, was air enthusiast from 1915. In 1925 he hired brilliant Agnew Larsen to design for awakening civil market. Resulting Fleetwing biplane (7 November 1925) had 3 open cockpits in line. Formed Pitcairn Aircraft Inc. at Philadelphia, with plant at Bryn Athyn, PA. Sesquiwing, Arrow racer, Orowing and Fleetwing 2 led to classic PA-5 Mailwing (August 1927) cargo carrier of which 20 were made in several versions. PA-6 Super Mailwing of 1928 again led to about 25 of several versions, ending with 300-hp PA-8S before Depression closed fixed-wing business, *see* next.

Pitcairn (USA). Pitcairn imported Avro-built Cierva C.8W autogyro January 1929 and set up

Pitcairn PA-36 (175-hp Warner), August 1934.

Pitcairn Autogiro Co., Willow Grove, PA. Larsen left, replaced by Paul E. Hovgard, producing PCA-1, similar to C.8W, PCA-2 3-seat 300-hp (1930), 21 built, PAA-1/PA-20/PC-2-30 all 110–125 hp, PA-18 180-hp 2-seater (about 20), PCA-3/PA-21/PA-34 all 300 hp with direct-control rotor, and ending with about 6 PA-19 (420-hp) 4-seaters with fixed wing before liquidation 1940, ironically assets being taken over by former chief engineer to form Pitcairn-Larsen Autogiro Co., which shortly became Aga Aviation Corp.

Pitts (USA). Curtiss Pitts built Samson 450-hp racer 1945 followed by several Formula racers, but famous aerobatic biplanes began with 190 Special *Little Stinker* for Betty Skelton (1947). Built several more, and from 1953 made plans available for lower-powered (65–95-hp) versions. As demand grew **Pitts Aviation Enterprises** formed at Homestead, Florida, marketing plans for S-1 single-seater. Mr Pitts developed 2-seat S-2 (1967) available as factory-built only, produced for Pitts by Aerotek Inc. of Afton, Wyoming (also building S-1 if ordered). Pitts sold out December 1976 to Doyle Child of Afton, who formed **Pitts Aerobatics** at Aerotek address, continuing until sold November 1983 to Christen Industries.

Pittsburgh (USA). Pittsburgh Metal Airplane Co. took over Thaden 1929 but were themselves bought 1931 by Metalair.

Pivot (France). M. Pivot built and flew monoplane 1912–13 notable for aileron system.

Plage & Laskiewicz (Poland). Zaklady Mecaniczne E. Plage & T. Laskiewicz formed 1864 at Lublin, and aviation division formed 1920 as soon as country independent. Began by licence production of Ansaldo SVA Balilla (70) and A.300 (80), followed by Potez XV (about 200) and Fokker VIIB/3m (11). M. Rudlicki taken on as chief engineer, produced R.VIII biplane recon-bomber (usually 650-hp Lorraine), R.IX 8-seater (Jupiter), R.X trainer (Whirlwind), R.XIII trainer or observation parasol monoplane (1931, over 220 built in many versions), P.XIV parasol trainer, R.XVI 5-seat monoplane with XVIB ambulance version, and R.XIX conversion of R.XIII to test Rudlicki's butterfly tail (which was flown 1925 on licence-built Hanriot).

Plan: *See* Max Plan.

Planadores Neiva (Brazil). Original name of Neiva, when built gliders only.

Planet (UK). Planet Aircraft Ltd formed 1946 to build outstandingly advanced Satellite 4-seater made of magnesium. Prototype made by Redwing at Croydon, but structural problems led to ARB refusing permission to fly 1948.

Platt-Le Page (USA). Platt-Le Page Aircraft Co. formed about 1941 at Eddystone, PA, producing XR-1 (USAAF 41-1) and -1A (42-6581) helicopters with side-by-side rotors.

Player (USA). William E. Player, Salt Lake City, flew PN-55 Player sport parasol 1940.

Poberezny (USA). Paul H. Poberezny, president of EAA, produced series of homebuilts including *Little Poop Deck* 1957, *Little Audrey* 1958 and *Pober Sport* (1959), latter making 13,000-mile flight to 72 US cities during May 1960. Later types include Acro-Sport and Super Acro-Sport biplanes and Pober P-9 Pixie. Mr Poberezny also redesigned Baby Ace and refined EAA Biplane.

Pobjoy (UK). Engine company adjacent to Short Brothers at Rochester in 1934 commissioned Harold Boultbee (from failed Civilian Aircraft) to design aircraft to use single Niagara engine, resulting Pobjoy Pirate (3 March 1935) extensively flown by Short test pilot Lankester Parker and used as company hack. Pobjoy reorganized May 1935 as Pobjoy Airmotors & Aircraft Ltd, exclusive licence to build Short Scion light transport, building 7; did not take up licence to build Scion Senior.

Podlaska: *See* PWS.

Poletecnico di Milano (Italy). In 1946 designed CVV 200 Alea 5-seater (220-hp Alfa), completed 1948.

Polikarpov (USSR). Nikolai Nikolayevich Polikarpov was, with Tupolev, most prolific, most senior and most famous designer before 1941. Handled first major programme by turning D.H.4 and later D.H.9a into R-1, over 2,800 built. I-1 monoplane fighter was failure, and several other early prototypes failed series adoption, but U-2 light biplane (February 1927, improved U-2 7 January 1928) sustained production of believed 41,000 in countless versions to 1953 (after Polikarpov's death 1944 called Po-2 in his honour). Another giant programme was R-5 biplane (1928) with 680- or 715-hp engine, 4,995 of basic version plus 32 other variants, often conversions. Biplane fighters included I-3 (400), I-5 (800 +), I-15 (733), I-15bis/152 (2,408) and I-153 (3,437), followed by tricky I-16 monoplane (7,005 single-seat and 1,639 + 2-seat trainers). At least 32 prototypes built of other Polikarpov designs, ending with BDP assault glider (and MP powered version) and outstanding NB bomber (23 May 1944). Nikolai Nikolayevich collapsed at his desk 30 July 1944.

Polliwagen (USA). Polliwagen Inc. have sold over 2,000 sets of plans for fast all-composites 2-seater (July 1977).

Polyarn: *See* KB-7.

Polyteknikkojen: *See* PIK.

Pomilio (Italy). Ottorino Pomilio enlisted in Battaglione Aviatori 1913, becoming designer together with Savoia to Direzione Tecnica dell'Aviazione Militare. Produced SP 1 and improved SP 2 pusher 2-seaters, with Fiat A12 engine. With permission to set up factory, resigned December 1915, forming SA per Costruzioni Aeronautiche Ing. O. Pomilio & C. February 1916. New factory and airfield built outside Turin, first prototype SP 2 flying there 10 July 1916. In parallel produced C 1 (later PC 1) tractor 2-seater (September 1916), with radiators forming inverted V on front cabane struts. PD followed with ventral fin and better armament (545), followed August 1917 by PE with frontal radiator (1,071).

Poncelet: *See* SABCA.

Ponnier (France). Louis Alfred Ponnier, director of Hanriot factory at Reims, founded Avions Ponnier 1912, producing racing monoplane (2nd place in Coupe Internationale at Reims 1913 flown by Vedrines). Produced M.1 biplane fighter 1915 (believed by Hanriot designer E.E. Dupont) characterized by giant spinner and span hardly greater than length. Larger 2-seat M.2 (January 1916) remained prototype, but Ponnier formed SAFCA (Société Anonyme Française de Con-

structions Aéronautiques) which built possibly 50 M.1s, at least half for Aviation Militaire Belge.

Pope (USA). Leon Pope built P-2 Thunderbird sporting biplane (April 1959).

Porokhovshchikov (Russia, USSR). Aleksandr Aleksandrovich Porokhovshchikov built trainers for Tsarist Imperial air service, for Bolsheviks, Red Army and several neighbouring countries. All were derived from 1914 Caudron designs with biplane wings of unequal span and short nacelle with pusher or tractor engine. Single examples of first 3 designs led to substantial production of pusher P.IV tandem-seater, tractor P.IVbis side-by-side and tractor P.IV 2bis tandem. More powerful P.VI and VIbis were built 1921–4.

Porsche (USA). Porsche founded a US subsidiary 1986 at Galesburg, Illinois, to re-engine Cessna Skylanes and Skyhawks with its PFM 3200 aero engine. Scheme abandoned 1988 when engine discontinued.

Porte (UK). Though John Porte had a distinguished career he never made aircraft. Thus, giant Porte Baby flying-boat was actually built at Felixstowe Seaplane Experimental Station.

Porterfield (USA). In 1934 E.E. Porterfield, former president of American Eagle Aircraft, formed Porterfield Aircraft Corp. at Kansas City. At about same time students at Wyandotte High School built Wyandotte Pup 2-seat cabin monoplane designed by Noel Hockaday. Porterfield bought aircraft and designer, marketing former as Porterfield Flyabout February 1935, production of several models exceeding 250. In 1936 lighter version produced as Zephyr, later called CP-40, developed into CP-50 Collegiate of which 7 versions were built with different 50–65-hp engines to total of about 400, ending with Pearl Harbor.

Portholme (UK). Portholme Aerodrome Ltd, St John's St, Huntingdon, built substantial numbers of Camels and Snipes, and a batch of Wight 840 seaplane torpedo bombers.

Portsmouth (UK). Founded 1932 as Wight Aviation to operate air services to Isle of Wight, major repair/overhaul centre in Second World War, changed name to **Portsmouth Aviation Ltd** 1943 and managed city airport. Planned 4 versions of Aerocar with 4/6-seat nacelle under high wing and twin booms with 101-hp Cirrus Minors or 155-hp Cirrus Majors, latter powering prototype (18 June 1947). Excellent aircraft, other factors prevented production.

Port Victoria (UK). To distinguish Royal Navy Aeroplane Repair Depot (January 1915) from large RNAS station on Isle of Grain it was named Port Victoria. In 1916 Experimental Construction Depot began producing modified or even completely new aircraft. PV.1 was Sopwith Baby with high-lift wings. PV.2 was new-design anti-Zeppelin seaplane (June 1916), excellent aircraft. PV.4 was pusher 2-seat fighter seaplane (1917). PV.5 and 5a were single-seat fighter-bomber seaplanes (1917–18). The PV.7 Grain Kitten and PV.8 Eastchurch Kitten were small biplanes for operation from destroyers. PV.9 was single-seat fighter seaplane (December 1917). Last products were 8 Grain Griffin reconnaissance landplanes (early 1918).

Pöschel (W. Germany). Pöschel Aircraft GmbH, Ulm-Allewind, built P-300 Equator 5/6-seat pressurized amphibian (tractor 310-hp Lycoming on top of fin) 1970. Turboprop P-400 crashed 1977.

Potez (France). In 1913 Henry Potez was Dorand's assistant at STA. After war broke out he and Bloch were assigned to help Capt. Etévé, but in 1916 they teamed up with Louis Coroller to found **Société d'Etudes Aéronautiques** at Suresnes, making Spad VIIs and designing SEA.1. Neither this nor SEA.2 and 3 were improvements on existing types, but SEA.4 was excellent. Potez, Bloch and Bessonneau formed Compagnie Anjou Aéronautique at Angers to build 1,000, but Armistice cut output to 115, and company wound up. Potez believed in a market for civil aircraft, so in 1919 formed **Aéroplanes Henry Potez** at Aubervilliers. Refurbished SEA.4s, and produced improved SEA.7, soon called Potez VII, with cabin for 2 passengers, 25 going into service on Compagnie Franco-Roumaine. This was start of 40 years in which number of fresh designs probably exceeded in number and variety those of all other constructors. Many were produced in remarkable quantity. Original VIII 2-seater ran to 100, 4-passenger IX reached 33, XV reconnaissance biplane reached 334 plus 135 built in Poland, improved XXVII reached 72 plus 155 built by

PWS in Poland, and XXV, better known as Potez 25, 2-seat military biplane, beat all other between-the-wars types with production of about 3,770 in France by Potez, ANF Les Mureaux and Hanriot, and at least 597 made under licence in other countries. Other types were 29 5-passenger biplane (157), 32/33 monoplane (206), 36 light monoplane (about 300), 37/39 fighter-reconnaissance (262), 43 3-seat monoplane (161), 54 heavy bomber (147 plus 49 for Spain and 59 improved 542s), 56 twin-engined monoplane (72), 58 ambulance/observation (214), 60 simple 2-seater (155), 62 airliner and 65 military version (23 + 15), and 63 series of modern twin-engined fighter/bomber/recon aircraft (1,384). This list ignores scores of other types, from flying-boats (*see also* CAMS) to racers, nor does it mention substantial business in Potez aero engines. Under 1936 nationalization Potez factory at Sartrouville (Paris) and Méaulte (Potez's home town) were taken over by SNCA du Nord, Potez becoming head of group. Berre, near Marseilles, went to SNCASE.

Potez (France). Henry Potez began again 1953, with **Société des Avions et Moteurs Henry Potez**, with works at Argenteuil (Paris). Potez 75 tank killer (10 June 1953) was ahead of its time, and Potez 91 observation aircraft also remained prototype. In 1958 Potez bought Fouga, forming Potez Air-Fouga to build last few of Magister line. Last Potez type was 840 18/24-passenger airliner (4 × Astazou, 29 April 1961). This failed to find buyers, and company's last factory, Air-Fouga at Toulouse, was taken over by Sud-Aviation 1967.

Pottier (France). Jean Pottier at Les Mureaux markets plans for a wealth of sporting monoplanes and biplanes, mostly metal construction.

Poulet: *See* Dalotel.

Powell (USA). Powell Aircraft, Detroit, formed by Prof. C.H. Powell (ex-NPL Teddington), producing light biplane with 32-hp Bristol Cherub (7 June 1925).

Powell (USA). John C. Powell, former Cdr. USN, had sold 600 sets of plans for P-70 Acey Ducey parasol 2-seater (20 June 1970) by 1986, some being seaplanes.

Potez 62.0 Ibis, late 1935.

Powers Bashforth (USA). Produced Mini Master 2-seater with twin tail booms (push/pull Rotax), markets plans N. America, international marketing by Sonoran Aviation, Scottsdale, AZ.

Practavia (UK). Practavia Ltd formed 1970 to take over from *Pilot* magazine management of Sprite aerobatic 2-seater (16 June 1976), many flying, plans/kits marketed.

Praga (Czechoslovakia). Formed 1915 as Breitfeld, Danek & Co. to build Hiero aero engines. Expanded to design own engines, trade name Praga, and also produce armaments. Changed name to **Ceskomoravska-Kolben-Danek** and opened Aviation Dept. April 1931 to produce aircraft of own design, adopting name CKD-Praga and aircraft known simply as Praga. Benes and Hajn joined from Avia and designed BH.39 biplane trainer (several versions). Other military biplanes included E.36 bomber, E.40 primary trainer, BH.41 advanced trainer and E.44 and 45 fighters. First to be built in numbers was E.114 2-seat ultralight, but few were built of twin-pusher 4-seat E.210, single-tractor E.214 and E.241 biplane trainer. On German occupation 1939 company became **Böhmische-Mährische Maschinenfabriken AG** on general war production. Factory re-established 1947 as **Závody Letecké Praga**, producing small number of E.210/211 and 114, and Doris B flat-6 engine.

Pratt-Read (USA). Produced training gliders for Navy (LNE-1) and AAF (TG-32) in 1942.

PRB (Italy). Pegna-Rossi-Bastianelli flew large biplane flying-boat, 2 push/pull pairs Fiat A12bis total 1,200 hp (11 May 1921).

Predappio (Italy). Member of Caproni group, produced several prototypes 1936–40, plus limited production of Ca 602 biplane trainer.

Potez (CAMS) 141, 21 January 1938.

Premier (UK). Premier Aircraft Constructions Ltd, Maylands aerodrome, Romford, built 3 Gordon Dove ultralight monoplanes 1937.

Prescott (USA). Produced prototypes of brilliant Pusher high-speed 4-seater (9 July 1985).

Procaer (Italy). Formed at Milan 1957 as Progetti Costruzioni Aeronautiche SpA, Procaer produced single Cobra 400 4-seater (1 × Marboré turbojet), but concentrated marketing on F.15 Picchio 3-seater (180-hp Lycoming) designed by Stelio Frati (7 May 1959). Developed to F.15E and F.15F (prototype built by General Avia 1977) but attempts to find partner failed.

Procter (UK). Formed at Camberley by name-change from Mitchell-Procter Aircraft November 1968 to continue Kittiwake and Petrel.

Promavia (Belgium). Formed 1980 by powerful industrialists and investors, with substantial Government backing for jet trainer; 1985 agreement with General Avia to co-operate in developing F.1300 Squalo, but in event Italian firm was withdrawn and Stelio Frati designed aircraft as all-Belgian Promavia Squalus F1300 (30 April 1987), global marketing in progress. Also proposing tandem-seat version and single-seat attack version with double power. Production planned 1993 at **PIC** (Promavia International Corp.) at Saskatoon, Canada.

Prop-Jets (USA). San Antonio company formed to resurrect Interceptor 400A pressurized turboprop 4-seater (ex-Myers, Aero Commander and Interceptor).

Protech (USA). Have marketed 100 + kits for PT-2 Sassy side-by-side high-wing aircraft.

Provence (France). Provence-Aviation, Berre/Vitrolles, was formed 1924 as aviation branch of Chantiers de Provence dockyard. Produced CPA.1 bomber-transport (2 × 450-hp Lorraine).

Prowler (USA). Redding, CA, Prowler Aviation Inc. flew prototype Morse 364P Prowler 17 March 1985. Tandem-seat fighter-like aircraft to be marketed with 350-hp Chevrolet, giving 300 + mph.

Prudden (USA). Prudden-San Diego Airplane Co. established in that city 10 November 1927 to build TM-1 6-passenger monoplane (3 × 120-hp Ryan-built Siemens SH.12) and Super TM-1 (with nose engine a 200-hp Wright J-5C).

Prva Srpska: *See* next entry.

PSFA Rogojarsky (Jugoslavia). Prva Srpska Fabrika Aeroplana Zivojin Rogojarsky was established 1925 in Belgrade, first Serbian aircraft factory. Built for Jugoslav air force Brandenburg biplane trainer, RWD.8, and indigenous Rogojarsky types. First was undesignated reconnaissance biplane designed by Rudolf Fizir (1932), followed by SIM-II parasol trainer by Sima Milutinović. PVT parasol advanced trainer (1934) designed by committee of 5 including Milutinović and Fizir was very successful; including improved P-100 over 220 built, some being seaplanes. Milutinović designed SIM-X primary trainer (1936, 190 in several versions), SIM-VI, VIII and IX light tourers and trainers, SIM-XIV-H twin-engined reconnaissance seaplane (8 February 1938, 30 delivered before German invasion) and R-313 twin-engined bomber/recon aircraft (1940, prototype crashed escaping from Germans April 1941). A committee designed IK-3 fighter (May 1938), 12 built, claimed 11 Luftwaffe aircraft before having to be destroyed on ground during retreat 1941.

PT: *See* Protech.

PTA (Russia). First Russian aero firm was Peterburgskii Tovarishchyestva Aviatsii (St Petersburg aviation company), which among other things built PTA No. 1, based on Farman IV but made in easily disconnected sections to meet army requirement. Retained 50-hp Gnome, but seat in streamlined nacelle. Completed 26 January 1911, flown by V.A. Lebedyev, 'not inferior to Farman'.

PT Nurtanio (Indonesia). PT Industri Pesawat Terbang Nurtanio (Nurtanio aircraft industry Ltd) formed 23 August 1976 by combining Pertamina's Advanced Technology and Aeronautical Division with Nurtanio Aircraft Industry (LIPNUR). Changed name December 1985 to IPTN, which *see*.

Puget Pacific (USA). Donald J. Wheeler won *Popular Science* competition for personal aircraft with Wheelair IIIA 4-seater (pusher 190-hp Lycoming); Puget Pacific Planes Inc. formed at

Tacoma, prototype tested late 1947.

Putilov (USSR). Aleksandr Ivanovich Putilov designed fuselages and landing gears under A.N. Tupolev at CAHI, but was enticed away 1928 to head Stal (steel) group at VVA academy, which became OOS (section for experimental aircraft construction) 1930. Produced Stal-2 high-wing 6-seater (11 October 1931), improved Stal-3 (1933), Stal-5 18-passenger flying wing with 2×900-hp M-34F (late 1935) and Stal-11 high-speed transport (autumn 1936), all with steel airframes.

Pützer (W. Germany). Post-war glider firm at Bonn which in 1957 produced improved Doppel-raab motor-glider developed into Elster (magpie); Elster B production version 1961 in all respects side-by-side aeroplane (95-hp Continental), and final Elster C (150-hp Lycoming) designed as glider tug. In 1966 Alfons Pützer helped form Sportavia-Pützer.

P-V (USA). Frank Piasecki's first company was P-V Engineering Forum Inc., organized 1941 at Sharon Hill, PA, building PV-2 and PV-3 (XHRP-1) helicopters before becoming Piasecki in 1946.

PWS (Poland). Podlaska Wytwórnia Samolotów (Podlasian aeroplane factory) was established 1923 at Biala Podlaska, with extensive facilities which grew with large orders for licensed aircraft, notably Avia and Potez. From 1926 produced

PZL TS-8 Bies, 23 July 1955.

own prototypes, PWS.1 parasol 2-seat fighter, PWS.3 light 2-seater, PWS.4 ultralight, PWS.7 advanced trainer biplane, PWS.10 parasol fighter (1927, 80 built), PWS.11 fighter trainer, PWS.12/14/16/26 biplane advanced trainers, PWS.20 8-passenger transport, and PWS.21/24 6-passenger transports. From 1934 PWS built licensed designs, and was almost out of business by 1939.

PZL (Poland). Państwowe Zaklady Lotnicze (national aviation establishment) was set up as Poland's main aircraft design and production organization 1 January 1928, having previously been CZL (central aviation establishment) and originally in 1919 CWL (central Warsaw aviation establishment), handling repair and maintenance only. Para-military government of 1926 urged better defences, and PZL concentrated on fighters with brilliant team of young graduates led by Zygmunt Pulaski. First, classic design, P.1 fighter introduced 'Pulaski wing' with inner section tapered in chord and thickness and sloped sharply down to join top of fuselage; led to more than 760 fighters of P.7, 11 and 24 basic types, majority for Romania, Turkey and Greece. Other types: L.2 STOL observation, L.3 bomber, L.4 and 27 trimotor airliners, PZL.5 2-seat biplane, P.19 3-seat tourer, P.23 and 43 Karaś bomber/recon, P.26 fast 3-seater and, not least, P.37 Loś heavy bomber, outstanding aircraft of which 70 delivered but only 36 combat-ready on 1 September 1939. Increased demand led to original Warsaw-Okecie factory being augmented by much larger factory at Mielec 1938. This was undamaged in 1939 and in 1940–44 was giant slave-labour plant managed by Heinkel.

PZL (Poland). After 1945 Polish industry was reconstructed, with many false starts and changes in organization. At first overall management was vested in ZPL, with PZL under original name assigned series production at Mielec, Rzeszów and Wroclaw (Breslau) of aircraft designed and flown as prototypes by CSS and LWD. After several changes today's much larger industry is managed by ZWSLS PZL (association of aircraft and engine industry), with foreign trade handled by Pezetel, which *see*. Industry comprises 3 major centres plus IL, which *see*. Two centres are Mielec and Swidnik: see **WSK**, both entries. Third is titled **PZL Warsawa-Okecie**, and is on site of original 1928 factory. Assigned to agricultural, training and utility aircraft, producing 3,600 since

PZL-Okecie PZL-130T Turbo-Orlik, December 1989.

1955, main programmes are: PZL-104 Wilga STOL 4-seat and utility, PZL-105 Flaming STOL 6-seat utility, PZL-106 Kruk ag-aircraft (piston or turboprop), PZL-110 (based on SOCATA Rallye), PZL-126 Mrówka ag-aircraft, PZL-130 Orlik and Turbo-Orlik multirole trainer, and PZL-230 Skorpion pusher turboprop trainer/ attack aircraft. National industrial development agency urgently seeking funds, and objective is to privatize industry.

Q

Qantas (Australia). Queensland & Northern Territory Aerial Service built 7 D.H.50A under licence 1926–8.

Quad City (USA). Quad City Ultralight Aircraft Corp., Moline, Illinois, market single-seat Challenger and 2-seat Challenger II certificated as micros or as FAA Experimental depending on engine chosen. Many options including floats.

Quaissard (France). GQ.01 Monogast high-wing single-seater flew 15 November 1983.

Quasar (France). Philippe Jean and Pierre Montel built Quasar 200 aerobatic single-seater 1984.

Queirolo (Italy). Luigi Queirolo set up company at Milan to build light aircraft. One family were single-engined and designated QR.2, initially (1935) with 60-hp CNA D.IV, 2bis (November 1939) had 95-hp Fiat A50bis and A.22 had 130-hp Fiat A54. He designed QR.14 light twin for CAT.

Questair (USA). Questair Inc., Greensboro, NC, produced Venture side-by-side long-range tourer, 288-mph cruise (1 July 1987).

Quickie (USA). Formed 1978 by Gene Sheehan and Tom Jewett, Quickie Aircraft Corp., Mojave, CA, produced distinctive Quickie single-seater (15 November 1977) with main wheels in spats on tips of long-span foreplane; over 2,000 kits delivered. Leg-Air built prototype of 2-seat Quickie Q2 (1 July 1980), 250 kits sold in first month.

R

Raab (Germany). Raab-Flugzeugbau GmbH formed by Anton F. Raab at Karlsruhe-Durlach February 1959 to take over Italian premises of late Col. Mario de Bernadi and produce MdB Aeroscooter in Germany. Also bought world rights (except Italy) to Ambrosini Rondone.

Raab (Greece). Raab Flugzeubau GmbH was Raab-Katzenstein reorganized 1934 at Riga, Latvia, but moved 9 months later to Athens, and yet again renamed as Société Anonyme Pour la Fabrication et l'Exploitation des Avions Raab. Built Tigerschwalbe IV military biplane, Pelikan light 2-seater and prototype R.27 fighter monoplane.

Raab-Katzenstein (Germany). Raab-Katzenstein Flugzeugwerke GmbH formed November 1925 at Kassel by former chief pilot and assistant managing director of Dietrich Flugzeugwerke. First product Schwalbe sport/training biplane, followed by larger RK.2 Pelikan biplane, RK.9 Grasmücke ultralight biplane and RK.25

Raab-Katzenstein RK.2a Pelikan, April 1927.

tandem-seat sporting low-wing monoplane. Sold licence to Pintsch of Austria and reorganized company in Riga, *see* above.

Raach (USA). Built baby (later Formula) LR-1 racer 1946.

RAAF (Australia). Royal Australian Air Force Experimental Station, Randwick, Sydney, produced prototypes of 5 types of aeroplane designed under supervision of Sqn/Ldr L.J. Wackett 1925–9.

RACA (Argentina). Representaciones Aero Comerciales Argentinas SA, previously agent and dealer, concluded agreement December 1972 for licence manufacture of at least 120 Hughes 500D and 500E helicopters.

Radley England (UK). Remarkable Waterplane (9 April 1913) built for pilot James Radley to design of E.C. Gordon England at Huntingdon, twin-hull biplane (3 × 50-hp Gnome in tandem on centreline), 3 seats in each hull. Rebuilt into Waterplane 2 (150-hp Sunbeam) with clinker-built hulls, 10-hr endurance.

RAE: *See* under Royal Aircraft Factory.

RAE Aero Club (UK). Staff of Royal Aircraft Establishment, Farnborough, formed Aero Club after 1918 which produced 3 ultralights: Zephyr pusher biplane (6 September 1923), Hurricane monoplane (July 1923, though started later, and then rebuilt 1925) and Scarab parasol, also known as PB Scarab from designers Peters/Brewer (February 1932). Scirocco abandoned 1926.

RAF: *See* Royal Aircraft Factory; Rutan.

Rafaelyants (USSR). Aram Nazarovich Rafaelyants was chief engineer at GVF repair/mod shops at Bykovo on Volga 1929–59. Major improvements 1929 to transports, PR-5, U-2L and Li-2, and own-design RAF-1 ultralight 1925, RAF-2 2-seat monoplane 1926, RAF-11 twin-engine transport 1938 (production prevented by war) and Turbolyet jet-lift test rig designed with Prof. Matveyev 1957.

Raine (UK). Two-seat ultralight (Cherub) believed left complete but unflown 1924.

Raisbeck (USA). James D. Raisbeck left Boeing 1969 and formed Raisbeck Engineering, Van Nuys, 1974, moved to Seattle, specialists in high-tech improvements to GA aircraft to increase speed, reduce fuel burn, field length, noise or vibration, or confer other advantages; over 120 programmes certificated.

Ram (Costa Rica). Ram Aircraft Co., San Jose, produced TI-Ram microlight, exhibited Vancouver Expo '86.

RAM (USA). RAM Aircraft Corp., Waco, TX, specializes in 'modification of selected single- and twin-engined GA aircraft for improved performance and efficiency'. Majority Cessnas, changes usually include new engine and installation.

Ramor (Austria). Ramor Flugzeugwerke built handful of light aircraft 1919–33, including own-design KE.14 4-seater.

Ramsey (USA). Ramsey Aircraft formed

Minneapolis January 1933 to build Flying Bathtub single-seat primitive ultralight (20/30-hp Aeronca).

Rand Robinson (USA). Huntington Beach, CA, producer of high-performance homebuilts: KR-1 single-seat (February 1972), many thousands of plans sold, 200 + flying; KR-2 2-seat (July 1974), 7,000 + plans, 350 + flying; KR-100 composite structure single-seat, kits marketed.

Ranger (USA). Ranger Aircraft Co., Oklahoma City, were not related to Fairchild's Ranger Engineering which built engines. Produced 3 small sport aircraft 1928–31, including Hunt Racer (90-hp Cirrus) of 1930.

Rankin (USA). Rankin Aircraft, Maryville, Missouri, took over rights to Porterfield Collegiate and produced improved model to 1987.

RANS (USA). RANS Inc., Hays, Kansas, offers wide range of homebuilts, including S-4 and -6 micros, S-7 Courier high-wing 2-seat, S-9 Chaos aerobatic, S-10 Sakota 2-seat derivative of S-9, S-11 Pursuit, low-wing and twin-fins, S-12 Airaile side-by-side pusher, and derived single-seat S-14.

Ransome, Sims & Jeffries (UK). Famous ag-company at Ipswich which built D.H.6, F.E.2b and ABC Dragonfly engine 1916–18.

Rausch (USA). Rausch Engineering Inc. built light aircraft 1959.

Rawdon (USA). Rawdon Brothers Aircraft Inc., Wichita, built T-1 tandem low-wing monoplane 1949 and T-1S spraying version, adding SD spraying/dusting model 1962.

RB, R&B (USA). R&B Aircraft Co. built light aircraft 1976.

RBVZ (Russia). Russkii Baltiskii Vagon Zavod, Russo-Baltic Wagon Works, moved from Riga to St Petersburg, decided to build aircraft April 1912 and hired I.I. Sikorsky as chief designer. Built giant aeroplane named *Grand*, span 88 ft 7 in (27 m) (2 × 100-hp Argus), flown 2 March 1913. This later given 4 engines and developed into Ilya Mourometz series of reconnaissance-bombers, 80 built 1913–18, many going on to serve after Bolshevik revolution.

RD (USA). RD Aircraft, Mayville, NY, produce family of Skycycle micros, as well as Little Dipper Replica, modernized version of Lockheed lightplane of 1944.

R.E.: *See* Royal Aircraft Factory.

Rearwin (USA). Rearwin Airplanes Inc. established by Ray Rearwin (whose sons were Kenneth and Royce) at Kansas City April 1928. Hired Fred Landgraf as designer, producing Rearwin Ken-Royce 2000C 3-seat biplane, about 12 built with various 165–170-hp engines. Dug Webber and Noel Hockaday designed Junior 3000 parasol monoplane, handful of versions during Depression. Sportster 2-seat high-wing cabin monoplane (30 April 1935) led to about 350 of several versions, which funded derived Speedster, Cloudster and Ranger, built in fair numbers. Taken over 1935 by partnership which in 1937 bought assets of Le Blond Aircraft Engine Corp., these engines being renamed Ken-Royce. Rearwin sold out 1942 to Commonwealth.

Red Bird (USA). Red Bird Aircraft Co. incorporated Oklahoma City 1928, but never achieved goal of 1 per day of 2-seat and 3-seat biplanes and 2-seat and 4-seat cabin monoplanes.

Redwing (UK). Formed April 1931 by name change of Robinson Aircraft Ltd at Wallington, Surrey. Moved to Blue Barns aerodrome, Colchester, 10 March 1932, also (1 July 1932) bought Gatwick, but production of Robinson Redwing side-by-side biplane remained at Colchester. Later firm moved to Redhill, doing subcontract work in Second World War and building Planet Satellites 1945–7.

Regent (UK). Regent Carriage Co., Fulham, London, built 20 Avro 504B 1915.

Regent (USA). Regent Aircraft built light aircraft 1950, 1954.

Reggiane: *See* Caproni.

Regia (Romania). IAR, which *see*, changed name 1940 to Regia Autonoma Industria Aeronautica Romana, still being known as IAR.

Regioliner (International). DAA renamed 1992 Regioliner GmbH; still 50% DASA, 25%

Aerospatiale and 25% Alenia.

Regional Aircraft (Germany). This Strategic Business Unit of DASA produces Do 228 and 328. HQ at Dornier airfield, 8031 Wessling.

Reid (Canada). W.T. Reid became chief designer at Bristol when Barnwell left in a huff to find a new career in Australia. He failed to do so, returned to Bristol and was given back his old job, to Reid's chagrin. So Reid went to Canada and in 1928 formed Reid Aircraft Co. at Montreal, building Rambler tandem-cockpit biplane. December 1928 merger with Curtiss resulted in Curtiss-Reid, which *see*.

Reid & Sigrist (UK). Important producer of instruments, especially for aircraft, formed aircraft department 1937, built RS.1 Snargasher 3-seater (2 × Gipsy Six) flown January 1939, and RS.3 Desford (named for location of works) 9 July 1945.

Reims (France). Agreement of 16 February 1960 gave Cessna 49% of Avions Max Holste, each having right to make other's aircraft. Cessna never made Max Holste aircraft, but French company was renamed Reims Aviation, building Cessna 172, and in 1964 prototype Reims/Cotelle JC 10 Scolair trainer. Latter never happened, and Reims became 100% licence-builder of single-engine Cessnas, apart from contributing parts for various Dassault programmes. In 1969 began assembly of Skymaster twin (push/pull), developing Reims' own FTB337G and Milirole versions. In 1989 Cessna disposed of shareholding to Compagnie Française Chaufour Investissement, but in line with Cessna Reims ceased production of piston aircraft, with 6,350 delivered. Apart from subcontract to Dassault, Airbus and ATR, sole production now is F 406 Caravan II twin-turboprop.

Remington-Burnelli: No company of this name existed: *see* Burnelli.

Renard (Belgium). Société Anonyme des Avions et Moteurs established 1927 by Georges and Alfred Renard at Evère, Brussels, to produce engines, starting with 100-hp radial. Soon designed aircraft, starting with Epervier parasol-wing fighter built by Stampe et Vertongen 1928. Three improved versions failed to dislodge Firefly, and completely new Constructions Aéronautiques G. Renard formed 1931 built R.17 4-seat cabin monoplane and R.30-300 5-passenger transport (3 × Gipsy), R.31 parasol recon monoplane (1933, RR Kestrel), R.32 (based on R.31 with GR.14 radial) and R.33 parasol trainer (120-hp Renard). R.31 built in quantity by Renard and SABCA. Company's final products were prototypes of R.35 pressurized 20-passenger airliner (3 × GR 750-hp radials), crashed on first flight 1 April 1938, and prototypes of single design of low-wing monoplane fighter built as HS12Y-engined R.36 (5 November 1937),

Renard R.37, July 1939.

R.37 (GR.14 engine) and Merlin-engined R.38 (4 August 1939).

Renaudau (France). Roger Renaudau built Avia-Sport ultralight January 1946.

R.E.P.: *See* Esnault-Pelterie.

Repair (Switzerland). Repair AG, subsidiary of FFA, handled marketing of Bravo series.

Replica Plans (Canada). Richmond, BC, company devoted to scaled warbirds, notably S.E.5a (1970).

Replogle (USA). Myrle Replogle produced Golden Bullet single-seat biplane 1958.

Representaciones: *See* RACA.

Republic (USA). Republic Aviation Corp. formed June 1939 by name change of Seversky, all personnel and Farmingdale location remaining unchanged. Built 120 EP-1 fighters for Sweden, final 60 requisitioned as P-35A for US Army, which also procured 272 P-43 Lancers of several versions. Derived P-44 cancelled in favour of bigger P-47B (6 May 1941) later named Thunderbolt, leading to 15,677 P-47s built at Farmingdale and at Evansville, Indiana (vacated 1945). At war's end P-72 and impressive XF-12 Rainbow (4 × 3,250-hp Wasp Major) remained prototypes, but RC-3 Seabee 4-seat amphibian (pusher 215-

hp Franklin) sold over 1,000 1945–7 because sold below cost. Alex Kartveli considered a jet P-47 but wisely started afresh with XP-84 Thunderjet (28 February 1946), leading to 3,368 'straight-wing' F-84 fighter-bombers, 2,713 swept-wing F-84F and 715 RF-84F. Odd jet/rocket XF-91 Thunderceptor and fantastic XF-103 turbo-ramjet fighter designed for Mach 3.7 (2,446 mph) both terminated, but AP-63 design for USAF attack fighter-bomber led to F-105 Thunderchief (22 October 1955) and to 830 production F-105s of various kinds. Company bought by Fairchild Hiller September 1965, initially as Republic Aviation Division, from 1971 as Fairchild Republic Co.

Republic of Korea (S. Korea). ROKAF (Republic of Korea air force) built small number of Pazmany PL-2 1973–6.

Repülö (Hungary). Repülö Müszaki Intézet (technical institute for aviation) designed world's first turboprop aircraft, RMI 1 (also called X/H) fighter-bomber (2 × Jendrassik Cs-1), aircraft complete 1942 but bombed before first flight.

Revolution (USA). Same president and almost same location as Air Command, Revolution Helicopter Corp. offers kits for Mini 500 light single-seater.

Rex (Germany). Flugmaschine Rex Gesellschaft established at Cologne-Bickendorf 1912 as flying

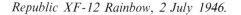

Republic XF-12 Rainbow, 2 July 1946.

F. J. Rey R.1, late 1949.

school, beginning licence-production of Morane-Saulnier monoplanes soon after. In 1915 designer Friedrich Hansen turned to fighters, D.6 (80-hp Oberursel) flying early 1916. D.7 of 1917 had variable-incidence lower wings.

Rex (USA). Rex Aviation built several tractor biplanes 1913–15.

Rey (France). François Rey formed Société des Avions F.J. Rey 1935 to develop wings able to flex and reduce incidence automatically when flying through gusts. Built aircraft 1938, destroyed Second World War, then R.1 rigid wing (16 December 1949) and flex wing (3 January 1951).

RFB (W. Germany). Rhein-Flugzeubau GmbH formed 1956 at Krefeld with licence from RWF to produce RW-3a Multoplane and 3b long-span version. Built own-design RF 1 STOL 6-seater 1960, progressively moving to Mönchengladbach. In 1968 VFW-Fokker bought 65% holding. In 1969 RFB bought holding in Sportavia, leading to Sportavia-Pützer (and Elektro-Mechanischer Fluggerätebau) becoming subsidiaries 1981. With Grumman American built Fanliner (114-hp ducted propeller) 1973, leading to Fantrainer (ducted 420- or 650-shp Allison 250), 47 for Thailand 1984–8.

Rhein-Flugzeugbau: *See* previous entry.

Rheinische: *See* Raab-Katzenstein.

Rhein-West: *See* RWF.

Rhodes Berry (USA). Los Angeles company which rebuilt B-26 into Silver Sixty executive transport with up to 14 seats, prototype 25 June 1960, first production 11 February 1961.

Ricci (Italy). Brothers Umberto and Ettore Ricci opened aircraft branch of giant shipbuilding firm at Naples, Industrie Aviatorie Meridionali, in 1919, building series of indifferent aircraft including R.1b twin-hull seaplane (3 × 280-hp), R.6 baby triplane and R.9 2-seat triplane. Work ceased about 1924.

Richard (France, USSR). Paul Aimé Richard was invited to replace D.P. Grigorovich as designer of Soviet marine aircraft (nobody else had experience). Gathered first-class team at OPO-4 within CCB August–December 1928, produced 'fantastic number of projects, eager to do all at once'. Only 1 major achievement TOM-1 heavy torpedo seaplane with 2 × BMW VI, later 2 × M-17 (1 January 1931). Too costly and complex, and remained prototype, Richard then returning to France.

C.H. Richard (USA). Lancaster, CA, company which produced 125 Commuter side-by-side high-

Richardson N-1 (2 × OX-5), early 1916.

wing aircraft 1968, 190 Sportplane aerobatic single-seater and two-thirds scale Fw 190 1972.

Richard Warner: *See* Warner.

Richardson (USA). Built N-1 seaplane 1916.

Richmond (USA). Richmond Airways Inc., Staten Island, NY, built Sea Hawk 5-seat flying-boat (160-hp Curtiss C-6) for their joy-ride business 1928.

Richter (Germany). In 1925 produced odd single-seater with pusher propeller behind grotesquely gulled monoplane wing.

Riddle (USA). Riddle Airlines, Miami, produced series of C-46R improvements to C-46 to add 1-ton payload, add 40-mph speed and allow 1-engine climb, 1958–61.

Rieseler (Germany). Sportflugzeugbau Rieseler founded 1921 at Berlin-Johannisthal to produce ultralights, including R.III single-seat (30-hp Haacke) and R.IV 2-seat. Production assigned to Mark, which *see*.

RIIGA (USSR). Riga (now capital of Latvia) institute of civil aero engineers produced series of ultralights from formation in 1962.

Rikugun (Japan). Not company but word meaning army, as distinct from Kaigun, navy. Rikugun Kokugijutsu Kenkyujo (army aerotechnical research institute) produced several projects in Second World War but flew only one type, Ki-93 heavy attack fighter (notable for 6-blade propellers on 2,400-hp Ha-214 engines), 2 prototypes built by Dai-Ichi Rikugun Kokusho at Tachikawa, 1945. Ki-202 advanced rocket-powered interceptor (derived from Mitsubishi J8M) never completed.

Riley (USA). Jack M. Riley formed **Riley Aircraft Corp.**, Ft Lauderdale, TX, 1952, specializing in improving existing aircraft. Put 2 engines in Navion to produce Twin Navion, sold rights to Temco. By 1961 turned Cessna 310 into Riley Rocket, Dove into Turbo-Exec 400 and Heron into Turbo Skyliner. By 1970 company renamed **Riley Turbostream Corp.**, Waco, TX, and by 1979 **Riley Aircraft Corp.** again, at Carlsbad, CA, concentrating on Cessna twins. Sold out to Advanced Aircraft 1983, which *see*; Riley then

formed **Riley International Corp.**, still at Carlsbad, still upgrading Cessna twins.

Ringhoffer-Tatra (Czechoslovakia). Tatra automotive and railway combine formed aviation department 1935 at Koprivnice, Moravia, building about 40 T.131 (licensed Jungmann) and T.126 biplane trainers and handful of T.1 2-seat cabin monoplanes. Taken over by Nazi Bohemia-Moravia administration 1939.

Rinne (Germany). Albert Rinne Flugzeug-Werke contributed to production 1916–18, notably by licence-production of Rumpler C.I.

Rio Claro (Brazil). Rio Claro aero club spent 1980–90 building prototype Super Surubim aerobatic trainer, 2 Carcará trainers (Jungmanns made of freijó wood) and gliders.

Rivers (USA). C. Rivers Stone (Greenville, SC) built Rivers R-1 single-seat canard (15 July 1983) with tail immediately behind pusher propeller.

Riverside (USA). Company at Riverside, CA, built Penguin non-flying trainer biplanes for Army 1917, with Ford engine, but one example was repeatedly flown (and subjected to various changes to try to improve it).

RLU: *See* Roloff.

RNAS: *See* Port Victoria.

Robertson (USA). Robertson Aircraft, Lambert St Louis airport, built Ro-1504 Rovaire 4-seater 1945.

Robertson (USA). Robertson Aircraft Corp. formed 1965 at Renton (Seattle) to produce STOL modifications, initially of CallAir and Cessna aircraft, later of Piper, Beech and other types. Assets acquired 1985 by R/STOL Systems, Raleigh, NC.

Robertson (USA). Robertson Aircraft Corp. built microlights 1982–5.

Robertson (USA). Robertson Development Corp., unconnected with previous, built light aircraft 1954.

Robey (UK). Robey & Co., Lincoln, was another engineering firm roped in to build aircraft

Robin HR.100, 1976.

1914–18, including Vickers Gun-carrier and Short 184. Robey-Peters RRF.25 was designed by J.A. Peters, biplane with 250-hp Rolls-Royce and gunner (Davis or Lewis) in each of 2 nacelles on top wing, Mk I (September 1916) and Mk II (January 1917).

Robin (France). Avions Pierre Robin formed at Dijon 1969 by changing name of CEA, Centre-Est Aéronautique. Continued production of DR series wooden 2/3/4-seat low-wing monoplanes originally derived from Jodel, over 3,000 by January 1991. All-metal R 3000 series (8 December 1980) since added in smaller numbers, marketed by Socata 1983–8. ATL (avion très léger) wood/composite 2-seater (17 June 1983) sold in modest numbers. Company acquired July 1988 by CFCI (Chaufour Investissement), M. Robin leaving to form Robin SA to provide after-sales support to existing customers.

Robinson (UK). Robinson Aircraft Co. formed October 1929 by Capt. P.G. Robinson at Stafford Rd, Wallington, Surrey, to produce Redwing side-by-side biplane designed by John Kenworthy (June 1930) and Redwing II (ABC replaced by Genet). Reorganized late 1930 as Redwing Aircraft Ltd, in former ADC hangar at Croydon: *see* Redwing.

Robinson (USA). Robinson Helicopter Co. formed 1971 at Torrance, CA, to produce light helicopter competitive in price with aeroplane. Resulting R22 (28 August 1975) seats 2, with Lycoming O-320 flat-rated 131-hp, 2,000th delivered by 1992. Four-seat R44 (31 March 1990) to be in production 1993.

Roche (France). Roche-Aviation SA formed 1945 at La Courneuve (Paris), building aircraft called Guerchais-Roche from chief engineer who pre-war had produced Guerchais-Hanriot and other designs. Main types T.35 (mid-1946) low-wing 2-seater and T.39 (1947) 3-seater (175-hp Mathis).

Rock (W. Germany). Glider manufacturer Rock Segelflugzeugbau produced Krähe powered sailplane 1957.

Rocket (USA). Rocket Aircraft Corp. formed 1946 by takeover of Johnson Aircraft Inc., Fort Worth.

Rock Island (USA). Rock Island Oil & Refining Co., Hutchinson, Kansas, formed Aircraft Division 1961 to produce Monarch 26 executive rebuild of B-26 Invader.

Rockwell (USA). On 16 February 1973 North American Rockwell was merged into Rockwell Manufacturing Co. to form Rockwell International Corp. Precisely a year later former NA Aerospace Group was replaced by NA Aircraft Operations and NA Space Operations. Aircraft Operations comprised Atomics International, B-1 Division, Los Angeles Aircraft Division, Columbus Aircraft Division (T-2 Buckeye, XFV-12A, OV-10 Bronco), Sabreliner Division (El Segundo, all Sabreliners), General Aviation Division (Bethany, Oklahoma, all Commander business and ag-aircraft) and Tulsa Division. In September 1978 North American Aerospace Operations was streamlined into Space Systems, Energy Systems and an Aircraft Group comprising North American Aircraft Division (with LA plant and Columbus plant), General Aviation Division, Tulsa Division and Sabreliner Division relocated at St Louis. In 1977 ag-aircraft were purchased by Ayres, in 1981 Commanders went to Gulfstream Aerospace and in 1983 Sabreliner went to a bank which formed Sabreliner Corp. This left North American Aerospace Business (which among other things manages Shuttle and Space Transportation Systems), and North American Aircraft with 2 facilities, Palmdale and Tulsa, which delivered 100 B-1Bs, upgrade OV-10, AC-130 and F-111, produced X-31A with MBB and participate in X-30 National AeroSpace Plane.

Rocky Mountain Helicopters (USA). Produce All-Star AS350 by conversion of Aerospatiale helicopters with 650-shp Allison C30M.

Rocourt (Belgium). Michel Rocourt produced ultralight in Mignet style 1986.

Rodenburg-Sanders (USA). William Rodenburg and Harold Sanders produced light aircraft 1959.

Roe: *See* Avro.

Rogers (USA). Rogers Aircraft Inc. formed 1921 after parent Rogers Construction Co. of NJ had taken over defunct Pacific Airplane & Supply Co., which *see*. Only known product called Pacific Standard C-1 racer.

Rogerson (USA). Rogerson Aircraft Corp. Irvine, CA, produces composite parts, control systems, fuel tanks and other aerospace components. In April 1984 purchased Hiller Aviation, renamed Hiller Helicopters and later **Rogerson Hiller Corp.**, producing RH-1100 and UH-12E at Port Angeles, Washington.

Rogojarsky/Rogozarski: *See* PSFA Rogojarsky.

Rohr (USA). Rohr Aircraft Corp., Chula Vista, CA world's biggest airframe component supplier in Second World War, took time off 1946 to produce totally odd MO-1 (Midnite Oiler) canard 2-seater with 2-control cockpit.

Rohrbach (Germany). Dipl.-Ing. Adolf Rohrbach, senior designer at wartime Zeppelinwerke Lindau, was world's greatest pioneer of metal stressed-skin construction. He could have stayed

Rohrbach Ro VIII Roland, October 1926.

with Dornier, but in 1919 he designed Zeppelin-Staaken E.4250, world's first modern airliner with 4 engines along leading edge of stressed-skin wing. In July 1922 he formed **Rohrbach Metall Flugzeugbau GmbH**, with subsidiary **Rohrbach Metall-Aeroplan A/S** in Copenhagen to evade Allied restrictions. Considering their superior structures, total number of aircraft produced (about 30) disappointing. All were high-wing cantilever monoplanes, some flying-boats with engines above wing (Ro II, Ro III and IIIa Roddra, Ro IV and Beardmore Inverness, Ro V Rocco, Ro VI Robbe and Ro X Romar) and others landplanes, notably Ro VIII Roland and VIIIa Roland II. By 1928 Allies no longer bothered. Kurt Tank designed final Copenhagen product, Ro IX Rofix fighter (1926), then went to Focke-Wulf. Tooling moved to Germany where Ro X boats were built before company taken over in April 1934 by Weser, Rohrbach becoming technical director.

Roks-Aero (Russia). Moscow corporation formed 1990 in Business Aviation Assoc linking Moscow Aviation Products Assoc, Myasishchyev factory, Yakovlev 'Skorost' plant, and factories at Komsomolsk, Luchovitsy, Novosibirsk, Smolensk and Ulan-Ude to built all except biggest aircraft plus Ekranoplans. Prototype T-101 Gratch multirole (1,000 hp turboprop) to fly May 93, seaplane, twin-engine and other versions; prototypes of six other designs building.

Roland: *See* LFG.

Rollason (UK). Rollason Aircraft and Engines Ltd, long-established sales/service firm at

Romaero Rombac 1-11 Series 560, 1983.

Croydon airport, later at Shoreham, took licence for Druine Turbulent and flew first of 25 (various sub-types) on 1 January 1958. Subsequently built 51 D.62 Condors, again several versions.

Roloff (USA). Three professional pilots, Charles Roloff (Palos Park, Illinois), Robert Liposky and Carl Unger, produced RLU-1 Breezy tandem 2-seater, 'vintage configuration with all modern facilities', some hundreds flying.

Romaero (Romania). Formed 20 November 1990 by changing name of IAv Bucuresti. Among other activities produces Rombac 1-11 (One-Eleven) and Islander. Previous names: ARMV-2 1951–7, CTIA 1958–61, IRCMA-IRMA 1961–78 and IAv Bucuresti 1978–90.

Romano (France). Etienne Romano, enthused by seeing French-built Wrights, built R-1 but it crashed on first flight. After First World War he found workshops at Cannes-La Bocca and in 1922 set up Les Chantiers Navales de la Croisette, changing name late 1920s to Chantiers Aéronavales E. Romano. Produced 130 types, concentrating on seaplanes (often with provision for catapulting), flying-boats and amphibians, but including various landplane fighters and trainers, some derived from seaplanes. Apart from a handful of R-83 fighters clandestinely supplied to Republican Spain, no series production resulted, with single exception of R-80 family of biplane trainers (February 1935), of which 147 were built for Armée de l'Air and

30 for Aéronavale, last in 1939 by which time company had been nationalized into SNCASE.

Rombac (Romania). Not a company but name of programme to build One-Eleven in Romania (*see* **Romaero**): formed from Romania and BAC.

Romeiko-Gurko (USSR). D.A. Romeiko-Gurko, assisted by D.N. Kolesnikov, built RMK-1 transport in 100-hp motor-glider class 1936. At same time was completing RG-1 high-speed transport with cockpit above shaft drive to propeller, 850-hp M-34 amidships and cramped 4-seat cabin at rear. Believed not flown.

Romeo (Italy). Società Anònima Industrie Aeronàutiche Romeo formed 1934 at Naples to take over activities of Officine Ferroviarie Meridionali, which thereupon abandoned aircraft construction. Chief types 1935–41 included Ro 26 biplane trainer, Ro 30 army-cooperation/recon biplane, Ro 37 2-seat fighter/recon biplane, Ro 41 biplane fighter and Ro 43 centre-float seaplane. By 1936 SAIA Romeo had again been renamed, becoming SAIMAM, or IMAM, aircraft being known as Meridionali (which *see*) but retaining Ro designations for Nicola Romeo.

Ronchetti: *See* RRA.

Roos Aircraft Co. (USA). In 1936 Victor Roos, president of American Eagle-Lincoln, bought out company and renamed it. Remained at Kansas

City building PT biplane and American Eaglet monoplane.

Roos-Bellanca (USA). Victor Roos established Roos-Bellanca Airplane Co. 1922 at Omaha to build to designs of Giuseppe Bellanca, starting with outstanding CF cabin monoplane. Within a year Bellanca resigned (joining Wright a year later). Roos later joined American Eagle.

Rootes (UK). Automotive tycoons Reginald and Billy Rootes (Hillman, Humber, Commer, etc.) were first to respond to Government's call for Shadow Factories, each intended to be shadow (duplicate) of parent, 1936. Shadow factories often larger than parent, with far better facilities for mass-production. Rootes plants included Speke (Liverpool) making Bristol Blenheims, Blythe Bridge (Staffs.) making Blenheims and Beaufighters, and 3 giant factories making poppet- and sleeve-valve engines.

Rose (USA). Rose Aeroplane & Motor Co. formed 1934 at 4415 E. Clark St, Chicago, to produce Parrakeet single-seat biplane. Rights purchased 1949 by Hannaford, which *see*.

Rosk-Aero (Russia). Private design bureau in Moscow whose first project is T-101 Gratch (rook), monoplane turboprop redesign of An-2; prototype (December 1992) built at LMZ.

Ross (USA). Ross Aircraft Corp., of Amityville, Long Island, NY, produced RS-1 Sportplane 1938, simple open tandem parasol. Modest production led to improved RS-21 1942, but war halted operations.

Rostvertol (Russia). Rostov-on-Don Helicopter Manufacturing Enterprise established 1991 to manage factories which built Mi-4, 6, 10 and 10K and now produce Mi-17, 26 and 34. Corporate member American Helicopter Soc., parent of Vertolservice operating/leasing company.

Rotary Air Force (Canada). Ponoka, Alberta, company marketing kits for GT 1000 single-seat high-speed autogyro and Series 2000 2-seater.

Rotec (USA). Rotec Engineering Inc., Duncanville, TX, have enjoyed massive success since in 1977 they began selling lightplanes (e.g. Panther Plus and 2-seat Panther 2 Plus) and range of microlights, all available in kit or ready-to-fly form.

Rotor-Craft (USA). Rotor-Craft Corp. formed by Gilbert Magill 1952 at Sun Valley, CA, to produce RH-1 Pinwheel helicopter strapped on to wearer. Later added Sky Hook, with 400-lb (181.4 kg) payload yet folding into suitcase. Navy/Army interest withered and in 1972 Mr Magill formed Aerospace General Co. to promote larger Mini-Copter using same peroxide-rocket tip drive.

Rotorcraft (S. Africa). Rotorcraft SA (Pty) Ltd formed February 1963 at Cape Town to develop Minicopter light autogyro. Sales confined to S. Africa, ending 1969.

Rotorcraft (UK). Rotorcraft Ltd formed 1959 by Servotec and Mitchell Engineering to produce 2-seat Grasshopper coaxial helicopter designed by J.S. Shapiro. Flown February 1962, but development petered out 1965.

RotorWay (USA). Formed 1970 by B.J. Schramm at Tempe, AZ (*see* Schramm) to produce improved helicopter named Scorpion Too. Subsequently moved to Chandler, AZ, and added RW-145 engine of 150-hp. By 1984 had produced completely new Exec helicopter. In 1990 moved to 300 S 25th Ave, Phoenix, going into liquidation, *see* below.

RotorWay (USA). Assets bought by Englishman John Netherwood, who formed **RotorWay International** 1 June 1990 (company name Cobb International), marketing Exec with 23 modifications for sale worldwide.

Rotorwing (USA). Rotorwing Aircraft Co., Birmingham, Alabama, produced Sportsman 2-seat autogyro (April 1960). Plans for 5 production versions not implemented.

Rouffaer (USA). Rouffaer Aircraft formed Oakland, CA, about 1932 to produce R-6 3/4-seat cabin monoplane with 80-hp engine designed by Chevrolet engineer, odd feature being perfectly streamlined nose of bullet form with windshield above engine immediately behind propeller.

Roussel (France). In mid-1930s Maurice and Jacques Roussel both designed a radial-engined fighter, Maurice with team at Bloch works and his brother privately. Latter worked on his own, but resulting Roussel 30 light fighter was built at

RAF BE.2 (No. 2 Sqn, RFC), 26 February 1913.

Bloch works at Courbevoie, flying April 1939; destroyed Bordeaux 1940. In parallel Jacques produced attractive Roussel 10 high-wing cabin 2-seater (July 1939). He never had his own company.

Royal Aircraft Factory (UK). Her Majesty's Balloon Factory was formed 1892 at Aldershot, moving 1905 to South Farnborough, where in 1910 Superintendent Mervyn O'Gorman made plans for future work on aeroplanes. Though known as 'The Factory' it had neither authority nor funds to construct any kind of aircraft—not even balloons—but O'Gorman laid down 6 types of aircraft (later published in *Reports & Memoranda* 59 in November 1911): BE, Blériot Experimental, meaning tractor aeroplane; BS, Blériot Scout, fast tractor single-seater; FE, Farman Experimental, pusher type; RE, Reconnaissance Experimental, 2-seat tractor; SE, Santos Experimental, tail-first or canard, but soon changed to Scout Experimental, replacing BS; and TE, Tatin Experimental, propeller behind tail. First aeroplane at Balloon Factory was Geoffrey de Havilland's No. 2, which he brought on his appointment December 1910 as Factory test pilot and designer (in theory he should have refrained from designing). This aircraft made acceptance test flight of 1 hr 14 January 1911, whereupon it was purchased and designated FE.1. Meanwhile, a crashed Blériot known as 'the Mankiller' was brought in for repair December 1910, emerging late January as completely rebuilt SE.1 canard (crashed 18 August 1911, killing Assistant Superintendent Lt. T. Ridge). On 1 April 1911 establishment renamed **Army Aircraft Factory**, and on 1 April 1912 prefix **Royal** added. On 11 April

1911 Factory received pusher Voisin donated to War Office by Duke of Westminster. It was totally rebuilt (only 60-hp Wolseley engine remained) into 2-seat tractor biplane BE.1 (1 January 1912). While BE.1 was being created de Havilland produced FE.2 (18 August 1911), and while this led to more than 2,300 FE.2a/b/d 2-seat pusher fighters, BE.1 led to more than 3,200 BE.2a/b/c/d/e 2-seat reconnaissance aircraft. Original BE.2 had not been allowed to compete in 1912 Military Aircraft trials (because Factory not supposed to build aircraft) but design was so obviously superior to winning Cody pusher that it became standard RFC type, built by 22 companies and soon equipping RFC Nos. 2, 4, 5, 6, 7, 8, 9, 10, 12, 13, 15, 16 and 21 Sqns. Subsequently developed into BE.8 and 12. E.T. Busk played part in applying theory of inherent stability in design of RE.1 (about May 1913) 2-seat reconnaissance biplane. From this came RE.5, of which Factory itself made 24 in 1914, followed by RE.7 (about 250) and RE.8 (4,077). Last major design began with BS.1, world's first high-speed single-seat scout (3 July 1912). This led via BS.2 (SE.2) to SE.4 (about August 1914), designed by Harry Folland to be world's fastest aeroplane and reached 135 mph. Next came SE.4a, after which Folland, assisted by John Kenworthy and Major Frank Goodden, designed fighter to be powered by new Hispano-Suiza V-8 engine. Result was 5,205 SE.5 and 5a fighters, plus others by Curtiss and Eberhart in USA. Factory produced many prototypes, total coming to 533 aircraft of 28 types by 1919. By this time formation of Royal Air Force 1 April 1918 had led to Factory being renamed **Royal Aircraft Establishment**, devoted solely to research in support of manufacturing industry.

Royal Army Aircraft Factory (Denmark): *See* Haerens.

Royal Army Aircraft Factory (Sweden): *See* FFVS.

Royal Dockyard (Denmark): *See* Orlogsvaerftet.

RRA (Argentina). Rochetti, Razzetti Aviación SA, Rosario, produced small number of J-1 Martin Fierro ag-aircraft (18 December 1975).

RTAF (Thailand). Royal Thai Air Force SWDC (Science and Weapon systems Development Centre) assembled 31 RFB Fantrainer 400s with composite wings, simultaneously producing alternative metal wings. Wings of 18 CT4 Air-trainers are being manufactured to extend life.

Rudlitsky (Russia). Georgii Valeryevich Rudlitsky built biplane with forward elevator and pusher 45-hp Anzani, flew well 1911. Possibly built further aircraft, with butterfly tail.

Ruffy-Baumann (UK). Ruffy, Arnell & Baumann Aviation Co. formed 1915 at Hendon by 2 pilots, Felix Ruffy (Italian) and Edouard Baumann (Swiss), who opened flying school and augmented their fleet by designing several biplane trainers, each built in very small numbers. Company taken over 1918 by Alliance, final trainer design becoming Alliance P.1.

Rumpler (Germany). E. Rumpler Luftfahrtzeugbau GmbH established at Berlin Johannisthal February 1909 by Austrian Dr Edmund Rumpler and R. Haessner. Began by building over 220 improved Taube monoplanes, adding from December 1913 2-seat biplanes leading to B.I trainer/recon built in land and seaplane forms (some by Pfalz). Early 1915 company restructured as **Rumpler Flugzeugwerke**, producing prototypes of C.I armed 2-seater, built by Rumpler, Hannoversche, Bayru, MFW, Pfalz, Rinne, Brandenburg and Germania. This led to C.IV and C.VII, latter highest-flying aircraft of war (23,950 ft [7,300 m] with gun and full load of cameras). Other types included G.I heavy bomber (about 60 built 1915–16), G.II, G.III and 7 types of fighters. Rumpler Limousine, passenger conversion of C.I, did not prevent liquidation 1920.

Runnels (USA). Russell W. Runnels built RR-1 Ruby 2-seat cabin aircraft (4 July 1967).

Ruschmeyer (Germany). Horst Ruschmeyer began design of MF-85 4-seater 1985, forming Ruschmeyer Luftfahrttechnik GmbH at Melle 1987. Loss of Porsche engine meant fresh start with R90-230RG (28 October 1990). Deliveries due 1992.

Rumpler C.IV No. 8186, March 1917.

RusJet (Russia). Joint-venture company set up in Moscow 1991 by several former Soviet design bureaux (including A.I. Mikoyan and Klimov Corp.), with 33.3% interest held by Marvol Projekt Consulting of Germany. RusJet immediately formed partnership with General Technologies (Russia) and AeroSud (S. Africa) and, with Marvol, paid Mikoyan OKB to design first joint project, LCPT (light cargo/passenger transport), twin turboprop. Two prototypes (1996) funded.

Russo-Baltic: *See* RBVZ.

Ruston, Proctor & Co. (UK). Large engineering firm at Lincoln which in 1915–18 built 200 BE.2c/e, 350 $1\frac{1}{2}$-strutters, 1,575 F.1 Camels and most of 600 Snipes ordered, as well as more than half of 1,500 Dragonfly engines ordered.

Rutan (USA). Elbert L. (Burt) Rutan began working on design of VariViggen canard tandem 2-seater 1963, formed Rutan Aircraft Factory Inc. (RAF) at Mojave Airport 1969 and flew VariViggen May 1972. There followed unique series of highly original designs, notably VariEze, LongEZ, Defiant, Grizzly tandem-wing STOL research aircraft and ultra-long-range Voyager (*see* Voyager). Consultant designs include NASA AD-1 slew-wing, Fairchild NGT (new-generation trainer), Quickie prototypes and numerous other prototype or research aircraft.

RWD (Poland). Warsaw technical high school produced aeroplanes which grew to support an industry: *see* Doswiadczalne Warsztaty Lotnicze.

All types were designated RWD from designers Rogalski, Wigura and Drzewiecki. RWD.1 (September 1928) was tandem 2-seat monoplane of 34 hp which won national competition. RWD.2 (May 1929) was 40-hp version which toured Europe and reached over 13,000 ft (3,962.4 m). RWD.3 was unsuccessful liaison aircraft. RWD.4 was 60-hp version of 2, 3 used by national team with much success. RWD.5 high-wing cabin 2-seater (7 August 1931) was built in quantity, one flying S. Atlantic (lightest aircraft ever to do so). RWD.7 was built to break speed and height records, which it did. RWD.8 tandem parasol trainer (November 1932) exceeded RWD productive capacity, about 100 being built plus over 500 by PWS. RWD.6 STOL high-wing cabin aircraft led to RWD.9, 6 being entered in 1934 Challenge de Tourisme and all finishing within top 10, later in 1934 taking first 3 places in Circuit of Europe. About 30 RWD.10 aerobatic trainers were followed by 110 RWD.13 STOL tourer/ambulance aircraft, over 30 of which survived war (in Romania) and were returned to Poland. LWS built 65 RWD.14b observation aircraft. By now an experienced team, RWD designed Types 15–25 before September 1939, but few were flown and even fewer survived war.

RWF (W. Germany). Rhein-West-Flug Fischer und Compagnie was formed at Porz-Westhoven, near Cologne, 1956, by H. Fischer to develop aircraft with pusher propeller in slot between fin and rudder. Tests on Fibo 2A led to definitive tandem-seat RW.3 with Porsche engine. Licence

RWD.5 (prototype flew 7 August 1931).

to build this was obtained by RFB which took over project.

Ryan (USA). Fighter pilot Tubal Claude Ryan left US Army 1922 and, unable to get job, formed small Ryan Airlines at San Diego, with workshops where small crew led by Harvey Bowlus converted 9 ex-war Standard J-1s into transports with pilot's cockpit behind cabin for 4 passengers. Airline prospered and grew, while, with B.F. 'Frank' Mahoney, Ryan carried out more ambitious conversions and, from 1925, original design. First was M-1 (14 February 1926), high-wing monoplane carrying 2 passengers or mail, 16 being built at San Diego. M-2 Bluebird was generally similar, 21 being built. In 1926 airline carried 5,000, mainly LA–San Diego, but Ryan and Mahoney had disagreements and for $25,000 Ryan walked out, leaving airline, M-1, M-2 and as-yet-unbuilt B-1 Brougham. Barely a week later (3 February 1927) Mahoney received a cable: 'Can you construct Whirlwind-engined plane capable flying nonstop between New York and Paris?' Chief engineer Donald Hall had already roughed out design, based on Brougham, when Lindbergh visited plant 23 February. Rest is history, Ryan NYP making flight 20–21 May 1927. Resulting demand for Brougham was such that 20 per month was inadequate, total topping 240. In 1928 company was renamed **Mahoney-Ryan** (which *see*), relocated at St Louis which had financed Lindbergh. This company was one of those swallowed by conglomerate Detroit to crash in Depression. T.C. Ryan had meanwhile been distributing imported Siemens engines and, above all, building up what was to become the Ryan School of Aeronautics at Lindbergh Field, San Diego.

Ryan (USA). In May 1934 Mr Ryan returned to manufacturing by forming **The Ryan Aeronautical Co.** at Lindbergh Field. His prosperous school needed a good trainer, and first product was S-T low-wing monoplane of mixed construction, with all-metal semi-monocoque fuselage with tandem open cockpits (8 June 1934). This led to large orders for derived civil and military versions, most numerous being Kinner-engined PT-22 Recruit (1,023 built in 1941). Ryan's interests were teaching and research, but in 1943 he responded to Navy specification calling for fighter with nose piston engine for range and tail turbojet for speed. Result was FR-1 Fireball (25 June 1944), but war's end limited production to

Ryan XF2R-1 Dark Shark, November 1946.

66. He produced Firebird, first air/air missile of USAF, followed by world's biggest family of targets, drones and RPVs derived from original Firebee of March 1951. In 1947 he bought rights to North American Navion, later selling out to Navion Aircraft. Whilst building fuselage barrel sections for KC-97, KC-135 and 707, Ryan produced X-13 Vertijet tail-standing VTOL (RR Avon, 10 December 1955), VZ-3 Vertiplane V/STOL with 2 propellers blowing on giant flaps (12 January 1959), XV-5A fan-in-wing high-speed VTOL (a far bigger project, 25 May 1964) and XV-8A Fleep Rogallo-type flexible-wing vehicle. Ryan sold assets to Teledyne 1969, which retained name as Teledyne Ryan. *See* next.

Ryson (USA). T. Claude Ryan formed Ryson Aviation Corp. for his son Jerome D. Ryan, producing STP-1 powered sailplane 1973. Other projects never happened.

SA (Singapore). Singapore Aerospace was formed as Singapore Aircraft Industries Pte Ltd early 1982 as unit of MoD. Comprises 6 subsidiaries which among other things have remanufactured RSAF A-4S Super Skyhawks (F404 engine, new avionics) including trainer conversions, conversions of F-5E to RF-5E, assembly of Super Puma and S.211 jet trainer,

Saab B18B bombers (prototype 10 June 1944).

and upgrades of Hunter, Skymaster and various helicopters. Partner with Eurocopter and Catic on EC 150 (P 120L); supplier of doors for Fokker 100 and nosewheel doors for 777.

SAAB (Sweden). In May 1921 Carl Clemens Bücker set up **Svenska Aero AB** with works at Lidingö, and later at Skärsätra, Stockholm, to manufacture aircraft of Heinkel design. This incensed Heinkel, and lacking his co-operation business withered, final product being Pirat 2-seat biplane land/seaplane with Lynx engine for training or Jaguar for fighting. Bücker returned to Germany 1932, taking designer Anders Andersson with him. This company was not connected with AB Svenska, for which *see* ASJA.

SAAB (Sweden). In 1930 ASJA took over SAAB, putting it on a sound footing, adding Nohab (later Svenska Flygmotor) AB building Bristol Pegasus and Mercury engines, and building under licence at Linköping such aircraft as Hart, Tiger Moth, Fw 44 Stieglitz and Raab Tigerschwalbe. In 1936 Government wish to strengthen home industry resulted in formation 2 April 1937 of wholly new company, **Svenska Aeroplan AB**, incorporating previous SAAB and ASJA companies. To Linköping was added large new factory at Trollhättan which went into licence production of Ju 86K bomber powered by Pegasus engines. In addition to latter, Svenska Flygmotor obtained licence for Twin Wasp, both types of engine being used in Saab-17 bomber and recon aircraft. Linköping also built Northrop (Douglas) 8A attack aircraft and Sk-14 (NA-16) trainers. Saab-17 was followed by twin-engined

Saab-18 high-speed bomber/recon aircraft, 18A with 2 Twin Wasp and 18B with DB 605B engines from Germany. Design of superior fighter began 1941 leading to J21 (30 July 1943) with pusher DB605B, 299 being delivered in 3 versions. Configuration was adaptable to jet, resulting in Goblin-engined J21R (10 March 1947), 60 being delivered. Saab-29 was outstanding swept-wing fighter/recon aircraft with licensed Ghost engine, later with afterburner (1 September 1948), 661 being built. Designs got better and better, with Saab-32 Lansen (3 November 1952) leading to 450 attack, recon and night-fighter versions. Most remarkable of all in appearance, Saab-32 Draken was preceded by Saab (this style replaced SAAB around 1950) 210 research aircraft to prove so-called double-delta shape (21 January 1952), leading to first J35 prototype (25 October 1955) and eventual total of 606 of these Mach-2 interceptor, recon and training aircraft. Other major types prior to 1965 included SAAB-90 Scandia airliner (16 November 1946), SAAB-91 Safir 3-seat light aircraft and trainer, designed by Anders Andersson (10 November 1945), and Saab-105 twin-jet trainer (29 June 1963) with 190 built for Sweden and Austria.

Saab-Scania (Sweden). In May 1965 company name changed to **Saab AB** (Aktiebolag), reflecting breadth of activities in fields of cars, missiles, electronics (fire control, computers, autopilots, etc.), spacecraft and high-tech products for industry and medicine. In 1968 decision was taken to merge with Scania-Vabis, automotive company best-known for trucks. In same year MFI (*see* Malmö) and a non-aero company,

Nordarmatur, were purchased. MFI-15 was developed into Safari and MFI-17 Supporter, nearly 260 being built (still produced in Pakistan as Mushshaq). Company's biggest programme to date was Saab-37 Viggen (8 February 1967), 329 being delivered by 29 June 1990 in attack, recon and trainer versions. In partnership with Fairchild SF-340 twin-turboprop airliner was launched (25 January 1983), US company subsequently withdrawing and designation changing to Saab 340, sales exceeding 350 before 1992. This massive success has supported development of Saab 2000 combining stretched 340 fuselage with new wing (built by CASA) and much more powerful Allison engines driving Dowty 6-blade propellers, orders/options exceeding 250 in 1992. Saab-Scania is member of IG JAS group producing JAS 39 Gripen (9 December 1988). It produces major parts for MD-80 family and BAe 146. Local dealer for Schweizer helicopters.

SAAC (International). Sammi Agusta Aerospace Corp. incorporated in S. Korea 22 May 1989 by Sammi of S. Korea, a major industrial group, and Agusta of Italy. Purpose was to produce SF.600TP Canguru utility transport and market it throughout Pacific basin. New 4.3 million sq ft factory has been built, to which Agusta has transferred SF.600 tooling, but moribund 1993.

SAAC (Switzerland). Swiss-American Aviation Corp. formed St Gallen October 1960 by William P. 'Bill' Lear to produce prototype SAAC-23 Learjet. Latter was originally designed by team led by Dr.-Ing. Hans Stüder, at Aircraft Development Corp. of St Gallen. In 1963 assets transferred to newly formed Lear Jet Corp., Wichita, which *see*.

SAAF: *See* South African Air Force.

Saalfeld (USA). Saalfeld Aircraft Co. produced Skyskooter autogyro (12 October 1960), Mr H.A. Saalfeld later being killed in crash.

Sääski (Finland). Osakeyhtiö Sääski formed company at Tampere 1928 to build biplane for training, touring, ambulance or ag duties, later with cabin and wheel/ski/floats.

SAAV (France). Société Anonyme l'Aile Volante (flying-wing company) was formed 1935 by Charles Fauvel to exploit his patents. His first machine was built by Caudron in 1933, with 40-hp ABC Scorpion mounted above wing on tall pylon. Bigger second wing had nose-mounted 75-hp Pobjoy, built at Toussus (10 February 1935). Work interrupted by war; for post-war, *see* Fauvel.

SAB (France). Société des Avions Louis Béchereau formed jointly with Pierre Levasseur 1918: *see* Béchereau.

SAB (France): *See* Bordelaise.

SABCA (Belgium). Société Anonyme Belge de Constructions Aéronautiques was formed December 1920 with main factory at Haren, with undertaking to purchase (BF6m annually) by SABENA. During first decade built over 350 aircraft under licence: Avia BH.21, Avro 504K, Bre.XIX, Nie.29C1 and, for SABENA, Handley Page W.8F. Own designs began with DP 2-seat ultralight, SABCA.2 for 4 passengers, S.XI 20-passenger airliner (3 × 500-hp) and S.XII 4-passenger (3 × 120-hp). In 1930s built Renard R.31 and Savoia SM.73, S.20 3-seat cabin monoplane, S.30 light side-by-side monoplane and S.40E trainer built for air force. Major effort was design, helped by Caproni, of S.47 2-seat

SABCA S.XI, February 1932.

fighter/attack aircraft (October 1937), but too late for war. SABCA also built engines under licence. Original company resumed operations 1949 with overhaul, assembly of Jeeps and design of S.70 trainer (abandoned), later overhauling F-84s, assisting Fairey with Hunter production and supplying SNCASO with parts for Vautour. From 1961 SABCA participated in manufacture of Hawk missile, F-104G and Br.1150 Atlantic, adding factory at Gosselies to original Haren site. During 1960s parity holdings were obtained by Dassault-Breguet and VFW-Fokker, leading to participation in all versions of Mirage, Alpha Jet, F27, F28 and Puma, adding in 1980s F-5, A310, Ariane and complete assembly/test of F-16. Today company is bigger than ever, still at original address, owned by Dassault Aviation (53%), Fokker (40 +) and others.

Sablatnig (Germany). Austrian Josef Sablatnig was pilot and experimenter 1911–13, then moving to Germany and becoming director of Union Flugzeugwerke. When this failed Dr Sablatnig formed Sablatnig Flugzeugbau GmbH, Berlin, in October 1915. First product was naval seaplane, SF 1 2-seat biplane. SF 2–SF 8 followed, LVG making 10 of 36 SF 2 and Sablatnig making 101 SF 5. Only small numbers were made of various landplanes, including C.I and II armed 2-seaters, N.I night bomber and a 240-hp 2-seat night-fighter monoplane. Strenuous post-war efforts centred around a 4-passenger cabin aircraft with foldable parasol wings. Wound up 1921.

Sabreliner (USA). Sabreliner Corp. formed July 1983 as subsidiary of NY bankers Wolsey & Co. following latter's purchase of Sabreliner Division from Rockwell. Based St Louis, with another site at Long Beach, Sabreliner announced new Model 85 in 1984 but by 1992 had still made no commitment, preferring to support and update 600 aircraft previously in service. Investment partner sought for Model 85.

SAC (China). Shaanxi Aircraft Co. was formed at that city in 1977 to build road transport vehicles and transport aircraft; 10,000 workforce and largest assembly hall in China. Main aero product is Y-8 derived from An-12B (25 December 1974), about 45 so far in 9 versions.

SAC (China). Shenyang Aircraft Corp. is long-established fighter factory which in 1956–9 produced 767 J-5 (based on MiG-17F), later producing much greater number of J-6 (MiG-19) versions including 634 JJ-6 trainers. SAC design team produced twin-jet delta J-8 (5 July 1969), delivering over 100 J-8 I and now producing J-8 II. New fighter is being designed. Other work includes parts for 757, C-130, ATP, A320, Dash-8, Saab 340 and other Western programmes.

SAC (USA). Spectrum Aircraft Corp., Van Nuys, CA, produced SA-550 modified Cessna/Reims Skymaster for multiple utility roles 1982.

SACA (Italy). Società per Azioni Costruzioni Aeronavali formed in Rome about 1939, factory at Brindisi. Associated with airline Aero Espresso Italiano but concentrated on light aircraft, mainly to design of others (e.g. 65 SAIMAN 202/M). Post-war supported Italian Stinson L-5 fleet, but failed in attempt to resume SAIMAN 202 production.

SACAB (Sweden). Scandinavian Aircraft Construction AB was formed 1984 by Peter Ahrens, ownership by various Scandinavian companies. Following demise of Ahrens Aircraft (which see), Mr Ahrens' son Kim carried out basic design of KM-180 utility transport (4 × LT101 turboprops). In early 1986 first flight was predicted for December 1986, but it never happened.

Sackett (USA). Horace E. Sackett produced low-wing Special J-1 Jeanie using some parts of J-3 Cub (5 June 1955).

Sadler (USA). Sadler Aircraft Co., Scottsdale, AZ, produced A-22 LASA light armed surveillance aircraft (8 October 1989) with 300-hp Chevrolet pusher. OPV is smaller version.

Sadlier: See VTOL, 2nd entry.

SAF: See Dewoitine, 2nd entry.

SAFA (France). Société Anonyme Française Aéronautique formed about 1930 to build under licence Koolhoven FK 41 and 43 3-seat cabin monoplanes.

Safety Aircraft (USA). Safety Aircraft Corp., San Leandro, CA, formed about time of Depression as research centre, but became general subcontract and manufacturing firm, building several prototypes, e.g. Capelis.

Sage (UK). Frederick Sage & Co., Peterborough, were high-class woodworkers specializing in shopfitting. From early 1915 made airship parts, adding Short 184 torpedo/bomber seaplanes from June 1915, plus large numbers of BE.2c (Curtiss engined, installation by Sage) and Avro 504K. In September 1915 Sage hired E.C. Gordon England as designer/pilot. He led design of Sage 1, large bomber (2 × RR Falcon), but not completed. Sage 2, designed for Admiralty by C.W. Tinson, was 2-seat fighter with upper wing joined to fuselage by glazed cabin with Lewis gun on top; flew 10 August 1916, good performance. Sage 3 was Admiralty trainer biplane, 75-hp RR Hawk (5 January 1917). Sage 4a/4b/4c were patrol/trainer seaplanes with Hispano or Sunbeam engines, first flown 3 July 1917.

SAI (Denmark). Skandinavsk Aero Industri A/S formed Kastrup 1937 to produce light aircraft, taking over business previously run by Kramme & Zeuthen. Built several versions of KZ.II trainer (last variant for RDAF). KZ.III 2-seat high-wing was followed by 4-seat KZ.VII Lark built in fair numbers and developed into KZ.X observation type. Final design was KZ.VIII single-seat low-wing aerobatic. Production ceased 1955.

SAI (Italy). Società Aeronautica Italiana Ing. A. Ambrosini formed 1934, works at Passignano, to produce trainer, touring and competition aircraft: SAI.1 2-seat biplane, 2 cabin 5-seat (2S different engine), 3 tandem-seat sporting (3S different engine), 7 fast cabin tandem-seat, 10 Grifone parasol tandem-seater. Chief designer Capt. Sergio Stefanutti, having proved canard layout with S.S.3 (see SCA), produced S.S.4 fighter (1 May 1939). Better fighter was conventional-layout SAI.207 (1942) derived from SAI.7. Order for 2,000 was overtaken by even better SAI.403 Dardo (December 1942), 3,000 ordered (1,200 by Savoia, 1,000 Caproni, 800 SAI) but Armistice halted work. Company resumed business 1946: see Ambrosini.

SAIB (France). Société Anonyme d'Applications Industrielles du Bois built several prototypes to designs of others 1916–18, including Courtois-Suffit fighter.

SAIMAN (Italy). Società Anònima Industrie Meccaniche Aeronautiche Navali formed 1929 to take over Lido di Roma factory previously operated by SA Navigazione Aerea. Undertook construction and support of aircraft, engines and power boats, and design of aircraft. Produced C.10 variable-incidence monoplane 1932 and C.4 2-seat biplane 1934, developed into SAIMAN 200 trainer, about 250 built (115 by Caproni-Vizzola), most during war for Regia Aeronautica. SAIMAN 202 side-by-side cabin low-wing monoplane also built in large numbers, about 50 civil and 365 military 202/M (including 85 by CNA and 65 by SACA). LB.4 of 1938 had twin booms and tricycle landing gear. Company failed attempted comeback post-war.

St Louis (USA). St Louis Aircraft Corp. formed at that city 1928 as subsidiary (later division) of tram-builder St Louis Car Co. First product was Cardinal C2-60, side-by-side high-wing cabin monoplane with 65-hp engine, followed by more powerful C2-85, -90, -100 and -110. During Depression built parts for Air Corps including aircraft skis, but in 1936 flew PT-1W biplane trainer. This led to Army purchase of XPT-15 and 13 YPT-15. Wartime work included manufacture of 200 Fairchild PT-23. Built 1 XCG-5; larger XCG-6 was cancelled.

SAL: *See* Scottish Aviation.

Salina-Hoffman (USA). Louis Salina and Earl Hoffman produced SH-1 Susie Bee aerobatic sport biplane (2 July 1967).

Salmon (UK). Tandem-wing 3.5-hp monoplane by Percy Salmon built at Farnborough September 1923.

Salmson (France). Emile Salmson established Société des Moteurs Salmson 1912 to produce aero-engines, especially Canton-Unné water-cooled radials. In 1916 built S-M.1 biplane designed by Lt. René Moineau with shaft drives to 2 tractor propellers. Far more successful was conventional Type 2 or 2A2 armed reconnaissance biplane (January 1917) of which about 3,200 were built. Some dozens were converted to, or completed as, post-war 'Limousine' passenger aircraft. Others licence-built in Japan. Aircraft manufacture lapsed until in 1925 Béchereau appointed designer, producing SB5 (Salmson-Béchereau 5) monoplane fighter, modified to SB 6 (SRAP 2). Work again lapsed until in 1934 Paul Deville produced Phrygane high-wing cabin 3-seater followed by D.6 Cri-Cri parasol 2-seater (1936), latter built by Salmson, Kellner-

Salmson 2A2 (US 1st Aero Sqn, June 1919).

Béchereau, Fouga, SFAN and Blériot. Post-war Salmson designs by CFA, which *see*.

Salvay-Stark (USA). North American engineers M.E. Salvay and George Stark formed Skyhopper Airplanes Inc. to build sporting aircraft. Skyhopper low-wing monoplane (26 March 1945) flew 1,000 hr by 1948; plans marketed, one constructor completing as side-by-side with tricycle gear. Sport-Aire TT-1 side-by-side cabin aircraft first flew 9 November 1959.

SAMF (China). Shanghai Aircraft Manufacturing Factory, subsidiary of Shanghai Aviation Industrial Corp., has delivered main/nose landing gear doors for MD-80 series since 1979 (1,799 sets by end-1990). In 1984 announced co-production of MD-82, starting with 25 for Chinese operators. First flew 2 July 1987; by 1993 35 delivered, plus MD-83s to be sold by McDonnell Douglas.

SAML (Italy). Società Aeronautica Meccanica Lombarda, large firm of military contractors with factories in Milan area (notably Monza), decided to build aircraft 1913, principal early product being Aviatik B.I built under licence, SAML building 410 of 568 constructed in Italy. Their designer, Swiss Robert Wild, came to Italy and designed SAML S.1 (October 1916) and derived S.2 recon-bombers, of which 657 were built. No post-war activity.

Sammi Agusta: *See* SAAC (International).

Samsonov (USSR). Pietr Dmitriyevich Samsonov worked at Shchyetinin, later joint head of manufacturing at OMOS. Two principal designs: MBR-5 monoplane amphibian (August 1935),

failed to replace Beriev MBR-2; MDR-7 stressed-skin flying-boat, 2 × M-88 engines (25 July 1940), no production.

Samsung (S. Korea). Samsung Aerospace (SSA) has been increasingly providing local content in assembling Bell 212 and 412 helicopters since May 1988. From 1994 Samsung will deliver 36 F-16C assembled from kits plus 72 wholly made locally, Daewoo and HanJin as subcontractors.

J. Samuel White: *See* White, J. Samuel.

Samu-Geönczy (Hungary). Designers in nationalized industry responsible for SG-2 Kék Madár (blue bird) side-by-side low-wing tourer (June 1954).

SAN (France). Société Aéronautique Normande established by Lucien Querey 1948 at Bernay, flying prototype SAN.101 high-wing 2-seater a year later. Then concentrated on Jodel designs, Delemontez joining as chief engineer: built 250 D.117 Grand Tourisme 1953–8, followed by D.140 Mousquetaire 4/5-seat version (4 July 1958). D.117 replaced 1958 by DR.100 (later DR.1050) Ambassadeur, later joined by D.150 (in 1963 named Mascaret). Final designs were D.140C Mousquetaire III and 140R Abeille, D.1052 Excellence and 6-seat D.160. Despite good sales, liquidation 1969, factory passing to Mudry.

Sanchez-Besa (Spain). Lt. Sanchez built Voisin-style biplane late 1909, and in 1912–14 Sanchez-Besa built a few aircraft for sale, as well as licensed engines.

Sanderson (UK). Angus Sanderson & Co., engineering firm at Newcastle upon Tyne, built 250 Sunbeam-engined Bristol Fighters 1918, having previously delivered 200 AW FK.8 and a few FK.10 quadruplanes.

Santa Ana (USA). Santa Ana (California) Aircraft Co. produced small number of VM-1 high-wing 3-seaters, 80-hp Anzani or any other radial engine up to 150 hp (5 January 1928).

Santos-Dumont (Brazil). Domiciled in Paris, Alberto Santo-Dumont was first builder of successful aeroplane in Europe (strange tail-first No. 14bis, Oct/Nov 1906). Diminutive bamboo No. 19 (November 1907) led to series of Demoiselles, some built by designer but many by home constructors (which S-D encouraged).

São Carlos (Brazil). São Carlos engineering school of University of São Paulo took over former IPT work 1975, where IPAI-26, -27 (former SP-18), -28 Super Surubim, -29 and -30 light aircraft were produced in prototype or research form.

SAP (China). Shijiazhuang Aircraft Plant established at that city in Hebei province 1969 to take over from NAMC production of Y-5 (An-2), delivering 290 by late 1992. SAP also produces W-5 and W-6 microlights.

SAPFEAR: *See* Raab (Greece).

Sargent-Fletcher: *See* Fletcher, both entries.

Saro (UK). In October 1928 A.V. Roe, together with John Lord and Harry Broadsmith, resigned from A.V. Roe & Co.—lately taken over by Siddeley—receiving £42,500 for their shares. This they invested in S.E. Saunders Ltd (*see* Saunders [UK]), company being renamed **Saunders-Roe Ltd**, commonly abbreviated to Saro. With other investors this provided capital for switch to metal construction, initially with longitudinally ribbed (corrugated) hull obviating need for stringers, first with A.17 Cutty Sark monoplane amphibian and larger A.19 Cloud, A.21 Windhover and A.27 London biplane flying-boat (30 for RAF). A.33 (4 × Perseus) remained prototype, followed by S.36 Lerwick, with smooth stressed skin but a failure. East Cowes factory built 453 Walrus and all 290 Sea Otter amphibians, as well as wing of Short Shetland. Post-war work included SR.A/1 jet fighter flying-boat (July 1947), 3 SR.45 Princess large transport flying-boats (22 August 1952), SR.53 jet/rocket supersonic fighter (with de Havilland Spectre rocket engine and HTP auxiliary power system, DH having acquired interest in Saro in 1956) and Skeeter and P.531 helicopters (20 July 1958) developed at former Cierva works at Eastleigh. Saro also built SR.N1 (1959), world's first hovercraft, and had many subsidiaries, some going to de Havilland and main company to Westland 1959 which continued Skeeter and Black Knight rocket and developed P.531 into Scout/Wasp.

Sasebo (Japan). Sasebo/Omura location of 21st Naval Air Arsenal (Dai-nijuichi Kaigun Kokusho), which from 1941 built aircraft to established designs: 25 Aichi B7A2, 103 Mitsubishi A5M4-K trainers (to Arsenal's design), 236 A6M2-K trainers (also to Sasebo

Saro A.17 Cutty Sark (Australian; prototype 4 July 1929).

design) and 590 Mitsubishi F1M2 seaplanes.

SASO (France). Société Aéronautique du Sud-Ouest formed February 1935 when Potez took over SA Bordelaise. Directors Henry Potez and Marcel Bloch, location Bordeaux-Mérignac. Planned as unit in Potez-Bloch-CAMS group, but thwarted by nationalization into SNCASO 1936.

Satic (International). Super Airbus Transporter International Co. formed 1992 as joint subsidiary of Deutsche Airbus (DASA) and Aerospatiale to build A300-600ST Super Flipper outsize carriers to augment and then replace Super Guppy transporters. Lead contractor is Latécoère.

SATTCO: *See* Service.

Saturn (USA). Saturn Aircraft Engineering, Oxnard, CA, built Meteor 5-seat light twin (13 September 1960).

Saunders (Canada). Saunders Aircraft Corp. formed 1968 at Gimli, Manitoba, to convert Herons into ST-27 twin-turboprops. Never flew planned new-build ST-28.

Saunders (UK). Around 1890 S.E. 'Slippery Sam' Saunders studied Canadian-Indian canoe of birchbark stitched with sinews. He later patented Consuta construction in which hull is multiple thin plies of mahogany stitched tightly with copper wire. Established **S.E. Saunders Ltd** at East Cowes mainly to build motor boats. In 1911 built hydroplane for Roger Ravaud, followed late 1912 by hulls of sewn cedar ply for Sopwith's Bat Boats. From 1914 built large numbers of Avro 504A/J, Short 184, Norman Thompson and 100 F.2A flying-boats, and experimental hulls for Cdr. Porte at Felixstowe. Saunders also built single T.1 2-seat armed biplane of own design 1917. Designer H.H. Thomas died in flu epidemic 1918, but firm stayed in aircraft business, with Kittiwake amphibian (19 September 1920), hulls of Vickers Vikings and complete Vickers Valentia flying-boats. Last products were A.3 Medina 10-passenger boat (2 × Jupiter) of 1926 and A.3 Valkyrie for RAF (3 × 650-hp Condor) of 1927. Became Saro 1928, though A.10 fighter (1929) called Saunders.

Savage (NZ). C. Savage and D. Shaw built Savage Special single-seat parasol (40-hp Henderson) 1946.

Savages Ltd (UK). Woodworkers and agricultural engineers of Kings Lynn, Norfolk, and Stroud, Glos., who in 1915–18 delivered 50 Voisin LA, 100 Avro 504K, 73 D.H.1 and 100 D.H.6.

Savary (France). Established pre-1909 at Chartres by Robert Savary, building about 12 biplanes (almost all different) pre-1914, 1911 military biplane winning Savary Légion d'Honneur. Retired early 1914 but 2 years later formed R. Savary et H. de la Fresnaye, Levallois-Perret, building over 1,000 aircraft by Armistice, about half of them Nieuports.

Savelyev (Russia). Vladimir Fedorovich Savelyev, mechanic at 2nd Aviapark 1916, assisted by V. Zalevsky, used fuselage of Morane G in building quadruplane. Span increased progressively from bottom to top wing, flew well from 19 April 1916 with 80-hp Gnome, later 100-hp Clerget. Did not build planned 8-wing passenger airliner, but did build and fly 2-seat reconnaissance quadruplane 1923, with 120-hp Le Rhône; reached 164 km/h (102 mph) on skis.

Savoia-Marchetti (Italy). To present coherent picture this outlines whole pre-1943 history of company formed 12 August 1915 at Sesto Calende as SIAI (**Società Idrovolanti Alta Italia**) with orders to build FBA flying-boats under licence. Rafaele Conflenti was hired 1916 as designer, improving French boat as S.8, 172 built by Armistice of over 800 ordered. S.9 (mid-1918) was further improved, with 180-hp Isotta-Fraschini replaced by 300-hp Fiat A.12bis, some built by new CAMS in France. Further refinement led to S.12, 13 and 16, over 230 of latter being built, 80 going to Soviet Union and 1 flown by de Pinedo throughout Australia and Far East. SIAI S.17, 19, 21 and 22 were small racing flying-boats. Conflenti produced S.23 trainer boat and twin-engined S.24 (unfinished) before leaving to join CAMS May 1922. His successor, Alessandro Marchetti, brought with him from MVT (which *see*) his high-speed biplane design. Company added Savoia-Marchetti to existing title, aircraft all being known by this joint name. Marchetti started new numbers at 50, S.50 being 161-mph MVT biplane. This was modified 1923 as S.51 fighter. S.52 flying-boat came 2nd in 1922 Schneider race. S.53 bomber led to S.55 twin-hull boat with tandem engines, 2 × 300-hp in prototype (August 1924) increasing with successive

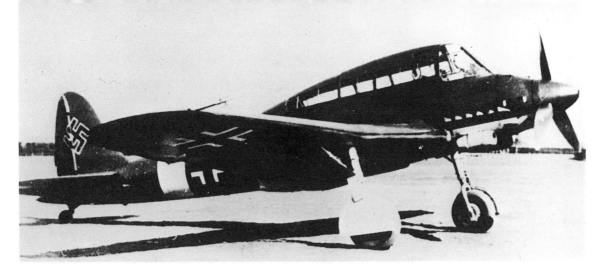

Savoia-Marchetti SM.93, 31 January 1944.

versions to 2 × 750-hp in S.55X, 25 of which, led by Gen. I. Balbo, flew to Chicago 1933 and back; about 245 of all versions built. Many other marine aircraft followed, including 22 S.66 (3 × 600-hp) twin-hull boats for airline Ala Littoria. From 1927 Marchetti began adding landplanes, and in about 1933 company name changed in consequence to **Società Italiana Aeroplani Idrovolanti 'Savoia-Marchetti'**. One early landplane, S.64, set impressive circuit records including 4,764 miles (7,665 km) in just under 59 hours. Final Schneider contender, S.65 with pilot sitting between push/pull 1,000-hp engines, crashed (as did 9 Savoia prototypes) into Lake Garda. Seven S.71 high-wing transports (3 × 240-hp) were followed by 6 larger S.72 (3 × 550-hp). This 'Fokker style' was obsolescent, and S.73 (3 × 800-hp) low-wing transport (4 July 1934) was much faster, 48 built (7 Belgian S.73s escaped to England May 1940, served with the RAF in N. Africa where 4 were captured by Italy!). Last high-wing fixed-gear type was S.74 (4 × 700-hp) with 22 passengers. SM.75 introduced 'Savoia-Marchetti' designations, 94 of these 226-mph (363.6 km/h) 30-passenger transports being built 1937–43, plus several variants including 4 SM.87 twin-float seaplanes. SM.78 was last biplane flying-boat, 49 built 1933–6. SM.79 Sparviero was most famous SM type, flown as long-range racer 1934 (3 × 780-hp) and 1,780 bomber and torpedo derivatives being built, most with 3 × 1,000-hp but a few 79B exported with 2 engines. SM.81 was bomber version of SM.73, 534 built 1935–42. SM.82 Canguru was large transport (3 × 950-hp), 720 built 1939–43. SM.83 was high-speed civil airliner, 23 built 1937–8. SM.84 bomber/torpedo carrier (5 June 1940) had 3 × 1,000-hp, 309 built. SM.85 and 86 dive-bombers were failures, and final prototypes

were SM.89 attack bomber, 91 twin-boom fighter, 92 twin-boom fighter with no central nacelle, 93 dive-bomber and 95 4-engined transport. Post-war, *see* SIAI-Marchetti.

Savoia Pomilio (Italy). No company of this name, but apart from licensed Farmans first aircraft mass-produced by SIA (Fiat) was called from designers U. Savoia and O. Pomilio; improved Farman pusher SP.1 (late 1914) led to SP.2 (*see* Pomilio), about 350 SP.3 and 146 SP.4.

Sawada (Japan). Lt. Sawada built Kaishiki-Go biplane 1916, believed 1st Japanese aircraft.

Sawano (Japan). Shiro Sawano built S25X modified Bowers Fly Baby 1976 and S25X II tandem cabin monoplane (21 October 1979).

Sayers (UK). Designed light monoplane 1923, 2 built by Handley Page as HP.22 and HP.23 (minor differences).

Kaishiki No. 7-Go. (U. Sawada), 1916.

SCA (France). Soc. Commercial Aéronautique produced SFR.10 low-wing cabin 3-seater (95-hp Renault) flown at Buc 16 October 1931.

SCA (Italy). Stabilimento Costruzioni Aeronautiche was government group based at Guidonia test centre, chief engineer Capt. S. Stefanutti, which *see*.

SCAL (France). Société de Constructions et d'Aviation Légère of Paris built F.B.30 ultralight 1936, pusher 40-hp Mengin, tandem open cockpits, several exported.

Scaled Composites (USA). Established 1980 by 'Burt' Rutan as independent R&D facility, handled research and design of several major aircraft but on receiving contract for scaled Starship purchased by Beech as subsidiary 1985. Sold back to Rutan November 1988, joint venture with Wyman-Gordon (heavy forging and metalworking giant), numerous current programmes.

SCAN (France). Société de Constructions Aéro Navales formed pre-1939, best-known product SCAN 20 designed by Bernard Devèze to meet 1942 specification for trainer flying-boat (Béarn, Potez or Salmson in 240/280-hp class). Prototype completed under Vichy authority but not flown until October 1945; 23 to Aéronavale 1951–2.

Scandinavian: *See* SACAB.

Scenic (USA). In 1977 Scenic Airlines, Las Vegas, acquired from AJI rights to Turbo Star 402 and 414 (Cessna turboprop conversions); in 1991 converted 8 Twin Otters with giant windows and quiet propellers.

Schaefer (USA). Schaefer & Sons established before 1917, then built RS fighting scout (9 December 1917), RS from designer N.B. Robbins and builder Schaefer. Prototype tested at San Diego by Signal Corps.

Schafer (USA). Schafer Aircraft Modifications Inc., formed 1977 at Waco, TX, produces conversions of Cheyenne II, Chieftain and pressurized Navajo with PT6A turboprops, and, with Aero Modifications International, rebuild of DC-3 with PT6A engines and other changes.

Schapel (USA). Schapel Aircraft Co. formed Reno, 1973, produced S-525 Super Swat ag-aircraft (pusher PT6A turboprop) 1980, SA-882 Flying Wing 1985 (180-hp Mazda).

Scheibe (W. Germany). Scheibe-Flugzeugbau established Dachau December 1951, initially producing Mü.13E Bergfalke glider designed by Dipl.-Ing. Egon Scheibe previously. Since 1951 built various sailplanes, plus 3 versions of SF.23 Sperling high-wing tandem cabin monoplane, various SF.24A Motorspatz single-seater and SF.25 Motorfalke (also built by Slingsby).

Schelde: *See* De Schelde.

Scheller (Germany). Formed at Celle prior to 1932, initially building S.IV.32b low-wing 2-seater of steel tube/fabric. Planned biplane and tailless monoplane (1936–7) not built.

Schempp-Hirth (Germany, W. Germany). Schempp-Hirth OHG established by Wolf Hirth at Göppingen 1935 to build sailplanes. Became world leader, and remains so today, but as Schempp-Hirth OHG, Kirchheim-Teck, also building light aeroplanes, initially Milan GS6 (May 1958) high-wing 2-seater, later licensed Piel Emeraude. Planned STOL aircraft abandoned, Piel license to Binder 1962.

Scheutzow (USA). Formed about 1963 by Webb Scheutzow to develop light helicopter with main rotor blades held in rubber bushes. Resulting Bee side-by-side 2-seater (180-hp) flew 1966. Money ran out 1977.

Schmeidler (Germany). Prof. Schmeidler at Breslau Technische Hochschule produced 2-seat STOL high-wing cabin monoplane with 60-hp BMW engine 1932.

Schmidt (W. Germany). Heinz Schmidt completed Zikade ultralight helicopter (65-hp) 1959. Never built planned 2-seater.

Schmitt (France). Paul Schmitt set up factory 1913 at Levallois-Perret (Paris) to build Morane-Saulnier monoplanes, continued during war. About December 1913 original design of biplane tested with entire wing cellule pivoted, incidence variable by pilot. Late 1917 produced prototype 2-seat 'corps reconnaissance' biplane with bombs and 3 guns (280-hp Renault), followed 1918 by centre-float armed seaplane (400-hp Liberty) said to have been tested by US Navy.

Schmuck (USA). Schmuck Aircraft Co., LA, formed 1928 to produce Monarch 3-seat biplane, marketed by Monarch Aerial Corp. Failed 1930.

Schneider (France). Société des Avions Schneider built series of large and powerful military aircraft made of Alférium light alloy, usually with close-pitch corrugated skin. Notable types included 'Henri Paul' BN6 (6-seat night bomber) of 1922 with 2 pairs tandem 370-hp Lorraine engines, and undesignated bomber of 1924 with central nacelle and twin fuselages each with 450-hp tractor Lorraine 12E. In 1926 firm renamed Aviméta.

Schneider (Germany). Swiss Franz Schneider, previously designer for Nieuport and, from 1912, LVG, formed Franz Schneider Flugmaschinen-Werke January 1917, mainly for repair but also producing innovative fighter 1918. Company reorganized as **Flugzeugbau Franz Schneider** at Siegefeld-im-Spandau 1920. Produced series of mainly light aircraft, Dr Gustav Lachmann, later of Handley Page, being designer 1924–5.

Schoettler (China). In 1922 F.C. Schoettler, assisted by E.O. Fuetterer, set up aircraft laboratory at Lungwha testing local materials. By 1924 had built S.I 2-seat biplane (160-hp Mercedes), test-flown and praised by ex-RAF W.E.B. Holland. Second Chinese aircraft.

Scholz (W. Germany). Manfred Scholz had his own company, and also operated as Scholz-Schmitz producing light aircraft 1979.

Schramm (USA). Schramm Aircraft built light aircraft 1967.

Schreck (France). *See* FBA; Donnet-Lévêque. Formed 1917 as Hydravions Louis Schreck-FBA, Quai de Seine, Argenteuil (Paris). Continued to produce flying-boats with FBA designations. Moribund 1932, acquired 1935 by Soc. des Avions Bernard, which itself failed 1935.

Schreder (USA). R.E. 'Dick' Schreder built at least 1 powered version of his many sailplanes 1962.

Schulze (Germany). Gustav Schulze Sport Flugzeugwerke ran pilot school and built own training aircraft 1912–14. In 1919 built light

Schreck FBA Type B, February 1915.

parasol monoplanes at Madel, Burg bei Magdeburg.

Schütte-Lanz (Germany). Famous airship builder established aeroplane subsidiary Schütte-Lanz Luftfahrtzeugbau 1915 at Zeesen, Königswusterhausen (Berlin); built C. class armed 2-seaters (Ago C.IV in quantity), D.I to D.VII fighters and 3 (R.27/29) of 6 Zeppelin-Staaken giants ordered.

Schwade (Germany). Otto Schwade Flugzeugwerke, Erfurt, built single examples of 2 pusher fighters, NR I and II, 1914–15.

Schweizer (USA). Famous sailplane builder formed 1939, Elmira, NY, built Grumman (later Gulfstream) Ag-Cat 1957–79; purchased rights to Ag-Cat 1981 and now markets several versions. Schweizer sailplanes were basis of Lockheed Q-Star and YO-3A 'quiet' aircraft, leading to SA2-37A (Army RG-8A) 2-seat multisensor quiet aircraft used by Army and today by Coast Guard. In 1983 took over manufacture of Hughes 300C Sky Knight helicopter, leading to turbine-engined Model 330 (14 June 1988), now in production. Also subcontracts for Bell, Boeing, Sikorsky and others.

Schweizerische (Switzerland). Schweizerische Flugzeugfabrik, Oberrieden (Zürich), alternative name from 1930 of Alfred Comte: *see* Comte.

Scicraft (Israel). Subsidiary of Cyclone Aviation Products. Produced Gambit side-by-side canard pusher homebuilt 1987, marketed complete or as kit with choice of 3 engines (Rotax, Hewland, Norton).

SCIM (France). Société Générale des Constructions Industrielles et Mécaniques was originally Etablissements Gabriel Borel (*see* Borel); new name from 1919.

Scintex (France). Scintex-Aviation SA was formed as aviation division of major producer of mechanical and electrical equipment, factories at Courbevoie (Paris) and Riom (Puy de Dôme). From 1959 exclusive licence for improved Piel Emeraude (225 by 1963) from which developed Super Emeraude (20 April 1962) and 4-seat Rubis (24 May 1961).

SCMP (Italy). Dornier subsidiary set up at Marina di Pisa January 1922 by Dornier to build Wal (6 November 1922) and other aircraft prohibited by Allies in Germany; Società di Costruzioni Meccàniche di Pisa built over 103 (probably 124) Wals; later renamed CMASA, which *see*.

Scottish (UK). Scottish Aviation Syndicate formed late 1910 to buy and operate aircraft, including Avis monoplanes designed 1911 by Howard Wright.

Scottish Aviation (UK). Formed at Prestwick 1935 to run new airport, flying school and other services. Built observation aircraft to A.4/45 (August 1947), developed into Prestwick Pioneer STOL transport (June 1950), 59 built, and Twin Pioneer (June 1955), 87 built. Took over Beagle Bulldog and HP.137 Jetstream: *see* British Aerospace.

SCTICSG: *See* Alliance (International).

SCWAL (Belgium). Office Brussels and plant at Baileux, produces SCWAL 101 ultralight side-by-side multirole (26 April 1984), as well as American Aircraft Falcon under SONACA licence.

S.E.5 etc.: *See* Royal Aircraft Factory.

SEA: *See* Potez.

SEA (Belgium). Société d'Etudes Aéronautiques formed Brussels 1936, in following year exhibiting SEA.1 5-seat monoplane (2 × Genet Major); believed flown later.

Seabird (Australia). Seabird Aviation Australia Pty Ltd, Pialba, Queensland, produced series of homebuilts, especially SB2 and SB3, but today concentrates on factory manufacture of SB5 Sentinel STOL observation aircraft (1 October 1989), marketed in several versions and followed by more powerful SB7 Seeker (1991).

Seair (Australia). In 1988 Seair Pacific Pty Ltd, Airlie Beach, Queensland, reported that it was building prototype 8-passenger seaplane with composite airframe and 2 pusher engines.

Seaplane Experimental Station: *See* Felixstowe.

Seaplanes Inc. (USA). Vancouver, Washington, firm carrying out STOL and/or performance improvements on Beech, Cessna, Maule, Piper, Stinson and Waco light aircraft.

Seawind (Canada). Seawind International, Division of Rodlen Aircraft at Haliburton, Ontario, produce Seawind 4-seat amphibian (23 August 1982), with GRP structure and 200-hp engine mounted on tail. *See* SNA.

SECA (France). Société d'Exploitation et de Constructions Aéronautiques, subsidiary of Aerospatiale at Paris Le Bourget, major overhaul and modification centre, produced many significantly altered aircraft e.g. F27 Friendship ARAT (Avion de Recherche Atmosphérique et de Télédétection).

SECAN (France). Société d'Etudes et de Constructions Aéro-Navales formed about 1939 as subsidiary of automotive giant Chausson. Post-war built aircraft parts and equipment, plus 144 SUC.10 Courlis 4-seaters with 200-hp Mathis pusher (February 1946).

SECAT (France). Société d'Etudes et de Constructions d'Avions de Tourisme established Boulogne 1938, produced RG.60 ultralight biplane, RG.75 2-seat high-wing cabin monoplane and S.4 and S.5 high-wing cabin aircraft. Briefly resumed post-war with LD.45 single-seat cabin biplane (January 1946).

SECM (France). Société d'Emboutissage et de Constructions Mécaniques formed 1916 at Colombes (Paris) by Félix Amiot, mass-producing Morane-Saulnier, Sopwith and Breguet aircraft. Post-war specialized in metal aircraft, including Lutèce 2-seat light biplane 1921, SECM 12 bomber later called SECM-Amiot 120BN2,

SECM 22 trainer, SECM 23 3-seat biplane and SECM 24 trainer. Then dropped original title in favour of Amiot during production run of Type 122 'Grosse Julie' bomber. *See* Amiot.

Security (USA). Security National Aircraft Corp. established by 'Bert' Kinner 1933 at Downey (LA), to build S-1-A Airster side-by-side low-wing 2-seater similar to Kinner Sportster. Suspended manufacture at No. 15 in 1935, formed new company Security Aircraft Corp. 1937 to build improved S-1-B but taken over 1939 by American Aircraft.

SEEMS (France). Société d'Exploitation des Etablissements Morane-Saulnier was name bestowed by Henry Potez after takeover of MS in 1963. Continued to develop MS.760 Paris twin-jet into 760C Paris III with 6 seats, and new versions of Rallye especially 4-seat Rallye Commodore (13 February 1964). Within a year programmes were entitled Potez, becoming SOCATA 1970.

Segrave-Saro (UK). Meteor light twin 4-seater (28 July 1930) was roughed out by Sir Henry Segrave (who for this purpose was technical director of Aircraft Development Corporation), actually designed by Saro, tested as prototype and then put into limited production by Blackburn.

Seguin (France). M. Seguin developed Adams-Wilson helicopter into significantly changed machine flown early 1980.

Seguin (USA). Seguin Aviation established 1967 at Seguin, TX, to produce Geronimo upgrade of Piper Apache.

Seibel (USA). Seibel Helicopter Co. established March 1948 by Charles M. Seibel (ex-Bell) to build S3 helicopter (1947) and 2 forms of S4, before selling out 1 March 1952 to Cessna, which retained Seibel to work on completely new CH-1 helicopter (July 1954).

Sellet-Pelletier (France). Christian Sellet and Jacques Pelletier formed company at Issy-les-Moulineaux to develop Griffon 120 light helicopter (8 September 1986), since 1989 2-seater.

SEMA (France). Soc. d'Etudes de Matériels d'Aviation produced 12 designs 1928–34, best-known being SEMA 10 and 12 multirole transport biplanes (Lorraine 240-hp 7Me or 350 hp 9Na) built by SA Bordelaise at Bordeaux-Bacalans 1933.

Sepecat (France/UK). Société Européenne de Production de l'Avion d'Ecole de Combat et d'Appui Tactique formed May 1966 by Breguet (France) and BAC (UK) to manage Jaguar strike/trainer programme (8 September 1968); principals became Dassault and BAe.

Sequoia (USA). Sequoia Aircraft Corp., Richmond, VA, market plans/kits for Model 300 Sequoia aerobatic 2-seater (300-hp), Model 302 Kodiak 4-seater and (700 + sets so far) improved version of F.8L Falco (ex-General Avia).

Seremet (Denmark). W. Vincent Seremet, Greve Strand, produced series of light rotary-wing aircraft designated up to WS.12 (1980).

Serv-Aero (USA). Serv-Aero Engineering, Salinas, CA, upgraded ag-aircraft, including replacement of R-1340 Wasp by R-1820 Cyclone or PT6A turboprop.

Servicair (USA). Glendale, CA, produced Loadmaster utility transport conversions of Convair L-13A.

Service (USA). Service Aviation Co. formed 1921 at Wabash, Indiana, chiefly to convert DH-4 aircraft and parts into 4-passenger transports; traded as SATTCO.

Servicios (Mexico). Servicios Aereas de America SA, Mexico City, service/repair firm which took licence to build Maule M-4 and instead built version with more power and c/s propeller, called Cuauhtemoc M-1, from 1964.

Servotec (UK). Formed 1952 by J.S. Shapiro to undertake R&D, and in 1960–63 built Cierva Grasshopper and CR Twin, becoming part of Cierva Rotorcraft 1969.

SET (Romania). Societatea pentru Exploatâri Technice formed Bucharest 1923, creating as manufacturing subsidiary **Fabrica de Avioane** to build aircraft to government order to designs of Grigore C. Zamfirescu. All single-engined biplanes, for training, observation and (SET.XV, 1934) fighting. Designing ceased 1937 but in 1941–2 built 30 He 111H-3.

Seversky (USA). Alexander P. de Seversky was Russian bomber pilot 1915, shot down and lost leg, became third-highest-scoring fighter pilot 1917, air attaché in USA 1917, wisely stayed on and became DoD test pilot and Gen. Mitchell's special advisor, US citizen 1927 and major in Air Corps reserve, whilst running **Seversky Aero Corp.** (June 1922) to manage consultancy and produce aero equipment. In January 1931 formed **Seversky Aircraft Corp.**, relying on brilliant stressed-skin designer Alexander Kartveli to translate founder's ideas into practice. Produced SEV-3 high-speed amphibian seaplane with landplane version, these leading directly to BT-8 trainer, Executive business transport, P-35 fighter (197, 1936–40), 2PA Guardsman 2-seat fighter (74) and AT-12 and XP-41 fighter prototype, but in October 1939 company, by now in large factory at Farmingdale, Long Island, NY, was renamed **Republic Aviation**.

Seville (Canada). Seville Aircraft Inc. formed 1985 by Sandy Sinclair at Milton, Ontario, to market Seville Two-Place tandem dual pusher ultralight as ready-to-fly or as kit.

SEVIMIA (France). Société d'Etudes Victor Minié Aviation (works at St Cyr) was separate firm from Victor Minié Aéronautique which made aero engines. Produced sailplanes and in 1950 masterminded installations of SNECMA Escopette pulsejets under wings in groups of 2 or 3.

Seyedo Shohada (Iran). Defence industries Seyedo Shohada project converts Bell 206A into Zafar 300 2-seat gunship attack helicopters (31 January 1989).

SFAN (France). Société Française d'Aviation Nouvelle was established 1935 by M. Chasseris (Nieuport director) to build lightplanes and gliders. Bought licence for BAC (Kronfeld) Drone, produced in modified form as SFAN 2, larger 2-seater being SFAN 4, and side-by-side cabin version SFAN 5.

SFCA (France). Société Française de Constructions Aéronautiques formed July 1934 to produce aircraft (initially to designs of M. Maillet) at Suresnes factory of Blériot-Aéronautique. First was Maillet 20 high-speed 3-seat low-wing monoplane, with fighter-type pilot canopy behind flush tandem enclosed passenger cockpits, Maillet 21 being production version. SFCA Lignel 10, 16, 20 and 30 were Renault-engined racers and advanced trainers in 230/260-mph class. Acquired licence for Peyret tandem-wing single-seater, building this as SFCA Taupin and 2-seat Taupin 5/2.

SFECMAS (France). Société Française d'Etudes et de Constructions de Matériels Aéronautiques Spéciaux was formed October 1952 by reorganization of Arsenal de l'Aéronautique, taking over design/production teams at Le Bourget, Villacoublay, Villeurbanne (Lyon) and former Brandt works at Châtillon sous Bagneux. SFECMAS 1402 Gerfaut series (15 January 1954) was first aircraft in world to fly supersonic on level without afterburner (3 August 1954). Led to Nord 1500 Griffon (20 September 1955). But in December 1954 merged into Nord, losing identity.

SGP (Austria). Long-established engineering and railway firm Simmering-Graz-Pauker flew prototype M-222 Flamingo 4-seater (2 × 200-hp) 15 May 1959.

Shaanxi: *See* SAC, 1st entry.

Shackleton (UK). W.S. Shackleton, major aircraft dealer, designed ANEC 1, Beardmore Wee Bee and Shackleton-Lee Murray (often called Shackleton-Murray) SM.1 tandem-seat parasol monoplane (70-hp Hirth) built by Airspeed at York (14 October 1933).

Shanghai: *See* SAMF.

Shapley (UK). E.S. Shapley produced 2 examples of Kittiwake side-by-side cabin aircraft notable for low gull wing, both built Torquay 1937–8.

Sharp (USA). Father/son team George and Loran Sharp, Newhall, CA, produced several aircraft, No. 7 being Meteora 2-seat helicopter (85-hp Continental).

Shavrov (USSR). Vadim Borisovich Shavrov joined OMOS 1925, and in 1928 began building simple 2-seat amphibian in his 1-room flat, flown 21 June 1929. Called Sh-1, led to Sh-2 (115-hp M-11, 11 November 1930), about 700 built by 1934. Sh-3 amphibian seaplane for 2 passengers or cargo never completed. Single Sh-5 photo/mapping aircraft (2 × 480-hp, 19 March 1934) had wheels/skis/floats. Sh-7 transport amphibian (330 hp, 16 June 1940) would have been series-built but for war.

Shchyerbakov (USSR). Aleksei Yakovlyevich Shchyerbakov produced several significant designs, but most important was Shchye-2 or TS-1 STOL utility transport (2 × 115 hp).

Shchyetinin (Russia). S.S. Shchyetinin, assisted by M.A. Shchyerbakov, started aircraft factory St Petersburg 1911, this soon becoming First Russian Aviation Works. Built Nieuport IV and Farman XVI, but plant manager D.P. Grigorovich (which *see*) soon began producing his own designs of pusher biplane flying-boat, based on a Donnet-Lévêque. This M-1 led to long series of M (Morskoi = naval) flying-boats built by Shchyetinin factory ending with M-20, MK-1 3-engined seaplane and GASN twin-engined seaplane 1917. Total output by October 1917 about 2,000, including 580 of M-9 type.

Shenyang: *See* SAC, 2nd entry.

Sheremetyev (USSR). Noted sailplane designer Boris Nikolayevich Sheremetyev produced several ultralights, including ShBM (ZAOR) developed from Mignet Flea with left/right rear wings individually pivoted, and Sh-13 (1939) noted for very high aspect ratio and range exceeding 1,500 miles on 388 lb (176 kg) of fuel/oil.

Shijiazhuang: *See* SAP.

Shin Meiwa (Japan). Kawanishi resumed operations October 1949 as Shin Meiwa Industry Co. Ltd., initially overhauling USAF aircraft, then produced re-engined DH Herons from 1964 and in 1966 received JMSDF contract for ASW flying-boat. Result was SS-2 (5 October 1967), 23 built as PS-1, followed by SS-2A amphibian (16 October 1974), 8 built as US-1 and -1A. Today has numerous contracts for parts: Kawasaki T-4, P-3C, 757, 767, 777, MD-11, MD-80, CH-47J, SH-60J, etc.

Shinn (USA). Shinn Engineering, Santa Ana, CA, produced about 50 modified Morrisey 2150 in 1959–62.

Shin Nihon (Japan). Company established December 1952 as Itoh Chu Koku Seibi KK to maintain and repair lightplanes. Reorganized 1960 as Shin Nihon Koku Seibi KK to produce N-58 Cygnet, later adding N-62 Eaglet. *See* Itoh; Nihon University.

Shishmaryev (Russia, USSR). Mikhail Mikhailovich Shishmaryev was early designer at Shchyetinin factory. After 1920 became major-general and professor at VVA (air force academy). Responsible at Shchyetinin works for GASN (seaplane for special duties), large twin-engined biplane (24 August 1917). In 1925 managed R-III improved version of D.H.9a.

Shiuchow (China). Shiuchow Aeroplane Factory was principal aircraft assembly and manufacturing centre in China 1936–8. 'Unofficial' volunteers arriving mainly from USA 1936 brought 30 Curtiss F11C-3, assembled at Shiuchow, closely followed by Curtiss BFC-2 Hawks and Curtiss A-8 and A-12 Shrike monoplanes (ex-US Army). By 1938 Flushing Type I Fighter was in production, based on BF2C but with many local modifications.

Shiukov (Russia). Aleksei Vladimirovich Shiukov built and flew gliders 1908–10 when student at Tiflis (Tbilisi), today capital of Georgia. Built powered Utka (canard, duck) September 1912, tail-first monoplane with 50-hp Gnome, repeatedly modified, eventually flew well. Utka 2 (Kanar-2), 80-hp Gnome, left incomplete 1914 because of war.

Shkolin (Russia). Luka Vasilyevich Shkolin ran out of money when his 1909 monoplane was almost finished. Anzani 25 hp had chain drive to 2 tractor propellers with inflight variable pitch, probably first in world.

Short (UK). 'The first manufacturers of aircraft in the world', brothers Eustace, Oswald and (later) Horace Short flew gas balloon 1897 and started making balloons for sale 1902, in 1903 setting up factory under railway arches at Battersea where customers could receive balloon already gas-filled. November 1908 formed **Short Brothers Ltd**, building Wright Flyers under licence (only source of such aircraft at that time, Wrights having no production facilities). Major contribution (gasbags, control surfaces) to Admiralty airship No. 1 1911, during war handled design/construction of several large rigid airships. From January 1909 built aeroplanes to design of others, starting with 6 Wright Model A, but soon concentrated on own designs, over 80 by

Short S.29 Stirling prototype, 14 May 1939.

1914, at Shellbeach and Leysdown, Isle of Sheppey, with new factory at Rochester added late 1914. Short Bomber (82) and Type 184 (over 900 by Short and 9 other companies) laid foundation for large company, adding Type 310 (124) and 827 (108), all long-span biplane bomber and torpedo carriers, 184, 310 and 827 being seaplanes. Large contracts for F.3 and F.5 pushed firm into flying-boats, but significant (small) design was Silver Streak 2-seat biplane (July 1920) made of aluminium alloy, which enabled majority of later products to be all-metal. Major flying-boats included S.8 Calcutta and military Rangoon (3 × Jupiter) used by Imperial Airways and RAF and produced under licence by Breguet; S.19 Singapore III of 1934 (4 × Kestrel), 33 for RAF; and above all S.23 Empire boat, used by Imperial as C-class, 4 × Pegasus or Perseus (July 1936), 42 of several versions. Superficially similar S.25 Sunderland, 4 × Pegasus or Twin Wasp (16 October 1937), was standard RAF patrol boat of Second World War, 739 built by 1945. Many were converted for civil use, and airline derivatives were Hythe and Sandringham, Solent being larger (4 × 1,690-hp Hercules). S.29 Stirling heavy bomber, 4 × 1,650-hp Hercules, proved disappointment (14 May 1939) but 1,759 Mk I and III bombers were built, plus 450 Mk IV glider tug transports and 150 Mk V transports, production being shared by Rochester, Belfast (see below), Austin Motor Co. at Longbridge and Rootes Securities shadow factory at Stoke. In 1934 took majority holding in Pobjoy, forming **Pobjoy Aircraft and Airmotors** with licence to produce Scion light transport (*see* Pobjoy). This helped clear Rochester for Sunderland and Stirling. In 1936 new airfield made at Sydenham (today Belfast Harbour airport), and Air Ministry built giant factory on airfield, adjacent Harland & Wolff shipyard, becoming **Short & Harland Ltd**, owned 50/50 by 2 companies. Began 1938 with 50 Bombay, then 150 Hereford, switching to Stirling production supplemented by Hucclecote, Gloucester, South Marston and Kidderminster. Government took over management March 1943, merging Short Bros. (Rochester & Bedford) with Short & Harland to form **Short Bros. & Harland Ltd** November 1947, all wartime factories being closed and operations concentrated at Queen's Island, Belfast, Rochester closing July 1948. Belfast built numerous prototypes (e.g., Sperrin, Sherpa, Sturgeon/SB.3, SB.4, SC.1, Seamews) and production Sealand, Canberra, Comet, Swift (soon cancelled), Britannia and 10 Belfasts, followed by Skyvan, 330/Sherpa and 360 and S.312 Tucano, with important missile and UAV/RPV and other divisions. Renamed **Short Brothers Ltd** 1977, becoming **Short Bros. plc** 1984, adopting shortened form Shorts (not a plural). Apart from large business in close air defence systems and other defence products, income almost wholly from subcontract: major parts for 737, 747, 757, 767 and 777, wing of Fokker 100, and complete nacelles and nose cowls for many turbofans. Company purchased by Bombardier of Canada June 1989, resulting in planned Shorts FJX being replaced by contribution to rival Canadair RJ.

Showa (Japan). Showa Hikoki KK formed 1939 at Tokyo suburb of that name, building L2D (licensed DC-3) and, from December 1942, 201 Aichi D3A2 dive-bombers. First Japanese aircraft company to restart after war, overhauling USAF aircraft 1951, name changed to Showa Hikoki Kogyo KK (Showa Aircraft Industry Co. Ltd). Supplied major parts to Shin Meiwa for PS-1/US-1 and participated in NAMC.

SIA (Italy). Outbreak of war 1914 spurred sudden need for aircraft. Lacking Italian designs, Fiat obtained licence for Farman 5b, produced at Fiat shops in Via Madama Cristina, Turin, and later at larger Locati coachbuilding factory on Via Nizza, first being flown at Mirafiori 7 October 1915 by Fiat test pilot 2nd Lt. Brach-Papa. Soon output reached 30 per month. Meanwhile Fiat collaborated on SP 1 (*see* Pomilio) and handled main production. Early 1916 switched to SP 2, and 5 June 1916 formed Fiat aviation company, Società Italiana Aviazione (SIA), occupying large new factory and hangars at Mirafiori. Produced 115 SP 2, followed early 1917 by SP 3, but needed more modern (tractor) aircraft, and late 1916 chief designer Ing. Torretta produced SIA 7b (June 1917), outstanding 2-seater, soon flown to Naples and back, and then to London, in each case non-stop. Meanwhile, Fiat produced massive A14 engine of 600 hp, 2 being used in SIA 14b (also called SIA 1200), flown November 1917 but not put into production. Instead 7b1 (260-hp A12) and 7b2 (300-hp A12bis, and strengthened cabane strut joints) were built to total of 505, followed by larger SIA 9b (700-hp A14), of which 62 delivered of 500 ordered by Armistice. In summer 1918 Celestino Rosatelli became chief designer, eliminating previous structural problems and with Ing. Gamba designing R.2 (30 July 1918) derived from 7b2. R.2 built post-war as Fiat BR.2, SIA being renamed early 1918 Fiat Aviazione.

SIAI: *See* Savoia-Marchetti.

SIAI-Marchetti (Italy). After September 1943 armistice original company (*see* Savoia-Marchetti) maintained its aircraft used by Allies, notably SM.79 and 82 transports, and began reorganizing as SIAI-Marchetti, with factories at Sesto Calende, Vergiate and Borgomanero. Built and tested prototypes of SM.101 6-seater (235-hp Walter Bora) and SM.102 8-passenger (2 × 520-

hp Ranger), whilst producing military and civil SM.95 transports, typically 30 passengers (4 × Alfa Romeo, Pegasus or Twin Wasp in 1,000-hp class). Eked out by making trucks and railway coaches but bankrupt September 1951. By 1953 withdrew from liquidation, began overhauling aircraft, and by 1962 started producing Nardi FN.333 (which *see*), from 1963 assisting SIPA with S.2510 Antilope. Startling expansion followed, flying Frati-designed SF.260 (250-hp Lycoming) 15 July 1964, leading to massive production of civil and (mainly) military versions, S.205 (180-hp Lycoming) February 1966, S.208 5-seater (260-hp Lycoming) 22 May 1967, SA.202 Bravo 2-seater joint development with FFA of Switzerland (115-hp Lycoming) 7 March 1969 FFA and 7 May 1969 SIAI, SM.1019 STOL observation/liaison (400-hp Allison turboprop) 24 May 1969, and S.210 6-seater (2 × 260-hp Lycoming) 18 February 1970. High-speed helicopter projects remained unbuilt. These aircraft supported massive expansion in activity, being followed by S.211 tandem light jet trainer (JT15D turbofan) 10 April 1981 and SF.600TP (developed from piston-engined 600 Canguro) utility transport (2 × 420-hp Allison) 8 April 1981. From 1977 increasingly worked with Agusta on helicopter production, and by 1983 had been taken over as Agusta subsidiary. In 1989 lost identity and today merely called Agusta Sesto Calende works.

SIAT (W. Germany). Siebelwerke-ATG GmbH formed 1952 by amalgamation of Siebel and ATG. When aircraft manufacture was permitted, in 1955, SIAT developed SIAT 222 4-seat tourer (August 1961), followed by 223 Flamingo 2-seater (1 March 1967). SIAT participated in manufacture of Noratlas, UH-1D, Bölkow 105, F-104G, Transall, Atlantic, HFB 320 and various prototype/research programmes. Became wholly-owned subsidiary of MBB 1968, losing identity.

Siddeley (UK). Siddeley-Deasy Motor Car Co. Ltd., Parkside, Coventry, produced engines from 1916 and D.H.10, BE.2c/2e, RE.7 and RE.8, and also designed and built Siddeley RT.1 (supposed improved RE.8), SR.2 Siskin (starting point for greatly improved Armstrong Whitworth Siskin) and Sinaia bomber built as Mks I, II and III respectively with 2 × 486-hp Siddeley Tiger (no relation to later Armstrong Siddeley Tiger), 600-hp Condor and 500-hp Galloway Atlantic. In 1919, despite having virtually no orders, John

Siebel Si 204A (NC.701 Martinet No. 121), January 1945.

Siddeley's board took decision to form Sir W.G. Armstrong Whitworth Aircraft and Armstrong Siddeley Motors.

Siebel (Germany). Flugzeugbau Halle (which *see*) was renamed 1936 for its newly appointed Generaldirektor Fritz W. Siebel, becoming Siebel Flugzeugwerke KG, producing Si 201 pusher STOL observation aircraft and Si 202 Hummel light 2-seater, main business being successive licence-production of Do 17, Ju 88 and Ju 188. Meanwhile developed Si 204 8-passenger transport flown 1941 and produced as Si 204D trainer (2×600-hp Argus) for navigation, radar and gunnery, built by Aero (515), BMM (492) and SNCAC (168 during war and 340 post-war designated NC 701 and 702 Martinet). Post-war became SIAT.

Siemens-Schuckert (Germany). Siemens-Schuck-

ert Werke GmbH, subsidiary of electrical giant, began building large non-rigid airships 1907, followed by aeroplanes from 1909, but discontinued 1911 after nephew killed flying. Aeroplane department reopened September 1914, Franz and Bruno Steffen joining as designers and creating series of R-types (*Riesenflugzeug* = giant aircraft). R.I (May 1915) had 2 tractor propellers driven by 3×150-hp engines in nose. R.II–R.VII were broadly similar in layout but larger, all with tail carried by rear fuselage in form of triangular booms, one inverted over the other. R.VIII had 6×300-hp Basse und Selve engines in fuselage with shafting to tractor and pusher propellers, and was largest aircraft of 1918. SSW Kann, never completed, was to have had 4×750-hp steam turbines. Fighters began with E.I monoplane (October 1915), 20 being built, followed by E.II and III, and more important D-types based loosely on Nieuport fighters: D.I.

Siemens-Schuckert R.III No. 3/15, late 1915.

(1916), 95 delivered, next to reach production being D.IV (1918) extremely fast-climbing interceptor with 160-hp Siemens-Halske, about 120 complete at Armistice plus prototypes of D.VI parasol monoplane.

Siemetzki (W. Germany). Alfons Siemetzki, 7951 Kirchdorf, trading as ASRO, produced and flew 3-T research helicopter (65-hp BMW turboshaft), leading to 2-seat ASRO 4 (100-hp BMW turboshaft), flown 1964.

Sierra (USA). Sierra Industries, Uvalde, TX, market wide range of (ex-R/STOL) performance/safety modifications to general-aviation aircraft.

Sikorsky (Russia). Igor Ivanovich Sikorsky studied Paris 1907, returning to Kiev with Anzani engine used in unsuccessful coaxial helicopter. Followed with better and more powerful helicopter, almost flew. Turned to aeroplanes; BIS-1 (Bylinkin, Iordan, Sikorsky) used 15-hp and then 25-hp Anzanis (ex-helicopter), rebuilt as BIS-2, flown by Sikorsky 11 June 1910. Modified into Sikorsky's own S-3 (November 1910), S-4 (December 1910) being larger version built for A.A. Gomberg who had 50-hp Anzani engine. S-5 (April 1911) had 50-hp Argus. With S-6 (100-hp Argus) Sikorsky took 3 passengers, and S-6A (March 1912) flew at 66 mph (106.2 km/h) with 4 passengers, later taking 1st prize at St Petersburg military competition. As result

Sikorsky appointed designer at new aviation department of RBVZ (Russo-Baltic Wagon Works), designing world's biggest aeroplane, *Grand*, 2 × 100-hp Argus, flown 2 March 1913. Later fitted with 2 extra engines as pushers and finally with 4 tractor engines, renamed *Russki Vityaz*. Led to unique series of 4-engined reconnaissance and bomber aircraft all called IM (from *Ilya Mourometz*), 80 being built 1913–18 in 6 main versions with 7 types of engine. At Revolution Sikorsky left with what he could carry, spent a year in Paris, where he would have produced aircraft but for Armistice, then to USA.

Sikorsky (USA). Impoverished Sikorsky taught in New York and scraped living before, with other Russian emigrés, formed **Sikorsky Aero Engineering Corp.** at Westbury, Long Island, 5 March 1923. As cottage industry built S-29 large biplane (2 × 300-hp Hispano), inadequate power but after fitting 400-hp Libertys flew well September 1924, varied career ending as 'German bomber' shot down in epic film. Series of one-offs, several for customers, led to S-38 amphibian (2 × 425-hp Wasp), usually 8-passengers, sold to PanAm, Army and Navy, eventual total 114. Sales of S-29A–S-34 enabled company to be restructured as **Sikorsky Manufacturing Corp.** in 1925, and S-38 enabled further reorganization to take place as **Sikorsky Aviation Corp.** 3 October 1928, becoming member of giant United Aircraft Corp. 1929 and moving into large new factory at Stratford, Connecticut. Here produced several

Sikorsky (Russia) S-16 (2-seat version), March 1915.

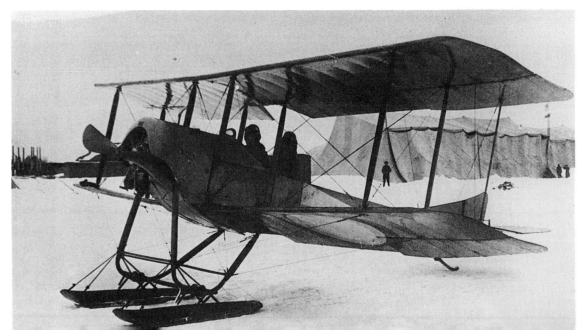

Sikorsky (USA) S-38A, June 1928.

major types including S-40 (4 × 575-hp Hornet) 44-passenger amphibians and S-42 (4 × 700-hp Hornet) long-range flying-boats for PanAm's Pacific route. S-43 was neat amphibian (2 × 750-hp Hornet) seating up to 19, 54 built. XPBS-1 was long-range flying-boat (4 × 1,050-hp Twin Wasp), flown August 1937, first US aircraft with tail turret. On 1 April 1939 merger with Vought resulted in **Vought-Sikorsky Division** of United Aircraft, so civil derivative of XPBS was designated VS-44A, 3 served transatlantic American Export Airlines. I.I. Sikorsky returned to helicopter, starting to test VS-300 14 September 1939. Led to VS-316, US Army XR-4 (14 January 1942), and to 233 production R-4/HNS/Hoverfly. Dynamic parts used in neater R-6, while XR-5 (450-hp Wasp Junior) flown on 18 August 1943 led to 379 S-51 variants, not including Westland-built Dragonfly versions. Designation S-51 reflected separation of Vought and Sikorsky January 1943, Sikorsky's main plant returning to Bridgeport. There followed famous series of logically developed helicopters:

S-55 (10 November 1949), S-56 (2 × Double Wasp, 18 December 1953), S-58 (8 March 1954), S-61 (2 × T58) initially flown as HSS-2 Sea King 11 March 1959, S-64 crane (2 × T73) 9 May 1962, S-65 (2 × T64) 14 October 1964 followed by CH-53E (3 × much more powerful T64) 1 March 1974, S-70 (2 × T700) flown as UTTAS UH-60A 17 October 1974, S-76 Spirit (2 × Allison, Turbomeca or P&WC) 13 March 1977 and, in conjunction with Boeing, RAH-66 Comanche (2 × T800) due August 1994.

Silvaire (USA). Silvaire Aircraft Co. formed Ft Collins, Colorado, 1954, in January 1955 purchasing rights to Temco (ex-Luscombe) Silvaire, producing slightly improved 8F version 1958–61.

Silvanskii (USSR). A.V. Silvanskii with partners formed OKB 1938 to build fighter (1,000-hp M88); amateurish effort made one perilous flight 1939.

Silvercraft (Italy). Silvercraft SpA formed 1962 at Sesto Calende, SIAI-Marchetti being shareholder and providing facilities for design/manufacture of SH-4 helicopter (October 1963), usually 235-hp Franklin and 3 seats; about 50 built, ending 1977 with single improved SH-200.

SIM: *See* PSFA Rogojarski.

SIMB: *See* Bernard.

Simera (S. Africa). Name adopted by Atlas Aircraft from 1992 for international civil market-

Sikorsky HH-60J Jayhawk, 8 August 1989.

Simplex K2S Red Arrow, March 1928.

ing, as division of Denel (Pty) Ltd. Defence contracts continue to use name Atlas within Simera division.

Simmering-Graz-Pauker: *See* SGP.

Simmonds (UK). Simmonds Aircraft Ltd formed September 1928 at Weston, Southampton, to build Spartan 2-seat biplane (95-hp ADC Cirrus), prototype flying with passenger non-stop to Berlin and then back, 49 built. *See* Spartan (UK).

Simplex (France). Société Simplex built small numbers of tailless monoplanes designed by M. Arnoux 1921–4, 2 being racers.

Simplex (USA). Simplex Aircraft Corp. formed January 1928 at Defiance, Ohio, to produce Red Arrow 2-seat monoplane (100-hp Kinner) with side-by-side open or enclosed cockpits. Ceased trading 1929 shortly after producing prototype Kite light monoplane, restarted as Sioux.

Sindelfingen (Germany). Subsidiary of Daimler-Benz outside Stuttgart where 3 prototypes were built 1918–19, followed by L.11 and sporting 2-seat L.14 parasol monoplanes 1919–20.

Sindlinger (USA). Frederick G. Sindlinger built 5/8-scale Hawker Hurricane (January 1972), plans marketed.

Singapore *See* SA.

Sioux (USA). From 1929 Simplex was reorganized as Sioux Aircraft Corp., brief existence building Red Arrow and Kite monoplanes.

SIPA (France). Société Industrielle Pour l'Aéronautique formed 1938 at Surèsnes (Paris) to support established companies (Morane-Saulnier, Lioré et Olivier and Amiot) by supplying mass-produced parts. In 1943 assigned responsibility for Arado Ar 396 advanced trainer, delayed until after liberation (29 December 1944), produced as SIPA S.10 (28), S.11 (50), all-metal S.12 (52) and refined S.121 (58), later modified as attack aircraft for Algerian war, total 234. Light 2-seat S.90 (1947) led to large numbers of S.901/902 trainer/tourers. S.200 Minijet (14 January 1952) and 300 (4 September 1954) were diminutive jet trainers. Final designs were 1000 Coccinelle light 2-seater, 1100 military multirole STOL armed transport and S.2150 Antilope 4/5-seater (7 November 1962) powered by Turbomeca Astazou turboprop. Income increasingly from subcontract to Sud-Aviation, losing identity.

Sisler (USA). Airline captain Bert Sisler built and sold Pipit 2-seater, formed Sisler Aircraft Co. and built SF-2 Whistler (EAA award 1973) and later marketed plans for improved version SF-2A Cygnet high-wing 2-seater.

SIT (Italy). In 1912 Ministry of War issued requirement for construction of 70 aeroplanes by spring 1913. One of very few firms with capability was SIT (Società Italiana Transaerea), formed 1912 at Turin, factory on Corso Peschiera, with capital from several big industrialists and technical assistance from Blériot. Initial production comprised 47 Blériot 80-hp and 2 of 50 hp, and 31 Farman 70-hp. Blériot-Sit saw much action 1913–16. Voisit (Sit-built Voisin LA) produced in limited number (36) 1915. Later built SP 2 and 3 (Pomilio), but single prototype of company's own Sit-biplane, Gnome-engined derivative of Farman F 20 (February 1913, only aircraft of SIT design). SIT wound up August 1917, factory taken over by Ansaldo following month.

Sitar (France). Formed by designer Yves Gardan at St-Florentin (Yonne) 1967 to produce low-wing light monoplanes GY 90 Mowgli 2-seater, GY 100 Bagheera 4-seat and larger more powerful GY 110 Sher Khan. Full title Société Industrielle de Tolerie pour l'Aéronautique et Matériel Roulant, ceased trading 1972 but GY 90 plans remained available.

Skandinavsk: *See* SAI.

Skoda-Kauba (Bohemia-Moravia Nazi protectorate). Austrian Otto Kauba interested RLM in proposal for flying-bomb, set up Skoda-Kauba Flugzeugbau Prague February 1942, building various piloted prototypes V1, V1A, V2, followed by unrelated V3 sporting aircraft. V4 single-seat fighter/trainer led to 4 excellent SK 257 prototypes built by Avia and RLM contract for mass-production, but workmanship at production plant at Trencín, Slovakia, caused rejection. S-K works produced many further projects including V5 advanced fighter, P 14 ramjet interceptor, twin-boom V6, canard V7 and conventional V8 trainer, flown on skis late 1944.

Skorost (Russia). Association (name = Speed) established by Yakovlev OKB and ZMDB 'Progress' engine association and aircraft factories at Saratov and Smolyensk. Collaboration sought 1992 with Hyundai (S. Korea).

Skycraft (Australia). R.G. Wheeler formed Skycraft Pty Ltd to manufacture Scout 'minimum aeroplane', ultralight single-seater (May 1974), 300 delivered by 1980.

Skycraft (USA). Skycraft Inc. formed 1960 Ft Worth by James L. Robertson. Built Skyshark, outstanding STOL high-wing aircraft with special

control system for flight down to 20 mph (32.2 km/h). Production versions never built, Robertson Aircraft Corp. being formed near Seattle to modify existing aircraft.

Skyfox (USA). Skyfox Corp. formed LA to rebuild T-33 jet trainers into Skyfox developed by Flight Concepts (23 August 1983). Rights transferred to BMAC (Boeing Military Airplane Co.) 1986.

Skyhopper: *See* Salvay-Stark.

Skylark (USA). Skylark Manufacturing Co., Venice (LA), produced Skylark 2-seater 1937–40, and several versions of Skycraft Model 445 twin-boom 4-seat pusher 1945–8.

Sky Sports (USA). Sky Sports International formed 1980 by Sky Sports Inc. and Gemini International to market late Klaus Hill's Humbug twin-engined ultralight, landplane or seaplane.

Skytrader (USA). Skytrader Corp. formed 1984 Richards-Gebaur AFB, Kansas, taking over Skytrader STOL transport previously produced by Dominion (q.v.); liquidation followed 1989.

Skyway (USA). Skyway Engineering, Carmel, Indiana, formed 1959, reaching agreement 1960 with Autogiro Co. of America for production and marketing of Skyway AC-35 roadable autogyro.

Slesarev (Russia). Vasilii Andrianovich Slesarev began building and altering aircraft 1913, producing modified versions of Nieuport IV and Farman XVI, before designing Svyatogor giant biplane, with 2 front wheels and 2 6 ft main wheels. Slesarev wanted 2×300-hp Mercedes engines to go in central engine room, driving pusher propellers by shafts and gears, but had to settle for 220-hp Renault. Construction began November 1914, and taxi tests began just 2 years later, but Svyatogor never got off ground.

Slingsby (UK). Famous glider manufacturer at Kirkbymoorside, Yorks, built 2 Motor Tutor single-seaters 1948, replicas of SE.5a and Rumpler C.IV 1969, Osbourne Twin Cadet 1970 and many other aircraft, major current product being versions of T67 Firefly derived from Fournier RF6B. Makes contribution to Westinghouse Sentinel airship, V-22 Osprey, 747 and Jetstream 41.

Slingsby T67M, 16 May 1985.

Sloane (USA). Sloane Aircraft Co. Inc. established New York July 1916, producing original designs for US Army: H-2 (October 1916) recon biplane designed by C.H. Day (ex-Martin), 125-hp Hall-Scott, 3 delivered, and 9 improved H-3 used as trainers. Company became nucleus of Standard November 1916.

Slyusarenko (Russia). Small factory at Riga opened 1913 by Vladimir Viktorovich Slyusarenko and wife Lidiya Vissarionova Zvereva, country's first woman pilot. Began building Farman IV and XVI for War Dept. Moved to larger premises at St Petersburg mid-1914, continuing to grow and building at least 197 aircraft of Farman, Morane or Lebed design. Farman-Slyusarenko was Farman XVI modified as short-span single-seater. Nieuport rebuilt with conventional stick/pedal controls. G.P. Adler designed fast monocoque fighter monoplane and twin-boom aircraft with 3-seat gondola and a 220-hp Isotta-Fraschini engine in each boom.

SMAN (France). Société Morbihannaise d'Aéro Navigation bought rights to Tisserand's 2 seat Hydroplum II amphibian; sold as factory-built (33 by January 1992) named Petrel, and in kit form.

Smedley (USA). Robert R. Smedley, Tulsa, OK, built racer 1959 modified from Lazor-Rautenstrach.

Smith (Australia). Allan C. Smith Developments Pty Ltd produced FSRW-1 2-seat amphibian (130-hp RR Continental driving 2 pylon-mounted tractor propellers) in 1983, flown land 16 March and water 2 December.

Smith (Canada). Ronald B. Smith markets plans for Bumble Camel, 3/4-scale Sopwith Camel.

Smith (USA). A.J. Smith built light aircraft 1981.

Smith (USA). Mrs Frank W. (Dorothy) Smith, Norco, CA, marketed DSA-1 Miniplane sport biplane designed by late husband (October 1956), 500 sets of plans sold by 1981.

Smith (USA): Herbert O. and Herbert V. Smith jointly produced light aircraft 1963.

Smith (USA). L.B. Smith Aircraft Corp. established Miami 1947, major overhaul/mod

centre, converted B-26 bombers into Tempo II pressurized executive transports (1959) and over 116 C-46 into Smith Super 46-C.

Smith (USA). Mike Smith Aero Inc., Johnson, Kansas, produced prototype XP-99 Prop-Jet (29 July 1982), 6 seats, pressurized, 1 × 850-hp PT6A-41.

Smith (USA). Ted Smith Aircraft Co. subsidiary of American Cement Corp., formed 1963 at Van Nuys, CA, to build Aerostar 6-seat twin (7 November 1966). Deliveries began August 1968. Assets acquired by Butler Aviation International 16 February 1970, all operations subsequently suspended. In 1972 **Ted R. Smith and Associates** formed and re-acquired from Butler all existing airframe parts, enabling production to continue. In 1973 name changed to **Ted Smith Aerostar Corp.**, producing larger Aerostar 700 (22 November 1972) and developing Model 4000 Turbofan Aerostar. On 24 March 1978 all assets and business transferred to Piper at latter's Santa Maria, CA, Division, increasing production of Aerostar 600/601/601TP. Piper terminated programme 1985.

Smith (USA). William M. Smith produced ultralight 1986.

Smŏlik (Czechoslovakia). First fighting aircraft produced in new country was ascribed to designer Alois Smŏlik, though built at what was then called Central Aircraft Works (June 1920). Sm 1 was Warren-strut 2-seater (220-hp Hiero). Excellent aircraft, Smŏlik subsequently being chief designer of Letov.

Smyth (USA). Jerry Smyth produced Model S Sidewinder side-by-side aerobatic monoplane (21 February 1969), marketed as kits/plans.

SNA (USA). SNA Inc., Kimberton, PA, purchased rights to Seawind amphibian, marketing kits (60+) with 300-hp Lycoming as option.

SNCAC: *See* Aérocentre.

SNCA du Midi (France). On forced nationalization of industry Dewoitine was assigned to SNCA du Midi, formed February 1937 and taking over main Toulouse factory a month later. Continued accelerated production D.520 fighter, and developed HD.730 seaplane (February 1940). In

December 1940 taken over by SNCASE, losing identity.

SNCA du Nord: *See* Nord (France).

SNCA du Sud-Est: *See* SNCASE.

SNCA du Sud-Ouest: *See* SNCASO.

SNCAM: *See* SNCA du Midi.

SNCAN: *See* Nord (France).

SNCAO (France). Société Nationale de Constructions Aéronautiques de l'Ouest formed under terms of Nationalization law January 1937, taking over a Breguet factory at Nantes, Loire-Nieuport at Issy-les-Moulineaux and Loire at St Nazaire. A major product was LN 140 series of naval dive-bombers, but under dictate of Vichy government SNCAO was merged into SNCASO March 1941.

SNCASE (France). Following forced nationalization Société Nationale de Constructions Aéronautiques du Sud-Est formed December 1936, taking over Levallois-Perret and Argenteuil plants of LeO (but not Rochefort), all Romano and SPCA and Sartrouville factory of Potez-CAMS. From 1 January 1941 took over SNCA du Midi, which went into liquidation. Continued production of D.520 and LeO 45. Post-1944 produced 27 prototypes, but staple products included Vampire (DH licence) and Nene-engined Mistral, Languedoc (ex-Bloch/SE 161), Caravelle (27 May 1955), S-55 and S-58

helicopters (Sikorsky licence) and Alouette helicopter (12 March 1955). Amalgamated with Ouest-Aviation 1 March 1957 to form Sud-Aviation. This amalgamated with Nord and SEREB 1 January 1970 to form Aerospatiale.

SNCASO (France). Following forced nationalization Société Nationale de Constructions Aéronautiques du Sud-Ouest formed November 1936, taking over Blériot-SPAD, LeO and SASO and a number of Bloch factories. After 1940 by far the most important group working under German direction, building Fw 189, He 111 and Ju 52/3m. Already largest group, made bigger by absorbing SNCAO in 1941. At Châteauroux Bloch 175 multirole bomber remained in production until Germans took over unoccupied zone, its engines thereafter being shipped to Germany for Me 323. Group of Châteauroux engineers formed Groupe Technique de Cannes, producing SO.90 transport (2 × 375-hp Béarn) which on maiden flight November 1942 took off with 9 on board, under noses of Italian guards, and crossed Mediterranean to Philippeville. Major post-war products included SO.30 Bretagne transport, SO.4050 Vautour attack and night fighter, Djinn helicopter and SO.9050 Trident rocket/jet interceptor. Renamed **Ouest Aviation** 1 September 1956.

SNECMA (France). Giant producer of engines built Atar Volant VTOL test rig (tethered flights under remote control began 22 September 1956) followed by piloted C.400 P-2 (14 May 1957) and C.450 Coléoptère VTOL annular wing aircraft (6 May 1959).

SNCA du Sud-Ouest SO.30P-2 Bretagne, September 1950.

Snoke (USA). R. Snoke built Swifty Jr. racer 1959.

SNOS (Italy). In 1911 Società Nazionale delle Officine di Savigliano supplied Turin Poly aero lab with reaction balance and equipment for testing engines, and in 1912–13 7 Maybach engines were produced under licence for airships. Works expanded 1914, with airfield added, and in 1915–18 SNOS produced 28 SP 2, 58 SP 3, about 50 Ca 33 and small batch of SIA 7b1.

Snow (USA). Snow Aeronautical Corp. formed 1955 by Leland Snow to build S-2B ag-aircraft, delivering 265 to 12 countries in first 10 years. Bought by Rockwell-Standard 1965, subsequently Olney (Texas) Division of Aero Commander.

Snow (USA). Snow Aviation International Inc. formed Columbus, Ohio, 1990 to build SA-204C or SA-210AT turboprop transports, not flown by late 1992.

SOBEH (Netherlands). Helicopter foundation set up 1952 to produce light ramjet tip-drive helicopter, designated SOBEH H-2 (12 May 1955). Later in 1955 programme taken over by NHI.

Socata (France). Société de Construction d'Avions de Tourisme et d'Affaires formed 1966 at Tarbes-Ossun (today Aérodrome de Tarbes-Ossun-Lourdes) as subsidiary of Sud-Aviation (today of Aerospatiale). Produced all versions of Rallye, Horizon (Gardan) and Socata's own Diplomate and wings for Magister. 1993 products are Epsilon, Oméga, Tampico/Tobago and Trinidad, and Socata/Mooney TBM 700 (*see* TBM). Socata makes parts for Airbus, Mystère/Falcons, Eurocopter France, ATR 42/72 and C-130.

Società Anonima Aeronautica d'Italia: *See* Ansaldo.

Società Anònima Industrie Meccaniche Aeronautiche Navali: *See* SAIMAN.

Società do Costruzioni Meccàniche di Pisa: *See* SCMP.

Società Idrovolanti Alta Italia: *See* Savoia-Marchetti; SIAI-Marchetti.

Società Italiano Aviazione: *See* SIA.

Société Aérienne Bordelaise: *See* Bordelaise.

Société Aéronautique du Sud-Ouest: *See* SASO.

Société Aéronautique Française: *See* Dewoitine, 2nd entry.

Société Aéronautique Normande: *See* SAN.

Société Anonyme Belge de Constructions Aéronautiques: *See* SABCA.

Société Anonyme Française Aéronautique: *See* SAFA.

Société Anonyme Pour la Réalisation d'Avions Prototypes (France). Established 1926 at Billancourt (Paris), mainly by Louis Béchereau (ex-SPAD), to build prototypes to his design. Began with C.2 2-seat monoplane and T.7 7-passenger transport.

Société Anonyme Pour l'Aviation et ses Dérivés: *See* SPAD.

Société Anonyme pour les Appareils Deperdussin: *See* SPAD; Deperdussin.

Société Bulte: *See* Guldentops.

Société Commercial Aéronautique: *See* SCA (France).

Société de Constructions Aéro Navales de Port-Neuf: *See* SCAN.

Société de Construction d'Avions de Tourisme et d'Affaires: *See* Socata.

Société de Constructions et d'Aviation Légère: *See* SCAL.

Société d'Emboutissage et de Constructions Mécaniques: *See* SECM; Amiot.

Société de Recherches et de Constructions Mécaniques: *See* SRCM.

Société d'Etudes Aéronautiques: *See* SEA (Belgium).

Société d'Etudes de Matériel d'Aviation: *See* SEMA.

Société d'Etudes et de Construction Aéro-Navales: *See* SECAN.

Société d'Etudes et de Constructions d'Avions de Tourisme: *See* SECAT.

Société d'Exploitation des Etablissements Morane-Saulnier: *See* SEEMS.

Société d'Exploitation et de Constructions Aéronautiques: *See* SECA.

Société Européenne de Production de l'Avion d'Ecole de Combat et d'Appui Tactique: *See* Sepecat.

Société Française d'Aviation Nouvelle: *See* SFAN.

Société Française de Constructions Aéronautiques: *See* SFCA.

Société Française d'Etudes et de Constructions de Matériels Aéronautiques Spéciaux: *See* SFEC-MAS.

Société Générale des Constructions Industrielles et Mécaniques: *See* Borel.

Société Industrielle des Métaux et du Bois: *See* Bernard.

Société Industrielle de Tolerie pour l'Aéronautique et Matériel Roulant: *See* Sitar.

Société Industrielle pour l'Aéronautique: *See* SIPA.

Société Nationale de Constructions Aéronautiques de l'Ouest: *See* SNCAO.

Société Nationale de Constructions Aéronautiques du Centre: *See* Aérocentre.

Société Nationale de Constructions Aéronautiques du Midi: *See* SNCA du Midi.

Société Nationale de Constructions Aéronautiques du Nord: *See* Nord (France).

Société Nationale de Constructions Aéronautiques du Sud-Est: *See* SNCASE.

Société Nationale de Constructions Aéronautiques du Sud-Ouest: *See* SNCASO.

Société Nationale d'Etude et de Construction de Moteurs d'Aviation: *See* SNECMA.

Södertälje Werkstäders Aviatikavdelning (Sweden). SWA formed by Baron Carl Söderström 1913 after he had qualified as pilot at Pau. Director of Scania-Vabis, new company had ample resources for producing variety of licensed (mainly French) designs. Closed 1917.

Sogepa (France). Société de Gestion de Participations Aéronautiques is state holding company to manage shareholdings in industry and effect mergers and other deals. In 1992 held 20% Dassault and 7% Aerospatiale, but arranging closer ties (perhaps as step towards a giant Aéroespace Française) and 1993 may own 36% Dassault and almost same Aerospatiale.

SOKO (Jugoslavia; Bosnia-Hercegovina). Destroyed in Second World War, Jugoslav industry slowly recovered under nationalized control. Preduzece SOKO formed 1951, building Westland Whirlwind and later Gazelle helicopters

SOKO G2-A Galeb, May 1961.

Sopwith Schneider No. 1 (2 floats), 8 April 1914.

under licence. In 1957 began design of G2-A Galeb jet trainer (May 1961), which led to J-1 Jastreb single-seat attack/recon aircraft, both made and exported in large numbers. P-2 Kraguj piston-engined attack aircraft (1966) built in small series, but 'Jurom' launched large programme: *see* SOKO/Avioane. G-4 Super Galeb jet trainer (17 July 1978) built in substantial numbers for home (136) and export. Novi Avion next-generation fighter seems unlikely to be built, Mostar factory destroyed in civil war 1991–2 and evacuated.

SOKO/Avioane (Bosnia-Hercegovina/Romania). International 50/50 programme for development of attack aircraft called Orao by former Jugoslavia and IAR-93 by Romania.

Solar (UK). Solar-Powered Aircraft Developments, SPAD, also known as TO or To from promoter Freddie To, built Solar One (19 December 1978).

Solar (USA). Edmund T. Price formed Solar Aircraft Co., San Diego, February 1928, to produce aircraft and accessories. George Prudden, ex-Stout, chief engineer, produced MS-1 8/10-passenger transport based on Prudden's TM-1 (21 January 1930), developed 1931 into MS-2 with 500-hp P&W Wasp. Later major force in gas turbines and afterburners, in 1958–60 sharing development of RON series naval light helicopters (Solar T62 engine).

Soldenhof (Germany). Produced at least 2 allegedly stallproof/spinproof tailless aircraft

1930–35, one being 2-seater with 40-hp Salmson.

Soloy (USA). Soloy Corp. re-engine Bell and Hiller helicopters, Beech Bonanza and Cessna 206, 207 and Caravan with various Allison 250 turbine engines.

Somers Kendall (UK). Somers Kendall Aircraft Ltd formed by J.N. 'Nat' Somers and W. Magalow to produce SK.1 light jet trainer (8 October 1955) designed by Hugh Kendall.

Sommer (France). Roger Sommer was outstanding pioneer aviator, flying at 1909 Reims meeting with Farman III (Vivinus), and building own-design biplane 1911 which flew with 13 on board. In 1914 formed company at Levallois-Perret (Paris), building under licence until 1918.

Sonaca (Belgium). Société Nationale de Construction Aerospatiale SA, Gosselies, incorporated 1 May 1978 to take over assets of Fairey SA. Biggest programme was F-16, others being most Airbus versions, C-130, Atlantique 2, Saab 340 and Aerospatiale and Agusta helicopters.

Sopwith (UK). T.O.M. Sopwith was important pioneer pilot, also famous for ballooning, car-racing and, especially, ocean yacht-racing. In 1912 formed Sopwith Aviation Co. at Kingston-on-Thames, assisted by engineer Fred Sigrist and pilot Harry Hawker (both Australian) and hiring draughtsman R. J. Ashfield. Design office and factory in former roller-skating rink, aircraft towed on own wheels to Brooklands for assembly and test or to Thames in case of seaplanes. Following series of undistinguished aircraft, built Bat Boat, very successful flying-boat, followed by 13 other types prior to war. Then $1\frac{1}{2}$-strutter 2-seat biplane, described as first aircraft ever to have synchronized front gun, gun for observer and well-arranged bombload, built in enormous numbers in UK and France. There followed Pup, Triplane, Camel, Dolphin and Snipe, all built in vast numbers by giant factory at Richmond Road, Ham, and several contractors. Post-war built Dove and Gnu, but large war-profit tax bill prompted liquidation September 1920. Business resumed under name of H.G. Hawker Engineering.

Sorrell (USA). Hobart Sorrell built Dr. I (Fokker triplane) $\frac{3}{4}$-scale replica 1957. Subsequently formed Sorrell Aircraft Co. Ltd, flying SNS-2 Guppy biplane (1967), SNS-7 Hiperbipe aerobatic biplane (March 1973) and SNS-9 Exp II 2-seat sport/trainer (22 May 1985); also produces microlights.

South African Air Force (S. Africa). Assembled 4 Hartbees at Cape Town and built 65 more at Roberts Heights 1937–8. Today is converting over 40 C-47 to stretched turboprop C-47TP Super Dakota.

Southern (UK). F.G. and G.H. Miles, D.L. Brown and H. Hull greatly modified an Avro Baby at Shoreham early 1929 into Martlet aerobatic single-seater. Further orders resulted in formation of Southern Aircraft Ltd, building 5 Martlets and 1 Metal Martlet.

Southern (USA). Southern Aircraft Corp. formed 1939 at Garland, TX, producing BM-10 biplane trainer 1940. Subsequently contributed parts for large wartime programmes. Flying Automobile (1946) never certificated.

Southern Cross (Australia). Southern Cross Aviation Ltd formed 1957 at Toowoomba, Queensland, and after much market study produced SC-1 4-seat all-metal low-wing monoplane (1 March 1961).

Sovromtractor (Romania). State enterprise under Soviet management which from Brasov controlled all Romanian aircraft manufacture 1947–56; types produced included IAR.811, 813, 814 and 817.

Soyer/Barritault (France). Claude Soyer and Jean Barritault produced trim SB.01 tandem-seat low-wing monoplane 1984.

SPAD (France). **Société Pour les Appareils Deperdussin** formed February 1910 at Bétheny, Reims, by wealthy silk merchant Armand Deperdussin (which *see*). Built numerous monoplanes and biplanes, most designed by Louis Béchereau and Andre Herbemont, but Deperdussin arrested for embezzlement 1913 and company in liquidation. Monoplanes with Béchereau monocoque fuselages set repeated series of world speed records, these early aircraft being known by principal's name rather than as SPADs. Assets taken over late 1913 by Louis Blériot, who renamed company **Société Anonyme Pour l'Aviation et ses Dérivés**, still SPAD. This company built over 2,500 aircraft by Armistice, including famous single-seat fighters SPAD VII/XII and XIII, over 15,000 of these being delivered by numerous subcontractors, chief SPAD plant during war being at Suresnes. In 1921 company again restructured by M. Blériot as Blériot-Aéronautique.

Sparmann (Sweden). Sparmann's Flyplanverkstad established 1935 Stockholm, producing S-1 single-seat low-wing advanced trainer, small series for Swedish AF 1937.

Spartan (UK). Success of Spartan aircraft built by Simmonds led to formation 1930 of Spartan Aircraft Ltd at original location (Weston, Southampton), moving February 1931 to East Cowes, IoW. There built Arrow 2-seat biplane (28), Three-Seater (19) and 3-engined Cruiser 6-passenger monoplane (17). Ceased work May 1935.

Spartan (USA). In September 1927 Mid-Continent Aircraft Co. at Tulsa, OK, taken over by group of investors, and Spartan Aircraft Co. formed 17 January 1928, building Spartan 3C-1 and various derived versions by late 1930. Production switched to C4-225 and derivatives, all 4-seat cabin monoplanes, followed by 5-seat C5 and C2-60 braced low-wing side-by-side sport/trainer (165-hp Wright 3-cyl). In 1936 7-X prototype led to 7W Executive low-wing retractable-gear 4-seater, 34 built by 1940 followed by 201 NP-1 trainers for Navy based on C3.

SPCA (France). Société Provençale de Constructions Aéronautiques formed 1924 at Marseilles and La Ciotat as aircraft subsidiary of SPC Navales and shipping line Messageries Maritimes. In March 1925 obtained rights to build Météore aircraft from CGCA, producing several Météore 63 3-engined flying-boats. Under Paulhan-Pillard licence built E.5 patrol or transport flying-boat (3 × Jupiter) and T.3-BN4 torpedo/bomber seaplane (2 × Jupiter). SPCA own designs included 30-M4 fighter with twin fuselages, central nacelle and crew of 4. Type VII was 3-engined Colonial transport, Type 81 a 4-passenger metal Colonial monoplane (300-hp Titan Major) and Type 90 another metal Colonial monoplane (3 × 350-hp) for passenger, cargo or ambulance duties.

Specialized (USA). Specialized Aircraft Co. produced rebuild of DC-3 (3 × PT6): *see* Tri Turbo.

Specialty (Canada). Specialty Aircraft Sales (1984) Ltd, Edmonton, produce Sea Thrush water bomber seaplane derived from Ayres S2R-600 Thrush.

Spectrum (USA). Spectrum Aircraft Corp. built light aircraft 1984.

Spencer (USA). P.H. Spencer, Pacoima, CA, pilot since 1914, designed Privateer (*see* Amphibions Inc.), Spencer-Larsens, Republic Seabees and Trident TR-1, all variations of basic Spencer Air Car configuration. This developed into S-12 4-seater, final version being S-12E (1 August 1974), marketed by Spencer Amphibian Air Car Inc. (also sold as plans). On 15 July 1988 company sold to Robert F. Kerans, *see* next.

Spencer (USA). Kerans formed Spencer Amphibian Aircraft Inc., IL.

Spencer-Larsen (USA). Formed 1937 by P.H. Spencer and V.A. Larsen (ex-Fokker, Standard and Sikorsky) to develop 2-seat amphibian with fuselage engine driving pylon-mounted pusher propeller.

Sperry (USA). Elmer Sperry's son Lawrence formed Lawrence Sperry Aircraft Co. June 1919 at Farmingdale, Long Island. First product sport biplane with folding wings and 2 × BMW motor cycle engines each driving tractor propeller, second triplane bomber amphibian (pusher Liberty 12). Third was Messenger, designed by Army Engineering Division for front-line liaison, tiny biplane with 60-hp Lawrance, 42 built of which most were designated M-1 or M-1A, 8 becoming radio-controlled MAT (Messenger aerial torpedo). Sperry drowned in Channel 1923 after Messenger force-landing.

Spezio (USA). Tony and Dorothy Spezio, Bethany, OK, built DAL-1 Tuholer (2 May 1961) tandem open-cockpit sport aircraft; many plans sold, business continued (name unchanged) by William Edwards, Northampton, Massachusetts, from August 1973.

Spirit One (USA). Spirit One Corp. market plans of Spirit 1 ultralight.

Spitfire (USA). Spitfire Helicopter Co. formed January 1975 to produce various marks of turbine-engined derivatives of Enstrom F-28A.

Spörrer (Germany). Only known product (1931) supposed foolproof monoplane with enormous rear wings which could pivot (trailing edge up) through 70° to prohibit spin and give steep approach at 20 mph (32.2 km/h).

Sport (USA). Sport Aircraft Inc., Lancaster, CA, took over Sunderland and market plans of S-18, over 134 sets sold January 1992.

Sport (USA). Sport Air Craft International, Hillsboro, Oregon, originally Chris Tena, market 2 versions of Mini Coupe.

Sport (USA). Sport Racer Inc., Valley Center, Kansas, sell plans for 230-mph 2-seat Sport Racer.

Sport-Aire (USA). George Stark (*see* Stark [USA]) designed Sport-Aire side-by-side low-wing monoplane (9 November 1959); plans marketed.

Sportavia (W. Germany). Sportavia-Pützer GmbH u. Co. KG formed 1966 by Comte d'Assche, Director of Alpavia, and Alfons Pützer to take over manufacture of Fournier RF4D and RF5 from Alpavia. Added RF6 and RS180, in 1969 RFB bought 50%, increasing holding to 100% January 1977, in 1981 making Sportavia-Pützer a branch without identity, RFB itself becoming subsidiary of MBB.

Spratt (USA). Spratt & Co. Inc. formed at Media, PA, by George G. Spratt to build Model 107 flying-boat (April 1979) to test patented scheme in which only movable surfaces are separately pivoted left/right wings.

Spyker (Netherlands). Nederlandse Auto u. Vliegtuig Fabrik, Trompenburg, built Spyker school biplane, 1-seat scout and 2-seat scout 1919–22, all related biplane designs.

SRAP (France). Société pour la Réalisation d'Appareils Prototypes active 1922–6 building one-offs to customers' designs.

SRCM (France). Long-time producers of aircraft hydraulics, Société de Recherches et de Constructions Mécaniques built aircraft under licence (various Minicabs, Supercabs and Jodels) as well as original design SRCM-153 Joigny (March 1969).

SSA: *See* Samsung.

Stabilaire (USA). Stabilaire Inc., Mass., produced supposed safe aircraft, unstallable, unspinnable, tested Portsmouth, New Hampshire, 1933 with 40-hp Szekeley, speed range 37–90 mph.

STAé (Belgium). Part of Ministry of Communications, Service Technique de l'Aéronautique produced bizarre Florine Project 4 helicopter 1947 with 75-hp engine driving through gears to 4 pylons, each with a wooden rotor.

Stahl: *See* OOS.

Staib (USA). Wilbur Staib built Airy-Plane light aircraft 1966.

Stampe et Renard (Belgium). Pre-war company restored at original Brussells-Evère site by J. Stampe and G. Renard, overhaul/mod service for SV.4 users and failing to find customers for new SV.4D and ex-Farman SR.7B Monitor. Ceased trading 1957.

Stampe et Vertongen (Belgium). Established 1922 at Antwerp Deurne-Sud by J. Stampe, M. Vertongen and designer Alfred Renard, early designs being designated RSV. Built small numbers of biplanes and monoplanes, all 2-seat trainers or tourers of 100–200 hp. Following Renard's departure (*see* Renard) designed further trainers, of which SV.4 (1933), with company's usual 4 ailerons, proved great success, nearly 1,000 being built in France post-war including 940 by Nord and AIAA. By 1934 S. et V. Were moving into high-powered military field with SV.7 recon bomber and SV.10 fighter/bomber/ recon (2 × 800-hp GR 14Krsd), but latter crashed, killing chief engineer and J. Stampe Jr. Never recovered, and little post-war activity.

Standard (UK). Standard Motor Co. Ltd, Coventry, produced BE.12, RE.8 and Sopwith Pup 1916–18.

Standard (USA). Standard Aircraft Corp. formed September 1916 at Plainfield, NJ, later adding

Stampe et Vertongen SV.10, November 1935.

RSV (Renard-Stampe-Vertongen) 26.100, April 1929.

plant at Elizabeth, NJ, in belief aircraft would be needed for war. Took over Sloane November 1916, building 3 Sloane H-2 biplanes as Standard H-2 for Army. Similar 2/3-seaters built as H-3 and Navy H-4H seaplane. About 800 SJ and J-1 trainers followed 1917; 2 M-Defense fighters were followed by 93 (of 460 ordered) E-1 single-seat fighter trainers. Elizabeth and Paterson plants also built 80 Curtiss HS-1 flying-boats, 140 (of 1,000) DH-4, and began mass-production of Caproni and O/400 heavy bombers. *See* Gates-Day.

Star (USA). Star Aircraft Co. formed by Phillips Petroleum at Bartlesville, OK, 1928, modifying aircraft for fuel/lubricant research by parent, and for executive transport and publicity. By 1936 had produced 38 Cavalier 2-seat high-wing cabin monoplanes (60-hp Velie, 82-hp Genet or 90-hp Lambert radial).

Star (USA). Star Aviation, New Braunfels, TX, market kits (50 +) for LoneStar sport helicopter (18 October 1990).

Starck (France). André Starck flew Chanute-type gliders pre-First World War, and a Mignet Pou 1935. Then designed AS.10 tandem-seat biplane, followed by AS.20 tandem-wing (narrow-gap biplane) flown 23 October 1942. Formed Avions André Starck 1945 to build conventional AS.57 low-wing side-by-side, similar AS.70 Jac, AS.71, AS.80 Holiday tandem-seat high-wing (available 1952 as factory-built at Boulogne-Billancourt or as kit), and AS.90 New Look single-seater (11 June 1950). Last designs were AS.37 (13 January

1977) with AS.20 wing arrangement (100 + plans sold) and Super New Look flown after his death in 1979.

Starfire (USA). Starfire Aviation Inc., Buckeye, AZ, market kits and plans of Firebolt Convertible 2-seat aerobatic biplane (15 May 1987).

Stark (USA). George Stark (of Salvay-Stark) gave his name to Sport Aire, prototype built by Al Trefethen and A. Thistle at Lomita. Later marketed as Sport-Aire.

Stark (W. Germany). Stark Flugzeugbau KG, Minden, formed to produce Stamo engines, bought licence to Druine Turbulent 1958 and built version with cosmetic changes.

Stark Ibérica (Spain). Successor to German company 1963, continuing development and production of Turbulent at Zaragoza until 1969.

Starling (USA). Starling Aircraft Co. established May 1928 at Minneapolis to build Starling Biplane, conventional 3-seater.

Starling Burgess: *See* Burgess.

Star-Lite (USA). Star-Lite Aircraft formed San Antonio, TX, to market kits/plans of brilliant (many awards) SL-1 sport single-seater (17 May 1983). Ceased production 1990.

States (USA). States Aircraft Corp., Chicago Heights, built B-3 tandem parasol monoplanes during Depression (about 1930–32).

Stearman (Boeing Wichita) XBT-17, 1 August 1941.

Statler (USA). William H. Statler, Northridge, CA, markets plans of Firefly tandem-seat low-wing monoplane (8 October 1976).

STDC (Japan). English-language name of 5-company Supersonic Transport Development Council acting since 1991 as liaison group for Japanese membership of Alliance programme.

Stearman (USA). Lloyd Carlton Stearman, architectural student and naval cadet pilot, worked for E.M. Laird in Chicago, moved with him to Wichita and stayed after Laird's return to Chicago, being appointed chief engineer of former Laird company after it was renamed Swallow (which *see*). Dispute with patron Moellendick led to Beech and Stearman setting up with Cessna to form Travel Air. In 1926 Stearman resigned and set up **Stearman Aircraft Co.** at Venice, CA, in premises of former Lyle-Hoyt (local Travel Air distributor), producing C-1 open 3-seat biplane (cheap with 90-hp OX-5, expensive with 240-hp Salmson) and derived C-2. In 1927 Stearman, with Hoyt, returned to Wichita to occupy plant at Bridgeport where Cessna had made first aircraft 1917. Better-capitalized, Stearman sold aircraft in large numbers, even in Depression, all biplanes for passengers, mail, training or sport. At time of giant conglomerates, 15 August 1929, company was bought by United Aircraft and Transport. Stearman opened large new plant at municipal airport (today McConnell AFB). Northrop briefly merged with Stearman, Stearman himself leaving to join Varney airline and later to be president of Lockheed. After dismantling of United, Stearman was re-formed

as division of Boeing September 1934. By this time Model 70 (December 1933) had been developed to X75, selected October 1934 as Army primary trainer. Subsequently total production of PT-13, PT-17, N2S and other versions amounted to 10,346, ending February 1945. Post-war 'Stearmans' have been most active, though company ceased to exist 1934.

Stearman (USA). Ariel Aircraft suspended production early 1942, but in February 1942 changed name to Stearman Aviation. Did not succeed in restarting production.

Stearman-Hammond (USA). Lloyd Stearman resigned from Lockheed, being replaced by Bob Gross and, after working at Wichita for 2 years developing Hammond Model Y twin-boom pusher, formed Stearman-Hammond Aircraft and built about 25 examples by 1939.

Steel Wing Co. (UK). Cheltenham firm, subcontractors in First World War, built wings of Bristol M.R.1.

Steen (USA). Steen Aero Lab. Inc., Rock Hill, SC, produced Skybolt 2-seat aerobatic biplane (October 1970), over 3,500 sets of plans sold; rights taken over by Stolp, but 1990 remarketed under original name.

Stefanutti (Italy). Sergio Stefanutti (*see* SCA) designed and built several canard (tail-first) designs: SS.1 light aircraft (1934), SS.2 (1935) and SS.3 Amitra (2 October 1937). These led to SS.4 fighter of 1939. *see* Ambrosini; Stelux.

Steglau (Russia). Estonian industralist Ivan Ivanovich Steglau designed and built at St Petersburg 3 excellent biplanes (No. 1, 4 May 1911), notable for welded steel structure and cantilever wings.

Stelux (Italy). Stelux Aircraft Corp., division of Spartaria, built Trenzo canard tandem 2-seater, last design of Stefanutti. Started 1984, first flight never announced.

Stephens (USA). C.L. Stephens designed Akro, first US aircraft designed around Aresti system (27 July 1967), plans marketed.

Stephens (USA). Robert D. Stephens, Wichita, built Special 1-A (December 1957), total cost $575, plans marketed at that time.

Stern (France). René Stern, 57730 Folschviller, flew ST 80 Balade low-wing single-seater 17 July 1983, plans and kits marketed.

Steward-Davis (USA). Flew a C-82 with added turbojet pod above fuselage November 1956, subsequently converted many C-82 and C-119 aircraft.

Stewart (USA). Donald Stewart marketed large numbers of plans of 2 single-seaters, Headwind (28 March 1962) cabin high-wing, and Foo Fighter (June 1971) resembling scaled 1917 scout.

Stinson (USA). As teenagers Katherine and Marjorie Stinson both became not merely pilots but exhibition pilots, giving displays through Midwest prior to 1914. Brothers Edward A. (Eddie) and Jack also became pilots and ran a

flying school at San Antonio, training numerous pupils including Canadians for service in Europe. Shut down on US entry to war, Katy raised over $2m flying Buffalo-Washington, and later set records non-stop San Diego–San Francisco. Eddie made first commercial flight NY–Chicago, in 1922 moving to Detroit whose chamber of commerce financed construction of 4-seat cabin biplane. This, first Stinson Detroiter, sold for $12,500 and triggered **Stinson Airplane Syndicate** February 1926, renamed **Stinson Aircraft Corp.** later same year. Detroiter sold well but redesigned to appear April 1927 as SM-1 high-wing 6-seater, over 120 being built in several versions. From 1928 3/4-seat Junior was added, production exceeding 380. In 1927 moved to new plant at Wayne, and 4 days before Wall St Crash controlling interest sold to Errett Cord, president of giant auto conglomerate which became AVCO. In July 1930 SM-6000 Airliner, first 'Stinson Tri-Motor', 10-seater, sold well (over 115), but Eddie Stinson force-landed in new Model R 25 January 1932, walked away and then died suddenly next day. Model R led to SR, first of Reliant family of high-wing (typically) 4-seaters, 39 civilian versions plus 7 new-build wartime including 500 AT-19 supplied as Reliant I nav. trainers to Royal Navy. Model 105 Voyager 2/3-seater sold well, 1,285 of 3 basic versions. In 1940 Victor Emanuel, president of Avco, placed Stinson under Vultee control, effective 30 June, preparatory to buying out Consolidated. Stinson remained at Wayne, where production went ahead on L-5 Sentinel, derived from Voyager but equipped for observation and casevac, total 3,590. Vultee's merger with Consolidated March 1943 made Stinson part of Vultee-Stinson Division. Post-war produced

Stinson Model A Tri-Motor, 5 December 1933.

Stout Air Sedan, October 1922.

Model 108 Voyager (August 1945) attractive 4-seater, 5,100 sold but on 1 December 1948 Convair disposed of Stinson division and 500 unsold Voyagers to Piper, who regarded acquisition as removed competition rather than as asset.

Stits (USA). Ray Stits produced 'world's smallest' aircraft 1948–52: Junior 8 ft 10 in (2.69 m) span monoplane and Sky Baby 7 ft 2 in (2.2 m) span biplane. Subsequently Stits Aircraft Corp., Riverside, CA, produced SA-3A Playboy single-seater, SA-3B 2-seater, SA-6B Flut-R-Bug, SA-7B Sky-Coupe high-wing 2-seat and SA-11A low-wing 3-seat. Final (1970) title Stits Aircraft Supplies.

Stoddard-Hamilton (USA). Stoddard-Hamilton Aircraft Inc., Arlington, WA, produce Glasair fast (cruise up to 284 mph) 2-seaters, over 1,300 plans sold by end 1992, nearly 350 flying.

Stolp (USA). Well over 2,000 sets of plans sold by Stolp Starduster Corp., Riverside, CA, for SA-300 Starduster Too 2-seat sport biplane. Many other designs flying including SA-500 Starlet 1-seat parasol, SA-750 high-power 2-seat aerobatic biplane, SA-900 V-Star, basically a biplane Starlet, Super Starduster for unlimited aerobatics and 4-seat 450-hp Cabin Starduster.

Stout (USA). William B. Stout established **Stout Engineering Laboratories** at Detroit 1919, producing Batwing 3-seat monoplane with blended wing/fuselage (200-hp Packard) and ST-1 torpedo bomber for Navy (2 × 398-hp Packard). In 1922 formed **Stout Metal Airplane Co.**, with strong design team led by George Prudden. Following year produced 1-AS Air Sedan, lumpy short-span corrugated high-wing transport with OX-5 and 4 passenger seats. This led to much better 2-AT Pullman (3 December 1924) with 400-hp Liberty and 8 passenger seats. Sold in

Ford 8-AT, 21 April 1931.

numbers, so firm bought August 1925 by Henry Ford (son Edsel had from start been director), producing 3-AT 8-seater with 3 engines. Ugly lash-up, soon replaced by outstanding 4-AT, first of the Ford Tri-Motors, but by this time (1928) Stout had been replaced by Howard Hicks: *see* next entry. Photo shows 8-AT.

Stout (USA). Stout Engineering Laboratories reactivated 1929, in 1931 exhibiting 2-seat Sky Car cabin monoplane, thereafter pursuing other fields. Sky Car prototype was flown by Stout through 1930s, and in 1945 was used to test Spratt pivoted wing.

Streak (USA). Streak Aero Corp. took over Aero-Flight, briefly producing Streak high-speed 2-seaters, including final model Streak 225 (1954).

Striplin (USA). Striplin Aircraft Corp., Lancaster, CA, produced FLAC rigid-wing ultralight from 1978, followed by Lone Ranger and Sky Ranger homebuilts.

Stroukoff (USA). Michael Stroukoff formed Stroukoff Aircraft Corp., Trenton, NJ, after controlling interest in Chase was bought by Kaiser-Frazer. Stroukoff had been VP and chief engineer, designing C-123. Subsequently his company thought up ways of improving C-123, which was being produced (KF having defaulted) by Fairchild. Results included YC-123E Pantobase, with sealed and strengthened fuselage fitted with land/water skis and wingtip floats; and YC-134 with many changes including boundary-layer control system and R-3350 engines. No production.

Sturtevant (USA). Long-established B.F. Sturtevant Co. (hydraulic pumps, etc.) formed Sturtevant Manufacturing Co. 1910 to produce petrol engines, biggest project being V-8 aircraft engine. To find a market for this, Sturtevant Aeroplane Co. formed 1915 at Boston, Mass., chief engineer Grover C. Loening. Result was handful of mostly 1- or 2-off own designs, including Model S 2-seat biplane seaplanes for Navy and disastrous Model B single-seat sesquiplane (vitually parasol monoplane) for Army. Successful products included Curtiss JNs and DH-4s.

Sud-Aviation (France). Formed 1 March 1957 by merger of Sud-Est Aviation and Ouest-Aviation. Largest programme SE.210 Caravelle (27 May

Sud-Aviation S.E.117 Fonceur, later Voltigeur, 5 June 1958.

1955); other important tasks completion of production of SO.4050 Vautour IIA, IIB and IIN, and development and production of Alouette II, Alouette III, Super Frelon and Djinn helicopters. In 1959–60 converted 220 T-28A into Fennec attack aircraft for Algerian war, and built 166 S-58 helicopters under Sikorsky licence. In 1960 agreed with Dassault to build Super Caravelle SST, which led to 29 November 1962 agreement between governments of France and UK to build Concorde. Contributed major components to Mirage IVA, Atlantic and VC10. On 10 July 1962 obtained licence for Gardan GY 80 Horizon, leading to SOCATA. In 1963 studied Galion short-range wide-body, leading to supposed political design leadership on Airbus A300. In 1968 collaborated with Nord-Aviation on SN 600 Corvette bizjet. On 1 January 1970 merged with Nord-Aviation and SEREB to form Aerospatiale.

Sud-Est Aviation (France). Formed by renaming SNCASE 1 September 1956. On 1 March 1957 merged with Ouest-Aviation to form Sud-Aviation.

Sukhoi (USSR, Russia). Pavel Osipovich Sukhoi born 1895, fought in First World War, joined CAHI 1920, designed tailskid of ANT-4 December 1924 and later led major AGOS brigade with entire responsibility for 8 ANT (Tupolev) designs from ANT-5 to ANT-51, working at Komsomolsk. In 1939 invited to take over defunct BOK offices in Moscow, and Sukhoi OKB has been here at 23A Polikarpov St ever since. Developed ANT-51 into BB-1, over 2,000 built as Su-2, but

Sukhoi Su-11 (first to have this designation) May 1947.

many other good aircraft (Su-1 and -3 fighters, Su-4, -6 and -8 attack aircraft, Su-7 interceptor, Su-5 piston/jet fighter, Su-9 and -11 twin-jet fighters, Su-10 4-jet bomber, Su-12 twin-boom multirole, and Su-15 and -17 swept-wing fighters) all remained prototypes, and OKB shut by Stalin 1 November 1949. Sukhoi himself then explored design of supersonic fighter, establishing 2 broad configurations designated S (62° swept) and T (57° delta). On Stalin's death OKB reopened 1953 in direct competition with MiG, producing series of S and T prototypes. S led to production Su-7 (fighter, changed to close-support) which, via Su-22I (2 August 1966), led to variable-sweep Su-17/20/22 family, 20 production variants. T led to Su-9 and -11 all-weather interceptors, which

led to Su-15 twin-engined interceptor. T-series also led to T-6 heavy attack aircraft very similar to TSR.2, but, on cancellation of this British aircraft, design changed to F-111 configuration with variable-sweep and produced at Komsomolsk 1973–91 as Su-24. T series also led to T-8 close-support attack (22 February 1975), produced in many sub-types as Su-25. Final T-series was T-10 (20 May 1977) leading to outstanding Su-27 multirole fighter, with naval versions. Other programmes include: Su-26, -29 and -31 competition aerobatic aircraft, S-21 (first to be designated for Mikhail P. Simonov, who succeeded Sukhoi as General Designer in 1975) supersonic bizjet which has led to very uncertain joint project with Grumman, S-51 project for

Sukhoi Su-27UB, June 1981.

SST, S-54 jet trainer, S-80M twin-turboprop STOL transport, S-84 single-turboprop 8/10-seater, S-86 pusher turboprop 6/8-seater and S-99 multirole 4/5-seater. OKB also important in large (Ekranoplan) surface-effect vehicles. Title **Sukhoi Aerospace Industries Association**, greater political power than any other former OKB and the only one to have its own mass-production plant (USPA). To be privatised by 1996.

Sullivan (USA). Sullivan Aircraft Manufacturing Co., Wichita, formed and died in Depression (1930–32) building K-3 low-wing 3-seat cabin monoplane, Kinner K-5 of 100 hp.

Summit (USA). Summit Aeronautical Corp., formed NY 1937 with works at Bendix Field, Teterboro, built HM-5 2-seat cabin monoplane (1941) in researching aircraft construction by Vidal thermosetting plastic-bonded veneer. Ceased 1941.

Summit (USA). Summit Aviation Inc., Middletown, Delaware, rebuilt Cessna T337 Skymasters (1979–87) into O2-337 Sentry military aircraft.

Sun (USA). Sun Aerospace Corp., Nappanee, IND, produced Sun Ray 100 single-seat pusher canard amphibian (4 September 1983).

Sunbeam (UK). Sunbeam Motor Car Co., Wolverhampton, major producer of aircraft engines 1916–18, with a trickle of post-war production, built Avro 504B, Short 827, Short 320 and Short Bomber aircraft for Admiralty. Also produced single Sunbeam Bomber (1917, 200-hp Sunbeam Arab) of 2 ordered.

Sunderland (USA). Sunderland Aircraft, NY, developed Thorp T-18 Tiger into S-18 with larger cabin and folding wings (1984): *see* Sport, 1st entry.

Sundorph (USA). Sundorph Aeronautical Corp. formed by Eiler C. Sundorph at LA, believed 1934, best known for Model 2 (XA-1) 200-mph (321.8 km/h) high-wing 4-seater (8 October 1937).

Sun Fun (Canada). Sun Fun Ultralight Aviation, Surrey, BC, markets Kestrel Hawk 50-hp ultralight 2-seater (1986).

Sunrise (USA). Sunrise Aircraft Corp. Of America formed 1964 by former Wagner personnel to produce S-1600 twin-turboprop STOL transport. Venture failed.

Sunrise (USA). Sunrise Ultralight Manufacturing Co., New Caney, TX, produced wide range of ultralights.

Super 580 (USA). Super 580 Aircraft Co., Carlsbad, CA, remanufactures CV-340/440 and earlier turboprop conversions to Super 580 standard (*see* Hamilton, 2nd entry).

Superior (USA). Superior Aircraft Co. formed mid-1956 at Culver City, CA, to acquire assets of Culver Aircraft and develop Model V into Superior Satellite (20 December 1957), but no further news.

Supermarine (UK). Noel Pemberton-Billing stood for Parliament in early 1916, and to avoid charge that he was a war profiteer sold his

Supermarine Walrus ASR.II (Saro-built), 1941 photo.

interest in Pemberton-Billing Ltd at Woolston, Southampton. Control passed to Hubert Scott-Paine, who became managing director. Since inception firm's telegraphic address had been 'Supermarine', and accordingly company was renamed **Supermarine Aviation Works Ltd.** Began with series of single-pusher flying-boats and amphibians (Channel, Sea Lion, Sea Eagle, Sea King), but first important type was Southampton flying-boat (10 March 1925), 2 × 500-hp Napier Lion, 68 built for RAF, Mk II having metal hull. R.J. Mitchell, who had joined original firm 1916, showed particular talent with S.4, S.5, S.6 and S.6B seaplanes which won 3 consecutive Schneider races 1927/29/31. Seal II pusher amphibian of 1921 led to Seagull of 1922, built in increasing numbers up to Mk V, which served as prototype of Walrus (pusher 750-hp Pegasus) of which 746 built in Second World War. Successor was Sea Otter (September 1938) with tractor 855-hp Mercury, 292 built 1944–5. RAF also received 14 Scapa (2 × 525-hp Kestrel) and 23 Stranraer (2 × 875-hp Pegasus) flying-boats. An additional 40 Stranraer were built by Canadian Vickers, links between Vickers and Supermarine resulting in Vickers taking 100% of equity of Supermarine in November 1928, name simply adding (Vickers) in front of Ltd. Mitchell's dissatisfaction with Type 224 fighter to specification F.7/30 (19 February 1934) led to his obtaining permission from chairman Sir Robert McLean to produce completely new design. This, Type 300 (5 March 1936), became Spitfire, 20,334 built plus 2,556 new-build Seafire naval fighters. Together with Vickers (Aviation), taken over by Vickers-Armstrongs October 1938, henceforth having clumsy title **Vickers-Armstrongs Ltd (Aircraft Section) (Supermarine Division)**. Before and during war design office moved to Hursley Park, near Winchester, large factory built at South Marston, Swindon, and Spitfire production also centred at other plants including Castle Bromwich and Chattis Hill. Mitchell died 11 June 1937, being replaced 1938 by Joe Smith, whose direction was responsible for all subsequent Spitfire development. Spitfire successor, Spiteful (June 1944), was in many ways inferior, but Spiteful wing was basis of jet Attacker (RR Nene, 27 July 1946), 181 built. This indifferent aircraft led in stages to Swift fighter for RAF, which proved unacceptable and was cancelled when large numbers were in production at South Marston and by Short at Belfast. This left only a series of twin-RR Avon naval fighters which

eventually led to Scimitar (1957), 76 built. Reorganization of Vickers December 1954 resulted in company becoming **Vickers-Armstrongs (Aircraft) Ltd (Supermarine Division)**. Final reorganization, which took VA (Aircraft) into BAC, resulted in formation of Vickers-Armstrongs (South Marston) Ltd, with little work except to build two Hovercraft.

Super Rotor (Brazil). MM Super Rotor Industria Aeronáutica Ltda, São Paulo, produce AC-4 Andorinha single-seat autogyro (December 1972) in both finished and kit form, and M-1 Montalvá (March 1985) 2-seater.

Surrey (UK). Surrey Flying Services Ltd, Croydon, built A.L.1 side-by-side biplane trainer (1929) to design of J. Bewsher. Used intensively until war.

Survol (France). Fauvel (which *see*) called his firm 'Survol' Charles Fauvel.

Svenska (Sweden). Established as Svenska Aero Aktiebolaget (not related to SAAB) at Lidingö by C.C. Bücker to build to Heinkel designs. Early products included S.1 and S.11 seaplanes, HD.14 torpedo bomber and HD.17 fighter-recon biplane. Own designs began with Pirat 2-seat biplane (1927) land- or seaplane, 200 or 400 hp, followed by light Falken trainer and Jaktfalk fighter (1932). Potentially important, Jaktfalk suffered from Bücker's departure and shaky state of firm, which in same year was taken over by ASJA. All work moved to Linköping but name remained Svenska, completing 5 J6 Jaktfalk built at Lidingö and building 3 more plus 7 J6B. See ASJA.

Sveshnikov (Russia). Aleksandr Nikolayevich Sveshnikov built 3 outstanding monoplanes at Kiev 1912–14 in general style of Blériot.

Swallow (USA). When E.M. Laird returned to Chicago September 1923, Wichita company was reorganized as Swallow Airplane Manufacturing Co., Lloyd Stearman designer and Walter Beech chief pilot. Redesigned Laird Swallow into more compact single-bay New Swallow with fully cowled OX-5 engine. Beech and L.C. Stearman left (*see* Stearman), leaving Jake Moellendick and W.M. Stearman to redesign into Swallow Commercial improved 3-seater with choice of 5 engines (usually 150- or 180-hp Wright-Hispano)

Svenska Viking I, June 1932.

up to 220-hp Whirlwind. This 1928 product was partnered 1929 by Swallow TP 2-seat trainer, about 200 built, followed by numerous other versions all killed by Depression. Moribund 1932, company reformed 1938 as **Swallow Aircraft Co.**, producing prototypes of LT-65 and Coupé 2-seat monoplanes, but work stopped by war.

Swanson (USA). Swanson Airplane Co. formed 1930 by S.S. Swanson, who had helped produce Swanson-Freeman biplane and later designed for Lincoln-Standard. Depression killed Swanson Coupe light 2-seat cabin monoplane (1931). In 1934 Sven Swanson developed Coupe into unnamed prototype built by Nicholas-Beazley, which in turn was basis of Fahlin Plymocoupe, Pobjoy R engine being replaced by Plymouth car engine.

Swanson-Freeman (USA). Subsidiary of S. Swanson & Co., Vermilion, S. Dakota; produced Model 3 Sport 1922, followed by SS-4 2-seat biplane late 1923 (80-hp Le Rhône).

SWDC (Taiwan). Science and Weapon-systems Development Centre of Royal Thai Air Force: *see* RTAF.

Swearingen (USA). Ed (Edward J.) Swearingen set up **Swearingen Aircraft Co.** as fixed-base operator at San Antonio 1953, and among other things built prototypes under contract (e.g. Piper Comanche, 24 May 1956). By 1960 had large business modifying aircraft to improve performance (e.g. Beech D50 rebuilt as Excalibur). Original designs began with Merlin IIA (13 April 1965), combining new fuselage with

Swallow (J-4), May 1926.

Swearingen SJ30, 1991.

Queen Air wing, Twin Bonanza landing gear and PT6A turboprops. This led to many derived Merlins and Metros, sales passing 500 by 1982. But in November 1971 Fairchild took over, buying 90% of stock and forming new subsidiary called **Swearingen Aviation Corp**. Predictably in 1981 this vanished, to be renamed Fairchild Aircraft Corp.: *see* Fairchild. *See also* next entry.

Swearingen (USA). Ed Swearingen started again, forming **Swearingen Aircraft Corp.** 1982, still San Antonio, building nacelles for Do 128 and marketing Taurus mod. of King Air 90 and kits of Swearingen SX300 275-mph 2-seater (July 1984). Later built prototype SA-32T for Jaffe and is developing SJ30 small bizjet (13 February 1991). In 1992 set up SJ30 production at Kent County AeroPark, Delaware (at Dover AFB).

Swiss-American: *See* SAAC (International).

Sylvaire (Canada). Sylvaire Manufacturing, Sylvan Lake, Alberta, market Bushmaster (1984) high-wing cabin monoplane, 1 or 2 seats.

Szaraz (USA). Arpad Szaraz, Bedford, OH, produced Daphne side-by-side high-wing aircraft (4 October 1961), 20 being built by 1969.

Szekeley (USA). Szekeley Aircraft Engine Co., needing work in Depression, produced Flying Dutchman low-wing single-seater 1930 to take their SR-3 engine.

Sznycer (Canada). Bernard Sznycer collaborated with Gottlieb in developing SG.VI light helicopter, prototype made by Engineering Products of Canada at Montreal (9 July 1947).

Szpak: *See* LWD.

T

TAC (Taiwan). Taiwan Aerospace Corp. established 27 September 1991 as basis for large aerospace industry including engines and avionics. Giant deal with McDonnell Douglas was replaced by 50% share in BAe Regional Aircraft, with production of RJ family in Taiwan and joint development of new versions.

Tachikawa (Japan). Tachikawa Hikoki KK (T. Aeroplane Co. Ltd) was originally Ishikawajima, renamed for city where main plant located. This factory expanded 1939–41 from 8,900 to 110,000 m² (about 1.2m sq ft), and during Second World War new factories added at Kofu and Okayama. Produced engines and numerous prototype aircraft, as well as major proportion of trainers (Ki-9/-17/-54/-55). Also important for Ki-36 close-support and for several transports, notably Ki-54 versions, LO (Lockheed licence) and nearly all Nakajima Ki-34. By 1944 prototypes developed of very advanced Ki-70 recon, Ki-74 high-alt recon/bomber, Ki-77 ultra-long-range and Ki-94 and -106 fighters. *See also* next entry.

Tachikawa (Japan). Though law permitting post-war manufacture of aircraft not published until 15 July 1952, company reformed as **Shin Tachikawa Kokuki** KK (New T. Aircraft Co. Ltd), with small but new factory at Sunagawa. Here were built Tachihi R-52 (September 1952), first post-war Japanese aircraft, parasol trainer, followed by revised R-53 (155-hp Cirrus Major) and Tachihi R-HM with improved 90-hp Mignet Pou. Subsequently devoted effort to overhaul of US and later JASDF aircraft.

Taganrog (Russia). On Don estuary, on border of Ukraine, vast facility for aircraft development and production, plus OKB originally formed by G.M. Beriev. Renamed 1990 Taganrog Aviation Scientific-Technical Complex (Russian: TANTK), named for G.M. Beriev.

TAI (Turkey). Tusas Aerospace Industries Inc. is English-language name for **TUSAS Havacilik ve Uzay Sanayi AS**, national aerospace company formed 15 May 1984, shareholders TAI 49%, other Turkish 2%, General Dynamics 42%, General Electric 7%, MD being appointed by GD. By 1992 TAI had delivered 100 of 152 F-16C/D and was building centre and aft fuselage and wings of USAF F-16s. Also building 34 SF.260D and 50 of 52 CASA/IPTN CN-235. Post-F-16 work being sought.

Talleres (Argentina). Talleres Al-Aire formed 1960 to produce light aircraft. Work in progress on AL-2 Tijerete twin-boom pusher and Turbay T-11 when proprietor killed 1975.

Talleres (Mexico). Internal disorder, difficulty of importing from Europe and strained relations with USA led November 1915 to establishment of Talleres Generales de Construcciones Aeronauticas at Valbuena, near Mexico DF. Produced engines (mainly Hispano) and various aircraft under licence, initially Blériot and Morane-Saulnier, followed 1918 by Microplano fighter and undistinguished series of 2-seat monoplanes and biplanes. BMW.III of 185 hp used in S-2 trainer biplane (January 1926) and Azcarate OE-1 (October 1928), both made in some numbers, followed by Whirlwind-engined Azcarate E, licensed Vought Corsair. Aircraft manufacture suspended 1930–42, when Teziutlan trainer

appeared, followed 1947 by TTS-5 6-seat transport (2 × 200-hp Ranger). *See* TGAM.

Tampier (France). René Tampier, inventor of Bloctube carburettor, produced roadable biplane 1921 and refined version 1922 with 300-hp Hispano for flight and auxiliary engine for land travel. In 1924 produced T.4 2-seat recon-bomber with 300-hp Hispano and auxiliary engine for starting and driving wireless generator; small series for Aéronavale as crew trainers. Heavy 'multiplace de combat' T.6 (1931) 3-seater with 2 × 600-hp Renault.

TANTK (Russia). Nearest English abbreviation for Taganrog, ex-Beriev.

Tarrant (UK). W.G. Tarrant Ltd, timber merchants and builders of Byfleet, Surrey, produced giant Tabor triplane (6 × 450-hp Lion), crashed on first take-off 26 May 1919.

Tatarinov (Russia). Vladimir Valerianovich Tatarinov, son of V.A. Tatarinov who in 1891 proposed jet aeroplane, built and flew gliders from 1908 and built unsuccessful 'Aeromobile' helicopter 1909.

Tatra: *See* Ringhoffer-Tatra.

Tawney (UK). Tawney Aircraft Ltd formed 1957 at Stapleford (previously called Stapleford Tawney) airfield to produce Owl 2-seat monoplane (75-hp pusher Porsche); damaged on first take-off 22 April 1960.

Taylor (UK). John F. Taylor produced JT.1 single-seater (4 July 1959), but was killed 16 May 1967 during testing of JT.2 Tich racer. Plans marketed, business continued by Mrs T. Taylor, about 130 JT.1 and 40 JT.2 flying, 800+ plans sold.

Taylor (UK). Richard Taylor built experimental monoplane at Hamsey Green, killed by wing failure on first flight 7 January 1937.

Taylor (USA). C. Gilbert Taylor and his brother Gordon founded **Taylor Brothers Aircraft Corp.**, 1929 at Rochester, NY, to market Chummy side-by-side monoplane (originally 62-hp Siemens u. Halske). At Bradford, PA, oilman William T. Piper was looking for investment opportunities, and chose Taylor. But firm withered, and when

Gordon died, C.G. Taylor moved to Bradford, Piper becoming secretary and treasurer. Firm finally crashed 1931.

Taylor (USA). Piper bought assets for $761 and started again as **Taylor Aircraft Co.**, still with C.G. Taylor as president and chief engineer and Piper as secretary and treasurer. It was entirely Piper's knowledge of market and eager drive that got Taylor to design totally new aircraft, smaller than Chummy: tandem-seat Cub (10 September 1930), with 50-hp Brownback Kitten, later 40-hp Salmson. With Piper's aggressive marketing over 300 Cub E-2 (37-hp Continental) sold during Depression, several new models appearing. But personality clash led to Taylor's departure 1936, Piper buying his shares. Walt Jamouneau replaced Taylor as designer, but just as company was really prospering (550 sales in 1936) factory burned down. Piper moved to Lock Haven and renamed company Piper Aircraft. *See* Taylorcraft.

Taylor (USA). Donald E. Taylor built light sporting aircraft 1976.

Taylor (USA). C. Gilbert Taylor, founder of original Taylor firm 1929, produced Bird 2-seater, 65-hp pusher watercooled Subaru (17 July 1979), outstanding aircraft. *See also* Taylor Aero.

Taylor (USA). Farmer M. Taylor produced Topper sport aircraft October 1956 and Tater Bug single-seater February 1963.

Taylor (USA). Ralph Taylor produced light aircraft 1972.

Taylor (USA). Ron Taylor produced light aircraft 1982.

Taylor Aero (USA). Taylor Aero Inc., Tipp City, OH 45371, today managed by Col. Robert H. Taylor (a son of C.G.) who with brother Bruce updated Bird and markets it with nose-or tailwheel or as plans.

Taylorcraft (UK). Taylorcraft Aeroplanes (England) Ltd formed November 1938 to build under licence from Taylor-Young at new factory at Thurmaston, Leicester. Initial production called Plus C (55-hp Lycoming) and Plus D (90-hp Cirrus Minor); 11th bought by RAF, named Auster I. Subsequently built 100 Auster I, 2 Mk II, 467 Mk III, 255 Mk IV and 780 Mk V. Company renamed Auster Aircraft 7 March 1946.

Taylorcraft (USA). When C.G. Taylor left 1936 he immediately set up **Taylorcraft Aviation Co.**, Alliance, Ohio, later in 1936 forming **Taylor-Young Airplane Co.** Produced side-by-side Model A 1937, achieving great success with refined B,C,D in many versions, total over 3,000. In 1941 tandem-seat D models appeared, leading to Army L-2 (1,940) and 250 TG-6 training gliders. Four-seat Model 15 Foursome prototype and 2,800 B-12B built 1945–6, but in latter year company bankrupt, possibly for tax reasons. *See also* next entry.

Taylorcraft (USA). C.G. Taylor started yet again 1949 as **Taylorcraft Inc.**, Conway-Pittsburgh airport, PA, buying assets of failed company at public auction. Built mainly side-by-side 2-seaters (various names) but closed down again 1958.

Taylorcraft (USA). Company again re-formed (not by C.G. Taylor) 1 April 1968 as **Taylorcraft Aviation Corp.**, occupying plant at Alliance, OH. Produced F-19 Sportsman based on pre-war Model B. This company bought by former Piper employees 9 July 1985 and relocated at former Piper home at Lock Haven, but failed 1986.

Taylorcraft (USA). In November 1989 assets bought by Aircraft Acquisition Corp. and restarted at Morgantown building various models of F22 series (*see* New Technik). In April 1992 secured independence and established at Lock Haven as **Taylorcraft Aircraft**; still (1993) producing F22 versions. *See also* Vector.

Taylor Kits (USA). Formed February 1990 at Morgantown by Aircraft Acquisition to market kits of T-Craft, a variant of F21B, similar to factory-built; light twin was due to fly 1992. Now Vector Aircraft.

TBM (France/USA). TBM SA formed (as TBM International) 1988 by Socata (70%) and Mooney (30%) to manage TBM 700 6/7-passenger aircraft (PT6A), Valmet joining to build wing. Prototypes flying since 14 July 1988 but dissolution likely.

Tchetverikov: *See* Chyetverikov.

TCM (USA). Teledyne Continental Motors is increasingly marketing conversions to liquid-cooled Voyager engines, first A36 Bonanza.

Teal (USA). Teal Aircraft Corp. formed 1976 (also in Canada), but failed to produce Thurston Teal for which rights had been bought from Schweizer.

Tebaldi (Italy). Ing. Tebaldi designed fighter 1918 which was built by Zari 1919, at least twice modified, from sesquiplane to high-wing monoplane (300-hp Hispano).

Technical Centre: *See* Civil (India).

Ted Smith: *See* Smith (USA), 15th entry.

Teledyne Ryan (USA). Successor to original Ryan, Teledyne Ryan Aeronautical are world leaders in drones, UAVs, RPVs, etc.; Model 410 for 24-hour surveillance was flown in manned form (27 May 1988) and is available in this form.

Tellier (France). Motorboat-builder Alphonse Tellier produced at least 6 aircraft 1909–16 before testing T.2 flying-boat (June 1916), developed into better T.3 (January 1917) with 200-hp HS8b, Tellier building 53 and Nieuport 47. Tc.6 version with 47-mm Hotchkiss in bow cockpit was ordered in large numbers, Tellier building 55 before Armistice. Fresh design T.4 was ordered in numbers with 350-hp Sunbeam, about 40 delivered. At least 5 fresh versions tested 1918, company being taken over August 1918 by Nieuport which sold about 12 Nieuport-Tellier boats before closure in 1920.

Temco (USA). In 1947 Texas Engineering & Manufacturing Co. Inc., Dallas, bought rights to GC-1B Swift, having previously made 329 for Globe Aircraft under subcontract. TE&M then formed Temco Aircraft Corp., developing TE-1 and T-35A trainer versions and prototypes of civil Model 33 Plebe. Sustained by massive aircraft subcontract and conversion business, Temco produced Model 51 Pinto jet trainer (26 March 1956), 11 for Navy as TT-1.

Temple: *See* Texas, 1st entry.

TENSA (Argentina). TENSA SA, Buenos Aires, reached 1979 agreement with Cessna that it would assemble 420 aircraft of various Cessna models by 1984, but did not do so.

Tereshchyenko (Ukraine). F.F. Tereshchyenko, Kiev factory owner, put his name to 2-seat monoplane 1914 which he financed and built. His factory built aircraft under licence 1916–17.

Termite (USA). Termite Aircraft, Bloomington, IL, marketed large numbers of kits/plans of Termite sport parasol (10 February 1957).

Terrill (USA). Howard L. Terrill, Torrance, CA, produced HLT-100 sport single-seater (September 1957) and HLT-101 racer (July 1962).

Tervamäki (Finland). Jukka Tervamäki produced JT-1 prototype autogyro 1958, JT-2 in 1965, Tervamäki-Eerola ATE-3 in 1968 and JT-5 in January 1973. Sold rights to Magni.

Terzi (Italy). Terzi Aerodine, Milan, specialists in glassfibre sailplanes, produced T-9 Stiletto (December 1990) very efficient 2-seater, in production by Sivel of Padua. T30 Katana 300-hp aerobatic aircraft (16 January 1991) available certificated or in kit form.

Texas (USA). Jay Ingram formed Texas Aeroplane Co 1914, built Ingram Foster (Curtiss type) pusher biplanes.

Texas (USA). Texas Aero Corp. incorporated 1927 at Temple, TX, to continue building Temple Monoplane, high-wing mail carrier (220-hp Whirlwind J-5). *See* Williams, 5th entry.

Texas (USA). Texas Agricultural & Mechanical College (Texas A&M) produced Ag-1 experimental ag-monoplane (1 December 1950) designed by Fred Weick with 21% thick wing and other unusual features. Ag-2 passed to Transland (which *see*), smaller Ag-3 was designed for low cost (November 1954).

Texas (USA). Texas Aircraft Manufacturing Co., Tyler, TX, built Bullet (ex-Johnson): *see* Aircraft Manufacturing.

Texas (USA). Texas Airplane Manufacturing Co., Addison airport, Dallas, acquired assets of Carstedt in 1974 and briefly continued marketing CJ600 stretched turboprop Dove.

Texas (USA). Texas Engineering & Manufacturing: *see* Temco.

TGAM (Mexico). Final title of Talleres was Talleres Generales de Aeronáutica Militar.

Thaden (USA). Thaden Metal Aircraft Co. established San Francisco 1927 to build Thaden Monoplane with 6/8 passengers (425-hp Wasp). Further versions appeared 1929, but later that year takeover made firm into Pittsburgh Metal Airplane Co.

Thalman (USA). Harry J. Thalman formed Thalman Aircraft Inc. at Salt Lake City in 1949, producing T-3B mid-wing 2-seater with geodetic construction and tailwheel landing gear, followed by T-4 mid-wing cabin 2-seater with retractable tricycle gear 1957.

THK (Turkey). Türk Hava Kurumu Uçak Fabrikasi established 1941 by Turkish Air League, factory at Etimesgut, Ankara. Produced over 100 Miles Magister, plus numerous proto-types, most Gipsy Major engined, before taken over 1952 by MKEK.

Thomas (USA). English engineer William Thomas Thomas joined Herring-Curtiss 1909, realized he could design and build on own account and with brother Oliver built first aircraft (10 June 1910). Went into production while W.T.T. toured eastern US giving demo flights. Moved from Hornell to Bath, NY, where with successful business established formed **Thomas Brothers Aeroplane Co.** May 1912. Also formed engine company and school. In 1914 moved to larger premises at Ithaca, where joined by B. Douglas Thomas (famed ex-Sopwith, no relation)

Thomas-Morse MB-6 racer, February 1921.

who designed T-2 trainer (24 for RNAS) and 15 similar SH-4 for USN and D-5 for Signal Corps. Needed to expand, hence Thomas-Morse.

Thomas-Morse (USA). Thomas Bros. had first real aircraft assembly line in N. America, but more rapid expansion was needed. Asked neigh-bour Morse Chain to take control; **Thomas-Morse Aircraft Corp.** formed January 1917, F.L. Morse president, doubled size of plant, built S-4 fighter and received order for 100 S-4A as ad-vanced trainers, followed by 1,050 S-4C of which 498 delivered. MB-1 and -2 fighters remained prototypes, but MB-3 (21 February 1919) seemed excellent fighter for post-war Army, but production of 200 went to low-bidder Boeing. T-M never really recovered, though produced numerous fighters and racers and, in 1928, XO-19 observation biplane which led to 180 of various O-19 versions. This business looked good to Consolidated, which bought T-M 1929.

Norman Thompson: *See* under N.

Thompson (USA). Thompson Aircraft, Philadel-phia, built strange tandem boxkite-like Boxmoth (November 1975).

Thompson (USA). John A. Thompson built light aircraft 1979.

Thompson (USA). Dr Norman Thompson also built light aircraft 1979.

Thöne u. Fiala (Austria). Major though unprofitable subcontractors in First World War, building several types, including Aviatik D.I, at Vienna.

Thorp (USA). John W. Thorp began developing T-111 Sky Scooter 2-seater 1946, based on Lock-heed Little Dipper. Formed **Thorp Aircraft Co.** 1949, Pacoima, CA, this design passed to Tubular Aircraft. In 1956 formed **Thorp Engineering Co.**, Burbank, CA, producing 2-seat T-18 (later called Tiger), by 1980 over 1,300 plans sold and 220 T-18 flying. Tubular built improved T-211 (1964), limited production by Adams Industries before rights bought 1985 by **Thorp 211 Aircraft Co.**; product-liability laws then restricted marketing by **Thorp Aero Inc.**, Kentucky, to foreign countries 1990 onwards.

Thruxton (UK). The Thruxton Aviation and

Engineering Co. Ltd formed 1962 to produce Gadfly 2-seat autogyro. Became Gadfly.

Thruxton Jackaroo: *See* Jackaroo.

Thulin (Sweden). In 1914 Dr Enoch Thulin acquired control of AVIS, renaming it AB Enoch Thulins Aeroplanfabrik. Became principal producer of aero engines, plus licensed Blériot, Morane-Saulnier and Albatros types. Own-design FA 2-seater built as land- and seaplane for Swedish Army and Navy. Type K (Blériot-derived) was fighter, 12 sold to Netherlands 1919, in which year Thulin killed in crash. TV (Thulinverken) was non-aviation company.

Thunderbird (USA). Thunderbird Aircraft Inc. established November 1927 at Glendale (LA) to develop Thunderbird biplane (July 1926) designed by Theo Woolsey, who became president. This 3-seater built with 90-hp OX-5 as Thunderbird W-14.

Thunder Wings (USA). Established as division of Thunder Developments Inc., Scottsdale, AZ, 1975, to produce 8/10-scale replicas of Second World War fighters, marketing P-40C, Spitfire IX and Fw 190A.

Thurston (USA). **Thurston Aircraft Corp.** established 1966 at Sanford, Maine, building HRV research hydrofoil aircraft and then Teal amphibian. Taken over by Schweizer, then Teal Aircraft. Meanwhile Thurston designed Explorer/Observer landplane versions produced (*see* Patchen), rights being transferred to Dr Maitland Reed's Air Nova. Thurston later designed improved 4-seat TA16 Trojan amphibian, called TA16 Seafire in production, forming International Aeromarine (*see* IAC [USA], 1st entry) at Sanford, Florida (not Sanford, Maine), 1982. This now superseded by **Thurston Aeromarine Corp.**, Maine.

Tikhonravov (USSR). Prof. Mikhail Kladiyevich Tikhonravov was on staff of NII scientific test institute 1940 when produced I-302 rocket/ramjet fighter; 2 built 1942, 1 flown on tow 1943.

Tilbury (USA). Without forming company, Tilbury Flash built by Owen Tilbury and Cecil Fundy, Bloomington, Illinois (March 1932); possibly smallest of all National racers (45-hp Church engine much modified), empty weight 270 lb (122.5 kg).

Timm (USA). Otto W. Timm took post of VP and chief engineer of the O.W. Timm Airplane Corp., Glendale, CA, 1926, to build Timm Biplane (July 1927) with open cockpit for 2 and 5-seat cabin behind (260-hp Menasco-Salmson), sold several, followed by at least 4 Collegiate parasol-wing trainers. Inactive 1930. *See* next.

Timm (USA). O.W. Timm formed Timm Aircraft Co., still at Glendale, 1935 to build T-800 high-wing transport (2 × 420-hp Whirlwind) with 2-seat cockpit and cabin for up to 10, using patented Aeromold process. This led to tricycle-gear T-840, but no production. Moved 1937 to Van Nuys, CA, building S-160 tandem low-wing primary trainer (22 May 1940), 262 of developed PT-220C version built for Navy as N2T Tutor.

Timmins (Canada). Timmins Aviation Ltd, Dorval, Montreal, large fixed-based operator, produced batch of Super Catalina conversions 1958–63 with 1,700-hp Wright R-2600 engines and many other changes.

Timofeyev (USSR). Viktor Timofeyev partnered Mikhail Artyumov in building AT-1 ultralight 1971 and channel-wing Omega (8 January 1975); he alone produced T-1 Mustang high-wing pusher 1975.

Tipsy (Belgium). Ernest Oscar Tips built twin-propeller biplane 1908, obtained Benelux agency for Gnome, served in FAB, escaped to England, joined Fairey and later managed Fairey SA at Gosselies. In spare time designed Tipsy S (September 1934) ultralight, produced by Avions Fairey and in UK, *see* below. Next came Tipsy B side-by-side, built from 1937 with open or enclosed cockpit, followed 1939 by Tipsy M tandem trainer. All these were flown in UK pre-war. Works at Gosselies destroyed 10 May 1940, rebuilt by October 1946 and work resumed on Belfair (refined BC) and new-design Avions Fairey Junior single-seater (1948), 7 of first and 2 of second built, factory then being used wholly for other work, notably Meteor production.

Tipsy (UK). Tipsy Aircraft Co. Ltd formed as sales organization February 1937 at London Air Park, Hanworth. Sold Tipsy S.2s built at Bristol (Kingswood), but manufactured B under Fairey licence, introducing many mods resulting in change of designation to Tipsy Trainer, 15 delivered by Second World War. In 1939 moved

Tipsy S. prototype, October 1934, with Swordfish (both Fairey).

to Liverpool Rd, Slough, building 3 there 1947. Some Bs brought up to Belfair (cabin) standard, a few Belfairs being sent from Gosselies to D. Heaton (Yorks) for completion.

TK: *See de Havilland.*

TM (USA). TM Aircraft, Pennsylvania, formed to market plans and part-kits of W. Terry Miller's TM-5 (1980) aerobatic 2-seat monoplane.

Todd (USA). Edward Todd built light sporting aircraft 1963.

Todhunter (Australia). Reg Todhunter built manpowered Skycycle 1979 and Blue Wren powered sailplane 1983.

Tokyo Gasu Denki Gasuden KR-1, March 1934.

Tokyo (Japan). Tokyo Gasu Denki Kogyo KK (Tokyo Gas and Electric Co. Ltd) built small numbers of KR-1 biplanes (March 1934) based on DH.83 Fox Moth, followed by about 30 KR-2 Chidori II 4-passenger developments. Also small number of TR.1 (January 1936) transports based on Envoy, 2 × 240-hp Tokyo GD Jimpu radials. In 1937 merged with Hitachi, losing identity.

Tokyo (Japan). Tokyo Koku KK built wooden Ki-107 Army trainer (October 1943), only about 30 completed when bombing halted work 1944.

Tomashyevich (USSR). Dmitri Lyudvigovich Tomashyevich worked for Kalinin and Polikarpov (deputy chief on I-180). Arrested late 1938, but in October 1941 assigned to run semi-free

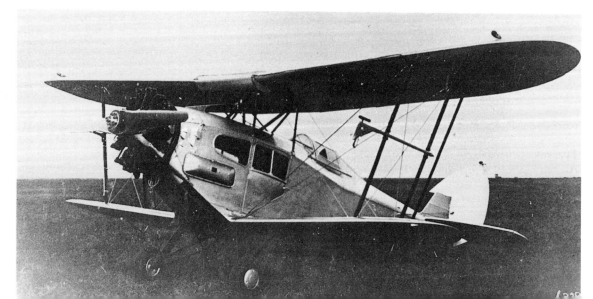

GAZ-266 (Omsk, Siberia). Here produced '110', conventional 379-mph (610 km/h) fighter/bomber (December 1942), but no productive capacity. Turned to problem of armoured close-support and anti-armour, several prototypes of Pegas flown 1942–3.

Tony Team (USA). Tony Team Industries produced sporting aircraft 1977.

Towle (USA). Towle Aircraft Co. incorporated 1928 at Detroit to produce TA-3 8-passenger amphibian (typically 2×220-hp Whirlwind).

Toyo (Japan). Toyo Koku KK (Toyo Aircraft Manufacturing Co. Ltd) formed 10 June 1952, a month before aircraft manufacture again permitted, with board made up of ministers, admirals and former Kawasaki MD and chief engineer. Built TT-10 tandem monoplane trainer (30 December 1952). Also held licence to Fletcher FD-25/25A.

Toyota (USA). Toyota Aviation USA, wholly-owned subsidiary of Japanese giant, hopes to enter lightplane market with all-composites aircraft powered by Lexus car engine, prototype designed and built by Scaled Composites (late 1991).

Tradewind (USA). Tradewind Turbines Corp. obtained from Soloy rights to Allison turboprop Bonanza October 1989, since marketed major conversion with B17D turboprop, wing radar and wingtip tanks.

Trago Mills (UK). Large retailers Trago Mills Ltd built prototype SAH-1 trainer (23 August 1983); superb aircraft, but never succeeded in sewing up a programme, sold to Orca.

Train (France). Etablissements E. Train formed at beginning of century to produce many light engineering designs, which in 1911 began to include a series of landplanes and (1912) seaplanes. From 1930, mainly aircraft engines.

Transall (International). Transall (Transporter Allianz) group formed January 1959 to build C-160 military airlifter (25 February 1963); original participants HFB, Weser and Nord. After several reshuffles these became MBB (DASA) and Aerospatiale. By 1972 built 172, followed by 35 upgraded aircraft 1982–5.

Transavia (Australia). Transavia Corp. Pty Ltd formed 1964 as subsidiary of large construction firm Transfield to market PL-12 Airtruk (22 April 1965) unconventional ag-aircraft, now called Skyfarmer; 120 delivered by 1987, none since.

Transcendental (USA). Transcendental Aircraft Corp., Glen Riddle, PA, formed about 1946 to produce 1-G convertiplane with 160-hp Lycoming driving tilting proprotors on wingtips (15 June 1954).

Transfield (Australia). Transfield Construction is parent of Transavia.

Trans-Florida (USA). Trans-Florida Aviation Inc., Sarasota, formed 1957 to market Cavalier 2-seat tip-tanked executive conversions of P-51D Mustang; became Cavalier 1967.

Transland (USA). Transland Co., subsidiary of Hi-Shear Rivet Tool Co. at Torrance (LA), produced air spraying/dusting equipment from 1950, from 1953 producing Ag-2 designed for Transland by Texas A&M (11 October 1956). Five prototypes only.

Travel Air (USA). Travel Air Manufacturing Co. formed at Wichita October 1924 by group including Walter H. Beech, Clyde Cessna and Lloyd Stearman. Travel Air 1000 (August 1925) 3-seat biplane was better than rivals and led to 15 variants with many engines. H. Rawdon designed subsequent high-wing monoplanes, including 6-seat 5000 (January 1927) and derived 6000, also built as seaplane, and 4-seat 10-D and 10-B (1929), but in early 1930 sought refuge from Depression by accepting takeover by Curtiss-Wright, which continued same designs.

Trecker (USA). Trecker Aircraft Corp. formed 1955 at Milwaukee as subsidiary of machine-tool giant, to assemble and distribute Piaggio P.136 as Trecker Gull. In 1960 added P.166 as Trecker 166, but inactive same year.

Trefethen (USA). In 1961 Al Trefethen took over Sport-Aire II (see Stark) and marketed plans.

Trella (USA). Assisted by 4 brothers, Frank Trella, Detroit, built 6 aircraft of original design from 1924. T-100–T-104 were biplanes, T-105 was high-wing monoplane and T-106 (September 1949) was side-by-side high-wing twin-boom pusher.

Travel Air Mystery S (Frank Hawks'), January 1930.

Tremaine (USA). Tremaine Aircraft, San Diego, CA, produced Humming Bird light aircraft 1926. First crashed La Brea but others followed plus HB racer version.

Tridair (USA). Tridair Helicopters, Costa Mesa, CA, market twin-engined conversions of Bell LongRanger called 206L-3ST Gemini ST.

Trident (Canada). Trident Aircraft Ltd, Sidney, BC, formed 1971 to develop TR-1 Trigull 6-seat amphibian (5 August 1973), fully certificated 1976 but funding for production not obtained.

Tri Q (USA). Produce tricycle landing gear mod. for Quickie Q2.

Tri Turbo (USA). Tri Turbo Corp., Camarillo, CA, produced for Specialized Aircraft conversion of DC-3 with 3 × PT6A-46 turboprops; inactive after Jack Conroy's death 1979.

TsAGI: *See* CAHI.

Tschetverikov: *See* Chyetverikov.

TsKB: *See* CCB.

TSPA (Georgia). Tbilisi Aircraft Manufacturing Association formed 1991 to manage former Dimitriov factory which produced MiG-21U and Su-25 families. Soon concluded licence to make GA-7 (Gulfstream, now Am. Gen.).

Tsybin (USSR). Pavel Vladimirovich Tsybin

was co-designer of Kolyesnikov KTs-20 and subsequently built Ts-25 assault glider and powered Ts-25M, LL and EP high-speed research aircraft (forward-swept, VG and oblique centre-pivot), ending with NM-1 research aircraft (1957) designed for Mach 2.8.

Tubular (USA). Tubular Aircraft Products Co., LA, produced improved Thorp Sky Scooter 1964-6.

Tucker (USA). L.G. Tucker produced light aircraft 1983.

Tucker (USA). Tucker Aircraft Co., Detroit, proposed lightweight fighter May 1940; design accepted as XP-57 but company failed before issuing drawings.

Tugan (Australia). Tugan Aircraft, Sydney-Mascot, formed 1934 to take over assets of defunct (Australian) General Aircraft, financed by South Sea island traders W.R. Carpenter & Co. Proposed to build 5 types, but produced only 1, LJW.7 Gannet 6-passenger or ambulance, derived from Codock, 9 completed, 6 for RAAF, before taken over late 1936 on formation of Commonwealth Aircraft.

Tunison (USA). M.C. Tunison, Santa Ana, CA, 1911, produced several one-offs ending 1928 with beautifully streamlined Scout with 4-seat cabin, 180-hp Hispano, 190 mph.

Tupolev (Russia, USSR, CIS-Russia). Andrei

Nikolayevich Tupolev was most senior designer in Soviet Union, managing largest OKB which from 1922 until his death December 1972 created more types (129) of more diverse aircraft than any other designer or company. Design engineer at Duks, co-founder with Zhukovskii of CAHI 1918, member of Komta, he headed state commission on metal construction 1922, building ANT-1 and ANT-2 cantilever monoplanes using corrugated Kolchug skin. Metal construction thus proven, formed AGOS as chief CAHI construction bureau, producing ANT-3 biplane (7 August 1925), many built including 70 as military R-3 with imported Lorraine engine. There followed amazing succession of mostly large and challenging monoplanes, often with major parts or even whole design carried out by Arkhangyelskii, Petlyakov, Myasishchyev or Sukhoi. Included ANT-4 (26 November 1925) leading to 218 TB-1 bombers and other versions; ANT-6 outstanding heavy monoplane bomber (22 December 1930) leading to 818 TB-3 and other versions; ANT-9/PS-9 airliner (about 83); ANT-20, largest aircraft in world 1934; ANT-25 long-distance (various); ANT-40, most modern bomber of 25 April 1934, leading to at least 6,656 SB-2; and ANT-58 (designed in a VT prison) leading to ANT-61 and 'about 3,000' Tu-2 during war. Designations then changed to Tu, a major project being dissection of B-29 and conversion into Tu-70/75 transports and then Tu-4 bomber, which via piston-engined Tu-80 and -85 led to giant swept turboprop Tu-95, produced as Tu-20 and -142 over 38-year period. Tu-88 (27 April 1952) led to about 2,000 Tu-16 in over 25 versions, plus about 200 of derived Tu-104 passenger transport. Bombers led to Tu-22 supersonic bomber and Tu-22M swing-wing bomber and missile-launcher, and to Tu-128 long-range interceptor. Transport led to turbofan-engined Tu-124, aft-engined Tu-134 (about 700 built) and Tu-154/164 (over 600 built 1968–91). On founder's death, OKB continued to bear his name, general designer now being founder's son Dr Alexei Andreyevich Tupolev, deputy Andrei I. Kandalov. Military aircraft mainly centred at vast Kazan complex, where Tu-160 produced 1981–92. Civil teams under Lev A. Lanovski develop aircraft for production at Kharkov and Ulyanovsk, notably Tu-204 which with British engines is marketed by Bravia. Tu-334 to fly 1993 with turbofans and possibly 1994 with propfans. 1993 attempt by OKB to proliferate into smaller aircraft. Title **ANTKI**

Tupolev Tu-8, ANT-69, December 1946.

(Aviation Scientific-technical Complex named for) **A.N. Tupolev.**

Turbay (Argentina). Ing. Alfredo Turbay produced T-1B Tucan parasol-wing single-seater. Turbay SA, Buenos Aires, formed January 1961 to undertake manufacture of T-3A 7-seater, 2×180-hp Lycoming (8 December 1964). Finally, T-11 aerobatic trainer was to be built by Al-Aire 1972.

Turbotech (USA). Turbotech Inc., Washington, hold over 30 STCs in respect of rebuilds and upgrades involving installation of more powerful engines, mainly to Cessna, Grumman and Stinson aircraft.

Turcat-Méry (France). Aviation subsidiary of car and engineering firm (Concorde test pilot André Turcat is same family) produced several early aircraft designed by Ing. Odier, several examples built of tractor biplane with ENV engine first flown June 1910.

Türk Hava: *See* THK.

Türk Uçak Sanayii Anonim Ortakligi (Turkey). This was original full name of TUSAS: *see* TAI.

Turner (USA). Turner Aircraft Inc., Grandview, TX, have sold many hundreds of sets of plans for various versions of T-40 sporting 2-seater, all developed from E.L. Turner's original T-40 (3 April 1961). Also produce microlights.

Turner (USA). Bill Turner, Riverside, CA, with Ed Marquart, built replica Gee Bee Model Z Super Sportster (450-hp Wasp); amazingly, only accident so far (in 1979) was due to brake problem on ground.

TUSAS: *See* TAI.

Twin Commander (USA). Twin Commander Aircraft Corp. formed Arlington, WA, December 1989 to support and manufacture former piston/turboprop Commander series from Gulfstream. New production not funded by 1992.

Tyndall (USA). E.L. Tyndall built sporting aircraft 1963.

Tyrov (USSR). Vsyevolod Konstantinovich Tyrov (thus pronounced, but written in Russian as Tairov, hence designations) was lecturer at MAI (Moscow Aero Inst.) 1930–39, and first deputy to Polikarpov. Formed OKO at Kiev, managing following until killed in crash December 1941: OKO-1 transport (October 1937), 7 passengers, 730-hp M-25A; OKO-4 sesquiplane fighter/bomber; Ta-1 (OKO-6) long-range escort (31 December 1939) with heavy armament and 2 × 1,100-hp M-88R, developed into excellent Ta-3 when Tyrov killed. OKO-7 heavy twin-engined fighter never completed.

U

UAC: United Aircraft Corp.: *see* United.

UAIK: Ulyanovsk Aviation Industrial Complex: *see* Aviastar.

UAT (UK). United Aerospace Technologies Ltd, on Dartmoor, marketed various forms of Ranger light canard pusher with either 1 or 2 190-hp Continental, 1987.

UATC: United Aircraft & Transport Corp.: *see* United.

UCC (USA). United Consultant Corp., Norwood, Mass., produced Twin Bee (1963) rebuild of Seabee with 2 × 180-hp tractor Lycoming.

Udet (Germany). Ernst Udet, 62 victories in First World War, lent his name to Udet-Flugzeugbau GmbH formed near Munich October 1922 by American William Pohl to build light aircraft to design of Hans Herrmann. In fact U 1–U 5 had flown previously, all small monoplanes. U 7

Udet (Aero Lloyd) U 11 Kondor (4 pusher Sh 12), June 1924.

Kolibri single-seat parasol was made in substantial numbers; U 8 was 4-passenger, and U 11 Kondor a 3-crew and 8-passenger (4 × 100-hp). By 1925 company financially in bad shape, and not even large demand for U 12 Flamingo biplane trainer could save it. Bankrupt when trying to meet U 12 demand 1925, premises taken over by BFW, which continued production.

UDRD (Philippines). Universal Dynamics Research and Development, Makati, Manila, produced Defiant 300 tandem trainer (February 1988) but local hardwood difficult to obtain. Switched to metal in Defiant 500 (950-hp PT6A turboprop), and hopes to build 1,800-hp Defiant 1000 as Co-In aircraft, but neither funded by 1992.

Uetz (Switzerland). Walter Uetz Flugzeugbau, at Speck, Zurich, produced numbers of both U2V (July 1962) derived from Jodel D119, and U4M Pelikan (21 May 1963) 4-seater.

UFAG (Austro-Hungary). Ungarische Flugzeugwerke AG formed 1915 at Albertfalva, Budapest, by Baron von Skoda, initially to build Lohner B-series and Hansa-Brandenburg C.II. Produced own design C.I late 1916, later building over 100, Phönix building 36 + .

Ufimtsev (Russia). In 1910–12 A.G. Ufimtsev built outstanding engines but hopeless aircraft (because they had circular 'Spheroplan' wings).

UFM (USA). One of many UFM groups in N. America, Ultralight Flying Machines of Santa Clara, CA (Larry Mauro), built Solar Riser solar-powered biplane (April 1979).

Ultimate (Canada). Ultimate Aircraft Corp. formed 1990 at Guelph, Ontario, to market plans, kits and factory-built Pitts S-1 and S-2 with many changes including larger and stronger wings, single-seat 10/100, /200 and /300 sport biplanes and 20/300 2-seater.

Ultimate Aerobatics (Canada). Market kits giving Pitts S-1 new wings, 200-hp Lycoming and other upgrades.

Ultra-Flight (Canada). Ultra-Flight Light Aircraft and Engineering Development, Sudbury, Ontario, formed 1960 to manufacture and market Sport-Aire: *see* Stark; Trefethen.

Umbaugh (USA). Raymond E. Umbaugh designed Model 18 2-seat autogyro in early 1950s, forming Umbaugh Aircraft Corp. at Ocala, Florida, about 1957 and flying prototype 1958. Developed Model 18A (June 1960), was to have been produced by Peace River. *See* Air & Space.

Umbra (Italy). Aeronautica Umbra (*see* AUT) re-formed post-war but did not begin design of aircraft until 1968 when AUM-903 3-engined STOL transport begun. This never built, but company briefly built Scheibe Motorfalke.

Ungarische: *See* UFAG.

Union (Germany). Union Flugzeugwerke GmbH formed 1956 by Heinkel/Messerschmitt as registered company for Flugzeug Union Süd.

United (USA). In 1928 Boeing, Pratt & Whitney and Vought formed **United Aircraft & Transport Corp.**, Frederick Brant Rentschler of P&W being president, office at Hartford, CT, where P&W and Vought had large and expanding plants. In 1929 added Hamilton Metalplane (soon becoming Hamilton Standard, leader in propellers), Sikorsky, Stearman, Standard Steel Propeller and 3 airlines which, with Boeing Air Transport, were merged 1930 into giant United Airlines. In 1934 Air Mail Act prohibited any one management from both manufacturing and operating aircraft; United Airlines was hived off and UATC became **United Aircraft**, comprising Pratt & Whitney, Vought, Sikorsky and Hamilton Standard, while Boeing went free again with Stearman as subsidiary. In June 1935 UAC split into **United Aircraft Manufacturing Corp.** and United Aircraft Export Corp., latter being international sales/marketing organization. In Second World War 11 companies built UAC products without royalty. On 1 May 1975 UAC changed name to **United Technologies** as result of progressive acquisition of additional divisions: Chemical Systems (rockets, previously UTC), Essex (automotive), Norden (mainly electronic) and Otis Elevator.

United Aerospace: *See* UAT.

United Aircraft (USA). United Aircraft Engineering Corp. formed New York February 1919 mainly to market war-surplus aircraft and engines, buying large stocks from Canada and UK. Did not survive to carry out avowed aim of building to others' designs.

United Consultant: *See* UCC.

United Eastern (USA). Formed about 1915 New York to run Eastern School of Aviation, built small number of biplane trainers for this school.

United Helicopter (USA). Brief successor to original Hiller Industries, building C-4 (UH-4) Commuter 2-seat coaxial helicopter (10 June 1946) followed by J-5 with single rotor and tail reaction jet. Then decided to use tail rotor, resulting in Model 360 by Hiller Helicopters.

United States: For Army *see* Engineering Division; for Navy *see* Naval Aircraft Factory.

United States Aircraft: *See* USAC.

United Technical Industries (USA). Built light aircraft and conversions 1967.

Univair (USA). Univair Aircraft Corp., formed 1946, moved to Colorado, holds rights to many classic types including Alon, Ercoupe, Forney, Mooney M-10 and Stinson 108. Mass-production of parts for older aircraft.

Universal Dynamics: *See* UDRD.

Universal Molded Products (USA). This corporation was successor to Monocoupe at Bristol, VA, building Monocoupe 90A including 20 for Army as L-7A.

Unruh (USA). Col. Marion D. Unruh, USAF, built Pretty Prairie Special (1 September 1957).

Upperçu-Burnelli: *See* Burnelli.

Urdaneta (Colombia). Urdaneta y Galvez Ltda formed Bogotá 1955 as general fixed-base operator and Cessna distributor, from 1969 assembling and increasingly manufacturing Cessnas including Ag-wagon and 310.

Urmston (UK). Dr J.H.B. Urmston built Currie Wot 2 1958 and later held rights, marketing small number of plans.

URMV-3 (Romania). Romanian acronym for Aircraft Component Repair Factory 3, this was designation of former IAR factory at Brasov (only one in country) from its rehabilitation March 1949 until in 1959 industry was reorgan-

ized, Brasov factory became IRMA and, in 1968, ICA-Brasov.

Ursinus (Germany). Oskar Ursinus, Editor of *Flugsport*, was from 1900 major figure in German aviation. In First World War designed at least 3 aircraft, largest being bomber/torpedo biplane with fuselage on upper wing and 2 × 160-hp Mercedes close together. Built as landplane at Darmstadt (1917) and as UWD seaplane by Gotha.

USAC (USA). United States Aircraft Corp., Burbank, CA, specializes in major conversions, notably Turbo Express rebuild of DC-3 (2 × PT6A turboprops).

USPA (Buryat region, Siberia). Ulan-Ude Aircraft Production Association formed 1991 under General Director Y.N. Kravtsov to manage production plant now part of Sukhoi AIA and previously associated with VNTKI Kamov, Mil and also formerly engaged in An production.

UTVA (Jugoslavia, Serbia). **UTVA Fabrika Aviona** established at Pancevo about 1952, first major product UTVA-56 4-seat monoplane (for over 30 years said flown 22 April 1959, now date given as 1956). Over 20 derived versions followed including ag, ambulance and seaplanes. In 1983 title **UTVA—Sour Metalne Industrije ro Fabrika Aviona**, main programme UTVA-75 2-seat multi-role (19 May 1976), 150 + built followed by 4-seat 75A not yet in production. Lasta military trainer (2 September 1985) being redesigned as Lasta 2. UTVA makes parts for 737, 747 and 757, Orao/IAR-93, Super Galeb and Optica and planned to make complete FLS Optica and Sprint and Croplease Fieldmaster.

V-8 Special (USA). This Colorado company market kits/plans of fighter-like tandem-seater (22 September 1978) with 125-hp mod. Buick car engine, 200-mph (320 km/h) cruise.

Vakhmistrov (USSR). Vladimir Sergeyevich

Vakhmistrov was greatest proponent of Z (*Zvyeno* = link) assemblages in which large aircraft took off with up to 5 smaller aircraft attached to it 1931–43.

Valentin (W. Germany). Valentin Flugzeugbau GmbH, 8728 Hassfurt, sailplane manufacturer, produced Taifun 12E (1985) short-span 2-seat aeroplane derived from Taifun 17E motor glider; further developed 1988 into 4-seat Taifun 11S.

Valkyrie: *See* Aeronautical Syndicate.

Valmet (Finland). State aircraft factory **Valtion Lentokonetehdas** (VL) established at Sveaborg, Helsinki, April 1921, to build under licence A.22 (Heinkel) seaplane and later over 30 types of which 18 of Finnish design, starting with D.26 Haukka fighter. Reorganized 1928 to incorporate IL (air force) depot, which was separated 1933 when VL became virtually private enterprise. Important types in 1930s were Tuisku and Viima II biplane trainers and Pyry advanced monoplane trainer, followed by Myrsky (1940) and Pyörremyrsky (1945) fighters. Lack of work 1945 resulted in title **Valtion Metallitehtaat**, state metal works, reorganized in 1950s with main aircraft works at Tampere, other plants handling repairs and engines. Built Vihuri advanced trainer (6 February 1951), series production being Vihuri III, and Tuuli III light aerobatic trainer, followed by Potez-Air Fouga Magister jet trainer. In 1958 title abbreviated to **Valmet OY**, expanding to build 12 Saab Draken followed by 46 BAe Hawks. Further reorganized 1974, separated from state metalworking group and taking name

Vakhmistrov Zvyeno: TB-3 and I-Z, first hook-on 23 March 1935.

Valmet Aviation Industries. Built L-70 Miltrainer, air force name Vinka (1 July 1975), leading to L-90 TP Redigo multirole turboprop trainer (1 July 1986). Valmet is assembling 57 F/A-18C Hornets and produces complete tails for Saab 2000.

Valsan (USA). Valsan Partners offer Quiet 727, with JT8D-217 outboard engines and other changes.

Valsts Elektrotechniska: *See* VEF.

Valtion: *See* Valmet.

Van Aswegen (S. Africa). C.H.J. Van Aswegen built Bergwind single-seater (1976) followed by Vansin 4-seater (May 1979).

Van Berkel (Netherlands). Van Berkel's Patent

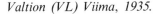

Valtion (VL) Viima, 1935.

Ltd, Rotterdam, built 4 types of Hansa-Brandenburg seaplane, biplane and monoplane, military and civil, 1920–23.

Vance (USA). Clair Vance formed Vance Aircraft Inc. at Oakland, CA, 1929, to produce Viking 'flying wing' mail/cargo carrier, with P&W Wasp or Hornet (450–660 hp) and tail carried on booms. Flew July 1932, but never made intended record distance flight.

Vancouver Aircraft (Canada). Briefly applied name (1938) of Boeing Aircraft of Canada.

Vancraft (USA). Vancraft Copters, Portland, Oregon, market kits for Vancraft 2-seat autogyro, and also Lightning Sport Copter single-seater.

Van Dine (USA). Peter D. Van Dine built light aircraft 1982.

Vanguard (USA). Vanguard Air and Marine Corp. formed 1958 to produce Omniplane fan-in-wing VTOL research aircraft.

Van Lith (France). Jean Van Lith produced Type VI 2/3-seat high-wing cabin aircraft (30 August 1959).

Van's (USA). Van's Aircraft Inc., Oregon, sold over 6,800 sets of plans for RV-3/4/6/6A sporting monoplanes.

VAPA (Russia). Voronezh Aviation and Production Association formed 1991 to manage large plants, formerly GAZ-18 and 64, on Il production (especially 86 and 96).

Vardax (USA). Vardax Corp., Bellingham (Seattle), convert DHC-3 Otters to PT6A turboprop power.

Varga (USA). Varga Aircraft Corp., Chandler, AZ, took over rights to Model 2150A (ex-Shinn, ex-Morrisey), building new examples from 1957 as 2150A Kachina.

VAT (USA). Vertical Aviation Technologies Inc., Sanford, Florida, developed Hummingbird (February 1988) from Sikorsky S-52, kits marketed.

Vazduhoplovna: *See* SOKO.

VEB (E. Germany). Under VVBF, national aircraft industry organized 1956 into 6 VEBs (Volkseigener Betriebe, publicly owned enterprise), each dealing with 1 type of product. Aircraft manufacture at VEB Dresden, others being gliders, engines, equipment, etc.

Vecto (USA). Vecto Instrument Corp., Houston, TX, produced Geronimo upgrade of Piper Apache, 180-hp engines and other changes, 1961–5.

Vector (USA). Vector Aircraft Co., previously Taylor Kits, formed at Morgantown by Aircraft Acquisition Corp. to market aircraft based on original C.G. Taylor design, starting with F21B. Completely new Twin-T light twin high-wing 3-seater about to fly 1993.

Veetol (Australia). Formed 1991 to attempt to put Phillicopter (*see* VTOL) into production.

VEF (Latvia). Valsts Elektrotechniska Fabrika (state electrical works) established aviation division 1935 to produce aircraft designated I from designer Karlis Irbitis. I-11 low-wing 2-seater (1936) led to I-12 built in series, plus prototypes of various trainers and fighters, halted by Soviet invasion 17 June 1940.

Vega (USA). **Vega Airplane Co.** formed 1938 by renaming AiRover. Affiliate of Lockheed, new plant built adjacent at Burbank to produce Vega Starliner light transport powered by Menasco Unitwin (22 April 1939), also built Vega 35 tandem trainer designed by North American as NA-35. Factory vastly expanded 1940, receiving massive orders, initially for Vega Ventura bomber for RAF. In 1941 became full subsidiary of Lockheed as **Vega Aircraft Corp.** Factory became Lockheed Plant 2, further expanded to build B-17 from June 1942. Produced PV-1 Ventura and PV-2 Harpoon, losing separate identity on merger into parent 30 November 1943.

Vegener (Russia). Capt. A.N. Vegener, director of Gatchina flying school, built training aircraft summer 1911 based on Farman but with streamlined nacelle and with ability for instructor to engage or disengage pupil's controls, first such in world.

Veljekset Karhumäki: *See* Karhumäki.

Velocity (USA). Velocity Aircraft, Florida, produce kits for 220-mph Velocity 2/4-seat tailless canard, 50 + flying.

Vendôme (France). Raoul Vendôme et Cie produced at least 12 different monoplanes and biplanes 1906–16, including 1909 Vendôme III with variable wing area. Final design 1916 observation biplane with 2 Gnomes in fuselage driving outboard propellers.

Venga (Canada). Venga Aircraft Inc. formed May 1985 at Montreal to produce TG-10 jet trainer; not flown by 1992.

Venture (Canada). Venture Flight Design Inc., Richmond Hill, Ontario, produced S1 Solarwind sport single-seater (30 June 1984).

Venture (USA). Venture Aviation produced P-51 Mustang scaled replicas until October 1984.

Vercellese (Italy). Vercellese Industrie Aeronàutiche formed 1936 at Vercelli to produce light aircraft, building over 500 FL.3 from 1937. Renamed AVIA 1939: *see* Azionari.

Vereinigte, etc.: *See* VFW.

Vereinigung (E. Germany). Vereinigung Volkseigener Betriebe Flugzeugbau, association of state-owned aircraft factories, formed 1955 to manage whole industry, aircraft manufacturing plant being VEB; occasionally abbreviated VVBF.

Verilite (USA). Verilite Aircraft Co., subsidiary of De Vore Aviation, formed October 1983 at Albuquerque, NM, to produce Model 100 Sunbird 2-seater (5 October 1987) with pusher 70-hp Emdair.

Verner (Czechoslovakia). Vlada Verner built W-01 Broucek single-seater 1970, followed by W-02 single-seat tailless canard (140-hp M 332).

Vertak (USA). Vertak Corp. produced light autogyro 1971.

Vertical Aviation: *See* VAT.

Vertidynamics (USA). Vertidynamics Corp. established March 1970 by Bruno Nagler (*see* Nagler) to continue work on VG-2 Helicogyro. Just a year later formed Nagler Aircraft Corp., but no further news.

Vertigyro (USA). Another of Bruno Nagler's companies, formed New York 1962 to produce VG-1, -2 and -4, all attempts to combine sustained hovering of helicopter with cruise mode of autogyro.

Vertol (USA). Formed March 1956 by renaming Piasecki Helicopter Corp.; no changes except in management, notably Frank Piasecki being replaced by Don R. Berlin (former chief engineer Northrop, Curtiss, Fisher and McDonnell). While in full production with H-21 and H-25/HUP, produced Model 107 (22 April 1958) reading to CH-46 Sea Knight and other versions, and Model 114 (flown as YCH-1B 28 April 1961) leading to CH-47 Chinook. Entire stock purchased by Boeing effective 31 March 1960, Vertol becoming Boeing Vertol Co. and now Boeing Helicopters Division.

Verville (USA). Alfred 'Fred' Victor Verville worked with Curtiss 1912, then designed at Army Engineering Division, producing unsuccessful aeroplane 1915. In 1918 worked with Virginius Evans Clark and Etienne Dormoy to produce

Verville 104-C Air Coach, early 1930.

VCP, Verville Clark Pursuit: outstanding performance, led to VCP-R racer (won 1920 Pulitzer) and 186-mph VCP-1. Even faster Verville-Sperry racer was fresh design. In 1925 began designing Buhl-Verville CA-3 Airster 2-seat biplane, in latter year forming **Buhl-Verville Aircraft Co.** at Detroit. Verville sold out 1927, formed **Verville Aircraft** 1928, built small numbers of Air Coach 104-C and (Packard diesel) 104-P, followed by Sportsman AT tandem biplane, 4 military trainers becoming YPT-10. In liquidation 1932.

Verwaltung der Luftfahrt-industrie (E. Germany). Interim (1955–6) organization to manage reconstituted state industry, replaced by VVBF.

Vest (Mexico). Vest Aircraft de Mexico SA, Mexico DF airport, modified DH.114 Herons with 340-hp Lycoming engines and other changes for hot/high take-offs 1959–62.

VFW (W. Germany). Vereinigte Flugtechnische Werke GmbH formed December 1963 at Bremen by merger of Focke-Wulf and Weser, other shareholders being United Aircraft, Friedrich Krupp, AG Weser and Hanseatische Beteiligungen. Continued work on Transall and F-104G, added Do 31 and Fokker F28 and produced VAK 191B jet V/STOL (10 September 1971). Later worked on own-design VFW 614 short-haul jet (14 July 1971). From 1968 acquired 100% of RFB and 50% of Henschel. With effect from 1 January 1969 VFW became equal partner with Fokker (*see* Zentralgesellschaft), VFW becoming **VFW-Fokker GmbH**. This association ended by mutual consent 11 February 1980, VFW becoming wholly owned by MBB 1 January 1981, and losing identity.

VGO: *See* Zeppelin, 2nd entry.

Viberti (Italy). Ali Viberti SpA formed 1946 at Turin by Dr Angelo Viberti to build light aircraft, starting with Musca I (1948) low-wing 2-seater. Planned successors never built.

Vickers (UK). In 1908 **Vickers Sons & Maxim Ltd**, one of giant shipbuilding, engineering and arms conglomerate's companies, built airship *Mayfly* for Admiralty, but it suffered structural failure. Built further airships, most notably R.100 designed and built 1924–30 at Howden, Yorks,

by team led by B.N. (later Sir Barnes) Wallis and N.S. Norway (later novelist Nevil Shute). In 1910 Capt. (later Major) Herbert F. Wood recommended licence for REP, and Vickers built 8 REP monoplanes 1911–12. On 28 March 1911 Wood became manager of **Vickers Ltd (Aviation Department)**, commercial and design office at Imperial Court, Basil St (near Harrods store), manufacture at existing works at Crayford, Bexley Heath and Erith, and testing at aerodrome at Joyce Green, all on SE outskirts of London. Monoplane No. 1 flew Joyce Green July 1911, original REP design being carefully altered by company designers A.R. Low, G.H. Challenger, pilot/designer Howard Flanders and pilot F. Macdonald. Late 1911 company opened flying school at Brooklands (Weybridge), where Vickers monoplanes trained 77 pilots 1912–13 and 36 in first half 1914. Own designs included EFB (experimental fighting biplane) pusher with Maxim gun in nose cockpit designed by Low/Challenger for Admiralty and exhibited Olympia February 1913. This led to numerous armed pushers, including FB.5 of which 241 supplied to front-line RFC (who nicknamed it Gunbus) plus 99 built by SA Darracq et Cie (France) and others by S/A Nielson & Winthers (Denmark), and 95 faster FB.9s, latter being first Vickers aircraft built in former Itala car factory at Brooklands (December 1915). Growing works built large numbers of BE.2 series, SE.5a and Sopwith 1½-strutter, plus over 25 different prototypes during First World War, design office moving to Crayford on outbreak of war, with former apprentice R.K. 'Rex' Pierson in charge. Little production of own designs until FB.27 twin-engined bomber flown (30 November 1917), later named Vimy and over 230 built with various engines 1918–20. This led to big-bodied Vimy Commercial (43), Vernon (55 for RAF), Victoria/Valentia (125 for RAF) and Virginia bomber (124 for RAF in 10 versions). After Armistice Pierson designed Viking amphibian (275-hp pusher RR Falcon), built in Weybridge dance-hall and towed to Brooklands, leading to 37 similar aircraft. All had Consuta hull of mahogany sewn with copper wire by S.E. Saunders, then Vickers subsidiary. Competition with Supermarine resulted in Aviation Department being elevated to status of company as **Vickers (Aviation) Ltd** August 1928, which 3 months later took over Supermarine, latter retaining its identity. B.N. Wallis used airship stressing in devising Geodetic metal-basketwork

Vickers-Armstrongs V.663 (E.4/49) Tay Viscount, 15 March 1950.

construction for aircraft, used in Wellesley bomber (19 June 1935), 176 for RAF, and in B.9/32 twin-engined bomber (15 June 1936) which, after much redesign, led to Wellington (11,461 built by October 1945, more than any other British aircraft except Spitfire and Hurricane). Wellington followed by larger Warwick (845) and 4-engined Windsor (3). Between wars company built further 43 prototypes, both it and Supermarine being taken over by parent Vickers-Armstrongs October 1938, further reorganization December 1954 resulting in **Vickers-Armstrongs (Aircraft) Ltd** being formed effective January 1955 to take over all Vickers and Supermarine aviation business. Viking airliner (22 June 1945) with 2 × 1,675-hp Hercules, 163 built, led to RAF Varsity transport and crew trainer (262) and Varsity crew trainer (160). Type 660 (18 May 1951) led to 107 Valiant bombers (4 × RR Avon), but much larger V.1000 transport was shortsightedly cancelled by RAF and BOAC November 1955. Viscount V.630 (16 July 1948) led to more capable V.700 and V.800 series, 444 built. V.950 Vanguard (20 January 1959) arrived just as turboprops appeared obsolete, only 43 built. Likewise VC10 (29 June 1962) tailored to foolish short-runway BOAC specification, so only 56 built. February 1960 Vickers became 40% shareholder in British Aircraft Corp., losing identity, in order to have half-share of TSR.2.

Victa (Australia). In 1953 Henry Millicer, of GAF Melbourne, won lightplane design competition by Royal Aero Club against 103 rival designs. Nobody showed interest in manufacture until in 1958 Pacific & Western Aviation built prototype (31 March 1959). Then non-aviation Victa Consolidated Industries undertook to build 50, also starting work on Millicer's all-metal R-2 4-seater, which remained one-off. Renamed Victa Ltd built 51 Airtourers redesigned in metal before selling out to AESL 1967.

Victor (USA). Victor Aircraft Corp. established 1916 at Freeport, Long Island, NY, but did not receive any large wartime contracts. Built 4 aircraft for designer Albert S. Heinrich, all extremely clean single-seat biplanes, 2 Scouts 1917 and 2 advanced trainers 1918.

Victory (Canada). Canadian government formed Victory Aircraft Ltd May 1942 to take over Malton (Toronto) plant of National Steel Car and accelerate production of Lancaster, producing 430 Lancaster X, 4 transport conversions and 1 York before being bought by Hawker Siddeley July 1945, becoming Avro Canada, later Avro Aircraft.

Vietnam (Vietnam). Vietnam Institute for Science and Technology, Hanoi, built 2 all-metal light aircraft C.1980, side-by-side TL-1 followed by tandem HL-1.

Viking (USA). Viking Flying Boat Co. formed 1928 at New Haven, CT, by Robert E. and brother Courtland S. Gross, mainly building

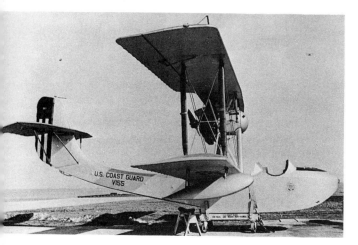

Viking (Lockheed) OO-1, modified FBA, April 1936.

FBA (Schreck) under licence. In 1932 both partners bought and ran Lockheed, but Viking continued to 1936 under their direction!

Viking (USA). Viking Aircraft Ltd, Eloy, AZ, formed late 1979 to build Dragonfly tandem-wing (or canard) sportplane (16 June 1980), over 1,800 sets of plans and 120 kits sold in 3 versions with differing landing gear.

Villiers (France). Ateliers d'Aviation François Villiers founded 1924 by previous proprietor of airline Les Grands Exprès Aériens. In 1925 leased most of Letord factory at Meudon, subsequently producing 26 types, most sesquiplanes or parasol monoplanes, 5 types for Aéronavale, including fighters with deck equipment, slats, jettisonable landing gear and flotation bags. Few sales after 1928, and when Vil.26 seaplane proved incapable of flight company collapsed 1931.

Vin-Del (USA). Vin-Del Aircraft, CA, built OR-71 Lil Quickie racer designed by Owl (6 June 1972), plans marketed.

Vinogradov (USSR). Ivan Nikolayevich Vinogradov built 3B/M Igrado 2-seat biplane January 1931 at FZU (Frunze) factory.

Vinot et Deguinard (France). Car manufacturer which after 1918 did various Government jobs, and in 1923–5 built Pescara Nos. 3 and 4 helicopters.

Vintras et Bouiller (France). At Aérodrome de Pau built VB-20 Isard 2-seat monoplane (9 August 1965). No news since 1969 of 5 aircraft of new type by Vintras, first supposed to fly 1969.

Vivian (Canada). L.R. Vivian Associates, Toronto, hope to build Helitruck-derived heavy-lift aircraft with helium-filled body and 4 tilting rotors.

VLI (E. Germany). To manage reborn aircraft industry in E. Germany (DDR), state organization created 1954 called Volkseigene der Luftfahrtindustrie, made up of VEBs, controlled by VVBF.

Vliôm (S. Africa). Vliôm Development, Randburg 2125, worked on unique VTOL with trike unit suspended from shrouded lift/cruise proprotor 1967–75.

VMZ (Bulgaria). Based at Sopot 1926–66 to produce mostly light aircraft and gliders. In 1983 set up Aviatsionna Tehnika, or Aviatechnica (which *see*).

Voisin (France). Gabriel Voisin, assisted by brother Charles, built kites from about 1895, using Hargrave-type boxkite configuration. Built gliders for their use and for sale from 1904, assisted by Ernest Archdeacon and Louis Blériot, forming what must be considered world's first aeroplane manufacturing company July 1905 as **Ateliers d'Aviation Edouard Surcouf, Blériot et Voisin** at Rue de la Ferme, Billancourt (Paris). Gabriel and Charles formed a more definite manufacturing firm at same location, **Appareils d'Aviation Les Frères Voisin**, on 5 November 1906. First aeroplane, Blériot III seaplane, failed to take off from Lac d'Enghien May 1906, and no successful machine until Delagrange I (aircraft were named for customers) made hops at Bagatelle from 16 March 1907. First good aircraft Farman I, tested at Issy from 30 September 1907. On 28 February 1908 obtained from Wilbur licence to build Wright Flyers in France. Reluctantly Voisin Frères removed forward elevator and added ailerons, and by time Charles killed September 1912 company—renamed **Aéroplanes G. Voisin**—had sold over 300 aircraft, about 100 more than Blériot. During First World War company delivered approximately 10,000 aircraft, almost all being pusher biplanes with 2 front and 2 rear wheels, 4 ailerons and cruciform tail, and robust airframe largely of steel. Few departures from same layout included large BN4, night bomber biplane with 4 × push/pull 300-hp Hispano, 1920. This was last aircraft built, Gabriel then turning attention to cars.

Vojenská (Czechoslovakia). Vojenská Tovarna na Letadla better known as Letov.

Volaircraft (USA). Formed 1958 at Aliquippa, PA, to produce Model 10 all-metal high-wing 4-seater, developed 1963–4 into Models 1035 and more powerful 1050. Bought by Rockwell-Standard 1965; 1050 continued as Aero Commander 100.

Volkseigener: *See* VEB.

Volmer (USA). Glider designer Volmer Jensen took over moribund Jarvis J-22 Jaybird 2-seat amphibian (85-hp pusher Continental) 1947, forming Volmer Aircraft at Glendale, LA, about same time; finally flew 22 December 1958, later moved to nearby Burbank, over 900 sets plans sold and C.120 VJ-22 Sportsman flying, almost unchanged from wartime Jarvis design.

Volpar (USA). Volpar Inc. formed 1960 at Pacoima, California, to market tricycle-gear kit for Beech 18, company owned by Volitan and Paragon. Moved Van Nuys and greatly expanded, over 30 major mod. programmes, latest being T-33 upgraded and re-engined as T-33V jet trainer and Falcon PW300-F20 Falcon 20 bizjet with PW305 engines plus reversers. In 1990 company acquired by Gaylord Holding (Switzerland).

Vos: *See* Helicopter Manufacturing.

Voisin-Farman I bis (3rd wing added), November 1908.

Vought (USA). Whole story here for convenience, despite major name changes. Chance (christened Chauncy) Milton Vought born 1890, learned to fly 1910 and qualified engineer (U. of Pennsylvania), fast and profane talker noted for instant decisions. Several important design appointments, including Wright-Martin chief engineer, before forming **The Lewis & Vought Corp.** June 1917 with father-in-law Birdseye B. Lewis. Began building VE-7 biplane trainer in 3rd floor of stocking factory at Long Island City, lowering parts by pulley-block from window for assembly in street, tethering to telephone pole for engine test. Despite circumstances 128 built, some by NAF. In 1922 Lewis retired, company becoming **Chance Vought Corp.**, father president, mother secretary/treasurer and Chance chief engineer. Outstanding success attended VE-7-derived VE-7SF fighter (64), UO-1 observation (141) and

Chance Vought F7U-3 Cutlass (128472), 1952.

FU-1 fighter (20). In 1925 F.B. Rentschler visited now properly laid-out plant to seek Vought's opinion on resigning as CEO of Wright in order to start Pratt & Whitney. Vought's reply: 'You're blasted right, things are in a helluva shape and getting no better fast'; but it was his promise of selection of the proposed Wasp to power the future Corsair that launched P&W. Corsair was another smash hit, 291 of O2U versions (from 11 October 1926) being followed by 289 O3Us. Such a firm looked attractive in an era of snapped-up conglomerates, and in 1929 Vought became division of United Aircraft & Transport; in fact prime instigators of UA&T were Vought, Rentschler and Boeing. First two moved 1930 into giant new plants at East Hartford, Connecticut, but on July 26 that year over-worked Vought died of blood poisoning. Rex Beisel became chief engineer, producing newer Corsairs, 140 SBU scout bombers, 245 SB2U Vindicator/Chesapeake dive-bombers, and 1,628 OS2U Kingfishers, mostly seaplanes. On 1 April 1939 Vought merged with Sikorsky to form **Vought-Sikorsky Division of United Aircraft** and occupy new plant at Stratford, where were built most Kingfishers. Beisel brought with him drawings of V-166 XF4U-1 Corsair carrier-based fighter with 2,000-hp P&W R-2800 (29 May 1940), 12,571 built by December 1952. At end 1942 unloved union with Sikorsky ended, company resuming previous title, building XF5U 'flying saucer' and F6U Pirate jet fighters. In 1948 division asked by Navy to move from Connecticut to Navy plant at Dallas, Texas, previously occupied by North American. Under new general manager Fred O. Detweiler company ceased to be division and was once more incorporated, as **Chance Vought Aircraft Inc.**, producing Regulus cruise missile, F7U Cutlass and F8U (F-8) Crusader jet fighters. Crusader exceeded Mach 1 on 1st flight (25 March 1955) and 1,259 built by 1965. Reflecting growing diversity, company became **Chance Vought Corp.** 31 December 1960, but 31 August 1961 merged with Ling-Temco Electronics to form LTV, **Ling-Temco-Vought**, Dallas plant becoming **LTV Aerospace Division**. In 1964 won VAX Navy attack competition with A-7 Corsair II (27 September 1965), building 1,545 by 1983. LTV aerospace/defence became subsidiary of LTV Corp. until 1 January 1976 when Dallas plant became **Vought Corp**. This endured until 29 September 1986 when it was renamed **LTV Aerospace and Defense Co.** with 2 divisions:

Vought Aero Products and, at Grand Prairie, TX, Vought Missiles and Advanced Programs. In 1990 these divisions renamed LTV rather than Vought, parent being unaltered. **LTV Aircraft Products Group** has A-7 update programmes and makes large portions of B-2, 747, 757, 767, C-17, Challenger and Regional Jet. Another division, Sierra Research, has major upgrade programmes on T-38, F-5, C-29A (BAe 125) and other aircraft. On 31 August 1992 sale completed to the Carlyle Group and Northrop, emerging as **Vought Aircraft Co**. Major programmes as before plus Panther 800, T800-engined Eurocopter EC565, and promoting FMA Pampa 2000 for USAF JPATS requirement.

Voyager (USA). Voyager Aircraft Inc. formed March 1981 by Dick Rutan and Jeana Yeager at Mojave Airport, CA, to produce aeroplane to fly non-stop round world near equator. Designed by Bert Rutan and built at Rutan Aircraft Factory, Voyager flew 22 June 1984 and flew round world 14–23 December 1986, 26,678 miles (42,925 km), 975 Imp. gal.

V.P. Chkalov (Uzbekistan). Name of famous pilot (killed 1938) chosen for production association managing Il-114 plant at Tashkent.

VT (USSR). Literally 'internal prison', Stalin's system of putting designers behind bars 1929–43, initially GAZ-43 Hangar 7, later Lubyanka and Butyrkii prisons and camps.

VTI (Jugoslavia, Serbia). Vazduhoplovno Tehnicki Institut, Zarkovo, near Belgrade, provided about half design engineers for Jurom Orao/IAR-93: see SOKO/Avioane.

VTOL (Australia). VTOL Aircraft Pty Ltd formed 1971 by D.A. Phillips to produce Phillicopter Mk 1 2-seat helicopter, flown 1971: see Veetol.

VTOL (Australia). VTOL Industries Australia Ltd (unrelated to previous) formed at Perth by Kim V. Sadlier to develop radical Air Bearing Fan vertical lift commuter aircraft 1990.

Vuia (Romania). Nationality of location a problem, as Trajan Vuia was Doctor of Law (Budapest, Hungary) and lived in Paris. Pioneer of flight, built unsuccessful tractor monoplane 1906, improved 1907.

Vultee V-1A, 19 February 1933.

Vulcan (UK). Vulcan Motor & Engineering Co. (1906) Ltd, Crossens, Southport, Lancs, built B.E.2c/d/e, D.H.4, D.H.9 and 9A in First World War.

Vulcan (USA). Vulcan Aircraft Co. incorporated 1928 at Portsmouth, Ohio, to produce American Moth 2-seat parasol monoplane.

Vulcan (USA). Vulcan Aircraft Corp. formed about 1985 to develop V2000 Starfire 6-seat fan-in-wing V/STOL business aircraft, hope to fly prototype early 1990s.

Vultee (USA). Jerry (Gerard) Vultee designed major parts of Lockheed Vega, Air Express, Sirius and Orion. When Lockheed-Detroit failed Vultee formed Airplane Development Corp. (*see* Airplane) January 1932, producing advanced stressed-skin cantilever monoplanes: assisted by Cord ($50,000), whose American Airlines was sponsor, built high-speed 8-passenger V-1 (19 February 1933), followed by V-11 attack bomber (June 1935), many versions; and in 1936 in giant new plant at Downey (LA) Vultee planned family of aircraft with common parts. Not many V-48 Vanguard fighters, but 11,537 Valiant trainers, Army BT-13 or -15. On move to Downey became **Vultee Aircraft Division of Avco**, and after Vultee's death (age 38 in crash of a Stinson in 1938) **Vultee Aircraft Inc.**, still division of Avco, in 1940 taking over Stinson whose Nashville plant was vastly expanded to produce Vultee Vengeance dive-bomber. In December 1941, just after Pearl Harbor, Vultee bought 34% controlling interest in Consolidated, with which it merged March 1943 to form Consolidated-Vultee Aircraft, later called Convair.

VVBF: *See* Vereinigung.

Vyzkumny a Zkusebni Letecky Ustav (Czechoslovakia). National aeronautical R&D institute founded 1922, major role in design programmes under general direction of Aero Vodochody.

VZLU: *See* preceding entry.

WAACO: *See* West Australian Aircraft Co.

Wackett (Australia). No company of this name, though W./Cdr. L.J. Wackett, previously CO of RAAF Experimental Station, Randwick, directed Codock, designed for Tugan and became Gen. Mgr. and designer of CAC.

Waco (USA). In October 1919 George 'Buck' Weaver and 6 others registered **Weaver Aircraft Co.** at Loraine, Ohio. Began to market Weaver Cootie 2-seat parasol monoplane, but quickly switched to Waco as initials of company. In 1923 reorganized as **Advance Aircraft Co.** at Troy, Ohio, with different management, to build Waco 7, 9 and Ten 3-seat biplanes (choice 85–220 hp), claiming 1928 'production greater than all other US commercial airplane manufacturers combined'. In 1929 renamed as **The Waco Aircraft Co.**, concentrating on biplanes in 2- to 5-seat class, using 3-letter codes to identify what by 1940 exceeded 110 different models. In 1935 still largest US producer, with 55 distributors and 175 dealers in USA and representatives in 26 countries, exports being over 40% of total. Chief families open

Waco Aristocraft (pusher 215-hp Franklin), March 1947.

tandem 2-seat aerobatic trainers and 4-seat cabin tourers, latter introducing models with nosewheel from late 1938. From December 1941 Waco cabin biplanes of 16 types impressed with designation UC-72 to UC-72Q, while company designed CG-3A training glider and CG-4A, CG-13A and CG-15A transport gliders. Waco built 1,075 of total 12,394 CG-4A and 427 CG-15A (one with 2 Jacobs R-755). In 1946 developed Aristocraft cabin monoplane, but liquidation followed 1947. Aristocraft passed to O'Neill.

Waco (USA). Unrelated to foregoing, merely having bought name, Waco Aircraft Co., subsidiary of Allied Aero Industries, formed San Antonio, TX, 1966, to market and produce under licence European aircraft. Works at Pottstown, PA, produced S220 Vela II (SIAI-Marchetti S.205) and TS250-5 Taurus (turbocharged version), and Meteor (SF.260). Marketed M220-4 Minerva (modified Socata Rallye Commodore) and planned production of T-2 Meteorite (SA.202). Company failed 1971.

Wag-Aero (USA). At Wisconsin, kits/plans for range of Sport Trainer high-wing side-by-side cabin aircraft (65–150 hp), Wag-a-Bond with convertible interior and 2 + 2 Sportsman multirole 4-seater.

Wagener (Germany). Hans Wagener formed Wagener Flugzeugbau, Hamburg, 1930, producing HW 3 and HW 4 parasol ultralights with DKW and Schliha 2-stroke engines.

Wagner (W. Germany). Having studied and tested ideas for torque-free helicopter, Josef Wagner formed Wagner Helicopter-Technik, Friedrichshafen, 1961. Early helicopters had coaxial rotors driven respectively by crankshaft and crankcase of engine. Later versions, called Sky-Trac, had conventional drive. Intended production vehicle, roadable 4-wheel, 4-seat Aerocar, completed 1968 but got no further.

Waitomo (NZ). Waitomo Aircraft Ltd formed at Te Kuiti by renaming Bennett Aviation. In 1968 rights to Airtruk acquired by Transavia.

Wallace (USA). Wallace Aircraft Co. formed Chicago 1927 to produce C-2 Touroplane high-wing 3-seater (choice 85–200 hp). Bought out 1929 by American Eagle.

Wallerkowski (W. Germany). Airline Capt. Heinz Wallerkowski, Munich, produced Hornisse sport single-seater (30 June 1978).

Wallis (UK). Wallis Autogyros Ltd formed at Cambridge, moving to Reymerston Hall, Norfolk, by W. Cdr. Ken Wallis 1959. First autogyro (August 1961) developed many patented features. Subsequently autogyros of several basic designs with 16 types of engine installation and wide variety of special mission equipment. Development only, no production.

Wallis (USA). Stanley B. Wallis produced light aircraft 1981.

Walraven (Netherlands E. Indies). Appointed chief engineer of NEI air force 1922, L.W. Walraven built 4 aircraft in spare time, forming Walraven & Co. 1933. Three of 4 used 1 or 2 Pobjoy engines.

Waltz (Mexico). Marketing of Vest Super Heron done by proprietor Francisco J. Waltz.

WAR (USA). War Aircraft Replicas, CA, marketed plans/kits for half-scale F4U, Sea Fury, Fw 190, P-47 and A6M, until president killed February 1989 in prototype WAR P-51.

Waring & Gillow (UK). Furniture maker of Cambridge Rd, London W6, built D.H.9 and assembled US-built O/400, 1918.

Warner (USA). Richard Warner Aviation Inc., Covington, Louisiana, bought all rights to Anderson EA-1 Kingfisher and W-1 Super Kingfisher amphibians.

Warwick (USA). William Warwick, Torrance, CA, produced Tiny Champ sport cabin monoplane (1 May 1960).

Wassmer (France). Société des Etablissements Benjamin Wassmer founded 1905, began aircraft production at Issoire 1945 building Jodel under licence. Developed De Luxe Jodel-Wassmer D.120 Paris-Nice, followed with WA-40 Super IV (or Sancy) 4-seat low-wing (8 June 1959), developed with fixed gear as WA-41 Baladou, glassfibre WA-50 (1966) and fixed-gear WA-51 Pacific, WA-52 Europa and WA-54 Atlantic. Final design WA-80 Piranha side-by-side trainer. With Siren formed CERVA. In liquidation 1977.

Watanabe (Japan). K.K. Watanabe Tekkosho (Watanabe Ironworks Co. Ltd) built aircraft parts from 1926 and complete aircraft, designed by others, from 1931. Major contribution to A5M, E14Y, K9W/Ki-86 and K10W. Own designs E9W submarine-based recon seaplane, WS-103S recon seaplane, and K6W and K8W trainer seaplanes. Designed K11W crew trainer and Q1W Tokai ASW aircraft but, before these were in full production, changed name to Kyushu Hikoki KK early 1943.

Waterhouse (USA). Waterhouse Aircraft Inc. formed by William Waterhouse and Lloyd Royer at Glendale, LA, 1928, building Romair biplane with 2 open cockpits, followed by Cruzair 3-seat monoplane.

Waterman (USA). In 1919 Waldo Waterman established W.D. Waterman Aircraft Manufacturing Co., Venice, LA, to design and build Gosling for Mercury. Waterman became designer/pilot for Bach, then manager Van Nuys Airport, finally starting Waterman Airplane

Corp., Santa Monica, LA, 1935, to produce simple tailless 2-seat monoplane; developed this into Arrowbile roadable aircraft with detachable swept wings and Studebaker belt-drive to propeller or 4 wheels. Moved to San Diego where in 1968 produced W-11 Chevy Bird ultra-simple single-seater with 140-hp Corvair engine.

Watkins (USA). Watkins Airplane Co., Wichita, produced small series of Skylark low-wing 2-seater with 60-hp Le Blond engine from 1930.

Watkinson (UK). C.T. Watkinson and C.W. Taylor built Dingbat ultralight monoplane at Teddington (June 1938).

Watson (USA). Gary Watson formed Watson Windwagon Co., Newcastle, TX, to market kits/plans of simple all-metal GW-1 Windwagon ultralight (19 April 1977).

Weatherley (USA). John C. Weatherley formed Weatherley Aviation Co., Hollister, CA, where 1961–5 produced WM-62C ag-conversion of Fairchild M-62 followed by improved W-201 family: see next entry.

Weatherley-Campbell (USA). Raymond Weatherley and William Campbell formed company pre-1946 at Dallas, TX, producing Colt high-wing 4-seater designed by Luscombe.

Weaver: See Waco, 1st entry.

Weber (Brazil). Willibald Weber built light aircraft 1982.

Wedell-Williams (USA). James Wedell was principal of Wedell-Williams Air Service Corp., Patterson, Louisiana, fixed-base operator. Built succession of low-wing braced monoplane racers 1928–33, notably 1930 Cirrus Racer, NR-54Y (Wasp) for Roscoe Turner 1932 and 2 Model 44 (Menasco) 1933. Leaped to fame with 3 monoplanes (supercharged P&W Wasp Junior) which won 1932 Bendix and set coast-to-coast records. Wedell himself set world landplane record (305 mph/491 km/h) September 1933. Many more wins and records with larger engines, but Wedell killed 1934 instructing in trainer, and racer-derived XP-34 fighter cancelled 1936 before completion.

Weedhopper (USA). Really micros, but classic

Wedell-Williams (Col. Roscoe Turner), January 1933.

design (reminiscent of 1907 Demoiselle) was 23rd by John F. Chotia; formed Weedhopper of Utah 1978–85, over 600 kits supplied, assets taken over by Weedhopper Inc., Clinton, Mississippi.

Weeks (USA). Kermit Weeks built light sporting aircraft 1981.

Wefel (USA). Ralph M. Wefel built modified HM-360 (Mignet Pou) 1963.

Weick (USA). F. Weick did not form company but took out several patents for foolproof aeroplane unable to stall/spin. In 1933 built W-1, modified 1935 as W-1A, high-wing twin-boom 2-seat, pusher Pobjoy, special flaps and aileron slots, rudders not used in normal flying. Patents transferred to Erco.

Weir (UK). G. & J. Weir, Cathcart, Glasgow, built B.E.2c, D.H.9 and F.E.2b 1915–18. In 1932–36 built W.1 to W.4 direct-control autogyros.

Weiser (Austria). A. Weiser und Sohn, Vienna 19, built small numbers of 3 types of Ö-UF Aviatik 1916–17.

Weiss (UK). UK by choice, Alsatian by birth, José Weiss was famed landscape artist and much-loved aviator; sought stable glider from 1900, pioneered thick aerofoil profiles (esp. 1905 glider), from 1910 built aeroplanes, assisted by Dr Alex Keith, Gerald Leak and pilot E.C. Gordon England (who set pre-1914 soaring record in Weiss glider); designed early Handley Pages.

Weiss, Manfréd (Hungary). Probably largest industrial group in country, Manfréd Weiss formed aviation subsidiary Weiss, Manfréd Flugzeug und Motorenfabrik AG 1928. Bought licences for Fokker C.V and F.VIII for clandestine LüH, plus 80 examples in 5 versions of Hungária (Udet U.12 Flamingo). WM's own Sport III 4-cylinder 136-hp engine powered later WM-10 and -13 2-seat biplanes. C.V. developed into WM-16A Budapest (550-hp GR Jupiter, for which WM had licence), but 16B had 860-hp GR K14 Mistral Major. This modified 1938 into WM-21 Sólyom multirole biplane, 25 built by WM, 43 by Mavag and 60 by MWG.

Welch (USA). Orin Welch built training biplanes (about 10) for his W. Virginia flying school 1927–30. Then moved to South Bend, Indiana, to produce simplest 2-seater; result, about 65 OW high-wing cabin monoplanes with Continental, Aeronca or Welch's own 45-hp engine.

Wells (UK). Wells Aviation Co. was small firm at Chelsea, London (30 Whitehead's Grove, later 10a Elystan St), built D.H.9, Sopwith 1½-strutter and company's own Reo single-seater (35-hp Green), all 1916–17.

Wells (USA). Eugene W. Wells, Hawaii, built Shama 'WW1' 2-seat biplane (August 1983).

Welsh (USA). George T. Welsh, Long Beach, built small run of Model A Welsh Rabbit (12 November 1965) high-wing cabin single-seater, followed by Model B 2-seat version with nose-wheel instead of tailwheel.

Wendt (USA). Wendt Aircraft Corp. registered January 1939 in New York to build W-2 Swift high-wing 2-seater (90-hp Le Blond or Warner Scarab Junior), radial often retrofitted.

Wendt (USA). Wendt Aircraft Engineering, La Mesa, CA, produced WH-1 Traveler low-wing tandem 2-seat cabin monoplane (15 March 1972); 70 sets of plans sold by 1980.

Werft Warnemünde (Germany). Werft Warnemünde des Flugzeugbau Friedrichshafen formed February 1917 as subsidiary of Friedrichshafen, building almost entirely marine aircraft including single- and twin-engined biplane and monoplane seaplanes. Dormant 1918, bought 1921 by Hugo Stinnes who produced boats, ice yachts and furniture, waiting for market to appear for aircraft. Hired designer Walter Rethel 1924 (in same year formed Ikarus as subsidiary), and began aircraft production 1925 renamed Arado, which *see*.

Werkspoor (Netherlands). Railway and diesel giant built 1 aircraft, Jumbo freighter, 480-hp GR9 (Jupiter), 1929.

Weser (Germany). 'Weser' Flugzeugbau Gesellschaft formed April 1934 by Deutsche Schiff- und Maschinenbau AG, Bremen, soon taking over Rohrbach, occupying Berlin factory and appointing Dr Rohrbach chief designer. Added second factory in Bremen 1935, and in Second World War produced almost all Ju 87 output in oval outer ring at Berlin-Tempelhof, plus (at Einswarden and Nordenham, Bremen), Do 18, He 60, He 114, He 115, Ju 52/3m and Ju 388L, plus numerous prototypes. Altogether 10 factories.

Weserflug (W. Germany). Original company resurrected 1956 as Finanz-und-Verwaltungs Gesellschaft 'Weser' GmbH, but renamed 'Weser' Flugzeugbau GmbH early 1957, controlling interest bought by United Aircraft resulting in link with Sikorsky (e.g. assisted S-60). Surveyed 10 wartime plants and restored Lemwerder, Einswarden and Varel. With Hamburger and Siebelwerke built Nord 2501. Handled readiness of 390 F/RF-84F and subsequent support. Major partner in Transall. Lost identity December 1963 on merger with Focke-Wulf to form VFW.

Wesley (USA). Joseph K. Wesley, Somerset, KY, built 15ft-span Special sport biplane (25 November 1957).

West Australian Aircraft Co. (Australia). Produced WAACO Staggerbipe backstaggered single-seat cabin biplane (November 1985).

Westermayer (Austria). Oskar Westermayer, A-2161 Poysbrunn, produced 4 single-seat rotorcraft, basically autogyros but WE 04 with helicopter-type cyclic/collective pitch, 1969–80. More recently produced Continental engine with liquid-cooled heads.

Western (Canada). Western Aircraft Supplies, Calgary, produced PGK-1 Hirondelle side-by-side low-wing cabin monoplane (27 June 1976).

Western (USA). Western Aircraft Corp., San Antonio, TX, produced Westair 204 high-speed 4-seater (November 1982), kits marketed.

Western (USA). Western Airplane Corp. formed at Chicago 1929 to build yet another 3-seat biplane with OX-5 engine.

Western Australian Airways (Australia). Formed 1921, like QANTAS and Larkin built D.H.50A under licence (3).

Western Wings (USA). Oregon company which since 1986 has marketed Hawk, modified from McDD 500D helicopters.

Westfall (USA). Miles Westfall produced light aircraft 1977.

Westland (UK). From mid-19th century John B. Petter produced ag-implements at Yeovil, where in 1895 2 of his sons produced first British motor car. Its oil engine was developed for production, becoming staple product of Petters Ltd, formed 7 July 1910. On outbreak of war Petters mass-produced these engines and electric generating plant to War Office, but grave situation in 1915 caused telegrams to be sent to War Office and Admiralty offering to make whatever might be required. Admiralty immediately said, 'We will send the drawings, get on with it.' To west of Yeovil was Westland Farm, where on 3 April 1915 chairman Ernest Petter opened door of tiny hut and said, 'This is the **Westland Aircraft Works**.' No new company formed, but quickly built factory and, under Robert A. Bruce, set up design organization. Built 808 aircraft before Armistice, mainly Short 166, Short 184, Sopwith $1\frac{1}{2}$-strutter, D.H.4/9 and 9A (Westland-designed), and Vickers Vimy. Bruce designed numerous aircraft from 1916, but no significant production apart from 36 Walrus naval biplanes (1920) until Wapiti multirole replacement for D.H.9A using 9A parts (March 1927), of which 517 built for RAF and 32 for export. Ten Wessex transports (3 × 140-hp) were followed by 68 conversions of Wapiti to Wallace I and 104 new Wallace II. Bruce had been succeeded by Arthur Davenport as chief designer, but what had been Westland Aircraft Works (Petters Ltd) was at last put on proper basis 4 July 1935 as **Westland Aircraft Ltd.** W.E.W. Petter became technical director (later famed for Canberra, Lightning and Gnat). First aircraft designed by Davenport's team under his direction was Lysander STOL army-coop monoplane (15 June 1936), 1,449 built by Westland and 225 by National Steel Car in Canada. Bulk of share capital bought July 1938 by John Brown shipbuilding group; rest later bought by AEI electrical group, but company not interfered with. Final fixed-wing designs Whirlwind twin-engine fighter (112), Welkin high-altitude fighter (84) and Wyvern carrier-based torpedo fighter (4,400-hp AS Python turboprop), total 103 plus 16 prototypes with 3,500-hp piston engine. Sikorsky licence 1947 led to WS-51/Dragonfly/Widgeon, WS-55/Whirlwind, WS-58/Wessex (most Whirlwind and all Wessex with turbine power), WS-61/Sea King/Commando, all produced in large numbers. In 1959 took over Saunders-Roe, adding Fairey Aviation and Bristol Helicopter Division 1960, cancelling Rotodyne but developing Gannet AEW.3, Belvedere and Scout/Wasp. Formed British Hovercraft Corp., and from 1965 produced Sioux (Agusta-Bell 47G2) under licence.

All helicopter business managed from May 1966 by wholly-owned **Westland Helicopters Ltd**. Agreement between UK/France 1967 led to joint production of Aerospatiale Gazelle and Puma (latter initially at former Fairey works at Hayes) and new-design Lynx (21 March 1971). Equal partner with Agusta in EHI; much-publicized financial battle February 1986 resulted in significant shares to United Technologies (resulting in market drive to sell S-70 Black Hawk) and GKN. Minor parts produced for Boeing, Airbus and McDonnell Douglas, and cowlings for Dash-8 and Do 328. Licence for Apache Longbow of June 1989 not yet taken up (1992).

Westphal (Germany). Westphalische Flugzeug-werke produced original design of Taube-type monoplane 1912, 4-inline engine.

West Virginia (USA). West Virginia Aircraft Co. formed at Wheeling 1919, produced at least 3 C-3 3-seat triplanes (150-hp Wright-Hispano).

Westwind (UK). Westwind Corp. Ltd, Edgware, Middlesex, produce Phoenix canard ultralight, with 50 hp for 'working' uses.

Wewyne (Lithuania). Built outstanding side-by-side high-wing cabin monoplane 1989.

Weymann (France). Charles Weymann built 2 biplanes 1916–18, one having all-metal wings. Formed Soc. Weymann Le Père 1929, equal partnership with Georges Le Père (see Engineering Division; Packard Lepère), taking

Westland Wyvern W.35 with RR Clyde turboprop, 18 January 1949.

over Avimeta premises at Courbevoie (Paris), building handful of light aircraft and at least 2 autogyros (Cierva licence). Le Père left 1930, little further activity.

WFI (USA). World Flight Inc., Cleveland, Ohio, formed by James Bede to develop BD-2 Love One (*see* Javelin) and attempt round-world non-stop.

W-F-W (USA). Registered in Los Angeles 1926, built at least 2 'Thunderbird, wings of the wind', yet another type of 3-seat open biplane.

Whatley (USA). Vascoe Whatley Jr., S. Carolina, built Special single-seat open biplane based on Gere Sport (23 June 1981).

WHE (UK). W.H. Ekin (Engineering) Co. Ltd, Aberdeen, formed March 1969 to produce 6 McCandless Mk IV autogyros, developed into Airbuggy with many changes (1 February 1973).

Wheeler (UK). Slymph single-seat monoplane built by Allen Wheeler at RAF Hinaidi, Iraq, 1931; preserved by Shuttleworth.

Wheeler (USA). Ken Wheeler formed Wheeler Aircraft Co. to build Express high-speed 4-seater, even prototype built from kit of pre-moulded parts (28 July 1987). Company restructured as Wheeler Technology Inc., Washington, marketing kits of enlarged CAD-designed production version (May 1990).

Whipporwill: *See* Laird, 2nd entry.

Whitacre (USA). Arthur G. Whitacre built sporting aircraft 1965.

Whitcraft (USA). Whitcraft Corp. produced light aircraft 1974.

White (USA). White Aircraft Co. formed by Burd S. and Harold L. White, Des Moines, Iowa, 1917, engaged in subcontract and repair, but produced Humming Bird 2/3-seat biplane 1926.

White (USA). White Aircraft Inc. formed 1939 at Buffalo, NY, by Donald G. White to produce modified (ex-Argonaut) Pirate.

White (USA). E. Marshall White, Huntington Beach, CA, produced Der Jäger single-seat sport biplane (7 September 1969), 100 + flying.

White (USA). William T. White, Dallas, TX, built Longhorn low-wing single-seater (June 1967).

White & Thompson: *See* Norman Thompson.

Whitehead (UK). Whitehead Aircraft Co., Old Drill Hall, Townshend Rd, Richmond, Surrey, built substantial numbers of B.E.2a, D.H.4 and Sopwith Pup, 1915–17. Also prototype Whitehead Scout single-seater 1916.

White, J. Samuel (UK). John Samuel White was flourishing boatbuilder at East Cowes, Isle of Wight, who on 1 January 1913 opened Aviation Department. All own-design aircraft called Wight, not only for location but also for company name and that of designer, Howard T. Wright. Pusher seaplane exhibited February 1913, at least 13 built, 11 for RNAS. Admiralty Type 840 seaplane, 2 only, but giant Wight Twin, 3; Trainer seaplane, 2; Baby, 3; landplane Bomber, 1; but Converted Seaplane (conversion of Bomber), 50. Firm also built AD.1000 seaplane and 110 Short 184 seaplanes.

White Lightning (USA). White Lightning Aircraft Corp. formed S. Carolina to produce high-speed 4-seater of that name (8 March 1986); despite graphite/glassfibre structure 39 aircraft and 32 kits by January 1992.

Whittlesey (USA). Whittlesey Manufacturing Co. formed August 1929 at Bridgeport, Connecticut, to build Avro Avian, but only C.12 before Depression.

WHL: Westland Helicopters Ltd: *see* Westland.

Wibault (France). When crippled Michel Wibault's home city of Lille was occupied 1914 he was permitted to stay, and passed time by building a wind tunnel and testing models. In 1917 he managed to cross front lines into French-held territory. Produced Wib.1 C1 fighter, 220-hp HS8b (8 November 1918), outstanding, but war over. Formed **Société des Avions Michel Wibault** at Billancourt (Paris) late 1919, produced succession of prototypes, at first all fighters, bombers or recon, all parasol monoplanes with totally Duralumin construction. A few were produced in series, notably Wib.72 (60 for Armée de l'Air 1928, plus 26 for Chile made by Vickers, and 25 built by PZL), and 18 Wib.74 and 18 Wib.75 for

Wibault-Penhoët 282 Le Diligent, *January 1933.*

Aéronavale. Penhoët (Chantiers St Nazaire) shipyard funded Wibault-Penhoët 280 low-wing transport (November 1930). In 1931 merged company registered as **Chantiers Aéronautiques Wibault-Penhoët**, producing derived Wib.281, 282 and 283 for Air Union and Air France. Small numbers made of Wib.360–367 as transports and racing aircraft, but 1934 Wibault-Penhoët taken over by Breguet, who built several Wibault projected designs. In 1956 Wibault was living retired in Paris as protégé of Winthrop Rockefeller, who funded small project studies. One, Le Gyroptère, was for 4 fans driven by a turboshaft engine to give vectored thrust for VTOL. Via Mutual Defense Aid Program it reached Bristol where, completely recast as neat single engine, it resulted in Pegasus and Harrier.

Wideröe's (Norway). Viggo Wideröe formed Wideröe's Flyveselskap og Polarfly A/S in Oslo 1933, first flying company in country. Built C.5 Polar utility seaplane (1948) designed by Birger Hönningstad, tough, versatile, several built.

Wiener Karrosserie-Fabrik: *See* WKF.

Wiener-Neustädter (Austria). Named for city which, despite name, is 40 miles south of Vienna, Wiener-Neustädter Flughafen Betriebs GmbH formed 1933 to run airport and provide services. Produced series of sport and light commercial aircraft, ending 1936 WN.16 twin-boom 2-seat pusher. After German takeover 1938 merged forcibly with Hirtenberg, renamed Wiener-Neustädter-Flugzeugwerke GmbH and vast new plant built specifically to mass-produce Bf 109.

Also built Doblhoff prototypes, hence WNF designations.

Wigal (USA). Fritz Wigal, Jackson, Tennessee, built autogyro with tractor propeller which, hinged to blow on main rotor, spun latter up to speed.

Wight: *See* White, J. Samuel.

Wikner (Australia). Geoffrey Wikner formed Wikner Aircraft 1929, rebuilding and improving Avians and other types and building prototype Lion and Wizard light monoplanes. Came to UK 1934: *see* Foster Wikner.

Wilden (W. Germany). Ing. Helmut Wilden built VoWi 8 and 10 light aircraft 1974–7.

Wiley Post (USA). Fabulous one-eyed aviator merely lent his name to the Wiley Post Aircraft Corp., formed 1935 at Oklahoma City to produce simple 2-seat biplane (designed and prototype built by Straughan) with 40-hp Ford A car engine. About 13 built.

Williams (UK). David Williams, designer of IML Addax, returned to UK to promote advanced devices 1985.

Williams (UK). Boatbuilder H. Williams, Littlehampton, built fuselages/hulls of various White & Thompson and Norman Thompson aircraft.

Williams (USA). Arthur L. Williams produced

W-17 Stinger Formula racer 1971, and with Carl Cangie WC-1 Sundancer racing biplane 1973, both very successful.

Williams (USA). Williams Aircraft Design Co. announced light aircraft 1976.

Williams (USA). Bob Williams built sporting aircraft 1973.

Williams (USA). George W. Williams credited with light monoplane 1908, formed Texas Aero Manufacturing Co. at Temple, TX, 1911, reorganized about 1920 as George Williams Airplane and Mfg Co., produced several Texas Temple single- or 3-seat parasol monoplanes 1926–9. Company renamed 1927 Texas Aero Corp.

Williams (USA). Williams Research, mass-producer of small turbojet and turbofan engines, built Bell-developed Jet Flying Belt and other personal lift devices, including Wasp (Williams Aerial Systems Platform) flying 2 men on single WR19 turbofan. Changed name to **Williams International** and proposed V-Jet small bizjet 1985 and X-Jet one-man VTOL 1986. Teamed with Rolls-Royce on bizjet engines.

Willoughby Delta (UK). Willoughby Delta Co., Witney, Oxon, built F experimental twin-boom 2-seater (2 × Menasco) early 1939.

Wilson (USA). Wilson Aero Products produced light aircraft 1968.

Wind Dancer (USA). Proof of concept autogyro, Santa Fe, NM, 1988.

Windecker (USA). Windecker Research, later Windecker Industries, Midland, TX, held Dow Chemical licence for glassfibre high-speed 4-seater developed by Drs L.J. and F.M. Windecker (7 October 1967), leading to production AC-7 Eagle (26 January 1969), also building for USAF 1 YE-5 as very first 'stealth' research aircraft.

Windryder (USA). Windryder Engineering, Colorado, produced Hurricane autogyro (August 1985), available with various options.

Windstar (USA). Built light sporting aircraft 1978.

Wing (USA). Design of Derringer fast 2-seater (2 × 160-hp) started at Hi-Shear factory June 1960, aircraft flying 1 May 1962. Wing Aircraft Co. formed 27 June 1968, still at Torrance (LA) but severed from Hi-Shear parent. Four aircraft used for certification (20 December 1966), but planned production at Coffeyville, Kansas, never funded.

Winther-Hollmann (USA). Winther-Hollmann Aircraft Inc. produced light aircraft 1982.

Winton (Australia). Scott Winton designed Sapphire ultralight, produced in 2 variants by J & P Heard, New South Wales.

Winton (Australia). Colin Winton, Queensland, produced Sportsman micro.

Wipaire (USA). Originally Wipline Inc., Minnesota, produces conversions to Super Beaver seaplane and amphibious Aztec.

Witteman-Lewis (USA). With ample backing, Witteman-Lewis Aircraft Corp. formed at Newark, NJ, 1919, building impressive airfield and factory at Hasbrouck Heights (later called Teterboro), where basic income was conversions of D.H.4 and DH-4 to post-war versions. A.F. Arcier (ex-Handley Page) designed FA-1 mail carrier (2 × Liberty), FA-2 5-seater (Liberty) and FA-10 flying-boat (2 × Cosmos Jupiter). As low bidder got job of building giant Barling Bomber as Witteman-Lewis NBL-1 (22 August 1923). Bought by Fokker 1924.

Wittman (USA). Steve Wittman, famed racing pilot from 1926, built numerous racing and touring aircraft including Special *Buster* (1933) which won 1947 Goodyear and 1934 *Bonzo* (won Continental 1949/50/52). Manager of Winnebago County Airport (Oshkosh) since 1931, Wittman produced Tailwind high-wing 2-seater 1953, subsequently about 390 built in over 40 local variants. Wittman moved to Ocala, Florida, plans and prefab parts still marketed 1993.

Wiweko (Indonesia). In 1948, Soepono Wiweko, then head of AURI (air force) design, produced WEL-1 parasol single-seater. Design resurrected, new prototype (13 August 1981) expected to lead to plans/kits available.

WKF (Austria). Wiener Karroserie Fabrik,

originally Dr W. Gutmann's bodybuilding firm, built Lloyd recon-bomber from July 1915, fitting 165-hp (instead of 145-hp) Austro-Daimler from December, calling result WKF Type 43. New 10-spar wing in Type 44, followed by prototypes of Knoller, Type 81, and then production of BA 8₂ designed autumn 1916 by Lloyd and Gasser (165-hp Austro-Daimler), but redesigned by WKF (Schieferl) with 220-hp Benz and from spring 1917 built in quantity. Various Type 80 prototypes, wholly WKF design, and triplane fighter. At Armistice designed civil sport biplane, prototype with 35-hp Hacke; planned 40-hp Hiero never installed.

WNF: *See* Wiener-Neustädter.

Wolf (USA). Donald S. Wolf produced W-11 Boredom Fighter biplane (30 August 1979), 130 being built by late 1986.

Wolf (USA). Steve Wolf built ultralight 1986.

Wolf (USA). William H. Wolf built light sporting aircraft 1981.

Wolfe (USA). Wolfe Aviation Co. built ultralights from 1985.

Wolff (Luxembourg). Ateliers Paul Wolff, L-8283 Kehlen, produced Flash-3 high-speed 3-seater with airframe entirely of composites (1985), followed by even more powerful 4-seat Sky-Wolff marketed in USA in kit form by Wolff Aircraft Engineering.

Wolseley (UK). Wolseley Motors Ltd, Adderley Park, Birmingham, pioneer car manufacturer, produced aero engines 1909–36, and in 1915–18 BE.2c and 2e and SE.5a (with Wolseley engine).

Wood (USA). Charles A. Wood produced single-seat high-wing Little Monster (5 July 1955), having designed since 1917.

Wood (USA). Stanley Wood produced SL-1 Formula V racer (8 June 1973).

Woods (USA). Harris L. Woods, Niagara Falls, had by 1969 designed and built 13 types of fixed- and rotating-wing aircraft and air-cushion vehicles, best-known being Woody Pusher tandem-seat parasol monoplane. In 1970 formed Aerosport.

Woodson (USA). O.L. Woodson designed aircraft from 1912. Formed Woodson Aircraft Corp. January 1926 at Bryan, Ohio, to produce Express biplane for mail or cargo (150- or 180-hp Wright-Hispano). Built 18, plus a Foto biplane and M-6 low-wing 2-seater. M-6 became Simplex Red Arrow, Woodson joining this firm as design engineer 1928.

Wood Wing (USA). Market plans and prefab parts of CJ-3D Cracker Jack light single-seat high-wing monoplane (6 October 1982).

Wren (UK). Wren Aircraft Ltd formed 1946 at Kirklinton, Carlisle, producing single Goldcrest aerobatic single-seat monoplane.

Wren (USA). Wren Aircraft Corp., Fort Worth, formed to produce Wren 460 STOL conversions of Cessna 182 (January 1963), showing dramatic low-speed behaviour; 33 conversions by 1966. Work ceased, but new Wren Aircraft Inc. formed February 1982 at Arizona, briefly resuming conversions.

Wright (Germany). Wright Flugmaschine GmbH formed January 1911 Adlershof, to build Wright F, H-S and L, modified for German (especially military) use.

Wright (UK). Brothers Howard and Warwick Wright took over Short Brothers works under Battersea railway arches late 1909, building Avis monoplanes and Voisin-style biplanes, many variations.

Wright (USA). Brothers Orville and Wilbur Wright flew gliders from October 1900 and powered Flyers from 17 December 1903. Sold Type A to US Army September 1908, gradually putting this model into production at Dayton, those for European customers being crated and assembled at Pau (other European customers purchasing machines licence-built by Short Brothers). Office-boy Clinton R. Peterkin sought financial backing and assembled formidable group of shareholders, forming **Wright & Co.** 22 November 1909 in NY City, with factory remaining at Dayton. Brothers assigned patents and exercised overall technical control, though rapidly being overtaken by rivals, one of whom was Glenn L. Martin. Company bought by syndicate 13 October 1915, Orville staying as consultant. On 17 August 1916 Martin, General

Aero and Simplex Automobile merged with Wright, forming **Wright-Martin Co.**, New Brunswick, NJ. Unhappy merger, though Martin's licence for Hispano-Suiza engines replaced aircraft as staple product. Martin resigned December 1917, and 2 years later company changed name to **Wright Aeronautical Corp.**, moving all engine production to initially small shop at Paterson, NJ. Built handful of passenger flying-boats (pusher Wright-Hispano or Liberty), various racers (notably F2W, 1923) and Navy fighters (XF3W Apache, 1926).

WSK-Mielec (Poland). Largest Polish aircraft plant, at 39-300 Mielec, produced over 15,000 aircraft 1948–92. Full title Wytwórnia Sprzetu Komunikacyjnego-PZL Mielec (transport equipment manufacturing centre, Mielec). Since 1960 delivered 12,000 An-2 in 11 main versions. In 1984 began production of An-28 STOL transport, and expect to add An-38 later. Ag-aircraft include M-20 Dromader (probably most capable in world), M-21 Mini and M-24 Super. Other types M-20 Mewa (Piper Seneca II) and M-26 Iskierka aerobatic trainer. Subcontract work includes major portions of Il-86 and Il-96, and parts for Socata Tobago.

WSK Swidnik (Poland). WSK Im Zygmunta Pulaskiego-PZL Swidnik, named for designer of famous PZL fighters. Began 1951 making parts of LiM-1 (MiG-15), followed by 1,700 SM-1 (Mi-1) helicopters, followed by 450 derived SM-2. Design office grew, today devoted entirely to turbine-engined helicopters: since 1965 over 5,300

Mi-2 and Mi-2B; prototypes of twin-Allison Kania/Kitty Hawk; 55 W-3 Sokól; and prototype SW-4 4/5-seater with 400-hp GTD-350. Parts made for Eurocopter, An-28, Il-86/96.

WTA (USA). WTA Inc., Lubbock, TX, acquired from Piper rights to PA-18-150 Super Cub and PA-36 New Brave, producing 250 of former 1982–6, plus 150 of latter.

Wytwórnia: *See* WSK-Mielec.

X

XAC: *See* Xian.

XAPA (Ukraine). Kharkov Aviation Production Association formed 1991 to manage plant previously engaged in Tu-134 conversions and support of other Tu programmes.

Xausa (Italy). Renato Xausa built light sporting aircraft 1984.

Xian (China). Xian Aircraft Manufacturing Co., Shaanxi 710000, established 1958, one of largest aircraft production complexes in China. Built 120 H-6 (Tu-16) bombers and B-6D maritime cruise-missile carriers. Current major production pro-

Xian Nin Hai, August 1934.

gramme derivatives of An-24 and -26 designated Y7-100/200/200A/500 with numerous changes from Soviet original. XAC has now developed JH-7 interdictor/strike aircraft. (Nin Hai naval seaplanes were built at Xian 1934–36.)

Y____

Yackey (USA). Yackey Aircraft, Forest Park, Illinois, built Liberty-engined transports based on Breguet Br XIV c1924.

Yakovlev (USSR). Aleksandr Sergeyevich Yakovlev born 19 March 1906, teenage aviation enthusiast, helped build glider at Koktebel 1923, with Ilyushin's help built successful own glider 1924, in same year became menial labourer at VVA but gradually learned every aspect of aircraft design and construction. Helped by Prof. V.S. Pyshnov built VVA-3 tandem-seat biplane (60-hp Cirrus) in spare evenings; jealousy caused investigations and delays, but Yu.I. Piontkovskii flew VVA-3 on skis 12 May 1927, outstanding aircraft. Yak gained admittance to VVA as proper student. VVA-3 flew 1,240 km (770 miles) in 15.5 hr, world class record, Yak redesignated

AIR-1 to please commissar A.I. Rykov. In 1928–9 built 4 AIR-2, similar to AIR-1 but various engines, many minor changes and at least first being seaplane. AIR-3 (June 1929) parasol monoplane version, followed by profusion of other light aircraft, notably including AIR-7 high-speed tourer with tandem enclosed cockpits (480-hp M-22 Jupiter). At 206 mph (332 km/h) fastest in USSR, and also comfortable, but loss of aileron through flutter put Yak in disgrace, evicted and forbidden to continue work. He was eventually offered derelict bed factory on Moscow's Leningradskii Prospect which has been Yakovlev OKB ever since. First major success AIR-14 (December 1935) single-seat advanced aerobatic trainer, 1,241 by 1940. Via racers and transports came Ya-20 (June 1937) which as UT-2 became standard air force and Osoaviakhim trainer, 7,243 by 1944. First really high-performance aircraft was Ya-22 (BB-22) long-range fighter (February 1939), leading to Yak-2 and Yak-4. Began design of No. 26 fighter November 1938, flown as I-26 1 January 1940, leading to vast and complex family Yak-1/7/7B/3/9 to total 1945 just exceeding 37,000. Yak-3 developed into lower-powered Yak-11 advanced trainer, 3,859 plus 707 by Let. Yak-12 high-wing STOL exceeded 3,300. Yak-15, 17 and 23 jets made in fair numbers, and Yak-18 (December 1945) led to several primary trainer variants adding up to 6,760 by 1967. These in turn led to today's Yak-50, 52, 53, 55, 55M and

Yakovlev Yak-3, July 1944; Yakovlev is now building 20 Allison-engined replicas.

56 trainers and aerobatic machines, trainers mass-produced by Condor. Helicopter work led 1952 to Yak-24 tandem-rotor transport (2 × 1,700-hp ASh-82V). Numerous jets then led to Yak-25 night interceptor (1953), leading to various Yak-25/26/27/28 derivatives for many roles. Yak-40 (21 October 1966) unusual 'slow jet', with unswept wing, 3 × 3,300-lb (1,497 kg) AI-25 turbofans, 24 seats and able to use 2,400-ft (732 m) strips, 1,011 built. Transport team next produced much bigger Yak-42, again with 3 turbofans at rear but with swept wing and 100–120 seats; flew 7 March 1975 but many changes and Aeroflot service delayed to late 1980; today 250 of many versions, leading via 42M to Yak-46, first (1993) with high-bypass turbofans, 1995 with advanced pusher version of D-27 propfan. Yak-36 jet V/STOL research aircraft led to Yak-36MP (1971) prototype of production Yak-38 naval strike/recon aircraft. This led to totally new and supersonic Yak-141 (March 1989), though halted 1993 through lack of funds, together with Yak-44 twin-turboprop 'AWACS'. New types: Yak-48 bizjet, Yak-58 pusher 6-seater, Yak-112 4-seater (20 October 1992) and Yak-130 jet trainer marketed with Aermacchi. Founder died 22 August 1988, succeeded by Aleksandr N. Dondukov, a deputy being son Sergei A. Yakovlev. OKB reorganized 1992 as **Yakovlev Aircraft Corp.**, Moscow, with associated factory **MMZ 'Skorost' I** (Moscow machine-building factory 'Speed' named for) **A.S. Yakovlev.**

Main production plant at Smolyensk, where prototypes (e.g. Yak-112) also now built. *See* Skorost. Agreement with Textron Lycoming for engines 1992.

Yates (USA). George Yates, Portland, Oregon, built series of 2-seaters from 1930, initially 90-hp Cirrus, then 100-hp Menasco. Followed single-seat parasol with 45-hp Salmson.

Yatsenko (USSR). Vladimir Panfilovich Yatsenko worked on Polikarpov's team, then replaced Kochyerigin on DI-6 programme. His own effort was I-28 fighter (about 1 May 1939), many good features, including tight group of 2 × 20-mm and 2 × 7.7-mm; eventually accepted for production, halted February 1940 with 5 delivered.

YDB (Ukraine). English-language abbreviation of **Yuzhnoye design bureau**, which seeks funds for An-124 conversion to launch ICBM at altitude, avoiding vulnerable fixed basing.

Yeoman (Australia). Yeoman Aircraft Pty Ltd formed 1958 as associate of Kingsford Smith to produce ag-aircraft, originally based on CA.6 Wackett, but production Cropmaster 250 was virtually new design.

Yermolayev (USSR). Vladimir Grigor'yevich Yermolayev worked on Stal-6 and -7, seized

Yokosuka D4Y3, captured 1944.

opportunity when Bartini arrested and became leading member of special KB to continue Stal-7 and produce bomber version. Stalin's interest January 1939 meant immediate large OKB, resulting in DB-240 (June 1940) leading to outstanding Yer-2 long-range bomber, 128 produced at Voronezh before evacuation, terrible difficulties but 300 more 1943, numerous proto-types and experimental engine installations, including 300 series Yer-2ACh-30B diesel-engined 1944, range over 3,110 miles (5,000 km) with 6,614-lb (3,000 kg) bomb. OKB run down after Yermolayev's death from illness 31 December 1944, taken over by P.O. Sukhoi.

Yokosuka (Japan). This city gave popular name to Imperial Navy's Dai-Ichi Kaigun Koku Gijitsusho (1st Technical Air Arsenal), whose designs were usually assigned to established manufacturers for series production, though some were also built by Dai-Juichi (11th) naval air arsenal at Hiro. Produced 6 prototype seaplanes 1916–18, 1 (Rogo-Ko) 2-seat recon (220-hp HS8b) being built by Aichi/Nakajima (219) 1918–20. In 1920–40 about 1,500 built of 10 designs of biplane trainer, mostly seaplanes, and K5Y (December 1933) was mass-produced, 5,770 by late 1944. Smaller numbers of recon aircraft included 126 E14Y monoplane seaplanes foldable for service aboard submarines. Small numbers built of bombers and flying-boats. B4Y biplane carrier-based torpedo bomber (late 1935) built mainly by Mitsubishi (135 of 205 total). D4Y Suisei (Comet) carrier-based dive-bomber (December 1940) was major type, 2,038 built, mainly by Aichi, 1942–5. Potentially one of best Japanese wartime aircraft, P1Y flown August 1943, 1,098 built, 996 by Nakajima. D3Y Myojo and R2Y Keiun never reached production, but MXY-7 suicide aircraft did (852, all by naval air arsenals).

York (S. Africa). T.R. York, Kempton Park, modified Globe Swift with 145-hp engine, fixed tricycle landing gear and many other changes (1974).

York (USA). York Research Corp. formed probably 1945 at NY City; chief engineer E. Brush produced Airmobile Model IIX (*sic*) Com-muter 4-seater with 2 × 114-hp Franklin (1946).

York (USA). Leon York, Midland, TX, produced June Bug low-wing sport single-seater (November 1954).

Youngman-Baynes (UK). L.E. Baynes designed special research aeroplane, based on Proctor IV, but with new wings incorporating R.T. Youngman's full-span slotted flaps, called Youngman-Baynes High-Lift, built by Heston (5 February 1948).

Younkin (USA). Jim Younkin built replica Travel Air Mystery S racer (March 1979).

Yuriev (Russia). Boris Nikolayevich Yuriev was, despite crippling lack of money, greatest Soviet pioneer of helicopter, of necessity carrying out most work on paper (though one experimental machine with 30-hp Anzani built 1912). His designs were adopted with few changes as basis for first CAHI (TsAGI) helicopter.

Z

Zacco: *See* Zeebrugge.

Zaidan (Japan). Zaidan Hozin Minkan Yusooki Kaihatsu Kyokai (civil transport development corp.) formed 1973 to manage YX (not built); may manage SST participation.

Zalewski (Poland/Russia). Polish designer W. Zalewski teamed up with V.F. Savalyev to design SZ No. 1 quadruplane (23 April 1916), built at 2nd Aircraft Park, Smolensk, using 100-hp Gnome Mono. Aircraft proved even more agile than Nieuport scouts, but only 1 built (saw active service).

Zander & Weyl (UK). At Dunstable, built Dart, Pup and Kitten; renamed Dart Aircraft.

Zaparka (Austria). Eduard Zaparka, later chief designer of Phönix, had Vienna design office 1914–15 where he produced fighting biplane built by army Flep.3, 100-hp Siemens rotary.

Zari (Italy). Factory of Zari Brothers near Milan built small number of aircraft 1917 to early 1920s to designs of others, including 1919 Tebaldi fighter.

Zavody (Czechoslovakia). Name merely meaning 'factory', in full Skodovy Zavody, largest engineering firm in country after First World War. Among vast range of products were aircraft (e.g. Dewoitine fighters under licence), aero engines, aircraft guns and controlling holding in Avia and airline CLS.

Zborowski (France). BTZ (Bureau Technique Zborowski) formed after Second World War by Count von Zborowski to develop various patented ideas, notably annular-wing VTOL aircraft; this realized in SNECMA Coléoptère (6 May 1959).

Zeebrugge (Belgium). Formed 1923 as Zeebrugge Aeronautical Construction Co. (Zacco), building several prototypes including 2-seat light trainer and 2-seat light cabin monoplane. Renamed 1925 Ateliers de Construction Aéronautique de Zeebrugge (ACAZ), building prototype of 2-seat reconnaissance fighter biplane (early 1926); survived to 1933.

Zenair (Canada). Zenair Aircraft Ltd, Midland, Ontario, formed 1974 to market Zenith 2-seat homebuilt; by 1991 well over 1,000 flying in 47 countries. Today almost unbelievable variety (CH-100/150/180/200/250/300/600/601/701/801/2000), all flown and many factory-built, e.g. 4-seat 801.

Zenith (USA). Zenith Aircraft Corp. formed 1927 at Santa Ana, CA, to produce 2 substantial commercial aircraft: Zenith Biplane, 5-passenger, 220-hp, and Albatross monoplane for 12 passengers (3 × 125-hp); latter tried to set new duration record. Moved to Midway City, CA, and in 1931–2 built more than 6 Z-6A and Z-6B commercial biplanes (420-hp Wasp) with 6-seat cabin ahead of open pilot cockpit.

Zentral-Aviatik (Austria). Full title Zentral-Aviatik und Automobil GmbH, linked with German Aviatik and from December 1914 produced Aviatik B.I, later built by others (e.g., Ö-UF). In 1922 built Ehrlich V biplane, open cockpit 2-seat cabin (180/200-hp Hiero).

Zentralgesellschaft (W. Germany). Registered in Düsseldorf but 50/50 a Dutch organization, full title Zentralgesellschaft VFW-Fokker mbH, formed May 1969 by VFW and Fokker and also directly controlling ERNO (spaceflight) and Avio Diepen.

Zephyr (USA). Formed 1933 by renaming Lenart, continued limited production of PT-2 tandem-cockpit trainer/tourer.

Zeppelin (Germany). Formed at Lindau, on Bodensee (Lake Constance), August 1914 near parent Zeppelin-Werke at Friedrichshafen. Chief designer Claudius Dornier charged with building largest possible metal flying-boats. Produced Rs I, completed October 1915, followed by Rs.II, III and IV, even bigger 8-engined Rs.V remaining on paper. Works at Lindau and Seemoos later formed part of Dornier empire renamed Dornier GmbH October 1922.

Zeppelin (Germany). Within 3 weeks of outbreak of First World War on 4 August 1914 Count (Graf) von Zeppelin had not only got Dornier started on giant flying-boats at Lindau but had also formed VGO (Versuchsbau Gotha-Ost GmbH), East Gotha Experimental Works, headed by Gustav Klein (of Robert Bosch electrical giant) and aviator Hellmuth Hirth. Design team headed by Prof. Alexander Baumann produced monster biplane bomber VGO.1, 1 tractor and 2 pusher 240-hp Maybach (11 April 1915), largest aeroplane in world. Improved VGO.II (September 1915) became first of remarkable series of R-Type (*Riesenflugzeug* = giant aeroplane) bombers, produced in series to Armistice. Company moved June 1916 to Staaken, Berlin, renamed Flugzeugwerft GmbH and, from January 1918, **Zeppelin-Werke Staaken**. Thus, R.IV–R.XVI known loosely as Staaken bombers. In 1920 built fabulous stressed-skin all-metal airliner, with 4 engines along leading edge of cantilever wing; this E.4/20 was designed mainly by Dr A.K. Rohrbach and flew 1920, but destroyed by Allied Control Commission.

Zherebtsov (USSR). Light helicopter with pulse-jet tip drive produced by B.Ya. Zherebtsov, assisted by Yu.S. Braginski and Yu.L. Starinin, flown 1950.

ZIG (USSR). ZIG-1 fast passenger transport, also designated PS-89, was designed by Laville 1933.

Zilina (Czechoslovakia). Zilina Transport Research Institute built Vazka (Dragonfly) autogyro, to design of student Vazek (1 April 1968).

Zlin 226T Trener 6, December 1955.

Zinno (USA). Joseph A. Zinno & Associates produced light aircraft 1977.

Zlatoust (USSR). Zlatoust Young Pioneers built sporting aircraft 1964.

Zlin (Czechoslovakia). Zlinská Letecká Akciová Spolecnost formed September 1935 as wholly-owned subsidiary of Bata Shoe Co., starting with series of 2-seat monoplanes built at Otrokovice: Zlin XII, XIII, XV and 212, as well as piston engines of 65 and 105 hp. In 1944 produced Bü 181D Bestmann and HM 504 engine, continuing after war as Zlin 281 (air force C.6) and 381 (C.106), sub-licensing Egypt to build Gomhouria. Post-war 12 types of trainers, tourers and competition aerobatic aircraft, major family stemming from Zlin 26 Trener of 1947, via 126 Trener II, 226 Akrobat, 326 Trener-Master and 326A Akrobat, 526A Akrobat and 526F and 726 (March 1973) and 726K, to total by 1977 of 1,452. In 1960 nationalized state industry began to be replaced by company names, and Otrokovice works became **Moravan Národní Podnik**, Moravian National Corp. Produced Zlin

42 side-by-side trainer/tourer (October 1967), Zlin 43 4-seater (December 1968) and 142, Zlin 50L aerobatic aircraft (July 1975) and Z 50M, and Z 37T Agro Turbo turboprop version of Let Z-37A Cmelák.

Zlokazov (USSR). Aleksandr Ivanovich Zlokazov was senior GVF (civil fleet) engineer at Irkutsk when he designed ARK-3 all-metal 10-passenger or cargo monoplane for Arctic transport (about 10 May 1935).

Zmaj (Jugoslavia). Fabrica Aeroplana I Hydroplana Zmaj (*Zmaj* = dragon) founded Zemun near Belgrade 1927 by Jovan Petrovic to produce Dewoitine D 27 parasol fighter, Hanriot 41 trainer biplane and possibly LGL B.3 bomber. Biggest production programme, FN trainer biplane, 600+ 1929–41. By far biggest development programme was R.1 twin-engined high-speed bomber and attack fighter (spring 1940); destroyed by German army late 1941.

Zodiac (France). Commercial company formed Paris 1896, which began constructing aeroplanes of general Voisin type 1909, designing S2 2-seater 1912.

ZOK (USSR). Factory for Special Construction, division of CAHI headed by Petlyakov 1936 until arrest 1937.

ZPL (Poland). Zjednoczenie Przemyslu Lotniczego, United Aircraft Industry, state overall management organization 1948–80: *see* ZWSLS.

Zrzeszenie: *See* ZWSLS.

Zurakowski (Poland). Designer of 2-seat helicopter built by GIL institute 1950.

ZWSLS (Poland). Since 1981 governing body of aviation industry has been Zrzeszenie Wytwórców Sprzetu Lotniczego I Silnikowego PZL, association of aircraft and engine industry.